César J. Ayala and Rafael Bernabe

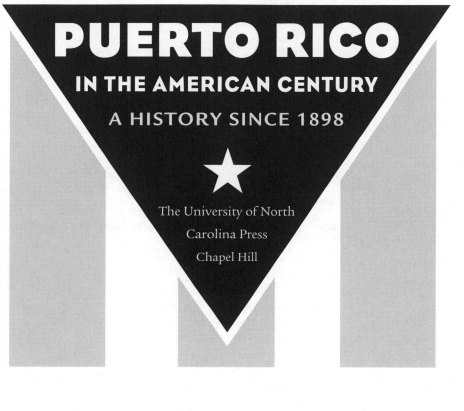

PUERTO RICO

IN THE AMERICAN CENTURY

A HISTORY SINCE 1898

The University of North
Carolina Press
Chapel Hill

Designed by Heidi Perov
Set in Legacy and Bureau Eagle
by Keystone Typesetting, Inc.

Publication of this book was aided by grants from the University
of California at Los Angeles and the University of Puerto Rico.

The paper in this book meets the guidelines for permanence and
durability of the Committee on Production Guidelines for Book
Longevity of the Council on Library Resources.

Library of Congress Cataloging-in-Publication Data
Ayala, César J.
Puerto Rico in the American century :
a history since 1898 / César J. Ayala and Rafael Bernabe.
p. cm.
Includes bibliographical references and index.
ISBN 978-0-8078-3113-7 (cloth: alk. paper)
1. Puerto Rico—History—20th century.
I. Bernabe, Rafael. II. Title.
F1975.A93   2007
972.9505′2—dc22   2006039830

11 10 09 08 07   5 4 3 2 1

For Félix Córdova Iturregui

CONTENTS

ILLUSTRATIONS, MAPS, TABLES, AND FIGURES

MAPS

TABLES

FIGURES

ACKNOWLEDGMENTS

Through all the stages of the preparation of this book, we received the unstinting support and guidance of Elaine Maisner, our editor at the University of North Carolina Press. We would like to thank anthropologist Arlene Dávila, economist James Dietz, and historian Francisco Scarano for their careful reading of the manuscript and detailed comments. Their suggestions did much to improve the final version of this work. Marithelma Costa also read portions of the manuscript and helped us avoid some unfair omissions.

Rafael Bernabe wishes to thank Marién Delgado and Melissa Figueroa for their help in finding materials at the José M. Lázaro Library at the University of Puerto Rico and Félix Córdova for the use of many hard-to-find books and materials.

César Ayala would like to thank Alisa Garni, Taekyoon Lim, and Charles Mahoney for their useful comments regarding chapters 9 and 13.

Subventions from the University of Puerto Rico and UCLA have contributed to reduce publication costs. At UPR, thanks are due to the Decanato de Estudios Graduados e Investigación. At UCLA, thanks go to Scott Waugh, dean of Social Sciences; Professor David López, chair of the sociology department; and Professor Randal Johnson, director of the Latin American Studies Center.

All shortcomings are, of course, our sole responsibility.

ABBREVIATIONS

AC	Asociación de Choferes
ACLU	American Civil Liberties Union
AFL	American Federation of Labor
AFL-CIO	American Federation of Labor–Congress of Industrial Organizations
AFT	American Federation of Teachers
ALP	American Labor Party
ASI	Acción Social Independentista
ATA	Asociación de Trabajadores Agrícolas
CAOS	Comité Amplio de Organizaciones Sociales y Sindicales
CEREP	Centro para el Estudio de la Realidad Puertorriqueña
CGT	Confederación General del Trabajo (in the 1940s); Concilio General de Trabajadores (in the 1980s and 1990s)
CIO	Congress of Industrial Organizations
CIS	Centro de Investigaciones Sociales
COG	Colectivo Orgullo Gay
COH	Concilio de Organizaciones Hispanas
CPI	Congreso Pro Independencia
CPT	Central Puertorriqueña de Trabajadores
ELA	Estado Libre Asociado (Commonwealth of Puerto Rico)
FALN	Fuerzas Armadas de Liberación Nacional
FLT	Federación Libre de Trabajadores
FRT	Federación Regional de los Trabajodores
ICP	Instituto de Cultura Puertorriqueña
ILGWU	International Ladies Garment Workers' Union
IWO	International Workers Order

MIA	Mujer Intégrate Ahora
MINP	Movimiento de Izquierda Nacional Puertorriqueña
MLN	Movimiento de Liberación Nacional
MOU	Movimiento Obrero Unido
MPI	Movimiento Pro Independencia
PC	Partido Comunista (Puerto Rico)
PCI	Partido Comunista Independiente (Puerto Rico)
PIP	Partido Independentista Puertorriqueño
PNP	Partido Nuevo Progresista
PPD	Partido Popular Democrático
PRC	Partido Revolucionario Cubano
PRCDP	*Puerto Rico Community Development Project*
PRRA	Puerto Rico Reconstruction Administration
PRSU	Puerto Rico Student Union
PRTC	Puerto Rico Telephone Company
PSP	Partido Socialista Puertorriqueño
ROTC	Reserve Officers Training Corps
UPR	Universidad de Puerto Rico
UTIER	Unión de Trabajadores de la Industria Eléctrica y Riego (Electrical Power Workers' Union)

PUERTO RICO
IN THE AMERICAN CENTURY

INTRODUCTION

In 1941, publisher Henry Luce announced the coming of the American Century from the pages of *Life* magazine. The moment symbolically marked the rise of the United States as a global power. It has been pointed out many times that American influence as proclaimed by Luce in 1941 and as built by U.S. strategists after 1945 did not imply the construction of a new colonial empire following the British or other European models. This is undoubtedly so, but it should not lead us to forget that there were exceptions. For some, the American Century had begun much earlier, on the eve of the twentieth century, when the Spanish-American War of 1898 led to the installation of U.S. colonial governments in the Philippines, Puerto Rico, and Guam. While the Philippines became independent in 1946, Puerto Rico and Guam remain under U.S. sovereignty to this day. Puerto Rico thus became an anomaly: a colony of a fundamentally noncolonial imperialism. It is this exceptional case that concerns us here.

The objective of this book is to acquaint the reader with the history of Puerto Rico since 1898. Such a project is never a neutral or value-free operation. We bring to it a particular perspective and set of interests. While we relay many findings of past contributions in this field, we also depart from some prevalent views regarding many of the events, processes, and historical figures discussed here. But before we go into these, it is appropriate to begin with some facts and a brief overview of the terrain we will cover.

Puerto Rico is the smallest and easternmost of the Greater Antilles (see Maps 1.1 and 1.2). Although often referred to as an island, it is in fact formed by three inhabited islands: Puerto Rico, Vieques, and Culebra, the latter two being much smaller than the former. The three islands have a combined area of roughly 3,500 square miles. Following convention, we will use the term "Puerto Rico" or "the island" to refer to the three insular territories taken as a unit. In 2006, Puerto Rico had close to four million inhabitants. It is therefore densely populated, with around 1,140 inhabitants per square mile. About one-fourth of Puerto Rico's surface is taken up by a coastal plain that encircles a mountainous interior, which in turn accounts for close to half of the island's territory. The remaining one-fourth of the insular surface corresponds to hilly areas between the flat lowlands and the central highlands. Puerto Rico's capital and largest city and harbor is San Juan, located on its northern coast.

At present, around half of those classified and/or describing themselves as Puerto Ricans reside outside Puerto Rico. Historically, most of them have lived in cities such as New York, Chicago, Philadelphia, and Hartford. In recent years, a new pole of Puerto Rican relocation in the United States has emerged around Orlando and other cities in central Florida. While Spanish is the vernacular of most Puerto Ricans who grew up on the island, English is the first language of many who were born in or grew up in the United States. The diasporic dimension of the Puerto Rican experience since 1898 forces anyone attempting an account of it to embark on a journey far beyond the confines of strictly insular geography. Yet a thorough history of Puerto Ricans in the United States entails going deep into the specific economic and political history of New York, Chicago, Philadelphia, and other North American cities. This is beyond the reach of a general overview. Therefore, while dedicating many of the pages that follow to developments in New York and, to a lesser extent, Chicago and Philadelphia, we know they are hardly enough to do justice to the richness of the history of the Puerto Rican diaspora.

Having gone through the twentieth century—and entered the twenty-first—under direct U.S. rule, Puerto Rico stands out as doubly exceptional. After being one of the few colonies of a fundamentally noncolonial imperialism, it remains, most observers would argue, a colony, long after most colonies in the world have moved on to either political independence or formal political integration with their metropolis, as in the case of some French colonies in the Caribbean. Not surprisingly, the question of the political relationship with the United States remains the central, constantly debated issue of insular politics.

The history of Puerto Rico after the onset of U.S. rule in 1898 breaks down into two distinct epochs: before and after World War II. Each epoch exhibits two distinguishable phases: an initial period of economic expansion in which productive and state structures, dominant political parties, and labor organizations are put in place, and a succeeding phase of economic slowdown in which established structures and institutions are subjected to increased stress. The early years of the century, 1898 to 1930, and the post–World War II decades from 1950 to 1975 were phases of expansion. They were followed by periods of slowdown or crisis between 1930 and 1950 and between 1975 and the present. Each phase of both expansion and slower growth has also exhibited distinct forms of population movement to and from the U.S. mainland.

Similarly, the succession of cultural policies and counterpolicies and literary debates over the twentieth century—from clashes over Americanization in the early 1900s to the debates on Puerto Rican identity in the 1930s, the "institutionalization" of Puerto Rican culture in the 1950s, and the new historiographical and literary currents of the 1970s, to name a few—can also be correlated, we will argue, to the alternating phases of Puerto Rico's economic and political evolution since 1898.

Not surprisingly, given Puerto Rico's rapid integration into the world capitalist economy from the late 1800s, the chronology of these phases coincides closely with the major stages in the evolution of international capitalism after the depression of 1873. Economist Ernest Mandel examined what he described as alternating expansive and depressive long waves of capitalist development. His dating of these phases coincides with the way historian Eric Hobsbawm and economist Angus Maddison break down the same 130 years in the history of international capitalism.[1] Table 1.1 correlates the epochs or phases of world capitalism since 1873 with some shifts in Puerto Rico's evolution. Mandel, Hobsbawm, and Maddison identify four major turning points in the evolution of the world capitalist economy: the beginning of economic expansion in the late 1890s, the crash of the late 1920s, the launching of a new boom in the immediate post–World War II period, and the shift toward slower growth in the mid-1970s. Each has also been a point of rupture in the economic and political life of Puerto Rico and of Puerto Ricans in the U.S. mainland. In the chapters that follow, we will consider each of these phases and turning points. Table 1.1 may serve as a quick reference as we progress through a complex century.

If the fit between general tendencies and the Puerto Rican itinerary is not perfect, it is because the world economy is not a piece of clockwork but rather an elaborate organism shaped by the general tendencies of capitalist accumulation that operate within specific contexts. It is not our job here to explore the debates regarding the inner mechanisms of these fluctuations, but we do wish to note the evident correspondence of the breaks in Puerto Rican history with this pulse of the world capitalist economy, and we will refer to the latter to the extent that it helps us to understand the former.

At the time of the Spanish-American War, the United States was a rising industrial power. Its dynamic industrial and financial lords ruled over a growing, largely immigrant, multi-ethnic proletariat, which was still nurtured by a

MAP I.I. The Caribbean

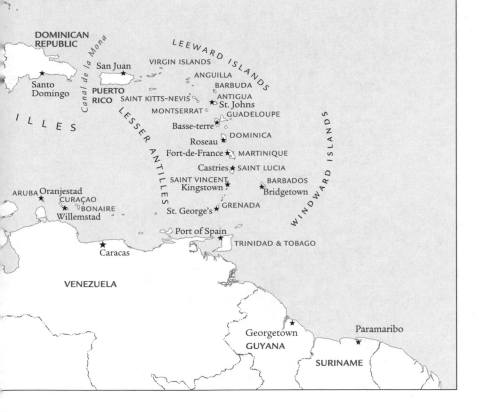

Atlantic

Ocean

TURKS & CAICOS ISLANDS

DOMINICAN
REPUBLIC

LEEWARD ISLANDS

VIRGIN ISLANDS

San Juan

ANGUILLA

Santo
Domingo

PUERTO
RICO

BARBUDA

SAINT KITTS-NEVIS

ANTIGUA

St. Johns

MONTSERRAT

Canal de la Mona

GUADELOUPE

I L L E S

Basse-terre

Roseau

DOMINICA

Fort-de-France

MARTINIQUE

Castries

SAINT LUCIA

SAINT VINCENT

BARBADOS

ARUBA

Oranjestad

Kingstown

Bridgetown

CURAÇAO

BONAIRE

Willemstad

St. George's

GRENADA

Port of Spain

Caracas

TRINIDAD & TOBAGO

WINDWARD ISLANDS

LESSER ANTILLES

VENEZUELA

Georgetown

GUYANA

Paramaribo

SURINAME

MAP I.2. Puerto Rican Municipios

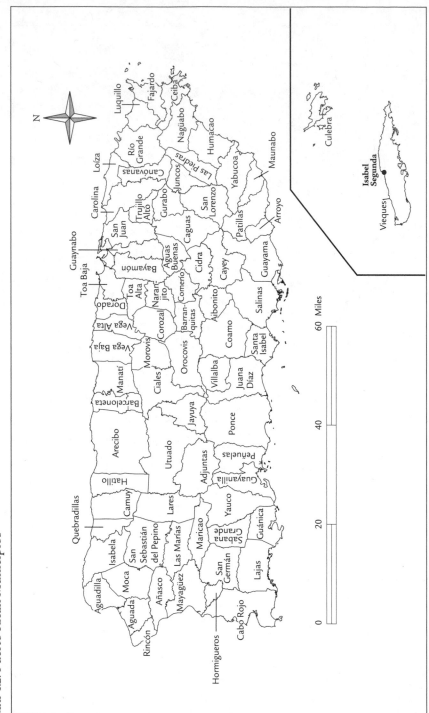

constant flow of new arrivals from abroad. The South had just lived through the consolidation of segregation in the 1890s and its judicial endorsement by the U.S. Supreme Court in *Plessy v. Ferguson*. In 1898, the war with Spain brought direct control over three colonial territories—the Philippines, Puerto Rico, and Guam—and inaugurated an era in which Cuba, Panama, the Dominican Republic, Haiti, and other formally independent republics became de facto U.S. protectorates.

Taking a step back, we can see a wider picture, a complex articulation and combination of diverse forms of political and economic forms of subordination, encompassing the people of the United States and its colonial possessions or semicolonial protectorates. We thus have (1) institutionalized racism and segregation in the Jim Crow South, combined with the disenfranchisement of many poor whites; (2) segmented labor markets and ethnic hierarchies of a largely immigrant working class in the industrialized or industrializing North and Midwest; (3) colonial subordination of overseas territories, such as the Philippines, Puerto Rico, and Guam; and (4) semicolonial control, including occasional occupation, of formally independent countries such as Cuba, Panama, the Dominican Republic, Haiti, and Nicaragua. All of these were in turn conditioned by the evolution and expansion of U.S. capitalism. Each one of these structures generated diverse forms of antiracist, anticolonial, antiimperialist, and even anticapitalist resistance, from Garveyism in the second decade of the twentieth century to the civil rights movement of the late 1950s and 1960s, from the craft unionism of Gompers's American Federation of Labor in the early 1900s to the insurgent industrial unionism of the Congress of Industrial Organizations in the 1930s, from the Filipino struggle for independence in the early 1900s to the Cuban revolutions of 1933 and 1959.

Puerto Ricans have been assigned to several locations within that larger architecture and have been affected by and/or have been direct participants in the struggles that emerged within it. They have gone through the twentieth century as inhabitants of a colonial territory that is both subordinate to and different from the United States. They have been defined as an ethnic group or a nonwhite people (or both) within the North American ethnocultural classification system. Meanwhile, most Puerto Ricans have been working people employed by capital both on the island and in the United States. Thus, at different points, our story crosses paths with developments in the Caribbean, the American labor movement, and black America.

This, we should point out, is not the usual approach to Puerto Rican history, which is more often than not discussed without much reference to global

TABLE I.I. Periods of Puerto Rican History since 1874

INTERNATIONAL PERIODS			PERIODIZATION OF PUERTO RICAN HISTORY
Mandel Long Waves	Hobsbawm Ages	Maddison Periods	Puerto Rican Economy
1874–93 depressive	Age of empire	Liberal world order	Crisis in sugar industry Boom in coffee economy
1893–1913 expansive			1898–1934: Boom in sugar industry Complete transition to central mills Inflow of U.S. capital into sugar, tobacco, banking, needlework industries
1914–39/47 depressive	Age of catastrophe	Conflict and anarchy	
			1930s: Crisis in sugar industry New Deal programs Sugar quotas/Plan Chardón Puerto Rico Reconstruction Administration
1940/48– 66/75 expansive	Golden age		Operation Bootstrap U.S. direct investments Growth in export light manufactures 1960s petro-chemical industrial project
1967/75–90 depressive 1	Crisis and uncertainty	Faltering growth/ deceleration	Crisis of Operation Bootstrap Section 936—Expansion of pharmaceutical industry Slow growth Growth in federal funds (welfare & other)
1990–2006 depressive 2	Global neoliberalism		Privatization policies Phasing out of Section 936 (1996–2006) State fiscal crisis

Puerto Rican State/Politics	Puerto Rican Diaspora	Cultural/Literary Debates
Spanish Restoration/ colonial absolutism Partido Autonomista	Political exiles— Partido Revolucionario Cubano	Liberal critique of Spanish colonialism
1898–1930: U.S. invasion/ Foraker and Jones acts Electoral dominance of Partido Unión Rise of FLT and Partido Socialista	1898–1914: Early labor migration to Hawaii 1914–34: Growth of El Barrio (East Harlem) Initial community activism	1898–1934: Debates over language/ Americanization 1920s: Literary vanguards
1930s: Crisis in colonial state/ political parties Rise of Partido Nacionalista, PPD, Partido Comunista Crisis of FLT Rise of CGT	Left activism in 1930s and 1940s Support for Vito Marcantonio, ALP, and Communist Party	1930s: Debates over Puerto Rican identity *Generación del treinta* Flowering of Puerto Rican music in New York City: Rafael Hernández, Pedro Flores
Creation of Estado Libre Asociado PPD hegemony Dominance of AFL-CIO unions	Mass migration—advocacy groups—ASPIRA Electoral politics— Democratic Party	PPD institutionalization of culture Oppositional literary efforts of *generación del cincuenta*
Rise of PNP PPD-PNP parity: rise and crisis of New Left/PSP Rise and fall of new labor: MOU/union fragmentation	Economic crisis Rise and crisis of New Left, Young Lords, and others	New History/Literature Nuyorican literature Salsa explosion
Push for statehood Privatization battles Mobilization vs. navy in Vieques PNP/PPD deadlock Labor movement divided over labor legislation	Integration of Democratic Party politics Fragmented community resistance to gentrification/ antiwelfare measures Growing migration to central Florida	Debates over nationalism, national identity, and postmodernism

trends or more than a passing consideration of political and social conflicts in the United States. While the text itself will bring out the particulars of our perspective, it may help the reader if we rapidly point out at least some of the more salient points where we depart from other accounts of the material covered here.

As we carried out our work, we have tried to avoid some of the one-sided conceptions that have often characterized similar efforts in the past. Thus, although we feel U.S. colonialism has deeply shaped Puerto Rican life since 1898, we do not think all key events or turning points of Puerto Rican history can be attributed to U.S. colonial policies. We thus allot considerable space to the initiatives and the ideas, the contradictions and limitations, of Puerto Rican actors in this intricate drama. Similarly, while U.S. policies have been colonial, they have not been monolithic or static. They cannot be reduced to the early heavy-handed attempts to impose English on a Spanish-speaking people, or to the idiocies of inept governors such as E. Mont Reily in the early 1920s, or to the brutal repression unleashed by Blanton Winship in the 1930s. They have also included flexible approaches, willing to tolerate Puerto Rican autonomy and even certain affirmations of Puerto Rican identity and culture. We have thus explored what we feel are the distinctive dynamics of a Puerto Rican political movement, namely the autonomist current, that has for over a century sought to install itself within that both subordinate and distinct politico-cultural space.

If U.S. intentions and policies have not been monolithic, neither has the impact of U.S. colonialism been of one piece. Thus, if sugar gained in economic importance after 1898, Puerto Rico's economy did not become a mere "sugar economy"; if much of the sugar industry was in U.S. corporate hands, half of the raw sugar was produced by mills owned by island residents; if U.S. capital and markets reshaped Puerto Rico's economy, most Puerto Ricans still worked for Puerto Rican employers. We thus attempt to nuance rather simplistic visions of Puerto Rico's economic and social evolution immediately after 1898 and beyond.

Throughout this work, we have benefited from the work of many researchers —sociologists, historians, literary critics, economists—both in Puerto Rico and the United States. Our account, however, is not a mere synthesis of secondary materials. At important points in the narrative, we have relied extensively on primary sources, such as contemporary newspapers, where we believe that it is necessary to fill voids in the existing literature or where our analysis is contrary to established notions.

Since the 1970s, much research has brought to light moments and figures of the Puerto Rican past that previous authors had largely ignored. This history "from below," as it was often called in the 1980s, and, more recently, oral history and personal testimonies have enriched our vision of the past and have firmly and deservedly implanted in our memory figures such as early labor leader Ramón Romero Rosa, pioneer labor-feminist Luisa Capetillo, suffragist Ana Roque, and chronicler of the early Puerto Rican community in New York Bernardo Vega, among many others. We fully sympathize with the retrieval of these forgotten figures and have stressed not only the struggles of the early labor movement but also what we argue were the no less significant labor organizing efforts of the 1940s and the diverse social and labor mobilizations of the late 1960s and early 1970s, as well as the resistances to privatization and neoliberal reform in the 1990s. But the attempt to write a history from below or from the margins has often led to a blurring of some of the divisions at the top, that is to say, within political and literary elites, which were nevertheless significant. We therefore dedicate more pages than readers may have been led to expect to the ideas of Rosendo Matienzo Cintrón, Nemesio Canales, Luis Lloréns Torres, and others, which we feel have been either ignored or misrepresented by past historians.

Through the twentieth century, Puerto Rican identity has been hotly debated on the island and arguably by Puerto Ricans everywhere. These debates occupy much space in what follows. We have nevertheless made an effort to single out some figures—figures often considered and treated as secondary, if at all, such as Rubén del Rosario and Nilita Vientós—who we feel combined a critique of U.S. colonial rule with a particularly open, dynamic, porous vision of Puerto Rican identity, a perspective that we believe is now more necessary than ever. They suggested the possibility of a non-nationalist critique of U.S. colonialism that we find very appealing.

As indicated above, we pay considerable attention to the Puerto Rican diaspora in the United States, but we have not allotted it a special chapter, a gesture that often turns it into an appendix to an otherwise island-centered text. Instead, we have tried to tell the history of the diaspora as it unfolded in constant interaction with events on the island. Or, to put it otherwise, we have tried to move toward a history of both the island and its diaspora as facets of a single historical process. This also helps in a recuperation of the itineraries of some well-known figures, such as poet Julia de Burgos.

While we feel the issue of Puerto Rican identity is important, we also consider that often key differences among Puerto Rican political actors—and their individual contributions, limitations, or contradictions—do not necessarily revolve around this issue. Such is the case, for example, with the ideas of the aforementioned Matienzo Cintrón, the trajectory of early labor leader Santiago Iglesias, the impact of revolutionary Nationalist Pedro Albizu Campos, and the colonial reformism of Luis Muñoz Marín, all of whose ideas and attitudes regarding U.S. rule and Puerto Rican self-determination we discuss in a manner that we hope does not simply repeat what has been said in the past.

Our presentation is organized in chronological order, according to the periodization outlined above. The first part, comprising chapters 1 through 8, covers the first phase of economic expansion and the Great Depression that followed it. The second part, which includes chapters 9 through 15, narrates the transformation that unfolded during the postwar economic expansion and the configuration that emerged during the subsequent period of slow growth and social crisis after the mid-1970s. In the conclusion, we offer some remarks regarding Puerto Rico's present dilemmas after a century of U.S. rule. Thematically, some of the chapters concentrate successively on economic, political, and cultural aspects of each period. We are aware that this division is somewhat arbitrary, and we often violate it ourselves. It is often impossible to speak about any of these areas without considering the others. Yet, one cannot write about everything simultaneously. Therefore, some of the chapters concentrate on one or another field of activity.

Of the triad economics-politics-culture, the term "culture" is perhaps the most problematic. It can include just about any aspect of human activity. Here we will center our attention on literary debates and developments, above all on those that have raised the issue of Puerto Rican identity, although other cultural phenomena, such as popular music, are also considered. Theater, painting, sculpture, and architecture as well as much literary production deserve a careful consideration that painfully exceeds the space at our disposal. Two aspects of Puerto Rican culture—religion and sports—have been largely left out. This is not a small subtraction, given the importance many Puerto Ricans have given to both. But we feel it is better to admit this deficiency than to attempt to hide it with a brief and thus superficial consideration. A similar caveat could be added regarding other aspects of the Puerto Rican experience, from many facets of the evolution of social mores or daily life to Puerto Rican participation in military conflicts as part of the U.S. armed forces, all of which deserve careful and critical consideration. But a general history such as this can cover only so much ground. Not a few among these areas are still waiting for an initial systematic exploration. Perhaps our mistakes and shortcomings will have the positive effect of stimulating new and better work in all these areas.

There are many good reasons to embark on a project such as the writing of this book. In our case, it has been the most direct of motivations: we are Puerto Rican, and the object of this work concerns us dearly. But we have done our best to keep our affections from dimming our critical faculties. It is for the readers to judge to what extent we succeeded or failed.

1898—BACKGROUND AND
IMMEDIATE CONSEQUENCES

On May 25, 1898, former secretary of the navy and future president Theodore Roosevelt wrote to Senator Henry Cabot Lodge urging him not to let the war with Spain end without seizing Puerto Rico for the United States: "I earnestly hope that no truce will be granted and that peace will only be made on consideration of Cuba being independent, Porto Rico ours, and the Philippines taken away from Spain." In Roosevelt's nuanced vision, if Cuba was to be independent and the future of the Philippines once taken from Spain was left unspecified, Puerto Rico had been chosen to become "ours." Others in the McKinley administration shared his perspective. On May 24, 1898, Senator Lodge had assured Roosevelt that "Porto Rico is not forgotten and we mean to have it."[1] Indeed, already by the 1890s Puerto Rico had been described as key for the protection of a future canal through Central America. In 1891, Secretary of State James Blaine advised President Benjamin Harrison: "There are only three places that are of value enough to be taken, that are not continental. One is Hawaii and the others are Cuba and Porto Rico."[2]

The advice of Blaine and Roosevelt was heeded: after bombarding San Juan on May 12, U.S. troops began landing in Puerto Rico on July 25, near the town of Guánica on the southwestern coast of the island. As Blaine had foreseen, the rise of the United States as a global power would not entail the construction of a colonial empire, but it would require the control of strategically located way stations. Puerto Rico was seized as such an outpost in 1898.

The military campaign of 1898 in Puerto Rico lasted nineteen days; the armistice of August 12 put a stop to the conflict while diplomats negotiated the terms of the peace treaty. The Treaty of Paris was eventually signed by U.S. and Spanish representatives on December 10, 1898, and ratified by Congress on April 11, 1899. Five U.S. and seventeen Spanish soldiers died in the course of the war in Puerto Rico. The "splendid little war," as John Hay—at the time U.S.

ambassador in London—famously called it, was indeed a relatively light affair in Puerto Rico.

U.S. troops found little resistance as they advanced through Puerto Rico. There were many indications that the new authorities could count on an initial favorable attitude from almost all sectors of Puerto Rican society. Several manifestos signed by the most prominent political leaders on the island welcomed the representatives of the U.S. republic, which many had long seen as an embodiment of democratic and progressive ideals. Local bands of "scouts" joined regular U.S. forces in the takeover of several towns, while others, organized in *cuadrillas* (small squadrons), tried to speed up the surrender of Spanish officials.

Captain General Manuel Macías, in charge of Puerto Rico's defense, cabled the Spanish minister of war on August 2: "The spirit of the country is generally hostile to our cause." On August 5, referring to recent reforms introduced by Spain, he added: "Not even with autonomy does the majority . . . wish to call itself Spanish preferring American domination." Whether Puerto Ricans desired U.S. "domination" was an open question, but it was now clear—bitterly so to Macías—that the country had ceased to think of itself as Spanish.[3]

Some authors would later recast 1898 as a traumatic moment, but this had more to do with their retrospective evaluation of the consequences of the U.S. rule than with the actual events at the time of the U.S. occupation.[4] All evidence indicates that in 1898, the invasion was seen by most as a positive break with the past.

A New Era: "Bandits," Women, Labor

The period between the collapse of the demoralized Spanish administration and the firm installation of U.S. authority opened a glimpse into the tensions that had shaped Puerto Rican society before 1898. In the mountainous interior, bands or *partidas* of rural poor men of diverse backgrounds (day laborers or *jornaleros*, sharecroppers, outlaws) staged attacks on *haciendas* and stores, in many cases in retribution for years of abuse at the hands of *hacendados*, foremen or merchants. The incidents were varied and complex and also included cases of rape and murder. The *partidas* were most active between August 1898 and February 1899. An informant of U.S. Commissioner Henry K. Carroll, author of a vast report on Puerto Rico, stated in 1899 that "there was a theory that property was going to belong to everybody. That was the opinion held by the country people."[5] If such was the hope of some, they were soon disabused of the notion. The outbursts of violence were rapidly quelled through the intervention of U.S. troops.[6]

But the *partidas* were not the only examples of how the collapse of Spanish rule brought into the open tensions that had until then been largely suppressed. The coming of U.S. rule, for example, led to a clearer separation between church and state as the Catholic Church lost the political and institutional privileges it had enjoyed under Spanish sovereignty. This permitted the legalization of divorce, although still under severe restrictions. Historian Eileen J. Suárez Findlay has shown how couples, and above all women, moved to take advantage of this new freedom that opened the way out of marriages in which many felt more like prisoners than partners.[7]

At the same time, people belonging to diverse currents began to openly promote their views, meeting together and publishing journals that would have been censored before 1898. Freemasons, *espiritistas*, and freethinkers extolled their anti-Catholic and anticlerical sensibilities. A witness informed Commissioner Carroll: "All men that have studied are freethinkers." To Carroll's question "Do you believe in the Scriptures as a revelation?," the informant responded, "Absolutely not." "Catholicism," commented another source, "was a religion by force. It was not permitted not to be a Catholic, and there were a great many people who were Catholics who are now freethinkers; there are . . . many Free Masons too."[8]

The invasion of 1898 also accelerated the rise of a vigorous labor movement. Initial organizing efforts in the shape of artisan associations, mutual-aid organizations, and reading circles emerged in the early 1870s during the period of political liberalism initiated by the revolution of 1868 in Spain. A first series of significant strikes took place in January–February 1895. Besides dockworkers who mobilized in San Juan, Arecibo, Arroyo, and Ponce, there were protests by tailors, masons, woodshop and construction workers, and railroad mechanics in San Juan, by street construction workers in Ponce, and by laborers in some sugar plantations in Ponce, Bayamón, and Añasco. The apparent reason for these simultaneous protests was a sharp increase in the prices of consumer goods. The press at the time described those initiatives as unprecedented: "This is how it starts," commented *La Correspondencia*, "such . . . is the start of the struggle between labor and capital that causes so much worry in the Old continent." Caught between two fires, the liberals of *La Democracia*, while supporting the strikers against the Spanish authorities, also lamented that workers would now discover the power they could muster through united action. One editorial concluded: "May God save Puerto Rico!"[9] The threats to "Puerto

Rico" were thus perceived by these liberals as not only coming from the Spanish authorities but also from within, as the demands of the dispossessed revealed tensions among the inhabitants of the island.

New efforts to organize urban artisans and laborers came soon after with the creation of the journal *Ensayo Obrero* on May 1, 1897, by Spanish-born carpenter Santiago Iglesias and typographers Ramón Romero Rosa and José Ferrer y Ferrer. In July, Iglesias organized the Centro de Estudios Económicos y Sociales. A first mass meeting of workers was convened on March 25, 1898. Led by Iglesias, Romero Rosa, Ferrer, and Eduardo Conde, the gathering was dissolved by the police. Iglesias was arrested soon afterward. Following the U.S. invasion, labor activists took immediate advantage of the new situation. A new publication, *El Porvenir Social*, edited by Romero Rosa, made its appearance, while Puerto Rico's first labor federation, the Federación Regional de los Trabajadores (FRT), was organized on October 23, 1898. This was followed by a strike of typographers in San Juan in November, the first significant labor action under U.S. rule.

This emergence of organized labor as an independent voice was to have a lasting impact on Puerto Rico's political landscape. The leading role in the early organizing efforts belonged to cigarmakers and typographers, groups who cultivated a strong sense of craft identity and pride in their role as labor's intellectual vanguard. The impact of the 1899 May Day celebration, organized by the FRT, was strong enough to prompt the U.S. military governor to decree the eight-hour day, a measure that remained unenforced. The FRT soon split over the question of labor's independence from bourgeois parties. Those insisting that the FRT remain politically independent organized the Federación Libre de Trabajadores (FLT) on June 18, 1899, which rapidly eclipsed its predecessor. The summer of 1900 witnessed new labor battles, which included a call for a general strike of all the skilled trades (bricklayers, painters, carpenters, among others) in San Juan. These efforts met fierce repression. Iglesias and more than sixty labor activists were arrested and charged with diverse violations. Harassment and the possibility of imprisonment led Iglesias and Conde to leave for New York in 1900. In New York, Iglesias came into contact with the American Federation of Labor (AFL), led by Samuel Gompers. By 1901, the FLT affiliated with the AFL.

Meanwhile, the sugar interests—mill owners, cane growers, and all those involved in the sugar trade—perceived the coming of U.S. rule as a step toward the realization of a cherished dream: gaining access to the tariff-protected U.S. sugar market.

Sugar: Dreams of Expansion

Sugar had twice been central to the Puerto Rican economy. The island went through an initial sugar boom in the sixteenth century, which included the growth of a slave-based plantation economy. Nevertheless, while retaining its military significance, the island soon became an economic backwater of the vast Spanish empire. Until 1800, most of the island's sparse population was made up of subsistence farmers, living beyond the reach of state or church. After the Haitian revolution closed down the world's largest producer in the early nineteenth century, Puerto Rico and Cuba—further stimulated by trade reforms introduced by Madrid—entered a sugar boom, again characterized by the expansion of slave plantations. As a result, Puerto Rico's economy was relinked to the world market. Sugar production spread in large parts of the coastal area, while subsistence farmers scurried to the interior where they sought to reproduce their independent mode of production away from the encroaching plantation economy.

Private property had been recognized in Puerto Rico in 1778, a measure that began the differentiation between titled private proprietors and the property-less. Yet many among the latter retained actual access to unused land. The state responded with attempts to coerce them into wage labor. After 1849, all those lacking property titles were required to either rent land or hire themselves out as day laborers. The latter were forced to carry a workbook (*libreta*) indicating their place of employment.

After the 1850s, the sugar plantation regime fell into crisis, caused above all by the fall of world market prices as beet sugar producers came into competition with cane sugar from the tropics. Meanwhile, in 1868 an anti-Spanish rebellion was launched in Puerto Rico. The Grito de Lares included the abolition of slavery among its demands, but it was rapidly crushed. Nevertheless, persistent abolitionist agitation—stimulated in part by the defeat of the Confederacy in the U.S. Civil War, the continued Cuban War of Independence of 1868–78, and slave resistance in the form of conspiracies, escapes, and individual acts of defiance—led to the abolition of slavery in Puerto Rico in 1873 in the context of political upheaval in Spain. There were around 30,000 slaves in Puerto Rico at the time of abolition. To survive in a highly competitive world market, sugar producers now had to modernize their operations while completing the transition to wage labor. This they were unable to do. The sugar industry entered into deep decline.

Meanwhile, the center of economic life shifted to the mountainous interior, where coffee producers enjoyed a thirty-year period of prosperity beginning in the late 1860s. By 1898, the island's principal export crop was coffee, and the western mountainous interior had become the site of a considerable accumulation of wealth in the hands of an *hacendado* class. The rise of the coffee economy dealt a new blow to the subsistence farmer economy as many formerly independent farmers were progressively subordinated to an emerging *hacendado* class, which was to a considerable extent made up of recently arrived immigrants. It was the tension between this impoverished mass and its exploiters that would later manifest itself in the *partidas* in 1898.

The expansion of the coffee economy stood behind the rise of the city of Ponce as an export center, vividly depicted in Manuel Zeno Gandía's 1922 novel *El negocio*. If San Juan remained the official center and the relay point of Spanish rule and church censorship, the southern city emerged as the site of an increasingly self-conscious *criollo* culture, liberal, freethinking, avid for more intense material and spiritual contact with the perceived centers of modern culture, such as the United States and Great Britain. By 1899, the two cities were almost equal in size (32,000–33,000 inhabitants each), and, although the contrast should not be overemphasized, according to U.S. Army physician Bailey K. Ashford, many saw Ponce as the site of the "spirit and culture of Puerto Rico" and despised San Juan's "bureaucratic airs."[10] It was in Ponce that the most significant early *criollo* political party, the Partido Autonomista, was launched in 1887. And it was in Ponce that in 1882 the *criollo* propertied sectors organized an agricultural fair without official support. The *feria-exposición* was an assertion of its sponsors' desire for a wider path toward economic modernization, which would include the end of trade monopolies and the promotion of industries. Spanish merchants were widely seen as the main obstacle to such reforms. They were denounced for their usurious lending rates and for selling at inflated and buying at depressed prices, thus squeezing the earnings of large and small producers. In 1899, the mayor of Guayama would complain to Commissioner Carroll that "on the ruins of agriculture there has risen a flourishing community of merchants." He added, "These merchants are nearly all peninsular Spaniards."[11]

The existing economic configuration was to be radically altered by the onset of U.S. rule. Sugar production rapidly expanded to become the dominant economic sector, marked by the presence of U.S. capital and a total orientation to the U.S. market. Coffee suffered the opposite fate. Coffee producers lost their protected markets in Cuba and Spain and had to compete in the U.S. market with the better established Brazilian coffee. Badly hurt by a devastating hurricane in 1899, the coffee industry recovered slowly, then stagnated and went into decline after 1914. But all this was still in the future. At first, coffee growers also hoped that U.S. rule would allow them to supplement their traditional outlets with easier access to the North American market while liberating them from the monopolistic abuses of Spanish merchants.

Liberal Hopes and the Model Republic

Given the hopes expressed by different currents of Puerto Rican society regarding the end of Spanish rule, it is not surprising that the first two political parties organized after 1898—the Partido Federal and the Partido Republicano—coincided in their basic demand regarding Puerto Rico's relation to the United States. Both parties favored the immediate transformation of Puerto Rico into an organized territory of the United States, in preparation for its eventual admission as a new state.

Both parties were reincarnations of different wings of the pre-1898 autonomist movement, which had gone through several mutations after the founding of the Partido Autonomista in 1887. During the nineteenth century, decisions taken in Madrid had tended to impress a specific dynamic on the island's political evolution. Of particular importance was the fact that in 1837, Spanish liberals, in one of their moments of ascendance in the peninsula, had excluded the colonies from the Spanish constitutional umbrella and decreed that Cuba, Puerto Rico, and the Philippines would be governed through "special laws" to be drafted at a later date. But the special laws never came. Thus, after 1837, through the many and complex fluctuations of peninsular politics, from monarchical reaction to moderate liberalism, the colonies remained under strict colonial administration, headed by all-powerful governors. Meanwhile, by making Puerto Rico and Cuba exceptional areas within the Spanish polity, peninsular liberals fostered the budding sense of distinct Puerto Rican and Cuban identities among their insular counterparts. Insular reformers gradually concluded that they had to place their liberalism outside the circle of Spanish patriotism or, at least, demand the recognition of an autonomous space within it.

It was only in 1865, in the aftermath of Spain's defeat at the hands of the resistance that had regained the independence of the neighboring Dominican Republic, that Madrid called on the colonies to propose possible ways of formulating the special laws promised in 1837. The liberal members of the Puerto Rican commission who made the trip to Madrid—José Julián Acosta, Segundo

Ruiz Belvis, and Francisco Mariano Quiñones—presented a brief in defense of the abolition of slavery as well as other reforms. Meanwhile, liberal, self-taught sociologist Salvador Brau argued for the elimination of the *libreta* or work-passbook system. But these efforts proved fruitless: the proposals were shelved. One of the commissioners, Ruiz Belvis, concluded that only revolution could bring about the desired changes.

Indeed, by 1867 a wing of this nascent liberalism had opted for the creation of clandestine clubs. Its main leader, Ramón Emeterio Betances, a physician, was an abolitionist and revolutionary democrat. As a student, Betances had participated in the upheavals of 1848 in Paris. The ideas of the projected revolution are best summarized by his 1867 manifesto "The Ten Commandments of the Free Man," which were (1) abolition of slavery, (2) the right to vote on all taxes, (3) freedom of religion, (4) freedom of speech, (5) freedom of the press, (6) freedom to trade, (7) freedom of assembly, (8) the right to bear arms, (9) the inviolability of the citizen, and (10) the right to elect authorities. In an emblematic literary effort, Betances translated into Spanish a biography of Haitian revolutionary Toussaint-Louverture, written by the radical American abolitionist Wendell Phillips.

Inspired from afar by Betances, an insurrection erupted and was rapidly crushed in the town of Lares in September 1868. A few days before, a far more powerful revolution had been launched in eastern Cuba, leading to a decade-long guerrilla war of independence. But 1868 was also a year of revolution in Spain, which eventually led to the short-lived Spanish republic of 1873-74.

It was in that context that Puerto Rico's first political party—the Partido Liberal Reformista—was formed in 1870–71, led by Acosta and José Ramón Abad, among others. The new party hoped to end Puerto Rico's status of colonial inferiority through integration into a liberal Spain. There were encouraging signs as Spanish liberalism decreed the abolition of slavery in 1873 and granted Puerto Rico representation in the Spanish parliament. But the repressive response to the Cuban insurrection tended to limit metropolitan tolerance of colonial demands for more rights. With the fall of the republic in 1874, Spain settled into the conservative, constitutional-monarchist regime of the Restoration, while its army pursued the crushing of the Cuban insurgency. In this context, Puerto Rican liberalism evolved toward the adoption of an autonomist program, a process that culminated in the founding of the Partido Autonomista in 1887 under the leadership of Román Baldorioty de Castro.[12]

In Puerto Rico, politics was then hardly differentiated from the world of journalism, which was in turn the monopoly of a thin literate sphere. The political class was made up of representatives of the *criollo* possessing classes and of an urban-professional milieu, imbued with the ideals of nineteenth-century economic and political liberalism and, in some cases, more radical democratic currents. Most of these men—and they were almost invariably men—had studied in Spain, France, or the United States, where they had assimilated diverse dosages of peninsular liberalism (including its admiration for British parliamentarism), French republicanism, and U.S. constitutionalism. To the authoritarian "I say so" typical of colonial governors, liberals counterposed "the clash of ideas through which enlightenment is attained."[13] Many returned home from their sojourns abroad sharply conscious of the backwardness of not only Puerto Rico but also Spain itself, when compared to some of its more advanced neighbors or to the United States. For example, the hero of Alejandro Tapias's 1882 novel *Póstumo el Transmigrado*, a man reincarnated in the body of a woman, escapes from Madrid to Paris and eventually travels to Boston for a feminist convention in search of more advanced ideas regarding women's rights.

A humorous representation of the vision that inspired this modernizing-liberal current is Tapia's brief text "Puerto Rico as Seen by the Half-Blind without Glasses," in which a nearsighted reader looks up Puerto Rico in an encyclopedia and is overjoyed to read a description of an island endowed with an active port, an efficient system of roads and railroads, diversified industrial and agricultural sectors, widely distributed landed property, a free press, several universities, and a prosperous peasantry that actively participates in local government. But this vision of a Puerto Rico internally differentiated into dynamic and interacting political, economic, and cultural spheres linked to the world through a diversified trade of products and ideas turns out to be a mirage: upon putting his spectacles on, the reader discovers that there was not even an entry for Puerto Rico in the encyclopedia. From the watchtowers of modernity, Puerto Rico was simply invisible. Ten years earlier, Baldorioty had similarly reported back from the Paris Universal Exposition of 1867 and dreamed of the time when Puerto Rico would be attractively represented on such occasions where an emergent modernity proudly displayed its achievements to itself.[14]

For the rural poor—the overwhelming majority of the population—these discussions were distant echoes, inaudible through the rigors of a harsh struggle for subsistence. Yet it was this shoeless, anemic, underfed, unschooled majority, reduced to the use of the coarsest clothing and utensils, who planted, tended, weeded, watered, harvested, processed, and transported the cane, coffee, and tobacco grown in the valleys of the coast and the highlands of the interior. Most of the income generated by the selling of the products of their labor in the world market did not make its way back to them: it was the substance of the profits of *hacendados* and traders. Nor did it return to them in the form of state services, such as health facilities or schools, which remained absolutely inadequate and in most areas nonexistent. They resisted the exactions of their employers as best they could, to the point that planters from Guayama, in a report examined by Luis A. Figueroa, described them as conducting "a passive but constant . . . strike," given their tendency to withdraw from waged work as soon as they earned enough for their subsistence or found other sources for it.[15]

After Baldorioty de Castro's death in 1889, the leadership of the Partido Autonomista passed into the hands of a younger generation: Luis Muñoz Rivera, José Celso Barbosa, José De Diego, and Rosendo Matienzo Cintrón, among others. These men would also dominate Puerto Rican party-politics through the first period of U.S. rule. While the autonomists insisted on reforms, Puerto Rican separatists continued conspiring from New York, the Dominican Republic, and St. Thomas in close collaboration with the Cuban independence movement. These efforts included the creation in New York of the Puerto Rico Section of the Partido Revolucionario Cubano. Some of its members adopted in 1895 what eventually came to be popularly and officially accepted as the Puerto Rican flag. This was an early emblematic indication of the key role that New York City would come to play in Puerto Rican life. But the New York revolutionaries were divided. They were all separatists with respect to Spain, but some tended to see separation from Spain as the preamble to annexation to the United States.[16]

In Puerto Rico, Partido Autonomista leader Muñoz Rivera elaborated a strategy based on a deep feeling of weakness. Puerto Rico, he argued in 1891, lacked an active peasantry, a militant youth, and a committed moneyed class. Reforms could be obtained only through alliances with metropolitan parties.[17] In this he did not exclude taking advantage of the need of Madrid to respond to the renewed Cuban insurgency after 1895. This led him to articulate an antirevolutionary but oppositional line that allowed him to both condemn the Cuban revolutionaries and blame Spanish misrule for the support they enjoyed. Reform, he argued, was the best antidote against revolution. In 1897, his efforts led to the signing of a pact with the Spanish Partido Liberal, led by Práxedes M. Sagasta, the largest opposition party to Antonio Cánovas's ruling Partido Conservador.

A wing of the autonomists led by Barbosa rejected the pact. They opposed dissolving their party into the Partido Liberal, which was furthermore a monarchist organization, while most autonomists were republicans. The party split, but Muñoz Rivera's maneuvering bore fruit when, on August 8, 1897, Italian anarchist Michele Angiolillo assassinated Cánovas and Sagasta replaced him as head of the Spanish government. Sagasta soon instituted autonomist reforms for Cuba and Puerto Rico in an attempt to appease Cuban resistance and postpone U.S. intervention, but it was too late. By the time Puerto Rico's autonomist cabinet was appointed, the United States had declared war.

The early demand for statehood formulated by the Puerto Rican autonomists in 1898 did not imply a repudiation of the autonomist ideal. Puerto Rico's autonomists imagined the United States to be, as they put it, a "State of states and a Republic of Republics."[18] For them, the U.S. occupation seemed to open a grand vista toward a prosperous future. Upon annexation, Puerto Rico's politically and economically dominant sectors hoped to enjoy all the advantages of integration, on an equal footing with the other states, into the most dynamic capitalist-industrial economy of the time. They would become the insular, Puerto Rican portion of the North American ruling classes.

Not all voices were as enthused with the coming of U.S. rule. Some leaders of the *separatista* movement, such as Betances and Eugenio María de Hostos, issued early warnings regarding the less than democratic imperial dynamics brewing within the "model republic."[19] But these early critical views were not representative of the initial reaction of the more influential Puerto Rican political currents, as we have seen.

The Foraker Act

Meanwhile, an intense debate raged in U.S. policy-making circles over which policies should be adopted regarding the newly acquired territories. Concerning Puerto Rico, Guam, and the Philippines, the Treaty of Paris provided that their "civil rights and political status . . . shall be determined by the Congress." What to do, then, with these islands? The question sparked an intense discussion. Two of the most popular authors in the English language entered the fray from opposite sides as Mark Twain denounced U.S. colonialism while Rudyard Kipling famously exhorted the U.S. to pick up the "White Man's Burden."[20]

Would the United States annex Puerto Rico and the Philippines as territories and future states? Would it facilitate their transition to independence? Or would it retain them without annexing them, turning them into colonies, and if so, what kind of government should it install there? Some observers warned that if the United States annexed them as new or future states, it would bring into the Union areas populated by "inferior races." If the United States, on the other hand, retained control over the new possessions without placing them on the path to statehood, it would break with its republican structures and traditions. This commitment to the preservation of a specifically white republic was both anticolonial and racist. Such was the position held by key Democrats, including presidential candidate William Jennings Bryan. Others, such as progressive, anticorporate South Dakota senator Richard Pettigrew, opposed colonial control as incompatible with democracy in the United States and contrary to the interests of the conquered peoples. To oppose the colonial option was to protect both the Filipino people and American democracy from the threat of empire.

A considerable portion of the opposition to the new colonial policies came from middle-class and labor currents, which also denounced the rise of the trusts and large corporations. The 1880s and 1890s had seen the emergence of protest movements aimed at what were perceived as abuses by banks, railroads, land speculators, and grain corporations, efforts that had coalesced in the creation of the People's Party in 1891. Many Populists opposed the war with Spain while favoring recognition of the Cuban rebels and of their government in exile. The Cuban rebels argued that recognition would guarantee Cuban independence without the need of U.S. military intervention. But as it moved toward intervention, the McKinley administration refused to recognize Cuban belligerency, which only increased the suspicion of many that its support for *Cuba libre* was a cover for U.S. imperial designs.

These middle-class and labor groups saw the imperial urge as another manifestation of the voracity of the corporations they had for years denounced at home. The trusts, they argued, were the enemies of democracy—of the farmer, the consumer, and the worker—at home, and they were the promoters of empire abroad.[21] This anticorporate indictment of U.S. colonialism was to influence the ideas of some of the early critics of U.S. rule in Puerto Rico, such as Matienzo Cintrón and Rafael López Landrón.

The possibility of free trade between the newly acquired islands and the United States, which would result from annexation, also worried American tobacco growers and the beet-sugar industry: cane sugar and tobacco from Puerto Rico, the Philippines, and Cuba would strengthen the sugar refining and cigar manufacturing trusts by giving them access to cheaper raw materials.

In mid-1900, Congress approved the Foraker Act, which organized a civilian government for Puerto Rico, thus replacing the military government that had ruled the island from 1898 to 1900. Among the features of the Foraker Act was the imposition of a temporary tariff on goods moving between Puerto Rico and the United States amounting to 15 percent of the duties applicable to foreign goods entering the latter. This apparently secondary disposition had profound implications. To understand them and the debate they generated, we must consider a few aspects of previous U.S. territorial expansion.

U.S. Territorial Expansion and the Insular Cases

Since its inception as a result of its war of independence, the United States had been an expanding republic. The expansion was carried out at the expense of the native inhabitants of the land, who were progressively dispossessed, as well as through the marginalization of Mexicans in the vast expanses taken from the republic to the south. Politically, the newly acquired lands were organized as territories under the supervision of Congress and the federal executive. As the white-settler population grew and as sectors of the economically and politically influential layers in each territory demanded it, the territories were admitted into the Union. Built on the graves of the Native American peoples and on the subordination of Mexicans by Anglos and accompanied until 1860 with the persistence and extension of slavery, this was nevertheless a republican form of expansion, insofar as the new territories were expected to and did successively join the Union under the same conditions as the founding states. It was the hope of the leaders of the Partido Republicano and the Partido Federal in Puerto Rico that this model of republican expansion (excluding, of course, the displacement of the native population) would be extended to the island, leading to statehood after a preparatory territorial stage.

Past U.S. Supreme Court rulings had furthermore determined that the U.S. Constitution covered U.S. territories, even if they were not yet states of the Union.[22] Among the constitutional dispositions that Congress could not depart from when organizing or administering the territories was the prohibition of tariffs (known as the "uniformity clause") between the parts of the United States. The significance of the temporary tariff included in the Foraker Act thus becomes evident: through the Foraker Act, Congress was organizing U.S. rule over Puerto Rico, but by imposing a tariff on goods coming from the island, it was treating it as *not* part of the United States. Through the Foraker Act, Congress both affirmed U.S. rule over Puerto Rico *and* defined the island as foreign territory.

For the anticolonialists, the Foraker Act was a constitutional scandal, a blow directed at the heart of the republic by the emergent imperial currents. The United States, the critics insisted, could legitimately govern Puerto Rico as a future state, or it could recognize its independence (as in the case of Cuba), but it could not, within the limits of the Constitution, retain control over it while demarcating it as not part of the republic.

The Supreme Court was soon forced to pass judgment on the constitutionality of the Foraker Act. Its decisions in the so-called Insular Cases, and above all in the case known as *Downes v. Bidwell*, became a key moment in the definition of the new relation between Puerto Rico and the United States.[23] In a 5–4 decision, the Court upheld the constitutionality of the Foraker Act, although the members of the majority offered different rationales for their votes. The decision of Justice Edward Douglass White proved to be the most influential.

White differentiated between incorporated and nonincorporated territories: it was up to Congress to determine whether it wished to incorporate or not incorporate a territory that had come under U.S. control. Mere possession by the U.S. did not imply incorporation into the Union. Incorporated territories were part of the Union, and its inhabitants were fully protected by the Constitution; unincorporated territories were possessions but not part of the United States. They were not foreign in an international sense, since they were under U.S. sovereignty, but they were "foreign in a domestic sense," since they had not been incorporated into the United States. They were "merely appurtenant there to as a possession."[24] The North American state in Puerto Rico thus became what Pedro Cabán has termed an "exceptional extension of the metropolitan state."[25] For the critics of the Foraker Act, the doctrine elaborated by Justice White was nothing but a judicial rationalization for empire, a bending of the Constitution to the imperatives of a colonial project. White tended to confirm such criticisms as he argued that rejecting the notion of nonincorporated territories would bar the United States from acquiring areas that were strategically important but that it did not wish to bring into the Union.

According to White's doctrine, basic individual rights had to be respected in such territories, even if incorporation or the extension of other aspects of the Constitution (a new distinction resulting from these decisions) was a prerogative of Congress. Colonialism was thus certified as constitutional as long as it was liberal, that is to say, as long as it respected certain basic individual rights. This combination of relative liberalism and colonial subordination has been a feature of Puerto Rican politics since 1900. As Richard Levins has pointed out, apologists of U.S. rule often refer to its liberal form while ignoring its colonial nature, while many critics only consider the colonial nature, as if the form were unimportant. But a comprehensive—in Levins's case, a Marxist—understanding of Puerto Rico's political evolution must take both features into account.[26]

There was an additional twist to Puerto Rico's new status. Through legislative and judicial actions, Puerto Rico had been defined as not part of the United States, yet Congress nevertheless organized its relation with it in a manner similar to the traditional territorial model. Instead of making the island subject to special colonial legislation, it made U.S. federal legislation extensive to the island (unless otherwise determined by Congress). Beginning in 1901, unimpeded trade was established between the island and the United States, while Puerto Ricans were made U.S. citizens in 1917. Thus, while determining that Puerto Rico was a possession but not part of the United States, Washington imposed on it much of the framework that had normally led to statehood. From the start, installed in what we may call the orbit of nonincorporation, the island was thus pushed and pulled in opposite directions: increasingly tied to the United States and insistently defined as not part of it.

Congress not only ignored the request for annexation formulated by insular political parties but also, through the Foraker Act, instituted an insular government that left little room for Puerto Rican participation. The Foraker Act created an insular government headed by a governor, a cabinet, and a five-member supreme court, all appointed by the president of the United States. A bicameral legislature was composed of an eleven-member executive council (including the six members of the cabinet) also appointed by the president and a thirty-five-member House of Delegates, elected every two years. The extent of the suffrage was left for the insular legislature to determine, which in turn established universal manhood suffrage in 1904. The House and the municipalities were the most significant forms of Puerto Rican participation in the new state structure.

Imperialism, Colonialism, and the Puerto Rican Anomaly

As the exhortation by Kipling reminds us, imperial models were not lacking at the time. The 1870s and 1880s were a period of crisis in the world capitalist economy. Imperial states scrambled to cordon off existing or potential commercial circuits, areas of investment, and sources of raw materials as well as the outposts needed to defend them and/or the routes linking them. Between 1870 and 1900, Britain acquired 4.7 million square miles, France 3.5 million square miles, and Germany 1 million square miles of overseas territories.[27] Ruling over a growing industrial power, the dominant sectors of the United States could, and did, disagree on how to respond to these developments, but they could hardly ignore them. In fact, similar expansionist tendencies were at work within the United States. The spectacle of growing unemployment and idle factories, combined with an unprecedented rise of social unrest—the labor rebellions of 1877, the rise of the Knights of Labor, the agrarian and populist insurgency, the Pullman strike—fed diverse versions of so-called glut theories, which argued that U.S. productive capacity had outgrown its internal market. It was this sense of a growing productive potential paralyzed by a hard-to-define barrier and not the reaching of some geographical limit that helped popularize Frederick Jackson Turner's notion, formulated in 1893, that the United States had entered a new epoch due to the closing of the frontier.

Since the 1880s, Secretary of State Blaine had proposed an active search for foreign markets, which he hoped to pry open by combining protectionist measures and the enticement of reciprocity treaties with the United States. If the consolidation of British world influence had the Suez Canal as one of its material supports, the vision of U.S. influence spurred on the project of a canal through Central America, an undertaking that also implied the construction of a new navy, capable of protecting such a strategic post.

Growing industrial capacity both suggested the need for commercial expansion and provided the technical basis for a new navy. Military theorist Alfred Thayer Mahan argued in turn that further industrial growth would depend on the projection of naval power. In the ideas and decisions of key policy makers, such as Roosevelt, Lodge, and Elihu Root, such inclinations coalesced into an active expansionist project. Its opening tour was the war with Spain.[28] Regarding Puerto Rico, Senator John T. Morgan (D-Ala.) summarized the views of many when he argued that Puerto Rico was too small to be independent and too strategically located to be left to others.[29]

The acquisition of Puerto Rico was followed by a series of actions that firmly evidenced U.S. hegemony over the Caribbean and Central America, including the imposition of the Platt Amendment on Cuba, which gave the United States the right to intervene in the new republic; the signing of the Hay-Pauncefote Treaty (1901), through which Britain recognized the right of the United States to construct and fortify an isthmian canal; the sponsoring of Panama's separation from Colombia in 1903 to facilitate the completion of that project; the formulation of the "Roosevelt Corollary" to the Monroe Doctrine in 1904, claiming for the United States the exclusive right to military intervention in the Caribbean on behalf of "civilized nations"; the establishment of a customs receivership in the Dominican Republic in 1905; repeated interventions in Cuba in 1906, 1912, and 1917, as well as the extended occupations of Haiti in 1915–34 and of the Dominican Republic in 1916–24; the acquisition of the Virgin Islands from Denmark in 1917; and intermittent interventions in Nicaragua leading to eventual occupation in 1927.

As can be seen from this list, U.S. imperialism, unlike its European predecessors, did not set out to build a formal *colonial* empire. Its rise to global influence implied a decoupling of economic and territorial expansion, a fact that was to deeply affect the world architecture of the American Century. But we should bear in mind that in its complex route to noncolonial yet global hegemony, the United States did carry along with it a few colonies. Puerto Rico has thus been a colony of the American Century: an exception to the rule, neither part of the United States nor of its informal empire.

Racism and Imperialism

The North American state that took over Puerto Rico in 1898 did not rule over a homogeneous social formation, nor was it the color-blind exemplar of civic ideals that many *criollo* liberal autonomists imagined. As Rogers Smith has shown, definitions of American citizenship had in the past reserved it for those endowed with certain capacities, which the articulators of such visions in turn associated with whiteness.[30] More immediately, the 1890s witnessed the consolidation of Jim Crow in the South, a process that should not be overlooked when examining U.S. colonial policy. Two processes intersected during this crucial period in the evolution of the American republic: the rise of southern reaction against the efforts of Radical Reconstruction to reshape the South between 1867 and 1877 coincided with the growing conservatism of the Republican Party as it attuned itself to the consolidation of big business and reacted to the growth of social unrest in the industrializing North. The context was thus created for federal acquiescence to the institutionalization of segregation in the South as the reinstated white oligarchies rewrote their state constitutions through the 1890s.

The racist Jim Crow doctrines accompanying segregation could have potentially served as sources of opposition to the taking of territories occupied by populations considered inferior. But to the extent that such territorial expansion did occur, racist views advised against incorporating alien populations as equals into the Union and favored instead the institution of some form of colonial tutelage over them. Conversely, the justifications formulated by northern expansionists of colonial control over other lands based on the alleged political immaturity of their inhabitants seemed to legitimate southern visions of a castelike hierarchical social order. Wall Street and Jim Crow could thus clasp hands as reconciled associates of a nascent imperialism. Social Darwinism, popular at the time, could also be brought into this ideological mix as a doctrine compatible with racial hierarchies, colonial projects, and the competitive logic of capitalist accumulation.

Besides being an epoch of nascent big business, southern counterrevolution, and new imperial projection, the Gilded Age witnessed the remaking of the American working class through mass migration over the Atlantic and to a lesser extent the Pacific. The perceived need to control this growing urban population, often seen as culturally inferior by the older ruling sectors of U.S. society, was another sphere where antiegalitarian orientations could, and did, emerge. As Eric Foner has argued, "The retreat from the ideals of Reconstruction went hand in hand with the resurgence of an Anglo-Saxonism that united patriotism, xenophobia, and an ethnocultural definition of nationhood in a renewed rhetoric of racial exclusiveness." All this implied a retreat from the "egalitarian vision of citizenship spawned by the Civil War."[31] Mark S. Weiner refers to what he calls "teutonic constitutionalism," an influential judicial doctrine that justified the limitation of the enjoyment of certain rights to "superior races." Such theories, he argues, had an important role in the formulation of the doctrine of nonincorporation.[32]

Indeed, the U.S. Supreme Court, presided over by Justice Fuller, which legalized Puerto Rico's and the Philippines' new colonial condition, had not long before declared racial segregation constitutional in its infamous *Plessy v. Ferguson* decision. Besides validating racial segregation within the Union and colonialism beyond it, the Fuller court also blocked anticorporate and labor reforms by limiting the potential scope of the Sherman Anti-Trust Act, certifying the use of injunctions against strikes and labor unions, and annulling social and labor legislation (which limited daily working hours, for example).

General George W. Davis, military governor of Puerto Rico in 1899–1900, had events in the South very much in mind when considering future U.S. policies toward its new possession: "It is well known that many of the Southern States . . . are proceeding to disenfranchise the illiterate colored population. . . . If the disenfranchisement of the Negro illiterates of the Union can be justified, the same in Porto Rico can be defended on equally good grounds." Nor did he forget the policies regarding "Indians" and immigrants: "The vast majority of the people are no more fit to take part in self-government than our reservation Indians, from whom the suffrage is withheld unless they pay taxes. They certainly are far inferior . . . to the Chinese, who for very good reasons are forbidden to land on our shores." Seen as dark and "only a few steps removed from a primitive state of nature"[33] and/or as products of a decrepit Spanish-Catholic obscurantism, Puerto Ricans were considered by many to be incapable of self-government.

Yet U.S. visions of Puerto Rico and of the Philippines were not identical: Puerto Ricans, Lanny Thompson has argued, tended to be "othered" as whiter, less alien subjects.[34] This may help explain why, from the start, U.S. rule of the Philippines was seen as temporary, if not necessarily brief, while Puerto Rico was seen as probably easier to assimilate and destined to remain under permanent control of the United States.

Not surprisingly, how to respond to this situation became a central aspect of Puerto Rican politics after 1900. Diverse responses could and would be articulated: Puerto Ricans could claim equal rights and self-government either as would-be Americans or through affirmations of Puerto Rican self-worth or through combinations of both. They could demand statehood, independence, or some form of autonomy. But such debates, as the rise of the labor movement or the hopes pinned on access to the U.S. market remind us, did not revolve only around questions of political equality, government structure, or national identity. Bitter conflicts about the production of wealth and the distribution of income, the profits of capital and the wages of labor, and the contrasting fortunes of different crops were no less significant. Indeed, in the immediate aftermath of 1898 and within the newly created relation of non-incorporation, the island was to undergo a profound economic transformation. The invasion of 1898 remade Puerto Rico's social classes and connected them to the world in new ways, thus conditioning future responses to U.S. colonial rule. It is to this transformation that we turn in the following chapter.

2

RESHAPING PUERTO RICO'S ECONOMY, 1898–1934

The first transformation of the Puerto Rican economy during the American Century took place in the immediate aftermath of the Spanish-American War. After a brief transition period, the Foraker Act of 1900 allowed for unrestricted trade between Puerto Rico and the United States. "An economic revolution from above and from the outside," as Miguel Guerra Mondragón put it, looking back from 1947, "was about to take place."[1]

Given the extraordinary productivity advantage of U.S. industry and agriculture, the installation of "free trade" between both regions had several immediate and medium-term consequences in Puerto Rico. Export activities with an ample market in the United States, such as raw sugar, tobacco, and needlework industries, expanded tremendously. The income thus generated was increasingly spent on imports from the United States. The expanding sugar plantation economy reshuffled social relations in the coastal plains. Tobacco growing and cigar and cigarette manufacturing also expanded and, like the sugar industry, attracted considerable U.S. capital investments. The needlework industry, which employed mostly women and children in their homes, also grew, above all after 1914. The principal market—indeed, practically the only market—for these products was the United States. By 1930, almost 95 percent of Puerto Rico's external trade was with the United States. By contrast, coffee production entered a period of stagnation, crisis, and, after 1914, collapse.

These shifts entailed changes in land tenure, income distribution, internal migration, and settlement; shifts also occurred in the relative weight of Puerto Rican and foreign owners of productive assets. Between 1900 and 1910, the population of Puerto Rico grew by 17.3 percent, but population in the cane-growing municipalities increased an estimated 45.4 percent while population in the coffee-growing municipalities decreased by 4.2 percent. Guánica, the area where the largest sugar mill was erected, experienced phenomenal

MAP 2.1. Crop Distribution and Demographic Growth, 1900–1935

Coffee region: 28%
Cane region: 72%
Tobacco region: 103%

0   20   40   60 Miles

population growth of 121.4 percent in the same period.[2] This tendency continued into the 1930s (see Map 2.1). The working and domestic environment of most Puerto Ricans was deeply transformed as market relations penetrated into the core of the social fabric.

If most rural dwellers had been propertyless before 1898, arrangements that in the past had allowed them some access to land for subsistence purposes now gave way to a starker condition of wage dependence. The situation of wage earners was particularly precarious, since the sugar industry could offer employment only during five or six months of the year. Nevertheless, basic improvements in urban sanitation and health management helped reduce the death rate considerably, from 30 per 1,000 in 1899 to 18 per 1,000 in 1940–41. This, combined with a consistently high birth rate (around 40 per 1,000), led to rapid population growth during the decades following the U.S. occupation.

Sugar, it should be underlined, was the decisive but not the only sector of the Puerto Rican economy. By 1935, sugarcane was grown in around one-third (34.5 percent) of all cultivated land (up from 15 percent in 1899). Coffee and tobacco combined accounted for another third of the total cultivated land. The remaining third was dedicated to food crops for local consumption. The undeniable centrality of sugar should not lead us to reduce the insular economy to a mere "sugar economy."

Looking at the transformations of this period, World War I emerges as an important moment of change. The war coincided with the most prosperous period ever of the sugar industry, a deepening of the crisis in the coffee region, the beginning of a rapid expansion of a needlework industry, the largest and most successful labor mobilizations to date, and a quickening of migration to the United States, stimulated by the recruitment of Puerto Rican workers to war production activities in the United States.

Colonial Initiatives, Native Hopes

The economic consequences of U.S. policies toward Puerto Rico were not unexpected. Sugar interests in Puerto Rico, for example, eagerly demanded the lifting of all tariffs on Puerto Rican sugar going into the United States. Their woes during the three decades prior to 1898 explain their wager on free trade with the United States.

World capitalism went through a long depression after 1873. The sugar industry was hit by falling prices, a symptom of the problem of overcapacity that affected many other sectors. Competition between tropical cane sugar and

European beet sugar sharpened. In Puerto Rico and other cane-growing areas, this context demanded a transition from the old *ingenio* to the modern sugar mill, or *central*. This implied not only a complex technical evolution but a differentiation of the *hacendado* class, as some became *centralistas* while others lost their *ingenios* and became mere cane growers, or *colonos*. The installation of the costly *centrales* and the creation of stable and reliable coordination between the *centrales* and the *colonos* in turn demanded the consolidation of a rural proletariat, available above all during the crucial period of the cane harvest, or *zafra*. This financial, technical, and social transition would have been a considerable challenge under any circumstances, but it was further hindered by the restrictions on exports to the peninsula imposed by the Spanish government, a policy that sought to protect Andalusian producers. As a consequence, already before 1898 the United States had become the main market for Puerto Rico's sugar.

By 1897, it was evident that Puerto Rico's sugar producers were drowning in the rough waters of a depressed world market. They had not managed to make the transition from the *ingenio* to the *central*. Not surprisingly, they became progressively convinced that their future depended on gaining freer access to the U.S. sugar market. The American market was a protected market. In other words, foreign raw sugar paid a tariff upon entering the U.S. market. As long as the United States needed to import sugar to satisfy its needs, the tariff guaranteed domestic producers a price higher than the world market price, since the price of raw sugar in the United States was the world market price plus the tariff paid by foreign sugar. It was this privilege that Puerto Rican producers were seeking through free access to the protected U.S. market.

For the very same reason that Puerto Rico's *azucareros* requested unrestricted trade with the United States, North American beet-sugar interests opposed it: they wished to keep Puerto Rican, Cuban, and Philippine cane sugar out of the U.S. market. But insular sugar had a key ally in the struggle for "free trade": North American cane-sugar refining corporations, such as the American Sugar Refining Company and the National Sugar Refining Company—the so-called Sugar Trust—interested in obtaining cheaper raw sugar and in directly investing in production in the newly acquired cane-growing areas. Not surprisingly, U.S. antitrust activists denounced the plans of the American refiners, who they were convinced had their eye on the land and labor of the new possessions.

In the end, Congress arrived at what seemed like a compromise. After a brief transition, the Foraker Act allowed for the free entry of Puerto Rican goods into the U.S. market. But, pressured by the beet lobby, Congress imposed a 500-

acre limit on the amount of land a corporation could own in Puerto Rico. The measure was intended to limit the expansion of large-scale cane production. But the compromise was only apparent: while free trade went into effect in 1901, the 500-acre law remained unenforced for almost four decades. Such disregard for the law was an indication of the favor sugar interests enjoyed among the U.S. officials assigned to administer the newly acquired territory. In 1917, the Jones Act, which replaced the Foraker Act, retained the 500-acre limitation and ordered a study of the holdings violating it. The study concluded that 477 partnerships or corporations held more than 500 acres. It was submitted to the Committee of Pacific Islands and Puerto Rico, which took no further action.[3]

In 1899, while conducting his survey of conditions in Puerto Rico, U.S. Commissioner Henry K. Carroll argued to his Puerto Rican interlocutors that "it seems to me extremely important . . . that you should diversify your industries." Carroll commented that the experience of the United States "shows that if you want to establish a new industry, you have to protect it."[4] The recommendation regarding diversification through tariff protection as opposed to overspecialization as a result of "free trade" went unheeded. By the 1920s, U.S. capital had occupied key areas of Puerto Rico's economy, which had not followed the diversified path favored by Carroll.

But through this process, the state did not limit itself to establishing unimpeded trade and ignoring the 500-acre disposition. It also engaged in the creation of an infrastructure for the expansion of the sugar industry. The construction of a vast irrigation system on the southeastern coast, which began operating in 1914, was the most spectacular example of this. Irrigation payments were within the reach of only the most productive farmers. The system thus promoted the replacement of extensive or underutilized farms with more capitalized operations.

The Hollander Act of 1901 introduced a tax of 2 percent on the assessed value of rural property. Property value assessors for tax purposes were to be appointed by the governor. This measure sparked a wave of protests, and the tax was subsequently reduced to 1 percent. However, the governor retained the power to appoint the assessors, while in the United States this was typically done by elected municipal officials. Governor Charles H. Allen was explicit about his intentions: "I'd tax a little life into them. Every Portorican has a right to demand that every acre of rich sugar land should be developed, and I'd tax it until they had to put up or shut up."[5] High assessments would force large landowners with idle lands to sell. They also forced many small property owners to enter the market economy, either as small producers or as wageworkers, in order to obtain dollars to pay the tax. Consequently, the tax measure promoted both the rise of capitalist agriculture based on the exploitation of a vast sea of wage laborers and the fragmentation of some existing large landholdings. Thus, the impact of both the irrigation and property taxes was compatible with a rise in the actual number of active farms in Puerto Rico, a point we return to below.

Sugar: Reversal of Fortune

Along with a world capitalist economy that entered a new period of expansion in the late 1890s, the economy of Puerto Rico grew rapidly after 1900. The sugar industry went from depression to boom. The transition from the *ingenio* to the *central* was rapidly completed. Between 1900 and 1910, sugar production grew 331 percent, from 81,000 to 349,000 tons. By the early 1930s, Puerto Rico was providing around 15 percent of the raw sugar in the U.S. market. A sector of Puerto Rican mill owners, cane growers, traders, and others involved in related industries (construction materials, iron works) benefited from this 1898 expansion, thus forming the nucleus of a new colonial bourgeoisie.

While Puerto Rican or resident (Spanish, French) mill owners and many *colonos* prospered, they nevertheless had to adapt to the growing presence of U.S. corporate capital. By the early 1930s, almost half of Puerto Rico's cane was ground by *centrales* owned by the four U.S. sugar companies: the South Porto Rico, the Central Aguirre, the Fajardo, and the United Porto Rico sugar companies. This inflow of U.S. capital was linked to the changes occurring within the United States. There, a few enterprises known as the Sugar Trust had gained oligopolistic control of the sugar refining business during the 1890s. The four U.S. corporations operating in Puerto Rico were vertically integrated with U.S. sugar refineries—such as the American and National sugar refining companies—which also owned *centrales* and other sugar operations in Cuba and the Dominican Republic.[6]

A snapshot of the sugar industry by the early 1930s looked as follows. There were forty-one *centrales* in Puerto Rico; eleven were owned by four North American sugar companies. In 1937, Esteban Bird estimated that the four U.S. sugar companies administered (owned or leased) around one-fourth of the cropland in cane farms.[7] These were the more advanced installations and processed around half of Puerto Rico's raw sugar. Half of the cane harvest was milled by the thirty *centrales* owned by Puerto Rican or resident interests. Around 6,000 *colonos*, including large employers and medium and small farmers, were in turn linked to the *centrales* in a relation of both conflict and dependence.

The whole edifice of the sugar industry, and the wealth of the mill owners and all but the smallest *colonos*, was of course built on the labor of the sugarcane proletariat. At the height of the *zafra*, the industry employed between 100,000 and 120,000 laborers, 90 percent as field workers. Anthropologist Sidney Mintz described the process as he observed it in the 1940s: "At that time most of the work was still done by human effort alone. . . . I would sometimes stand by the line of cutters, who were working in intense heat and under great pressure, while the foreman stood (and the *mayordomo* rode) at their backs. . . . The lowing of the animals, the shouts of the *mayordomo*, the grunting of the men as they swung their machetes, the sweat and dust and din easily conjured up an earlier era. Only the sound of the whip was missing."[8]

Indeed, while it generated formidable profits for the mill owners and largest *colonos*, the expansion of the sugar industry coincided with continued poverty for those who labored in the fields and mills. Even in the best of times, the idle season or *tiempo muerto* represented a period of precarious survival, barely assured through the combination of different activities such as cultivation of food crops, crab hunting, and employment in construction or in the needlework industry. During the harvest or *zafra*, workers received a steadier income while enduring long hours, often a twelve-hour day. In 1919, Joseph Marcus described their basic diet as rice, beans, coffee, bread, and, if things were good, codfish. A study conducted by historian Erick Pérez Velasco concluded that real wages of sugarcane workers remained roughly the same between 1900 and 1914, increased in the war years, but fell back to the 1914 level by 1920. Thus real wages failed to increase significantly between 1900 and 1920. A study conducted by Frank Tannenbaum in the late 1920s reached the same conclusion.[9]

It was not easy for sugarcane workers to organize. In fact, many workers were not directly employed by the *centrales* or *colonos*. Employers often contracted out the cutting of a cane area or *colonia* to bosses known as *rematistas*, who in turn subcontracted the job to heads of crews known as *encabezados*. There were thus in many cases several intermediaries between the workers and the owner of the cane being cut. On balance, more land was planted under the management of the non-U.S. *centrales* and *colonos* than under the direct supervision of U.S. sugar companies.

The fortunes accumulated by the Georgetti, Cautiño, Roig, Serrallés, Valdés, Mercado, Bird, Aboy, Goudreau, Benítez, García Méndez, Fabián, Fonalleda, and other families are ample evidence of the participation of a Puerto Rican or resident capitalist class in the prosperity of the sugar industry after 1900. Their prosperity was wholly dependent on privileged access to a protected U.S. market. Not surprisingly, most of the sugar interests opposed political independence or any change that could possibly endanger or limit that access. When in 1913 the Wilson administration threatened to remove the tariff on raw sugar, the Puerto Rican *azucareros* immediately denounced the measure.[10] Given fierce international competition, the Puerto Rican *azucareros* could hope to prosper only within the carapace of U.S. tariff protection.

Given their attachment to the U.S. market, the *azucareros* tended to support statehood or, failing that, some form of self-government under U.S. rule. Many joined or supported the pro-statehood Partido Republicano organized in 1899, whose evolution we trace in the following chapter. Nevertheless, and contrary to what is often asserted, prominent *azucareros* also belonged to the rival Partido Unión, which by 1922, after several zig-zags, settled for a program of insular self-government within the existing relation with the United States.

Recognition of the fact that Puerto Rican *azucareros* benefited from unrestricted trade with the United States has led some historians to question the notion of colonial subordination as a category to understand Puerto Rico after 1898. Carmen González Muñoz, for example, concludes from it that the Foraker Act was not the "result of an unilateral imposition" but rather "a dispositive produced within the space of negotiation that opened in 1898." Within that "space of negotiation," she adds, there is no "subordinator and subordinated, but an interplay of forces in which conjunctural agreements based on difference are attained."[11] But this conclusion, which the author describes as inspired by postcolonial theory, is as unilateral as the narrative of unmitigated U.S. control. While some authors offer a simplistic vision of colonialism, their postcolonial critics would deny its existence. In either case, the complexities of colonialism are lost. In fact, dependent colonial bourgeoisies have existed and prospered in many places. This does not negate the existence of colonialism, nor does it dilute the phenomenon to a mere "space of negotiation."

The processes we have described were in no way unique to Puerto Rico. They followed patterns unfolding in the world sugar industry, which can be briefly summarized as a considerable increase in the presence of metropolitan capital in the overseas sugarcane growing areas, the generalization of the modern mill, and the formation of new sugarcane proletariats, processes that in many cases (Puerto Rico, the Philippines, Java, and Taiwan) unfolded in the context of old or new colonial relations. These tendencies within the sugar industry were in turn concrete forms of four features typical of imperialism in its classical moment between the late 1800s and World War II: the rise of oligopolies in the metropolitan economies, growing export of capital to underdeveloped areas, specialization of the latter in the production of raw materials or food products for export, and the construction of new colonial empires.

The effect of these changes in the configuration of the world sugar industry was the dramatic comeback of cane sugar, partially reconquering the terrain it had yielded to beet sugar in the previous period. A significant aspect of that comeback was the expansion of production in the U.S.-controlled sugar islands: Puerto Rico, Hawaii, and the Philippines, all of which were annexed or taken over in 1898, and Cuba, also invaded in 1898 and placed under a protectorate after its formal independence in 1902. This sugar circuit also included the Dominican Republic, occupied from 1916 to 1924 by U.S. troops; the Virgin Islands, sold by Denmark to the United States in 1917; the sugarcane growers of Florida and Louisiana; and the beet-sugar industry in the western states. Integrated into the world capitalist economy, these provinces of the American Sugar Kingdom were affected by the creeping crisis of the world sugar market during the 1920s.

Puerto Rican participation in this expansion of a cane-sugar proletariat was not limited to the growth of Puerto Rico's sugar industry after 1898. The first significant episode of Puerto Rican migration under U.S. rule was the transportation of 5,000 workers to the cane fields of Hawaii alongside Japanese, Filipino, Portuguese, and other laborers. Contracted by the Hawaii Sugar Planters Association with the approval of the new colonial government (which was already deploying the theory that Puerto Rico's poverty was caused by overpopulation), Puerto Rican workers found conditions so harsh that many refused to go beyond San Francisco, or returned there as soon as they could. While the distinction would soon be claimed by New York City, the largest Puerto Rican population outside Puerto Rico (around 3,000) in 1910 was still located in Hawaii.[12]

U.S. Investments and the Tobacco Industries

Sugar production was not the only sector marked by the growing presence of U.S. capital after 1898. Such was also the case with the tobacco industry, the banking sector, railroads, and electric power generation, to mention the more visible examples.

The banking sector was dominated by four U.S. and Canadian concerns (the American Colonial Bank, the Royal Bank of Canada, the Bank of Nova Scotia, and First National City Bank), which according to a 1930 study held half of the "banking capital" in Puerto Rico. The Puerto Rico Railway Light and Power Company, also a Canadian concern, operated the electric grid in roughly the eastern third of Puerto Rico as well as the trolley system in San Juan. The railroad line running along the northern, western, and southern coast connecting San Juan and Ponce was owned by the American Railroad Company. The telephone system was operated by the Puerto Rico Telephone Company, owned by foreign but at the time resident Danish entrepreneurs Hermann and Sosthenes Behn, founders of the International Telephone and Telegraph.[13] Weighty as the presence of North American capital was, it should be borne in mind that in many sectors, Puerto Rican capitalists were also able to expand. Insular banks, for example, handled a considerable amount of business around the island, and locally owned companies provided electricity in Ponce and Mayagüez.

The tobacco industry in particular was characterized by the significant presence of U.S. cigar manufacturers, who employed a largely urban labor force to process the tobacco leaves purchased from a mass of small and medium farmers. Tobacco farming was largely located in the hilly areas or in the valleys of the interior. The average tobacco-producing farm in 1909 had a mere 2.7 acres planted in tobacco. The corresponding figure for 1929 was 3.1 acres. Tobacco was and remained a small farmer's crop.[14] Unlike coffee, it did not require an initial period of several years before plants came into production; it also required less capital outlay than sugarcane-growing.

Nevertheless, the emergence of an expanded class of small tobacco farmers was linked to the intrusion of the American Tobacco Company—the so-called Tobacco Trust—that became the main buyer and processor of tobacco leaves in Puerto Rico. In other words, the new layer of tobacco farmers was, like the colonos, subjected to a situation of dependency and subordination to commercial and manufacturing capital.

In the United States, the Tobacco Trust had been formed principally on the basis of the manufacture of cigarettes. The Trust had faced problems in controlling cigar production on the mainland, where many established local brands and local marketing arrangements blocked its path. In 1910, the Tobacco Trust controlled only 14.4 percent of the cigar output of the United States. This is in contrast to cigarette production, where the Trust's market share ranged between 75 and 90 percent, depending on the year.

In Puerto Rico, the relative weakness of the pre-1898 cigar industry and the Trust's connections with the U.S. market combined to give the Trust a monopoly on *both* cigarette and cigar production. The Tobacco Trust opted not to buy out existing operations outright in order to avoid the danger that some of their experienced leaders would create competing enterprises. Instead, it preferred to obtain a controlling interest in existing concerns while at least initially keeping the previous owners as partners or directors of the reorganized enterprises. Through this procedure, the Porto Rico American Tobacco Company established itself on the island in 1899 by taking over factories of Toro & Compañía in San Juan and Ponce and of Rucabado & Portela in Cayey and San Juan.[15]

The Trust's control of the market for tobacco leaf gave it a tremendous advantage in its dealings with farmers. After 1921, when the international prices of agricultural raw materials in general and of tobacco in particular began to decline, farmers in Puerto Rico felt the squeeze of the Trust. Through the 1920s, authors Francisco M. Zeno and Miguel Meléndez Muñoz (who had owned tobacco farms in Cidra and Cayey, respectively) acted as intellectual representatives of the tobacco growers. They denounced the evils of corporate control, the pressure on the small farmer or *colono* by the sugar and tobacco companies, and the misery of the rural laborers.

The contradictions of the colonial tobacco industry are vividly portrayed in some of Meléndez Muñoz's short stories. "Portalatín's Uncertainty," "Prosperity," and "Portalatín in Bankruptcy," for example, tell the story of one farmer's evolution from coffee to tobacco grower and eventually to landless laborer. In 1913, Meléndez Muñoz produced one of the earliest studies on the condition of the Puerto Rican peasantry after 1898, in which he favored social and labor reforms and the creation of cooperatives to confront the abuses of the Trust.[16] Zeno, on his part, dreaded the rise of a militant labor movement, but unlike the larger Puerto Rican and U.S. sugar and tobacco interests, he felt it was necessary to neutralize labor with timely reforms from above, such as the implementation of the 500-acre limit.[17]

The 1920s were years of falling agricultural prices internationally, but the onset of the Great Depression in 1929 further worsened the situation of the tobacco farmers. By 1931, Puerto Rican growers decided to organize a boycott of the Porto Rico American Tobacco Company. Enforcement of the boycott entailed burning the storehouses of farmers who broke it, which led to the emergence of "night riders" similar to those who at times operated in U.S. tobacco-growing regions. But the Tobacco Trust was an international cartel with several sources of raw material. It could withstand the impact of an isolated boycott by Puerto Rican growers. This small-farmers' protest petered out by 1932.[18]

The perception of the growers was sound enough: there was too much to-bacco in the market, and perhaps a limitation of production could bring prices up. By the mid-1930s, as we shall see, they not surprisingly embraced the New Deal agricultural programs organized through the Agricultural Adjustment Act, which precisely sought to combine crop reduction and compensatory payments for farmers.

But changes and tensions emerged, not only in the relation between farmers and tobacco companies but also in the manufacturing phase of this industry. Cigar and cigarette production expanded rapidly after 1900. By 1910, it employed more workers than the *centrales* of the sugar industry. Before 1914, some of Puerto Rico's key labor battles were organized or led by cigarmakers, while in the early 1930s, women tobacco operatives staged several mobilizations in the midst of the Great Depression. Between these two dates stood a complex transformation of the tobacco industry in general and of the manufacturing process in particular.

Cigarmakers made up a leading sector of the early Puerto Rican labor movement, deriving their education at least in part from the institution of the reader, which characterized much premechanized cigar production. Workers paid a comrade to read to them novels, political tracts, newspapers, and labor journals while they worked. Luisa Capetillo, Prudencio Rivera Martínez, Bernardo Vega, Jesús Colón, and Antonia Pantoja, among others who would play key roles in working-class and community initiatives in Puerto Rico and the United States, were shaped by the world of the *tabaqueros*.

But the world of the reader and the skilled and proud cigarmaker progressively succumbed under the blows of repression and of the decomposition of the craft as a result of advancing mechanization. By 1905, the tasks of making a cigar were already being broken down into detailed operations. The manufacturing division of labor and mechanization advanced in the following years. In 1921, a finished cigarmaking machine was introduced.

While the old craft had been dominated by males, the growing division of labor leading to mechanization coincided with the increasing feminization of the labor force. Other areas of the tobacco industry, such as cigarette production and, above all, the stemming of tobacco, had employed a largely female labor force from the start. Whereas in 1910, 30 percent of the 11,118 workers employed in tobacco manufacturing were female, by 1935, 73 percent of the 14,712 employees in the industry were women.[19]

After 1920, the value of cigar exports began to decline, and tobacco exports increasingly took the form of tobacco leaves. Premanufactured tobacco represented 22 percent of the value of all tobacco exports in 1910, 53 percent in 1920, and 77 percent in 1930. By 1940, practically all tobacco exports from Puerto Rico were in the form of tobacco leaf. As in the case of sugar, the island was progressively led to specialize in the production of raw materials for metropolitan industries. Such an economic dynamic can hardly provide a launching pad for further economic advance or the basis for cumulative, self-sustaining growth.

Crisis in Coffee and the Rise of the Needlework Industry

While the sugar industry had gone through a deep crisis in the last decades of the 1800s, coffee had enjoyed a veritable belle epoque in the western and central mountain region. The late nineteenth century is the only period in Puerto Rican history in which the most dynamic sector of the insular economy was located in the interior highlands. The coffee boom was stimulated by difficulties confronted by growers in Brazil and Java and by the opening of the Cuban market to Puerto Rican coffee. Before the coffee expansion of the 1880s, the central mountain region had been an internal frontier of independent subsistence production, in many areas beyond the reach of government authority. The expansion of the coffee *haciendas* implied the end of such freedoms, fragile and miserable as the lives they sustained may have been.

As lands dedicated to subsistence farming were turned to export production, economic differentiation advanced, bringing prosperity to some but loss of property or of access to land to others. Former subsistence farmers, both titled owners and squatters, now lost their property or land and became subordinated to the rising *hacendado* class, either as *arrendatarios* (tenants), *agregados* (tenants-at-will), or *jornaleros*. While tenants paid rent in kind or money, *agregados* worked for wages during harvesttime or whenever necessary while also being allowed to live on the land of their employer. They often tended small plots as a source of subsistence or cash crops under diverse sharecropping arrangements with the landowner.

As the coffee boom advanced, the condition of these *agregados* deteriorated. The amount of land at their disposal shrank. The golden age of coffee, which would later nurture myths of a lost, glorious past, was in fact an epoch of declining living standards for many.[20] The spread of market relations generated tensions between farmers and merchants, debtors and creditors. The laboring classes were largely native-born, descendants of the peasantry who had initially populated the interior. The emergent *hacendado* class was culturally split: besides the *criollo* layer, there also emerged a stratum of Spanish, Corsi-

can, Mallorcan, and other recently arrived immigrants. The relentless exploitation of the day-laborers and the marginalization of the poorer farmers gradually spawned the resentments that later exploded in such incidents as the
partidas sediciosas of 1898.

One of the classics of Puerto Rican literature, the novel *La charca* by Manuel
Zeno Gandía, published in 1894, vividly documents the social conditions of the
coffee region, above all the widespread misery that contrasted with the wealth
of the *hacendados*, on the eve of the U.S. invasion. Zeno does not refrain from
criticizing even the more conscious sectors of the *criollo* propertied classes
(represented by the character of the *hacendado* Juan del Salto) for not being
able, or willing, to take concrete action to solve the social ills they denounced.
It is not surprising that Zeno was among those that early on pinned his hopes
on the changes that U.S. rule could bring.

Coffee growers themselves expected to obtain easier access to the U.S. market, which, they hoped, would complement their European outlets. This was
not to be. Indeed, one could say that after 1898, sugar and coffee traded places:
as sugar went from bust to boom, coffee sank into ever-deeper crisis, slowly at
first, and much more rapidly after 1914. U.S. rule did not bring any distinct
advantages, as coffee was not protected by U.S. tariffs, and Puerto Rican producers found it almost impossible to penetrate a market already occupied by
coffee imported from Brazil. The disruption of European markets after 1914
as a result of World War I dealt another blow to an already weakened *hacendado* class.

It is often argued that, given the hard times they encountered after 1898, the
coffee *hacendados* became increasingly critical of U.S. rule and gradually drifted
toward support for political independence. It is true that coffee growers were
unhappy with their situation under U.S. rule. But rhetoric aside, their discontent translated into rather meek and futile requests for remedies from the
colonial authorities. The Association of Coffee Growers organized in 1909 led a
languid existence, its officers complaining about the passivity of its members.
When the start of the war in 1914 closed the coffee growers' European markets,
the association reacted by asking Congress to impose a tariff on coffee imports
into the United States. Coffee growers thus aspired to what the sugar interests
already had: access to a protected U.S. market. This, the newspaper *La Democracia* explained, was their golden dream.[21] Such views were not compatible
with a consistent *independentismo*.[22]

It was in this impoverished central and western coffee area that the needlework industry spread after World War I cut off the United States from its

sources of embroidered cloth and drawn linen, such as France, Belgium, and Japan. The needle trades expanded rapidly through the 1920s. By the early 1930s, they employed more than 60,000 mostly female workers, a figure surpassed only by the sugar industry during harvesttime.

As it expanded, the needlework industry created two types of productive arrangements. Hundreds of agents put out work to thousands of families who worked at home. This mechanism was typical of embroidery, lace-making, and drawn work. Meanwhile, garment manufacturing was often carried out in large and small urban workshops. In 1918, for example, four large establishments in Mayagüez employed a combined total of 1,000 workers, and two large establishments in Ponce employed 1,400 workers. However, most shops were small. By 1930, there were 166 shops with an average workforce of around 40 workers each. The larger shops paid better wages and made it easier for the workers to organize. The poorer household producers, however, were responsible for around 90 percent of the output. Estimates of the number of people working at home in this industry were approximations, because such estimates registered only the transactions between the women and their employers. A report of the U.S. Department of Labor is thus closer to the truth when it states that 40,000 families, not individuals, were employed in home needlework in 1933.[23]

Small Farmers, *Agregados*, and Landless Laborers

As the Puerto Rican economy was remade after 1898, diverse observers began to denounce the evils resulting from the concentration of landownership and the displacement of the small farmer by large, often North American corporations. There were many variations of the critique, but the underlying vision was simple: from a land of small property holders (*pequeños propietarios*), Puerto Rico had been turned into a mass of dispossessed and impoverished wage-workers. Thus, Nationalist leader Pedro Albizu Campos famously denounced how after 1898 a veritable "legion of proprietors" had succumbed under the wheels of the corporate juggernaut.[24] But this appreciation was not a monopoly of the nationalist movement. Most commentators at the time shared the notion, with very few exceptions. If anything, it may be described as more of a national than a nationalist myth. Zeno denounced how 80 percent of the *pequeños propietarios* of 1898 had been turned into peons. Prominent leaders of the two main political currents of the time, Antonio R. Barceló and José Tous Soto, affirmed in a joint statement that before 1898, "Puerto Rico was a country mainly composed of the owners of small *haciendas*."[25] Luis Muñoz Marín, future governor of Puerto Rico, argued in 1929 that the "recreation of a large independent yeomanry is the will of the people."[26] One of his close collaborators, Samuel R. Quiñones, insisted that before 1898, "a generous agrarian fragmentation assured the equitable distribution of the fruits of the land."[27]

Independence activist José Enamorado Cuesta and social scientist Clara Lugo were among the few who questioned this consensus. Enamorado thus pointed out in 1929 that widespread landlessness "was already there under Spanish rule." Lugo, for her part, indicated that census figures did not reveal a drastic reduction in the number of farms in Puerto Rico after 1898.[28]

Indeed, as Enamorado and Lugo argued, rural landlessness or, more accurately, propertyless-ness, was already massive at the time of the U.S. occupation. Commissioner Carroll described the situation in 1899 as follows: "There are three classes of property holders here—those who have large estates, those who have small estates, and those who live on a borrowed piece of land. . . . The latter class is the most numerous." Carroll explained that "those who depend upon daily wages for support constitute the great majority of the people."[29] In other words, those "who depend upon daily wages," including those "who lived on a borrowed piece of land," constituted the majority of the rural population. Thus, concentration of landownership in a few hands was a legacy of Spanish rule, not the result of the impact of the U.S. occupation on a mass of small property holders. The vision of a nation of yeoman farmers was a retrospective idealization, not a realistic description of Puerto Rican society before 1898.

Furthermore, census figures do not indicate a catastrophic fall in the number of farms in Puerto Rico after 1898. In fact, the number of farms in Puerto Rico jumped from 39,021 in 1899 to 58,371 in 1910. By 1930, at the onset of the Great Depression, the number of farms stood at 52,965. If compared to 1910, this represented a fall of 9 percent. This was a significant but hardly catastrophic reduction, and it still represented an increase if compared to 1899. The number of farms reported in the 1920 census (41,078) has led some observers to conclude that there was a sharp reduction in the number of farms between 1910 and 1920; however, this reduced number was largely due to the fact that the 1920 census did not count farms under three acres that produced less than $100 in cash crops.[30] The 1930 census, which reverted to previous practices, registered the number of farms at 52,965.

Further calculations published elsewhere and based on the tax records of a significant number of representative municipalities confirm the estimates from census reports regarding the increase in the number of farms and the decrease in the average farm size in Puerto Rico between 1899 and 1915. Similarly, the Gini index calculated on the basis of this material points to a reduction in the degree of concentration of landownership during this period.[31]

The possibility that the number of farms may have increased between 1899 and 1910 should be neither surprising nor seen as exceptional, unless one were to mechanically equate the initial implantation or the course of capitalist accumulation in agriculture with a necessary reduction of the number of farms. In fact, while capitalism in agriculture implies a tendency toward more capitalized production, this need not always imply larger farms in terms of acreage or a shrinking number of farms. The decomposition of precapitalist landholdings and the evolution of capitalism in agriculture can take diverse forms, including reduction in average farm size and increase in the number of farms in any given area. The equation of the emergence and development of capitalism in agriculture with ever-larger farms is sometimes formulated in Marxist terms, as a manifestation of the tendency toward the concentration and centralization of capital inherent to capitalist accumulation. In fact, no less an authority than Lenin, in his theoretically orthodox and empirically detailed study of U.S. agriculture, warned against such a simplistic approach. He insisted, on the contrary, that the introduction of capitalist and commercial agriculture, above all in the areas of former plantation economies, implied a growing dependence on wage labor but not necessarily an increase in average farm acreage or a decrease in the number of farms.[32] In 1898, the Puerto Rican countryside was characterized by the sizable presence of extensive, underutilized properties, such as former cane lands that had been turned to pastures. Against that background, the increase in the demand for raw material (raw sugar or tobacco leaves) by new sugar mills or cigar companies and the need to pay new property or irrigation taxes could very well foster the subdivision and selling of undercultivated holdings. These trends implied the creation of farms that were smaller yet large enough to require wage labor. Meanwhile, some formerly landless households also acquired land to be cultivated with family labor.

But idealized visions of the past, and particularly persistent and widely shared misrepresentations, must draw sustenance from some aspect of social reality. There are several dimensions of the evolution of Puerto Rican agriculture that help explain why it was described by many observers at the time as the disappearance of a yeoman peasantry. It should be remembered that while the majority of the rural population was already propertyless in 1898, many enjoyed access to land under diverse conditions as squatters, sharecroppers, or *agregados* in what were often large but underutilized, undercapitalized, or idle landholdings. This now began to change, above all in the coastal cane-growing region. Former *agregado* subsistence plots were transferred to sugarcane production. Food once grown or gathered by the *agregados* now became a commodity to be bought with their miserable wages. The number of proprietors remained fairly constant while the usufruct rights enjoyed by many deteriorated.

Moreover, land tenure was neither stable nor secure. The rise of the sugar and tobacco industries created a market for cane and tobacco farmers, but it also implied that they existed in close dependence and subordination to commercial and manufacturing capital. As late as 1940, less than 1 percent of small farmers obtained credit from a bank. Tobacco farmers borrowed money principally as advances from the merchants who purchased their crops. The largest lenders to the small *colonos* were the sugar mills. For small farmers, low prices for their products and the high cost of credit and inputs implied that their hold on the land was always precarious. A study conducted in the late 1930s revealed that a majority of small farmers (57 percent) had purchased and not inherited their land, indicating dependence on the market for land acquisition and lack of an entrenched, small farmer class passing down properties to their descendants.[33] This suggests that the frontier between the rural wageworker and the small farmer was very porous. If land acquisition was a realistic possibility for many, descent from the condition of small farmer to that of rural wageworker was not uncommon.

Critics were therefore wrong in deploring the displacement of an alleged pre-1898 mass of rural *property* owners or in describing the process as a massive reduction in the absolute number of farm owners. But they were not mistaken in diagnosing a reduction in usufruct rights or the precarious hold of small farmers over their properties. It was that context that nurtured the widespread demand for the "restoration" of the small farm, given the hardships of wage labor in sugar, coffee, and other sectors.

Furthermore, it should be underlined that Puerto Rican agriculture did exhibit tremendous levels of inequality. By 1935, there were 52,790 farms. Farms holding more than 200 *cuerdas* (1,259) were 2.4 percent of the total number of farms, but they held 45.2 percent of all land under cultivation. On the other side of the spectrum, farms holding less than 10 *cuerdas* (27,108) were 51 percent of all farms, but they held only 11 percent of the land under cultivation.[34]

The call for agrarian reform, beginning with the enforcement of the 500-acre limitation, was to play a key role in the rise of the Partido Popular Democrático (PPD) in the context of the Great Depression. The PPD, in turn, was to dominate Puerto Rican politics until the late 1960s. But before we address those developments, we must first take a look at Puerto Rico's political struggles as they unfolded between 1900 and 1930, in the midst of the economic changes we have just described.

3

POLITICAL AND SOCIAL STRUGGLES IN A
NEW COLONIAL CONTEXT, 1900-1930

In 1899, the two political parties that had been organized soon after the onset of U.S. rule—the Partido Federal and the Partido Republicano—called for the transformation of Puerto Rico into a state of the United States. Their programs reflected the hope of the Puerto Rican possessing classes of joining the U.S. federal state structure as equals, with the corresponding representation in Congress and control of their own state government. But this request for annexation had been ignored. A new colonial structure was instituted through the Foraker Act of 1900. Puerto Rico was to be a "possession" of the United States, with no assurance of a future as either an independent republic or a state of the Union. The Puerto Rican possessing classes were not admitted as equal partners into the Union but rather turned into colonial subjects.

This turn of events placed Federales and Republicanos in a paradoxical situation. If they denounced U.S. policy, they ran the risk of seeming anti-American, eroding their political credit with the new authorities and making their objective—statehood—less viable. But if they chose to demonstrate their pro-Americanism by muting their discontent and adapting to the new political structures, they would help install and sanction a regime that pointedly defined Puerto Rico as a "possession" and not as a territory in preparation for statehood. Political trends linked to Puerto Rico's professional and possessing classes may be classified according to how they responded to this dilemma.

One Republicano leader, Rosendo Matienzo Cintrón, concluded that it was necessary to denounce the new colonial regime, even at the risk of seeming anti-American. Initially formulating his critique from a pro-statehood perspective, he gradually evolved to a pro-independence position: if self-government could not be attained under U.S. rule, it would be necessary to constitute an independent republic. But Matienzo Cintrón, whose ideas we explore below, was an exception. The Partido Republicano followed the opposite path. Instead of denouncing U.S. colonial rule, it adapted to it while hoping its uncritical pro-Americanism and the gradual integration of Puerto Rican life to that of the United States would lead to eventual annexation as a state.

The Partido Federal and its successor, the Partido Unión, organized in 1904, followed a third course, criticizing U.S. colonial policies and eventually relinquishing statehood as impractical given opposition to it in Washington while also shirking away from a consistent push for independence. It thus settled on a policy of gradual reforms within the relation of nonincorporation. In Puerto Rico, this policy came to be known as "autonomism."

Puerto Rican politics thus came to be dominated by two parties, the Partido Republicano and the Partido Unión, whose stated objectives—statehood and autonomy/independence—were not matched by a will to challenge the limits of the relation of nonincorporation imposed on them in 1900. This behavior corresponded to the accommodation of the Puerto Rican propertied classes, including both the prosperous *azucareros* and the struggling coffee growers, to the political limits decreed by their new colonial ruler.

Meanwhile, the labor movement, organized in the Federación Libre de Trabajadores and, after 1915, in the Partido Socialista, developed its own version of reformist colonial politics. What follows is a brief chronicle of these parallel routes to accommodation as the Puerto Rican possessing and laboring classes settled into the orbit of nonincorporation assigned to them by Washington.

The Partido Republicano and the Early Years of U.S. Rule, 1900–1904

After 1898, U.S. military governors faced the task of organizing a new insular administration. The project could not be completed in an orderly fashion without obtaining the collaboration of the better-trained sectors in Puerto Rico. Indeed, the first U.S. military governor initially retained the prewar autonomist cabinet presided over by Luis Muñoz Rivera. Muñoz Rivera, leader of the Partido Federal, undoubtedly saw this as a chance to consolidate his influence over the ongoing political transition. Not surprisingly, the reorganization of government structures by the new rulers, including the dismantling of the autonomist cabinet, led to growing tensions. U.S. officials turned to the Republicanos in search of support against a disgruntled Muñoz Rivera.

The Partido Republicano drew support from sectors of the emergent sugar interests, firmly addicted to the U.S. sugar market. But at this early stage, the party also served as a vehicle for professional, democratic currents, linked to large propertied interests, to be sure, but also committed to the ideals they associated with the American republic. It was also able to attract some defiant plebeian expressions unleashed by the end of Spanish rule. The party received the support of the Comité de Defensa Republicano, better known as the *turbas*, which physically attacked the supporters of Muñoz Rivera's Partido Federal.

Some authors have presented them as a popular democratic agency, helping to dismantle the leftovers of Spanish authoritarianism.[1] This is a useful corrective to the reduction of the *turbas* to an expression of irrational pro-Americanism. But it goes too far in the opposite direction. The *turbas*, while plebeian in composition, were tied to a party of the propertied classes—the Partido Republicano—and enjoyed the complicity of the San Juan municipal government and of sectors of the police. Moreover, the *turbas* targeted not only the rival Partido Federal but also the emergent labor movement, organized in the FLT. While the *turbas* expressed a leveling impulse from below and a desire to get back at figures associated with social or racial privilege, they were soon turned into irregular troops for the imposition of a new hierarchical order from above.

The main leader of the Partido Republicano, José Celso Barbosa, best represented the reformist democratic current, able to relate to some aspirations of the dispossessed but ultimately and firmly committed to the existing order of class privilege. Barbosa was a U.S.-trained black physician. The son of an artisan, he graduated from the University of Michigan in 1877, where he acquired a deep admiration for the U.S. Republican Party. To the end of his life, it remained for him the party of emancipation. He criticized segregation in the U.S. South but saw it as a regional blemish in an otherwise democratic federation.[2] Barbosa's views on race did not differ significantly from those of his fellow white professionals. He insisted that the "race problem" did not exist in Puerto Rico and that if blacks and whites remained separate "socially," this was logical and appropriate. Blacks should help perpetuate racial peace by not raising demands in terms of color. Race mixing, he added, tended to whiten the insular population: race division would dissolve through the withering away of blackness.[3]

Denouncing the followers of Muñoz Rivera as anti-American, Barbosa and the Republicanos gained the favor of American officials by 1900 while the *turbas* harassed the more vocal critics of the new authorities. Ironically, the Republicanos thus helped install a new colonial relation, which many in the United States saw as a break with U.S. constitutional and republican traditions. As early as 1902, party cofounder Matienzo Cintrón criticized Barbosa and his collaborators, not because they favored statehood (an aspiration he shared at the time), but rather because they did not defend it consistently, in practice adapting to a new colonial structure.[4]

Barbosa himself took this policy of adaptation a step further by insisting that Puerto Rico's political status was to be determined not by its inhabitants but by the U.S. Congress. His agenda was not premised on growing self-activity but on passive acceptance of the right of Congress to decide Puerto Rico's future. "Regarding us," he wrote in a characteristic statement, "the definitive political solution depends on the will of Congress."[5] What flowed from this was not an active struggle for statehood but accommodation to colonial rule until Congress saw fit to make Puerto Rico a state.

At times, Barbosa referred to the situation of neighboring republics under U.S. influence as an argument for statehood. He warned that these republics were not truly independent, their sovereignty often violated by the United States. He concluded it was better to be part of the "American family . . . and not a humble republic subjected to the whim and will of Congress."[6] But if he pointed to U.S. interventionism as an argument against independence, he did not allow this to lead him into an interrogation of the nature of the "American family" he wished to join or into an inquiry—even while struggling for statehood—into the forces behind the inability of the United States to relate democratically with "humbler" republics. Such critical attitudes, of course, would have soured his relation with Congress. Having made a lasting wager on metropolitan favor, Barbosa and his party thus reiterated their uncritical pro-Americanism in the hope that Congress would eventually free them from colonial (and spare them semicolonial) subordination and bestow upon them the privilege of joining the Union.

The Rise of the Partido Unión

While reaffirming its support for U.S. rule, the Partido Federal, led by Muñoz Rivera, protested what it perceived as support by U.S. officials for the Partido Republicano. By 1904, a dissident wing of the Partido Republicano, including Matienzo Cintrón, joined with the Partido Federal and the leaders of the labor coalition launched in 1899, the FLT, to organize the Partido Unión under a program of opposition to the Foraker Act. Its catch-all program included statehood, autonomy, and independence as equally acceptable options.

Meanwhile, U.S. policies had led Muñoz Rivera to readjust his manner of seeking support in Puerto Rico and of speaking to the new authorities. While in the past he had espoused universal suffrage, in 1899 he argued against it, since "it would be extremely dangerous to hand over our future to the masses, who are entirely without civic education and who might be wrongly directed by . . . agitators."[7] By 1900 he shifted back to a defense of universal suffrage. There was an inner logic to such fluctuations.

Muñoz Rivera sought incorporation into the United States. To the extent that he felt it could be attained as he and his collaborators were recognized as the civilized portion of an otherwise backward people, he was willing to describe the "masses" as unprepared for suffrage. Yet to the extent that the alleged incapacities of the dispossessed majority became a justification for limiting the participation of even the propertied and professional classes in a restrictive colonial regime, Muñoz Rivera felt compelled to reformulate his demand for self-government, not in the name of Puerto Rico's "civilized" minority but in the name of a capable and wronged Puerto Rican people. Such would be the preferred patriotic discourse after 1900.

Still, in 1903, an American observer formulated the following description of Muñoz Rivera's Partido Federal: "To it belong the more conservative elements. . . . Their horror of Negro domination, coupled with fear of the results of a further extension of the suffrage to the poorer whites, has largely determined their attitude toward public affairs. They welcome American rule, but look with considerable misgiving upon the probable effects of American democratic ideas on the institutions of the island."[8]

The creation of the Partido Unión with the support of the Federales, dissident Republicanos, and the labor movement worked well for Muñoz Rivera. His current became the dominant tendency within the party, and the party, after obtaining a majority in the House of Delegates in 1904, dominated Puerto Rico's politics until the late 1920s. From the start, its evolution was shaped by internal tensions, but on balance its trajectory was that of accommodation to the existing relation of nonincorporation while lobbying for reforms within its limits.

The program of Muñoz Rivera's current fluctuated as he and his collaborators tried to synchronize their aspirations with the constraints imposed by the unfamiliar political system of the new colonial power. The intentions of the U.S. government, given the diverse paths being followed in Hawaii, Cuba, and the Philippines, and the ongoing debates regarding colonial policy were not easy to discern. Was the Foraker Act a temporary measure? Was statehood feasible? Could the demand for U.S. citizenship be an attainable first step toward it? Should the party concentrate on reforming existing structures (obtaining an elected governor) while postponing other demands? Could there be some form of self-government, a sort of British dominion status, under the U.S. Constitution?

Regarding these issues, Muñoz Rivera insisted that statehood was the best option for Puerto Rico. Referring to statehood, "home rule," and independence, he argued in 1911: "We prefer the first; propose the second and keep the third in reserve as the last refuge of . . . our honor."[9] Yet by 1912 the Partido Unión removed statehood from its program. For Muñoz Rivera this was more an act of compliance than of rebellion. Statehood was preferable but impossible, since Congress was not willing to grant it. He argued, furthermore, that independence was a "purely abstract ideal. It cannot be realized. It will never be realized. We register it, . . . because some things are above any calculation."[10] If both statehood and independence were beyond reach, the only realistic option was the search for reforms within the existing political framework. After 1913, a more vocal *independentista* wing did emerge within the party, headed by José De Diego. But in 1914, the party adopted the "Miramar rules," which restricted current efforts to the attainment of autonomist reforms.

By 1915, several positions coexisted within the Partido Unión. Some leaders, such as Félix Córdova Dávila, opposed independence and favored autonomy. Muñoz Rivera supported autonomy and paid lip service to eventual independence. De Diego favored independence but would settle for autonomy if the former was not possible in the short run.[11] To top it off, the party had an annexationist wing, which included Martín Travieso and Juan B. Huyke, among others. Far from providing a strategic perspective for the possessing and professional classes, the clash of currents within the Partido Unión embodied their perplexity in the face of U.S. colonial rule.

The Jones Act of 1917

The reforms that Muñoz Rivera, who died in 1916, and the Partido Unión had long waited for took the form of the Jones Act, approved by Congress in 1917. The urge to reform was at least in part due to the coming entry of the United States in the European war, which nurtured a desire to affirm U.S. control over Puerto Rico.

The most far-reaching aspect of the Jones Act was the extension of U.S. citizenship to Puerto Ricans. In 1912, the Partido Unión had opposed extension of U.S. citizenship if it did not come with a promise of future statehood. If Puerto Rico was not to be a state, U.S. citizenship could be interpreted only as an attempt to block independence and perpetuate Puerto Rico in its colonial status. Such was indeed the purpose of the measure, as explained by its proponents. For them, the extension of U.S. citizenship did not constitute a promise of statehood but rather an attempt to exclude any consideration of independence. As Governor Arthur D. Yager put it, it meant "that we have determined . . . that the American flag will never be lowered in Puerto Rico." The same point was made by William A. Jones (D-Va.), head of the House Committee on Insular Affairs; General Frank McIntyre, head of the War Department's Bureau of Insular Affairs; and former governor Beekman Winthrop, among other participants in the congressional hearings. The House Committee report on the proposed legislation affirmed that "Porto Rico has become permanent territory of the United States." What Puerto Ricans desired was "to legislate for themselves in respect to all purely local affairs."[12]

For the Partido Unión, this was a bitter pill to swallow. Informed that statehood was impossible, it was being deprived of even the "last refuge of . . . our honor" that adorned its program. It was being ordered to trim its aspirations to that of legislating over "purely local affairs." The Jones Act did expand Puerto Rican participation in the insular government. An elected bicameral legislature (a Senate and a House of Representatives) was installed. The president of the United States, however, would still appoint the governor, the commissioner of education, the auditor, the attorney general, and the supreme court.

On balance, the extension of U.S. citizenship was an ambiguous gesture. It was seen by its proponents as affirming the permanence of U.S. rule over Puerto Rico without entailing a promise of statehood. Yet, it did seem to create a sturdier legal basis for requesting statehood. If Puerto Ricans were deemed worthy of U.S. citizenship, could they be consistently denied the fullest form of self-government available to U.S. citizens? Not surprisingly, Barbosa and the Partido Republicanos interpreted the measure as a boost to their aspirations. Citizenship, they felt, would eventually lead to annexation, whatever the intentions of Congress in 1917.

After 1917, the programs of the Partido Unión focused on the reform of the existing colonial structures. U.S. policy makers insisted that the party formally abandon any mention of independence. Horace M. Towner (R-Iowa), president of the House Committee on Insular Affairs and future governor of Puerto Rico, advised Partido Unión leaders in 1921 that "there is legitimate ground for a larger measure of self-government, but that has been greatly injured by the active independence propaganda." Former governor Regis Post offered similar advice.[13] Meanwhile, Governor E. Mont Reily announced that he would not appoint Partido Unión members to government posts as long as the party had an *independentista* program. By 1922, the Partido Unión, yielding to these pressures, removed independence from its program and adopted the vague idea of a "free associated state" as its objective. Meanwhile, the U.S. Supreme Court dispelled any doubts regarding the implication of U.S. citizenship to Puerto Rico's status. In 1922, it concluded that Puerto Rico remained an unincorporated territory.[14]

By then, the actual practice of the Unión and Republicano parties differed much less than their programs. In 1913 and 1914, both the Partido Unión and sectors of the Partido Republicano had proposed an alliance to lobby for reforms of the existing regime.[15] By 1924, these inclinations matured to the point of making possible the creation of the Alianza, an electoral bloc of a wing of the Partido Republicano and the Partido Unión. The leaders of the Alianza felt that opposition in Washington made both statehood and independence unfeasible. It was necessary to formulate a third "autonomist" option. Needless to say, they hoped for the widest possible autonomy. But their past trajectory indicated that they would accommodate to whatever their reading of congressional tolerance led them to consider realistic. In 1926, visiting Spanish journalist Luis Araquistáin commented that Puerto Rico's leading politicians demanded neither independence nor statehood "since they suppose that the Americans will not grant either." He added, "This . . . has led them to almost reconcile themselves to the existing regime. If they could elect their governor their reconciliation would be complete."[16]

Coffee, Sugar, and the Partido Unión

It is often argued in historical literature that the Partido Unión evolved toward an anti-American or even *independentista* position, an orientation that corresponded to the views of the coffee *hacendados*, who had been badly hit by the U.S. invasion.[17] There are three misconceptions present in that appreciation.

The first is that the Partido Unión became a defender of independence. In fact, the party followed a tortuous course, adapting itself to the limitations imposed by the new colonial power. After 1904 it remade itself, through a series of approximations, into an autonomist party interested in immediate reforms to the existing regime.

The second misconception is to attribute a militant *independentismo* to the coffee *hacendados*. As we saw in chapter 2, although the latter were unhappy about their situation after 1898, they were unable to formulate anything but bland petitions to the new authorities. The Partido Unión served as a vehicle for their requests, which included lower taxes, cheaper credit, and special tariff measures. The *hacendados* did provide a narrative of past glories, which was part of the requests for political reforms, but this did not amount to an *independentista* program.

A third misconception is to reduce the Partido Unión to a vehicle of the coffee *hacendados*. In fact, the sugar interests, firmly oriented to the U.S. market, were well represented in the leadership of the party. Sugar baron Eduardo Georgetti was president of the party, and *azucareros* Ramón Aboy and Eduardo Cautiño, for example, were among its candidates in the 1912 elections. The party consistently defended the *azucareros*. When in 1913 the Wilson administration threatened to eliminate the tariff on sugar, the Partido Unión and the House of Delegates presided over by De Diego rapidly mobilized against the measure. Its discourse was that of the sugar barons: Puerto Rico's prosperity depended on sugar, and sugar depended on the tariff. Muñoz Rivera had argued that if "free" sugar were decreed, Congress should grant Puerto Rico the right to negotiate commercial treaties or, perhaps, independence. But this was the path that he and his party wished to avoid, since they favored the perpetuation of the existing tariff.[18]

By 1919, young Partido Unión legislator Benigno Fernández García penned a scathing description of his party. Corporation lawyers, he argued, controlled it. Working on behalf of the Tobacco Trust, they had blocked labor legislation he introduced in 1913. Working on behalf of the sugar interests, they built an irrigation system to benefit U.S. corporations in the southern coast.[19] This description is hardly compatible with the notion of the Partido Unión as representative of a traditional agricultural world. Whatever links its leaders had with the receding world of the *hacienda*, the party was also able to attach itself to the economic trends introduced after 1898.

This is also true of De Diego, often seen as the embodiment of a conservative *hacendado* and/or traditional Hispanophile rejection of U.S. rule. Not only was he part of the commission that in 1913 lobbied on behalf of the sugar interests, but, in 1910, he had also favored the elevation of the legal limit of land a corporation could own in Puerto Rico (from 500 to 5,000 acres). It was, he argued, a right of each owner to sell his land at a price fixed by the market. He added, "The land conceived as fatherland, will always be ours, no matter who possesses it."[20] De Diego held traditional views on some issues, but his defense of the sovereignty of the market as determinant of productive specialization and property shifts made him a prophet, not of precapitalist but of capitalist society.

There were dissident voices within the Partido Unión. Mariano Abril argued in 1913 that while "free" sugar would destroy part of the insular sugar industry, it would also allow Puerto Rico to diversify its agriculture and export markets, a transformation for which independence would be the best framework. But the views that prevailed in the Partido Unión were not those of Abril's anti-sugar critique, as we have seen.

To summarize, the Partido Unión was able to encompass the defense of both coffee and sugar propertied interests, neither of which was willing to go beyond a policy of colonial reform. Such colonial reformism, as we explore in the following chapter, was compatible with affirmations of Puerto Rican identity and protests against the most egregious colonial injunctions, such as the imposition of English as the language of instruction. What we have here is the dynamic that has defined Puerto Rican autonomism under U.S. rule: a practice and a discourse that affirms a Puerto Rican identity and seeks to increase insular political participation within the limits imposed by colonial rule and the competitive pressure of U.S. capital.[21]

The Emergence of the Partido Socialista

Across the class divide and through bitter clashes with employers, the labor movement followed a parallel path toward the articulation of its own colonial reformism. From the start, the emergent labor movement understandably took a position favorable to the new authorities. Whatever its shortcomings, the new regime could hardly be worse than Spanish rule, which had outlawed all unions and harassed and jailed labor activists.

Between 1900 and 1904, the FLT—the federation of craft unions organized in 1899—suffered the attacks of the *turbas* associated with the Partido Republicano. The *turbas* also directed their wrath against the Partido Federal, led by Muñoz Rivera. By 1904, this led the FLT to join the Partido Federal and the dissident Republicanos headed by Matienzo Cintrón to form the Partido Unión. As a result of the victory of the Partido Unión in 1904, five labor activists were elected to the House of Delegates. But the link did not last long. The FLT broke with the Partido Unión by 1905–06.

Given the antilabor attitude of many Partido Unión leaders, labor activists developed a healthy suspicion of their demand for self-government. Santiago Iglesias, labor's most influential leader, denounced the demand for self-rule by the Partido Unión as an attempt to institute a government that would curtail labor rights. But Iglesias stopped short of applying this class analysis to the

U.S. state. While denouncing the class interests lurking behind the Puerto Rican propertied classes' patriotic declarations, he embraced American patriotism as a seamlessly democratic impulse. The more crippling aspect of this vision was not so much his rejection of independence, for which *independentistas* would later criticize him, but rather the way it precluded a critical perspective on the U.S. political system, which he saw as a benevolent, classless democracy.

This feeling of dependence on the protective shell of U.S. rule was a product of the precariousness of a harassed labor movement in need of all the allies it could find. In that sense, struggling against the Puerto Rican propertied classes while remaining politically independent of the North American state would have been facilitated by the presence and support of a strong anticapitalist wing within the U.S. labor movement. Indeed, the first contacts of FLT leaders in the United States were with the radical Socialist Labor and Socialist parties. However, the followers of Daniel De Leon or Eugene Debs were not to be the shaping contacts of the FLT but rather the American Federation of Labor, led by Samuel Gompers.

The link had been made by Iglesias in New York, where he lived during most of 1901. By the fall he had been appointed AFL organizer in Puerto Rico. Thanks to his association with Gompers, Iglesias met with both Presidents William McKinley and Theodore Roosevelt. Arrested upon his return to the island in November 1901 (on charges pending since 1900 under a not-yet-repealed Spanish antiunion law) and convicted soon afterward, he was at the time carrying a letter from Roosevelt, requesting no obstacle be placed in the way of his lawful organizing efforts.

In December 1901, a meeting of 500 workers voted to affiliate the FLT with the AFL.[22] By early 1902, the campaign led by Gompers had pushed Governor William Hunt to recommend the repeal of the laws under which Iglesias had been jailed. In April 1902, the insular supreme court overturned Iglesias's conviction.

As the events around the Iglesias case demonstrate, the link to the AFL brought distinct advantages to a nascent labor movement. But this also meant that the AFL brand of conservative business unionism, not conducive to a radical questioning of U.S. political structures, would exert considerable influence on the FLT. Gompers thus helped turn the quest for international allies by Puerto Rico's labor activists and their need to take advantage of the democratic openings resulting from U.S. rule into a growing identification with the American state.

If early labor leaders struggled, as Angel Quintero Rivera has argued, to liberate the workers from a paternalistic culture that taught them to obey their traditional social superiors, many proved unable to do so without fomenting a sense of dependence on the new colonial authorities.[23] Opposition to the patriotic pieties of the Partido Unión was formulated not from an internationalist perspective but from a version of American nationalism, similar to that of Gompers's. Iglesias explained in 1901: "My mission is most eminently American. . . . The Porto Rican people will know how America treats the laborers." Flying in the face of a history of violent labor conflicts in the United States—the epic Pullman strike had occurred only seven years earlier—Iglesias, in jail at the time, argued that in North America "not a single case of such uncalled for persecution is recorded against a laborer."[24] Such uncritical support of U.S. rule led Iglesias to endorse U.S. foreign interventions as both democratic and beneficial. By 1925, this mix of collaboration with the AFL and support for U.S. influence in the hemisphere enabled his appointment to head the AFL-sponsored Pan American Federation of Labor, which sought to keep Latin American workers from nationalist or socialist orientations.

Despite the pledges of Americanism, the early history of the FLT was a tale of violent confrontations. It was only as a result of insistent mobilization that labor was able to secure the effective recognition of the right to assemble and to strike. In fact, in spite of valiant efforts by unpaid activists, the FLT never organized a significant number of agricultural workers—the main contingent of the Puerto Rican working class—and thus remained an organization of craftsmen, among which cigarmakers and typographers stood out for their militancy and intellectual preparation. Among the pioneers of the labor movement, Juan Vilar, Prudencio Rivera, Pablo Vega Santos, Alfonso Torres, and Moisés Echevarría were cigarmakers. Ramón Romero Rosa, Julio Aybar, José Ferrer y Ferrer, and Rafael Alonso were typographers. Luisa Capetillo was a reader in tobacco workshops. Esteban Padilla was a tailor and a cigarmaker; Manuel Rojas, a barber; and Juan S. Marcano, a shoemaker. Eduardo Conde worked as a binder and in many other trades. Santiago Iglesias was a carpenter and Eugenio Sánchez López a blacksmith.

Quantitatively, the evolution of the FLT can be divided into two periods: between 1903 and 1915, it fluctuated from a low of 5,500 to a high of 8,700 members; during World War I and its aftermath, it more than tripled in size to 28,000, a number that remained fairly constant through the 1920s.[25]

Among the efforts of the early labor movement were the sugarcane workers' strikes of 1905 in Arecibo, Carolina, Río Grande, Guánica, Ponce, and Guayama, followed by a dockworkers' strike in San Juan, all of which included violent clashes with the police. Strikes continued in 1906 in Arecibo, a center of early labor activism. But, as indicated, these mobilizations did not lead to the creation of durable union structures among agricultural workers. The 1905–06 actions were followed by sporadic cigarmaker strikes in San Juan, Río Piedras, Bayamón, Caguas, Cidra, and Cayey. Worker protests gained in intensity between 1911 and 1914. Clashes during the tobacco strikes led to a government campaign to disarm workers by confiscating revolvers and other weapons: "It is now very difficult for the natives to obtain or carry weapons of any sort without being apprehended."[26] Moreover, in 1911–12, the government cracked down on reading centers and anarchist activists, such as Juan Vilar, a fact that strengthened the weight of the moderate wing within the FLT, led by Iglesias.

Labor was able to generate its largest mobilizations during the wartime economic boom. In 1915, 17,000 cane workers went on strike. "Martial law," Iglesias reported, "has been practically declared." At least seven workers were killed (six in Vieques, one in Ponce) during these actions. This was followed by the 1916 strike, in which 40,000 workers participated. Workers in the fields were joined by railroad, foundry, trolley, dock, and construction workers and by around 2,000 women operatives of the Porto Rico American Tobacco Company. Meat cutters and garbage collectors staged protests, above all in San Juan and its periphery.[27] More strikes by cane cutters and tobacco and dockworkers, often involving clashes with the police, followed between 1917 and 1921. Governor Arthur D. Yager responded with repressive measures, which in 1920 included banning gatherings in rural areas and prohibiting the use of the red flag. The Partido Unión supported these measures. During a 1919 sugarcane workers' strike in Fajardo, Antonio R. Barceló, main leader of the Partido Unión, proclaimed that if it were in his power, he would deport Santiago Iglesias. It is not surprising that labor activists had little enthusiasm for the demands for self-government formulated by Barceló.[28]

The FLT was no mere replica of the AFL. While the latter rejected the idea of an independent party of labor, the FLT eventually helped to build such a party. This initiative was preceded by the creation of a labor party in Arecibo, which won the municipal elections in 1914. It was this party, led by Esteban Padilla, that issued the call for the founding convention of the Partido Socialista, held in Cayey in March 1915.

The FLT both sustained the Partido Socialista and imbued it with its blind trust of the U.S. Congress. Its program called for the enactment of labor legislation, the abolition of the death penalty, enforcement of the "500-acre law," state ownership of basic services, and women's suffrage. In 1919, socialist leader Manuel Rojas proposed that the party adopt the creation of an independent republic as its objective. The proposal was defeated. The program retained its vague aspiration to a "Social Democracy of Labor" while warning the U.S. Congress, seen as labor's protector of last resort, that all petitions for self-government were attempts to enhance the privileges of the insular ruling classes.

The party, led by skilled workers and supported by the sugarcane proletariat, rapidly became a significant force. In the elections of 1920, it received 23 percent of the vote. It elected four legislators and controlled eight municipalities. The eastern coastal area from Río Grande to Yabucoa remained a bulwark of socialist electoral strength through the 1930s.

As early as 1923, labor leader Sandalio Alonso denounced the growth of a layer of "socialist functionaries of a bureaucratic style" who had never belonged to a union but now joined the party to further their individual ambitions.[29] Indeed, the demobilization of the rank and file during the 1920s nurtured the integration of party leaders to the state apparatus at a municipal and insular level. This bureaucratic drift led to alliances with traditional parties. In 1920, the Partido Socialista experimented with an electoral alliance with the Partido Republicano in Ponce. This combination became the preamble to the Coalición, an electoral alliance between the Partido Socialista and a wing of the Partido Republicano for the elections of 1924. The other, more conservative Republicano wing, as we saw above, organized the Alianza with the Partido Unión. (See Fig. 7.1.)

Evidently, there was no unanimity among the political leaders of the possessing classes about how to respond to an independent party of labor. While the Republicanos, led by Rafael Martínez Nadal, who formed the Coalición with the Partido Socialista, felt comfortable with its mild reformist orientation and pro-U.S. views, the organizers of the Alianza still considered it too threatening. José Tous Soto, leader of the Republican wing of the Alianza, explained how in Washington he had been made to understand that no alliance including a party bearing the name "Socialist" would be considered a legitimate interlocutor by U.S. policy makers.[30] Whatever fears existed in Puerto Rico or Washington, Martínez Nadal's appreciation proved correct. The Partido Socialista was to rapidly abandon the radicalism that may have animated some of its founders.

In spite of a less than glorious end, the Partido Socialista was an extraordinary achievement. It was not only the embodiment of a political program but an expression of a rich autonomous cultural sphere of labor, which included social centers, journals, and study groups. Although fundamentally male and skilled, the labor movement was more open to female participation and women's demands for equality than other political currents. The FLT, for example, embraced the demand for women's suffrage in 1908, long before either the Unión or Republicano parties.

The life of Luisa Capetillo brought together many strands that went into the making of Puerto Rico's early labor radicalism: the leading role of cigarmakers, the ideas of anarchist and utopian socialism, and, in her case, the struggle for women's emancipation. Born in 1879 in Arecibo, she worked at times as a reader in cigar workshops and was active as an FLT agitator in the 1905–06 cane workers' strikes. In 1911, she published her first long text in defense of women's rights, which for her included suffrage as well as economic and sexual rights. Her rejection of gender stereotypes made her well known beyond the labor movement. Years later she would be remembered as the first woman to have "worn pants" in Puerto Rico.

During the second decade of the twentieth century, Capetillo moved between Puerto Rico, New York, Havana, and Tampa, an itinerary through the world of the cigarmakers in the Caribbean and the United States. Her strategic vision was limited to the notion of a general strike, which would dismantle the existing order and lead to communal forms of life. Like others in the labor movement, she seems to have been indifferent to Puerto Rico's "status question," insisting that only the dismantling of bourgeois society and state could liberate humanity. This radical but abstract vision could coexist with Iglesias's reformist unionism insofar as both tended, for different reasons, to concentrate on immediate workers' struggles.

The Birth of El Barrio and Puerto Rican New York

The world of Puerto Rican labor activism, as the travels of Capetillo indicate, was not restricted to the island. Cigarmakers had since the 1890s formed much of the nucleus of the budding Puerto Rican community in New York.

Economic expansion during World War I and the 1920s and the closing of the door on European migration improved the chances of Puerto Ricans seeking jobs in the United States.[31] There were around 45,000 Puerto Ricans in New York City by 1920. In Manhattan, Puerto Ricans tended to concentrate in East Harlem, soon to be known as El Barrio, and in Chelsea. In Brooklyn, they settled around Boro Hall and the Navy Yard. Chelsea attracted cigarmakers, while the Brooklyn waterfront became a home for maritime workers. The

Labor, feminist, and anarchist activist Luisa Capetillo participated in working-class struggles in Puerto Rico, Tampa, Havana, and New York City in the first two decades of the twentieth century. (Laboratorio fotográfico Biblioteca José M. Lázaro, Universidad de Puerto Rico – Río Piedras)

Puerto Rican diaspora was heavily proletarian and largely employed in un-skilled and low-paying manufacturing jobs in garment, biscuit, pencil, and rope factories and in service occupations as porters, janitors, and maids. But their wages, however low, were higher than those prevalent on the island. As on the island, many women were employed as home needleworkers.

Riots in the summer of 1926 during which stores in El Barrio were ransacked by gangs (allegedly sponsored by non–Puerto Rican merchants), followed by clashes with the police, led to the creation of the Liga Puertorriqueña e His-pana, an umbrella organization of smaller groups that sought to represent Puerto Ricans to a wider public. Puerto Ricans were also active in non–Puerto Rican organizations, from socialist clubs to mainstream parties. Brooklyn storekeeper and community leader Carlos Tapia, active in the Democratic Party, exemplified the second option. In 1918, Bernardo Vega, Jesús Colón, Lupercio Arroyo, and others organized a Spanish language committee of the U.S. Socialist Party. In the early 1920s, they organized the Alianza Obrera, which brought together Spanish-speaking radicals. In 1924, they supported farmer-labor candidate Robert M. La Follette for president.[32]

Unlike Iglesias and other leaders of the Partido Socialista, Vega and Colón combined their opposition to the Puerto Rican propertied classes with denun-ciations of U.S. capitalism. They thus objected to Iglesias's uncritical support of U.S. officials in Puerto Rico and U.S. policies in Latin America. In 1922, for example, they took exception when Iglesias sided with Governor Reily against the Partido Unión. They agreed that the Partido Unión was an enemy of labor, but they saw no reason why the recognition of that fact should lead to blanket support for the governor.[33] In their case, opposing the privileges of the Puerto Rican propertied classes did not lead into support of U.S. colonial rule.

The Women's Suffrage Movement

The second decade of the twentieth century saw the rise of a women's suffrage campaign led by Ana Roque, Mercedes Solá, Beatriz Lassalle, Carmen Gómez, and Olivia Paoli, among others. This was a movement of middle-class women active in the professions open to them, such as nursing, pharmacy, and teach-ing. Roque had been writing on women's rights since the 1890s.[34] The move-ment lobbied the political parties after the founding of the Liga Femínea in 1917, which in 1921 became the Liga Social Sufragista. The prevalent ideology of this current, as studied by María Barceló Miller, was that of "social feminism," a perspective that demanded rights for women but did not question their association with motherly and domestic occupations. This limited but did not annul the break that suffrage represented with the notion of women as subordinate, dependent, and infantilized beings.

After the passage of the Nineteenth Amendment in the United States in 1919, many entertained the hope that the measure would be extended to Puerto Rico. Genara Pagán, labor activist and one of the leaders of the 1914 tobacco workers' strikes, returned from New York (where she had moved) and attempted to register to vote in the 1920 elections. But colonial administrators determined that the new constitutional provision did not apply to the island, given its status as unincorporated territory.

After 1920, the issue of women's suffrage could not be detached from the impact of the rise of the Partido Socialista. Barceló, leader of the Partido Unión, admitted that the vote of poor, illiterate women would favor the Partido Socialista. There were around 300,000 potential women voters, of which 250,000 were illiterate. With universal suffrage, argued Barceló, "the Partido Socialista would overwhelm us." A wing of the movement concluded that suffrage restricted to literate women was a more realistic immediate objective.[35] While some saw this as a tactical maneuver, others shared Barceló's antisocialist fears: their link to the men of their class was stronger than their solidarity with lower-class women. Others refused to abandon the call for universal women's suffrage. As a result, the movement split in 1924.

The Liga Social Sufragista grew closer to the Coalición, which included the Partido Socialista. It demanded voting rights for all women. The Asociación Puertorriqueña de Mujeres Sufragistas worked with the Alianza, limiting its demand to the vote for literate women. Furthermore, while the latter restricted its campaign to Puerto Rico, the Liga asked Congress to promulgate the desired reform over the head of the insular legislature. Criticized as unpatriotic, the Liga responded that its hand had been forced by the inaction of the insular legislature. Indeed, it was the threat of congressional action that finally shamed the Alianza into enacting a limited suffrage measure in 1929. Literate women were able to vote in 1932, a right extended to all women in 1936 as a result of legislation approved by the Coalición after it won the elections of 1932.

Hostos, Matienzo Cintrón, and the Partido de la Independencia

The largely forgotten ideas and initiatives of former autonomist leader Rosendo Matienzo Cintrón and of separatist thinker Eugenio María de Hostos and of their collaborators demand some attention as the most sophisticated early attempt to confront critically the onset of U.S. rule from a consistently democratic perspective.

After 1898, Matienzo Cintrón became a supporter of "Americanization." By this he did not mean aping U.S. customs to somehow seem "American" but a transformation of Puerto Rican society through reforms he associated with the United States, such as the recognition of democratic freedoms, the separation of church and state, public education, greater independence for women, and the institution of self-government. For him, "Americanization" was shorthand for democratization and modernization. He initially supported statehood because he saw it as the most adequate political vehicle for such a project. Hostos, a veteran separatist, took a more cautious position. While favoring independence, he proposed a united front to demand the right of Puerto Rico to determine its status. To do so was both to act and demand recognition as a collective subject capable of self-direction.[36]

Consistent with their initial views, both Matienzo Cintrón and Hostos rejected the Foraker Act. Hostos denounced how it created a "hybrid" regime: a mixture of "American-style" government and "Spanish-style" colonialism."[37] But Hostos died in 1903 after a lifelong struggle for Antillean independence. Meanwhile, Matienzo Cintrón abandoned the Partido Republicano. Unswerving in his commitment to Americanization as he understood it, he now denounced U.S. colonial policy, not because it was Americanizing Puerto Rico but rather because it was imposing a "false Americanization." "True Americanization," he now bitterly realized, would have to be attained not in collaboration with but in opposition to U.S. policy.[38] "In the twentieth century," he wrote in 1911, "the American flag represents . . . the same as the flag of King George in the eighteenth century! . . . What a degeneration!"[39] By 1912, he took this logic to the limit and concluded that Americanization, given the mutation of the American republic into a colonial empire, would paradoxically require the constitution of an independent Puerto Rican republic.

While Matienzo Cintrón and Hostos criticized U.S. colonial policies, they also asked themselves why the admired republic had betrayed the democratic practices they attributed to it. Both linked what Matienzo Cintrón called the "grave alteration" in the "fundamental rules" of "American democracy" to the rise of the "plutocracy," of the "trusts," of "monopoly companies," of the "great coalitions of capital." The trusts not only were propelling the United States into colonial adventures but also threatened democracy within North America: a clash was thus brewing in the United States between the forces of democracy and the plutocracy. The outcome of that struggle, Hostos had argued

Rosendo Matienzo Cintrón in 1905. An early supporter of annexation,
Matienzo Cintrón evolved toward a pro-independence position as he
became disillusioned with U.S. colonial rule.

earlier, would largely determine the future of the Caribbean.[40] The struggle for
Antillean self-determination and the battle to salvage U.S. democracy had the
same antagonist: the emergent American plutocracy.

In 1904, Matienzo Cintrón joined in the creation of the Partido Unión. But,
as the party settled into a policy of accommodation with the colonial authorities, he grew increasingly distant from its leading sector. He thus became part
of the legislative fraction known as the *radicales*, which also included Manuel
Zeno Gandía and Luis Lloréns Torres.

In 1909, the *radicales* succeeded in briefly shifting the policies of the Partido
Unión toward a more militant, anticolonial direction. Through a stormy legis-

lative session, they repeatedly clashed with House president De Diego, who, in spite of his later fame as an *independentista*, insisted then on a policy of collaboration with Governor Regis Post. But in 1909, the executive went so far in blocking legislation approved by the House that even the sector led by Muñoz Rivera felt the need to register something stronger than verbal objections to colonial misrule. The moderates thus yielded to the *radicales'* proposal of closing the legislative session without approving the budget bill, thus threatening the government with administrative paralysis.

In response, the U.S. Congress amended the Foraker Act to allow for the rolling over of the budget of any given year if the legislature failed to approve a new one. But Governor Post was removed. By 1910, a new governor adopted a more amicable attitude toward the Partido Unión, which in turn—and to the dismay of the *radicales*—abandoned the idea of pursuing the protest begun in 1909. In 1910, Matienzo Cintrón and Lloréns Torres clashed again with the leaders of the Partido Unión over diverse issues. While the *radicales* opposed the death penalty and defended women's suffrage, pro-labor and pro-*colono* legislation, and the 500-acre limitation, De Diego, Georgetti, and other leaders of the Partido Unión repeatedly took the floor to defend the opposite positions.[41]

In 1912, Matienzo Cintrón and the *radicales* came together to organize the Partido de la Independencia, the first party that under U.S. rule embraced independence as its sole objective. Its program was written by Rafael López Landrón, a lawyer with links to the labor movement who had collaborated with Matienzo Cintrón in cooperativist and other campaigns in the past. The program proposed state ownership of banks, railroads, and telephone and telegraph services and guaranteed employment, minimum wage laws, the eight-hour day, old-age pensions, equal rights for women, and the promotion of cooperatives.[42] While favoring growing state regulation of the economy, it also proposed closer citizen control over elected officials and government functionaries through the institution of reforms taken from the program of American progressives of the time, including the recall of elected officials, citizens' legislative initiatives, and referendums on specific measures. For them, the aspiration for a socially progressive Puerto Rican republic and the struggle against the plutocracy in the United States were interdependent and hopefully mutually reinforcing impulses.

López Landrón saw the struggle in Puerto Rico as part of a wider clash: "Capitalism," he warned, "is marching . . . toward its international organization." Only the "cosmopolitan movement of labor" could counteract the "cosmopolitan movement of capital." Mere political democracy was obsolete: to control "the Rockefellers, the Morgans and the Harrimans," the republic of Jefferson and Washington was insufficient. For that, a new "social" democracy was indispensable.[43]

López Landrón applauded the progress attained under U.S. rule, such as productive advances, health reforms, wider opportunities for women, and freedom of speech. But, unlike Iglesias and other labor leaders, this did not lead him to idealize the United States as a classless democracy. The United States, he argued, had replaced the "aristocracy of birth" with an "aristocracy of money." Puerto Rico, transferred from Spanish to U.S. rule, had moved from a "theocratic-military monopoly" to the "monopoly of the external plutocracy."[44]

It is not hard to see why the Partido de la Independencia—created by professionals not linked to the world of labor (López Landrón excepted) but endowed with a program that could hardly attract support from the possessing classes—led a short life, disappearing after 1914. Matienzo Cintrón died in 1913, and López Landrón died in New York in 1917 after having participated in the founding of the Partido Socialista in 1915.[45] Other members of the party, such as Lloréns Torres, left active politics. Some returned to the Partido Unión, which after 1913 at least nominally had adopted an *independentista* program.

Puerto Rican politics, given the demise of the Partido de la Independencia, thus came to be dominated by the clash of versions of colonial reformism, which included the accommodation of the Partido Unión to the limits of the relation of nonincorporation with the United States, the collaboration of the pro-statehood Partido Republicano with U.S. colonial rule, and the colonial-reformist drift of the Partido Socialista. Linked to different classes or sectors, each party confronted its rivals while hoping to gain Washington's favor and support for its short- or long-term objectives.

Since the strictly political debates between 1900 and the mid-1920s are complex enough, we have somewhat artificially divorced them in our discussion from cultural issues arising from the onset of U.S. rule. We must now repair this omission by going over some of the literary and related developments in which many of the figures we have already met, including Matienzo Cintrón, De Diego, Lloréns Torres, and Zeno Gandía, were active participants.

4

AMERICANIZATION AND ITS
DISCONTENTS, 1898–1929

The nineteenth century witnessed the emergence of a sense of cultural distinctiveness and national consciousness in Puerto Rico. This was a graded and uneven process. The largely island-born dispossessed majority must have increasingly seen Spanish merchants and bureaucrats as belonging not only to another social class or rank but to another people or culture. But in a country that in 1887 had a literacy rate of 8.8 percent, the more conscious, written formulations of this emergent sense of collective self were elaborated within the precarious literary-journalistic circles of a thin layer linked by family ties to the *criollo* possessing classes. Within that sector, furthermore, differentiation from Spain was a gradual and complex process.

As the *criollos* began to see themselves as other than Spaniards or as Spaniards of a different kind, some began to identify with those whom Spain had once conquered, the pre-Columbian inhabitants known as Tainos. An elaborate example of this was Eugenio María de Hostos's 1873 novel, *La peregrinación de Bayoán*, whose protagonist, Bayoán, bore a Taino name and identified with the island's country folk. Bayoán declared that he had no compatriots in the cities or among the wealthy *hacendados*. It was among the *jíbaros* (working farmers or rural wageworkers), presented in typical romantic style as "philosophers of nature," that true men could be found, instead of among city dwellers, who were "reptiles." Only *jíbaros* constituted a solid basis for an emergent "national character."

Africa and blacks occupied an ambiguous place in the emergent map of a Puerto Rican identity as formulated by many liberal *criollos*. While *criollo* liberals embraced the cause of the abolition of slavery and sought to push it through against the resistance of recalcitrant slave-owning planters, many retained racist notions of black inferiority while some feared that blacks would outnumber whites if slavery were allowed to expand. Most liberals aspired to a future bourgeois order based on the collaboration of labor and capital regulated by the market, freed of past state restrictions and commercial monopolies. But even this project was implicitly colored, literally, by the race question: blacks were normally envisaged as belonging in the future to the subordinate laboring classes.[1]

These debates interacted in a complex way with the issue of the political relation to Spain. Puerto Rican white liberals could defend incorporation into a liberal Spain, insisting on their identity as Spaniards, implicitly or explicitly excluding nonwhite islanders from their imagined community. They could, more radically, demand incorporation into a liberal and multiracial Spain that would also include nonwhite islanders as equal participants in the life of the Spanish nation. Or they could demand autonomy or independence for a Puerto Rican people or nation with specific and distinct characteristics, which then opened the issue of the definition of those characteristics and the place allotted to nonwhites within it.

Salvador Brau, for example, author of the most sustained attempt to analyze Puerto Rican society and culture from a liberal autonomist and reformist perspective, praised the work of black women teachers and of black educator Rafael Cordero as examples of racial harmony, in turn the best means of avoiding the bloody confrontations that had occurred in other lands.[2] Such exaltations of white benevolence and black moderation implied a rejection of the more virulent racist views, but they also discouraged a consistent questioning of racial hierarchies that perpetuated the connection of blackness with socially subordinate positions. The revolutionary separatist wing held more definite antiracist views. Ramón Emeterio Betances, for example, proudly admitted his "mixed" racial provenance, while Hostos penned furious attacks on racism.

While the *separatistas* embraced political independence, which many combined with a vision of an Antillean identity, the *autonomistas* still tried to define Puerto Rico as a regional entity within the larger Spanish polity. Thus, autonomists more often than not referred to Puerto Rico as *el país*, with its own interests that they wished to protect, and to Spain as the *nación*, to which they pledged allegiance. This tension between *país* and *nación* was still present in their texts in 1898, as U.S. troops began landing in Guánica.

Against that background, the coming of U.S. rule had a complex, even contradictory, impact on Puerto Rican culture and sense of identity. From the start, U.S. colonial authorities sought to reshape the islanders in their own image, a project that prominently included the attempt to impose English through its use as the language of instruction in an expanding public school system. But the imposition of English and Americanization through the school system was not coupled with censorship or institutionalized persecution of Spanish or other cultural forms. Nor were Puerto Ricans displaced by U.S. or English-speaking settlers. Demographically, the new colonial rulers were restricted to a small group of functionaries and entrepreneurs, who nevertheless occupied key positions of power and influence. Puerto Rican possessing classes were politically subordinated but retained considerable material resources. Neither them nor the dispossessed majority exhibited an inclination to abandon Spanish for English. The press and public sphere that now came into the open and thickened in the context of the wider freedoms allowed by U.S. rule had Spanish as its medium. Puerto Ricans used these wider freedoms to protest the more offending aspects of U.S. rule, including the imposition of English. The net result of this configuration was the fact that while official business and schoolwork was conducted in English, Puerto Rico remained a Spanish-speaking society with a literary field more attuned to Spanish, European, or Latin American letters than to U.S. literary trends.

The same may be said of a wider feeling of Puerto Ricans as a distinct people. By the 1920s, the vitality and persistence of that feeling were evident enough to be recognized even by some who had earlier denied its existence. In 1899, U.S. functionary Victor S. Clark described the Puerto Rican people as "plastic and malleable."[3] Thirty years later, visiting the island as researcher for the Brookings Institution, Clark described Puerto Rico as "vividly conscious of its individuality."[4] Paradoxically, through the arrival of an English-speaking colonial power, Spanish acquired an added significance as it suddenly became available as the most evident marker of a distinct Puerto Rican identity, a role it could not play under Spanish colonial rule. Simply put, the initial project of Americanization of a "plastic and malleable" human material had failed. By the 1920s, if not earlier, the issue of Puerto Rican identity, of the need to relaunch a national project interrupted in 1898, was making its way into the center of concern of a new literary generation.

Nevertheless, since the term "culture" encompasses such a broad array of phenomena, here we must of necessity restrict the scope of our analysis. In this chapter, we first examine official U.S. Americanization policy and the diverse responses it elicited among prominent political and literary figures. We then turn our attention to three concurrent processes: the autonomous cultural sphere generated by the organized labor movement, the incessant work of popular cultural creation among the dispossessed, and the beginning of Puerto Rican cultural expressions in New York. To conclude, we examine the stirrings of younger, relatively well-off students who after World War I sought to renew Puerto Rican literature and gradually moved toward posing the problem of Puerto Rican identity with unprecedented energy, a process that, in their case, came to fruition in the 1930s.

Contrasting "Americanizations," Contrasting Identities

After 1898, most members of Puerto Rico's political leadership, veterans of the Partido Autonomista that had been organized in 1887, took a decidedly favorable view of U.S. rule. As we saw in chapter 3, Rosendo Matienzo Cintrón in particular elaborated a defense of Americanization, by which he meant the remaking of Puerto Rican culture in a democratic and modern direction, not the servile imitation of American culture. This implied a dynamic, open vision of Puerto Rico's culture as something to be both affirmed and constantly reelaborated. His objective, both as an early supporter of statehood and eventual supporter of independence, was not to "protect" Puerto Rican culture as a finished object but to transform it and to mix it with all that he considered progressive in American and other cultures. "To not accept an advance," he wrote in 1911, "because it comes from a country that we consider our enemy is . . . idiotic[,] and to applaud without reservation . . . everything that comes from ourselves, is equally stupid."[5] Matienzo Cintrón was as confident of the durability of the Puerto Rican "personality" as he was convinced of the futility of a return to the past: "Just as we cannot cease being Puerto Rico no matter how much time goes by, nothing in the world can turn us into the Puerto Rico that we were."[6] For Matienzo Cintrón, the fact that the Puerto Rican "personality" had crystallized slowly had been an advantage, not a drawback, since "it had given us time to take from all foreign winds, thoughts, goals, institutions, culture, tastes, even dresses and fashions."[7]

Matienzo Cintrón envisaged the coming together "of all peoples, all civilizations, all creeds."[8] As part of that process, Latin America and Puerto Rico, cross-fertilized by "opposite currents," would eventually bring forth "the fruit of universality."[9] Such was the cultural orientation that corresponded to his radical democratic opposition to U.S. colonial rule. To the extent that he proclaimed an attachment to Spain, it was to the Spain that he described as going from the "heroes of Villalar to Ferrer," that is to say, from the early opponents of absolutism to semi-anarchist anticlericalism preached by radical educator Francisco Ferrer.[10]

Yet, in spite of his dynamic notion of Puerto Rican culture, the logic of

Matienzo Cintrón's growing opposition to U.S. rule did lead him to attempt a definition of a national type, a symbolic embodiment of the Puerto Rican people that he called "Pancho Ibero," the first of many literary attempts at national definition that were to follow through the century. The very name of this fictional character allowed for little appreciation of the African dimension of Puerto Rican culture. While Matienzo Cintrón emphatically rejected racism, he tended to see and define Puerto Rican culture as strictly an extension and differentiation within the Iberian tradition.

While Matienzo Cintrón used the term "Americanization" to refer to a democratic remaking of insular society and the creation of a modern Puerto Rican culture shaped by diverse influences, by the time of his death in 1913 the word was almost universally used to refer to the attempts to reshape Puerto Rican life according to the preferences of U.S. colonial administrators. For Victor S. Clark, one of the officials entrusted with the organization of the new school system, Puerto Rico was a blank page. Puerto Ricans were, he argued, "in our hands to create and mould."[11] In spite of such attitudes, U.S. education initiatives were not without merit. After 1898, thousands gained access to primary education. From 1901 to 1917, school enrollment grew from 30,000 to 150,000, or around one-third of all children of school age. But the nature of the education to be imparted became a point of bitter debate.

Policies followed during this period included the imposition of English as the language of instruction in high schools and, during certain periods, in primary schools. Even the names of schools and the punctuation of the year with U.S. holidays invited students to think of themselves as part of an American narrative going back to Washington, Jefferson, and Lincoln.[12] An irritating detail signaled how little time U.S. officials had for the island's culture: until 1932, U.S. authorities officially referred to Puerto Rico as "Porto Rico," a Portuguese term never used in the Island.

These policies generated both individual and collective resistance. Teachers and students diverged from official directives and conducted classes in Spanish. The Asociación de Maestros, organized in 1913, demanded that Spanish be adopted as the language of instruction. José De Diego, leader of the *independentista* wing of the Partido Unión after 1913, became associated with the defense of Spanish as the author of legislation that, in 1913 and 1915, requested it be made the language of instruction. But if De Diego, like Matienzo Cintrón before him, came over to an *independentista* position by 1913, he did so from a very different political and cultural perspective. Matienzo Cintrón opposed U.S. colonial rule as an anticlerical, freethinking, pro-labor democrat who wished to radically transform Puerto Rican culture. De Diego did so while formulat-ing a far more traditionalist notion of Puerto Rican identity, which included conservative views on labor and women's rights, for example, and did not look favorably on U.S. influences fostering either.[13]

U.S. policies of cultural imposition and above all the attempt to make En-glish the language of instruction deeply affected the early educational experi-ences of the rising generation, born in or around the time of the U.S. invasion. The economically better-off among these young men and women were to move on into professional careers by the early and mid-1920s. We will come to their initial literary efforts and their more mature work in the 1930s later in this chapter and in chapter 6.

Modernismo and Other Currents

Meanwhile, the elaboration by Matienzo Cintrón and De Diego of their respec-tively radical-democratic and conservative conceptions of Puerto Rican culture and identity coincided with the brief and late apogee of a new literary sen-sibility in Puerto Rico: *modernismo*. Two of its exponents, Nemesio Canales and Luis Lloréns Torres, rank among the more influential Puerto Rican authors of the twentieth century. *Modernismo* articulated three elements (in diverse pro-portions, according to each author): openness to cosmopolitan and moderniz-ing influences, an affirmation of Puerto Rican cultural identity and of its link with a Hispanic American cultural universe, and a challenge to U.S. arrogance. Proud but not narrowly nationalist, it allowed some of its practitioners to oppose U.S. imperialism while, for example, admiring Walt Whitman's poetic breakthroughs. Lloréns Torres's "Canción de las Antillas" combined the for-mal innovations that Nicaraguan poet Rubén Darío had popularized with a joyous, celebratory, self-confident tone and pleasure in self-description remi-niscent of Whitman's "Song of Myself." But this was more of a song of *our-*selves. It was an attempt to affirm a collective identity, which in this poem was presented as female, strong and beautiful, and rooted in both an Indian and Hispanic past, again to the exclusion of the African heritage.

The vehicles for these literary explorations were the short-lived journals edited by Lloréns Torres, Canales, and Miguel Guerra Mondragón, such as *Revista de las Antillas* and *Juan Bobo*. Lloréns Torres, Canales, and Guerra Mon-dragón were not only literary figures but also involved in the political battles of the time. Lloréns Torres had been part of the radical wing of the Partido Unión along with Matienzo Cintrón, discussed in the previous chapter. The political views of Lloréns Torres in the second decade of the twentieth century, like those of Canales, can be described as a variant of moderate socialism, inspired by a general rejection of social inequality and exploitation, without a systematic understanding or critique of capitalism. In 1913, Lloréns Torres wrote enthusiastically of Mexican *zapatismo*, assuring his readers that it entailed the beginning of the social revolution many had thought would begin in Europe. But he turned this into a call, not for revolution, but for the wealthy to understand it was better to enter the path of reform than risk a bloodier outcome if change came from below.[14]

In 1914, Lloréns Torres published *El grito de Lares*, a dramatic text about the 1868 revolution against Spanish rule. He can thus be credited with beginning the recovery of this event, which the autonomist tradition had largely disregarded. In it he includes a dialogue in which a wageworker likens himself to a slave and, while joining the insurrection, bitterly comments on the fact that its fruits would probably be enjoyed by the local possessing classes and not by the dispossessed like him. Such denunciations of inequality are also present in other texts by Lloréns Torres (for example, "Soliloquio del soldado," "Banquete de gordos," "Un sermón en la bolsa") but are often combined with elitist recriminations of the oppressed for passively accepting their fate.

After Matienzo Cintrón's death in 1913 and the collapse of the Partido de la Independencia by 1914, Lloréns Torres largely abandoned active politics. He remained Puerto Rico's best-known poet at least until the 1930s. His works would be subjected to diverse readings as the century advanced. They were respected by younger poets, even if they diverged from his literary preferences, in the 1920s and 1930s. They were subsequently enshrined after his death in 1944 as a poetic expression of Puerto Rican patriotism. By the 1970s, he came to be seen by the "new historians," whose views we examine below, as the poet of the old conservative *hacendado* class as it reacted to the U.S. invasion. Yet more recent readings have argued that his poetry articulates a vindication, for both men and women, of pleasures proscribed by repressive civilization that gives it a subversive, ludic, panerotic, liberating charge. His poetry in this reading should not be reduced to an affirmation of *hacendado* or of male privilege.[15] As we have seen, his views, at least between 1909 and 1915, favorable to agrarian and labor reforms, were hardly compatible with the interests or preferences of conservative *hacendados*. Through all these debates, his commitment to a poetry that is both modern and autochthonous, sophisticated and directed to a wide public, remained a model for many as late as the 1960s.

Canales and Guerra Mondragón, two of Lloréns Torres's collaborators in the brief life of Puerto Rican *modernismo* before it was overtaken by the literary avant-garde of the 1920s, were equally interesting figures. Canales's ideas are best summarized as a constant interplay of opposites. On the one hand, his democratic and egalitarian convictions and his faith in the promise of modernity led him to criticize any and all idealizations of the past. His ironic pen attacked the traditional subordination of women, the old notions of honor and chivalry, the Christian cult of poverty and renunciation, and the conservative fear of cultural change. In 1909, as a member of the House of Delegates, he introduced one of the earliest bills favoring women's suffrage. And yet he also felt that emergent bourgeois civilization, centered on the competitive accumulation of moneyed wealth, tended to debase or destroy social forms and the sensibilities they fostered, which he considered necessary for a true flourishing of the human faculties. Canales thus insisted on the need to bury the past and fully embrace modernity while often making use of the past to denounce the limitations of bourgeois society. He favored the growing participation of women alongside men in public life while at the same time praising "feminine" culture centered around fashion and gossip; those unproductive "frivolities" had the merit of at least not being subjected to the imperatives of efficiency that ruled the masculine world of business.

He similarly defended democracy and political equality but at the same time playfully chided the revolution of 1911 in China for instituting another drab and ugly government of presidents and ministers: if the deposed imperial court had been despotic and arbitrary, it at least had the merit of being elegant and full of ancient mystery, something which, he added, could not be said of President Taft. While praising the Futurist avant-garde for breaking with tradition, he also denounced it for embracing an ugly commercial world. Canales rejected both the vision of poverty as a virtue and the pursuit of ever-larger money fortunes; both attitudes, through either privation or the accumulation of wealth in a quantitative, abstract form, deprived humans of a true, concrete enjoyment of the world. Not a few of his texts are veritable reveries: they describe diverse states of lethargy and idleness, both sensual and spiritual enjoyment, and a loss of the self in a dream or daydream, which he saw as a refuge from his bourgeois existence.[16]

His sympathies for both anarchists and aristocrats, for socialist demands for equality and the elegance of the imperial court, for feminism and "feminine" frivolities, for the need for revolution and a desire to escape into a world of sensual enjoyment, converged in some of his texts into a vision of an irreverent and egalitarian—and simultaneously elegant and aristocratic—socialism,

Author, editor, and legislator Nemesio Canales. Canales held prolabor, feminist, and socialist views and was a key participant in Puerto Rico's literary milieu during the second decade of the twentieth century. (Laboratorio fotográfico Biblioteca José M. Lázaro, Universidad de Puerto Rico–Río Piedras)

something akin to the views found in Oscar Wilde's "The Soul of Man under Socialism." This socialism would emancipate the senses, liberating them from the imperatives of capitalist accumulation, which turns all use values and human faculties into a means of augmenting profits, into an exchange value. Typically, in 1915 Canales had favorably compared the war to normal bourgeois existence: war at least had an element of heroism that bourgeois civilization had obliterated. Yet he felt a deep aversion to war and its consequences. By 1922, he was forcefully arguing that only the abolition of capitalism, with its inherent tendency toward militarism, could save the world from a new conflagration. Pursuing his editorial projects, in 1918 Canales left for Venezuela, Panama, and eventually Argentina. He returned to Puerto Rico in 1921 and died in 1923.[17]

Like Canales, Guerra Mondragón sought in literature a refuge from the base world of bourgeois society. Rejecting what he called "photographic art" and the realism that according to him had stunted literature in Spanish, he embraced the notion of a literature of "imagination and fantasy," which he associated with the English tradition of cultural aversion to industrial society.[18] A translator of Oscar Wilde, his essays contain abundant references to John Ruskin, Matthew Arnold, and William Morris. He yearned for an art that would obey its own laws: "Our art, then, is not a reflection of this epoch, of this feverishly commercial San Juan; it is not a reflection of the things that are, but of those that should be and of those that in the end will come to be."[19]

But Guerra Mondragón, cosmopolitan as his interests were, also saw his work as part of a Puerto Rican cultural project. He was thus a precursor and in some cases the mentor of younger authors who in the 1930s were to sharply pose the question of Puerto Rican identity. Guerra Mondragón identified three epochs in the evolution of Puerto Rican culture. The first, up to the late nineteenth century, was dominated by the generations who, upon their arrival from Europe (he made no mention of those who arrived from Africa), concentrated all their efforts on the initial accumulation of a material fortune. The second epoch began at the end of the nineteenth century, which witnessed "the foundation of the Puerto Rican personality" and a struggle for its political rights. This was the generation of the autonomist movement, which Guerra Mondragón identified as the *generación del 1887*, the year in which Puerto Rican liberals and Autonomistas confronted a wave of repression by the Spanish authorities. Finally, a third epoch and a new generation—Guerra Mondragón's own—had emerged, a cohort imbued with the "noble spirit of modern culture" that could bring to fruition the project of "turning a factory into a fatherland."[20] This tripartite division of Puerto Rican history, as well as the desire to trace the evolution of the emergence of a "Puerto Rican personality" and even the privileging of the autonomist movement, were to forcefully reemerge in the work of Antonio S. Pedreira and other figures of the influential literary efforts of the 1930s.

But Guerra Mondragón, like Canales and Lloréns Torres, was no mere aesthete. A practicing lawyer and at times legislator for the Partido Unión, he wrote many pieces of legislation and reports on economic or social issues and, in the 1930s, helped put together the test cases seeking to enforce the 500-acre limitation on land tenure. While Lloréns Torres remained an *independentista*, Guerra Mondragón is credited by many with the first elaboration, for the program of Partido Unión in 1922, of the idea of a "free associated state" as a third alternative to both statehood and independence. Guerra Mondragón's literary antirealism was thus linked to a consistently reformist pragmatism in the political sphere.

The realism held in such low regard by Guerra Mondragón was alive in Puerto Rico as several novelists sought to portray an appalling social reality. Manuel González García's *Gestación* (1905), Ramón Juliá Marín's *La gleba* (1912), Miguel Meléndez Muñoz's *Yuyo* (1913), and Manuel Zeno Gandía's *Redentores* (1925), to mention a few, explore diverse aspects of the island's situation from the particular point of view of each author. *Gestación* and *La gleba* describe the exploitation of the agricultural laborer. In a utopian turn, the former has the *hacendado* transform his farm into a cooperative. In *Yuyo*, Meléndez Muñoz sympathetically describes his heroine's struggle to escape from her father's well-intentioned but repressive grip in a novel that includes a defense of women's rights. Zeno Gandía's *Redentores* counterposes U.S. officials who embody U.S. colonial policies and Americans who reject them, a construction that can be read as a novelized version of Matienzo Cintrón's opposition of "true" and "false" Americanizations. Zeno Gandía's novel—its author being a more conservative thinker than Matienzo Cintrón—incorporates racist imagery, conservative and moralistic rejection of big-city life as a den of perdition, and a portrait of the Catholic hierarchy as an agent of justice in a corrupt world. But Catholicism does not function in the text as a mark of a Puerto Rican identity (as it does in some texts by De Diego, for example) opposed to a Protestant colonizer. Some of the Catholic figures in the novel are American, and Catholicism functions along with a commitment to democracy—a somewhat incongruous combination—as a link between honest Americans and Puerto Ricans.

More striking is the evolution of the novel's main character, a newspaper editor and crusading critic of the colonial regime who progressively abandons his views and eventually becomes the first Puerto Rican colonial governor. This portrait was probably meant as a criticism of the collaborationist policies of the Partido Unión. With the passage of time, it came to be read by others as an uncanny prefiguration of the political evolution of Luis Muñoz Marín, the son of Luis Muñoz Rivera and Puerto Rico's dominant political figure after 1940. Like the novel's protagonist, Muñoz Marín evolved from a critic of colonialism to become the first elected colonial governor in 1948.

Labor's Alternate Cultural Initiatives

Before the coming of a mass culture industry, the labor movement generated its own literary and cultural circuit that included journals, study and theater groups, concerts and poetic recitals, and the writings of working-class authors. Essayists such as Ramón Romero Rosa, Juan S. Marcano, and Luisa Capetillo, novelists such as José Elías Levis, and editors such as Juan Vilar wrote and lectured about a varied set of social questions. Capetillo, as indicated, had a lasting impact through her labor as well as feminist activism. In his 1904 text *Musarañas*, Romero Rosa campaigned against superstitions and organized religions, which he saw as limiting the advance of the working class. Manuel Rojas denounced the Spanish legacy of "four centuries of ignorance and serfdom."[21] Dozens of local labor journals were launched between 1900 and 1930 in towns such as San Juan, Ponce, Mayagüez, Caguas, Arecibo, and Aguadilla, among others. *Unión Obrera*, organ of the Federación Libre de Trabajadores and, after 1915, of the Partido Socialista, was published from 1902 to 1935. Although many journals were short-lived, they are testimony to the lively intellectual life of the labor movement at the time.

Such politico-literary initiatives were equally present among Puerto Rican workers who left the island for North America. Activists Bernardo Vega and Jesús Colón, for example, imbibed the radical international traditions of the cigarmakers and mixed them with their experiences in cosmopolitan New York. In his memoirs, Vega describes a night in the Escuela Ferrer (named after the Spanish educator executed by the Spanish government in 1909): "Carlo Tresca, . . . editor of the newspaper *Il Martelo*, spoke in Italian about anarchism and the theories of Darwin; Elizabeth Gurley Flynn spoke in English about free communities and liberated relations among human beings; Pedro Esteves held forth in Spanish about war, peace, and the situation of the proletariat; and, finally, the Catholic anarchist Frank Kelly gave another talk in Spanish about Jesus Christ, the 'first communist.'"[22]

But the culture of labor should not be idealized. While entertaining a more open attitude toward women's demands, many labor leaders, as Eileen J. Suárez Findlay has argued, still saw the struggle against their exploitation by the bosses as means of freeing women for what was seen as their natural maternal tasks. Similarly, some artisans' search for respectability in terms of established cultural hierarchies led them to adopt practices associated with the literate whiter sectors while they "scorned *bomba* drumming . . . fearing that such African culture could destroy their carefully constructed refinement."[23]

Still, Afro–Puerto Rican culture did not cease to evolve and create new forms, in spite of its lack of prestige or invisibility from the vantage point of literate culture or even from the better-off sectors of the working class. One of the innovations whose influence would prove more lasting was the emergence of the *plena*, a danceable musical form in which *panderos* (tambourine-like drums) and sometimes other instruments accompany the interaction between a singer and chorus (constituted by the drummers and instrumentalists). Often attributed to John Clark and Catherine George, who had come to Ponce as part of a migrant flow from the non-Hispanic Antilles around 1900, the *plena* emerged within coastal working-class sectors and generated a first legendary interpreter in singer Joselino "Bun Bun" Oppenheimer. The fact that his assassination in 1929 was the topic of a *plena* was no coincidence: the *plena* is often a chronicle of and a commentary on current town, national, and even international events. In turn, the first recording of *plenas* were made in New York in the late 1920s by Manuel "Canario" Jiménez, an indication of the key role that city would play in the evolution of Puerto Rican music. By the 1930s, the *plena* found its first literary advocates in some members of the *generación del treinta*, whose work we shall examine below.

A Parallel (Trans)Nationalism: The Trajectory of Arturo A. Schomburg

As we consider the cultural initiatives of Puerto Ricans in the United States and debates regarding race and nationalism, it is necessary to give special attention to the work and exceptional life trajectory of Arturo Alfonso Schomburg. By 1920, Schomburg had lived in New York for almost thirty years, having moved there in 1891. But the specific way in which he engaged life in the metropolis made him a unique figure.

Schomburg was born in San Juan in 1874. His mother was from St. Croix in the then Danish Virgin Islands, and he was to spend part of his youth in St. Thomas. From the start he was immersed in the cultures of both Puerto Rico and the non-Hispanic Caribbean. While in Puerto Rico, Schomburg was a disciple of José Julián Acosta, elder figure of Puerto Rican moderate liberalism. In his youth, Acosta had joined with other students in Madrid to collect documents related to the island of Puerto Rico, an early indication of their budding envisioning of the island as the location of a distinct people and a desire to register its history.[24] Schomburg would later exhibit a similar passion for recuperating and recording a collective past. When Schomburg moved to New York, he joined the separatist clubs active in the struggle for Cuban and Puerto Rican independence. But Schomburg was to follow an uncommon itinerary: he progressively identified with the growing African American community in New York.

Schomburg thus became not a Puerto Rican socialist, like Vega or Colón, or a Puerto Rican nationalist but rather a black nationalist, or perhaps a black inter- or transnationalist. The community he preferred to imagine as his own was that of Africa and its vast diaspora. To his death in 1938 he remained an admirer of Marcus Garvey, whose contribution to the struggle of blacks for recognition and respect he consistently defended against his detractors.

Schomburg became the avid archivist of a shared African past, of its achievements and buried glories. By the 1920s he had built an extraordinary collection of books, manuscripts, and artworks related to African cultures. One of his texts, "The Negro Digs Up His Past," a programmatic statement of his life's work, was to be included in one of the inaugural anthologies of the Harlem Renaissance. "The American Negro," he argued, "must remake his past in order to make his future. Though it is orthodox to think of America as the one country where it is unnecessary to have a past, what is a luxury for the nation . . . becomes a prime necessity for the Negro. . . . History must restore what slavery took away. . . . So among the rising democratic millions we find the Negro thinking more collectively, more retrospectively than the rest, and apt out of the very pressure of the present to become the most enthusiastic antiquarian of them all."[25]

For Schomburg, the Harlem Renaissance was certainly not the occasion for exotic excursions uptown. Devoutly religious, somewhat old-fashioned, and dead serious about fighting white prejudice, he probably had a low opinion of the more bohemian and escapist aspects of that cultural movement. More significantly, he seems to have been troubled by the fact that the notion of a specifically North American black identity, favored by some protagonists of the Harlem Renaissance, tended to contradict his vision of an international African universe and, more personally, designated him as an outsider, as a "foreign black."

While unique in his commitment to a Pan-Africanist vision, Schomburg's vindication of black historical agency, as Jesse Hoffnung-Garskof has pointed out, was not foreign to the Cuban–Puerto Rican revolutionary clubs in New

York in the 1890s in which black and mulatto Cubans (such as José Gualberto Gómez) and Puerto Ricans (Sotero Figueroa, Francisco Marín) had very visible roles. These men openly underlined the decisive role of blacks in the struggle for Cuban freedom, most visibly exemplified in the person of Antonio Maceo, commander of the rebel armies. Schomburg's passage to Pan-Africanism thus had some continuity with his experience in the Cuban and Puerto Rican separatist movement that should not be overlooked.[26]

Between the Great War and the Great Depression: The Avant-Garde of the 1920s

Before World War I, the more prominent literary and political figures in Puerto Rico had reached adulthood before 1898: their lives had been split by the coming of U.S. rule and its complex consequences. By 1920, U.S. rule had already lasted two decades; the island had been economically transformed; and the world was undergoing wide, sometimes startling political, economic, and technological upheavals, from the generalization of the automobile and the coming of the airplane and of the cinema to the collapse of several European dynastic regimes and of the Ottoman empire and the reverberations of the Mexican and Russian revolutions. Meanwhile, a new generation of Puerto Ricans born around the time of the U.S. invasion were coming of age. They had little or no recollection of Spanish colonialism. Children of the new century, they had been fully reared under U.S. rule. By the early 1920s, many were graduating to professional careers or less prestigious white-collar jobs after going through a school system committed to their thorough Americanization. Members of this generation, such as Pedreira, Muñoz Marín, Vicente Géigel, Pedro Albizu Campos, Juan Antonio Corretjer, and Luis Palés Matos, among others, were to radically transform Puerto Rico's intellectual and political landscape in the 1930s.

While Matienzo Cintrón and De Diego debated in the legislature and Canales and Lloréns Torres tried to renew Puerto Rican letters in the second decade of the twentieth century, many among these young men quietly resented and some openly protested the imposition of English and the decreed Americanization they were made to suffer. The Department of Education had responded to expressions of discontent with varied forms of repression, including the suspension of students opposing its policies or criticizing U.S. rule. In 1915, for example, a group of students from the Central High School in Santurce were suspended after they expressed support for proposed legislation making Spanish the language of instruction. Supporters organized a special school for the suspended students, which they named Instituto José De Diego. In 1919, Commissioner of Education Paul Miller requested the names of the university students and aspiring teachers who had signed a petition in favor of independence: "I shall not," he explained, "appoint or approve the nominations by school boards of persons concerning whose loyalty to the United States there may be any doubt."[27] Between 1920 and 1922, conflicts marked every school year, as the authorities sought to prevent students from adopting certain names for their clubs (De Diego) or displaying the Puerto Rican flag, actions that were seen as critical of U.S. rule.

Such policies pushed the more alert protesters to sharper critical views on U.S. policies. Many became impatient with the vacillations of the Partido Unión. Some, including Géigel, Samuel R. Quiñones, and Emilio R. Delgado, joined the new Partido Nacionalista, which had been organized in 1922 after the Partido Unión removed independence from its program. But the new party remained a small, rather dormant organization as its youngest founders spent their abundant energies elsewhere. Between 1918 and 1929, members of this generation allowed themselves to be influenced, in diverse proportions according to each participant, by the ideas of Wilsonian recognition of the rights of nations to self-determination; Ghandian opposition to British rule; the anti-imperialism and student activism of the Latin American university reform movement, in turn nurtured by the ideas of the Mexican and Russian revolutions; Augusto César Sandino's resistance of U.S. occupation in Nicaragua and the sympathies it gathered all over Latin America; and, most prominently, the aesthetic vanguard agitating the Western artistic world through the 1920s. Although barely separated by a few years, these initiatives already seemed a world apart from the pre-1914 literary efforts of De Diego, Zeno Gandía, or Matienzo Cintrón, even if some of the younger poets admired the critical spirit of Canales or the cosmopolitanism of Guerra Mondragón.

Indeed, through the 1920s Puerto Rico sustained more than its share of literary manifestos and avant-garde calls to arms. In 1921, Palés Matos and José De Diego Padró founded Diepalismo (the name constructed by combining the names of the two young poets), while Vicente Palés and others created a current they called Euforismo. The *euforistas* rebelled against old and tired forms and called for a poetry that could speak to a world of machines and electricity. Yet another tendency, Noísmo, sought, as its name indicated, to negate all limits to the creative spirit. Some *noístas* were to play major roles in the literary and political initiatives of the 1930s and beyond: Quiñones, Géigel, and Fernando Sierra as leaders of the Partido Popular Democrático, which dominated Puerto Rican politics from 1940 to the late 1960s; and Juan Antonio Corretjer as a leader of the Partido Nacionalista in the 1930s and as *independentista* and socialist activist thereafter. Another *noísta*, Delgado, was to become a communist militant and participant in the Spanish Civil War. Clemente Soto Vélez, one of the inspirers of yet another avant-garde movement, Atalayismo, organized in 1928, would also be jailed in 1936, along with Corretjer, for his role as a leader of the Partido Nacionalista.[28] Muñoz Marín, son of Muñoz Rivera, participated in these literary efforts intermittently, since he spent much of the 1920s in the United States. He was to become Puerto Rico's dominant political figure of the post–World War II period.

During the 1920s, these varied currents shared a rejection of a stifling, stagnant, Puerto Rican literary scene and a desire to shock it out of its lethargy. They thus oscillated between a euphoric conviction that the old was on the verge of collapse under the impact of the new and the despair that nothing could ever upset the deadening routine of Puerto Rico's small-town life, as described in the poems "Topografía" and "Pueblo" by Palés Matos.[29]

But during the 1920s, the Puerto Rican avant-garde, while hoping to join the most advanced literary currents of the time, lacked a key element that would have aided their development: a literary establishment, an institutionally entrenched academic art, an authorized canon to rebel against. Lloréns Torres, the most respected poet of the time, and the informal *tertulias* he presided over offered a rather limited target for attack, all the more so since the poet himself was not devoid of sympathy for the younger authors. In a sense, then, Puerto Rico had its avant-garde before having its literary establishment.

The participants in these experiments, as indicated, mixed their poetic iconoclasm with an aversion to the imposed Americanization they had endured. They were convinced, furthermore, that U.S. colonial rule had impoverished most Puerto Ricans, from old coffee *hacendados* and small farmers to displaced artisans and the rural proletarians. In 1929, *noísta* poet Delgado wrote, for example:

> Today you are sad, Island
> The peasant sees you leave—resigned—
> In the smoke sent up by the *centrales*
> And in the bourgeois pipe of Uncle Sam.[30]

Through the 1920s, a perspective gradually crystallized within this milieu that envisaged Puerto Rico as a national project truncated by the invasion of

1898. This was not, of course, a recipe for unanimity, even among authors of a fairly similar social background. Debates immediately ensued, as we shall see, not the least on the racial component of the Puerto Rican identity to be defended. Plus, the promotion of such an identity proved to be compatible with more than one political orientation, from radical nationalism to autonomism and socialism.

Emissaries from the Old and New Worlds

Into these evolving orientations, several foreign visitors added new ingredients that should not go unmentioned. At the time, the closest thing to the absent cultural establishment opposed to the artistic avant-garde was provided by the ongoing transition of the University of Puerto Rico from a teacher's college, which it had been since its founding in 1903, to an institution of higher education. Younger intellectuals had an ambiguous attitude to this process. Some of the initiatives linked to it did not fail to attract their interest. Through them they came into contact with major Spanish intellectuals of the time, such as Tomás Navarro Tomás, Fernando de los Ríos, Américo Castro, and Federico de Onís and with well-known Mexican author José Vasconcelos, all of whom were invited to the university in the late 1920s.

Most of the visiting Spanish scholars had links with the Centro de Estudios Históricos in Madrid, where future Puerto Rican academics Pedreira, Margot Arce, Rubén del Rosario, and Francisco M. Cabrera studied in the early 1930s. The Centro de Estudios Históricos and the visiting scholars were exponents of a moderate-liberal intellectual tradition going back to the Instituto Libre de Enseñanza founded in 1886 and the Ateneo of Madrid organized in 1834. The creation of the Centro de Estudios Históricos in 1910 coincided with the establishment of the Residencia de Estudiantes in Madrid and with the launching of the series Clásicos Castellanos, which sought to reissue key literary texts. The elements of this mix of historical-literary research, the cultivation of an enlivened intellectual life among students, and the formation of a canon through the identification of classical texts became part of the objectives of the young authors of the 1920s as they matured during the following decade into what came to be known as the *generación del treinta*.

Yet, these rising intellectuals did not uncritically adhere to these institutional projects. The expansion of the university was marked by a "Pan-Americanist" ideology extolled by its new chancellor, Thomas Benner: the notion of Puerto Rico as a meeting place of Hispanic and U.S. cultures. For many young intellectuals, such as Géigel, Pedreira, Quiñones, and Emilio S. Belaval, this conception threatened to turn Puerto Rico into a cultural nonentity, a sort of empty space or neutral ground where others could meet, an empty platform to stage the encounter of Spanish, Hispanic American, and U.S. intellectuals. Many were thus drawn to the ideas of Vasconcelos, fresh from his work as Mexican minister of education in the immediate aftermath of the Mexican Revolution, with its nationalist and anti-imperialist undertones and its vindication of indigenous cultures. Vasconcelos wrote extensively about his stay in Puerto Rico in the introduction to his book *Indología* (1927) and spoke highly of the still relatively unknown young Nationalist leader he had met in Ponce, Albizu Campos, and of young poet and journalist Muñoz Marín, who invited him to write regularly for the newspaper *La Democracia*, which he was directing at the time.

While Vasconcelos articulated a defense of *mestizaje*—cultural and racial mixing—as the route to the emergence of a "cosmic race," other visitors favored decidedly racist interpretations of Puerto Rico's ills. Most prominently, in 1928 Spanish journalist Luis Araquistáin published *La agonía antillana*, an account of his trip through the Caribbean, including Puerto Rico, in 1926–27.[31] Araquistáin combined his observations with the ideas of Cuban historian Ramiro Guerra on the impact of the sugar industry in Cuba. Guerra denounced the displacement of the small farmer, squeezed by the rise of large corporations on the one hand and a landless proletariat on the other. But if the former meant growing North American influence, the latter included a considerable number of black Jamaican and Haitian immigrants: the Cuban nation, identified by Guerra with the (implicitly white) small farmer, was threatened from above and below. Guerra's critique of the plantation thus had a racist edge. It was this aspect of Guerra's work that Araquistáin underlined. In Puerto Rico, he argued, the *jíbaro*, which he took to be white, was still a dominant demographic presence. The island had been spared the wave of "Africanization" suffered by Cuba. The attainment of independence would depend on the *jíbaro*'s struggle for the land, which would lead him into a confrontation with the United States.[32]

In Puerto Rico, some of the younger authors borrowed from Araquistáin's racist tract, even if they later turned away from it. Géigel wrote a glowing review of Araquistáin's book, endorsing his views on black immigration as a threat to *hispanidad*.[33] In 1928, Muñoz Marín wrote a review of Araquistáin's book (for the U.S. liberal magazine *The Nation*) that came very close to accepting many of its main propositions. Muñoz Marín thus asserted that only in the Hispanic Caribbean had whites prevailed over blacks, since the former hold their own only as long as independent production survives. Slightly diverging from Araquistáin, Muñoz Marín argued that while Spaniards had mixed with the population of color, this had not Africanized them. The mulatto, he wrote, was in fact a "Spaniard of a different color." But Muñoz Marín agreed with Araquistáin that promoting Spanish immigration was a good idea, even if he tried to also use the notion to deflate American feelings of superiority. He thus reminded his readers that "Havana, with its enormous Spanish proletariat and middle class . . . holds its own culturally against not only Jamaica, W.I., but also against Jamaica, L.I." In a final burst, he insisted that in Puerto Rico, Americanization was a bigger threat than Africanization, even if "there is always the possibility that we shall be Africanized first and Americanized afterward. That would be hell."[34] Meanwhile, the young Palés Matos was writing the first poems that eventually became part of his 1935 landmark book of "black poetry," *Tuntún de pasa y grifería*, which he saw, among other things, as a vindication of the African component of Puerto Rican culture.

To conclude: by 1930, thirty years of Americanization had ironically led to the crystallization of a desire for national affirmation among a significant sector of Puerto Rico's rising literary generation. Most were young professionals with family links to large and small propertied sectors. As they left behind their avant-garde experiments of the 1920s, their work increasingly centered on the quest for a Puerto Rican identity, of which different participants in these efforts were to elaborate varied definitions through the 1930s and beyond.

The qualitative refocusing of this literary and political generation was dramatically proclaimed in 1929 by Géigel, Quiñones, Pedreira, and Alfredo Collado Martell when they launched *Indice*, the journal that set the tone for the literary debates and explorations of the 1930s. *Indice* placed the question of Puerto Rican identity at the center of its concerns and called for the preparation of a balance sheet of Puerto Rico's evolution after 1898.[35] Its initiators explicitly presented it as a break with the avant-garde aesthetic. *Indice*, they warned, would nurture no philias or phobias, it would not be a mouthpiece of any "group," it would exist beyond the limits of any "ism," and, inverting the avant-gardist preferences, it affirmed its desire to be more "useful" than "strange," more "beneficial" than "surprising."

But the debates of the 1930s initiated by *Indice* were framed by a radically changed political, economic, and social situation: the onset of the Great Depression and its impact on Puerto Rico. The Depression marked the end of the first period of U.S. rule over Puerto Rico and initiated a second stage characterized by sharpened social and political conflicts. The following chapters are devoted to these developments.

ECONOMIC DEPRESSION AND POLITICAL CRISIS: THE TURBULENT THIRTIES

The depression of the world capitalist economy in the 1930s shook Puerto Rican society to the core. No structure instituted after 1898 was spared: the sugar industry, political parties, and the labor movement all went into crisis. The dominance of the Partido Unión, renamed Partido Liberal, was broken as the Coalición of the increasingly conservative Partido Socialista and part of the Partido Republicano won the elections of 1932. A new current, led by Luis Muñoz Marín, crystallized within the Partido Liberal, which sought to promote social reforms and eventual independence, in coordination with the New Deal programs of the Roosevelt administration. A militant nationalist movement, inspired by Pedro Albizu Campos, burst into the political landscape and reshaped it. At the same time, the dominance of the Partido Socialista/Federación Libre de Trabajadores in the world of labor began to show signs of exhaustion. By 1940, a new labor federation, the Confederación General del Trabajo, emerged to challenge the FLT. In 1938, the current led by Muñoz Marín launched a new party, the Partido Popular Democrático, which dominated Puerto Rican politics until the 1960s. The Left also gained ground in the Puerto Rican *colonia* in New York. El Barrio in East Harlem was the strongest bulwark of New York's American Labor Party and the electoral base of its best-known leader, Italian American congressman Vito Marcantonio. In this chapter, we explore the period running from the crash of 1929 to the eve of the founding of the PPD in 1938. It is the most turbulent period of Puerto Rican history under U.S. rule.

Sugar Crisis

After enjoying a boom during World War I, the world sugar industry went into depression in the spring of 1920. Prices fell as European production regained prewar levels and came into competition with increased output elsewhere.

Lower prices did not immediately hit producers operating within U.S. tariff walls. Congress, pressured by domestic beet and cane interests, enacted repeated increases in the tariff paid by foreign sugar. The main beneficiaries of this policy turned out to be producers in the Philippines and Puerto Rico, who increased their share of the U.S. market through the 1920s.

The desire to remove Philippine sugar from the U.S. market compelled U.S. beet interests to push legislation through Congress that would lead to Philippine independence. President Hoover vetoed the measure in 1930, indicating that a broader consideration of U.S. interests dictated caution before creating a politically unstable republic. The measure was reenacted over his veto but rejected by the Filipino legislature. Yet it was evident that the idea of a change in the status of the Philippines was not about to go away.

Meanwhile, falling sugar prices converged in Cuba with the despotic government of Gerardo Machado to promote growing unrest. By mid-1933, a general strike, combined with a militant student movement and a "sergeants' rebellion," installed a new government headed by Ramón Grau. The government's Left, led by Antonio Guiteras, was soon fostering measures that raised many an eyebrow in Washington, from the nationalization of utilities to plans for agrarian reform. Washington never recognized Grau's government and was relieved when Fulgencio Batista, a rising military caudillo, overthrew it. But the fall of Grau did not erase the fact that the State Department faced a volatile situation in its Cuban protectorate.

In Puerto Rico, chronic poverty became more acute. Per capita income fell around 30 percent between 1930 and 1933.[1] Unemployment grew. Mobilizations shook the island between August 1933 and March 1934. The unemployed demanded work and relief. Dockworkers and laborers in the needle trades and tobacco and sugar industries struck for better wages. Consumers organized boycotts against gasoline and electric power companies. In August 1933, 7,000 tobacco workers were on strike in Caguas, 5,000 of which were women. By September, the protests spread to Santurce, where 838 workers were reported on strike; over 600 were women. In August, strikes in the needlework industry sprang up in the west in Lares, San Germán, and Mayagüez. In Mayagüez, more than 2,000 workers from close to seventy shops were involved in bloody street fights with the police. At least one woman striker was killed. By September, the movement spread to Santurce, where more than 500 workers were involved, again mostly women. Late in September, another striker was killed, this time in Gurabo, in a protest against the United Porto Rico Sugar Company.

These mobilizations were a prelude to the general strike of the sugar workers in January 1934. The strikers rejected the agreement signed by the FLT and called on Nationalist leader Albizu Campos to represent them. Meanwhile, the protests against gasoline and power companies were gathering strength. Drivers of *carros públicos* (car shuttles operating between towns) led the gasoline boycott. The committees heading the electricity boycott included small shopkeepers with a cocktail of varied radicals (nationalists, dissident left-socialists, and communists). In spite of the call by nationalist José Enamorado Cuesta for the creation of a "Strike Committee" to coordinate all these initiatives, those involved in the ongoing struggles failed to centralize their efforts.[2]

While the FLT played a rearguard role in most of these actions, it did push for the organization of factory workers in the needle trades. Led by Teresa Angleró, the FLT used the context created by Roosevelt's National Recovery Administration, which provided for codes regulating conditions in each industry, to bring workers into new unions.[3]

Given this context of depression and social unrest, it was evident to the Roosevelt administration that urgent action was needed both to reorganize sugar production in the areas supplying the U.S. market from the Philippines to the Virgin Islands and, more immediately, to address the situation in Cuba. In Puerto Rico, the first significant federal intervention came with the creation of the Puerto Rico Emergency Relief Administration under the provisions of the Federal Emergency Relief Act. This organization employed tens of thousands and distributed food to many more.[4]

But relief measures were combined with authoritarian initiatives. When the need to appoint a new governor arose in 1934, former governor James Beverly wrote to the Bureau of Insular Affairs in Washington: "I strongly favor an ex-army officer . . . one who has sufficient experience to know how to size up and handle delicate situations and who has the courage to do his duty whether it is popular or not. Is not General Winship available. . . ?"[5] Blanton Winship was available and was appointed governor in 1934. His willingness to "do his duty" led to some of the bloodiest moments of a dramatic decade.

Enter Muñoz Marín

This was the context in which Luis Muñoz Marín began to play a significant role in Puerto Rican politics. In 1933, Muñoz Marín was thirty-five. He was the son of Luis Muñoz Rivera, Puerto Rico's most influential political leader until his death in 1916. Born in 1898, Muñoz Marín lived mostly in the United States between 1910 and 1920. In 1915, he entered Georgetown University but soon dropped out. In 1916, visiting the island on the occasion of his father's death, he got acquainted with members of Puerto Rican literary circles such as Nemesio Canales and Miguel Guerra Mondragón. Back in the United States, he became a socialist, partly under the influence of the Russian Revolution. It was at this time that he attempted to study Marxism, but he never went beyond the briefer texts.

Returning to Puerto Rico in 1920, Muñoz Marín campaigned for the Partido Socialista. In 1921, he published two issues of the radical journal *Espartaco*. For Muñoz Marín, the Puerto Rican revolution would be enabled by the American revolution: "To be ready to overthrow the *criollo* bourgeoisie as soon as the American proletarians overthrow theirs. To be ready, above all, for the creation of the New Social Order. This . . . is the mission of *Espartaco*." In the second issue, Muñoz Marín penned a tribute to labor martyr Joe Hill of the radical Industrial Workers of the World "not because Joe Hill wrote verses. Any idiot can write verses. We say it because he was shot in Salt Lake City five years ago for being a soldier of the FUTURE."[6]

In 1921, Muñoz Marín moved to West Englewood, New Jersey. He began moderating his views but remained a left-wing reformist, participating in activities of labor groups in New York such as the Alianza Obrera and supporting independent presidential candidate Robert M. La Follette in 1924. In 1923, he worked in Puerto Rico preparing his father's selected works and represented the FLT at the convention of the American Federation of Labor in Portland. Meanwhile, he actively participated in the literary avant-garde of the time. Muñoz Marín was interested in the innovations of the newer American poets, as exemplified by Carl Sandburg's *Chicago Poems* (1916) and Edgar Lee Masters's *Spoon River Anthology* (1914). He was also attracted to poems of social protest, such as Vachel Lindsay's "Bryan, Bryan, Bryan" on the Bryanite agrarian-populist movement in 1890s. In 1919, he translated Edwin Markham's "The Man with the Hoe" into Spanish. A protest against the exploitation of the working farmer written in 1899, Markham's poem (inspired by Jean-François Millet's 1862 painting of the same title) had been widely popular in the U.S. labor movement. It became lastingly associated with Muñoz Marín and read in part:

> Bowed by the weight of centuries he leans
> Upon his hoe and gazes on the ground,
> The emptiness of ages in his face,
> And on his back the burden of the world.

Who made him dead to rapture and despair,
A thing that grieves not and that never hopes,
Stolid and stunned, a brother to the ox?
Who loosened and let down this brutal jaw?
Whose was the hand that slanted back this brow?
Whose breath blew out the light within this brain?

The text, as Cary Nelson has pointed out, presents the exploited as incapable of self-emancipation: Markham sees himself as speaking "on behalf of mute suffering."[7] Muñoz Marín did come to see himself as a privileged interpreter of the longings of a downtrodden, exploited rural worker, even if he was less dismissive of the culture of Puerto Rico's *jíbaros*. But Muñoz Marín was also drawn to the minimalist style of the imagist poets with which he experimented (in English) while not abandoning the topic of despair and future deliverance:

Do you grow weary of waiting in vain
For a bolt of song out of the silence of the stars?
Bend low with me
And listen to the dreams of the dry weeds-
The rain-dreams, the flower-dreams
Of our brothers the dry weeds![8]

In 1926, Muñoz Marín led his most ambitious political campaign yet. The Alianza, which had won the elections of 1924, was by then divided: its main leader, Antonio R. Barceló, and his supporters favored mild fiscal reforms (reassessing property values for tax purposes), which were opposed by the conservative wing of the Alianza, led by sugar baron Eduardo Georgetti. The organizations of the possessing classes, known as Fuerzas Vivas—the associations of farmers and of sugar producers and the chamber of commerce—campaigned against the reforms. Muñoz Marín returned to Puerto Rico at this point and was appointed by Barceló editor of the Alianza's paper *La Democracia*.

Muñoz Marín then put forth a vision of Puerto Rican politics as an interplay of three forces: the plutocracy (the Fuerzas Vivas); the reformist middle classes, represented by Barceló; and the labor movement, represented by the Partido Socialista and its main leader, Santiago Iglesias. Muñoz Marín argued that the middle-class sectors led by Barceló, mistaking the Partido Socialista for a revolutionary force, had fallen into the trap of an alliance with the "plutocracy," which would sabotage any attempt to introduce even the mildest reforms. Similarly, the Socialists, mistaking Barceló for an opponent of reform, failed to realize that, liberated from the embrace of the "plutocracy," he could be an ally in a struggle for gradual change. Muñoz Marín concluded it was necessary to bring Barceló and Iglesias, the middle and working classes, together in a joint front against the "plutocracy." Such an alliance, which he described as a "peaceful revolution," would include a dosage of affirmation of Puerto Rican cultural identity and use the existing political structures to introduce the desired reforms. Wages would still be lower than in the United States, and this would have to be the case as long as Puerto Rico needed to attract U.S. capital, but they would rise above their present miserable level.[9] All these ideas would resurface later as part of the efforts that led to the creation of the PPD in 1938.

But in 1926–27, the initiative of Muñoz Marín was premature. Barceló was not about to break the Alianza in the hope of an agreement with the Socialists. Yet in 1933, Guerra Mondragón, a close collaborator of Muñoz Marín, described their 1926 campaign as "our New Deal."[10] For him, at least, it was clear that their earlier efforts had been a trial run for the movement that eventually crystallized in the context created by the Depression and the reactions to it.

The New Deal, Sugar, and the Plan Muñoz Marín

By the time Muñoz Marín returned to Puerto Rico in 1931 after another sojourn in the United States, the Alianza had broken up and the wing led by Barceló had become the Partido Liberal, which Muñoz Marín joined. The younger wing of the party, which included Muñoz Marín, Ernesto Ramos Antonini, Samuel R. Quiñones, and Vicente Géigel, succeeded in pushing Barceló's current into adopting an *independentista* program, despite the objections of the *azucareros* like Georgetti and Jorge Bird, who favored an autonomist plank.[11]

But despite Muñoz Marín's efforts, the Coalición of the Partido Socialista and a reunified Partido Republicano won the elections of 1932. The Partido Liberal did obtain more votes than any other single party, and Muñoz Marín was elected to the Senate.

Muñoz Marín traveled to Washington, D.C., in the summer of 1933. There, he became aware of the sugar program being elaborated by the Department of Agriculture. The plan, later embodied in the Sugar Act of 1934, provided for the assignation of quotas to each producing region. It was to be expected that the State Department would demand a sizable quota for Cuba, in order to ameliorate the political situation there, while beet states would use their congressional clout to ensure an adequate quota for themselves. Hawaii, as an incorporated territory, came next in the pecking order. This left Puerto Rico and the Philippines to bear the brunt of the reduction in production.

The program provided for payments to farmers to reduce production. The necessary funds were to be obtained through a processing tax to be imposed on mills and refineries. But in the case of the insular territories, the program also allowed for the use of the tax to finance wider reform programs. Muñoz Marín was quick to realize that it was now possible to obtain support in Washington for reform measures in Puerto Rico as long as they contributed to the objective of rationalizing the sugar industry. One could even call for state intervention to rectify the workings of the "invisible hand" of the market, until then seen as unerring and self-correcting, without immediately provoking denunciations of communism. This regulatory ethos was especially strong in the Department of Agriculture led by Henry A. Wallace and Rexford G. Tugwell.[12]

Muñoz Marín now convinced himself that the New Deal would permit the creation of a more "independent economy," an economy—as he explained in a letter to Eleanor Roosevelt—that would be "as far as possible planned and autonomous."[13] For Muñoz Marín, there existed a perfect fit between curtailing sugar production, curbing the imbalances of unregulated capitalism, reconstructing the Puerto Rican economy, and preparing it for political independence.[14]

Upon returning to Puerto Rico, Muñoz Marín announced his first proposal, known as the Plan Muñoz Marín. The plan, further elaborated by agronomist Carlos Chardón, proposed that the government buy the properties of the United Porto Rico Sugar Company, which included five sugar mills and 30,000 *cuerdas* of land. Good agricultural lands thus obtained would be exchanged for a larger amount of poorer land in the hands of cane growers, or *colonos*. The poorer land would be withdrawn from sugar production, divided into small farms, and distributed to the landless. The plan would both reduce sugar overproduction and begin a controlled agrarian reform. In March 1934, Tugwell of the Department of Agriculture visited the island to explore ways in which the Sugar Act could be implemented. He embraced the ideas of the Plan Muñoz Marín as a welcome addition to the plans of the Roosevelt administration.

Plan Chardón

The desire of the Roosevelt administration to reorganize the American Sugar Kingdom was present in several initiatives besides the Sugar Act of 1934. Such measures included the Tydings-MacDuffie Act of 1934, which created the Commonwealth of the Philippines as a transition to independence, and the repeal of the Platt Amendment, which since 1903 had affirmed the right of the United States to intervene in Cuba and had poisoned the relation between the two countries. Puerto Rico was transferred from the jurisdiction of the War Department's Bureau of Insular Affairs to a new Division of Insular Territories and Possessions in the Department of the Interior. Ernest Gruening was appointed to direct it.

Gruening, former editor of the liberal magazine *The Nation*, was a critic of U.S. interventionism, including the occupations of Haiti and the Dominican Republic. A campaigner against private power interests in New England, he was a defender of public utilities. More immediately, as a member of a commission that had just studied conditions in Cuba, he had coauthored a report (*Problems of the New Cuba*) that favored land redistribution, crop diversification, and increased food production there. The Liberales hailed the transfer to the Department of the Interior and the appointment of Gruening as a victory for the New Deal in Puerto Rico.[15]

The next step in the confluence of the political current headed by Muñoz Marín and the New Deal was the creation by President Roosevelt of a Puerto Rico Policy Commission, composed of the rector of the University of Puerto Rico, Carlos Chardón; Commissioner of Agriculture Rafael Menéndez Ramos; and agronomist Rafael Fernández García. This commission was entrusted with the elaboration of a plan for Puerto Rico's economic reconstruction under the framework of the Sugar Act. It produced one of the key documents of the decade: the *Report of the Puerto Rico Policy Commission*, dated June 14, 1934. The report, better known as the Plan Chardón, followed the ideas outlined in the Plan Muñoz Marín while extending them beyond the sugar industry. The plan proposed the acquisition of sugar mills capable of processing 250,000 tons of sugar, or about 25 percent of insular production, and the creation of 24,000 homesteads through land redistribution. The premise of the document was the need to replace "blind development" with a "fundamental plan" capable of promoting a balanced economy. The Plan Chardón, Muñoz Marín hoped, would "decolonize" the Puerto Rican economy. It would create, Chardón argued, a "Puerto Rican economy for the Puerto Ricans."[16]

The plan led to the creation of the Puerto Rico Reconstruction Administration (PRRA). The PRRA, headed in Puerto Rico by Chardón, grew into a vast apparatus, staffed by a new generation of reform-minded professionals. Many went on to become the initial cadre of the PPD that Muñoz Marín organized in

1938. By 1936, the PRRA had initiated diverse programs, from public building, housing, and park construction to buying and operating Central Lafayette in Arroyo and Central Los Caños in Arecibo. In 1937, it purchased the facilities of the Ponce Electric Company; it also built and operated a cement factory in Cataño and initiated a rural electrification program. By 1936, the PRRA employed 52,000 persons, almost half as many as the sugar industry at the height of the harvest.[17] It sponsored Esteban Bird's *Report on the Sugar Industry*, which documented the misery of rural workers and small farmers.

Meanwhile, in March 1935, Guerra Mondragón, an associate of Muñoz Marín, was appointed by the PRRA to assist Attorney General Benjamin Horton in the preparation of a test case to enforce the 500-acre limitation. Horton had little sympathy for this effort. Gruening pressured him to resign. Benigno Fernández García, another collaborator of Muñoz Marín, was named attorney general.

Opposition to Reform

Two sectors denounced the Plan Chardón and the initiatives regarding the 500-acre limitation: large sugar interests, both Puerto Rican and North American, and the Coalición of the Socialistas and the Republicanos. The worries of the former grew as the elaboration of the sugar legislation progressed. Each draft further reduced Puerto Rico's quota. In the end, after fixing the beet quota, Congress left the quotas of the insular areas to be determined by the secretary of agriculture. The possibility that the Sugar Act would entail land redistribution and measures for the protection of the *colonos* increased the concern of sugar mill owners. Their sense of exclusion was heightened when, on Gruening's recommendation, they were denied representation in the commission that drafted the Plan Chardón.

The *colonos*, on their part, hoped that the projected legislation would include protections against perceived abuses by the mill owners. Muñoz Marín appealed to them to mobilize in favor of the New Deal. By August 1934, a sizable group of *colonos* created a new Asociación de Colonos. Its first president, Jesús T. Piñero, soon became Muñoz Marín's close collaborator and supporter.

Under fire from diverse quarters, the sugar interests felt compelled to finance a study of the sugar industry, published as *The Sugar Economy of Puerto Rico* in 1938 by Columbia University Press. The study emphasized the degree of efficiency attained by the industry. As the decade progressed, the debate on the role of the sugar industry continued unabated. Its critics, such as Esteban Bird and Antonio Fernós, denounced it as the cause of misery and mass unemployment. Its advocates argued it was the best antidote to poverty, which they attributed to overpopulation.[18]

But the mill owners were not the only ones upset in 1934. The Coalición had won the elections of 1932, yet Muñoz Marín's maneuvering had turned him into the perceived representative of the New Deal in Puerto Rico. By October 1935, the Coalición denounced how, through his control of the PRRA, Muñoz Marín had created a "supergovernment" beyond any control of elected representatives.[19]

Responding to the attacks by the Coalición, Gruening denounced them as only interested in turning the PRRA into a patronage machine.[20] For his part, during a visit to Puerto Rico in January 1936, Secretary of the Interior Harold Ickes, appalled at the poverty he had seen, debated Ponce entrepreneur José A. Ferré, accusing the sugar interests of being the cause of the existing situation.[21] Thus, the Coalición could not realistically have much hope that Wallace, Gruening, or Ickes would pay much attention to their denunciations of Muñoz Marín's "supergovernment."

But there were tensions within the New Deal coalition. When in 1936 Chardón and the PRRA opted to create cooperatives in the lands of Central Lafayette in Arroyo instead of exchanging it for the less productive land of colonos as originally planned, the Asociación de Colonos was quick to protest. It warned that such experiments insinuated that the colonos, and by implication all employers, were "superfluous and could easily be replaced" by the workers themselves. It was "a formula of a frankly communist character" since "all the agricultural workers of Puerto Rico will look to Arroyo as a new promised land and to the employer . . . as the monster that exploits their labor and holds their property." Chardón responded that cooperativism was the most effective way of preempting communism within the limits of capitalism. In fact, Chardón had closed a worker's education program that he felt promoted "class conflict" instead of seeking to reconcile capital and labor, thus avoiding divisions within the "Puerto Rican family."[22]

After engineering the creation of the PRRA in contact with the federal Departments of the Interior and of Agriculture and having gained the sympathy of landless workers, small farmers, colonos, and reform-minded professionals, Muñoz Marín seemed well placed for an electoral victory in 1936. But this was not to be, as the violent clash between a new nationalist movement and U.S. authorities radically upset the Puerto Rican political landscape between 1936 and 1938.

The Rise of the Partido Nacionalista and Pedro Albizu Campos

No movement in Puerto Rican history has been more controversial than the Partido Nacionalista led by Albizu Campos. Its profound impact cannot be denied. The adjectives used to describe it have run the full spectrum from patriotic to criminal, self-sacrificing to demented, proto-socialist to fascist. From a political and economic perspective, it articulated a sharp rejection of U.S. political and economic control and what it perceived as its consequences: the reduction of the island to a "sugar economy," absentee control, the displacement of the small farmer, the impoverishment of the rural working class, and the lack of protection for island industries.

The program of the Partido Nacionalista included proposals for lowering the limit on land tenure to 300 acres, state ownership of basic utilities, protection of industries oriented to the local market, and diversification of foreign trade. Although not socialist—the Nationalist social and moral ideal was the independent, self-employed producer—Albizu Campos and his party did sympathize with labor, both programmatically, as proponents of prolabor legislation, and in practice, supporting labor struggles. In 1934, for example, Albizu Campos accepted the invitation by a group of cane workers to lead their strike after they rejected the contract signed on their behalf by FLT leaders with the *centralistas*. He criticized the United States for its lack of minimum wage laws, the concentration of its wealth in a few hands, and what he called the "traditional Yankee way of solving strikes, machine gunning the people."[23] Yet the Partido Nacionalista did not see itself as a party of labor but rather as a patriotic vanguard.

In the case of Albizu Campos, these ideas coexisted with traditional Catholic views, including conservative notions regarding women and family and opposition to coeducation as well as an idealization of Puerto Rico's situation before 1898. In its inclination toward minority armed operations, its openness to labor's aspirations combined with Catholic and conservative views on diverse social matters, its aversion to the moneygrubbing pettiness of the bourgeoisie, and its severe moral code of self-sacrifice, the nationalist movement brings to mind some strands of Irish nationalism, with which Albizu Campos had contact while completing his bachelor's degree and a law degree at Harvard in 1913–17 and 1919–21.

Albizu Campos's itinerary was in many ways the opposite of Muñoz Marín's. Muñoz Marín was the white privileged son of Puerto Rico's best-known politician, born into a mesh of privileged connections. Dropping out of college,

Meeting of the Partido Nacionalista at the Plaza de Armas in front of city hall in San Juan in the early 1930s. This period witnessed the rise of a new and militant nationalist movement headed by Pedro Albizu Campos. (Proyecto digitalización fotos El Mundo–Biblioteca José M. Lázaro, Universidad de Puerto Rico–Río Piedras)

Muñoz Marín never held a formal job for long, shifting from one part-time or freelance occupation to the next, combining them with his literary or political enthusiasms. Albizu Campos, on the other hand, was the poor mulatto "illegitimate" son of a working woman (a laundress). Rising through the school system, he went on to the University of Vermont and then Harvard, propelled by a focused drive and a disciplined effort, in sharp contrast to the carefree, chain-smoking and hard-drinking bohemian lifestyle of Muñoz Marín's. While Muñoz Marín held only general religious views, favoring birth control, for example, Albizu Campos was a devout Catholic and looked askance on the loosening of traditional gender roles and morality.[24]

Upon his return to Puerto Rico in 1922, Albizu Campos joined the Partido Unión, hoping it would take a stand in favor of independence. In 1924, he favored inviting the Partido Socialista to the proposed Alianza. When his proposal was ignored, he denounced the Alianza as a party of the "plutocracy" and joined the small Partido Nacionalista. In June 1927, Albizu Campos departed on a long trip to the Dominican Republic, Haiti, Cuba, Mexico, and Peru to agitate in favor of Puerto Rico's independence. Two witnesses, Nationalist leader Juan Antonio Corretjer and visiting Mexican intellectual José Vasconcelos, felt that Albizu Campos's rise in the party was opposed by part of the old leadership on racist grounds. Albizu Campos was not white, and in their eyes not even a Harvard education and traditional bourgeois attitudes on many issues could compensate for that fact. Still, he enjoyed enough support to be elected president of the party in 1930, soon after his return to Puerto Rico.[25]

Unfortunately, Albizu Campos rarely cited authors or works that influenced his ideas. His stay in Cuba coincided with the publication of Ramiro Guerra's very influential *Azúcar y población en las Antillas*, a classic indictment of the sugar monoculture and of U.S. economic influence. Guerra's views, including his positive portrait of Spanish colonialism as more favorable to the constitution of new nations than British rule and of the "independent farming class" as the "backbone of the nation," cannot but remind the reader of some of Albizu Campos's texts.[26] But Albizu Campos, it should be underlined—as opposed to some of his contemporaries—never gave credence to or repeated the racist undertones of Guerra's defense of the small farmer.

Not all members of the Partido Nacionalista in the early 1930s shared Albizu Campos's Catholic nationalism. At that time, the party attracted *independentistas* holding diverse views on social matters. Ramón S. Pagán, for example, a Nationalist killed in a confrontation with the police in 1935, considered himself a socialist. Enamorado Cuesta sought to combine his nationalism with a prolabor perspective. In 1930, Clemente Soto Vélez, another Nationalist with socialist inclinations, recruited fellow socialist Luis Vergne Ortiz, who was soon made vice president of the party. Vergne Ortiz's proclaimed objective was to fight for the "socialist republic of Puerto Rico."[27] In 1934, Nationalist student Martín Avilés Bracero explained that, while rejecting Marxism's tendency to see spiritual endeavors as a "superstructure," he agreed with its understanding of social divisions. Albizu Campos, he added, had been more willing to defend the workers' interests than "so-called socialists" such as Santiago Iglesias.[28] But the range of views within the party became narrower as it became more tightly knit around Albizu Campos. Soto Vélez, Enamorado Cuesta, Vergne Ortiz, Avilés Bracero, and many others eventually moved on to other organizations.[29]

Albizu Campos on U.S. Territorial Policy and Puerto Rican Politics

While Albizu Campos became a central political figure during the 1930s, he wrote some of his most interesting texts in or before 1930. In them he argued, for example, that statehood was not the objective of U.S. interests in Puerto Rico: U.S. corporations preferred the existing colonial regime, which he characterized as an "irresponsible system of government." Albizu Campos thus concluded that by collaborating with U.S. corporate interests and subordinating themselves to Washington, statehooders were doing the opposite of what was needed to attain their goal. Former U.S. territories had not obtained statehood as a result of subservience to Congress or to extraterritorial economic interests but through the emergence of autonomous regional forces willing to demand equal treatment within the Union. To give themselves a chance, statehooders had to confront Washington and even be willing to force their way into the Union, as some territories had done, calling a constitutional convention, for example, and electing a congressional delegation. Unwillingness to act independently would condemn them to a colonial purgatory.

Yet Albizu Campos also considered that the promise of statehood as a means of curtailing the power of external economic interests was by then a fiction. Congress was under the control of Wall Street. No state government could hope to take significant action against its interests. This left only independence, he concluded, as a means of escaping the power of the U.S. "plutocracy."[30]

But Albizu Campos felt that, along with the annexationists, the autonomists also had some hard choices to make. They could demand truly significant autonomous powers, such as the power to protect island industries through tariffs, or they could settle instead for cosmetic changes to the existing regime, such as electing more insular officials. In the first case, their politics would be anticolonial, if not *independentista*. In the second, autonomism would just help give U.S. colonial rule a Puerto Rican face.

Albizu Campos's analysis had interesting implications. Puerto Rican politics, he suggested, was characterized by the clash of two variants of accommodation to U.S. rule: an annexationist current unwilling to defy Washington in its quest for statehood, which was thus condemned to administer the colonial regime established in 1898, and an autonomist movement intent on widening its niche within—but not on defying the limits of—the colonial relation. This, we would argue, is a fairly accurate description of the dynamics of Puerto Rican politics throughout the American Century.

Albizu Campos's warning to both statehooders and autonomists that, if they wished to attain their respective goals, they had to commit themselves to the emergence of an active political force, willing to act independently of Congress, corresponds to the dimension of the Nationalist discourse that distinguished it from all other movements in Puerto Rico after 1898. Albizu Campos was the first to address Puerto Ricans as subjects capable of collectively remaking their polity independent of, or even against the will of, the United States. Before him, Rosendo Matienzo Cintrón, Luis Lloréns Torres, José De Diego, Muñoz Marín, and others had defended independence, but they took it as self-evident, as José Celso Barbosa had done with statehood, that it would be realized if and when Washington granted it. It was Albizu Campos who first insisted that independence was something for Puerto Rico not to receive but to make through its own activity. It is this notion of self-determination and self-activation underlying his vision of independence that made his intervention such a radical departure in the Puerto Rican political landscape of the 1930s.

Gordon K. Lewis and Luis Angel Ferrao have described the Partido Nacionalista as fascist on the basis of its nationalist ideology, its conservative side, and other traits, such as the black shirts worn by its paramilitary formation, the Cadetes de la República.[31] There are, of course, coincidences, even influences, as the shirts were perhaps taken from the Italian model. While still a Nationalist, party secretary Corretjer confessed to both early sympathies and rapid disillusionment with fascism. But fascism was both militantly antilabor and committed to imperialist conquest, neither of which describes the discourse or actions of the Nationalists.[32] We have already mentioned Albizu Campos's participation in the 1934 strike in the sugar industry. The party adopted the same position during the 1938 dockworkers' strike. Party president Ramón Medina Ramírez called the strike "the prelude of . . . the liberation of our fatherland" while applauding the emergence of a new militant labor federation in the United States, the Congress of Industrial Organizations (CIO), whose maritime affiliate, the National Maritime Union, was actively supporting the strike in Puerto Rico.[33]

Albizu Campos's perspective was best summarized in a 1937 letter in which he denounced U.S. colonial control over Puerto Rico, British rule over India, French atrocities in Algeria, Japan's invasion of China, Italy's occupation of Ethiopia, and Germany's treatment of the Jews.[34] Author José Luis González was thus mistaken when he argued that Albizu Campos had never condemned fascism or other empires besides the United States.[35] Albizu Campos similarly rejected the Soviet regime as a new form of despotism. His position was that of a nationalist anti-imperialism, informed by a vision of Catholicism as an alternative to the contending blocs of "democratic" imperialism, fascism, and communism.

During World War II, the Nationalists continued to denounce U.S. colonialism while underlining that they were equally opposed to its imperialist rivals.[36] Criticized by others, and most prominently by the Communists, as weakening the antifascist front, the Nationalists were on the other hand praised by Stalin's main Marxist critic, Leon Trotsky. From his Mexican exile, Trotsky commented that the Puerto Rican Nationalists were among the few participants in international antifascist congresses who remembered to denounce imperialism in other than its fascist form.[37]

The Turbulent Year: 1936

In spite of its poor showing in the 1932 elections, Albizu Campos's denunciations of the island's economic situation and his support of popular protests, such as the general strike of cane workers of 1934, made him a visible figure. His party's militant discourse and advocacy of armed struggle, including recruitment by the Cadetes, made it an object of government surveillance. If police reports filed in court are reliable, close to 1,000 *cadetes* marched in commemoration of De Diego's birth on April 16, 1934, while 900 marched in 1935 and 700 in 1936.[38] In October 1935, policemen in Río Piedras detained the car of Nationalist Ramón S. Pagán. A gun battle ensued, during which four Nationalists and a bystander were killed. Police Commissioner Francis E. Riggs vowed he would not allow any Nationalist violence. Albizu warned that police violence would be answered in kind.

On February 23, 1936, Nationalists Hiram Rosado and Elías Beauchamp shot and killed Commissioner Riggs. Arrested, they were taken to a police station and shot. While many lamented the assassination of Riggs, the killing of the Nationalists was universally condemned. Gruening later wrote that, meeting with Muñoz Marín in Washington at the time, he was unable to obtain even a "simple statement of sorrow" from him regarding Riggs's death.[39]

Even before the attack on Riggs, Federal Justice Department agents had visited Puerto Rico to investigate the Nationalists. Following up on this, the combined efforts of a federal grand jury and the U.S. Federal District Court in San Juan led to the indictment on April 4 of Albizu Campos, Corretjer, Soto Vélez, Luis F. Velázquez, and five other Nationalist leaders for "conspiring to overthrow the government of the United States" and recruiting soldiers for

Nationalist leader Pedro Albizu Campos (hand raised) speaks at the funeral of the Nationalists killed during a confrontation with the police in October 1935 (known as the Río Piedras massacre). Second from the right is Dionisio Pearson, Nationalist survivor of the confrontation. (Laboratorio fotográfico Biblioteca José M. Lázaro, Universidad de Puerto Rico–Río Piedras)

that purpose.[40] The indictment added a further explosive element to an already turbulent political situation.

Meanwhile, incensed by the assassination of Riggs, Maryland senator Millard Tydings, chairman of the Senate Committee on Territories and Insular Affairs, introduced a bill (S. 4549) on April 23, 1936, to grant Puerto Rico independence if Puerto Ricans voted for it in a plebiscite. But there was a catch: the bill provided for few transitional measures. For an economy totally oriented to the U.S. market, independence under such conditions would bring considerable hardship.

While associated with Tydings, the bill had actually been approved in a cabinet meeting on March 18, during which Secretary of the Interior Ickes suggested that a measure already drafted in the Department of the Interior be given to the Maryland senator. Some sectors, such as the beet sugar interests, favored independence, but for Ickes and Gruening, the objective of the measure was to dampen the demand for it, reminding its proponents that the United States had the power to make Puerto Ricans pay dearly for it.[41]

The bill was denounced in Puerto Rico as an attempt to discredit independence. Yet during May, pro-independence meetings were held across the island. American flags were lowered from city halls, plazas, and schools. Students at Central High School in Santurce staged repeated marches and, when confronted by the police, rioted. Meanwhile, an assembly held on May 4 and attended by several hundred delegates organized a Frente Unido Pro-Constitución de la República, presided over by linguist Rubén del Rosario.

But there were differences among the *independentistas*. Géigel felt that the reaction of the Partido Liberal had been too timid: "We seem too concerned with what Washington may say or want."[42] It was necessary to seize the moment to attain independence. Meanwhile, Albizu Campos had called for the organization of a constituent assembly. Puerto Ricans, he argued, had to organize themselves as a sovereign body. Others such as Rafael Arjona Siaca warned that convening such an assembly would place its organizers before a hard choice if Washington refused to recognize it: either backing down or declaring a "revolutionary war." Barceló, president of the Partido Liberal, joined Arjona Siaca in opposing the "revolutionary procedure" proposed by Albizu Campos.[43]

If anything, the conjuncture evidenced the limited organizational capacity of the Nationalists, who, put to the test, were not able to take practical steps to realize their program. Albizu Campos, furthermore, called on students and women not to risk possible confrontations with the authorities.[44] This is an example of how some of his conservative views on women and the young had a negative impact on possible mobilizations.

While the debate on the Tydings bill raged, the trial of the Nationalist leaders began in the federal district court in San Juan. After a first jury failed to agree on a verdict, a second group (ten Americans and two Puerto Ricans "clearly associated with the American business interests," as one juror described them) found the accused guilty.[45] Albizu Campos was sentenced to ten years in a federal penitentiary with the possibility of probation after six years. On June 7, 1937, he and the other prisoners were transported to Atlanta, Georgia. Albizu Campos remained there until his release in June 1943. He then resided in New York until his return to Puerto Rico in December 1947.

A Forgotten Critique: Clara Lugo and
the Economic Dilemmas of the Republic

The most articulate response to the Nationalist position from a perspective of the New Deal *independentistas* appeared in the newspaper *El Mundo* in late June

1936 in an article written by economist Clara Lugo.[46] Regarding the past, Lugo objected to Albizu Campos's view of the period before 1898 as a time of prosperity in which land had been widely distributed. In fact, Lugo argued, a depressed economy and an impoverished population had characterized Puerto Rican society in 1898. In 1898, only a minority owned land while an abyss separated the rich from the poor. Regarding the present, Lugo explained that the number of landowners had remained relatively constant between 1897 and 1930. The main calamity since 1898 had been corporate control of new land brought under cultivation. Regarding the future, Lugo argued that the Nationalists simplistically felt that tariff protection and land redistribution would automatically result in economic prosperity.

Lugo did not reject the need to protect the local market or redistribute land, but she warned that they were no panaceas. The island needed to export in order to pay for its imports. Even if growing diversification should be a goal, a sudden collapse of the sugar industry had to be avoided. It was necessary to negotiate adequate access to the U.S. market. Lugo objected to the Nationalist view that Puerto Rico was not overpopulated and that to promote birth control was to "collaborate with the enemy." She insisted that an ever-growing mass of workers seeking employment greatly benefited U.S. capital. To teach workers to control their reproduction was to help create a healthier, stronger people.

Lugo envisioned a republic with a capitalist economy in which foreign capital would be "strictly controlled," a project to be conducted, furthermore, in collaboration with the United States.[47] But what if the hopes of such collaboration were to be dashed? Puerto Ricans would then have to choose between conducting a struggle to remake their economy against the will of the United States or settling for a perpetuation of some variation of the existing colonial economic structure. This was a dilemma that Lugo, Muñoz Marín, and his collaborators would indeed face in the early 1940s.

Vito Marcantonio and Puerto Rican New York Activism

In the context of the turmoil generated by the trial of the Nationalist leadership and the Tydings bill, left-wing New York congressman Vito Marcantonio traveled to Puerto Rico to join Albizu Campos's defense team but was unable to reach the island before the trial concluded. His return to New York was the occasion of a march of more than 10,000 in support of the jailed Nationalists.[48] Before coming to Puerto Rico, Marcantonio had introduced a generous independence bill as a counterproposal to the Tydings bill. Marcantonio's bill imposed no tariff restrictions for Puerto Rican goods or migratory limits for Puerto Ricans. It also committed the United States to ample support for the insular economy's reconstruction as "indemnification" for decades of colonialism.

Marcantonio's interest in Puerto Rico was linked to the fact that his congressional district included both his home turf of Little Italy and the Puerto Rican area in East Harlem.[49] While his support in the former was largely a matter of ethnic identification, his support in El Barrio reflected the popularity of his leftist views there. The American Communist Party was also growing in El Barrio. Through the 1930s, it issued diverse Spanish language periodicals and organized clubs and lodges of the International Workers Order (IWO), an insurance cooperative. Juan Emanuelli was one of its main organizers and Jesús Colón one of its key propagandists. Colón, who had come to New York in 1918 and joined the party in 1933, headed the Spanish section of the IWO, which had around 10,000 members, half of whom were Puerto Rican.[50] The IWO described itself as a "multinational organization" committed to the struggles of a united, multicultural working class. In 1934, the Communist Party nominated Puerto Ricans Pedro Uffre for Congress and Armando Ramírez for state assemblyman.[51] It has been estimated that by 1938, the party had 400 members in El Barrio.

Communist influence and support for Marcantonio were linked. Marcantonio was close to, if not a member of, the party. He was first elected to Congress in 1934, lost his seat in 1936, regained it in 1938, and held it until 1950. El Barrio was the only area in which his American Labor Party (ALP) displaced both Democrats and Republicans as the largest party. In 1937, Oscar García, running as a Republican candidate with ALP endorsement, was elected to the New York State Assembly. He was the first Puerto Rican elected to public office in the United States. In 1938, he ran and won as an ALP candidate.

Joint Communist and Nationalist activities in 1936 constituted a reconciliation of sorts. In 1932, a scuffle in New York between Nationalists and Communists resulted in the death of Nationalist Angel María Feliú. Even then Albizu Campos went out of his way to warn that "authentic international communism and socialism are not enemies of the nationalism of the colonies because it represents an anti-imperialist opposition."[52] In August 1936, Nationalists (such as Lorenzo Piñero of the Junta Nacionalista) and Communists (such as A. Rodríguez Berríos of the Communist Party in Lower Harlem) joined many others to repudiate a Partido Liberal leader for supporting Marcantonio's rival in the coming election and for his links to the *azucareros*. Meanwhile, one of Marcantonio's staffers, Communist Harry Robinson, was in Puerto Rico in July–August 1936 and joined diverse activities in favor of independence while denouncing the power and influence of the *azucareros*.[53]

Yet, there were differences between Nationalists and Communists. The latter felt Puerto Rican migrants had to join social and political struggles in the United States. The former tended to see themselves as exiles focused on the struggle for independence. This was to be a recurrent debate between Puerto Rican activists in New York.

Crisis of the New Deal in Puerto Rico and Its Consequences

The events following the attack on Riggs provoked a break between Muñoz Marín and the New Deal establishment. Gruening began to see anything short of complete support as a sign of disloyalty. For his part, Muñoz Marín felt that the Tydings bill perversely sought to obtain a mandate for the "present colonial status" under "threat of literal starvation."[54]

But, if Muñoz Marín did not denounce the Nationalists to ingratiate himself with Gruening, neither did he want to endorse their call for a constituent assembly. Independence not preceded by an economic agreement with the United States would spell disaster. Yet simply opposing the Tydings bill threatened to weaken Muñoz Marín's influence among many Liberales, who were in no mood for politics as usual. How could he take a clear stand for independence while avoiding the more defiant Nationalist proposals? Seeking a way out, Muñoz Marín startled the Liberales with the idea that they boycott the elections. Let the Coalición do as it pleased. Independence was imminent, and the Liberales should concentrate on the search for adequate conditions for it. Such conditions were possible, since it was not in the interest of the United States that the economy of an important trading partner be ruined. Barceló and other party leaders resisted Muñoz Marín's proposal. On July 25, a tumultuous general assembly of the Partido Liberal rejected the boycott by one vote. Muñoz Marín refused nomination to the post of resident commissioner while objecting to the composition of the new party leadership. On September 10, he and his supporters organized Acción Social Independentista (ASI), thus becoming an official faction within the party.

In the elections of November 1936, the Coalición defeated a divided Partido Liberal. Barceló blamed ASI and denounced it as a party within the party. Muñoz Marín, on his part, warned that Gruening would try to divide the

Liberales by offering reforms if they dropped the demand for independence. Such had been the sterile road, he added, followed by the Partido Unión in 1922 when it had adopted the idea of a "Free Associated State." Barceló, in turn, warned against "nationalist influence" and called for a return to the "patient" politics of Muñoz Rivera.[55] Muñoz Marín demanded an assembly to determine the orientation of the Partido Liberal. Instead, on May 31, 1937, Barceló expelled Muñoz Marín and his main supporters from the party. A wit commented: "Barceló has expelled the Partido Liberal."[56] Future events proved this appreciation correct.

By then, the most dramatic event of the decade had shaken the island. In Ponce, an attempt to prevent a Nationalist march led to twenty-one deaths as the police opened fire on an unarmed column of the Cadetes de la República. More than 10,000 attended the funeral of the Nationalists, which featured speeches by Nationalist Julio Pinto Gandía, Communist José Lanauze, and Ernesto Ramos Antonini, a close collaborator of Muñoz Marín's. In New York, 3,000 gathered in the Park Palace ballroom in East Harlem to hear Albizu Campos's lawyer Gilberto Concepción and Congressman Marcantonio denounce what came to be known as the Ponce Massacre.[57]

Muñoz Marín, in Washington at the time, blamed Winship and Gruening for the massacre. But even then he combined his attacks on them with positive references toward Roosevelt. Gruening was presented as undermining the spirit of the New Deal. Muñoz Marín, furthermore, tried to use the American Civil Liberties Union (ACLU) investigation of the events, which criticized the Nationalists but blamed the police for the massacre, to mend Puerto Rican faith in the North American state. He presented the ACLU as the true face of U.S. liberalism, which *La Democracia* admitted had failed Puerto Rico once but, it assured its readers, would "not fail it a second time."[58]

But the 1930s, economic depression and political upheaval were matched by a sharp intensification of literary and cultural debates, to which we now turn.

CULTURAL DEBATES IN AN EPOCH OF CRISIS: NATIONAL INTERPRETATIONS IN THE THIRTIES

The 1930s coincided with the coming of age of a group of men and women of letters who redefined the Puerto Rican intellectual landscape in a lasting way. They came to be known as the *generación del treinta*. What is most distinctive about this cohort is the urgency with which it debated the question of Puerto Rico's cultural identity. The questions formulated by the journal *Indice* in 1929—"Is our personality as a people completely defined?" and "Which are the defining signs of our collective character?"—encapsulate the central issue posed by key authors during this crucial decade.[1]

Antonio S. Pedreira was the guiding spirit of *Indice*, and his essay *Insularismo* published in 1934 ranks among the most influential texts in Puerto Rican intellectual history. Tomás Blanco's response, *Prontuario histórico de Puerto Rico*, and the parallel poetic efforts of Luis Palés Matos gathered in *Tuntún de pasa y grifería* have similarly cast a long shadow over Puerto Rico's intellectual field. Over the years, they have been the object of different, even opposite readings—a running polemic that continues to this day. Puerto Rican fiction also experienced a revival at this time through the impact of works by Emilio S. Belaval and Enrique Laguerre. Meanwhile, from academic Margot Arce to poet Julia de Burgos, women made an initial significant inroad into the Puerto Rican literary sphere.

If the question of Puerto Rican identity occupied a central place in the work of this generation, the questions of race and of the African dimension of Puerto Rican culture were a source of debate, with each author plotting his or her own path through or around it, as we shall see. As we trace the contours of these and related contributions, it is appropriate to begin with Pedreira, initiator of *Indice* and the most prolific author of his generation.

The Impact of Antonio S. Pedreira

Between 1929 and his death in 1939, Pedreira wrote editorials for *Indice* (1929–31), literary reviews in the mainstream press, a collection of essays, a biography of Eugenio María de Hostos, a bibliography of Puerto Rico, his influential essay *Insularismo*, an essay on the image of the Puerto Rican peasant, a study of the repression suffered by the autonomist movement in 1887, a biography of annexationist leader José Celso Barbosa, and a massive history of journalism in Puerto Rico. Meanwhile, except for a brief interlude in 1931–32, he was director of the Department of Hispanic Studies at the University of Puerto Rico.

Pedreira's work was not only vast but also impressively coherent. Through it he hoped both to animate a public sphere of cultural debate in Puerto Rico and to shape it through his representation of Puerto Rico as an emergent distinct cultural entity. His work sought to define the turning points as well as the traumatic moments and unresolved impasses in the evolution of what he called the "Puerto Rican personality."[2]

Pedreira's attempt to construct a Puerto Rican personality exhibits the features of what John Hutchinson calls "cultural nationalism." Its articulators, argues Hutchinson, typically "combine a 'romantic' search for meaning with a scientific zeal to establish this on authoritative foundations. . . . These histories typically form a set of repetitive 'mythic' patterns, containing a migration story, a founding myth, a golden age of cultural splendor, a period of inner decay and a promise of regeneration." This "quest," Hutchinson adds, "has resulted in an explosion in the genetic sciences, including archeology, folk-lore, philology and topography."[3] Pedreira's project was indeed a genetic investigation into the origins and dynamics of the "Puerto Rican personality," which combined a "'romantic' search for meaning" with a "scientific zeal" to document its evolution.

In *Insularismo*, Pedreira periodized Puerto Rico's evolution into three epochs. The first was an epoch of "formation and passive accumulation" (Hutchinson's "migration story"), from 1493 to the start of the nineteenth century, in which Puerto Rico was a "prolongation of Hispanic culture." Africa, according to Pedreira, entered this process as a degrading agent within the transplanted Hispanic cultural body. A second period of political and cultural "awakening" (Hutchinson's "golden age") followed from the early nineteenth century to 1898. A third period of "indecision and transition" (Hutchinson's "period of inner decay") ensued after 1898.

Pedreira's *Insularismo* was openly racist. According to it, racial mixing—the "fusion" of races—was at the root of Puerto Rican "confusion." The text included a gallery of racial stereotypes: the passivity of blacks, the indecisiveness of the mulatto, the impulsiveness of the *grifo* (light-skinned mulatto). *Insularismo* was also sexist. It argued, for example, that primary education largely imparted by women inhibited Puerto Rico's evolution as a distinct and forceful culture. Pedreira combined these opinions with a laudatory biography of black political leader Barbosa. For some critics, this indicates a shift away from his earlier views; for others, it is congruent with them. According to this view, Pedreira offered Barbosa as an example of how blacks could escape their race, so to speak, through the assimilation of white European culture.[4]

Against the background of his periodization, Pedreira announced the beginning of a fourth moment (Hutchinson's "promise of regeneration"), the completion of the agenda interrupted in 1898. Pedreira focused on texts that could be read as explorations of Puerto Rican identity as well as political movements that had promoted gradual change, as opposed to revolutionary initiatives. He privileged the events of 1887, in which the autonomists played a central role, over the Lares separatist insurrection of 1868. This perspective was compatible with the reformist project from above that was then emerging under the leadership of Luis Muñoz Marín in the context of the New Deal. Indeed, *Insularismo* criticized the spread of large landholdings and of the sugar monoculture, the resulting pressure on the small farmer, and the impact on the land (deforestation, erosion, drying up of rivers), topics also covered in the contemporary Plan Chardón sponsored by the PRRA.

But *Insularismo* was also informed by an aversion to certain aspects of bourgeois culture, as Pedreira placed himself in what he described as a tradition that went from Jean-Jacques Rousseau to José Ortega y Gasset: a heterogeneous current, defined by its skepticism regarding aspects of modern, urban, capitalist, industrial civilization. This is the broad sensibility that Michael Löwy has described as the "cultural-romantic" critique or aversion to diverse aspects of capitalist modernity. We already encountered a variant of this outlook in the work of Nemesio Canales in the second decade of the twentieth century and shall encounter it in other authors of the 1930s and beyond. It has been, we would argue, a major dimension of Puerto Rican letters through the twentieth century. Pedreira in particular lamented the displacement of the "teacher" by the "professor," by which he meant the replacement of what he considered the careful cultivation of a many-sided personality by a stunted professional specialization. He similarly decried the advance of the anonymous and easily discarded creations of mass production at the expense of the durable product of the master-artisan, the generalization of a mindless rush represented by the motto that "time is money" at the expense of the enjoyment of time and place. Pedreira objected to an emergent civilization in which "everything is measured," "everything is charged for," which behaves as if "all things and all attitudes had a price in American gold." In the work of Pedreira (as opposed to Canales), this critique of bourgeois culture had a sharp elitist edge as he also rejected the leveling tendencies of universal suffrage. Defending the prerogatives of "superior men," he denounced how "with equal opportunity for all, the mob has been quite content to see the ascendancy of its values at the cost of the decline of the cultured."[5]

Puerto Rico, Pedreira concluded, had become more "civilized" but less "cultured." The more direct source of these ideas within the wider romantic-cultural current is not hard to detect. The echoes of Oswald Spengler's vision of the decline of civilization, which largely reached Pedreira through Ortega y Gasset, were evidently present in *Insularismo*. Spengler was, of course, the conservative tail-end of German romantic sociology, which goes back to the work of Ferdinand Tönnies in the 1880s. Pedreira's opposition of culture and civilization can be seen as one of the many reelaborations of the well-known opposition of community and society (*Gemeinschaft* and *Gesellschaft*) formulated by Tönnies. But progress, Pedreira warned his readers, was inevitable. Nor had everything been well in the past. One could only hope, he argued, for example, that the *jíbaro's* hut (*bohío*) be replaced by a modern dwelling as rapidly as possible. The task, then, was not to counterpose but to reconcile "culture" and "civilization." Furthermore, culture functioned in his text as both a sphere opposed to the basest aspects of civilization and as the content of Puerto Rico's particular identity. His affirmation of culture in both senses was a call to reconcile aesthetics with economics, poetry and the dollar, Puerto Rican culture with U.S. influences.

Many elements of this vision—excluding the more blatant racism and sexism —would become part of the cultural-political project of the Partido Popular Democrático after 1940 while also informing the work of some of its sharpest critics, such as René Marqués, a testimony to the pervasive influence of Pedreira.

Pedreira's Interlocutors: Emilio S. Belaval and Tomás Blanco

The publication of *Insularismo* coincided with that of Belaval's *Los problemas de la cultura puertorriqueña*. This essay and the stories collected in Belaval's

Los cuentos de la universidad also revolved around the question of Puerto Rican identity.[6]

Like Pedreira, Belaval set out to elaborate the "diagram of our culture" and divided Puerto Rico's evolution into three stages: a preparatory stage between 1511 and 1813, a period between 1813 and 1898 in which a Puerto Rican culture and politics emerged, and the ensuing period of "disorientation." In the formation of Puerto Rican culture, Belaval privileged two sectors: the white *hacendado*, who, he argued, ruled over women and slaves with a loving but strict hand, and urban privileged sectors, which made sure to import modern cultural trends from the metropole. The African element, explained Belaval, had been too small to truly contribute to the emergence of a new culture. It had added only "a dark, fatalist uneasiness" to it. In the final analysis, he argued, Puerto Rican culture was essentially Spanish. It was to that source—the Hispanic tradition remade in the world of the *hacienda*—that Puerto Ricans had to turn to discover their origins and to better define their personality.

Belaval thus proposed a conservative "cultural nationalism" that would furthermore abandon all obsessions with the outside world. This was where he most clearly departed from Pedreira's perspective. While *Insularismo* insisted that Puerto Rico had to open itself to the world, Belaval argued that notions such as universalism, Hispanoamericanism, Antilleanism, or Iberoamericanism had to be abandoned once and for all. It was time to concentrate on making a Puerto Rican culture centered "on its own geography."

Belaval had broached these issues in stories he began writing in 1923 and collected in *Los cuentos de la universidad* in 1935.[7] These texts revel in ridiculing the aping by Puerto Rican students of U.S. college life, as seen in the portrait of student Antonio Pérez, who changes his name to Tony and, having adopted the wide pants fashionable at the time, exaggerates their width to a grotesque dimension. The desire to imitate U.S. culture has produced results that deserve caricature, but Belaval chose to counterpose it to a conservative version of Puerto Rican identity. Another story, for example, offers a sympathetic portrait of Bebe Pacheco as she abandons her interest in jazz, leaves Tony, declines the opportunity for casual premarital sex, and instead embraces a "feminity" that is "rooted in the soul of the land." Bebe thus readies herself for "a life of patience and of many births," a life that would have the traditional large house (*casona*) as its "emotional horizon." Similarly, the young nationalist students, as well as some of the female characters, are presented as attractive defenders of a traditional concept of honor and masculinity. For them, debates on changing relations between men and women are just "bedroom gossip." Feminism is invariably seen as trivial and referred to in mocking terms. Belaval was no puritan. He upset many readers, including Pedreira, with his description of the centrality of the erotic in the minds of his young characters. His ideal of traditional womanhood did not imply a renunciation of the flesh. But his sensual characters are also the most traditional. There is enough "sensuality and eroticism," the narrator argues at one point, in "four centuries of Don Juanism, Catholicism and sexual rhetoric" to not require any importations (meaning feminism).[8]

The stories in *Los cuentos de la universidad* are further testimony to the pervasiveness of racist views among key authors of this generation. The only black present in the book is the character of Antoñón, pimp and marijuana provider, who operates from a cavelike hangout visited by the students. The latent hostility of the students toward Antoñón is revealed through the prefacing of references to him with an insult ("Pig, Antoñón!") and the initial proclamation by one of the students: "Antoñón, tonight I want to kill you." As the smokers become intoxicated, they ask Antoñón for a woman. Their hostility erupts when he presents them with a young white *jíbara*. The students immediately react to "liberate" her as one of them shouts, "Thou shall not eat white meat, Antoñón." If the students' dimmed reflexes add a farcical tone to the encounter, this does not erase the fact that it includes an explosion of violence without parallel in the rest of the collection in which the students insult, beat, and attempt to burn Antoñón. The story is told in the amused tone with which an adult would refer to the escapades of the young, chiding their excesses and yet sharing some of their exhilaration. Magali Roy-Féquière has pointed out that the first edition of *Los cuentos de la universidad* included a story ("Un craneo chato se arrima a la luna"), removed by Belaval from later editions, that also presented the mulatto as a resentful, negative presence.[9] Far more Hispanophile and at least as racist as the worst passages of *Insularismo*, as well as promoting cultural self-centeredness, Belaval's early texts were, if anything, more conservative than Pedreira's.

In the mid 1940s, Belaval published a new collection, *Cuentos para fomentar el turismo*. These stories, devoid of the blatant antifeminism and racism of *Los cuentos de la universidad* and perhaps the most accomplished narrative texts of this period, portray a whole series of social problems: the exploitation of the rural worker, the displacement of the small farmer, the abuses of merchants and usurers, the drift of the impoverished *jíbaro* to the city slums, the policies of cultural imposition through the school system, among others. The title is an ironic comment on the attempt by Governor Blanton Winship to promote

Puerto Rico as tourist site, an idea that struck many as grotesquely out of touch with the spectacle of misery Puerto Rico could offer at the time.[10]

In 1935, Tomás Blanco published *Prontuario histórico de Puerto Rico*, the most influential counterpoint to Pedreira's *Insularismo*. *Prontuario* was free of *Insularismo*'s evident racism. Blanco's analysis was informed by his familiarity with texts, largely North American, critical of the politics and economics of U.S. imperialism. He thus decried the naïveté of the Puerto Ricans who in 1898 had applauded the U.S. invasion. They had not detected the expansionary economic dynamic that had led to the war with Spain, thus confusing the idealism that may have inspired the American public with the particular interests behind the actions of their government. Blanco's political perspective was best summarized in an article in which he rejected fascism and communism as well as "laissez-faire capitalism" and embraced the idea of a reformed capitalism, as embodied in Roosevelt's New Deal or the embattled Spanish Republic.[11]

But in spite of differences on the racial question and of his greater interest in economic and political questions, Blanco's views had many points of contact with Pedreira and Belaval, beginning with the division of Puerto Rican history into three periods: an epoch of formation until the end of the eighteenth century; the nineteenth century, which witnessed the "transformation of the inhabitants into a well defined people"; and finally a period of "disorientation" after 1898. Similarly, although he gave more space to the Lares insurrection as a sign of a growing sense of identity, he nevertheless insisted on the greater significance of the liberal-reformist current and its two main achievements, the abolition of slavery in 1873 and the Autonomist Charter in 1897.

Beyond his *Prontuario*, Blanco addressed the racial question in other texts such as *El prejucio racial en Puerto Rico* (1937–38) and "Elogio de la plena" (1935). In them he rejected racism but did so from a perspective that tended to block a deeper exploration of the problem. Blanco argued that Puerto Rican racism was nothing more than a harmless prejudice, a notion he tried to demonstrate by contrasting it with the practices of the Jim Crow South. Blanco not only minimized the problem but also attributed the alleged mildness of Puerto Rican racism to the almost complete absence of "pure blacks" in Puerto Rico and to the fact that blacks had become culturally Hispanicized. Blanco's antiracism was of a very peculiar kind, as it minimized the problem as well as the African contribution to Puerto Rican culture.

Even Blanco's vindication of the *plena*—an Afro–Puerto Rican musical form —is marked by these ambiguities. While Blanco insisted on the *plena* as a more vibrant part of Puerto Rican culture than the upper-class *danza*, he also explained that, setting aside its rhythmic pattern—which he passed over rapidly—the *plena* is not "black" but "white," not African but Spanish.[12] Thus, while celebrating it, Blanco also tended to whiten the *plena*, a gesture that seems to contradict his antiracist intentions.

Alternate Visions: The "Black" Poetry of Luis Palés Matos

Meanwhile, the poetry of Palés Matos provided a more complex contrast, or parallel, depending on the critic, to Pedreira's or Belaval's implicit or explicit racism. While Palés Matos published his volume of so-called black poetry, *Tuntún de pasa y grifería*, in 1937, he had completed and published many of the poems included in it as early as 1926.

Palés Matos's road to *Tuntún* was complex. His interest in Afro-Caribbean culture had diverse motivations. After a *modernista* period influenced as much by Edgar Allan Poe as by Rubén Darío, the Nicaraguan poet initiator of *modernismo*, he participated in the literary avant-garde of the 1920s. In 1922, he explained that Dadaism was to literature what Bolshevism was to the social order: it wanted to overthrow all established categories.[13] This opened a possible path to the vindication of African culture as an alternative to the tired European aesthetic tradition or as means to scandalize a conservative public. An example of this is his poem "Ñam Ñam." If European culture makes cannibalism the embodiment of the utmost savagery, Palés Matos builds his playful poem around the sound and rhythm of chewing African teeth as they joyfully feast on white meat.

He was also imbued by the Spenglerian pessimism regarding the "decline of the West," which suggested the need for a return to the vital cultures of the "primitive."[14] The advance of civilization was creating an overintellectualized woman at the cost of her sexual drive and fertility: it was only necessary, argued the young Palés Matos, to compare Henrik Ibsen's cerebral heroines to Helen of Troy to perceive this decadence of the "white race."[15] The racist association of Africa with the primitive could thus be redefined as a sign of its promise instead of its inferiority. The Spenglerian notion of the decay of culture due to the advance of civilization was also present, as we have seen, in the work of Pedreira. The idea was a shared reference for many authors of this generation, even if each took it in different directions.

Through these *modernista*, avant-garde, and Spenglerian moods, Palés Matos approached the world with a sense of exile, a romantic longing for an alternate existence liberated from the imperatives of bourgeois civilization. This was also present in the work of Pedreira, who decried a world ruled by the motto "time is money." But in the case of Palés Matos, Africa became the refuge from surrounding social reality. The poem "Pueblo negro" constructs a dream place ("pueblo de sueño") that lies deep within the poet's conscience ("tumbado allá en mis brumas interiores"), an alternate world of sensuousness and relaxation. In another poem, the word "Kalahari" inexplicably comes to the poet's mind: a call from an unknown, dimly sensed alternate sphere.[16]

But besides their avant-garde search for a new aesthetic, Spenglerian despair concerning the West, and romantic aversion to bourgeois routine, Palés Matos's poems also offered themselves as vindication of the overlooked, often maligned African component of Puerto Rican culture.[17] Thus, as the poetry of a white poet about black culture, a celebration of eroticism and pleasure in a repressive culture, an evocation of the female black body by a white male, an affirmation of an Afro-Caribbean identity for Puerto Rico, the poetry of Palés Matos has lent itself to many varied, even opposite readings. Some have seen him as accepting and reproducing traditional racist stereotypes (blacks as sensual, sexual bodies). Others see his work as subverting racist culture from within, provocatively celebrating precisely what it has constructed as inferior.

At least initially, the poetry of Palés Matos was attacked as artificial and contrived.[18] Yet by the 1950s, if not earlier, he had been accepted as one of Puerto Rico's major poets, a status made official by the publication of some of his texts by the Instituto de Cultura Puertorriqueña in beautifully illustrated editions. The 1960s and early 1970s brought yet another bifurcation of opinions as some critics, such as Arcadio Díaz Quiñones, claimed him as a poet of anti-imperialist Antillean identity and as an alternative to Hispanophile nationalism while others rejected his work as perpetuating racist views.[19]

"Ñáñigo al Cielo," to take an example, describes the transformation of heaven from an ethereal and solemn place into a festive scene as a result of the arrival of the black man. Is this a celebration of the capacity of African culture to subvert white/Christian categories and open a path to a freer enjoyment of our humanity, or is it a reproduction of typical stereotypes regarding African culture? While we find the first reading more convincing, others have certainly disagreed.[20] Palés Matos's "Mulata Antilla," which closes the 1937 edition of *Tuntún*, was perhaps the best summary of his vision of an oppressed yet vibrant Afro-Caribbean culture of resistance. But again, this use of the *mulata* has been, and is, controversial: while some see it as a rejection of racism with its pretensions of racial purity, others argue that the "*mulata* myth" evades a history "of slavery, oppression, sexual violence, and turns it into an emblem of pleasure."[21]

Literary critic and academic Margot Arce (left) and poet Luis Palés Matos in the mid-1930s. Both were key figures of the *generación del treinta*, which posed the problem of Puerto Rican identity with unprecedented intensity in the midst of the Great Depression. (Proyecto digitalización fotos El Mundo–Biblioteca José M. Lázaro, Universidad de Puerto Rico–Río Piedras)

Less controversial, and not directly connected to the racial question, Palés Matos's work in the 1940s and 1950s was to include some of the best poetry ever written in Puerto Rico, a facet of his trajectory that we cannot explore here.

Civilization's Further Discontents

The debates regarding Puerto Rican culture in the 1930s attracted many authors besides the better known Pedreira, Blanco, Belaval, and Palés Matos. Some Nationalists turned the opposition to a utilitarian civilization into a more openly conservative defense of Catholicism as an essential aspect of Puerto Rican identity. But this implied a tension within Nationalist thought, which saw itself as continuator of nineteenth-century separatists, such as Hostos and

Ramón Emeterio Betances, who had been anticlerical republicans. At least two authors, José Paniagua Serracante and José Toro Nazario, openly resolved this tension by rejecting what they considered had been the mistaken views of Hostos. They felt Hostos's heterodox, positivist, materialist placing of science above faith had opened the way to U.S. colonialism by undermining a possible spiritual resistance to it. Canales's critique of traditional notions of honor and courage were similarly denounced as the expression of a crass materialism that had led to acceptance of U.S. rule.[22]

Interestingly, although Pedreira would later be described as a Hispanophile author, militant Hispanophiles such as Paniagua Serracante did not see him as a fellow thinker. Conservative as Pedreira's views may have been, he was considered to be too dismissive of the Spanish past, too unconcerned with the religious dimension of culture, and not critical enough of some of the changes resulting from U.S. rule. Pedreira was thus criticized for reducing the Spanish conquest to a sordid affair conducted by uncultured adventurers, thus ignoring its spiritual impact. He was also wrong when he argued that Puerto Rico had progressed materially after 1898. Schools had been built, but they were "atheist schools." Ironically, by the end of his response to Pedreira, Paniagua Serracante's religious perspective, in spite of his Nationalist credentials, had all but eclipsed any mention of Puerto Rican particularity. While Pedreira keenly sought the manifestations of the "Puerto Rican soul," Paniagua Serracante's discourse tended to reduce it to the insular manifestation of a universal Catholicism.

A different form of aversion to modernity in its bourgeois form may be found in some texts of Nationalist leader Juan Antonio Corretjer. In an article written in 1936, as he awaited trial, his rejection of market civilization took the form of an exaltation of medieval cultural forms (such as monastic life) and of pre-Columbian cultures. He thus saw the Renaissance, the Enlightenment, and capitalism as gradually weakening the spiritual energy of medieval Christianity. This was, of course, yet another version of the notion of the conflict between "culture" and "civilization," echoes of which we encountered in the work of Pedreira and Palés Matos. Corretjer, on his part, had borrowed from the ideas of Slavophile and both antibourgeois and anticommunist author Nicholas Berdyaev, taking from him the notion of a future beyond the bourgeois present as the arrival of a New Middle Age in which a religious, mystical impulse would engulf all social activities: yet another version of the cultural-romantic critique of capitalist civilization. Corretjer admitted that he had initially seen fascism as embodying such an impulse, but he soon realized that it was a new version of a degraded materialist civilization. He similarly rejected the Soviet Union as a new form of the reigning materialism. "Here and there," he argued, "under the imperialist 'trust' or under the administrative state—man disappears . . . under a deluge of golden manure." He thus embraced a religious, mystical aversion to bourgeois society combined with a militant anti-imperialist nationalism, ruled by a strict ethic of self-sacrifice and influenced by the model of religious asceticism.[23]

Literary Landmarks and Explorations

Puerto Rican authors of the 1930s were concerned with other issues besides the question of identity. Realist narrative took up the main social questions of the time. Enrique Laguerre's *La llamarada* (1935) tells the story of a young university graduate who gets his first job as a supervisor in a sugar plantation, an experience in which he is confronted with the injustices within Puerto Rico's largest industry at the time. Through the novel, the narrator suggests an opposition between the past prosperity of the coffee industry in the interior and the miseries of the coast, gripped by the iron hand of the *centrales*. The nostalgic-romantic recovery of the coffee *hacienda* is accentuated at the end of the novel as the protagonist returns to the interior, which in his case also implies reconciliation with his father.

In 1943, José Luis González, an author whose work would span several literary generations, from the 1940s to the 1980s, published his first book of stories, *En la sombra*. The story line of the main text of the collection resembles Laguerre's *La llamarada*. Its protagonist is a young man employed in a sugar mill, soon after graduating from the university. But here his rejection of the injustices he discovers does not conclude with a return to the coffee interior but rather with an encounter in which two men are heard speaking about the need for social reforms. If *La llamarada* and "En la sombra" suggest different solutions, they denounce similar injustices. Their readers were probably young educated men and women committed to social, labor, and agrarian reform who could easily identify with the protagonists. Not surprisingly, *La Democracia*, the newspaper identified with Muñoz Marín, serialized *La llamarada* beginning in January 1938 during the initial campaign of the PPD.

During the 1930s, women began to enter the intellectual arena in greater numbers as literary critics, such as Margot Arce and Concha Meléndez; as poets, such as Julia de Burgos and Clara Lair; and as social workers and scientists, such as Carmen Rivera de Alvarado and Clara Lugo. The growth of the university played a role in this, as women found a more accessible, if still male-dominated, intellectual circuit than the traditional late-night politico-literary gatherings at cafés or restaurants of journalists, political leaders, and poets. By 1940, the Asociación de Mujeres Graduadas de la Universidad de Puerto Rico, organized in 1936, had 368 members. Between 1938 and 1942, it published its own journal, and in 1945 it launched *Asomante*. Under the leadership of Nilita Vientós, *Asomante* was to become the island's best-known literary journal of the 1950s and early 1960s.[24]

Some women authors were neither professionals nor academics, and some led precarious lives, as exemplified by poets like Burgos and Lair. Lair's name was Mercedes Negrón Muñoz. She was a niece of Luis Muñoz Rivera and a cousin of Muñoz Marín. Her sister, Angela, was a well-known journalist. Both Lair and Burgos questioned traditional views on women. Lair signed her first articles in the journal *Juan Bobo*, edited by Canales, with the pseudonym Heda Gabler. Her poetry spoke of an eroticism freed from the limits of marriage or convention. Similarly, in a well-known poem, Burgos counterposed two Julias: an authentic Julia, eager to join the struggle for human emancipation, and an artificial Julia, ruled by the reigning "social conventions." As opposed to Burgos, who strongly condemned racism in some of her best-known poems, Lair chided Palés Matos for his interest in black culture: as we have seen, she was hardly alone in holding such views.[25]

Burgos had been politically active since 1934, when she met Nationalist leader Pedro Albizu Campos. In 1936, she was elected secretary general of the Frente Unido Femenino Pro Convención Constituyente and participated in activities of the Partido Nacionalista during that crucial year. As the Spanish Civil War erupted, she took a decided stand in favor of the Spanish Republic. Hers was a left-nationalism. Between 1938 and 1943, she wrote poems not only about Albizu Campos but also about San Juan's best-known slums (La Perla and El Fanguito), in support of the 1938 dockworkers' strike, in memory of Cuban anti-Machado fighter Rafael Trejo, in praise of Soviet Russia (at the time of the battle of Stalingrad), and against fascism and aggression in Spain and China. In 1938, she published her first book, *Poema en veinte surcos*, followed by *Canción de la verdad sencilla* in 1939. The former contains poems often recited to this day: "Yo misma fui mi ruta" and "A Julia de Burgos," two eloquent declarations of independence from social convention and traditional women's roles and a declaration of adherence to social and labor struggles. "Ay Ay de la grifa

Poet Julia de Burgos was active in pro-independence, labor, and antifascist movements in the late 1930s and early 1940s. (Proyecto digitalización fotos El Mundo–Biblioteca José M. Lázaro, Universidad de Puerto Rico–Río Piedras)

negra" is a protest against racism and "Río Grande de Loíza" an evocation mixing erotic yearning and patriotic attachment through the poetic fusion of the river and a lover's embrace.

Burgos moved to New York in 1942. Like other members of the *generación del treinta*, she thus joined what soon became a mass migration of Puerto Ricans to New York and other North American cities. During 1943–44, she worked with *Pueblos Hispanos*, the left-wing New York journal sponsored by the American Communist Party and edited by former Nationalist prisoner Corretjer, a project we discuss in chapter 7. She died in New York in 1953, a victim of privation and alcoholism. Her last anguished poems were in English:

It has to be from here,
right this instance,
my cry into the world.
My cry that is no more mine,
but hers and his forever,
the comrades of my silence,
the phantoms of my grave.
It has to be from here,
forgotten but unshaken,
among comrades of silence
deep into Welfare Island
my farewell to the world.[26]

Songs from Afar: El Barrio's Growing Importance

The presence of Burgos and Corretjer in New York in the 1940s reminds us of the importance which that city had already attained in the lives of many Puerto Ricans. By the 1930s, El Barrio, an area in upper Manhattan east of black Harlem, had grown into a bustling Puerto Rican enclave replete with restaurants, *bodegas*, political and social clubs, and theaters and movie houses. Puerto Rican music had been played in New York ever since islanders had begun to move there.[27] Key composers and interpreters, such as Rafael Hernández, Pedro Flores, Manuel "Canario" Jiménez, Pedro Ortiz "Davilita" Dávila, and Francisco López Cruz, had gone to New York in the late 1920s.

Hernández wrote some of his best-known compositions, including "Lamento borincano" (1929) and "Preciosa" (1935), in New York. They were representations of Puerto Rico as influential as any essay or novel. "Lamento borincano" is a vindication of the ruined small farmer in the midst of the Depression and "Preciosa" a loving, idealized depiction of insular geography. It describes its people as combining the traits of Hispanic and Indian traditions. The African dimension goes unmentioned. "Lamento borincano" became associated with Muñoz Marín's movement for social reform; "Preciosa," after the reference in the original version to the "tyrant" who ruled Puerto Rico was replaced by a more innocuous complaint about "destiny," became a favorite of autonomist patriotism. Before New York, Hernández, the son of a cigarmaker from Aguadilla, had spent some time in Cuba, and before that, in another international formative experience, he and more than a dozen young Puerto Rican musicians had been part of the 369th Infantry "Hellfighters" Jazz Band led by James Reese Europe, which toured Europe to great acclaim as part of the U.S. expeditionary force in World War I. The U.S. Army's black band was in large measure Afro–Puerto Rican. The insular themes of Hernandez's songs (the plight of the small farmer, for example) and the references to him as "el jibarito" tended to erase everything but his being born on the island as determinant elements in his life and work. But "el jibarito," as we have seen, had in fact gone through a fairly cosmopolitan experience, which he was to further enrich when he left for Mexico in the mid-1930s.

The 1930s also saw the first combination of the American big band model with Latin music, as exemplified by Augusto Coen y sus Boricuas, organized in 1934. Puerto Rican musicians such as Juan Tizol, Fernando Arbello, Ramón Usera, and Ralph Escudero explored the expanding universe of jazz firsthand while playing or arranging for Duke Ellington, Fletcher Henderson, and other ensembles. Tizol composed "Caravan" and "Perdido," pieces that became Ellington and jazz standards. Meanwhile, the thirties were also the golden age of Puerto Rican trios and quartets in New York, such as the Trío Borinquen and the Cuarteto Victoria organized by Hernández in 1926 and 1932, respectively. Flores closed the 1930s with his "Despedida" sung by the young Daniel Santos, in which a Puerto Rican soldier takes leave of his friends and loved ones on the eve of his departure for the front. By then, compositions by Hernández and Flores had become part of the popular musical repertoire all over Spanish-speaking America.[28]

New York became the residence of several members of the *generación del treinta*, such as Soto Vélez, Graciany Miranda, and Emilio R. Delgado, who shared a path through the literary vanguard of the 1920s to political radicalization in the 1930s and relocation in New York in the 1940s. Their itineraries constitute a forgotten dimension of the *generación del treinta*, which is often unilaterally reduced to a set of elitist, Hispanophile, racist, and conservative authors. Soto Vélez and Miranda had been the founders of the current known as Atalayismo. They combined iconoclastic literary initiatives with support for the Partido Nacionalista. Soto Vélez was jailed with Albizu Campos in 1936. After his release, he settled in New York and worked with Vito Marcantonio's American Labor Party.[29] Still active in the 1970s, Soto Vélez welcomed the emergence of a Puerto Rican literature in English.

Meanwhile, like other Nationalists, such as Corretjer, Miranda expressed some early sympathies for fascism, but he turned against Mussolini at the time of the Ethiopian campaign, siding with the African state against the Italian invaders.[30] His work as poet, editor, and journalist awaits a careful examination. After many twists and turns, including stretches of *independentista* and labor activism, he too settled in New York in the late 1940s or early 1950s, where he lived a life of relative obscurity but of continued literary efforts. Like Burgos, Miranda eventually ventured into the writing of poetry in English, some of it collected in his book *Hungry Dust*.[31]

Delgado, after participating in the literary vanguard of the 1920s, went to Spain in the early 1930s. As political polarization edged Spain toward civil war, he joined the Spanish Communist Party and eventually became editor of its paper, *Mundo Obrero*. Barely escaping the fall of Madrid to Franco's army in 1939, he settled in New York, where he labored for more than two decades of the Cold War as a correspondent for the Soviet news agency Tass. During the 1950s, he wrote on Puerto Rican questions, arguing, for example, against those who insisted that there was no racism in Puerto Rico.[32] During the 1960s, he was heartened by two developments: the Cuban Revolution and the "black revolution" in the United States, which he saw as the harbinger of the "social revolution."[33] "It seems," he wrote to a friend, "that I am destined to witness (and act) in all the critical movements of our time: the Spanish revolution, the Cuban revolution, and, now, the social revolution in the United States." An opponent of the imposition of English, he did not allow this to interfere with his admiration of the poetry of e. e. cummings, Robert Frost, Carl Sandburg, or William Carlos Williams.[34]

Unfortunately, most accounts of the *generación del treinta* center on the admittedly more influential work of Pedreira, Blanco, and Palés Matos and some aspects of the work of Burgos and rarely mention the work and trajectory of this expatriate wing.

Balance Sheet in 1940

In what can be read as a summary of the intellectual efforts of the decade, in 1940 the Ateneo in San Juan, headed at the time by Vicente Géigel, organized a wide-ranging forum on Puerto Rican culture. The gathering was an unprecedented initiative. It included multiple interventions on economic, political, literary, educational, historical, religious, and other issues. Such an event would have been unthinkable ten years earlier, when Géigel, Pedreira, and others had launched the journal *Índice*. It was an occasion for the members of a maturing intellectual generation to recognize themselves as part of a collective project and reaffirm their claim as articulators of a Puerto Rican identity. Laguerre spoke on the novel, Belaval on drama, Arce on the university, Jaime Benítez on the definition of culture, Muñoz Marín on culture and democracy.

The forum took place against an ominous background. The war in Europe had begun in September 1939. There were real if understated tensions among the participants. Several future debates can be detected in some of the counterposed presentations. Two were evident: the debates on the war, democracy, and independence, and on culture and the role of the university. Thus, Rafael Arjona Siaca argued that dictatorship had to be resisted but (in obvious reference to U.S. rule over Puerto Rico) added that democracy would not be complete as long as one "people" kept another under its "omnipotent will." Muñoz Marín, on his part, avoiding the issue of colonialism, spoke of Puerto Rico as a sanctuary where, in a world overrun by barbarism, the idea of a democratic culture could be preserved. These positions foreshadowed the clash between those among Muñoz Marín's collaborators, like Arjona Siaca, who favored a push toward independence and those who, like Muñoz Marín himself, were to turn away from that orientation.

Equally distant were the views of Arce and Benítez on culture and the university. Arce wrote, in terms reminiscent of Pedreira, of the need to create a "cultured man" instead of a specialist, of cultivating the spirit of "service to others" instead of a desire for "economic gain." But her concept of culture included a focus on the "Puerto Rican circumstance: our geography, our history, sociology, politics, language, art, tradition."[35] Benítez, on the other hand, insisted that culture should be seen as a set of "goals to be attained," inspired by certain universal values that had four sources: Greek and Renaissance culture, Christianity, and modern science.[36] These interventions were the first shots of the clash between the cultural "universalism" Benítez would make the official ideology of the University of Puerto Rico, which he headed between

1942 and 1966, and the views of Arce and others, who saw such universalism as a grandiloquent name for the typical colonial disdain for Puerto Rican culture.

But these debates came into the open only later, in a political context transformed by the emergence of a new political movement: the Partido Popular Democrático. It is to this development that we now turn our attention.

TURNING POINT IN THE FORTIES: RISE OF THE PARTIDO POPULAR DEMOCRÁTICO

The period between 1938 and 1948 marked the beginning of a new epoch in Puerto Rican politics. It was dominated by the rise of the Partido Popular Democrático and by the struggle of diverse currents within it to determine its orientation. The end result of this process was the consolidation of a new autonomist project under the leadership of Luis Muñoz Marín. These years also saw the brilliant rise and tragic fall of a new labor federation, the Confederación General del Trabajo, which was at first allied with the PPD but came into conflict with it by 1945. In this chapter, we cover the initial victory and internal evolution of the PPD and its evolving relation with the labor movement. This period includes one of the most hotly debated moments in twentieth-century Puerto Rican political history: Muñoz Marín's break with his past pro-independence position.

As we saw in chapter 5, in May 1937, Muñoz Marín and his supporters had been expelled from the Partido Liberal. On July 22, 1938, they launched the PPD. The party's emblem was a red profile of a *jíbaro* against a white background, and its motto was Bread, Land and Freedom (*Pan, Tierra y Libertad*). The PPD was launched with some initial assets. Muñoz Marín still controlled *La Democracia*, the newspaper founded by his father in 1890. The post of attorney general was still held by PPD supporter Benigno Fernández García. Four liberal legislators went over to the new party. Consequently, the PPD had a legislative presence even before its first elections. In August 1938, its legislators opposed Governor Blanton Winship's proposal to reinstate the death penalty, an action they described as the "first work of the Partido Popular."[1]

The *populares* threw themselves into the 1939–40 campaign with extraordinary energy. Muñoz Marín traversed the island speaking at dozens of large and small roadside gatherings. The PPD's constituent assembly, held on July 21, 1940, brought together 4,000 delegates. Muñoz Marín insisted that candidates

PPD leader Luis Muñoz Marín addresses a gathering during the founding convention of the PPD in 1940. The PPD was to dominate Puerto Rican politics until the late 1960s. (Proyecto digitalización fotos El Mundo–Biblioteca José M. Lázaro, Universidad de Puerto Rico–Río Piedras)

be representative of the party's constituency, which he defined as workers, farmers (*agricultores*), and the middle class.[2] The PPD issued drafts of the main bills it intended to introduce. In a rally on September 15, 1940, in Santurce, its candidates were sworn to support the measures the voters were being asked to endorse. Foremost among these were the proposed land and labor reforms. The party published *El Batey*, a small newspaper, and the pamphlet *Catecismo del pueblo*, which explained its ideas in an agile and accessible format.

Regarding the status question, Muñoz Marín made a momentous decision. He announced that a vote for the PPD would not be interpreted as a vote for any status but rather for immediate social reforms. He added, "I have as always my personal conviction in favor of independence through peaceful means and in friendship with the United States."[3] PPD leader Vicente Géigel criticized both the decision to postpone the status issue and the unilateral manner in which Muñoz Marín had taken it.[4] Yet he soon yielded to Muñoz Marín, a pattern that repeated itself several times until a final break between both men occurred in 1951.

Muñoz Marín's campaign had a clear leftist inclination. He emphasized that his party would not buy votes, a common practice at the time. Parties that bought votes, he argued, served the wealthy who gave them the money to do so. Muñoz Marín hoped to attract socialists, trade unionists, non-Nationalist *independentistas*, socially minded professionals, and small farmers. Trying not to leave anybody behind, he had the PPD's constituent assembly send greetings to Puerto Rico's most admired poet at the time, Luis Lloréns Torres, and to its best-known composer of popular music, Rafael Hernández.[5] Of particular importance was Muñoz Marín's success in gaining the support of a renewed labor movement.

New Labor Activism and Left Influence in the Late 1930s

By 1940, Puerto Rico's labor movement had undergone a significant transformation ushered in by two labor battles in 1937: the strike of 600 operatives at the Red Star Manufacturing Co. (a button factory) in Sunoco (near today's Villa Palmeras), and a strike of the drivers of the White Star Bus Line in San Juan. Four workers were killed during the drivers' strike.[6] Meanwhile, workers in other sectors exhibited a renewed militancy. In 1938, a strike of 7,500 dockworkers shook insular commercial and productive activity. The strike was led by a newly formed union of office and warehouse workers, which received the support of the sailors organized by the National Maritime Union, affiliated with the new North American federation, the Congress of Industrial Organizations.

Members of the Communist Party of Puerto Rico played a key role in these mobilizations. Activists coming from both the Partido Socialista and Partido Nacionalista had organized a communist current in 1932. José Lanauze Rolón was an example of the first trajectory and Luis Vergne Ortiz of the second. Lanauze Rolón was a black physician who had graduated from Howard University in Washington, D.C., the premier center of higher education for African Americans at the time.[7] Vergne Ortiz was a lawyer who began his political life in 1915 as a student opposing the imposition of English as the language of instruction. He had been a disciple of prolabor lawyer Rafael López Landrón, one of the founders of the Partido de la Independencia in 1912. Vergne Ortiz joined, then left the Partido Socialista in the 1920s. After a sojourn in the Partido Nacionalista in 1930–32 (during which he described himself as a Marxist), he joined Lanauze Rolón and others to create an organizing committee for a Communist Party.[8] In 1932, Lanauze Rolón ran as a write-in candidate for resident commissioner. Through 1933 and 1934, both men were active in the strikes and boycotts of the time. In 1934, Alberto Sánchez, a worker who had gone to the United States in 1926 and entered the Communist Party there, joined the effort to create an insular party.

The new movement differentiated itself from both the Partido Socialista and the Nationalists. Against the former, it favored a revolutionary break with capitalism and independence for Puerto Rico. Against the latter, it proposed anchoring the struggle for independence on the organization of labor. Lanauze Rolón criticized the Nationalists for their nostalgia for the past, their conservative Catholic views, and their failure to link up with the labor movement. The bourgeoisie, he added, is "the worst enemy" of independence. The Nationalists, with no links to labor and no support from the bourgeoisie, were destined to move in a void. But there were, he added, points of contact between Nationalists and Communists: support for independence and for the nationalization of basic services. Lanauze Rolón hoped that, in their struggle against U.S. rule, the Nationalists would evolve toward "a socialist economic policy."[9]

But the issue of the relation with the Communist International provoked a split in the nascent movement. In September 1934, militants from San Juan, Cataño, Santurce, and Hato Rey led by Vergne Ortiz rejected affiliation with the International.[10] Thus, two parties were organized in 1934: the Partido Comunista (PC), led by Sánchez and Lanauze Rolón, and the Partido Comunista Independiente (PCI), led by Vergne Ortiz. The former tried, without success, to apply the policy favored by the Comintern at the time, the construction of red unions parallel to the existing labor organizations.[11] Meanwhile, through 1935 and 1936, the PCI carried on its agitation and propaganda activities. The sites of these meetings read like a list of the poorest urban neighborhoods in San Juan at the time: Shanghai, La Perla, Campo Alegre, Tras Talleres, Parada 15, Sunoco.[12] By January 1935, the PCI was expressing sympathy for Trotsky's critique of Stalinism. Vergne Ortiz also recruited a young man who sought him out in his house in Villa Palmeras, César Andreu Iglesias, who was to become Puerto Rico's best-known Marxist as well as a prominent journalist and novelist.

Somewhat surprisingly, given the expressions of anti-Stalinism, in 1936 Vergne Ortiz and his comrades joined the rival PC. By mid-1937, Vergne Ortiz had

CGT and Communist Party leaders Juan Santos Rivera (left) and Juan Sáez Corales during a meeting in the mid-1940s. (Proyecto digitalización fotos El Mundo–Biblioteca José M. Lázaro, Universidad de Puerto Rico–Río Piedras)

reconstituted the PCI, which did not take off as a viable organization.[13] Andreu Iglesias remained in the PC. Meanwhile, leaders and militants of the PC came to occupy important posts in the labor movement. Its influence reached far beyond the 600 members one of its leaders claimed in 1943.[14] By 1940, Juan Sáez Corales was the head of the Unión Protectora de Desempleados, which had been organized in February 1939 in an assembly of close to 600 delegates at the Municipal Theater in San Juan. Juan Santos Rivera was a leader of the Unión de Trabajadores de la Construcción. Sánchez had become a top official of the Asociación de Choferes (AC), the new drivers' union, organized in 1937.

By 1940, the AC had become the backbone of the new labor upsurge. Besides Sánchez, the AC was led by Ramón Barreto Pérez, a PPD militant from Ponce, and Gerardo Ferrao, a veteran organizer among drivers.[15] The AC's legal counsel was entrusted to Francisco Colón Gordiany, former Partido Socialista legislator, who had played a leading role in the White Star Bus Line strike.

The AC published a yearly *Album de la Asociación de Choferes de Puerto Rico* that reflected the influence of the Left. The *Album* for 1940, for example, contained articles by Communists Lanauze Rolón and Andreu Iglesias and a PPD leader sympathetic to socialism, Eugenio Font Suárez. Font Suárez had also been, like Vergne Ortiz, a disciple of Rafael López Landrón. His text in the *Album* pointed out the affinity between workers' struggles of the time and the Partido de la Independencia, organized by Rosendo Matienzo Cintrón and López Landrón in 1912. The *Album* also carried a selection of poems, including two ("Soliloquio de un soldado" and "Banquete de gordos" against war and social inequality) by Lloréns Torres (who had also been a founder of the Partido de la Independencia), as well as Muñoz Marín's translation of Edwin Markham's "Man with the Hoe." The inclusion of the Markham–Muñoz Marín text is not surprising, given its theme and the budding alliance between the AC and the PPD. The use of texts by Lloréns Torres would not be surprising if critics had not tended in recent years to reduce his views to that of a conservative *hacendado*; many of his pronouncements were in fact quite compatible with the demands and outlook of the labor movement.[16]

On May 31, 1940, at a meeting in the offices of the Asociación de Trabajadores de Hoteles y Restaurantes in Santurce, 112 delegates from forty-two unions organized a new labor federation: the Confederación General del Trabajo (CGT), headed by Communist Juan Sáez Corales. The following month, the founding of the CGT was saluted at a gathering in New York where Jesús Colón of the International Workers Order and Congressman Vito Marcantonio joined Alberto Sánchez and Colón Gordiany of the CGT on the speaker's platform. Such interactions between the New York Puerto Rican Left and their island counterparts were common at the time. In 1938, for example, American Communist Party organizer Juan Emanuelli had joined with Pedro Albizu Campos's lawyer Gilberto Concepción and left-nationalist José Enamorado Cuesta to organize a committee in solidarity with the 1938 dockworkers' strike.[17]

The PPD, for its part, was well attuned to this labor upsurge. Through 1939 and 1940, two PPD leaders, Ernesto Ramos Antonini and Víctor Gutiérrez Franqui, helped bring to court employers violating the Federal Labor Standards Act, the first federal minimum wage law, enacted in 1938. Similarly, in 1938 striking dockworkers benefited from the actions of Attorney General Fernández García, who prevented Governor Winship from using legislation covering "emergency" situations to repress the strike. Muñoz Marín attended the congress of unemployed workers in March 1939. He supported the protests of *público* drivers and attended their 1939 and 1940 congresses.[18] Ramón Barreto Pérez, leader of the AC and the CGT, and Pedro J. Dumont, a leader of the construction workers' union, were PPD candidates for the Senate. When a rival political alliance described itself as the "union of the Puerto Rican family," Muñoz Marín riposted that there existed two families in Puerto Rico: a "small and privileged family" of the exploiters and the "large family of the exploited." The statement drew immediate praise from Communist Lanauze Rolón.[19] Thus, by 1940 the sympathy of the new labor movement for the PPD was evident. The leading bodies of the CGT and of several unions functioned as a de facto alliance between the rising labor movement, the PPD and the PC.

1940 Elections

On its way to the 1940 elections, the PPD was helped by two developments. The historic leaders of both the Socialist and Liberal parties—Santiago Iglesias and Antonio R. Barceló, respectively—had died in the period preceding the elections. And both the Partido Socialista and Partido Republicano, which made up the Coalición, had suffered debilitating splits. While Senator Bolívar Pagán kept control of the Partido Socialista, Commissioner of Labor Prudencio Rivera, with the support of much of the Federación Libre de Trabajadores, organized the Partido Laborista Puro. The *laboristas* and the dissident republicans joined with the Partido Liberal to create the Unificación Puertorriqueña Tripartita. The elections of 1940 thus became a threeway race between the Coalición (the Republicans and the Socialists), the Unificación Puertorriqueña Tripartita (dissident Republicans, dissident Socialists, and the Partido Liberal), and the new PPD (see Figure 7.1).

In his campaign closing speech, Muñoz Marín proclaimed the elections would launch a new epoch in Puerto Rican history. He described the first epoch as the "time of the patriots," personified by his father, Luis Muñoz Rivera, whose death in 1916 had ushered in an epoch of political "managers," a "dead time," equivalent to the dire jobless period between sugar harvests. A victory of the PPD in 1940 would inaugurate the age of "the people."[20] The tripartite periodization (golden age, decadence, promise of revival) typical of the texts of the *generación del treinta* was thus deployed to present the PPD as the synthesis of the legacy of Muñoz Rivera and the aspirations of "the people."

The elections produced a mixed result. Overall, the Coalición received more votes than the PPD and thus controlled the post of resident commissioner. But the PPD won a majority in the Senate. In the House, the Coalición and the PPD elected an equal number of representatives, with the three elected candidates of the Unificación Puertorriqueña Tripartita holding the deciding votes. The

FIGURE 7.1. Political Parties in Puerto Rico, 1899–1940

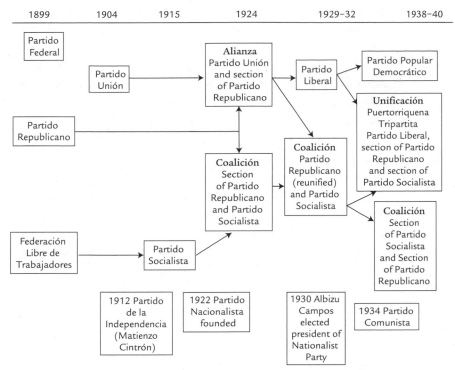

PPD could thus initiate its reform program as long as it could count on the votes of the "tripartite" minority in the House.

Three factors enhanced the PPD's ability to put its initial program into practice: the upholding of 500-acre legislation by the U.S. Supreme Court; the naming of Rexford G. Tugwell as governor; and the increase in government revenues during the war.

In 1935, the insular legislature had created the judicial means for enforcing the 500-acre limitation, which had been a dead letter since 1900. Rubert Hermanos, the first corporation to be prosecuted, challenged the authority of the insular government to intervene in the enforcement of a federal disposition. The insular supreme court upheld the statute, but the U.S. Court of Appeals for the First Circuit in Boston revoked that decision in the fall of 1939. On March 25, 1940, the U.S. Supreme Court revoked the appellate court's decision, thus opening the path to the implementation of the 500-acre limitation.[21]

But the PPD reform plans required financial means. These were also forthcoming. The Jones Act of 1917 established that excise taxes paid by exports to the United States be returned to the insular government. This fund grew rapidly after 1941 as Puerto Rican rum became a substitute for decreased U.S. liquor production (given the use of distilleries for war production and the inability to increase imports from Europe and other areas). Plus, the PPD benefited from wartime military projects as new U.S. installations were established on the island and older ones expanded. We explore these developments in more detail in chapter 9.

The PPD might have confronted a major obstacle had it faced an uncooperative governor. This difficulty was also averted. The Supreme Court ruling on the 500-acre law prompted the Department of the Interior to send Tugwell to Puerto Rico to report on the impact of enforcing the statute. Tugwell's mission led to his appointment as governor in 1941. This was a fortunate turn of events for Muñoz Marín: Tugwell was an acquaintance from the early New Deal and a supporter of agrarian reform and planning. Tugwell himself saw his task as ensuring that U.S. military bases in Puerto Rico would not find themselves isolated in a "hostile environment."[22]

Such views were shared by other federal functionaries who felt broad reforms were needed in Puerto Rico in order to avoid a major political crisis. As early as November 1936, Secretary of the Interior Harold Ickes had privately recorded his concern regarding the collapse of the reform program in the wake of the Riggs assassination. Regarding Ernest Gruening's turn against Muñoz Marín and his "former liberal friends in Puerto Rico," he had written that "it is a poor time, in view of the substantial progress that we have made in bringing about better feelings toward the United States on the part of the Spanish-American countries, to resort to extreme measures in Puerto Rico."[23] Thus, while cautious, Ickes probably welcomed the possibility of rebuilding a loyal reform coalition in Puerto Rico through the Tugwell–Muñoz Marín connection.

The PPD Wartime Bloc

In 1941, Muñoz Marín was elected president of the Senate. The PPD legislative team, coordinated by Géigel, soon produced a series of far-reaching measures. Between 1941 and 1945, an agrarian reform was launched. A planning board, a government bank, and an industrial development company were created. New public utilities (water and power) were organized. Labor, wage, and other social legislation was enacted. By 1941, sectors of the American press were referring to these transformations as a "peaceful, ballot-box revolution."[24] But not all sectors were equally supportive. As the PPD began to put its program into practice, Muñoz Marín found himself fighting several battles. His trajectory during those years was shaped by his need to combine initiatives on diverse fronts.

Muñoz Marín had to first neutralize his enemies to the right. The Coalición remained a significant force. Coalitionist resident commissioner Bolívar Pagán led a campaign in the U.S. press denouncing the PPD and Tugwell. Prominent employers such as José A. Ferré of Ponce Cement, Celestino Iriarte of the White Star Bus Line, and *centralista* Antonio Roig and groups such as the Association of Sugar Producers and the Chamber of Commerce denounced Muñoz Marín and the PPD. Merchants in the import business joined sugar interests in opposing programs to promote local food production. Puerto Rico's largest daily, *El Mundo*, was hostile to the PPD and Tugwell. Attorney General George A. Malcolm and former auditor Patrick J. Fitzsimmons were similarly denounced by the *populares* for sabotaging the 500-acre law and for joining the anti-Tugwell campaign.[25]

During 1943, U.S. congressional committees from both the House and the Senate visited Puerto Rico. The House Committee, led by Jasper Bell (D-Mo.), had a clear anti-Tugwell and anti-PPD agenda. Meanwhile, bills were introduced in Congress in 1943 to unseat Governor Tugwell, annul legislation creating the Land Authority and other agencies, and to reassign rum-tax funds to federal projects on the island, thus diverting them away from PPD reform projects. Resolutions were introduced in 1944 calling on the president to remove Tugwell. Concurrently, the main sugar interests, such as the Fajardo Sugar Company, contested the 500-acre law in court.

Against such enemies, Muñoz Marín could draw on two sources of institutional and political support in Washington and in Puerto Rico. In Washington, he and the PPD leaned on those sectors within the Roosevelt administration willing to stand by them and Tugwell. In Puerto Rico, Muñoz Marín sought the support of the *independentista* and the more active trade union wing of the PPD coalition.

The CGT grew rapidly, claiming 80,000 members in 59 unions by October 1940.[26] Its First Congress in May 1942 was attended by 1,115 delegates from 159 unions claiming 150,000 members. FLT leaders accused the Department of Labor, now headed by former attorney general Fernández García, of siding with the CGT. Indeed, not a few members of the new staff of the Department of Labor were members of or close to the PC and/or open supporters of the CGT.[27]

Collaboration between the PPD and the CGT reached its peak in the 1942 strike in the sugar industry. Secretary of Labor Fernández García sided with

PPD leader Luis Muñoz Marín (with cigarette), at the time president of the Senate, speaking to Governor Rexford Guy Tugwell during a gathering in the early 1940s. (Proyecto digitalización fotos El Mundo–Biblioteca José M. Lázaro, Universidad de Puerto Rico–Río Piedras)

the strikers and attacked the "sugar barons." Muñoz Marín attended the funeral of one of the two workers killed during the strike. Both the CGT and the FLT claimed to represent the strikers. When the FLT signed a contract on their behalf, the CGT called on workers to continue the strike. This division mirrored the conflict in the United States between the conservative AFL and the more radical CIO. The FLT insisted that the government was siding with the CGT; Sáez Corales and Colón Gordiany of the CGT in turn praised Tugwell for not repressing the strike as had been customary in the past.[28] Eventually, the CGT agreed to call off the strike while a new Minimum Wage Board evaluated wages in the sugar industry. The board imposed wages higher than those obtained by the FLT, further discrediting it.

The Puerto Rican Left in New York: The Case of *Pueblos Hispanos*

While a new labor movement emerged in Puerto Rico, the weekly *Pueblos Hispanos* was launched in New York under the directorship of freed Nationalist Juan Antonio Corretjer. The effort reflected the strength of the Left in the Puerto Rican community in New York. The paper's masthead committed it to support the independence of Puerto Rico and the Philippines, "trade union unity in the Americas," the rights of Puerto Ricans, Mexicans, and Filipinos in the United States, and the struggle against Franco in Spain.

Corretjer had been favorably impressed by Communist Party leader Earl Browder while they were both imprisoned in Atlanta. On its part, the American Communist Party was evidently interested in cultivating a link with the Puerto Rican independence movement. *Pueblos Hispanos* was a joint venture of *independentistas* and the American Communist Party. From New York, the paper carried texts by Puerto Rican Communists Jesús Colón and Consuelo Lee, former nationalist prisoner Clemente Soto Vélez, and poet Julia de Burgos. From the island, it published texts by Communists Andreu Iglesias and José Luis González. The paper also carried statements by Browder and American Labor Party congressman Marcantonio. Soto Vélez also became an organizer of Marcantonio's ALP.

Since some authors have described the views of Nationalist leader Albizu Campos as close to fascism, it should be noted that he reacted favorably to the support received from the American Communist Party. In 1943, he and Corretjer were elected to the national committee of the Communist-led International Labor Defense, while Browder and Albizu Campos exchanged cordial letters. Albizu Campos warmly thanked the American party, and in particular Browder and William Z. Foster, for their defense of Puerto Rico's independence. He summarized his perspective as "no slavery among the nations of the New World; no imperialism over any nation of this hemisphere; the Americas open to all humanity."[29]

But there were tensions within this project, such as the differences between Corretjer and Albizu Campos, for example, over the former's dual participation in Communist and Nationalist structures. Corretjer left or was expelled from the Partido Nacionalista in or around 1943.[30] There were also different emphases among the contributors to the paper. While Colón's columns focused on the situation of Puerto Ricans in New York, Corretjer was more concerned with the struggle for independence.

Colón had been writing columns in the New York Spanish and radical press since the late 1920s covering a very ample set of topics: Puerto Rican independence, workers' struggles in the United States, racism against and among Puerto Ricans, women's rights and sexual liberation. In a 1943 contribution to *Pueblos Hispanos*, he drew attention to the fact that a Puerto Rican, Luis Rodríguez Olmo, had been recruited as an outfielder by the Brooklyn Dodgers. This, he explained, could have a significant impact, not only in terms of the visibility of Puerto Ricans in the U.S. public eye but also as a step toward the eventual breaking of the color line barring African American players from the major leagues. He called on Puerto Ricans to fill Ebbets Field whenever Rodríguez Olmo played and invited them to write letters to the Dodgers organization urging it toward desegregation.[31]

Distancing himself from a nationalist logic that counterposed Puerto Ricans to Americans, Colón explained that "there are two United States, just as there are two Puerto Ricos." Puerto Rican workers had to "make common cause with the PEOPLE of the United States" while struggling against U.S. imperialism.[32] This was crucial, and not only for Puerto Ricans in the United States. To contribute to the democratic struggles in the United States was to also create more favorable conditions for a Puerto Rican republic.[33]

But Colón's internationalism was shaped by the policies of the Communist parties of the time, which subordinated working-class agendas in the pursuit of the broadest possible antifascist front. This led him to side with President Roosevelt against labor leader John L. Lewis when the latter defied the wartime no-strike pledge favored by the Communists.[34] This was another source of friction: Corretjer was not comfortable with the Communists' inclination to lavish praise on Roosevelt and Tugwell and to tone down denunciations of U.S. imperialism in the context of the "war against fascism." Yet, he did join them in calling for a vote for the PPD in the elections of 1944.[35]

Pueblos Hispanos stopped publication in 1944 for reasons that may have been financial or political. It donated its printing materials to the CGT in Puerto Rico. Furthermore, the context in which it was launched would soon be overtaken by the coming of the Cold War and the liquidation of the Communist-influenced U.S. labor Left that had nurtured it.

Muñoz Marín and the Status Dilemma

Meanwhile, by 1943–44 Muñoz Marín was shifting his view on the status question: he was evolving away from his *independentista* position. This was a gradual process completed only in 1946. No shift in perspective by a Puerto Rican political leader has been more debated. It has been alternatively described as a breakthrough from past dilemmas or as a betrayal of fundamental principle. For a more dispassionate consideration, it is convenient to look back and forward from the mid-1940s.

For more than two decades, Muñoz Marín had been a critic of the colonial relation with the United States, both of the type of political subordination it implied and of what he felt were its economic consequences: overspecialization, mass unemployment, low wages, absentee control, and systematic outflow of profits. Puerto Rico's plight was for him as much a result of the throwing open of its economy to U.S. competition and capital as of overpopulation (although he felt the latter was a contributing factor to insular poverty).

But Muñoz Marín believed independence offered no easy exit. Precisely because Puerto Rico had acquired a one-sided economy, dependent on privileged access to a protected U.S. market, a sudden break with the metropole would result in an impoverished republic.[36] Colonialism had terrible economic consequences, not the least of which was the fact that it did not tend to create an economic foundation for independence.

The New Deal had seemed to offer a way out: the Roosevelt administration had launched a program of state-led rationalization of the sugar industry and had vindicated public intervention to correct the inadequacies of an unfettered capitalism. Muñoz Marín felt it would now be possible to equip Puerto Rico with a more balanced economy. Absentee control would be reduced; production would be diversified and some of it redirected to the insular market. Such changes would then be consolidated by political independence within a collaborative interaction with the United States.[37]

Muñoz Marín recognized that since the mid-1930s, Puerto Rico had received a sizable amount of economic aid from the United States. But that only meant, he added, that the exploitation of the Puerto Rican people by U.S. corporations was also a burden on the U.S. taxpayer. It was in the interest of the American people to help Puerto Rico reorganize its economy on a different basis, freed from the exploitation of absentee capital and able to develop its own industries to the point of not requiring relief efforts.[38]

Yet by 1943–44, if not earlier, Muñoz Marín became convinced that independence as he had envisaged it was impossible. Puerto Rico could not hope for generous commercial agreements with the United States after independence. "Most favored nation" treaties signed by the United States would force it to grant its cosignatories whatever it granted Puerto Rico, foreclosing any preferential treatment to facilitate the island's emergence from colonialism.[39] Muñoz

Marín concluded that independence had to be abandoned as economically unviable. These ideas, he would later explain, had simmered in his mind since at least 1940 but took definite shape only in 1944–45, after he studied the conditions under which the Philippines were to be granted independence and after conversations with U.S. Tariff Commission economist Benjamin Dorfman.[40]

In the past, doubting the viability of independence had not prevented Muñoz Marín from denouncing the negative effects of free trade and the dominance of absentee capital over the Puerto Rican economy, such as overspecialization and mass unemployment. Concern about independence did not turn him into an apologist of free trade or U.S. capital. But as he definitely abandoned independence as unviable, he proceeded to also jettison his critical views on this matter, exchanging them for an increasingly unqualified trust on the beneficial effects of free trade and absentee capital on the Puerto Rican economy. "Overpopulation" now became the fundamental cause of Puerto Rico's poverty and unemployment, while free trade and the reliance on U.S. capital came to be regarded as forces helping to ameliorate problems that Muñoz Marín and his collaborators increasingly described as strictly demographic. Muñoz Marín thus went over to the perspective that the sugar interests had articulated in the past against his and his collaborators' critique of the political and economic structure put in place after 1898.

Furthermore, in 1946, a U.S. Tariff Commission report on the possible consequences of statehood and independence argued that in recent years, incoming U.S. government funds had exceeded outgoing profits and dividends. For Muñoz Marín, this now became proof that the United States did not "exploit" Puerto Rico. The United States was a sort of "harmless imperialism" that had stumbled into Puerto Rico in 1898 and mismanaged it since then. Gone was his past consideration that the need for relief was testimony to the one-sided economic structure generated by the impact of U.S. production and capital on an unprotected Puerto Rican economy. It was necessary to change the system of political misrule while retaining the existing economic relation with the United States, which was now redefined as fundamentally beneficial.

Muñoz Marín's early explanations of his new course still included some criticism of U.S. trade policies and echoed some of his past fulminations against metropolitan corporate interests. As the case of Cuba demonstrated, he warned, an independent Puerto Rico would be vulnerable to predatory North American finance capital.[41] But if he denounced independence as hospitable to such capitalist interests, he did not do so to better challenge the latter's prerogatives within the North American polity or to further the quest for a planned reconstruction of the Puerto Rican economy under U.S. rule. On the contrary, he soon embraced U.S. capital investment as the main agent of Puerto Rico's future industrialization. Nor did he abandon independence to become a consistent critic of U.S. trade policies or of the actions of U.S. corporate capital around the world. Such a stand was hardly compatible with his emphasis on developing amicable relations with the U.S. foreign policy establishment and U.S. investors.

Domestic capitalists were of course satisfied with this shift, which they had supported all along. Muñoz Marín's only other option at the time was to break with the more timid sectors of the PPD coalition and pursue a state-centered/*independentista* orientation with the support of the pro-independence wing of the PPD and the labor movement. His trajectory since the mid-1920s made it very unlikely that he would choose that path.

Indeed, underneath the many twists and turns, there is an evident continuity to Muñoz Marín's trajectory. It can be described as an unshakeable attachment to the North American state as the only possible guarantor of Puerto Rico's progress. As he put it in 1929, Puerto Rico "is fundamentally dependent for the solution of its increasingly grave problems upon the American sense of noblesse oblige."[42] This reasoning initially supported a transition to independence in collaboration with the New Deal. In the 1940s, it became associated with something other than independence, a nonindependent path that would be the political shell of a projected market-propelled modernization. This is the dimension of the trajectory of Muñoz Marín and the PPD that most clearly distances them from Latin American populism, with which they are often uncritically associated.

Latin American populism includes the governments of Perón in Argentina, Cárdenas in Mexico, Vargas and Goulart in Brazil, Arbenz in Guatemala, and the Movimiento Nacional Revolucionario in Bolivia. Each of these at some point implied an increase in political and economic independence and a confrontation with at least some of the metropolitan powers. Washington had a role in the overthrow of the Arbenz and Goulart governments. Cárdenas's oil nationalizations and his agrarian reform generated hostility from both Britain and the United States, curbed by the need to cement alliances for the coming war. Perón and the Movimiento Nacional Revolucionario were harassed for their unwillingness to subordinate themselves to Allied policies during the war. In the case of Muñoz Marín, all his reform plans were structured in connection with U.S. government policies, from the time of the New Deal to wartime mobilization and, later on, the Cold War.

This inclination also clearly demarcated Muñoz Marín from the more prominent trait of Albizu Campos's and the Nationalists' discourse, discussed in chapter 5: their willingness to interpellate Puerto Ricans as a collective subject capable of remaking its political and material situation independent of and, if necessary, against the will of the North American state.

Some authors have argued that Muñoz Marín initially pursued an independent state-based capitalist development, which he abandoned in 1945–47.[43] Others, such as Emilo Pantojas-García, have pointed out that at no point did Muñoz Marín challenge United States' political control.[44] José Padín has argued that the project of a "developmental state" was undermined from the start by the sabotage and resistance of the domestic capitalist sectors. It was not, according to him, abandoned due to imperialist pressure.[45] We would favor a nuanced combination of these approaches. While Muñoz Marín may have hoped for political and economic independence at one point, which would have required breaking the resistance of some absentee or domestic capitalists, he always felt it could only be attained in close collaboration with the metropolitan state. As soon as he realized the former could not be pursued with U.S. state support, he redefined his objectives accordingly. Domestic capital had pushed him along this course all along. Thus, imperial constraints and domestic pressures pushed him in the same politico-economic direction.

But if by 1945–46 Muñoz Marín concluded that independence had to be abandoned, what was to be done regarding the status question? He recognized that statehood ensured access to the U.S. market, but it brought with it an added tax burden. Muñoz Marín also believed that the flourishing of a distinct Puerto Rican culture was incompatible with annexation.

Over the years, Muñoz Marín had argued—against the autonomist wing of the Partido Liberal—that anything but statehood or independence would keep Puerto Rico, as a territory and possession, under the plenary powers of Congress.[46] Here he now also readjusted his views. By 1946, he concluded that it was possible for Puerto Rico to cease being a colony without becoming independent or a state of the Union. It was only a question of devising some form of noncolonial self-government mutually acceptable to Congress and the Puerto Rican people.

With hindsight, one must conclude that Muñoz Marín succeeded in bringing about considerable changes by moving down the path he charted in 1946–

47. His new economic orientation led to the launching of Operation Bootstrap in 1947, under which Puerto Rico did undergo a rapid economic expansion in the context of the global postwar economic boom that resulted in significant improvements in living standards. Similarly, his political reorientation led to the creation in 1950–52 of the Estado Libre Asociado (Commonwealth of Puerto Rico), framed by a constitution ratified by the insular electorate.

But hindsight also enables us to point out that half a century after the launching of Operation Bootstrap, and in spite of mass out-migration, Puerto Rico still suffers from high unemployment rates, dependence on federal government subsidies, and lack of a self-sustaining economic dynamic. The key problems Muñoz Marín set out to solve still characterize Puerto Rico's economy. Many would also argue that politically, Puerto Rico remains a colony. Material conditions in the island are no longer desperate, and this is a major achievement, but the problems that shaped the debates of the 1940s are still unsolved sixty years later. Muñoz Marín's chosen strategy modernized the Puerto Rican polity and economy but did not alter its colonial nature, and an evaluation of his trajectory cannot afford to ignore either aspect of his legacy.

The Breakup of the PPD Bloc

By 1943, tensions were surfacing within the PPD. That year, *independentistas* from within and without the PPD joined to create the Congreso Pro Independencia (CPI), a non-party pro-independence coalition.[47] The First Congress, convoked under the slogan "Defend Democracy Struggling for Independence," met on August 15, 1943, at the Sixto Escobar Stadium. It was an impressive event featuring 1,800 delegates and 15,000 spectators. Most prominent among the PPD leaders participating was Géigel, who was elected vice president. Also present were Communists Sáez Corales, Lanauze Rolón, Andreu Iglesias, and Santos Rivera, left-nationalists such as Enamorado Cuesta, and unaffiliated *independentista* academics and professionals such as Rubén del Rosario, Clara Lugo, and Rafael Soltero Peralta, among others. Muñoz Marín did not attend but sent a cordial if noncommittal greeting.[48] Pressed by U.S. senator Millard E. Tydings to define his position, Muñoz Marín insisted he was for whichever noncolonial option was more economically advantageous, a position that failed to embrace independence while not precluding it.[49]

But the *independentista* wing was becoming impatient. Tensions exploded in the PPD nominations assembly for the 1944 elections, a stormy meeting of 1,200 delegates held in La Perla Theater in Ponce. The main point of contention was the selection of the candidate for resident commissioner. The *independentistas* favored Rafael Arjona. Muñoz Marín demanded that he be allowed to designate the candidate. It took hours for the gathering to come to a decision, as Muñoz Marín refused to put the point to a vote. In the end, an exhausted assembly yielded to Muñoz Marín's wishes, who chose conservative *colono* leader Jesús T. Piñero as PPD candidate.

In November 1944, the PPD obtained a spectacular victory. Its share of the vote exploded from 38 percent in 1940 to 65 percent. It was a massive show of confidence for its social reform measures. Muñoz Marín would no longer have to contend with a hostile commissioner in Washington or legislative obstructions in Puerto Rico. Nor could there be any question in Washington as to which insular party enjoyed wider support. Muñoz Marín could now move against his *independentista* and labor allies if they insisted on advancing their agendas. Thus, in the fifteen months from late 1944 to February 1946, the leading wing of the PPD turned in rapid succession against the labor movement, represented by the CGT, and against the independence movement, structured around the CPI.

As early as 1943, tensions emerged within the CGT between the PPD on the one hand and the sector led by Communist Sáez Corales and labor lawyer Colón Gordiany on the other. The pro-PPD sector, led by legislator Ramón Barreto Pérez, was centered in the unions of sugarcane workers, strongly influenced by PPD leader Ernesto Ramos Antonini. The struggle within the CGT was linked to the status question. Barreto Pérez and Ramos Antonini sought to keep the CGT from taking a definite stand on it, while Colón Gordiany and Sáez Corales favored a clear position in favor of independence.

This growing conflict within the CGT led to a split during its Third Congress in March 1945. The split produced two organizations: the CGT, allied to the PPD, and the CGT-Auténtica, led by Colón Gordiany and Sáez Corales. Government harassment of the latter was enhanced by the extension to Puerto Rico of the Taft-Hartley Act of 1947. Its restrictions on labor activism and anticommunist dispositions were used to demobilize and purge the union movement. By the early 1950s, the wartime union movement was no more. Radicals had been isolated. Others, like Alberto Sánchez, joined the PPD.

Undoubtedly the ease with which the PPD isolated the Communists had much to do with their policies during the war. Since 1941, the Communists had supported the PPD. By 1944, party leader Santos Rivera explained that the PPD represented "the interests of the Puerto Rican national bourgeoisie," which, he explained, "in this historical moment, coincide with the immediate interests

CGT leader and labor lawyer Francisco Colón Gordiany, who was active in the bus drivers' strike of 1937 and other struggles, at a meeting in the mid-1940s. (Proyecto digitalización fotos El Mundo–Biblioteca José M. Lázaro, Universidad de Puerto Rico–Río Piedras)

of the working and peasant class." But Santos Rivera warned that the PPD also included reactionary forces. Thus, it was necessary for the labor movement to retain its independence; otherwise, he added, if a break with the PPD were to occur, workers would be in danger of suffering a "major defeat." Yet the PC reiterated its support for the PPD. It went further and concluded it was better to dissolve itself into an "association" to hinder conservatives from red-baiting the PPD.[50] The American Communist Party, as part of its support of President Roosevelt, had done likewise a few months earlier.[51] When the PPD turned against it, an unprepared CGT suffered the "big defeat" that Santos Rivera had predicted and probably facilitated. Whatever its causes, the destruction of the CGT was a historic turning point in the history of the Puerto Rican working class. Instead of entering the postwar period with a strong, unified union movement, capable of playing a significant and independent political role, it was burdened with a fragmented and bureaucratic union structure.

Meanwhile, the clash between Muñoz Marín and the *independentistas* intensified. Muñoz Marín fired a first shot after the second pro-independence congress on December 10, 1944. The congress, held at the Quintana racetrack in Hato Rey, was again a grand occasion with 1,600 delegates and ample participation by low-, mid-, and high-level PPD leaders. But now Muñoz Marín issued a warning. Some leaders of the CPI wished to turn it into a party within the PPD. Ironically, he was formulating against the CPI the same accusation that Antonio R. Barceló had leveled against him in 1936, when he had organized Acción Social Independentista to promote independence against Barceló's vacillations.

Tensions grew after Senator Tydings introduced a new bill (S. 227) on January 10, 1945, allowing for the celebration of a plebiscite on independence. The measure drew considerable support from within the PPD (eleven of its seventeen senators, twenty-two of its thirty-seven representatives, forty-two of its seventy-three mayors).[52] Faced with an *independentista* offensive, Muñoz Marín reiterated that the PPD had no mandate on the issue. Plus, Puerto Rico had other options besides independence, which should be part of a plebiscite.[53] He thus favored a three-way contest between independence, statehood, and some form of "dominion government." A bill along these lines was introduced by Commissioner Piñero in the House and by Tydings in the Senate on May 15, 1945 (H.R. 3237 and S. 1002).

The polemic regarding the counterposed bills intensified. By February 1946, Muñoz Marín announced that the CPI had become a party within the PPD. Following his lead, a majority of the top body of the PPD declared membership in the party incompatible with membership in the CPI. Muñoz Marín still insisted it was legitimate to defend independence within the PPD; only membership in the CPI was unacceptable.[54]

Meanwhile, while trying to defuse the *independentista* threat, Muñoz Marín did not abandon his efforts to move the U.S. Congress in the direction of the reforms he now advocated. If the Tydings independence bill had not progressed, neither had his own Tydings-Piñero bill. New initiatives had to be taken if Congress was to be made to take action. Thus, in February 1946, a few days after expelling the CPI, the PPD-controlled legislature adopted a bill providing for a three-way plebiscite on the status question. Governor Tugwell vetoed the measure. He could not, he explained, allow the celebration of a plebiscite that included options Congress may find unacceptable. The legislature, seeking to dramatize the need for reform, readopted the measure over the governor's veto. It then went to President Truman, who vetoed it on May 16, 1946.

It was then that Muñoz Marín announced that he was no longer an *independentista* and embraced the idea of some form of noncolonial association as a substitute for independence.[55] Muñoz Marín's new orientation was debated in a marathon meeting of the PPD's leading bodies in Barranquitas on the night and dawn of July 3–4. Géigel and other *independentistas* objected to Muñoz Marín's position. The PPD, argued Géigel, should not surrender before the battle. Why was Muñoz Marín certain that it was impossible to negotiate adequate terms for independence if he had not even tried? Muñoz Marín's new formula, he added, was a rehash of the "Estado Libre Asociado" plank the Partido Unión had adopted in 1922, which Muñoz Marín had always rejected. It was during this debate that Antonio Fernós emerged as the ablest defender of the "new road." After debating for ten hours, the conclave adopted Muñoz Marín's new orientation by a vote of 50 to 9.[56]

A new set of *independentistas* now abandoned the PPD. By October 1946, they joined those who had left earlier and others who had never been in the PPD to organize a new Partido Independentista Puertorriqueño (PIP). But Muñoz Marín, insisting that his goal was still a noncolonial status that in the long run did not preclude other options, was still able to retain the loyalty of some *independentistas*, such as Géigel, who had been the most eloquent opponent of his new course in the Barranquitas meeting.

Fortunately for Muñoz Marín, reforms were on the way. They came both as a response to pressures from the island and as result of wider considerations. Indeed, some officials within the Truman administration had argued against vetoing the PPD-sponsored plebiscite bill. Denying Puerto Rico the right to vote on its status, they argued, would help anti-American states and movements denounce the United States as a colonial power. Policy toward Puerto Rico had to be fit into a global equation. As Gabriel Kolko and other scholars have explored, during the war and its aftermath, the U.S. government pursued a policy that favored the opening of the British, French, Dutch, and other competing empires to U.S. goods and investments. This would be followed by a slow, gradual transition of most colonies to independence, which would leave the institutional guarantees to private investors untouched. To manage such a shift, the United States needed to build the legitimacy of moderate anticolonial forces around the world, a task that required establishing its own anticolonial credentials. Thus, as the Philippines moved on to independence, Puerto Rico's situation and the Jim Crow South stood out as potential sources of embarrassment. The more radical anticolonial/anti-imperialist currents and governments, as well as Communist parties and Soviet diplomats, could be expected to present Puerto Rico as proof of Washington's less-than-consistent commitment to self-determination. Last but not least, Puerto Rican *independentistas* could be counted upon to use any available international forum to publicize their cause. Thus, there was some pressure on U.S. policy makers to demonstrate that the island was moving toward some form of self-government.

Muñoz Marín was aware of this dynamic. Not unlike his father, who after 1895 leaned on the Cuban insurgency to pressure Spain for autonomy, he now sought to take advantage of the need of the United States to address the worldwide rise of anticolonial and anti-imperialist sentiment. In 1945, for example, in a CBS broadcast for a North American audience, he warned that the Soviet Union had staked its claim as a leader of the colonial world. The United States had to act decisively if it did not wish to lose ground to its wartime ally. Its behavior in Puerto Rico, he argued, would be a key element in either enhancing or weakening its reputation among "oppressed humanity."[57]

By 1946, the demand for reform led President Truman to appoint Jesús T. Piñero governor of Puerto Rico. He thus became the first Puerto Rican ever to hold the highest post in the insular government. The following year, Congress enacted legislation making the governorship an elective post.[58] Against his critics, Muñoz Marín could point to real if limited steps toward self-government. In the process, he had again leaned on the pressure of more radical sectors to extract the desired reforms. He wrote to Undersecretary of the Interior Oscar Chapman in June 1947: "With an Independence Party being registered, with the

A march past the front gates of the University of Puerto Rico during the 1948 student strike, sparked by the barring of Nationalist leader Pedro Albizu Campos from the Río Piedras campus. (Proyecto digitalización fotos El Mundo–Biblioteca José M. Lázaro, Universidad de Puerto Rico–Río Piedras)

extreme Nationalist Party expecting the return of Mr. Albizu-Campos, . . . it will become increasingly difficult to maintain an attitude of good sense in Puerto Rico. . . . Only prompt action on the elective governor bill can free us of very bad potentialities."[59] Muñoz Marín's apologists often refer to the achievements of his pragmatic approach, contrasting them to the impractical ideals of *independentistas* and radicals and the less than brilliant results of anticolonial struggles around the world. It is thus sobering to remember that Muñoz Marín's bargaining power was greatly enhanced by the pressure exerted on U.S. policy makers by the rise of anticolonialism internationally and by the militant *independentista* and Nationalist minority in Puerto Rico.

Meanwhile, conflicts did emerge when Albizu Campos returned to Puerto Rico at the end of 1947. The raising of the Puerto Rican flag at the university on the day of his arrival led to the expulsion of several students, including future *independentista* leaders Juan Mari Brás, Jorge Luis Landing, and José Gil de la Madrid. A strike ensued after permission was denied for a student-sponsored talk by Albizu Campos.[60] In the aftermath of this conflict, the PPD-controlled

PIP leader Gilberto Concepción de Gracia (right) is greeted in October 1949 by ALP congressman Vito Marcantonio. Marcantonio was a longtime supporter of Puerto Rico's independence. In the context of the Cold War and anticommunist persecution, Concepción de Gracia traveled to New York City to support Marcantonio in the race for mayor.
(AP photo)

legislature enacted Law 53 of June 10, 1948, often called the Gag Law, modeled on the Federal Smith Act, which made it illegal to advocate the violent over-throw of the government of the United States. The law was amply used after the Nationalist insurrection of 1950.

The PIP carried out its constituent assembly on July 25, 1948. It was an impressive gathering with 5,216 delegates in attendance and 15,000 spectators. Muñoz Marín, running for governor, warned that every vote for the PIP, which he demagogically described as "fascist," endangered Puerto Rico's future, since it would increase the doubts of U.S. investors about coming to the island.[61]

Muñoz Marín's right turn was not limited to the island. In New York, El Barrio remained a center of support for ALP congressman Marcantonio. In 1948, Henry Wallace, running for president on a third party ticket against the rightward shift of U.S. politics, obtained 2.4 percent of the vote nationwide but won El Barrio with 42 percent. In 1949, Marcantonio ran for mayor in an attempt to save the ALP's ballot status. He had defended the PPD from the attacks of the Right but had denounced it when it turned against the CGT and expelled its *independentista* wing. Muñoz Marín in turn joined the anticommunist attacks on Marcantonio. In 1949, he sent San Juan mayor Felisa Rincón to New York to campaign against him. Gilberto Concepción, head of the PIP, also traveled north, in his case to support Marcantonio.[62] Marcantonio won in El Barrio by a big margin. When Marcantonio, the only congressman to oppose the Korean War, lost his seat in 1950, he still won El Barrio, receiving 60 percent of its votes. His fellow ALP candidate for the Senate, black intellectual W. E. B. Du Bois, got 6.5 percent of the vote citywide and around 45 percent of the votes in El Barrio.[63] But El Barrio was about to be remade by the onset of mass migration, the other side of the island's economic upheaval after 1945. In the context of economic change and Cold War repression, previous forms of labor, community, and political activism, both on the island and in New York, fractured. New forms of mobilization would emerge, both on the island and in its diaspora, in the 1960s.

In November 1948, Muñoz Marín became Puerto Rico's first elected governor as the PPD sailed to another overwhelming victory, garnering 61.2 percent of the vote. During the next four years, Muñoz Marín concentrated on the elaboration of a new set of status reforms, which led to the creation of the Commonwealth of Puerto Rico in 1950–52. We explore the conflicts that shaped its emergence in the following chapter.

BIRTH OF THE ESTADO LIBRE ASOCIADO

Since 1945, Luis Muñoz Marín had argued that the status issue should be resolved in a special election or plebiscite. But during the electoral campaign of 1948, in which he was to be elected governor for the first of four terms, he put this idea aside. He now asked voters to endorse a new status through their vote for the Partido Popular Democrático in the regular elections. Specifically, Muñoz Marín proposed to ask the U.S. Congress to allow Puerto Rico to adopt its own constitution.[1] The result of this process was the creation of the Estado Libre Asociado (ELA), or, as the term is officially translated, the Commonwealth of Puerto Rico. The nature of the ELA has been in debate since its inception. This chapter covers its birth as well as the reactions that its creation elicited from its opponents, which ranged from forceful written critiques to the Nationalist insurrection of October 1950 and the heated debates at the United Nations in 1953. To conclude, we summarize some recent developments regarding the constitutional definition of the arrangement created in 1950–52.

The creation of the ELA was shaped by the actions of several actors and their different agendas. Muñoz Marín and Antonio Fernós sought to finesse the U.S. Congress into relinquishing its plenary power over Puerto Rico while avoiding any confrontation with any sector of the Washington establishment. They thus sought to minimize the reach of the proposed reforms in the hope of making them more palatable to the Department of the Interior functionaries and congressmen opposed to any weakening of U.S. claims over Puerto Rico. Meanwhile, they privately hoped that the courts would eventually certify that as a result of the new arrangement, Puerto Rico was no longer a territory of the United States.[2] The U.S. State Department, on the other hand, looked favorably upon legislation that would allow the United States to argue Puerto Rico was no longer a colony while not reducing its ultimate rights over the island. While Washington wished to get the new arrangement certified by the United Nations as noncolonial, Muñoz Marín hoped to extract a noncolonial status from Congress without it realizing it. Both positions stood to benefit from a vague definition of Puerto Rico's territorial or nonterritorial status in the proposed legislation. In the end, as some of Muñoz Marín's close collaborators would eventually admit, the State Department was far more successful than the PPD leaders in furthering its agenda. While the former was, at least until the late 1960s, able to present the ELA internationally as a noncolonial status, the PPD's unwillingness to demand a clear definition of the new relation ensured its ambiguous, limited, and static nature.

The elaboration of the new arrangement was largely the work of Fernós, the PPD's resident commissioner since 1946. He had replaced Jesús T. Piñero, who had in turn been appointed governor. Fernós and Senator Joseph O'Mahoney (D-Wyo.) introduced the corresponding bills in March 1950. They eventually became Public Law 600 signed by President Truman on July 3, 1950.[3] The process instituted by P.L. 600 can be briefly summarized. Puerto Rico residents would vote to accept or reject the terms of P.L. 600. If they voted in favor, they would elect a constitutional assembly, which would draft a constitution for Puerto Rico. This constitution would be submitted to Puerto Rico's voters for ratification. If ratified, it would be sent to the president for transmittal to Congress, which would certify that it complied with several dispositions included in P.L. 600. The most important specification established that the constitution was to deal only with the structure of the insular government, not with any aspect of the relation with the United States. Once certified by Congress, the constitution would come into effect, and the insular government would be reorganized under its dispositions.

Regarding the continuity of U.S. federal jurisdiction in Puerto Rico under P.L. 600, there was—and there is—little dispute. The text of P.L. 600 is quite explicit on this. All the existing prerogatives of the U.S. federal government in Puerto Rico remained unchanged. Federal legislation, not explicitly made inapplicable by Congress, would apply in the island, and federal courts would continue to operate in Puerto Rico. In fact, all the features pertaining to the relation between Puerto Rico and the United States in the Jones Act of 1917 (renamed the Federal Relations Act) were demarcated by Congress as off-limits for the constituent assembly to be convoked under P.L. 600. Fixed unilaterally by Congress in 1917—in fact, earlier, since they were mostly carryovers from the Foraker Act of 1900—those areas were to remain beyond the reach of the Puerto Rican voters or their elected representatives. They included citizenship, immigration, coastwise shipping, commercial treaties and foreign relations, and all matters related to military activity, currency, and tariff policy. Furthermore, in the case of conflict, federal acts would prevail over the insular constitution.

Yet in spite of this, Muñoz Marín and the PPD still claimed that P.L. 600 implied a profound change in the nature of the relation with the United States. This claim hinged on the phrase included in P.L. 600 that indicated that the law was to be adopted "in the nature of a compact" and in recognition of "the principle of government by consent." These phrases were interpreted by the PPD as meaning that the terms of the relation with the United States, although still unchanged as far as their concrete content was concerned, had been redefined as no longer being the result of the exercise by Congress of the plenary powers that the Constitution grants it over U.S. territories but as the conditions agreed upon and stipulated through a pact between Congress and Puerto Rico.

To better understand the doctrine of the "compact," it is useful to remember that before 1946, Muñoz Marín, Fernós, and other PPD leaders had argued that no form of noncolonial autonomy was possible under the U.S. political system.[4] The U.S. Constitution, Fernós had argued, provides only for the existence of states and territories. Congress has complete authority over the latter under the "territorial clause" of the Constitution (Article IV, Section 3). As long as Puerto Rico remained a territory, it would be under the complete authority of Congress. It could escape that authority only by becoming something other than a U.S. territory, that is to say, either a state or an independent republic. But Fernós now argued that P.L. 600 implied the invention of a third way out of the territorial status. When the United States admits a new state, he explained, two things happen simultaneously that are nevertheless distinct: Congress approves legislation enabling a territory to constitute itself as a state, and the new state is admitted into the Union. In the case of Puerto Rico, Congress had enabled it to constitute itself as a state by drafting its own constitution, but then, instead of proposing to admit it into the Union, it had offered to enter into a "compact" with it. Puerto Rico had ceased to be a territory of the United States, but it had not become a state or a republic. Instead, in the process of becoming a self-governing entity, it had entered into the aforementioned "compact." While federal laws continued to apply to the island, this was no longer by virtue of the "territorial clause" of the Constitution but due to the consent of Puerto Rico to the terms enunciated in P.L. 600.[5] Since a "compact" now existed and the relation had been placed on a new footing, Congress could no longer alter the structure of the insular government unilaterally.

The notion that P.L. 600 kept intact the concrete *terms* of the existing relation with the United States while changing the *nature* of the relation allowed Muñoz Marín to alternately emphasize, as he deemed it convenient, one or the other aspect of the measure. When reassuring congressmen, he underlined that the terms of the relation remained unchanged; when responding to those who in Puerto Rico argued the measure changed nothing, he insisted on the re-definition of the existing relation as a "compact." As indicated, he and Fernós hoped that U.S. courts would eventually interpret the new status along the lines closer to the second description.

Nationalist Insurrection

It was in this context that the Partido Nacionalista launched an armed revolt. The Nationalists denounced P.L. 600 as a sham: a constituent assembly that could not address the issue of the relation with the United States was no constituent assembly; it was a means of reforming the colonial government. Puerto Rico remained an unincorporated territory. Congress was simply allow-ing Puerto Rico to rewrite part of the Jones Act.

Since the late 1940s, the Nationalists, under the intellectual leadership of Pedro Albizu Campos and the practical coordination of Tomás López de Victoria, had begun preparations for an armed insurrection. The plan, ac-cording to participant Elio Torresola, consisted of attacking police stations and U.S. government installations in diverse towns. After the initial incur-sions, the detachments would withdraw to a town in the interior (probably Utuado), where they would entrench themselves and attempt to hold out for as long as possible. The objective was to cause a political crisis in Puerto Rico and to embarrass Washington internationally in the hope of creating a con-text in which the United Nations and foreign governments would be less likely to accept the process initiated by P.L. 600 as a legitimate means of decolonization.[6]

But this was a project of a group of patriots with little support beyond their own party. As often happens with such endeavors, a few accidents were able to unmake ongoing preparations before they were completed. Between October 27 and 30, a series of searches and an initial shoot-out between Nationalists and the police led the former to conclude that mass arrests were imminent. It was necessary to act immediately, or arms and militants would be lost without a fight. Nationalist commandos attacked police stations in Arecibo, Jayuya, Utuado, and the governor's mansion in San Juan. Groups fought gun battles in several spots in San Juan as well as in the town of Naranjito. Two Nationalists, Torresola and Oscar Collazo, attempted to shoot their way into the Blair House in Washington, D.C., where President Truman was residing while the White

Nationalist leaders Ramón Medina Ramírez (left) and José Rivera Sotomayor under arrest after the Nationalist insurrection of 1950. (Proyecto digitalización fotos El Mundo–Biblioteca José M. Lázaro, Universidad de Puerto Rico–Río Piedras)

House underwent reparations. It was in Jayuya that the Nationalists accomplished the most, burning the police station and federal post office and holding out in the surrounding fields until November 2. By then, except in Naranjito, fighting had all but stopped. Twenty-five persons died in the course of these actions, more than in the Spanish-American War in Puerto Rico. In terms of social composition, of the 140 combatants whom historian María Seijo Bruno studied, 69 percent were wageworkers of one sort or another.[7]

During and immediately after the rebellion, more than 1,000 Nationalists as well as *independentistas* and Communists not connected with the insurrection were arrested. The so-called Gag Law, enacted in 1948, proved useful for jailing or intimidating many not connected to the insurrection. The Partido Independentista Puertorriqueño both praised the valor and the capacity for self-sacrifice of the Nationalists and affirmed its commitment to a peaceful struggle for independence. The fact is that material improvements under the PPD were more tangible than the Nationalists' patriotic call, above all in a context in which the desperate economic situation that had framed the Nationalist upsurge in the 1930s was giving way to the postwar economic expansion.

The crackdown on dissident voices even reached the functionary formally in charge of repressing the rebellion. Attorney General Vicente Géigel had been one of the founders of the PPD. He had led the PPD on the Senate floor between 1940 and 1948 and wrote much of its social legislation. He had been attorney general since 1949. While not hiding his *independentista* views, he had remained loyal to Muñoz Marín after 1946. In the elections of 1948, for example, combining his support for independence with the PPD's new orientation, he had argued that economic growth through U.S. investments would create the material basis for independence. In the meantime, U.S. corporations would no longer be able to exploit Puerto Rico, given the social and labor legislation enacted by the PPD.[8]

Nevertheless, Muñoz Marín, afraid that Géigel's *independentista* sympathies could make him unreliable, fired him in February 1951.[9] Géigel now entered the debate on the status question with redoubled energy. In a series of polemical texts published in May and June 1951 and later collected in *La farsa del Estado Libre Asociado*, he argued that P.L. 600 left federal control of Puerto Rican life untouched. Far from altering the nature of the existing relation, P.L. 600 would help perpetuate it by dignifying it with the appearance of a contract between equals. Géigel was indignant, not because Muñoz Marín had abandoned independence, a step taken in 1946 and which Géigel had been willing to live with, but rather because Muñoz Marín had embraced a reformed colonial model. Muñoz Marín had betrayed not independence but any meaningful—that is to say, noncolonial—concept of autonomy.

The plebiscite on the proposed reform took place on June 4, 1951. The only choice offered was acceptance or rejection of the terms included in P.L. 600. The first option received an overwhelming majority (76.5 percent) of the votes cast, but around 35 percent of the registered electors failed to vote. The PIP boycotted the plebiscite, while the statehood party gave no official indications as to how to vote. The delegates to the constitutional assembly were elected on August 27, 1951, and the constitution they elaborated was ratified with the support of 80 percent of those voting. The PIP again boycotted the ratification plebiscite. This time, around 40 percent of the electors failed to vote. Flawed as the process was, given the limited options—and that fact should not be glossed over—there is no question that the new arrangement enjoyed considerable support at the time.

But the enactment of the new status was not yet complete. The constitution still had to be sent to Congress for final revision. Congress, significantly, did not limit itself to considering whether the constitution complied with the terms formulated in P.L. 600, which, according to the defenders of the theory of the "compact," should have been its only determination. Instead, it passed judgment on dispositions related to the areas that P.L. 600 had purportedly given the Puerto Rican people the right to organize through a constitution of their own making. Several congressmen rejected as "socialistic" Section 20 of the new constitution, which established employment and an adequate standard of living as rights to be guaranteed in step with future economic progress. The repeated explanations by PPD leaders that Section 20 was not "socialistic" (it was inspired by the Universal Declaration of Human Rights adopted by the United Nations) were to no avail. Thus, the resolution approved by Congress and signed by President Truman on July 3, 1952, provided the constitution would not go into effect until Section 20 was removed and until a disposition was added, stating that no future amendments to the constitution could alter the relation with the United States as defined by P.L. 600, the Federal Relations Act, the U.S. Constitution, and the resolution imposing the new conditions.[10]

The amendments were soon adopted by a reconvened constitutional convention. The ELA was proclaimed on July 25, 1952. The date chosen was no coincidence: July 25 was the date of the first landing of U.S. troops in 1898. The image of Muñoz Marín raising the Puerto Rican flag was expected to complement that of the landing in Guánica: U.S. rule had led to Puerto Rican self-government.

The mishaps during the ratification process in Congress lent themselves to opposite interpretations. For Fernós, the fact that Congress had not unilaterally amended the proposed constitution but had allowed Puerto Rico to approve the amendments was further demonstration that the process had transformed the relation with the United States from a unilateral exercise of congressional power to a bilateral "compact." Critics of P.L. 600 could riposte that under the dispositions approved by Congress, Puerto Rico had no way of rejecting the amendments without also relinquishing the opportunity of having its own constitution. The constitution would come into effect only if and when Puerto Rico yielded to the new conditions enunciated by Congress. Fernós's satisfaction that the amendments were approved by the constitutional assembly was but an extreme example of his delusion that having Puerto Rico consent to congressional impositions somehow turned the latter into something other than impositions.

The same objection, of course, could be applied to P.L. 600 as a whole. Fernós had argued that Congress had allowed Puerto Rico to organize itself as a self-governing entity and had offered a "compact" to it, which Puerto Rico had accepted. The problem was that, had Puerto Rico rejected the proposed "compact" by not ratifying P.L. 600, it would have by the same token declined the opportunity to write its own constitution. The possibility of Puerto Rico writing its own constitution, of its emergence as an allegedly self-governing entity, had been conditioned by Congress on previous consent to the existing forms of federal jurisdiction. The asymmetrical and indeed colonial nature of the process that had brought forth the alleged "compact" is hard to deny.

In fact, the reality of the "compact" was more ambiguous than we have allowed for so far. Muñoz Marín and Fernós, in their desire to reassure Congress, had at times argued that not only the terms but also the nature of the relation with the United States would remain unchanged as a result of the proposed legislation. Congress, they argued in such occasions, would retain its plenary powers over Puerto Rico but would agree not to use them. In that case, the "compact" became more of a moral commitment on the part of Congress than a legal alteration of Puerto Rico's status. The "bill's importance," Muñoz Marín argued at one point, "is moral rather than practical."[11] Questioned about the possibility of Puerto Rico using the power to amend its constitution to create an entirely new document, Muñoz Marín answered: "You know, of course, that if the people of Puerto Rico should go crazy, Congress can always get around and legislate again."[12] But if Congress could "always get around and legislate again," that meant Puerto Rico was still under its plenary powers.

Congress, on its part, was guilty of its own ambiguities. P.L. 600 and the resolution ratifying the constitution neither asserted nor denied that Puerto Rico would remain an unincorporated territory. Some congressmen committed to the retention of Congress's plenary powers over Puerto Rico sought to press the issue, to no avail. Thus, Congressman George Meader (R-Mich.) introduced an amendment during the consideration of the constitution that clearly stated that Congress retained all plenary powers over Puerto Rico. The amendment was rejected. This could be taken as an argument in favor of the "compact" theory or the nonterritorial nature of the new status. Unfortunately for this view, as a thorough study of the debate indicated, the amendment was rejected as untimely, unnecessary, or unclear, but "no speaker urged rejection . . . on the ground that Congress was granting an irrevocable delegation of power to Puerto Rico."[13] The result of a parallel debate on the other side of Capitol Hill around an amendment introduced by Senator Olin D. Johnston (D-S.C.) had an equally ambiguous outcome: while Congress declined to explicitly reassert its plenary powers over Puerto Rico, neither did it explicitly nor even implicitly renounce them. On balance, an early and very thorough study of these debates by David Helfeld concluded that "in Constitutional theory, Congress continues to possess plenary authority over Puerto Rico which, in status if not in title, remains a territory." Indeed, privately, Undersecretary of the Interior Oscar Chapman had assured Congressman O'Mahoney in May 1950 that the new legislation did not "preclude a future determination by the Congress of Puerto Rico's ultimate political status."[14]

The international reputation of the United States in a world moving toward decolonization had been a concern of U.S. officials during adoption of P.L. 600. The State Department had argued that "in view of the importance of colonialism and imperialism in anti-American propaganda," the new legislation would "have great value as a symbol of the basic freedom enjoyed by Puerto Rico, within the framework of the United States of America." The House Committee report concurred: "The passage of this bill . . . would stand as . . . evidence . . . that the United States practices as well as preaches the doctrines of democracy and self-determination."[15] According to some historians, it was this desire to shield the United States from anticolonial denunciations that stood behind the rejection of the amendments proposed by Meader and Johnston. Too bold an assertion of continued congressional authority would validate the argument that the new constitution had, at best, produced a reformed colonial regime. The more prescient U.S. policy makers preferred formulas that allowed them to pass a fundamentally unchanged colonial relation as a major transformation.

Muñoz Marín was aware of this. Indeed, he tried to use the fact that an admission of colonial control would bring embarrassment to the United States to coax his North American interlocutors into yielding to his interpretation of the "compact." Thus, whenever a senator or representative suggested that Puerto Rico remained a possession of the United States, Muñoz Marín would respond that he felt no group of U.S. citizens could be a possession of other U.S. citizens.[16] He thus placed his interlocutor in the position of either accepting the fact that the United States was still a colonial power or yielding to the notion that Puerto Rico was no longer a possession. But again, to his critics it would seem that Muñoz Marín was only reminding rather provincial congressmen of the need to use more acceptable language to refer to what was in fact a less than acceptable colonial situation. The debate at the United Nations in 1953 was by far the most important episode in which the need to present the new arrangement as noncolonial led U.S. officials to embrace the PPD notion of the "compact."

The Debate at the United Nations in 1953

Since 1946, the United States and other colonial powers had sent reports to the secretary general of the United Nations on the situation in the nonindependent territories. In 1953, the U.S. government informed the U.N. that Puerto Rico was no longer a non-self-governing territory. It would thus cease rendering the corresponding reports. This generated a complex debate at the U.N. in which the evaluation of the Puerto Rican situation was mixed with the debate on whether it was the U.N. or the colonial powers that could determine when the reports ceased to be necessary and which body within the U.N. should attend to such matters. During this debate, Resident Commissioner Fernós was made part of the U.S. delegation at the U.N. to help articulate the defense of the ELA.

Muñoz Marín, Fernós, and their collaborators approached the debate at the U.N. as the first opportunity to push their vision of the ELA as a nonterritorial status on the U.S. ruling circles. Thus, Muñoz Marín's draft of the letter to President Truman asking for a cessation of the reports to the U.N. asserted both that Puerto Rico had "ceased to be a territory of the United States" and that insular "laws cannot be repealed or modified by external authority." But Department of the Interior functionaries insisted from the start, in negotiations that were not made public at the time, that Puerto Rico remained a territory under the plenary powers of Congress and that at the most, U.S.

delegates at the U.N. should state that Puerto Rico's judicial status was to be determined by the courts.[17] Similarly, State Department attorneys privately argued that through P.L. 600, Congress had not divested itself of the powers enunciated in the "territorial clause." But if officials of the Department of the Interior argued privately that Puerto Rico was still a territory of the United States, at least some also indicated that it was better to downplay the fact at the United Nations. In January 1953, Undersecretary of the Interior Chapman advised Secretary of State Dean Acheson that "it would be preferable to emphasize the uniqueness of the Commonwealth's status rather than to continue to apply to it the label of 'territory.' "[18] It was a way of diverting discussion away from Puerto Rico's continuing status as a U.S. territory. Nevertheless, the debate at the U.N. eventually forced the U.S. delegation to come over to the argument that there now existed a "compact" between Puerto Rico and the United States. But this proved to be a hollow victory for the PPD. Policy makers in the United States soon forgot the declarations they had felt compelled to make at the U.N.

The debate at the United Nations raised interesting issues regarding Puerto Rico and colonialism in general that historians have largely ignored. Two general positions emerged at the U.N. that could be labeled the subjective and objective perspectives on colonialism. The U.S. delegation articulated the subjective approach. According to it, no restrictions of Puerto Rico's sovereignty could be described as colonial if Puerto Rico had consented to them. Once it had been determined that the Puerto Rican people had consented to the existing structure, no further proof was needed to demonstrate that self-determination had been attained. Thus, against the argument that Congress still controlled many areas of Puerto Rican life, Fernós invariably answered that such control was now part of a "compact" that Puerto Ricans had freely endorsed.

Against this, the delegates from several governments formulated what may be called an objective approach. According to them, the basic criteria to be considered was not—or was not only—the expression of consent but rather whether the new arrangement made it possible for the population concerned to govern itself. If under the new arrangement key areas of Puerto Rican life were still in the hands of Congress, then it followed that Puerto Rico was still a colony. From this perspective, it was possible to recognize that the ELA represented progress over the previous situation while still arguing that Puerto Rico was not yet able to govern itself. New steps toward self-determination were needed, and the U.S. government should continue to render the corresponding reports. Such was the position articulated by Lakshami N. Menon, delegate from the largest former colony, India. Similar views were expressed by the delegates of Socialist but not pro-Soviet Yugoslavia and of the government of Guatemala, then headed by the leftist Jacobo Arbenz. If reports were appropriate in the past, argued the Yugoslavian delegate, then they continued to be justified, since the Federal Relations Act explicitly kept Puerto Rico's relation with the United States unchanged. Variations of the same analysis were formulated by the delegates of the governments of Mexico and of the former Dutch colony of Indonesia.

Faced with such criticism, the U.S. delegation now embraced the PPD's preferred definition of the ELA as a "compact" through which Congress had relinquished its plenary powers. Delegate Frances P. Bolton thus explained that "there exists a bilateral compact of association between the people of Puerto Rico and the United States which has been accepted by both and which in accordance with judicial decisions may not be amended without common consent."[19] Fellow U.S. delegate Henry Cabot Lodge Jr. felt compelled to obtain from President Eisenhower the following statement, which he read into the record: "I am authorized to say on behalf of the President that if at any time the Legislative Assembly of Puerto Rico adopts a resolution in favor of more complete or even absolute independence, he will immediately thereafter recommend to Congress that such independence be granted."[20] These assurances, plus support from allied governments, allowed the United States to obtain its objective. On November 27, 1953, the U.N. General Assembly, through Resolution 748 (VIII), voted 26–16 in favor of relieving the United States from having to report on Puerto Rico's progress toward self-government.

The Unending Debate: The ELA since 1952

The debate on the nature of the ELA continues to this day. Its defenders argue that through it, Puerto Rico ceased to be an unincorporated territory, although most of those who hold this position also argue that there are many areas in which a wider autonomy would be desirable. For most statehooders and *independentistas*, the ELA is a thinly disguised form of territorial and/or colonial government. Puerto Rico remains an unincorporated territory to which Congress has delegated more government functions than in the case of past territories (election of the insular governor, its own constitution).

Over the years, U.S. courts have made contradictory pronouncements regarding the nature of the ELA. In 1956, in *Figueroa v. People of Puerto Rico*, the U.S. Court of Appeals for the First Circuit (in Boston) concluded that the

ELA constitution was not "just another Organic Act of the Congress," as the Foraker and Jones acts had been. To argue otherwise, warned Chief Justice Calvert Magruder, was to charge Congress with fraud: "We find no reason to impute to the Congress the perpetration of such a monumental hoax."[21] The First Circuit reiterated the conclusion that the ELA constitution is not a federal statute (and thus not unilaterally revocable by Congress) in 1984 in *Hernández Agosto v. Romero Barceló* and in 1985 in *United States v. Quiñones*. Yet in 1980, in *Harris v. Rosario*, the U.S. Supreme Court determined that Congress could treat Puerto Rico differently than the states regarding certain welfare programs by virtue of its powers under the territorial clause, a decision that implied that Puerto Rico was still a territory of the United States. In 1987, in *U.S. v. López Andino*, the First Circuit again found that the ELA "is a sovereign separate of the United States," and its laws emanate from a source other than federal laws.[22] But in 1993, the U.S. Court of Appeals for the Eleventh Circuit (in Miami) concluded in *United States v. Sánchez* that "Puerto Rico is still constitutionally a territory" and added that "Congress may unilaterally repeal the Puerto Rican constitution or the Puerto Rican Federal Relations Act and replace them with any rules or regulations of its choice."[23]

What this amounts to is the fact that U.S. policy makers retain a wide range of options regarding Puerto Rico. If they wish to maintain the status quo, they can leave the present ambiguity untouched. If they opt to perpetuate or strengthen the ELA, past court decisions that endorse its unique status can be turned into the ruling precedents. Conversely, if they were to favor replacing the ELA with another arrangement (statehood, independence, associated republic), decisions asserting Puerto Rico's status as a territory and Congress's plenary powers over it can become the accepted interpretation.

The latest installment in this ongoing debate has been the *Report by the President's Task Force on Puerto Rico's Status* issued in December 2005.[24] Without bothering to examine the complex tangle of court decisions constructed around the ELA in the past, the report firmly sides with the opinion that Puerto Rico is a territory of the United States and is thus under the plenary powers of Congress, which may at any time alter its government. If this were to become the accepted view in Congress, the White House, and the courts, Washington would be removing the floor on which the PPD has stood since 1950. It must be added that if such were the case, the Nationalist, PIP, and Communist *independentistas* who in 1950–52 argued that under the ELA Puerto Rico remained a territory under the plenary powers of Congress would stand vindicated, while the assertions to the contrary made at the U.N. by U.S. delegates take on the contours of the "monumental hoax" that Justice Magruder referred to in 1956.

But as the position of several participants in the debates at the U.N. in 1953 suggests, perhaps too much time is spent discussing whether the "compact" exists or not or whether Puerto Rico freely consented to it. After all, one could grant both claims while still arguing that Puerto Rico remains a non-self-governing territory, that is, a colony.

Some supporters of the ELA reached this conclusion very early. In 1953, Pedro Muñoz Amato diagnosed that "the reality of the 'free associated' state is incomplete." Muñoz Amato criticized PPD leaders for curbing their demand of self-government in order not to embarrass the United States internationally.[25] In 1958, Carl Friedrich of Harvard, an ELA supporter and advisor to the 1951 constitutional convention, argued that "self-government means government not only by consent, but by participation in the process of legislation." Seen from that angle, he concluded that Puerto Rico enjoyed a "measure of local home-rule"[26] but was not self-governing. He listed some of the reforms necessary to reach self-government. They included a clarification of the "compact" as "incontestably inalterable" without the consent of Puerto Rico, the right of Puerto Rico's legislature to declare federal legislation inapplicable to the island, the transfer of the administration of federal programs to insular agencies, and participation of Puerto Rico in diverse international bodies. Regardless of whether these changes were enough for the attainment of self-government, the fact is that fifty years after the creation of the ELA, not one of them has been implemented.

All efforts to alter the terms of the alleged "compact" have failed. In 1959, Resident Commissioner Fernós and Senator James Murray (D-Mont.) introduced bills (H.R. 5926 and S. 2023) that would have replaced the Federal Relations Act with the "Articles of Permanent Association of the People of Puerto Rico with the United States." In support of this effort in March 1959, the Puerto Rico legislature approved a Joint Resolution asking Congress to clearly state that Puerto Rico was no longer a possession (an implicit admission there was still confusion regarding this point).[27] But in spite of Eisenhower's promise at the United Nations, the 1959 initiative died in committee.

By 1962, even Muñoz Marín had to admit (privately) that the ELA had not removed the onus of colonialism from the U.S.–Puerto Rico relation and that many in Congress and the federal government acted as if no "compact" existed.[28] A process of negotiation with the Kennedy and Johnson administrations ensued, but its sole concrete result was the celebration of a plebiscite in 1967. The ELA as a status to be further developed won handily, but the attempts to negotiate any changes to its original structures again failed.

Furthermore, while no changes have been introduced to the purported "compact," the extension of federal legislation has the effect of constantly redefining the reach of the federal government within Puerto Rican society without any bilateral negotiation. The limits imposed by P.L. 600 imply that federal legislation can overrule the constitution approved in 1952. Thus, although the constitution forbids wiretapping, federal agencies may engage in this practice in Puerto Rico: the restriction applies only to the insular police and justice system. Similarly, and more dramatically, the ELA constitution states that there "will be no death penalty." But the most recent decision by the U.S. Court of Appeals for the First Circuit has determined that U.S. federal courts in Puerto Rico may impose the death penalty given the extension to Puerto Rico of federal legislation that allows for capital punishment in certain cases. The prohibition regarding the death penalty applies only to insular legislation. Fernós's disciples could riposte that this situation was a result, not of colonial imposition, but of the terms of the "compact" Puerto Rico had entered into in 1950. Be that as it may, the question still poses itself as to whether the terms of that alleged "compact" are such that one can speak of Puerto Rico as self-governing.

Through the 1980s, José Trías Monge, former chief justice of the Puerto Rico Supreme Court and one of the architects of the ELA, published his *Historia constitucional de Puerto Rico*, a treatise that includes a balance sheet of his own trajectory, as well as that of Muñoz Marín and Fernós, on the status issue. While clinging to the theory of the "compact," Trías Monge admitted that the island was not self-governing. Muñoz Marín's unwillingness to demand a clear definition from Congress or to embarrass Washington with denunciations of colonialism impeded the fight for a more meaningful autonomy. Muñoz Marín, he argued, missed the chance to clearly define the new status during the process of adoption of P.L. 600 and later failed to use the legitimacy of the 1951 constitutional assembly to extract a clear demarcation of the powers of Congress over Puerto Rico. The attempt to gain congressional favor by insisting that colonialism, if it had ever existed, had ceased in 1950–52 was, according to Trías Monge, another concession that came to haunt the PPD as it made the struggle for further reforms more difficult by making them seem less urgent.

It should be remembered that after abandoning the goal of independence in 1946, Muñoz Marín had still advocated a noncolonial relation with the United States. In this, as Géigel had denounced in 1951 and Trías Monge admitted by the 1980s, he failed.[29] After 1946, he had in fact settled, not for some form of free association, but for what looked very much like a de facto reorganization of the insular government within the limits of the relation of nonincorporation. It is thus necessary to conclude that the evolution of Muñoz Marín had come full circle. In 1937, in the wake of the Tydings bill, he had warned Antonio R. Barceló and the Partido Liberal not to abandon independence to seek reforms to the existing relation under the label of "Free Associated State," a formula that the Partido Unión had adopted in 1922. By 1952, Muñoz Marín had embraced the very same position he had warned Barceló against: like the Partido Unión in 1922, and like Barceló and his wing of the Partido Liberal in 1937, Muñoz Marín in the end opted to limit his program to what he deemed acceptable to Congress, which turned out to be a reformed territorial status.

Looking further back, it may be noted that the colonial policy of nonincorporation had been formulated in 1901 by members of the same U.S. Supreme Court—the Fuller court—that in 1896 had endorsed racial segregation in its notorious decision in *Plessy v. Ferguson*. Yet while in the United States the doctrine of separate but equal was revoked in 1954, Puerto Rico's colonial status and arguably its definition as unincorporated territory has survived into the twenty-first century.

In spite of its limitations, until the late 1960s the ELA enjoyed overwhelming support in Puerto Rico. The reason is not hard to find. To begin with, the ELA, while falling short of a true process of self-determination, still represented an advance over previous forms of colonial administration. But the support it enjoyed corresponded to an even greater degree to the fact that after 1940, many Puerto Ricans began to detect an improvement in their standards of living, due in part to the programs initiated by the PPD and more generally to the fact that the world capitalist economy was embarking on its postwar expansion. Puerto Rico was to partake of that expansion—of its contradictions certainly, but also of its benefits—to an extent initially not replicated in other areas of the colonial world.[30]

In fact, the vigor of the economic expansion was such that political scientist Carl Friedrich could confidently predict in 1959 that by 1975, Puerto Rico would attain a standard of living at least equal to that of the poorest state of the Union and that it would have an economy able to "provide from national savings enough growth to take care of all Puerto Ricans."[31] Reality, as we shall see in the following chapters, failed to match this prediction. In 2006, thirty years after the date in which Friedrich expected it to catch up with the poorest state and to be able to finance its own growth, Puerto Rico's per capita income is still a third of the U.S. average and half that of the poorest state, and its economy is still dependent on the influx of U.S. private investments and public funds.

Dissatisfaction with the ELA has so far resulted in the growth of the statehood and not of the independence movement. The more evident reason for this is the fact that half the per capita income of the poorest state of the United States is still considerably higher than the standard of living of the independent republics of the region. The severe economic hardship into which the latter are driven by the workings of the world economy controlled by the developed states, such as the United States, imply what may be called a constant "Tydings effect" on Puerto Rico, informing its people that independence is possible but miserable. One could think of different ways of organizing the world economy—indeed, one must, if most of the world's population is to ever escape underdevelopment. But that has not been the direction in which the world has moved in recent decades. Placed in an intermediate position in a world and regional economy increasingly polarized between rich and poor countries, most Puerto Ricans have tended to favor a continued political relation with the United States. By 2005, that majority is evenly split between those favoring statehood and those upholding autonomy. But that is now. In the 1950s and 1960s, the ELA still enjoyed overwhelming support. The economic shifts it presided over were to completely transform both island society and the Puerto Rican diaspora in New York and beyond. We explore these changes in the following chapter.

TRANSFORMATION AND RELOCATION: PUERTO RICO'S OPERATION BOOTSTRAP

Both politically and economically, the evolution of Puerto Rico after 1945 is a study in continuity and discontinuity. Politically, the creation of the Estado Libre Asociado marked a significant reformulation of the claims to legitimacy of the insular government within a persistent colonial framework. Similarly, in the economic sphere, changes unfolding since before the creation of the ELA radically transformed the insular productive landscape without altering its underlying colonial and dependent nature.

Puerto Rico's postwar economic transformation took place in a specific international context. While decolonization began to gather speed, by the late 1940s world capitalism was embarking on a long period of expansion that lasted until the late 1960s. The reorganization of the world economy during the postwar boom included the semi-industrialization of some underdeveloped and raw material–producing areas as well as considerable migration from less to more developed regions. Puerto Rico was a very visible participant in these trends. After 1947, the economic shifts that reshaped Puerto Rican society were propelled by a new wave of U.S. investments in an expanding manufacturing sector, almost exclusively oriented to the U.S. market. U.S. capital was attracted to the island by a mix of incentives that included exemption from insular and federal taxes, relatively low wages, and open access to the U.S. market. If wages remained low by U.S. standards, they were higher than those paid by the sugar, needlework, and tobacco industries before World War II. At the same time, beginning in 1945–46, a massive number of Puerto Ricans, unable to find employment in Puerto Rico, left for the United States in search of jobs and higher pay.

While Partido Popular Democrático leader Luis Muñoz Marín presided over this process as governor between 1948 and 1964, it was Teodoro Moscoso, head of the government program to attract U.S. investors, who came to embody the official drive to increase manufacturing and export production. Originally groomed to pursue his family's drugstore business, Moscoso began his career in government as one of Governor Rexford G. Tugwell's young collaborators in the early 1940s. The material shape of modern Puerto Rico was to come closer to the vision of this rather colorless technocrat than to that of any other single PPD leader, including Muñoz Marín.

The features of the postwar period in Puerto Rico are hardly unique. This epoch, according to Eric Hobsbawm, witnessed "the most dramatic, rapid and profound revolution in human affairs of which history has record."[1] All aspects of this shift were in exhibit in Puerto Rico: the generalization of literacy and urbanization, the shrinkage of the peasantry, the incorporation of women into new areas of public life, and the transformation of domestic work and of leisure by consumer durables. The urban layout was altered by the automobile; sex and reproduction were transformed by contraception. Views on the family evolved with the growing acceptance of divorce and of sex out of wedlock. These were not instant changes, nor were they welcomed by all, but they gained ground relentlessly.

In twenty years, the island was transformed from a largely agricultural district into an export-oriented manufacturing platform with decaying agricultural activity. This inversion bypassed the possibility of a more balanced and complementary relation between industry and agriculture. The adoption of the North American model of an automobile-centered life meant a rapid passage from rural and semirural settlement to suburban sprawl. By 1970, photographs of pre-1940 and even pre-1950 Puerto Rico had acquired the aura of images from a distant past, and the lived experience of the younger generations felt a world apart from that of their grandparents and even their parents, who had reached adulthood as Operation Bootstrap picked up pace in the 1950s.

Meanwhile, mass migration transformed the Puerto Rican *colonia* in New York. By the mid-1970s, 12 percent of the population of New York was Puerto Rican. Puerto Rican areas in New York, which were never limited to East Harlem, emerged in new locations, with sections of the Bronx becoming large and visible *boricua* neighborhoods. By the 1970s, almost 40 percent of the Puerto Ricans in New York lived in the Bronx, followed by 33 percent in Brooklyn and 23 percent in Manhattan. But Puerto Ricans did not settle only in New York. Many found employment in the manufacturing sector in the mid-Atlantic, New England, and midwestern states: the garment industry in Philadelphia and the steel and related mills and factories in Chicago; Gary, Indiana; and Lorain, Ohio.[2] Other Puerto Ricans, mainly women, became domestic workers in well-to-do households, while a significant number of men worked in the farms and food processing plants in New Jersey, Pennsylvania, New York, Connecticut, Illinois, and other nearby states. Some settled in adjacent cities, creating the initial nucleus of future Puerto Rican *barrios* in Boston; Paterson and Camden, New Jersey; and Hartford and Bridgeport, Connecticut. By the early 1970s, there were more than thirty cities in the United States with a population of 10,000 Puerto Ricans or more.[3] The largest concentrations were in the Northeast, along a corridor roughly running from Boston through New York to Philadelphia.

The dynamics underlying this mass migration are no mystery. While the main feature of the economic shift after 1950 had been the expansion of factory production, until the mid-1960s the growth of factory employment on the island failed to compensate for the rapid reduction in agricultural and home-needlework employment. Some areas did better than others. Since most of the new industrial plants established were located in San Juan and a handful of urban areas (near Ponce, Mayagüez, Bayamón, Guaynabo, and Carolina), the disparity between the jobs destroyed in agriculture and home-needlework and those created in factory manufacturing was particularly acute in the countryside and in the interior of the island. Unemployment and shrinking economic options became the defining features of many small towns and rural areas, pushing many of their inhabitants to the larger towns and, ultimately, the United States.[4]

This was, nevertheless, an epoch of improving living standards for most Puerto Ricans. The average real weekly salary in manufacturing increased from $18 for men and $12 for women in 1953 to $44 and $37 respectively in 1963.[5] Not only were wages higher for those able to secure jobs, but new government water, electricity, housing, road, basic health, and education services improved the living conditions of even the poorest Puerto Ricans. Life expectancy, to take just one index, increased from forty-six to sixty-nine years between 1940 and 1960.

By the early 1960s, the Puerto Rican government identified what it saw as four deficiencies of its industrialization project: persistent high unemployment, which never fell below 10–11 percent; the volatility of labor-intensive operations of U.S. companies, able and willing to move to other low-wage areas; the over-concentration of industrial activities in a few urban areas; and the particularly acute problem of unemployment among men. By the late 1950s, government planners formulated a grand petrochemical project that sought to address these problems. New capital-intensive oil processing operations and related "satellite" industries would provide high-wage employment largely for males along the southern and western coast. But this petrochemical dream never materialized.

By the mid-1970s, the world capitalist economy entered a new period of slow growth, and the Puerto Rican economy lost much of its dynamism. It now became evident that Puerto Rico's material progress after 1950 had not abolished the imbalances of its colonial, dependent economic structure. All the main problems that had been debated in the 1930s—high unemployment, dependence on U.S. capital and U.S. government funds, persistent differentials in living standards between the island and the United States—came to the fore once again. In fact, complete reliance on U.S. capital investments and full orientation to export production had not been the PPD's initial perspective when it was organized in 1938. The PPD had emerged as a party of the New Deal, largely dedicated to the ideas of planning, state enterprise, and a more autonomous development in preparation for political independence. This orientation was abandoned by 1946–47. The story of this shift is the prelude to Puerto Rico's postwar transformation.

The PPD and Social Reform

The PPD rightfully interpreted the votes it received in the 1940 elections as a mandate for social reform. Its program had several interconnected elements. The PPD had promised an agrarian reform, which would break up large holdings and diversify production. New state-owned industries would reduce absentee control while providing sorely needed employment. New laws were expected to guarantee minimum wages, maximum hours, and union rights. Potentially, implementation of the 500-acre limit would have placed a considerable amount of land under the control of land reform agencies. In 1940, there were 55,519 farms in the island of which 342 had over 500 acres. These large farms held 31 percent of the land in farms and 44 percent of the farm value (land and installations).[6] Yet the PPD's project had several features, which must not be overlooked, that help explain its evolution and inconsistencies.

The PPD was neither radical nor revolutionary. It was committed to respecting existing legal-judicial procedures and property rights. All land expropriated, for example, was compensated. This meant that reforms would be limited to the state's ability to pay for them. Here, as in other areas, the war came to the rescue of the PPD. Existing legislation established that federal excise taxes collected on Puerto Rican goods exported to the United States be returned to the insular treasury. Just before the war, remittances had averaged around $4 million a year. But during the war, mainland shortages of distilled beverages increased demand for Puerto Rican rum, and remittances rose to as high as $55.6 million in 1944. All told, the insular government received around $160 million in extra revenue between 1941 and 1946. But it was evident that financing would become a severe problem when the special wartime circumstances came to an end.

Furthermore, the PPD at no time contemplated a challenge to, much less a confrontation with, the U.S. government. On the contrary, Muñoz Marín and his associates were confident that they could bend U.S. government policies to their own advantage. Unlike the Nationalists, they were confident that independence would be obtained through collaboration and with the political and economic support of the United States. The PPD would thus face some hard choices if the federal government proved less responsive than expected to insular development projects.

Conceived within strict legal limits and in collaboration with the federal government, PPD reforms had a clear top-down dynamic. The changes brought about were not the result of a broad social movement of the rural population from below. While the PPD supported the sugar workers' strike of 1942, it never sought to collaborate with the new and growing labor federation, the Confederación General del Trabajo, to turn the agrarian reform or the new state-owned factories into experiments of alternate participatory politics or management. Plus, the PPD coalition included social sectors that were wary of radical social experiments. Foremost among these were the *colonos*, large sugarcane growers, who since 1936–37 had indicated they would oppose any measure that they felt went against the logic of private property and private initiative.

The PPD was committed to the promotion of industries, hopefully directed to the insular market and using island raw materials. Since private capital was unable or unwilling to initiate these projects, it would be necessary for the state to establish an initial nucleus of industries. Nevertheless, many functionaries, such as Moscoso, head of the government industrialization program, still saw private enterprise as the natural and most adequate vehicle for economic development.

These features of the PPD reform project—its respect for existing property rights, its commitment to collaboration with Washington, its top-down, nonparticipatory dynamic, and its inclusion of conservative sectors opposed to cooperative experiments or to radical inroads into the prerogatives of the market or private enterprise—restrained it in its confrontation with opposing social and political sectors.

Opposing forces were active from the start. Sugar corporations challenged the implementation of the 500-acre law in the courts. They joined with importers to oppose plans to increase food production. The idea that Puerto Rico could be less dependent on sugar exports and food imports was perceived by both groups as a threat to their interests. Private insular interests refused to buy goods (bottles, paper, cardboard) produced by government-owned industries. Puerto Rican banks applied pressure to limit the scope of the Development Bank of Puerto Rico. Confronted with such opposition, respectful of the existing legal framework, committed to appeasing the *colonos*, hosting sectors who agreed that private enterprise was preferable to public agency, and unwilling to mobilize the dispossessed against economic privilege, the PPD was from the start timid in its response to attacks from the Right. Propertied interests were able to deeply compromise PPD reforms from their inception.[7] The agrarian reform law enacted by the PPD was applicable only to corporate holdings, thus exempting the *colonos*. The planning board was given only advisory functions and did not constitute an attempt to curb the decisions of the market in a consciously determined direction. The Development Bank's ability to intervene in the private economy as a promoter of strategically determined economic choices was likewise curtailed.[8]

The PPD's Agrarian Reform

In 1941 a new land law (Law 26 of April 12, 1941) created the Land Authority. Initially led by Carlos Chardón, former head of the Puerto Rico Reconstruction Administration, it was entrusted with carrying out a program that had three basic features: the creation of small family farms, the distribution of plots for homes (*parcelas*), and the organization of "proportional profit farms." Of the three, the *parcelas* program (Title V of the law) affected the largest number of rural dwellers.

The *parcelas* were conceived as a means of transforming the situation of the *agregados*, those landless laborers residing on landowners' lands or squatting on public lands. There were around 150,000 *agregado* families in Puerto Rico.[9] The *parcelas* program allowed for the distribution of small plots of up to three acres (most were smaller) where the former *agregados* could build a house and engage in some food production. *Agregados* received the farms in usufruct. Offspring could inherit usufruct rights, but the *parcelas* could not be sold or mortgaged.

The amount of land provided did not allow the *parceleros* to escape waged labor, but it did transform their situation as rural proletarians. The acquisition of small plots signified the creation of a living space not subject to the author-ity, or power of eviction, of the landowners. The acquisition of a *parcela*, there-fore, signified freedom from the all-encompassing world of plantation life. The party that granted the *agregados* the *parcelas* was thus seen as the agent of partial emancipation from landlord power. By 1945, 14,000 families had been settled in *parcelas*, and the visibility of the program undoubtedly had a role in the Popu-lares' landslide victory in the elections of 1944. By 1959, 52,287 families had been resettled in *parcelas*.[10]

While the *parecelas* program continued through the 1940s, the small farm component of the PPD land reform (Title VI of the law) never took off. This pro-gram entailed the distribution of farms of 5 to 25 acres. By 1951, only 437 farms with a total of 6,283 acres had been created, representing only 0.33 of the land in Puerto Rico.[11]

In fact, some proponents of land reform, including Chardón, head of the Land Authority, had doubts about the creation of small farms. They felt that income inequalities had to be reduced while higher productivity attained in large-scale operations had to be maintained.[12] This was the origin of the most innovative aspect of the agrarian reform program. Instead of distributing land to small farmers, the state would retain it and lease it to semicooperatives to be known as proportional benefit farms (Title IV of the law). State-appointed managers would lead the farms. Managers and workers would receive wages and a share of the profits. The program sought to combine the egalitarian ethos of land distribution with the efficiency of large-scale production. This was the type of scheme that the *colonos* had opposed since the time of the PRRA as contrary to the principle of private property.

Furthermore, as indicated, PPD projects were conceived as administered re-forms and not as a social revolution. This was evident in the case of the propor-tional benefit farms. For workers, they signified a change of employer, not a radical shift in their forms of labor or social participation, besides an improve-ment in the wages received.[13] As one critic pointed out in 1951: "The most disheartening development has been the bureaucratic manner in which these state enterprises . . . have been managed. Lacking any socially constructive, not to mention socialist, ideology, the managers . . . have maintained the same attitudes toward the land and the people working it as prevailed before the reform."[14]

Expected both to show a profit and to help reduce unemployment, the pro-portional benefit farms were subjected to contradictory imperatives. They tended to employ more workers than private concerns, with the immediate effect of both increasing their production costs and reducing the portion of profits received by each worker.[15] Unpopular with the *colonos* and other opponents of state-run schemes, the proportional benefit farms were to be progressively abandoned by a PPD officialdom that had turned to industrial promotion as the road to Puerto Rico's modernization.

Indeed, by 1949, the government made its last purchase resulting from the initial 500-acre litigation, limiting itself after that to moral pressure on those violating the law to sell the lands in excess of the legal limit. One student of the agrarian reform found in 1977 that "there are currently over 100,000 acres in open violation of this law."[16]

To summarize, the PPD's stunted agrarian reform—the centerpiece of its 1938–40 campaign—failed to affect the overall structure of land tenure. Few small farms were created, proportional benefit farms were relatively large, and the *parcelas* and all farms under three acres were not counted as farms for census purposes. Thus, a look at the comparative data for land tenure in 1940 and 1950 in Table 9.1 hardly leads to the conclusion that an agrarian reform—indeed, any change at all—occurred in the intervening period. The PPD's agrarian reform did not create a layer of independent farmers or a state-owned or cooperative agriculture, did not break up most existing latifundia, and did not diversify production or redirect it to an expanding internal market. But it freed thousands of *agregado* families from the politico-economic clutches of the landowners, thus constituting a formidable, loyal electoral base for the PPD, the party responsible for the distribution of the *parcelas*.

The sugar industry, it should be pointed out, did not suddenly collapse after 1945. In fact, sugar production continued to increase until the early 1950s and then began to gradually decline. Smaller mills began to shut down in the 1950s. The larger *centrales*, which had been established in the first decade after 1898, collapsed last. Central Fajardo ceased production in 1978. Central Guánica, which in the first decade of the century had been the largest sugar mill in the world, closed in 1982. Central Aguirre followed in 1991. As the industry became less profitable, the government bought many of the decaying installations, a move that allowed many *azucareros* to shift their capital elsewhere while the state inherited the costly job of managing the declining industry.

This reduction of sugar production in and of itself was not a fact to be lamented. What was troubling was the missed chance, as indicated, of creating a more diversified agriculture and a healthier link between rural and urban development on the island. Agricultural overspecialization was thus replaced, not by a modern, diversified agriculture, but by even greater dependence on

TABLE 9.1. Land Tenure in Puerto Rico, 1940 and 1950

SIZE OF FARMS (CUERDAS)[a]	NUMBER OF FARMS (%)		ALL LAND IN FARMS (CUERDAS) (%)	
	1940	1950	1940	1950
Under 3[b]	—	—	—	—
3–9	28,172 (51.86)	27,985 (52.29)	143,284 (7.61)	143,008 (7.75)
10–19	11,288 (20.78)	10,538 (19.69)	151,510 (8.04)	144,449 (7.83)
20–49	8,575 (15.79)	8,687 (16.23)	258,563 (13.73)	263,720 (14.29)
50–99	3,200 (5.89)	3,166 (5.92)	215,540 (11.44)	216,148 (11.72)
100–174	1,504 (2.77)	1,440 (2.69)	191,678 (10.18)	186,539 (10.11)
175–259	646 (1.19)	627 (1.17)	135,568 (7.20)	133,055 (7.21)
250 and over	936 (1.72)	1,072 (2.00)	787,577 (41.81)	757,967 (41.08)
All farms	54,321	53,515	1,883,720	1,844,886

Source: U.S. Department of Commerce, Bureau of the Census, *United States Census of Agriculture: 1950: Alaska, American Samoa, Guam, Hawaii, Puerto Rico and Virgin Islands, Territories and Possessions* (Washington, D.C.: GPO, 1952), vol. 1, pt. 34, p. 176.

Note: Gini index decreased from .730 to .724 between 1940 and 1950, an insignificant change. Most of the *parcelas* distributed by the Land Authority were of less than 3 acres and thus do not figure in the table.

a A Puerto Rican *cuerda* equals .9712 acres.

b Not enumerated or counted as farms in 1950. Figures for 1940 (1,198 farms with total area of 2,154 *cuerdas*) excluded from the table for comparison purposes.

food imports. Furthermore, with the reduction of the agrarian reform to the distribution of residential plots, land came to be seen by government planners, and by most Puerto Ricans whose life was shaped by these social transformation, as a mere ground for erecting structures and not as a productive asset. This in turn prepared the ground—literally—for an urbanization process characterized by the adoption of the North American model of suburban automobile-based horizontal sprawl that has progressively spread over fertile lands.[17]

The Coming of Operation Bootstrap

The evolution of PPD industrial policy followed a pattern similar to that of its agrarian reform: an initial push for change undermined by external enemies and internal inconsistencies. As indicated, the PPD sought to launch an industrialization project that would combine production for the internal and/or export market using local raw materials while increasing insular control over a

FIGURE 9.1. Federal Expenditures and Excise Tax Income, 1940–1949

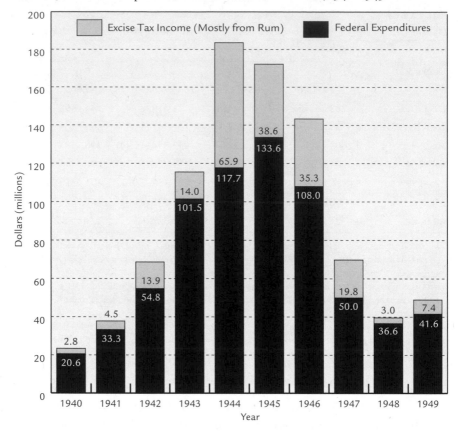

Source: James Dietz, *Economic History of Puerto Rico: Institutional Change and Capitalist Development* (Princeton: Princeton University Press, 1986), 206.

self-financing development project. A reduced but productive sugar industry would help finance the inputs needed for industrialization. There were considerable obstacles in completing this project.

First of all, island industries could not be protected from the competition of North American producers. Not surprisingly, Puerto Rican entrepreneurs were not willing to risk challenging well-established U.S. competitors. Under colonial conditions and given the dispositions of the Jones Act, import substitution thus confronted severe limitations. The state, hoping to jump-start an industrialization process, organized the Puerto Rico Development Company

(Law 188 of May 11, 1942) and entrusted it with the creation of a series of state-run enterprises. A glass and bottle factory began operations in January 1945, followed by a paper/box factory in 1946 and, in 1947, a ceramics/clay products plant and a shoe factory.

Even this limited attempt at state enterprise was fiercely attacked by entrenched private interests. Newspapers and rum producers refused to buy the products of the paper and the glass factories. The state did not respond to this sabotage with popular mobilizations or administrative measures, which would have defied existing legal frameworks or political structures. The very limited impact of this state-industrialization project can be ascertained from the fact that manufacturing's share of the national income barely increased from 11.8 percent in 1940 to 13.6 percent in 1949.[18]

Yet the years of World War II did witness a significant impact of government economic initiatives. This was the result, not of the insular state–led industrialization effort, but of a rapid increase in federal war-related expenditures. This can be appreciated in Figure 9.1. The stimulus provided by federal investment in military and related civilian infrastructure, such as highways, greatly benefited the PPD in this initial crucial period.[19]

As we saw in chapter 7, by 1946 the PPD and Muñoz Marín had come to the conclusion that an independent Puerto Rico intent on remaking its economy by reorienting part of it to local consumption, diversifying its agriculture, creating new industries, and substituting imports could not count on favorable trade or aid agreements with the United States. Muñoz Marín thus abandoned the objective of political independence, arguing that access to the North American market was the key for Puerto Rico's future development. Export production and reliance on foreign (fundamentally U.S.) direct investment now became the central features of the PPD's economic strategy.

Cumulative changes in economic orientation finally reached a defining moment with the passage by the insular legislature of the Industrial Incentives Act of 1947 (Law 346 of May 12). The measure granted private firms exemption from insular income, property, and other taxes and the payment of fees for licenses until 1957. Since U.S. corporations operating in Puerto Rico paid no federal income taxes, this offered them an almost tax-free environment. Moreover, federal minimum wage laws were not automatically applicable to the island. Instead, minimum wages were fixed on an industry-by-industry basis and revised periodically. In the late 1940s, wages on the island were considerably lower than in the United States. Tax exemption, lower wages, and open access to the U.S. market became the three pillars of the new industrialization project.

Meanwhile, the five state-owned factories were sold to private concerns by 1949–50. In 1950, the Puerto Rico Development Company was made part of the Economic Development Administration, popularly known as Fomento, which was put in charge of promoting the new development strategy. That strategy was given the name Operación Manos a la Obra and, in English, Operation Bootstrap.

The state now redefined its role as promoting and facilitating investment in whichever operations private U.S. capitalists wished to establish. Such a policy implied the emergence of an industrial sector characterized by weak internal links. No integrated industrial sector arose, since many operations functioned as enclaves bringing in raw materials and shipping out their output. Little or no taxes were paid to the insular government. Meanwhile, income generated in Puerto Rico was not spent on island products or invested in their production but spent on imports from the United States.

Not surprisingly, once embarked on a policy of self-perpetuating hyper-dependence on foreign capital, as José Padín has termed it, the government was led to expand the incentives to U.S. companies at every sign of faltering investments. Thus, the initial 1947 law granting tax exemption until 1957 was followed by a 1948 law (Law 184 of May 13) that extended tax exemption until 1959. In the midst of the recessionary impact of the end of the Korean War, this was followed by Law 6 of December 15, 1953, which granted a ten-year tax exemption to all firms from the moment they started operations, provided they began operating before the end of 1963. In 1963, Law 57 of June 13 removed the deadline on the concession of tax exemptions and granted longer exemption periods (up to seventeen years) to firms locating outside the metropolitan areas.[20]

The policies adopted by the PPD did bring impressive immediate results. By the summer of 1950, 80 new industrial plants were in operation; by 1952, that number increased to around 150. In 1956, the income generated by the manufacturing sector exceeded that of agriculture for the first time.

As had occurred with the needlework and tobacco industries between World War I and World War II, women accounted for a considerable portion of the new industrial workforce. By the early 1960s, women held about 60 percent of the new jobs. Since industrialization coincided with the decline of the home-needle industry, its initial impact was a modest increase in labor force participation rates for women: from 23.4 percent in 1950 to 24.4 percent in 1960. In

Women employed in light manufacturing in the 1930s. Women have played a key role in all stages of the evolution of capitalist manufacturing in Puerto Rico. (Proyecto digitalización fotos El Mundo–Biblioteca José M. Lázaro, Universidad de Puerto Rico–Río Piedras)

the next two decades, the labor force participation rates for women continued to increase, to 30.8 percent in 1970 and 36.5 percent in 1980. Meanwhile, the labor force participation rate of males dropped from 70.6 percent in 1950 to 65.8 percent in 1960.[21]

Since the industries attracted to the island were labor-intensive operations that required relatively low investment in fixed capital, it was easy for them to pack up and leave if more profitable opportunities emerged elsewhere. State planers worried about the volatility of these operations, the absence of linkages between them and much of the surrounding economy, and persistently high unemployment rates (among males in particular). Fomento strategists sought a new industrial project that would more firmly ground capital investments on the island, provide higher-paying jobs (above all for men), and serve as the nucleus of an integrated industrial grid. This was the origin of Fomento's petrochemical project.

Operation Bootstrap Matures and Wilts: The Petrochemical Project

In 1961, Fomento began to promote the idea of a petrochemical complex that would include oil refining, synthetic fiber and fertilizer plants, and other industries, including plastics. Oil refining and its satellite industries would become the axis of a new stage of industrialization. Presidential Proclamation 3663 of December 10, 1963, changed the limitations on oil imports to Puerto Rico, allowing the island to import a larger quota of foreign oil to be processed for export to the United States. The new quotas would initially benefit the operations of the Commonwealth Oil Refining Company, Caribbean Refining Corporation (a subsidiary of Gulf), Union Carbide, Philips Petroleum, and Sun Oil. Thus, the "petrochemical boom," as Emilio Pantojas-García has underlined, marked the shift in the type of investor attracted to Puerto Rico, from the relatively small-scale capitalists in the consumer goods sector to large transnational corporations in more capital-intensive operations. By the late 1960s and early 1970s, Fomento strategists in Puerto Rico announced the plan to build a deep-water oil facility (*superpuerto*) capable of handling tankers bringing in the raw material for the oil-related plants.

Meanwhile, government officials believed they had discovered another axis of economic development. By the mid-1960s, prospecting operations led to the discovery of copper deposits in the Utuado–Adjuntas–Lares area in the interior of the island. Several U.S. mining companies, including American Metal Climax and Kennecott Copper, sought concessions to exploit these findings. This project generated strong opposition, fueled both by environmental concerns and by resistance to the handing over of a potentially valuable resource to foreign investors. The impact of these and other social movements will be discussed in chapter 11. The struggle over mining activities continued through the early 1970s and succeeded in stopping the projected operations.

A similar fate befell portions of the government's grand petrochemical project. The planned *superpuerto* drew widespread resistance from the same coalition that since 1964 had questioned the projected mining operations. Rejection of continued reliance on foreign capital and the possible environmental consequences of highly polluting oil refining, processing, and transport operations fed an opposition that went far beyond the environmental and *independentista* groups initiating and largely leading it.

After the 1973 Arab-Israeli War, the international oil industry was shaken by the embargo imposed on the United States by the Arab oil-exporting states and the consequent rise in the international price of oil. U.S. import policy shifted.

Presidential Proclamations 4219 and 4297 of April and June 1973 now allowed importers to bring oil into the U.S. after paying an import fee. Puerto Rico's extended import quota ceased to be an advantage over its competitors. The petrochemical project stalled. The satellite industries never materialized, and the existing refining operations reduced their scope. The Commonwealth Oil Refining Company went bankrupt in 1978, leaving a depressing panorama along the southwestern coast, where its rusting remains can be observed to this day. Not too far away, the shell of the old Central Guánica presents a similar vestige from an earlier epoch: a vivid composite image of the sharp discontinuities of Puerto Rico's economic evolution as determined by the shifting needs and preferences of the U.S. market and the pressure of U.S. capital.

Meanwhile, since the launching of Operation Bootstrap, the insular government actively promoted the rise of a tourist industry. Tourism affected urban development along some of the more attractive coastal areas, shaped official and commercial representations of Puerto Rico and its people, and contributed to the image of Puerto Rico as a model of noncommunist development in the context of the Cold War.[22] In this sector, the government did not rely on the initiative of private investors seduced by tax incentives but directly made significant initial outlays of its own. In 1947–49, it built a modern hotel near old San Juan to be administered by the Hilton Company. Under the name Caribe Hilton, it was turned into a showcase of Puerto Rico's ongoing modernization. By the early 1960s, the government also built what became the San Juan and La Concha hotels, which were also run as joint operations with U.S. corporations. Gambling was legalized in 1948, and a modern airport was completed in 1949. Improvements in air travel enabled a growing number of tourists to reach the island. The budding industry received a major boost when the Cuban Revolution redirected the Havana tourist trade to Puerto Rico, making it the Caribbean's premier tourism site at the time.

Even during Operation Bootstrap's best years, the official unemployment rate remained above 10 percent. The figure would have been much higher had it not been for another feature of Puerto Rico's transformation after 1945: mass migration to the United States. Simply put, the creation of employment in the new industries was not able to compensate for the ongoing reduction in employment in the sugar and the needlework industries. Between 1950 and 1960, factory employment increased from 55,000 to 81,000. But this was canceled by the reduction in home needlework employment from 51,000 in 1950 to 10,000 in 1960. Meanwhile, employment in the sugarcane industry declined from

87,000 in 1950 to 45,000 in 1960. In fact, the total number of jobs in Puerto Rico fell by 60,000 between 1950 and 1959 (see Table 9.2). The "golden age" of Operation Bootstrap was actually characterized by a shrinking economy in terms of employment.[23] But, as indicated, the limits of the PPD's industrial miracle were partly hidden by the other side of the postwar expansion: the massive relocation of Puerto Ricans to the United States.

Mass Migration

The movement of Puerto Ricans to the United States had begun in the 1890s and accelerated after 1898. Puerto Rican workers headed north in search of higher wages and greater economic opportunities. Wages were indeed higher in the United States, but this differential by itself did not produce massive outward migration before 1945. The number of Puerto Ricans moving to the United States fell during the 1930s when massive unemployment deterred migration.

It was only in the 1950s that the outflow of population reached gigantic proportions. The prospect of finding better-paying jobs was now a reasonable wager, since the North American economy had entered a period of rapid expansion. Plus, migration became more accessible and easier. Advances in air transportation greatly reduced traveling time between Puerto Rico and New York. Action taken by the Puerto Rican government with the Civil Aeronautics Board broke the monopoly of air travel to the island and brought down fares to New York from $180 to as low as $35.[24] Net migration between 1950 and 1970 was equal to 27 percent of the population of the island in 1950. Table 9.2 provides the figures for out-migration. Figure 9.2 shows the general pattern of migration from Puerto Rico to the United States throughout the twentieth century.

The role of the ELA government in this process has been the subject of debate. Descriptions of its role have ranged from official claims to a neutral stance (neither for nor against migration) to visions of mass migration as a state-sponsored and organized process. Neither of these appreciations does justice to the role of the state in this process. Migration was not caused by a conscious state decision.[25] It is true, nevertheless, that once the process got underway, the insular government did much to assist it. Its policies can hardly be described as neutral. Government planners blamed "overpopulation" for Puerto Rico's persistent unemployment and took a favorable view of migration. In the 1950s, for example, Harvey S. Perloff's influential study *Puerto Rico's*

TABLE 9.2. Employment, Unemployment, Labor Force Participation, and Out-Migration in Puerto Rico, 1950–1965

Year	Agri-cultural	Non-agri-cultural	Total	Labor Force Participation[a]	Un-employment Rate[b]	Out-migration
1950	203,000	400,000	603,000	55.50	15.40	34,155
1951	192,000	379,000	571,000	53.50	16.00	41,920
1952	172,000	378,000	550,000	50.90	14.80	61,658
1953	174,000	366,000	540,000	50.10	14.50	74,603
1954	164,000	375,000	539,000	49.00	15.30	44,209
1955	161,000	396,000	557,000	48.30	13.20	31,182
1956	152,000	400,000	552,000	47.50	13.20	61,647
1957	151,000	404,000	555,000	47.20	12.80	48,284
1958	137,000	409,000	546,000	46.30	14.20	25,956
1959	125,000	417,000	542,000	45.40	13.30	37,212
1960	135,000	430,000	565,000	45.70	11.80	23,742
1961	135,000	433,000	568,000	45.50	12.70	13,800
1962	132,000	429,000	561,000	44.20	12.80	11,363
1963	122,000	464,000	586,000	44.40	11.00	4,798
1964	108,000	496,000	604,000	44.60	11.20	4,366
1965	99,000	535,000	634,000	45.40	11.70	10,758
Total						529,653

Sources: Junta de Planificación de Puerto Rico, *Serie Histórica del Empleo, Desempleo y Grupo Trabajador en Puerto Rico, 1984*; Center for Puerto Rican Studies, *Labor Migration under Capitalism* (New York: Monthly Review Press, 1978), 186–87.
a Percentage of noninstitutionalized civilian population who belonged to working group.
b Percentage of working group who were unemployed.

Economic Future spoke of 50,000 migrants a year as a means of stabilizing population growth.[26]

In 1947, the insular government created a Migration Office, which in 1951 became the Migration Division of the Puerto Rico Department of Labor. The division functioned in part as a labor recruitment agency for industrial, agricultural, and domestic workers, collecting information on workers and their levels of education and skill and referring workers to employers. While helping to defend workers (above all, seasonally contracted agricultural laborers) from some blatant abuses, it also sought to regularize and facilitate the flow of workers to the North American labor market. Through the 1950s and 1960s, the

FIGURE 9.2. Emigration from Puerto Rico, 1900–2000

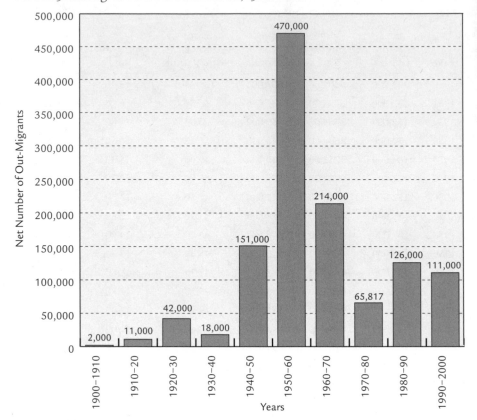

Sources: Data for 1900–1970 are from José L. Vázquez Calzada, *La población de Puerto Rico y su trayectoria histórica* (Río Piedras: Escuela Graduada de Salud Pública, Recinto de Ciencias Médicas, Universidad de Puerto Rico, 1988), 286; data for 1970–80 are from Francisco L. Rivera-Batiz and Carlos E. Santiago, *Island Paradox: Puerto Rico in the 1990s* (New York: Russell Sage Foundation, 1996), 45; data for 1980–2000 are from Matthew Christenson, "Evaluating Components of International Migration: Migration between Puerto Rico and the United States," Population Division, U.S. Bureau of the Census, Working Paper Series No. 64 (December 2001): <http://www.census.gov/population/www/documentation/twps0064.html> (accessed Feb. 1, 2005).

Puerto Rico Department of Labor negotiated agreements with agricultural employers' associations in Connecticut, Massachusetts, and other states. It thus functioned as de facto facilitator of the system of contract labor that redirected Puerto Rico's reserve army of labor to U.S. employers desiring to replenish their sources of relatively cheap labor power.

Puerto Rico secretary of labor Fernando Sierra Berdecía (left) posing with the staff of the Migration Office in New York City in 1948. The office tried to regulate Puerto Rican migration to New York City during the postwar boom. (Proyecto digitalización fotos El Mundo–Biblioteca José M. Lázaro, Universidad de Puerto Rico–Río Piedras)

Most Puerto Ricans were still drawn to New York City, but a growing number also settled in other midsize northeast, mid-Atlantic, and midwest cities. They were incorporated into the lower rungs of the U.S. labor market: as unskilled, low-wage operatives in light manufacturing (garment, food processing), as service and maintenance workers (in restaurants, hotels, laundries, delivery services), and as farm laborers (mostly men) and domestic workers (mostly women). In Chicago, Gary, and Lorain, some found better-paying jobs in the steel mills and related operations.[27] In New Jersey, Puerto Ricans worked as farm laborers and in canneries and processing plants. In the Connecticut River Valley, they harvested and processed tobacco. The point of incorporation of Puerto Ricans into the U.S. economy augured a grim future: manufacturing was a shrinking sector of the economy of New York and other northeastern cities. The gradual decline of the 1950s and 1960s would become a steep fall in the 1970s, with catastrophic effects on Puerto Ricans. The same was true of agricultural employment, which was to be hard hit by the ongoing process of mechanization.

Puerto Rican farm workers in the United States in the 1950s. Migrant labor to farms in the United States was a major part of the economic transformation of the 1950s. (Proyecto digitalización fotos El Mundo–Biblioteca José M. Lázaro, Universidad de Puerto Rico–Río Piedras)

Sea Change in the 1970s

By 1974–75, the long postwar expansion of world capitalism came to a close. Puerto Rico's economy was no exception. While the gross domestic product of the island grew at an average yearly rate of 7.7 percent between 1959 and 1974, over the next decade, GDP growth slowed down to 1.9 percent yearly. Manufacturing employment fell, and real wages declined.[28] It suddenly became much harder to attract new investors. But during the whole preceding period, no basis for a new development project had been created. The island was as dependent as ever on attracting foreign capital for its prosperity.

The PPD and Muñoz Marín had set out in 1940 to reduce Puerto Rico's unemployment, free it from reliance on U.S. relief funds, and attain living standards comparable to those in the United States. By the time the period of postwar expansion ended, Puerto Rico's per capita income was still half that of

Mississippi, the poorest state of the Union. Enduring poverty and unemployment made the island no less dependent than in the past on federal funds to maintain a minimum of purchasing power.

Meanwhile, between 1947 and 1974, the PPD presided over a growing denationalization of the Puerto Rican economy. In 1928, a Brookings Institution report had calculated that around 25 percent of Puerto Rico's total wealth was in the hands of absentee interests. As we saw, at the height of the sugar industry, U.S.-owned mills processed around half of the sugar produced in Puerto Rico. By 1974, according to James Dietz, 70 percent of all productive wealth in Puerto Rico was owned by "external investors."[29] This was a particularly ironic turn of events for a party that had emerged as an opponent of absentee control of Puerto Rico's economy.

The government, locked into its reflexes as a promotional state, proceeded to devise new incentives to attract a new generation of foreign investments. The epoch of the sugar companies, which had been followed by light industry and the petrochemical project, was to be replaced by the growth of the capital-intensive pharmaceutical industry, attracted by the dispositions of new tax legislation embodied in Section 936 of the U.S. Internal Revenue Code enacted in 1976. We come to these developments in chapter 13.

Puerto Ricans in the United States were also hit by the end of the rapid postwar boom. One of the consequences of the creeping crisis of U.S. capitalism in the 1970s was the contraction of light manufacturing in New York, Philadelphia, Chicago, and other cities, areas, and economic sectors where many Puerto Ricans had found employment in the postwar boom. The situation was already critical by the mid-1970s. Most Puerto Ricans remained at the bottom of the North American social pyramid. In 1975, the median yearly income for all U.S. families was $12,836; the corresponding figure for Puerto Rican families was $7,629. While 11.6 percent of all U.S. families lived under the poverty level, 32 percent of all Puerto Rican families found themselves under that threshold. In 1959, the average earnings of Puerto Rican families had been 71 percent of the U.S. average; by 1974, this had dropped to 59 percent.[30] Since then, conditions have worsened as Puerto Ricans were particularly hard hit, as indicated, by the collapse of the urban manufacturing sectors in the states where they had relocated during the postwar expansion.

Yet, as Carmen T. Whalen has underlined, such structural determinations of persistent poverty were to be brushed aside by many commentators. Instead, Puerto Ricans came to be seen as part of an underclass, stuck in poverty as a result of a culture of indolence and/or dependency. The welfare and other budget cuts justified by such theories were to further worsen the situation of many Puerto Ricans through the 1980s and 1990s.[31]

But that frustrating balance sheet was still in the future. In the 1950s, Puerto Rico was undergoing a rapid material transformation. Most Puerto Ricans saw their living standards improve due to higher wages, upgraded public utilities, and expanded government educational, health, and housing services. The insufficiency of these advances and the persistence of high unemployment did not countervail the general feeling of gradual progress shared by many. The drama of mass migration brought the pains of separation and of adaptation to a new social environment. But it would be one-sided to see this process as an unadulterated tragedy. While Puerto Rican workers had to continue their hard struggle for an adequate livelihood, many did so under less desperate conditions. There was then ground for both optimism, which semiofficial ideology turned into an apology of the political and economic status quo, and for criticism of the many not-so-bright aspects of the new Puerto Rico arising under the aegis of Operation Bootstrap.

Moreover, the initiatives of the PPD were not limited to agrarian reform and Operation Bootstrap in the economic sphere or to the creation of the ELA in the political sphere. Both were connected to a no-less visible institutional cultural project. In the next chapter, we turn to the cultural policy and academic and literary debates that accompanied the PPD's economic and political initiatives during the 1950s.

POLITICS AND CULTURE IN THE
EPOCH OF PPD HEGEMONY

By 1960, the Partido Popular Democrático and Luis Muñoz Marín were at the height of their popularity. Economic growth was improving the living standards of many Puerto Ricans. The more offending aspects of colonial rule, such as presidentially appointed American governors or the imposition of English, had been eliminated. Progress was no mere slogan but took on tangible forms, which for many turned debates about colonialism into a less than urgent question.

The very texture of daily life was changing. Beginning with the construction of a vast individual home development project in the area of Puerto Nuevo in San Juan in the late 1940s and the opening of the first supermarkets and the initial shopping malls in the late 1950s, Puerto Rico took the route of growth on the U.S. suburban model. Slum areas subsisted, even grew, as thousands were left jobless by decaying agricultural production. But new *urbanizaciones*, which replaced wood with cement as the basic building material, also spread further and further, beginning with what now came to be known as the San Juan metropolitan area. But the process was not immediate: it would take several decades before the growth of suburban space, highway networks, malls, and eventually megastores strangled life in most old town centers.

During the 1950s, the PPD was able to isolate not only the Partido Nacionalista and the Communists but also the moderate Partido Independentista Puertorriqueño. The PIP obtained 19 percent of the vote in the 1952 election, yet by 1960 this figure dropped to 3.3 percent. Meanwhile, Nationalist leader Pedro Albizu Campos, enfeebled and hospitalized, although technically in jail, had become a living symbol of independence but ceased to be an active political force. The Nationalists still launched spectacular attacks, such as the shots fired at Congress by Lolita Lebrón, Angel Figueroa Cordero, Irving Flores, and Rafael Cancel Miranda in March 1954. But the immediate result was further vigilance of a weakened movement.

Although gradually gaining strength, the statehood movement did not yet project itself as a serious rival to the PPD. The Catholic hierarchy failed in its attempt to organize a party, the Partido Acción Cristiana, to oppose government promotion of family planning. The Confederación General de Trabajo had split and disintegrated. Ongoing transformations had a disorienting effect on the union movement. A new working class, with no organizational continuity with past struggles, took shape. U.S. unions, themselves undergoing rapid bureaucratization after the upsurges of the 1930s, controlled the organizing that did take place. The PPD faced no serious opposition.

In New York, the Puerto Rican *colonia* was undergoing a similar transformation. Past activism and left-wing influence were sidelined with the rest of the U.S. Left in the era of McCarthyism and overwhelmed by new migrants from the island with no connection to past struggles in New York.

Muñoz Marín was now celebrated in the pages of *Time* and *Life*. Puerto Rico became a showcase of the benefits of the American way.[1] Puerto Ricans were appointed to visible posts as U.S. representatives. Most prominently, Teodoro Moscoso, head of Operation Bootstrap, became coordinator of the Alliance for Progress, launched by the Kennedy administration in response to the Cuban Revolution.

Meanwhile, Muñoz Marín had been able to attract a good part of the Puerto Rican intellectual field. For many, the work of the PPD was nothing short of the realization of the aspirations of the *generación del treinta*. Writing in 1943, Fernando Sierra Berdecía, playwright and essayist, and secretary of labor between 1947 and 1961, argued that Antonio S. Pedreira, author of the influential essay *Insularismo*, had found the "root" of Puerto Rican culture in the peasant and asked his readers if this was not the same figure described in Edwin Markham's poem "The Man with the Hoe," which Muñoz Marín had translated into Spanish in 1919. For Sierra Berdecía, the rise of the PPD was the awakening of the man described by Markham, Muñoz Marín, and Pedreira.[2]

In that context, Puerto Rican literary and cultural debates generated several interacting trends: social science research projects, at first largely conducted by North American experts; a semiofficial cultural apparatus, which included more than one current; public debates on some of the consequences of modernization and government policies (on migration or birth control, for example); oppositional literary and artistic activity, sometimes uneasily embedded in official institutions; and emergent forms within popular culture in a changing material context.

Social Science and the New Optimism

Writing in 1950, Jaime Benítez, rector of the University of Puerto Rico (UPR), remembered how in 1938 he had analyzed the poetry of Luis Palés Matos as a symptom of the pessimism that engulfed Puerto Rico. But through his poetry, Palés Matos turned his pessimism into a splendid aesthetic achievement. Those incapable of such artistry, Benítez warned in 1938, had to either embrace a new "faith" or succumb to unproductive frustration. Twelve years later, Benítez proclaimed that the defeatism of the 1930s was in retreat. Puerto Rico was going through a "spiritual reorientation" led by Muñoz Marín. Palés Matos had created great art out of his pessimism; Muñoz Marín had led the way to a new optimism.[3]

Benítez was no mere commentator. The expansion of the UPR under his leadership became a premier example of Puerto Rico's progress. Reform of the university had been a student demand for years. In the early 1940s, several positions had emerged as to which form it should take. Regarding structure, PPD cofounder Vicente Géigel favored a participatory model, with student and faculty electing some of their administrators. Regarding orientation, Margot Arce and other *independentista* faculty favored a "Puerto Rican university" open to diverse influences but willing to affirm a distinct national identity. Benítez opposed both positions. Against Géigel, he favored a hierarchical structure. In contrast to Arce, he saw any preoccupation with things national as a symptom of provincialism. Legislation introduced by the PPD followed Benítez's model. Plus, as the new rector of the university, Benítez was empowered to push his particular vision of "universal culture."[4] This perspective was promoted not only through literary interventions. Benítez ruled the UPR with an iron fist, particularly after the 1948 student strike, prohibiting political activities and abolishing representative bodies.

Benítez took advantage of the availability of Spanish intellectuals, whose opposition to Franco's regime turned them into exiles while their moderate liberalism made them acceptable to the PPD. The UPR attracted luminaries such as Juan Ramón Jiménez, Pedro Salinas, and Jorge Guillén. World-famous cellist Pablo Casals also moved to the island. The Estado Libre Asociado government financed an annual festival led by him and sought to place his fame at the service of promoting Puerto Rico as a site for investment.

Much intellectual work linked to the PPD project was carried out in UPR research centers such as the Centro de Investigaciones Sociales (CIS), organized in 1945. The CIS sponsored ethnographic, demographic, sociological, and economic surveys that sought to both define Puerto Rico's problems and to orient state policy. Through it John K. Galbraith, Wassily Leontief, and Carl Friedrich, among other prominent scholars, were brought to Puerto Rico during the 1950s.

The CIS sponsored Harvey S. Perloff's 1950 study *Puerto Rico's Economic Future*. As a register of the shifting official diagnosis of Puerto Rico's problems, it was the successor to the Brookings Institution report of 1930 and the Chardón report of 1934. While the first was informed by laissez-faire orthodoxy and the second by the New Deal's planning ethos, Perloff's work reflected the new prevalent mixed-economy Keynesian synthesis: while allowing for government intervention and guidance, it yielded to the key role of private capital in Puerto Rico's future development.

The perspective that best corresponded to the PPD's project of industrialization was that of modernization theory. Henry K. Wells's *Modernization of Puerto Rico* (1969) and Charles T. Goodsell's *Administration of a Revolution* (1967) were representative examples of the work done within that perspective.[5] Wells framed his study as an examination of the obstacles to the advance of modern culture, defined as pragmatic, democratic, and innovative. Traditional Hispanic culture was conceived as conservative and fatalist. He thus conflated U.S. influence with modernity and anti-Americanism with traditional rejection of modernization. The question of what kind of modernization Puerto Rico had undergone since 1898 remained out of sight. Reducing Puerto Rican nationalism to conservative elite resistance to modernity, Wells excluded the possibility that such critical sensibilities could contain prescient denunciations of the contradictions of Puerto Rico's particular colonial, dependent, uneven modernity.

Goodsell's text, a study of the Tugwell governorship, was an unabashed apology of the PPD and its political project. According to it, Puerto Rico had undergone a "peaceful revolution." Sugarcane monoculture had given way to a diversified industrial economy, and self-government had replaced colonial subordination. The growing control of the Puerto Rican economy by U.S. capital, the fragmented, dependent nature of its industries, and the limits of Puerto Rican self-government were conveniently overlooked. While the work of Wells and Goodsell had a more general sociological or historical bent, other studies were animated by very practical concerns. Such was the case of population, migration, and related research through the 1950s and 1960s.

From "Overpopulation" to the "Culture of Poverty"

In the past, many PPD leaders had argued that Puerto Rico's unemployment and poverty were the result, at least in part, of an unbalanced colonial economy subordinated to U.S. capital. By 1947, they had embraced the perspective that export production and U.S. direct investments were part of the solution and not the problem. Overpopulation now came to be seen as the fundamental—indeed, the only—source of insular poverty. What the island needed was further U.S. investment combined with an attempt to limit population growth. The latter could be attained through a reduction in the birth rate and increased migration. Not surprisingly, the cultural determinants of fertility, family structure, and women's reproductive choices, as well as the dynamics of Puerto Rican migration, were key areas studied by the CIS at the UPR.

The need to manage migration had been felt since 1947, perhaps earlier. By the late 1940s, Puerto Rican movement into New York had turned Puerto Ricans into an increasingly visible feature of New York life. Xenophobic reactions, combined with anticommunism, were not lacking. Puerto Ricans were said to migrate to New York to vote for left-wing congressman Vito Marcantonio in exchange for a place on the relief rolls. By 1947, warnings were being issued of Puerto Ricans overwhelming schools and health facilities, stealing jobs, spreading disease, and corrupting morals. In 1947, with a mixture of sympathy for the situation of the migrant and fear of a backlash that could block further migration, the insular legislature created a Migration Office, which in 1951 became the Migration Division of the Puerto Rico Department of Labor.[6]

Anxious to respond to some of the attacks on Puerto Ricans, the Puerto Rico Department of Labor hired the Bureau of Applied Social Research of Columbia University to carry out a study on the Puerto Rican migrant. The project was led by future left-wing critic of U.S. society C. Wright Mills and published in 1950 as *The Puerto Rican Journey*. There were, according to this study, no community institutions integrating the Puerto Rican migrant to the surrounding metropolis. Puerto Rican activism in New York, going back to the 1920s, was simply ignored. Despite this blindspot, the study suggested some interesting dynamics emerging from the process of migration. It argued that migration was often an opportunity to move beyond restrictive cultural patterns. Women, for example, were able to claim a greater degree of independence. As one of the women interviewed argued: "Here I belong to myself."[7] Yet the sense of greater freedom was combined with a feeling of loss of community, as the individual now found himself or herself in a more impersonal, hostile world. The study, the first to call Puerto Ricans "a people on the move," suggested that this dilemma was not unique to Puerto Ricans, even if they were forced to experience it more intensely. The "isolation of the individual" was after all a "characteristic of modern metropolitan society" as a whole.[8] Nevertheless, *The Puerto Rican Journey*, as Edgardo Meléndez Vélez has underlined, did also suggest that Puerto Rican culture was the source of the Puerto Rican's failure to integrate successfully to metropolitan society.[9]

Moving along the path opened by *The Puerto Rican Journey*, other works helped shape the perception of Puerto Ricans in the United States. Beginning with the first edition of *Beyond the Melting Pot* in 1963, Nathan Glazer and Daniel P. Moynihan perpetuated the vision of Puerto Ricans as culturally disadvantaged and lacking organizing traditions in New York while, in later editions, praising the self-help orientation of their community groups: such was the path to success in American society, as opposed to the route of protest attributed by the authors to African Americans. In 1966, anthropologist Oscar Lewis offered a harrowing portrait of life among poor Puerto Ricans in *La Vida: A Puerto Rican Family in the Culture of Poverty, San Juan–New York*.[10] Lewis, in spite of a sensationalist presentation, still ambiguously presented what he called the "culture of poverty" as both the result and cause of poverty. But if Mills and Lewis could nuance their more problematical judgments, such subtleties were lost on many other commentators and state functionaries.

Thus, as Carmen T. Whalen has argued, the problems confronted by Puerto Ricans in the United States (low pay, lack of job security, discrimination) were to be reframed as the "Puerto Rican problem," that is to say, as the islanders' inability to avail themselves of the opportunities inherent in American society. The Puerto Rican experience was not seen as rooted in patterns generated by metropolitan capitalist society. Instead, many observers saw the migrants' persistent poverty as the product of some alleged Puerto Rican cultural particularity, such as the illusion of a future return to the island, fatherless families, overprotective mothers, or Hispanic aversion to labor.[11]

By the 1980s and 1990s, the mechanization of agriculture, the collapse of manufacturing in the cities of Puerto Rican concentration, and the reduction in state social services had increased the levels of unemployment and poverty of many Puerto Ricans. But the structural causes of these phenomena were ignored as Puerto Ricans were turned, in works such as Linda Chavez's *Out of the Barrio* (1991), into an example of an "underclass" trapped in a self-inflicted condition of dependency, poverty, and illegality.

The notions of Puerto Rican poverty in the United States as a result of cultural factors and of island poverty as a result of overpopulation had one thing in common: they largely ignored the workings of capitalism and colonialism as relevant factors in the study of the Puerto Rican condition. Indeed, there was no need to examine the latter insofar as all problems resulting from economic development or migration could be ascribed to overpopulation or culture. The "culture of poverty," "underclass," and overpopulation theories were thus, as Laura Briggs has argued, racialist paradigms that blame the poor—and in this case, the Puerto Rican poor—for their own poverty.[12]

Given the centrality of overpopulation in explanations of Puerto Rico's poverty, women's bodies and their sexuality became objects of state and academic intervention during the 1950s and 1960s. Issues related to reproduction and contraception provoked controversies during this time, but, in the absence of a women's movement, these debates were conducted in terms other than women's right to control their fertility. Promoters of contraception argued that it was necessary to address the problem of overpopulation. The Catholic Church rejected contraception as the gateway to immorality. Many *independentistas* denounced it as a threat to the nation.[13]

Nevertheless, not all *independentistas* shared such views. In fact, the early defenders of birth control had been *independentistas*. PIP leader Carmen Rivera de Alvarado had defended women's access to birth control since the 1930s. In 1925–28, Communist José Lanauze Rolón organized a birth-control group called Liga para el control de la natalidad. Lanauze Rolón accepted the notion that Puerto Rico was overpopulated, opposed abortion, and frowned on extramarital sex. But he argued that women had a right to information that could help them make choices regarding their lives and health. No moral catastrophe would ensue if sex were to be taken as a legitimate aspect of human existence, even when not geared toward reproduction. Variations of these ideas were advanced by Rivera de Alvarado and Celestina Zalduondo, social workers concerned with the situation of poor women, even if they sometimes accepted Malthusian overpopulation explanations for poverty.

To complicate matters further, the story of birth control in Puerto Rico cannot be detached from the initiatives of Clarence J. Gamble's American Birth Control League or its links with U.S. pharmaceutical corporations. Over the years, Gamble helped create groups in Puerto Rico, such as the Asociación

Puertorriqueña Pro-Bienestar de la Familia in 1954, which lobbied the government to lift legal restrictions on contraception and promoted "family planning."[14] Through the 1950s, programs sponsored by these associations in collaboration with U.S. pharmaceuticals distributed newly developed contraceptive gels, foams, pills, and devices such as diaphragms and IUDs and closely monitored the results. Many have criticized the use of Puerto Rican women to test means of contraception, yet many women sought participation in birth control programs as a means of better controlling their lives.

The most controversial aspect of the population programs was the use of sterilization as a means of birth control. As this type of operation became available, critics argued that many women were forced or misled into having the procedure performed. The charge has been made from Catholic, nationalist, and feminist perspectives. Some authors, such as Briggs, have called for some caution regarding these appreciations. According to Briggs, regardless of the intention of government planners or private institutions, many women saw the availability of sterilization as an attractive option. There is little evidence of forced sterilizations, although some private hospitals did refuse services to multiparous women if they did not agree to be sterilized. The issue is complex: while sterilization may have been pushed by private institutions and looked upon favorably by the state, it was nevertheless sought by many women as a means to limit reproduction. Whatever the abuses perpetrated by private and state organisms, they were rarely, if ever, denounced at the time in terms of women's right to govern their bodies and lives. Overpopulation, Catholic morality, or the nation provided the vocabulary used to debate fertility.

From "Americanization" to the Institutionalization of Puerto Rican Culture

Institutional culture did not take the form of sociological and demographic studies only. The epoch of PPD hegemony also included an institutional attempt to construct a distinct conception of Puerto Rican identity. As indicated, for many PPD intellectuals, the party's efforts were a continuation of the work of the *generación del treinta*. Thus, in 1954 Eugenio Fernández Méndez explained the cultural project of the PPD in terms of the categories formulated by Pedreira in *Insularismo*.[15] If anything had prevented Puerto Ricans from solving the question formulated by Pedreira, "What are we?," it had been the unending debate between annexation and independence. The creation of the ELA allowed Puerto Rico to go beyond that sterile discussion. It could now pursue its "cultural self-determination" within the limits of the existing relation to the United States.[16]

Partly inspired by this perspective, in 1946 the Centro de Investigaciones Históricas was created at the UPR under the leadership of Arturo Morales Carrión. Lidio Cruz Monclova, Labor Gómez, Luis Díaz Soler, and Morales Carrión became known as the *generación del cuarenta* in Puerto Rican historiography. In the case of Morales Carrión, Gómez, and Díaz Soler, the continuity with some aspects of the work of Pedreira is evident. Like him, they wished to trace the evolution of a Puerto Rican "personality" and underlined the role in that process of nineteenth-century autonomism. The PPD's "gradualism" was for them the modern analogue of the nineteenth-century autonomist current. Gómez, for example, sought to exorcise any notion of revolutionary rupture from the Puerto Rican collective soul: "Nothing in Puerto Rico," he wrote, "is brought about violently, nothing has a drastic, inorganic or explosive character."[17]

The clearest example of *puertorriqueñista* policies, which characterized a wing of the PPD, was the creation in 1955 of the Instituto de Cultura Puertorriqueña (ICP). Over the years, the ICP reissued out-of-print books, promoted artisanal traditions and musical forms, and organized a national archive, among other activities. The development of the ICP was placed in the hands of Ricardo Alegría, a moderate *independentista* who became one of the more visible articulators of the PPD's cultural policy.

At the same time, between 1948 and the creation of the ELA, Puerto Rico was acquiring other elements associated with nationhood in the postwar world: an official flag and anthem and representation in international sport competitions, whose impact in generating a sense of collective self in a world of nations has been underlined by several historians. As Eric Hobsbawm has argued, "The imagined community of millions seems more real as a team of eleven people."[18] In Puerto Rico, the sport was not soccer but baseball, basketball, or boxing. The effect was nevertheless the same.

The PPD's cultural initiatives did not unfold without internal tensions, as can be seen in its problematic relation with the term "nation." While affirming Puerto Rico's particularity, the PPD sought terms other than "nation," which smacked too much of *independentismo*, to designate Puerto Rico as a differentiated entity. "People," "culture," "identity," "personality," and "community" were among the terms recruited to this effort. But, despite the PPD's occasional qualms, it can be argued that autonomist cultural affirmation of some sort was, and is, the more adequate cultural superstructure to Puerto Rico's status as a nonincorporated territory. The relation of nonincorporation defined Puerto Rico as a possession of but not part of the United States. In other words, it defined it as both subordinate to and different from the United States. The closest analogue to this definition would not be a politics that denied all differences or asserted a total identity between Puerto Rico and the United States but rather a stance that both affirmed that difference while acquiescing to a subordinate status. Seen from the perspective of the metropole, insofar as the relation of nonincorporation defined Puerto Rico as subordinate, it could, and at first did, correspond to a policy of cultural imposition and "Americanization." But insofar as it also defined it as different, it was also compatible with a more flexible practice, capable of allowing for certain affirmations of Puerto Rico's particularity, in turn linked to larger Puerto Rican participation in the colonial administration. Autonomism seized this possibility as it rejected the most evident forms of cultural imperialism. It filled that nonincorporated space with a particular vision of Puerto Rico's cultural difference. Autonomism has thus been a contradictory, Janus-faced vehicle for constructing Puerto Rico as both distinct from and subordinate to the United States.

But there is another dimension to this type of cultural affirmation besides its compatibility with colonial rule. At any given moment, there are several national narratives available for official promotion. The official conception of the ICP not only avoided the question of colonialism but also attempted to reconcile past and present class and racial conflicts. A history of conquest, enslavement, and exploitation became the history of the emergence of a Puerto Rican culture through the mixing, in harmonious synthesis, of the Taino, Spanish, and African traditions. Affirmations of a Puerto Rican identity have thus been double-edged. They have claimed an autonomous space vis-à-vis the colonial ruler and have led to significant democratic achievements, such as the end of the imposition of English. But they have also sought to neutralize tensions within Puerto Rican society, glossing over or seeking to harmonize persistent class and racial hierarchies.

A shared non-*independentista* cultural identity was not the only type of reconciliation yearned for by the PPD's official cultural organs. In 1955, Muñoz Marín announced Operación Serenidad, arguing that progress should not be reduced to its material aspects.[19] It was as if Pedreira's program of reconciling aesthetic sensibilities and economic progress, "culture," and "civilization" while retrieving Puerto Rico's "fragmented" soul was now embodied in the diverse initiatives of the PPD. While Operation Bootstrap promoted the growth of production and the advance of "civilization," Operación Serenidad insisted they had to be subordinated to the enrichment of human culture. While Operation Bootstrap relied on incentives to U.S. capital, the ICP insisted on the affirmation of a distinct Puerto Rican culture, all of this within the shell of the ELA, a regime that was portrayed as resolving the tension between the contradictory impulses toward annexation and independence. But not all were taken in by this *muñocista* or autonomist synthesis.

Variations of Oppositional Culture

Some members of the *generación del treinta*, as we have seen, fully supported the project of the PPD. Others distanced themselves from it with varying degrees of militancy and from diverse perspectives.

Vicente Géigel first played a key role within the PPD but was eventually pushed aside. In 1942, he published *El despertar de un pueblo*, a series of essays that explicitly sought to establish a continuity between the concerns of the *generación del treinta* and the objectives of the PPD. Like Pedreira, Tomás Blanco, and Emilio S. Belaval, he divided Puerto Rico's evolution into three stages: formation, emergence, confusion. To this he added the conviction that the rise of the PPD constituted the end of the period of disorientation that had followed 1898. Géigel tried to remain within the PPD while clinging to his proindependence perspective. In the long run, his flexibility and patience were not reciprocated. In 1951, Muñoz Marín fired him from the post of attorney general. A decade after *El despertar de un pueblo*, Géigel now penned *La farsa del estado libre asociado*, one of Puerto Rico's classic political pamphlets and a scathing critique of the ELA.

But it was Margot Arce (director of the Department of Hispanic Studies at the UPR between 1943 and 1965) who produced an initial balance sheet of her generation, in 1943.[20] It was framed as a comment on Pedreira's *Insularismo*. Arce accepted Pedreira's periodization and extended it to the present. If 1898 had broken Puerto Rico's historical continuity, the year 1929, with the launching of the journal *Indice*, had marked the beginning of a "renaissance." But the "renaissance" had faltered in 1936. Arce linked this to several factors, including the lack of a leader ("an exceptional man") and the impact of the Spanish Civil War. While support of the Spanish Republic had been justified, it had also "distracted us from ourselves." Anticipating the international realignments that would follow the end of World War II, Arce insisted that Puerto Rico had to act if it did not wish to have its situation determined by others, as in 1898.

Like Pedreira, Arce formulated a cultural critique of certain aspects of capitalist society, such as its tendency to impose a commercial rationality on all social activities. Independence would be a vehicle for consolidating not only Puerto Rican culture against Americanization but culture in general against the debasing pull of commercial society. In her case, this was combined with a strong but understated Catholicism and with elitist conceptions, which, at least in her youth, led her to raise doubts regarding the desirability of universal suffrage.[21] Yet her practice seemed to contradict some of her more traditional opinions. Thus her work as a pioneer woman academic ran contrary to her own views on the desirability of women's concentration on the domestic sphere.

The combination of a critique of colonialism in the name of Puerto Rican culture and of certain facets of capitalist society in the name of a beleaguered cultural sphere resurfaced in the work René Marqués.[22] Marqués was the best-known exponent of a conservative cultural critique of the Puerto Rico created by Operation Bootstrap. In terms akin to Pedreira's opposition of "culture" and "civilization," he denounced how being a poet had become a stigma within the dominant, aggressively utilitarian conception of progress. Marqués's work is full of characters left behind or crushed by progress: the poet as well as the isolated Nationalist leader, the *jíbaro* and the *hacendado*, the impoverished survivor of an aristocratic past and the humiliated father of a disappearing traditional family. The protagonist of one of his best-known stories, modeled on Albizu Campos, summarizes this outlook: "I do not belong to this epoch in which I live."[23] This alienation from the present corresponded, in the case of Marqués, to conservative views. Marqués, for example, rejected women's growing participation in many fields, which he described as the imposition of the "anglo-saxon matriarchal pattern" on the island.[24]

Yet, in part as a result of his feeling of alienation from the present, Marqués was able to point out many ironies of Puerto Rican reality in the 1950s. He thus denounced the destruction of agriculture and industrialization dependent on U.S. capital, all under the aegis of a party created in the name of agrarian reform and an end to absentee economic control. Marqués did not allow himself much hope that the culture he vindicated could survive the advance of progress. Progress, he argued, created a docile "average man" enamored with the comforts of the American way of life.

In 1959, Marqués edited *Cuentos puertorriqueños de hoy*, a sampling of the work of narrators of his generation, including José Luis González, Pedro Juan Soto, and Emilio Díaz Valcárcel. These authors explored the underside of the postwar expansion—the continued exploitation of the working class, the miseries of life in the urban slums, the discriminations encountered in New York, the traumatic experiences in the U.S. Army and the Korean War, the effects of the U.S. military presence in Puerto Rico. Opposition to U.S. colonialism did not prevent them from assimilating formal innovations pioneered by North American artists. Thus Marqués was influenced by Tennessee Williams, and Hemingway served as a model for González, who cultivated an unadorned, straightforward prose. In similar fashion, graphic artist Lorenzo Homar, who lived in New York from 1928 to 1950, became acquainted with modernist works and New Deal public art initiatives. Puerto Rican artists thus reworked trends coming from a rich variety of sources, including the metropole whose political control they opposed.

Many works and efforts of the 1950s and early 1960s could be mentioned, but we must limit ourselves to a few representative examples. Around 1950, Marqués and González published two emblematic texts: *La carreta* and *Paisa*. The common itinerary of their protagonists—countryside, San Juan slum, New York—is an indication of the social dynamic that attracted their attention, in spite of their ideological differences. Marqués's play ends with a call for a return to the land. González starkly depicts the realities of urban life but rejects all nostalgia for an agrarian past. One of his early stories, "El ausente" (1943), presaged the transformation that Puerto Rico was to undergo after 1945. "El ausente" tells the story of Marcial, son of a small farmer, who abandons his father's house after he is beaten for missing work. Marcial labors first in the cane fields and later in a quarry. He eventually returns to the farm but is no longer able to live there; town life and industrial work have made him a different man. The story ends as he leaves for a second time. This was indeed to be the destiny of thousands of Puerto Ricans in the 1950s. González, while denouncing the exploitation through which this transformation was completed, still felt it was the likes of Marcial—children of an emergent urban-industrial Puerto Rico—who embodied an alternative to the existing colonial capitalist order.

Soto's 1961 novel, *Ardiente suelo, fría estación*, may be singled out as one of the more accomplished attempts to offer a portrait of Puerto Rican society in transition, both on the island and in New York. The novel constructs a mercilessly pessimistic image. Puerto Ricans are becoming Americanized, their language collapsing into a degraded mix of English and Spanish. Modernization is turning their life-world into a standardized landscape, which one character describes with one word: "Levittown," referring to the emblematic U.S. suburb. Progress is presented in a bleak light. Older, dignified houses are being turned into desolate gas stations. Sordid attitudes dominate. A garden built to honor fallen soldiers becomes a flower-selling business.

The novel inconsistently criticizes island prejudices against those returning from the United States while also presenting cultural hybridity as a mark of degradation. The migrant, having advanced further down that road, was the clearest emblem of the terrible destiny awaiting all Puerto Rico. This was made all the more evident by the presentation of the world of such returnees as a subculture of prostitutes, drug addicts, and, above all, homosexuals, seen as the clearest embodiment of degenerate hybridity. While the migrant represented a terrible destiny, island Puerto Ricans were not far behind. "New York has defeated us," explains one character, referring to all Puerto Ricans. Puerto Rico was "a ship adrift, a plant without roots."[25]

Not all authors portrayed migration in such a negative light. González avoided transforming migrants into emblems of cultural degeneration. Instead, his stories, such as "La noche que volvimos a ser gente," link the situation of Puerto Ricans in New York to the exploitation they share with other working people and to the vision of a remaking of the capitalist metropolis— literally paralyzed in the story during one night, due to the New York blackout of 1965—in a more human and egalitarian direction.

One of the most interesting narrative texts of the 1950s was written by a figure who did not move in a literary or academic milieu. César Andreu Iglesias was a Communist leader and labor activist who retired from the party in the early 1950s. In 1956 he published the novel *Los derrotados*, a portrait of the nationalist movement. Andreu Iglesias presented the Nationalists' commitment to a patriotic ideal in the midst of a world in which everything "has its price" as the source of both their most admirable traits and their greatest weaknesses. It was their aversion to a world in which commercial interests ruled that both elevated them above all opportunism and the petty interests of a bourgeois mentality and also made it impossible for them to link up with the struggles of the working class, thus ensuring their heroic isolation and eventual defeat.

Andreu Iglesias formulated a similar vision in a 1961 essay on Albizu Campos. In it he defined a common ground with the Nationalist leader, not only on their shared defense of independence but also on Albizu Campos's refusal to live according to the prevailing values of market society. Agreeing with those who argued that Albizu Campos was a man from "another time," Andreu Iglesias added that this did not necessarily mean he was a man of the past. It all depended, he explained, "on whether the dollar or dignity will prevail in the

Marxist labor activist, journalist, and novelist César Andreu Iglesias at the time of hearings on "un-American activities" in San Juan in the mid-1950s. (Proyecto digitalización fotos El Mundo–Biblioteca José M. Lázaro, Universidad de Puerto Rico–Río Piedras)

man of the future. If what awaits us is a world in which everyone will have a price . . . then the life of Albizu Campos will be sealed by his death. But if another kind of world awaits us, in which people will not be seen as exchange values, then . . . it would be perfectly clear that, far from belonging to the past, he belongs to the future."[26]

While the authors of the postwar generation took on the world created by Operation Bootstrap, Nilita Vientós Gastón edited *Asomante*, Puerto Rico's best-known literary journal of the time. A forceful polemicist, Vientós Gastón was the author of hundreds of book reviews, later included in the collection *Indice Cultural*. Like Marqués, she rejected the dominant perspective that reduced progress to its material aspects, the individual to "an economic entity," and society to a "mere conglomerate of producers and consumers."[27] But Vientós Gastón was a liberal thinker, unlike Marqués. Her works are devoid of nostalgic references to the past. Her vision was both *independentista* and cosmopolitan, grounded in Puerto Rico but open to diverse, including North American, cultural influences.[28]

Yet, Vientós Gastón's critique of the "spiritual miseries" of an "affluent society," even if devoid of nostalgias for the past, shares Marques's antipathy for many features of a utilitarian bourgeois culture. They are both variants of what we have already referred to as a cultural-romantic aversion to modern society.[29] Nor are they exceptions. This aversion has been one of the prevalent responses to modernity in Puerto Rican letters since the second decade of the twentieth century, although its manifestations have not been uniform. The romantic sensibility implies a rejection of the market as the fundamental organizing principle of social life, from the perspective of past social forms or of alternative cultural spheres. It can correspond to elitist or egalitarian yearnings as well as reformist or revolutionary inclinations. It can be found associated with the nostalgia for very different social formations, from tribal society to *hacendado* hierarchies, the independence of the small farmer, or the privileges of literate elites.

Variants of such cultural-romantic aversion to modern capitalist society can be detected, to mention some of the authors discussed in this work, in Nemesio Canales's aesthetic critique of bourgeois existence, Pedreira's opposition of culture to civilization, Palés Matos's poetic search for alternate worlds, Albizu Campos's idealization of Puerto Rico before 1898, Juan Antonio Corretjer's 1936 vision of the future as a "new middle age," Marqués's evocative narrations and essays, Andreu Iglesias's appreciation of Albizu Campos's aversion to market values, and even in Muñoz Marín's launching of Operación

Essayist, reviewer, lawyer, and editor Nilita Vientós published Puerto Rico's best-known literary journal, *Asomante*, during the 1950s and 1960s. (Laboratorio fotográfico Biblioteca José M. Lázaro, Universidad de Puerto Rico–Río Piedras)

Serenidad to combat the reduction of progress to a mere quantitative accumulation of material goods. Part of the work of graphic artist Homar was shaped by this sensibility, as exemplified by his prints inspired by Kafka's aphorism "We were expelled from paradise, but paradise was not destroyed," which invite the viewer/reader to recognize his or her dissatisfaction with the present as a half-conscious desire for a plenitude that was lost but may still be recovered. Meanwhile, stretching herself thin over the divergent duties of a divorced mother in the 1940s and 1950s and the world of bohemia (classical site of the romantic sensibility), composer Silvia Rexach brought forth a dozen exquisite masterpieces of the bolero, a melancholy counterpart to the roaring progress of Operation Bootstrap.

A key poetic work of this period, Francisco Matos Paoli's *Canto de la locura*, may be placed under the same rubric. Matos Paoli, secretary general of the Partido Nacionalista, had been jailed under the Gag Law in 1950–52 and 1954–55. While incarcerated, he went temporarily insane. His text was a result of that experience. It is a meditation on madness by a participant in a movement that PPD ideologues often described as demented. *Independentista* literary critic Josemilio González argues that in a colonial context where "reason and science" have been used to "justify the slavery of an entire people," it is not strange to find protest "associated with madness."[30]

In a more optimistic epic register, Corretjer's long poem *Alabanza en la torre de Ciales* (1951–52) attempts, like so many others before him, to define a Puerto Rican identity. The poem presents the birth of the Puerto Rican nation as the creation of Taino, African, and white working people. Corretjer's nationalism was now informed by Marxism, which he had embraced in the early 1940s. The most dramatic portion of the poem was both a reminder of the exploitation suffered by generations of the dispossessed and a celebration of their labor as the true source of the Puerto Rican nation. It was to be musicalized by protest singer Roy Brown in the 1970s and became a popular emblem of Puerto Rican Left patriotism.

Undercurrents within the Institutions

There is a tendency to reduce cultural institutions created or promoted in the period of PPD hegemony to their official or semiofficial intentions. Actual practice was more complex. In some cases, critical voices and works emerged within official organisms, such as the ICP, the UPR, and the Department of Education. Thus, at one point or another, *independentista* authors such as Marqués, Soto, and Díaz Valcárcel and graphic artists such as Homar and Rafael Tufiño were linked to the Department of Education or the ICP. Similarly, *independentista* scholars continued to work in the university, producing, for example, the first general history of Puerto Rican literature by Francisco Manrique Cabrera and the first dictionary of Puerto Rican literature by Josefina Rivera in 1956.

Cabrera's history of Puerto Rican literature conceived its task as that of tracing the evolution of "our personality" in terms close to those used by Pedreira. In that sense at least, his project was compatible with PPD cultural policy, even if the author was an *independentista*. Cabrera's text coined the description of 1898 as a "trauma." The phrase "trauma of 1898" became one of the most repeated and, we would argue, misleading descriptions of the impact on Puerto Rico of the Spanish-American War.

The Community Education Division of the Department of Education, organized in 1949, was an emblematic cultural project of the early PPD. Conceived as a means of reaching a wide public with didactic messages, it recruited the talents of graphic artists Homar, Tufiño, Carlos Marichal, and Irene and Jack Delano. Marichal was a republican exile from Franco's Spain. Jack Delano first came to Puerto Rico in 1941 as a photographer for the Farm Security Administration. In 1957, Homar went on to organize the Taller de Artes Gráficas at the ICP. Artists working in these venues, along with the independent Centro de Arte Puertorriqueño created by Tufiño, Homar, José Torres Martinó, and others in 1950, brought forth a torrent of masterful works—woodcuts, drawings, paintings, posters, short films, stage sets, book illustrations—which combined a pursuit of artistic excellence and a desire to communicate with a wider public.

A sign of the cooperation of writers and graphic artists, the two portfolios produced by the Centro de Arte Puertorriqueño in 1951 and 1952, *La estampa puertorriqueña* and *Estampas de San Juan*, were paired with texts by Marqués, who emphasized their importance as alternative representations of Puerto Rican life. This was not the Puerto Rico of tourist brochures.[31] Meanwhile, Delano's photographic work spanning five decades allowed him to create a visual registry of Puerto Rico's transformation from a largely agricultural to a semi-industrialized urban society.[32] Delano's images of working people almost invariably present laborers as isolated if dignified individuals and hardly ever as collective, much less organized or mobilized, subjects. Delano took photos of trade union meetings, strikes, and picket lines, but he did not include them in his published collections.[33] These choices may reflect both Delano's sympathy with working people and their welfare and his close ties with the PPD cultural establishment.

Cortijo's Revolution

Beyond the purview of official cultural policies and institutions and hardly mentioned by intellectuals at the time, other initiatives were having a lasting impact on Puerto Rican culture, both on the island and in New York. Puerto Rican ears and feet were being retrained to the musical innovations emerging in the context of mass migration north and the rapid urbanization of the

Puerto Rican working class, with its strong Afro–Puerto Rican musical traditions. By the late 1940s, U.S. capitalism entered a new epoch of expansion, Cuban band leader Pérez Prado launched the era of the mambo, and Puerto Ricans flowing massively to New York turned dance halls such as the Palladium on 53th Street and Broadway into the mecca of the new musical trends, best exemplified by the rich mixture of Afro-Cuban and jazz forms by Cuban band leader Frank Grillo (Machito) and Tito Puente. Puente, born of Puerto Rican parents in New York in 1923, grew up listening to both Cuban and Puerto Rican music as well as the sounds of Goodman, Ellington, Basie, and Hampton, among other stars of big band swing.[34] He was soon joined by island-born Tito Rodríguez at the center of a bubbling Puerto Rican and Latino nightlife that defied the more dreary aspects of life in the lower rungs of the metropolitan social edifice. Younger performers, including Ray Barreto and Eddie Palmieri, were not far behind and would come to the fore in the 1960s.

Meanwhile, popular music was also evolving on the island, which was itself undergoing a rapid economic transformation. There, bandleader Rafael Cortijo and singer Ismael Rivera were key figures in the creation of a new type of Afro–Puerto Rican musical expression, drawing from the rich traditions of the *plena* and the *bomba* as well as from other Caribbean rhythms such as calypso. Cortijo and Rivera, with the support of well-known composer and singer Bobby Capó, for the first time pierced the unofficial but effective exclusion of blacks from many venues and television. Other ballroom orchestras of the past had incorporated stylized versions of Puerto Rican Afro-Caribbean forms into their repertoire, but the work of Cortijo signaled an unprecedented intrusion of these proletarian inventions into the mainstream.

The hits of Cortijo and Rivera became enduring favorites. Their impact, as indicated, on the visibility of Afro–Puerto Rican culture, on the projection of Puerto Rican music through Latin America and beyond, and on the sounds and movement of Puerto Rican life are undeniable. But this recognition was far from immediate. At the time, Cortijo's music was still considered by many an unsophisticated, disreputable expression, an appreciation intensified when the first epoch of Cortijo's band and Rivera's career were interrupted by their arrests in 1962 for drug possession. But their influence grew, and the offshoots of their group, such as the Gran Combo with its singers Andy Montañez and Pellín Rodríguez, and later Roberto Roena y su Apollo Sound and Ismael Rivera's own group (Los Cachimbos, organized in 1972), became equally popular. By that time, the further musical transformation of the late 1960s, commonly associated with the term "salsa," was underway, and a new generation of authors and historians had begun to pay attention to the vitality and richness of these creative efforts.

Rubén del Rosario's Critical *Independentismo*

Rubén del Rosario was one author who did not share an attachment for threatened elite cultural forms. Del Rosario, Puerto Rico's first academically trained linguist, writing as a minority of one, produced some of the most interesting reflections on Puerto Rico's culture in the 1950s and 1960s.

Del Rosario's starting point was the notion of language as a changing structure. Language was not a reflection of the "spirit of the people"; it was an evolving means of communication. There was no evidence that Spanish was degenerating in Puerto Rico. What some saw as signs of decay were changes inherent to the evolution of any language, which inevitably included borrowing from foreign tongues. Puerto Rican Spanish was impure because it was changing, and it was changing because it was alive. Suggesting a link between linguistic purism and racism, he argued, "Neither the value or the usefulness of a language depends on its purity of blood."[35] Purist attitudes, he added, often implied disdain for actual, living Puerto Rican culture and language, in all its fertile impurity. *Independentistas*, he felt, should embrace that dynamic and evolving language, not some abstract purist norm, as their ever-changing patrimony. His was an *independentismo* imbued with a radically dynamic vision of Puerto Rican culture.

According to del Rosario, purist attitudes toward language were often symptoms of conservative attitudes toward culture: "Changes in customs are always attributed, like changes in language, to a pernicious foreign influence. Purists and traditionalists have always condemned innovations in the name of morality."[36] For del Rosario, the ideas of Spanish linguist Germán de Granda were a case in point. According to del Rosario, de Granda's notion that Puerto Rico was losing its culture and language was in fact a reflection of de Granda's aversion to phenomena such as "divorce, migration, family planning, women's work outside the home, industrialization, Protestantism, the weakening of the Catholic Church, . . . and many other things which he thinks are the product of Americanization." Such views, argued del Rosario, implied not so much a rejection of colonialism as a refusal to come to terms with "real modern Puerto Rican life."[37] Such attitudes had to be abandoned, along with the related notion that Puerto Rican culture was disintegrating, when it was, in fact, much like a living language, constantly being remade under changed circumstances.

Arguing that there is no necessary one-to-one correspondence between language and nationality, del Rosario added that it was a mistake to think of the evolution of a Puerto Rican identity as inseparable from Spanish. Even in the unlikely eventuality that English displaced Spanish, such an outcome would not imply the end of a Puerto Rican identity, "if our people do have something new to say to the world."[38] A hypothetical speculation, since he felt Spanish was not disappearing, the argument shows how his perspective admitted the possibility of a Puerto Rican literature in English.

But del Rosario's attack on purism had another dimension. A conservative dead end for *independentistas* (burdening them with a static vision of language and culture), purism was also compatible with the PPD's autonomist mix of Puerto Rican culture and colonial subordination. PPD policy makers, he warned, could and did combine the defense of Spanish against invading anglicisms while perpetuating Puerto Rico's colonial status. If *independentistas* allowed themselves to be seduced by such gestures, they risked becoming a cultural appendix to PPD colonial politics. Against autonomist and *independentista* purisms, del Rosario thus favored both anticolonialist and antipurist perspectives favorable to independence but opposed to a static conception of culture: "What we propose, then, is an open culture, . . . open to all foreign influences."[39]

Developments since the 1950s have confirmed del Rosario's perspective. Puerto Rican Spanish has not disintegrated. English has not displaced it. Writers have mined the richness of Puerto Rican street language and have used it to renew Puerto Rican literary discourse. In the United States, a Puerto Rican literature in English has emerged. New critical currents have vindicated the notions of cultural hybridity and permeable identities. Last but not least, the PPD has shown a consistent ability to link its colonial politics with affirmations of a Puerto Rican identity. All of this tends to confirm del Rosario's prescient claims. His brief, crisp essays remain an example of a critical non-nationalist *independentismo* that has rarely received the attention it deserves.

PPD HEGEMONY UNDERMINED: FROM MOBILIZATION TO RECESSION, 1960-1975

The 1960s are remembered around the world as a moment of insurgent social movements, sudden cultural shifts, and, in many cases, political fracture at the top. Puerto Ricans on the island and beyond were part of that general trend. By 1965, the life of most Puerto Ricans had been deeply altered by the economic reconfiguration of Puerto Rican society. Agriculture went into rapid decline, and industry increased its share of employment. Jobs requiring a high school education or technical skills grew. Mass primary education became a reality. An expanding university produced a growing number of professionals and skilled workers, including thousands of women. Puerto Rico now had a new working class, an expanded student population, and a rising layer of professionals.

But Puerto Rico's party structures and leadership teams had been put in place in the 1940s. They now came under strain to adapt to a changed social context. Currents calling for renewal emerged within the autonomist, state-hood, and *independentista* movements, all of which went through splits and mutations during the 1960s. In the elections of 1968, a new statehood party defeated a divided Partido Popular Democrático, ending a string of victories stretching back to 1940. Meanwhile, the late 1960s and early 1970s witnessed the rise of social movements that challenged diverse aspects of Puerto Rico's economic and/or political dynamics, from the environmental consequences of industrialization to the U.S. military presence. Other initiatives sought redress from injustices, from sexism to the lack of adequate housing for the poor. Students mobilized against the draft into the U.S. armed forces. Between 1969 and 1975, labor unions fought several major battles, and new coordinating efforts were attempted.

No less visibly and with lasting implications for Puerto Ricans everywhere, the 1960s signaled the emergence of a new political activism in the Puerto Rican diaspora, from the rise of the Young Lords and the Puerto Rican Student

Union to community service groups such as ASPIRA and the election of the first Puerto Rican to Congress. These upheavals had a profound cultural impact, as they redirected debates about Puerto Rican history and identity and created a new context for literary departures on the island and among Puerto Ricans in the United States. We explore these shifts in chapter 12. This chapter discusses the social and political aspects of this process.

The Division of the PPD and the Elections of 1968

Two decades after the landmark election of 1940, the internal life of the PPD had become a sordid struggle for the control of municipal governments or state agencies. The crusading New Dealers that once followed Luis Muñoz Marín in the battle for labor and agrarian reform had by now become part of a top-heavy political machine—fairly honest, by later standards, but devoid of vision besides the continuation of existing policies. Yet the PPD could claim credit for a still vigorous pace of economic expansion.

The status issue remained a source of frustration, in spite of public pronouncements to the contrary. After the failure of the Fernós-Murray bill of 1959, which sought to expand the autonomous powers of the Estado Libre Asociado, Muñoz Marín shifted strategies. He now first sought an agreement with the Kennedy administration on new legislation, which would then be presented to Congress. This initiative was frustrated when the White House unceremoniously withdrew its support for the proposed legislation (H.R. 5945, known as the Aspinall Bill of 1963). Congress limited itself (through P.L. 88-271 of 1964) to the creation of a commission to study the status options and issue recommendations.

Eventually, the status commission proposed the celebration of a plebiscite, which was held on July 23, 1967. The ELA received 60.4 percent of the vote to statehood's 39 percent. The *independentistas* boycotted the plebiscite, arguing that it did not constitute a true process of self-determination, since its results would not be binding on Congress, which thus retained the power to determine what to do with Puerto Rico.

Despite the 1967 plebiscite victory, growing frustration within the PPD due to the lack of progress on the status question and the persistent control of the old guard aggravated internal tensions. Early indications of discontent had emerged as early as 1959, when some voices began to question what they felt was the loss of the social reform orientation that had originally inspired the PPD.[1] By 1964, discontent was spreading to wider sectors. Economist Jenaro

Baquero, for example, criticized over-reliance on foreign capital.[2] In June, the growing differences blew open when twenty-two members of the reform sector called on PPD committees to exercise their right to renew the party's candidates for the coming elections. Meanwhile, a more impatient wing, led by Gerardo Navas, José Santori, Noel Colón, and others, organized Vanguardia Popular in April 1964. They warned that the PPD had to make major adjustments to meet the challenge of the statehood movement. It had to abandon its one-sided emphasis on permanent union with the United States and its reluctance to consider wider forms of autonomy.[3]

In 1964, partly in response to the calls for renewal, Muñoz Marín declined to run for governor, but he remained the dominant figure in the PPD. He designated Roberto Sánchez Vilella as his successor, who was elected governor in November. Sánchez Vilella had the support of the reformers, some of whom—Baquero, for example—were made part of his administration. Sánchez Vilella soon ran into conflict with sectors of the PPD machine. Tensions grew, even if Sánchez Vilella stuck to the PPD's existing political and economic orientation (pursuing the attempt to shift the axis of Operation Bootstrap from light to heavy industry, centered on oil refining and petrochemical plants). At the same time, Vanguardia Popular was moving left. In 1965, it opposed the U.S. intervention in Santo Domingo as well as the draft of Puerto Ricans into the U.S. Army. In 1967, it called for a boycott of the plebiscite held that year, as a result of which it was expelled from the PPD.

By the summer of 1968, Sánchez Vilella, denied renomination by the PPD, opted to run for governor against the candidate chosen by the PPD. The division of the PPD opened the path to its defeat in the 1968 elections by a new statehood party: the Partido Nuevo Progresista (PNP), whose main leader, industrialist Luis A. Ferré, was elected governor. A chain of almost three decades of uninterrupted PPD victories had been broken, even if the party retained control of the Senate and thus the ability to hinder Ferré's initiatives.

The PNP was itself the product of the parallel division of the statehood movement, provoked by the 1967 status plebiscite. That year a majority of the leaders of the pro-statehood Partido Estadista Republicano had opted to boycott the plebiscite. A group led by Ferré disagreed. They organized Estadistas Unidos to participate in the plebiscite, and the group became the nucleus of the PNP.

The growth of the statehood movement had been a visible trend since the mid-1950s. The statehooders' share of the vote had steadily grown from 12.9 percent in 1952 to 34.7 in 1964. While statehood gathered support from diverse sectors, most analysts agree that it benefited considerably from the consolidation of a relatively well-off salaried, professional, and entrepreneurial group whose income level allowed it to think of itself as a "middle class." The group's material aspirations and forms of consumption and leisure resembled and were modeled on their North American, largely suburban, automobile-centered counterparts. Moving in the orbit of the "American way of life" at its most prosperous and self-confident, often working for U.S. corporations or the federal government, this sector was receptive to the PNP statehood message.[4] The triumph of the Cuban Revolution of 1959—in opposition to many of the ideals this group had come to embrace—and the emergence of new radical sectors in Puerto Rico enhanced statehooders' insecurities and their desire for protection through association with the United States.

But the PNP could hardly win with the votes of the better-off alone. The PNP was able to exploit the fact that Puerto Rico's living standard was both higher than that of neighboring independent countries and lower than that of even the poorest state of the Union. While the former consideration acted as an argument against independence, the second allowed for an association of statehood with improved living standards.

But in 1972, the PPD was able to retake the governor's mansion. In other words, the consolidation of the PNP as an equal partner/opponent of the PPD was to occur in the 1970s in a deeply changed economic climate. We will explore these developments in chapter 13. In 1968, the first PNP administration, curbed by its lack of control of the legislature, had to contend not only with PPD legislative obstruction but also with a renewed and militant independence movement, whose relatively small size was partly compensated by its influence in a diverse array of emergent labor and social movements.

La Nueva Lucha, 1959–1975

By the late 1950s the independence movement was much reduced in numbers, but initiatives were not lacking. Three were particularly significant: the creation of the Federación de Universitarios Pro Independencia in 1956 and the launching of the Movimiento Pro Independencia (MPI) and of the newspaper *Claridad*, both in 1959. The MPI was initiated by veteran *independentistas*, including Juan Mari Brás, Lorenzo Piñero, Carmen Rivera de Alvarado, and César Andreu Iglesias, as well as by younger activists dissatisfied with the existing *independentista* organizations. Returning to Puerto Rico after four decades in New York, socialist activist Bernardo Vega became the MPI's secretary of organization in 1961.[5] These initiatives soon acquired a dynamic point of reference in the Cuban Revolution, which provided an example of vibrant anti-imperialism and socialism in a country culturally and historically linked to Puerto Rico. A radicalized *independentismo* now entered a period of quantitative growth, increased visibility, and ideological redefinition.

The MPI dedicated much effort to denounce U.S. rule internationally, seeking to reopen the case of Puerto Rico at the United Nations. In 1960, the U.N. General Assembly, which by then included a growing number of former colonies, formulated several resolutions on colonialism. This opened the possibility of a return of Puerto Rico to the U.N. agenda. By 1972, the *independentistas* obtained what was at least a symbolic victory when the U.N.'s Decolonization Committee decided to begin hearings on the situation in Puerto Rico. While no practical actions were taken as a result, the U.S. State Department was forced to maneuver diplomatically regarding Puerto Rico in a manner that had not been necessary since the 1950s.

Both the MPI and the more moderate Partido Independentista Puertorriqueño faced constant harassment by federal agencies.[6] Aggressive tactics were used, for example, to disrupt the campaign to boycott the 1967 plebiscite. Letters were sent in the name of nonexistent organizations such as "Committee against the Foreign Domination of the Struggle for Independence" calling on *independentistas* to vote and accusing their leaders of being under the control of the Cuban government.[7] In 1987, it was officially confirmed that for three decades, the intelligence division of the insular police had kept files on thousands of *independentistas*. The *carpetas*, as the files were known, demonstrated a systematic pattern of vigilance and harassment of *independentista* groups.

Still, through its participation in labor, student, and other struggles, the MPI grew in size and influence. The march of some 20,000–30,000 in September 1971 on the occasion of a U.S. governors' conference in Puerto Rico was a clear expression of the rise of the new independence movement. This growth coincided with an ideological shift. The MPI, which at first labeled itself a "patriotic vanguard," by 1969 adopted Marxism-Leninism as its "guide to action" and in November 1971 reconstituted itself as the Partido Socialista Puertorriqueño (PSP). A significant politico-cultural milieu emerged around it and its newspaper, *Claridad*. At its height in November 1975, the PSP was able to hold a 10,000-strong congress in San Juan's largest indoor venue, the Coliseo Roberto Clemente. By 1977–78, the party could claim considerable influence in key labor unions (power, education, telephone, university, and oil and petrochemical workers, among others).

Juan Mari Brás (left), leader of the MPI/PSP, and Rubén Berríos, leader of the PIP, in the early 1970s. Both were key figures in the rise of the new independence movement at the time. (Proyecto digitalización fotos El Mundo–Biblioteca José M. Lázaro, Universidad de Puerto Rico–Río Piedras)

Meanwhile, the PIP went through a transformation of its own. After the death of party founder Gilberto Concepción de Gracia in 1968, a new generation of PIP activists, led by Rubén Berríos, pushed the party away from its Christian Democratic leanings. Berríos argued that Puerto Rico's ills were the result both of colonialism and of capitalism. Independence was necessary but not sufficient; socialist reforms were equally urgent. In 1972, the PIP doubled its votes in the general elections, and Berríos was elected to the Senate. But tensions simmered within the PIP between Berríos and the party's Left, known as the *terceristas*. The Left espoused diverse versions of Marxism. Berríos defended his vision of the PIP as "democratic socialist," which he and his followers saw as a left, but non-Marxist, alternative to traditional social-democracy.[8]

The PIP's economic project included the promotion of import substitution combined with the extension of the state sector and redistributive policies to reduce social inequalities. Foreign capital would be sought, but strict controls would be enforced, requiring more reinvestment of profits in Puerto Rico. The PIP's program failed to explain how it would respond if such policies generated a hostile reaction from U.S. corporations or government. The *terceristas* felt that carrying out such a program would require mass mobilization to confront inevitable sabotage and aggression by its internal and external opponents. Moreover, obtaining support for such a program required making the organization of the working class the axis of the party's activity.

By 1973, *terceristas* and other dissidents were expelled from the PIP. Some joined the PSP, while others created new organizations, such as the Movimiento Socialista Popular, identified with the Latin American non-Stalinist revolutionary Left. But all *independentista* organizations remained numerically small and weak in electoral terms. The PIP obtained close to 70,000 or 5.4 percent of the votes in the 1972 elections. The impact and visibility of *independentista* parties was largely due to their significant role in the rising social and labor mobilizations of the time.

New Social Movements, 1965–1975

Internationally, the 1960s witnessed the rise of mass student movements from Mexico to Prague, Paris, and the campuses of the United States. Puerto Rico was no exception. As in other countries, the movement had the authoritarian structure of the university as one of its immediate targets. Since the student strike of 1948, the University of Puerto Rico had been pacified under the direction of Rector Jaime Benítez. The budding student movement now demanded a new university law, which its leaders hoped would create a more democratic UPR.

As in the United States, the student movement also grew around the opposition to the Vietnam War, the draft, and the presence of the U.S. military on campus, especially the Reserve Officers Training Corps (ROTC). Hundreds of pickets, marches, forums, and concerts were organized around these and related issues. Needless to say, in Puerto Rico the issue of recruitment to the U.S. armed forces raised the problem of the island's relation to the United States. Rejection of the draft often led to denunciations of colonialism.[9] Beyond opposition to U.S. intervention in Vietnam and support for independence, the fact that island youths were being drafted into the U.S. armed forces while island residents had no representation in Congress or vote in presidential elections struck many as incompatible with one of the classic tenets of U.S. democracy: the principle of "no taxation without representation." The draft was often denounced as a blood tax, unfairly imposed on Puerto Rico.

Beginning in October 1964, with the first on-campus marches since 1948, the movement against the ROTC intensified. A new university law approved in 1966 by a PPD legislature and the appointment of a more tolerant rector, Abraham Díaz González, stimulated student activism. Serious clashes ensued as pro-statehood groups mobilized in response to attacks on symbols of U.S. presence. In May 1967, students and members of the *independentista* Federación de Universitarios Pro Independencia clashed with ROTC cadets in the Río Piedras campus. In September, confrontations spilled into the streets of Río Piedras. In the process, a bystander—taxi driver Adrián Rodríguez—was killed by a stray bullet. By then, the tensions within the PPD were leading to its division. The processes were not unrelated: the demand for university reform both strengthened and drew support from the reformers within the party, while rejection of student radicals stiffened opposition to reform by the party's conservative wing.

The division of the PPD allowed the PNP to win the elections of 1968. Thus, in 1969 a pro-statehood governor took office just as a growing number of young activists were moving left. It was a recipe for additional confrontations. Student mobilizations reached another high point in September 1969, when protesters partially burned the ROTC installation in Río Piedras. On November 7, further clashes unfolded as statehood militants led by PNP senator Juan A. Palerm attempted to enter the Río Piedras campus and attacked the offices of the MPI. Four months later, on March 4, 1970, new confrontations led to the death of student Antonia Martínez, shot by the police as they chased anti-ROTC protesters. The following day a clandestine *independentista* group killed one U.S. Navy sailor and wounded another in San Juan in response to the death of Martínez. A year later, on March 11, 1971, as the insular police entered the Río Piedras campus, shots fired from within the university killed two police officers and an ROTC cadet. By then the student and antiwar movement had polarized public opinion. It had become a central piece of the Puerto Rican political landscape and a major preoccupation of Governor Ferré.

Along with the student and antiwar movements, additional activist fronts emerged at this time. Foremost among these, at least in terms of its role in reshaping Puerto Rican public debates, was the nascent environmental movement. Some early voices, such as author Enrique Laguerre, had denounced the destructive effects of Operation Bootstrap on Puerto Rico's soil, water, and air.[10] By 1966, Tomás Morales, Arsenio Rodríguez, and José del Castillo issued a "Conservation Manifesto," an initial formulation of environmental awareness. In 1967, the Episcopal Church financed the creation of Misión Industrial, a project that after 1970 was to play a leading role in many environmental struggles. As in the case of the student movement, the growing split within the PPD became a factor in the debates regarding the environment. In 1964, Vanguardia Popular had made public the ongoing secret negotiations with U.S. multinationals interested in obtaining licenses to exploit copper deposits in the central region of the island. Meanwhile, the PPD old guard clung to their longstanding commitment to foreign investment and growth at any cost.

Beginning in 1965, the MPI and Vanguardia Popular, as well as other left organizations, campaigned against the mining concessions. The movement gathered considerable support, including sectors within the PPD leadership and professional organizations. In the end, these mobilizations forced the government to abandon the proposed mining projects.

Overlapping with the new independence, student, and environmental movements, the late 1960s witnessed initiatives to protest the presence of the U.S. Navy in Culebra. The navy had used the island of Culebra for amphibious landing practice since 1923. During World War II, it was incorporated along with Vieques and the Roosevelt Roads base in Ceiba into a vast military complex on the eastern coast of Puerto Rico. In January 1971, dozens of activists occupied navy-held lands in Culebra, and many were arrested, including PIP leader Berríos. Protests continued until President Ford ordered the navy to abandon Culebra in 1975. But the navy then intensified the use of neighboring Vieques as a bombing range. The struggle against the navy in Vieques would continue with ups and downs until its transformation into a mass movement during 1999–2003.

Meanwhile, the late 1960s saw the rise of another form of social protest in the form of land occupations or *rescates*. By the early 1960s, the rapid growth of the urban population, along with the effects of persistent unemployment, had generated a housing crisis.[11] This was the context in which thousands of families took it upon themselves to occupy privately or publicly owned land to build sorely needed homes. Between 1968 and 1976, around 80,000 persons participated in such *rescates*. The Left and *independentista* organizations as well as religious groups influenced by the "theology of liberation" joined, publicized, and supported these actions. In 1972, the Ferré PNP government yielded to the demands of thousands of squatters but not without legislating stiffer fines and jail terms for future actions, a measure that helped weaken the movement after 1972. But *rescates* did not completely disappear. The early 1980s would witness one of the most visible battles by a squatter community—the struggle of Villa Sin Miedo in Río Grande. Similarly, inadequate housing conditions remained a problem for thousands of Puerto Ricans, a fact tragically exemplified by the mud slide that in October 1985 killed at least ninety-four persons in the Mameyes community located in the hilly areas around Ponce.

By the late 1960s, sectors of the labor movement had also begun to stir. Indeed, the years 1969 to 1975 stand out as a period of remobilization within its century-long evolution.

Labor Upsurge, 1969–1975

After the division of the Confederación General del Trabajo in 1945, the union movement had entered a period of fragmentation. The independent CGT, hounded by the PPD, disintegrated. As Operation Bootstrap took off, PPD leaders insisted that labor had to limit its demands. But the emphasis on enticing investors with low wages led the U.S. labor federation, the AFL-CIO, to denounce the island as a haven for runaway plants in 1955.[12]

At this time, several AFL-CIO unions began to organize in Puerto Rico. Prominent among these was the International Ladies Garment Workers' Union (ILGWU). By the end of 1959, it had organized 7,000 or close to 22 percent of garment workers in Puerto Rico. These numbers peaked at 14,000 and close to 40 percent in 1970. As early as 1955, Muñoz Marín had come to an agreement with ILGWU president David Dubinsky. While the latter agreed to tone down his objections to the industrialization program based on relatively low wages, Muñoz Marín agreed not to antagonize ILGWU organizing efforts.

By 1963, twenty-six AFL-CIO unions had moved in and accounted for about two-thirds of Puerto Rico's organized workers. A new ingredient was added by the aggressive tactics of the International Brotherhood of Teamsters, which had been expelled from the AFL-CIO in 1957. Beginning with the strike at the *El imparcial* newspaper in 1960 and led by Mexican American organizer Frank

Chávez and former student leader José Gil de la Madrid, the unruly teamsters faced the opposition of employers, the government, and AFL-CIO unions, such as the Seafarers International Union.

By the late 1960s, calls for reactivation were coming from other quarters as well. The new wave of labor activism began with the strike of 1,200 workers at the General Electrical plant in the area of Palmer in Río Grande from October 1969 to July 1970. Workers confronted repeated acts of police aggression but were supported by *independentista* activists as well as the surrounding community, which joined them in mass pickets and marches.

Joint initiatives by several unions in support of the Palmer strike led to the creation in 1971 of the Movimiento Obrero Unido (MOU). Between 1971 and 1974, the MOU was the most visible coordinating effort of the new wave of labor activism, which at first included both independent unions and locals of the AFL-CIO. The two main promoters of the MOU were Pedro Grant, PSP militant and leader of the International Brotherhood of Boilermakers, and Peter Huegel of the Amalgamated Meatcutters Union.

MOU raised issues that were of interest not only to unions but also to the working class as a whole, such as the rising cost of living. It played a central role in supporting the seven-month strike in 1972 at *El Mundo*, Puerto Rico's largest newspaper, a key labor battle of the early 1970s. The conflict was marked by violent clashes between strikers and the police. Strikebreakers were transported and supplied by five helicopters that on February 12 were partially destroyed by bombs placed by an *independentista* clandestine organization. These events were the more spectacular aspects of a wider swell of activism. By 1972, Governor Ferré was replaced by PPD governor Rafael Hernández Colón, while the wave of labor actions continued unabated. In July 1973, the new governor mobilized the National Guard in response to simultaneous strikes by electrical-power workers, firemen, and garbage collectors of San Juan. Strike activity peaked in 1974 when almost 40,000 workers were involved in strikes, including teachers of the public school system, university nonteaching staff, and the employees of the water services agency.[13] Some important labor battles occurred in the private sector, such as the violent 1975 strike at Puerto Rican Cement, owned by former governor Ferré. But these proved to be the tail end of the wave of labor militancy that we have traced from the Palmer strike in 1969.

In 1974, the international recession hit the Puerto Rican economy with devastating effect. Unemployment rose appreciably, a fact that probably had a dampening impact on labor activism. But the policies of the Left also contributed to the meager organizational harvest of these hard-fought labor battles.

Electric system workers who were members of UTIER in a picket line in front of a power station during a protest in the mid-1970s. (Proyecto digitalización fotos El Mundo–Biblioteca José M. Lázaro, Universidad de Puerto Rico–Río Piedras)

Before his departure from the MPI in 1970, veteran activist Andreu Iglesias had pushed for joint actions by all labor organizations, regardless of their international affiliation: such was the road toward class, and eventually anticapitalist, consciousness. Other currents within the MPI-PSP were keener on reducing the influence of U.S. unions through the creation of independent unions.

There were different versions of this perspective, which in some cases corresponded to a socialist impatience with conservative AFL-CIO unions and in others to a nationalist desire to create Puerto Rican unions. Furthermore, many within both currents felt that union leaders should follow party directives. As Pedro Grant recognized later, the PSP almost "functioned as a second government." In 1977, Grant admitted that the push for a labor federation linked to the PSP had led to divisions and the loss of much of what had been achieved after 1969.[14] As had occurred with the division of the CGT in 1945, a major chance to forge a united, democratic, and politically independent labor movement had been lost.

Second-Wave Feminism in Puerto Rico and Other Initiatives

The early 1970s also saw the rise of a new wave of feminist activism, with the creation of the first women's organizations since the suffragist groups of the 1920s. The movement was led by university students and young professionals who had become frustrated with the lack of interest in women's issues exhibited by traditional parties, unions, and even the new left. Journalist Norma Valle would later remember, for example, how she and other women felt marginalized while participating in the 1972 strike at El Mundo.[15] In 1971, the Association of Women Journalists invited U.S. feminist Gloria Steinem to Puerto Rico, a visit that elicited hostile reactions from conservative sectors and served as public notice that a new movement was in the making.

In 1972, women activists organized Mujer Intégrate Ahora (MIA). MIA and individual feminists raised issues that were soon being debated beyond the small circle of activists: discrimination and harassment, restrictive family legislation, contraception and abortion rights, women's sexuality and sexual orientation. There were tensions within the movement between those wishing to link (some argued this in fact meant subordinate) women's demands to other political/social struggles and those favoring a more independent feminist agenda, as well as between those willing to embrace lesbian rights and those worried about fomenting too close a connection in the public mind between feminism and lesbianism. Relations with the Left were close, since many feminists were *independentistas* and/or socialists, but problematical, since left organizations were not consistent in embracing the feminist agenda.

In 1973, abortion, with certain restrictions, became legal in Puerto Rico as a result of the decision of the U.S. Supreme Court in *Roe v. Wade*. Instead of celebrating this as the extension to Puerto Rico of an achievement of the North

American women's movement, prominent *independentista* intellectuals (Bishop Antulio Parrilla, president of the Ateneo Eladio Rodríguez Otero, and Vicente Géigel, among others) denounced it as a colonial imposition. There were variations within this orientation. While some combined it with conservative opposition to contraception and a "hedonist" and "materialist" culture, others warned against such "reactionary" views and denounced instead the alleged role of abortion as a form of colonial population control along with sterilization.[16] Yet neither group was willing to articulate a defense of abortion rights as part of a Puerto Rican struggle for self-determination. Feminists were thus almost alone in defending the legalization of abortion as a step forward for Puerto Rican women as well as in defending the legitimacy of feminism against those who saw it as a North American intrusion.[17]

Meanwhile, in 1973 gay and lesbian activists formed Puerto Rico's first gay organization, which in 1974 adopted the name Colectivo Orgullo Gay (COG). COG had a brief but fruitful life, which included the issuing of the journal *Pa'fuera*. The emergence of a gay activism was prompted by the push to demand the elimination of antigay statutes (prohibiting "contra natura" acts) as part of the revision of the penal code in progress at the time. The prohibitions were nevertheless retained and were repealed only in 2003.[18] Most left groups ignored gay struggles or held homophobic views, but there were exceptions. During the late 1970s, the Trotskyist Liga Internacionalista de los Trabajadores consistently raised the issue as part of its agenda.

Both MIA and COG, as well as other new labor and left organizations, went into decline in the late 1970s. The pioneer feminist groups were to be replaced by small but persistent collectives such as Taller Salud and the Organización Puertorriqueña de la Mujer Trabajadora, among others. Through the 1980s, the gay movement began to revive around the demand for an adequate government response to AIDS (the first case in Puerto Rico was diagnosed in 1982). As in other countries, the struggle for visibility included the organization of annual Gay Pride parades, the first of which was held in 1990. Through the 1990s, both feminist and gay activists had to face the backlash of conservative religious groups, which on the model of the North American New Right actively campaigned against abortion and gay rights.

Puerto Rican gay activism also emerged in the United States. Puerto Rican transvestite Ray "Silvia" Rivera was an important participant in the 1969 Stonewall riots, the initial flash point of the struggle for gay rights. Rivera was active in other pioneering initiatives such as STAR (Street Transvestite Action Revolutionaries) and the Gay Liberation Front.[19] In 1977, literary critic and

Socialist Efraín Barradas created Acción Socialista Pro-Educación Gay as part of the PSP activities in the United States. Puerto Rican gays in the United States faced the double task of demanding recognition as Puerto Ricans in a largely white gay movement and as gays in a historically homophobic Puerto Rican culture.[20] In 1978, the Comité Homosexual Latino tried to participate in the Puerto Rican Day parade but was unable to complete the route due to constant and violent harassment. A gay contingent gained a stable foothold in this highly symbolic parade only in 1989.

The impact of the relatively small feminist and gay organizations should not be underestimated. Through their efforts, women's issues as well as questions of reproductive and sexual orientation acquired an unprecedented visibility in Puerto Rico. A similar judgment is warranted regarding the impact of student, environmental, labor, and community activism of the late 1960s and early 1970s. The concerns expressed by such groups regarding a long series of related issues (such as growing air and water pollution, over-reliance on the automobile, unplanned suburban expansion, land speculation, housing shortages for the poor, destruction of agriculture, growing reliance on food imports, subservience to U.S. corporations, the potential giveaway and environmental misuse of mineral resources, persistent low wages and tax exemptions to large investors, and lack of government resources to finance adequate services) amounted to a many-sided questioning of the PPD's model of economic development since the launching of Operation Bootstrap. While those indictments remained a fragmented critique, like the movements that sustained them, they still implied a significant shift away from the consensus regarding the blessings of progress in its existing forms.

But the rise of new activist currents on the island was not the only means through which Puerto Ricans worked their way onto the map of the worldwide labor and social mobilizations of the late 1960s and early 1970s. The 1960s was a period of emergent movements and struggles of oppressed peoples in the United States. Puerto Rican communities in New York, Chicago, Philadelphia, and other cities were active participants in these upheavals. The mobilizations on the island in 1965–75 thus coincided with the rise of a new Puerto Rican social and political activism in the United States.

New Activism in New York and Beyond

Most Puerto Ricans arriving in the United States were wage-laborers. They suffered diverse forms of discrimination by state officials (from welfare bureaucrats to police officers), employers, and landlords. Against that background, four basic distinct forms of Puerto Rican political and public intervention and activism emerged through the 1960s and early 1970s: (1) the creation of "self-help" and/or advocacy organizations, largely committed to middle-class values of social advancement; (2) integration into mainstream politics within the existing (largely Democratic Party) electoral machines; (3) the launching of nonprofit, often federally funded community projects designed to address housing, health, education, recreation, drug rehabilitation, and other needs; and (4) the creation of radical activist organizations and mobilizations. These currents and initiatives did not evolve independently of each other but rather interacted in complex ways while over the years individuals migrated from one sphere of activity to another.

In New York in 1956, activist Gilberto Gerena Valentín and others formed the Congreso de los Pueblos with the objective of fostering the creation of hometown associations as a first step toward organizing Puerto Ricans in the city. Gerena Valentín had come to New York in 1936 and had been active with Vito Marcantonio's American Labor Party. He had worked, for example, along with Communist Juan Emmanuelli organizing tenants to resist abuses by landlords (including direct actions to stop evictions). An experienced union organizer, he had been expelled in 1951 from the Hotel and Club Employees Union because of his identification with the Left. Most members of the associations created by the Congreso were working-class people, women garment workers being the largest group.[21] The Congreso was instrumental in launching what became the most visible ceremony of Puerto Rican affirmation in New York City: the Puerto Rican Day parade, first held in 1958. The activity was of course modeled on the existing patterns of "ethnic" affirmation in the United States, such as the Irish St. Patrick's Day parade.

This initiative roughly coincided with the creation of the Puerto Rican–Hispanic Leadership Forum in 1957 (which later changed its name to Puerto Rican Forum) and ASPIRA in 1961. ASPIRA was led by Antonia Pantoja, probably the best-known Puerto Rican community activist in this period. Her memoirs, like those of New York socialist activists Jesús Colón and Bernardo Vega, include an evocation, through the figure of her grandfather, of the world of the early-twentieth-century cigarmakers, further testimony to the lasting impact of that sector of the early labor movement in Puerto Rico. Her narrative moves on to her arrival in New York in the mid-1940s, her growing consciousness of racism in Puerto Rican culture, her studies in the Communist Party–sponsored Jefferson school, and the launching of the Puerto Rican–Hispanic

A meeting of ASPIRA in 1965. Created as a counseling service to promote the educational progress of Puerto Rican students, ASPIRA became one of the best-known community self-help efforts among Puerto Ricans in the United States. (Proyecto digitalización fotos El Mundo–Biblioteca José M. Lázaro, Universidad de Puerto Rico–Río Piedras)

Leaderhip Forum. The Forum and ASPIRA were consciously modeled on the National Association for the Advancement of Colored People, the Urban League, and the American Jewish Congress.[22] Their implicit objective was the promotion of a liberal professional Puerto Rican middle class committed to the further advancement of Puerto Ricans within the existing political and economic structures. ASPIRA was created as a bilingual counseling service that sought to reduce school dropout rates among Puerto Ricans and enable a growing number to enter college.

While not radical, ASPIRA took exception to official insular government views. It insisted that the insular government should stop claiming to represent Puerto Ricans in the United States. As opposed to the ELA government's policy of avoiding controversy, it emphatically denounced the many forms of discrimination faced by Puerto Ricans. It favored the institution of bilingual education in schools and the creation of university-level programs of Puerto Rican studies. In 1972, ASPIRA was among those suing the New York City Board of Education for not providing adequate services for Spanish speaking students. The suit led to the ASPIRA consent decree of 1974, which mandated that bilingual education be provided for Spanish-speaking students.

Meanwhile, by the early 1960s, major parties could hardly ignore the sizable Puerto Rican community. In 1962, New York City mayor Robert Wagner named Herman Badillo, a member of the Puerto Rican–Hispanic Leadership Forum, as Commissioner of Relocation (in charge of relocating poor families to housing projects). In 1965, Badillo, by then the most prominent Puerto Rican political player in the city, won the presidency of the borough of the Bronx. In 1970, he became the first Puerto Rican elected to Congress.[23]

By the late 1960s, the federal programs launched by the Johnson administration, known as the War on Poverty, created the basis for new institutional and funding links between the federal government and ethnically defined community organizers in the inner cities. This created the context for the emergence of federally funded community projects led and/or staffed by Puerto Ricans. The need for these initiatives was documented by the study entitled the *Puerto Rican Community Development Project* (PRCDP), a near equivalent of the Plan Chardón on the island during the New Deal. The PRCDP had been initiated by the Puerto Rican Forum. The document demonstrated that Puerto Ricans "are not making it once they learn English."[24] Most Puerto Ricans remained trapped in low-paying jobs and lived in decaying and crowded buildings while the Puerto Rican community as a whole exhibited low levels of educational attainment and high rates of unemployment. These problems reinforced each other as low wages led to conditions that hindered educational pursuit, which in turn limited access to better-paying positions. In the context of the expansion of federal antipoverty programs, the document proposed the creation of a citywide development project to promote varied self-help community efforts, largely staffed by Puerto Ricans.

The question of Puerto Rican identity played a central but ambiguous role in the proposal elaborated by the Puerto Rican Forum. On the one hand, it asserted quite explicitly that its objective was the "acculturation" and "integration" of Puerto Ricans into American life through the elevation of an increasing number to a middle-class status. It presented as a model what it described as the passage of other ethnic groups (and in particular Jews) from the ghetto, through a "guilded ghetto" (as they improved their living standards), to eventual migration to the suburbs "to be like any other American."[25] Yet, while at times suggesting the future integration of the more prosperous Puerto

Ricans into the suburban middle class, the project also emphasized that the key means to Puerto Rican self-reliance and material advance was the assertion of Puerto Rican pride and identity. Differences soon emerged among the many participants in the preparation of this project. The Puerto Rican Forum itself pulled out, dissatisfied with the adoption of what it felt was a top-down bureaucratic structure.

But the antipoverty initiatives of the Johnson administration were soon overtaken by the urban rebellions of the time. The years 1964 to 1968 witnessed major urban riots or uprisings in most major cities in the Northeast, Midwest, and California. Whereas on the island the embracing of the slogan of "black power" by the Student Non-violent Coordinating Committee and the emergence of the Black Panther Party were distant stimulants, within the Puerto Rican communities in the United States the impact of this radicalization of the struggle against racial oppression was more direct. Indeed, counterposed to the model of moderate "ethnic associations" and ethnic politics based on the time-tested pattern of U.S. politics, a new street-wise and direct action Puerto Rican activism emerged in the late 1960s.[26]

The first explosion occurred not in New York but in Chicago. The Puerto Rican population of Chicago had grown over the years to approximately 80,000 by 1970. Its original nucleus had been formed during the postwar economic expansion by male steel-mill workers and female domestic laborers. By the late 1960s, the Logan Square, Humboldt Park, and West Town neighborhoods had acquired a distinct Puerto Rican imprint.[27]

In the summer of 1966, the killing of Puerto Rican youth Aracelis Báez by the Chicago police led to three days of rioting, remembered as the Division Street Uprising. These protests accelerated the politicization of the Young Lords street gang, led by José "Cha Cha" Jiménez. The Chicago Young Lords joined the Black Panthers and other groups in community initiatives and protest actions. Other more moderate vehicles of political intervention also emerged. The city directed federal funds to create War on Poverty programs incorporating community leaders, or, as radical critics claimed, co-opting and neutralizing them. Others created the Spanish Action Committee of Chicago and Latin American Development Organization with an orientation similar to that of ASPIRA or the PRCDP in New York City.

By the early 1970s, many Puerto Ricans mobilized around what was to be a political battleground in Puerto Rican Chicago for the next two decades: the policies and curriculum of the high school serving the largely Puerto Rican areas. Activists demanded that Tuley High School adopt a profile in tune with its largely Puerto Rican student body. This battle was initially successful. School installations were renovated, and it was renamed Roberto Clemente High School in memory of the Puerto Rican Major League Baseball star killed in a plane crash in 1972 while on a relief mission to Nicaragua.

Meanwhile, the Young Lords Organization had acquired a New York branch. The latter came out of the Sociedad Albizu Campos. Organized in 1969 and named after Puerto Rico's Nationalist leader, it had a stronger student component than its Chicago counterpart. These young activists, including Felipe Luciano, Juan González, Pablo Guzmán, and Miguel Meléndez, were active in the antiwar and other student mobilizations of the time. By 1970, the New York group separated from Chicago and became the Young Lords Party.

The Lords embraced the ideas of Third World anticolonialism and socialism, mixing the example of the Black Panthers with the ideas of Frantz Fanon's anticolonial classic *The Wretched of the Earth*, Ernesto Guevara's "Socialism and Man in Cuba," and the writings of Mao Tse-tung. The Young Lords were active not only in New York City but also in Newark, Bridgeport, Philadelphia, Boston, and Detroit and attracted Puerto Ricans in the military and in prisons. By the early 1970s, the group had close to a thousand members, but its influence reached much further. The Lords staged marches and sit-ins, blocked streets, and organized community actions, raising issues such as garbage collection, inadequate health services, lead poisoning, police harassment, abuses by landlords, and the right to bilingual education. They published the tabloid *Palante* and sent a strong and defiant message that the "spics" were very much upset at the way the American Dream had turned out for them. Among their more spectacular actions, attracting wide media attention, were the eleven-day takeover of the First Spanish Methodist Church of East Harlem, the commandeering of a Department of Health X-ray truck to provide services in El Barrio, and the occupation of the Lincoln Hospital School of Nursing in the Bronx to demand adequate health installations.

Student activism also played a role in the new Puerto Rican movement in New York. The Puerto Rican Student Union (PRSU) arose in the City University of New York system. In 1969, the PRSU fought, along with the rest of a largely nonwhite student movement, for an open admissions policy and for the creation of Puerto Rican studies programs, among other measures. Puerto Rican enrollments at the university skyrocketed from 5,425 in 1969 to 16,352 in 1974, largely as a result of the open admissions policy attained through student activism.[28] Both the Young Lords and the PRSU took a stand in favor of the independence of Puerto Rico. In October 1970 (in commemoration of the Nationalist uprising of 1950), both groups led a 10,000-strong march to the U.N. headquarters to demand an end to Puerto Rico's colonial status.

The early 1970s also witnessed significant organizing efforts among Puerto Rican agricultural workers, above all in Connecticut. Misión Industrial, an organization sponsored by the Episcopal Church and active in island environmental struggles, created the Comité de Apoyo del Migrante Puertorriqueño, while PSP militants and other activists organized the Asociación de Trabajadores Agrícolas (ATA). ATA defied harassment and threats by employers to reach farm workers and objected to the ELA government's claim to represent Puerto Rican workers in relation to employers in the United States. ATA lost vitality by 1975 but helped lay an important basis for Puerto Rican activism in the state and in the city of Hartford in particular.[29]

After 1972, both the Young Lords and the PRSU went into rapid decline, the former becoming an isolated Maoist sect. The new activism continued, nevertheless, embodied in diverse groups, such as the Movimiento de Izquierda Nacional Puertorriqueña (MINP) and the U.S. branch of the island-based PSP. The MINP, led by Noel Colón, Iris Velgara, Esperanza Martell, Americo Badillo, Frank Velgara, and Federico Lora, among others, grew out of El Comité that led the struggle against the replacement of low-income housing with expensive high-rises in the Upper West Side of Manhattan. By 1975, El Comité decided to become a party-like socialist organization—the MINP.

On the island, the MPI, which in 1971 became the PSP, gave considerable importance to the creation of a foothold in the United States. In 1973, more than 3,000 supporters participated in the founding of its New York branch. The party soon had groups active in New Jersey and in cities such as Hartford, New Haven, Boston, Worcester, Philadelphia, and Chicago.

But the PSP and the MINP analyzed the situation of the Puerto Rican diaspora differently. The PSP's general declaration on this was marked by an island-centered orientation, resistant to an acknowledgment of the particular situation of Puerto Ricans in the United States. While it denounced the problems faced by Puerto Ricans in the United States, it emphasized the struggle against the "assimilation" of the Puerto Rican nation, which, it argued, could be stopped only through independence. Attaining that goal should be the priority of all Puerto Ricans.[30] This orientation led it to emphasize the organization of actions such as the National Day of Solidarity with the Independence of Puerto Rico (October 27, 1974), which brought around 20,000 to New York's

Madison Square Garden. While impressive in terms of the number of participants, critics felt these efforts did little to promote the struggles of Puerto
Ricans in the United States.

In contrast, the MINP saw Puerto Rican struggles in the United States as part
of what it hoped would become an anticapitalist movement of a multiracial/
national North American working class.[31] Puerto Rican activists had to build
an internationalist anticapitalist movement in the United States in collaboration with all oppressed sectors. The debate at times took the form of some
activists defending the notion that Puerto Rico was a "divided nation," while
others argued that Puerto Ricans in the United States constituted a distinct
"national minority" within the North American social formation.

Nevertheless, in spite of their initial impact, neither the PSP nor the MINP
lived up to its promise. The PSP (as we explore in chapter 13) went into a
growing crisis on the island after 1976. Its U.S. branches also went into decline.
The MINP broke up in 1981 as a result of internal disputes, linked to differences
regarding the weight that Puerto Rican issues or general working-class concerns should be given in the organization's work. Thus, not unlike what occurred on the island, by the early 1980s much of the new U.S. Puerto Rican Left
had gone into recession, but not without leaving its mark on the way Puerto
Ricans in the United States were seen by others (both non–Puerto Ricans and
Puerto Ricans on the island) and how they saw themselves.

Meanwhile, as the 1970s progressed, tension brewed in Puerto Rican Chicago.
Humboldt Park, one of the neighborhoods heavily populated by Puerto Ricans,
was the site of an epidemic of arson fires as landlords sought to remove low-
income tenants and to profit from the elimination of run-down structures.
Frustration with official inaction led to riots in the summer of 1977. Community and political activism around this time included the creation of the pro-
independence Movimiento de Liberación Nacional in 1977 and its support for
initiatives such as the Puerto Rico Cultural Center and the Pedro Albizu
Campos High School. A few years earlier, in 1974, supporters of independence in
Chicago organized the Fuerzas Armadas de Liberación Nacional (FALN), a clandestine organization. Like other groups of the American new Left moving in the
same direction (such as the wing of the Students for a Democratic Society
turned Weathermen), the FALN sought to "bring the war home," placing bombs
in government and corporate offices. We explore these actions in chapter 13.

On a smaller scale, Puerto Rican activism in Philadelphia, where the third-
largest Puerto Rican community in the United States was located (close to
25,000 in 1970), exhibited the same differentiation as in New York and Chicago:

ethnic associations/advocacy groups, publicly funded agencies, mainstream party-politics, and radical activism. Some of these modalities were embodied in diverse stages of the evolution of the Concilio de Organizaciones Hispanas (COH) organized in 1962. Initially a social club, the COH evolved into an advocacy coalition involved in housing and other issues. It helped initiate the Puerto Rican Day parade in Philadelphia, first held in 1964. In 1968 funds from the Philadelphia Anti-poverty Action Commission fostered its change into a community service agency. Its leaders tended to favor Puerto Rican political activism in the Democratic Party machine. Parallel to these efforts, both ASPIRA and the Young Lords came to Philadelphia in 1969 and 1970 respectively. According to Carmen T. Whalen, if the Chicago Lords emerged out of a street gang and the New York branch from the student movement, the Philadelphia group had considerable affinity with progressive Catholic currents.[32] As in other cities, the Young Lords organized both protests and community actions, such as breakfast programs and child care services. In 1979, former Young Lord and PSP activists who opposed the support by other Puerto Rican organizations of Philadelphia major Frank Rizzo created the Puerto Rican Alliance. The Alliance sought to combine community mobilizations and electoral politics. During the 1980s, it ran candidates for the city and state assemblies while also leading sit-ins, marches, and other protests. But in general, by the late 1970s the wave of Puerto Rican activism was on the wane.

End of an Era

The generalized recession of 1973–74, ecompassing both the United State and Europe, had an immediate impact on Puerto Rico and the metropolitan areas where Puerto Ricans had settled during the postwar boom. As the Puerto Rican economy failed to grow for the first time in decades, Puerto Ricans were also hit by layoffs in New York, Chicago, Philadelphia, and other cities' manufacturing sectors. In Puerto Rico, the recession wrecked the PPD administration of Governor Hernández Colón.

In 1972, it will be remembered, after four conflictive years, PNP governor Ferré had lost his bid for reelection. Initially, the incoming Hernández Colón administration still hoped to pursue the more ambitious phase of Operation Bootstrap: the construction of an oil-processing complex including refineries, petrochemical plants, satellite industries, and a deep-water port facility (the *superpuerto*) on the west coast of Puerto Rico. Environmental groups, such as Misión Industrial, and *independentista* organizations generated a wide opposition to the projected *superpuerto*. Moreover, in 1973–74, Governor Hernández Colón was confronted with new eruptions of labor militancy, mentioned above, largely among public sector employees.

Then the international economic slump hit with full force. For the first time in more than three decades, the Puerto Rican economy failed to grow. By January 1976, unemployment passed the 20 percent mark. One of the historically specific aspects of the 1974–75 recession—the oil-embargo imposed on the United States by the Arab oil-exporting states and its reverberations through the international oil industry, combined with environmentalist opposition in Puerto Rico—pushed the Hernández Colón administration to abandon the proposed *superpuerto*, a prelude to the demise by the early 1980s of the once-grandiose petrochemical project. The golden era of Operation Bootstrap was now definitely over.

Meanwhile, the ever-present status question was to be another source of frustration for the Hernández Colón administration. Pursuing what it considered had been the mandate of the 1967 status plebiscite, Governor Hernández Colón convinced the Nixon administration to create an ad hoc committee with members named by the federal and ELA governments to study possible changes to the existing status. It formulated the proposal for a "New Compact of Permanent Union."[33]

The "New Compact" would have exempted Puerto Rico from federal wage and environmental regulations while giving it a role in the negotiation of commercial agreements that could affect it. Federal legislation would not apply to Puerto Rico unless explicitly extended by Congress, and the Puerto Rican government could formally petition Congress to exempt the island from proposed legislation. A joint commission would be named to oversee the transfer of selected federal operations to insular hands.

But even this rather limited reform, which barely suggested a path to an attenuation of federal control of many areas of insular life, was not to be. The Ford administration had taken no action on it by the time of the 1976 elections, which the PPD lost. In a further blow to the PPD, President Ford, who had also lost his bid for the presidency, rejected the "New Compact" proposal as constitutionally unviable and politically unworkable. Then, as one of his last actions in office, he issued a statement proposing that Congress and Puerto Rico "begin now to take steps which will result in statehood."[34]

The stage was thus set for a major offensive by the statehood movement, now headed, in a changed economic context, by Governor-elect Carlos Romero Barceló.

RETHINKING THE PAST, BETTING ON THE FUTURE: CULTURAL DEBATES FROM THE SIXTIES TO THE EIGHTIES

The rise of new student, labor, antiwar, environmental, and independence currents in the late 1960s and the economic sea change of the early 1970s had their counterpart within the long-running debate on Puerto Rico's history and identity. In a manner reminiscent of the rise of the *generación del treinta* in the context of the Great Depression, a new cohort of historians, social scientists, and artists now sought to remake the inherited visions of the past, offer new analyses of the present, and renew literary and artistic expressions and discourse. A salient aspect of the new literary wave was the participation of women in leading and prominent roles and in unprecedented numbers. Furthermore, this was the moment of the "Nuyorican explosion" as the children of the postwar mass migration came of age in the midst of persistent poverty and discrimination and in a period of mobilization and unrest in North American inner cities. Mixing English and Spanish, asserting their identity and denouncing racism, Nuyorican poets and historians now challenged not only white American but also Puerto Rican island-centered representations of migrants as demoralized cultural hybrids. Varied as these efforts were, most of them shared a newfound passion for history from below; an enthusiasm for popular struggles, culture, and language; and a desire to pose class, racial, and gender issues largely overlooked by both official culture and its fundamentally nationalist-*independentista* critics of the past.

Opposition to U.S. intervention in Vietnam soon became a unifying focus of diverse challenges to the structures often described by this insurgent sensibility as the "establishment," a word that soon made its way into Puerto Rican Spanish. The influence of the Cuban Revolution was equally significant, and it was not only political. The refreshingly undogmatic revolution (perhaps best represented by the admired figure of Argentinean revolutionary Ernesto

Guevara) also created new cultural reference points through such institutions as the literary center Casa de las Américas, the work of its graphic artists and filmmakers, and the rise of the new song movement, as well as through the formulations of new literary visions of Latin American unity.

This coincided with the international success of a new generation of Latin American authors, known in Latin America as *el boom*. Aspiring young Puerto Rican writers thus felt the urge to join what was perceived as a continental upsurge of cultural renewal and political resistance. Authors of the international new Left also had an impact: Herbert Marcuse as a critic of the "American way of life" and consumer society and Frantz Fanon as a theorist of colonial mentality and of decolonization, to mention two prominent examples.

The journal *La escalera* (1966–73) was an early vehicle of new critical views. It was sustained by veteran Marxist César Andreu Iglesias and younger leftists such as Gervasio García, Georg Fromm, Samuel Aponte, Annie Fernández, and resident North American biologist Richard Levins, among others. The journal's name emblematically referred to the ladder used by its founders to address the participants at a teach-in that had been forbidden by the University of Puerto Rico administration. It was within this radicalized milieu that new representations of Puerto Rico's history and identity and a new literary and artistic sensibility emerged in the late 1960s and the 1970s. These newer voices differentiated themselves from their immediate predecessors, who in some cases had also represented an attempt to elaborate nonofficial perspectives or alternative literary orientations beginning in the early 1960s. Political scientists Manuel Maldonado Denis and Gordon K. Lewis and the poets grouped around the journal *Guajana* were the most influential of these transitional figures.

Before the Explosion: Voices from the Early 1960s

Through the late 1960s, the uneven but influential work of Maldonado Denis stood out as a counterpoint to official versions of Puerto Rican history. At a time when many described the latter as a hugely successful process of modernization, he provided a critical reading of U.S. rule, a reminder of the repression used to sideline its opponents and of the shortcomings of Operation Bootstrap. He thus rejected the description of Puerto Rico's transformation as a peaceful "revolution" as well as the theory put forth by Luis Muñoz Marín of an American "dumb imperialism" (*imperialismo bobo*), which had stumbled into an expansionist adventure in 1898. Imperialism, he argued, is an inherent aspect of advanced capitalism, as the historical record of the United States in the Caribbean demonstrated.

Maldonado Denis's perspective can be described as a combination of a typically nationalist problematic, including coincidences with some of the luminaries of the *generación del treinta*, such as Antonio S. Pedreira, with diverse strands of Marxism and anticolonial or anti-imperialist thought. In 1963 he argued, for example, that the destruction of Puerto Rican culture was one of the aims of U.S. colonialism: cultural assimilation, he insisted, is an essential aspect of any colonial project. Puerto Rico was going through a process of "denaturalization" and "hybridization." This perspective led to the vision of the "mixed" culture of the Puerto Rican migrant as the embodiment of the destiny to be avoided. The struggle for independence was "a desperate race to stop the process of cultural assimilation."[1] Intellectuals and students had a key role to play in that struggle against "assimilation" since they were the ones more keenly aware of it. In the counternarrative he constructed to Partido Popular Democrático ideology, it was the autonomism of Luis Muñoz Rivera and Muñoz Marín that repeatedly sabotaged the efforts of patriots such as José De Diego and Pedro Albizu Campos and prevented the attainment of political independence.

It is not difficult to see why the work of Maldonado Denis has been largely forgotten. In our epoch, social thought has learned to valorize hybridity as culturally productive, has recognized the vitality of both Puerto Rican and Nuyorican culture, and is suspicious of the idea of the intellectual as the privileged representative of national culture. But the historian is forced to recognize the impact of Maldonado Denis's work at the time. It would also be unfair to reduce his approach to a repetition of Pedreira's problematic from an *independentista* perspective. Maldonado Denis distanced himself from Pedreira's racial theories as well as from his elitist rejection of "mass society." If he exalted the figure of Albizu Campos, he still criticized his lack of connection with the labor movement. Maldonado Denis furthermore insisted that U.S. civilization could not be reduced to a crude utilitarianism. Well-read in U.S. progressive thought, his articles are peppered with references to U.S. social and economic historians such as C. Wright Mills, William A. Williams, Paul Sweezy, Walter Lafeber, and many others whose contributions to anti-imperialist thought he evidently appreciated.

The other outstanding attempt to reconsider the Puerto Rican past and present at the time was Gordon K. Lewis's 1963 *Puerto Rico: Freedom and Power in the Caribbean*. Ambitious in reach (the author familiarized himself with Puerto

Rican writing to an unprecedented extent for an English-speaking scholar), the text was politically ambiguous. While ostensibly anticolonial, Lewis dismissed the nationalist movement as a version of fascism and painted an admiring portrait of Muñoz Marín. He still hoped for a return to the PPD's original reformist élan. The book was in that sense compatible with the critical currents within the PPD in the early 1960s.

Meanwhile, the rise of the new independence movement found an early literary counterpart in the work of the poets grouped around the journal *Guajana*, launched in 1962.[2] *Guajana* proposed a politically committed poetry that would speak of and to "the people" as part of a patriotic and social struggle. Poets moving in this current were not identical, nor were all their texts explicitly political. Nevertheless, most participants in these efforts exhibited some combination of anticolonial, patriotic, and socialist inclination.

In some instances, the desire to take poetry to a wider public led into songwriting and singing. Such was the case of Antonio Cabán Vale, known as El Topo, who became one of the founders of the "new song" current in the early 1970s. The *nueva canción* grew out of the *canción protesta*, a trend connected to the student activism of the time. The titles of the first albums, Roy Brown's *Yo protesto* (1970) and Noel Hernández's *De rebeldes a revolucionarios* (1970), convey the spirit of this work. These and other interpreters combined Latin and North American models and traditional Puerto Rican forms into agitational, critical, satirical songs avidly taken up by many activists. Through the musicalization of texts, Brown and others transformed works by *independentista* poet Juan Antonio Corretjer into popular songs, which along with newer creations, such as El Topo's "Verde Luz," became popular emblems of national pride in the 1980s and 1990s. But song was not the only cultural field renewing itself at the time. A "new history" now endeavored to reconsider the Puerto Rican past.

A New Past for a Different Future

Many elements that would characterize the work of Puerto Rico's "new historians" can be detected in Gervasio García's 1970 review, published in *La escalera*, of Maldonado Denis's *Puerto Rico: A Socio-historic Interpretation*. García criticized Maldonado's book for its overemphasis on politics and the colonial question, its tendency to reduce politics to the clash of prominent leaders, and its lack of primary research, particularly regarding the lives of working or oppressed sectors.[3] In contrast, new historians would insist on the need to pay closer attention to social and economic dynamics and to recover the history of the laboring classes.

Marxist Georg Fromm had already formulated a call for a more rigorous reconsideration of the past in the pages of *La escalera* on the occasion of the 100th anniversary of the Lares insurrection of 1868. Fromm criticized socialist and former Nationalist leader Corretjer for presenting Lares as a protosocialist insurrection as well as historian Lidio Cruz Monclova for limiting himself to constructing a list of factors that could have triggered the insurrection. Fromm thus rejected both the arbitrary forcing of the events into a desired mold (Lares as socialist revolution) and the positivist reduction of history to an accumulation of facts devoid of any effort to differentiate between key and secondary determinations.[4]

Even earlier, Richard Levins, who had moved to Puerto Rico in the 1950s, had called for a Marxist reconsideration of Puerto Rican society in his 1963 review of Lewis's *Puerto Rico*. Insisting on the need for a Puerto Rican revolution, Levins argued that Lewis's Fabian socialism still hoped to transform Puerto Rican society through the collaboration of Puerto Rican and U.S. liberals. This, argued Levins, was the root of his mistaken appreciation of the nationalist movement. For Lewis, anything that could disrupt the collaboration with metropolitan liberalism was seen as reactionary. Against this, Levins riposted that U.S. liberalism was a wing of the U.S. imperialist establishment and hardly a reliable ally for social transformation in Puerto Rico. Moreover, he argued that the family resemblance of Puerto Rican Nationalism was not with fascism but with Irish republicanism. Despite its limitations, Puerto Rican Nationalism was an anticolonial and anti-imperialist movement. Levins did argue that the Nationalists failed to acknowledge the fact that U.S. colonial rule not only was based on coercion but also enjoyed considerable support. The roots of that support had to be studied if the Left wished to ever have an impact beyond itself. Pursuing this orientation, Levins argued for a careful study of Marxism as an indispensable step toward the consolidation of a new radical critique of the present. The Puerto Rican Left had to move from nationalism to a truly anti-imperialist and socialist perspective, a shift that required a sustained study of the specific contradictions of capitalist society.[5]

In 1970, García, Angel Quintero Rivera, and others organized the Centro para el Estudio de la Realidad Puertorriqueña (CEREP), a research collective that became the main proponent of new historical interpretations. The Centro de Estudios Puertorriqueños at Hunter College, established in 1973, played a similar role in New York, promoting a reexamination of the Puerto Rican migration from a class and largely Marxist perspective. A third element contributing to the new interpretations was the work of older Marxists, longtime critics of Nationalism, and former members of the Partido Comunista José Luis González and Andreu Iglesias. A colloquium organized at Princeton by critic Arcadio Díaz Quiñones in 1978 brought together representatives from each of these tributaries to the then emergent current of historical reinterpretation.[6]

Beginning with the publication of *Lucha obrera en Puerto Rico* by Angel Quintero Rivera in 1972, CEREP attempted a recovery of the history of the Federación Libre de Trabajadores and of the Partido Socialista. While past historians had largely ignored these movements or, in the case of many *independentistas*, dismissed them given their pro-U.S. positions, the "new historians" saw them as valid expressions of working-class resistance and sought to explain their ideological evolution as a result of specific historical contexts. These historical reconsiderations were prepared with the present in mind. Most "new historians" saw their work as a contribution to the rise of a new labor movement in Puerto Rico, which, as we have seen, was undergoing a significant upsurge at time. The same type of commitment was present in the work of women historians, such as Yamila Azize and Norma Valle, who by the late 1970s published some initial contributions to the recuperation of women's struggles and women's participation in the workers' movement.

As they retrieved the history of forgotten labor struggles and initiatives, "new historians" also denounced the antilabor, sexist, and racist views held by some of the most admired figures both of the *independentista* tradition and of the literary canon built by the *generación del treinta*. While past *independentista* historians had privileged figures such as De Diego, new historians now counterposed to him forgotten working-class activists such as feminist-socialist Luisa Capetillo and radical typographer Ramón Romero Rosa.

The work of Quintero Rivera integrated these views into a new interpretative framework that over the years became extremely influential. According to him, Puerto Rican politics after 1898 should be seen as a struggle of three social sectors: a coffee "patriarchal" and precapitalist *hacendado* class badly hit by the onset of U.S. rule; a professional layer and Puerto Rican sugar interests who benefited from, and thus favored, U.S. rule; and an emergent labor movement faced with the conservatism of the first group and antilabor practices of the second bloc in the context of a new colonial relation. According to Quintero Rivera, the coffee *hacendados*, as they reacted to U.S. rule, tended to formulate a reactionary patriotism infused with a hierarchical and traditionalist social and cultural perspective. This was a conservative *independentismo* that Quintero Rivera identified with the Partido Unión, whose staying power he linked to the survival of paternalist relations between the weakened landowners and their social subordinates in the world of the *hacienda*. Quintero Rivera described the perspective of the old *hacendado* class as the vision of Puerto Rico as a "large family," with the role of protective father reserved for the old landed ruling classes.[7] Quintero Rivera's notion of the "large Puerto Rican family" as the metaphor at the center of the paternalistic ideology of the Puerto Rican possessing classes was to be embraced by other authors who progressively re-envisioned De Diego, Pedreira, Albizu Campos, Luis Lloréns Torres, and René Marqués as political or literary bearers of this worldview.

In chapter 3, we explored some of the more questionable aspects of this vision of class conflict in early-twentieth-century Puerto Rico. They include the reduction of the Partido Unión to a representative of the coffee *hacendados*, the attribution of *independentista* positions to the *hacendados*, the conflation of very different thinkers such as Lloréns Torres and De Diego as ideologically equivalent, and the invisibility to which this interpretive framework condemns the initiatives of an admittedly small, radical democratic tendency formed by Lloréns Torres, Rosendo Matienzo Cintrón, and Rafael López Landrón, among others.

By the late 1970s, historians were also taking a new look at the coffee economy before 1898. Fernando Picó documented the miserable working conditions of the highland laboring poor in the late nineteenth century under the rising *hacendado* class.[8] Such a vision was a corrective to the notion of that period as a golden age of coffee-based prosperity truncated by the war of 1898. Somewhat unilaterally, Picó tended to exclusively ascribe that idealized vision to the Nationalists, while, as we saw in chapter 2, it was in fact shared by many of their contemporaries.

Not long after Picó, Laird W. Bergad produced a further contribution to the study of the late-nineteenth-century expansion of coffee production. But Bergad's study raised serious doubts regarding key tenets of the framework proposed by Quintero Rivera. Bergad's study concluded that the *hacienda* was hardly a "patriarchal" arrangement "where," as Quintero Rivera had claimed, "traditional values such as social prestige rather than profit maximization determined economic behavior."[9] While the coffee *hacienda* was not yet fully capitalist, due to the combination of wage with other forms of labor subordination, it was driven by the profit imperative, as evidenced by the grinding down of the working poor, the transformation of land into a commodity, and the investments in productive technology due to competitive pressures.

While Quintero Rivera provided the analytical grounding for new readings, González, a member of the previous literary generation, formulated some of the more polemical interventions in defense of the new orientations. González's life had followed a unique itinerary. He had been a member of the Partido Comunista since the early 1940s. With the coming of the Cold War and McCarthyism, González left Puerto Rico and eventually settled in Mexico. After he became a Mexican citizen, he was repeatedly denied entrance into U.S. territory, including Puerto Rico. But his influence in the Puerto Rican literary scene persisted. In 1976, in a book-length interview conducted by Arcadio Díaz Quiñones, he argued that Albizu Campos's conservative nationalism had hindered the growth of the struggle for independence. This frontal attack on the main icon of Puerto Rican nationalism generated a lively debate within *independentista* sectors. The *Conversación* was also the inaugural text of a new publishing house, Huracán, led by Carmen Rivera Izcoa, which became the main editorial vehicle for the new critical, literary, and historical currents. Huracán published Quintero Rivera's initial articles in 1976 under the title *Conflictos de clase y política en Puerto Rico*, as well as the works of Picó.

In 1980, Huracán published one of the most influential essays of the period, José Luis González's "El país de cuatro pisos." Elaborating on the metaphor contained in the title, González presented a new vision of Puerto Rico's historical evolution. A first floor was laid by the first Puerto Ricans, not *peninsulares* who still thought of themselves as Spaniards, nor Tainos who, argued González, had disappeared, but blacks who could no longer think of themselves as African and certainly did not think of themselves as European. A new distinct culture was forming well before the 1840s, not as an elite literary culture but as a popular culture of a distinct Afro-Caribbean flavor. According to González, the white migrants who arrived in the nineteenth century built a second floor to the island's cultural edifice, which made Puerto Rico's evolution diverge from that of the Lesser Antilles. González differentiated the often recently arrived and coarse *hacendados*, devoid of literary sensibilities, from a professional urban layer, responsible for the first literary constructions of Puerto Rico as a distinct entity. A third stage was initiated by the coming of U.S. rule and the diverse responses to it. Here González's argument built on Quintero Rivera's notion of a "triangular struggle." For González, while the Puerto Rican possessing classes elaborated a conservative political-literary perspective obsessed with the loss of the land and the retrieval of the past, the popular sectors continued to resist as best they could, building a vibrant popular culture often ignored by the literary elites. A fourth stage had begun with the creation of the Estado Libre Asociado in 1950–52, an era in which the culture of the old possessing classes yielded its final literary expressions as rural Puerto Rico receded into the past. But the void generated by this collapse was not filled by an incoming American culture but rather by an emergent Puerto Rican popular culture, rooted in its Afro-Caribbean dimension. The independence movement, he concluded, had to unburden itself of its Hispanophile, elitist, backward-looking inclinations and reconstruct itself as part of a project of Antillean solidarity. In his 1976 novel *Balada de otro tiempo*, González presented the same or related ideas in a narrative form.

Roughly coinciding in time with González's "El país de cuatro pisos," Juan Flores in New York produced an influential critique of Pedreira's 1934 classic *Insularismo*. Flores's work was partly inspired by *Calibán*, a commentary by Cuban author Roberto Fernández Retamar on the influential essay *Ariel*, published in 1900 by Uruguayan essayist José Enrique Rodó. Rodó had portrayed Latin America as a spiritual force counterposed to an emphatically material North American civilization. Ariel referred to one of the forces at the command of Prospero in Shakespeare's *The Tempest*. In his essay, Fernández Retamar chose Ariel's opposite, the deformed Caliban, to identify Latin America with its dispossessed and despised black, mestizo, and indigenous majorities. Flores extended this analysis to Pedreira. Pedreira, he argued, had worked within the Rodó framework of opposition to an advancing materialist modernity, to which he had added elitist elements taken from José Ortega y Gasset and, through him, Oswald Spengler and other irrationalist, even semifascist currents. This was a reactionary bourgeois mixture that had little to offer Puerto Rico's working class and popular sectors. Flores underlined how Pedreira's vision of the past privileged autonomism over the separatist revolutionary currents. He also criticized Pedreira's dismissal of pre-Columbian Taino culture as irrelevant to an understanding of Puerto Rican culture, a result of Pedreira's reduction of culture to written culture, which also blinded him to the importance of popular culture. While warning against any "romantic idealization," Flores, taking the work of Peruvian Marxist José Carlos Mariátegui as model, vindicated the memory of Taino communal culture as a "persistent symbolic" alternative to capitalist civilization. Such a vision, combined with a long tradition of slave, peasant, and proletarian resistances, "contains the anticipation of a radically different cultural field," of a future communal, classless culture. Flores praised Corretjer's 1950 poem "Alabanza en la torre de Ciales" as an attempt to evoke that continuum of "indigenous, slave and working class cultural life."[10]

Racism Reconsidered

The impact of Africa's decolonization during the 1960s, the American civil rights and black liberation movements, and the rise of a new Left fostered a reexamination of the racial question in Puerto Rico.

Race, of course, is a cultural construction, and racism has to do not only with the way "races" relate to each other but also with the definition of the "races" as part of a specific system of classification. The Puerto Rican racial system is different from that of the United States. While the latter tends toward a white/black binary opposition, the Puerto Rican system allows for a third "mixed category," which many would describe as being the largest. Within this system, not being white does not necessarily make a person black. Most Americans would thus classify as black many people who in Puerto Rico do not think of themselves as such. Puerto Rico's racism is therefore different from that of the United States, but it is nonetheless real. In fact, the very insistence on differentiating mixed from black can be read as a symptom of how blackness (or certain physical characteristics associated with blackness) is seen as the less desirable pole within a continuum of shades.

In 1975, Isabelo Zenón published *Narciso descubre su trasero*, a scathing indictment of Puerto Rican racism.[11] Zenón denounced the dominant literary and historiographical currents for their construction of an image of Puerto Rico as essentially white. This view, he argued, opposed *jíbaro* peasant culture to African culture and, after thus whitening the *jíbaro*, turned him into the fountainhead of Puerto Rican culture. Zenón piled example upon example of the implicit or explicit racism present in much of Puerto Rican literature and historiography. He pointed out how historians had praised the Cádiz Constitution of 1812 as the source of Puerto Rican liberalism but had failed to indicate that descendants of Africans had been excluded from its dispositions. Liberals such as José Julián Acosta and Francisco M. Quiñones were remembered as opponents of slavery, but historians overlooked that they opposed the extension of suffrage to free blacks. In the 1930s, historian Rafael W. Ramírez, writing in the influential journal *Indice*, had retrospectively justified an 1848 decree that restricted the rights of free blacks as a means of maintaining order and of keeping "unhealthy" ideas at bay. The "order" in question, Zenón pointed out, was that of slavery and the "unhealthy" ideas those of emancipation. Luis Palés Matos's "black" poetry was taken to task for fomenting, in Zenón's reading, the stereotype of blacks as infantile, hypersexual, and primitive beings and the notion of an immutable "black soul." Zenón similarly rejected the assertions by Nationalist leader Albizu Campos that racism had been introduced after 1898 to divide Puerto Ricans. Puerto Rican racism, he argued, long predated the U.S. invasion, and the Puerto Rican people had been anything but united before 1898. Historians, according to Zenón, consistently overlooked the fact that key figures of the Puerto Rican past had not been white. Accounts that failed to mention that Albizu Campos, Ramón Emeterio Betances, or Román Baldorioty de Castro were seen by their contemporaries as either mulatto, mixed, or black tended to perpetuate the dominant view of Puerto Rico as essentially white.

The vast two-volume text was at times disorganized and repetitive and the reading of some passages less than convincing, but it had the undeniable merit of defiantly demanding a place for the problem of racism in the debates concerning Puerto Rican culture and society.[12] Zenón was a Socialist and an *independentista*, but he insisted that Puerto Rican anticolonialism had to break with its color blindness. It had to seriously confront the problem of Puerto Rican racism.

Zenón's text was well received by some *independentista* intellectuals, such as González, Andreu Iglesias, and Corretjer. Corretjer admitted that some of his poems had reproduced racist notions that Zenón had rightfully pointed out. Others were not as open minded and warned Zenón against fomenting racial divisions that, they argued, could weaken the Puerto Rican nation in its confrontation with U.S. colonialism.[13]

Meanwhile, many Afro–Puerto Ricans responded favorably to the example of North American blacks who now asserted a distinct identity and look. "Afro" hairstyles became popular on the island, to the chagrin of more traditional or racist sectors. Zenón mentioned the case of the director of the insular basketball tournament who in 1971 asked players to "trim their 'African look' cuts as much as possible."[14] Evidently, many visible and admired sports and music stars disagreed with such admonitions and embraced some version of the "African look," a contribution to Afro–Puerto Rican self-esteem that has been little recognized. Such was also the case of the musical revolution associated with band leader Rafael Cortijo, singer Ismael Rivera, and composer Catalino "Tite" Curet, whose late 1970s composition "Las caras lindas" is perhaps the best-known assertion of black pride in Puerto Rican popular music.[15]

Inspired, wholly or in part, by the desire to revise the views of past historians who underestimated the importance of slavery, at times described it as relatively mild, and ignored the resistance put up by the slaves, several young scholars opted to reexamine the history of slavery in Puerto Rico. Francisco Scarano studied the expansion of the sugar slave-plantation economy in the nineteenth century, demonstrating its considerable importance and lasting impact on Puerto Rican society as well as the high levels of productivity attained and the extremely harsh conditions under which the slaves were forced to labor.[16] Meanwhile, Guillermo Baralt sought to unearth the record of slave rebellions and protests as a forgotten undercurrent in the struggle for abolition. Since then, a handful of scholars have continued the exploration of this understudied aspect of Puerto Rican culture and society.[17]

Literary Insurgencies

Meanwhile, coinciding with the work of the new historians, a group of young authors entered the literary field. In 1972, Rosario Ferré and Olga Nolla launched the literary magazine *Zona de Carga y Descarga*. In typical avant-garde spirit, the editors proclaimed that Puerto Rican literature and criticism had become a tired repetition of old styles and approaches, from the political pamphleteering favored by some to the academic routinism practiced by others. Puerto Rican literature had to reinvent itself through undogmatic experimentation. By 1976, a series of works signaled the appearance of the new literature that *Zona* had so loudly demanded: *La guaracha del Macho Camacho* by Luis Rafael Sánchez, *Papeles de Pandora* by Rosario Ferré, *El ojo de la tormenta* by Olga Nolla, *Cinco Cuentos Negros* by Carmelo Rodríguez Torres, *La familia de todos nosotros* by Magali García Ramis, *La novelabingo* by Manuel Ramos Otero, and *Desimos désimas* by Joserramón Melendes, which had been preceded by *La renuncia del héroe Baltasar* by Edgardo Rodríguez Juliá in 1974. These works were followed by *Vírgenes y mártires* by Ana Lydia Vega and Carmen Lugo Filippi in 1981, *Las tribulaciones de Jonás* and *El entierro de Cortijo* by Rodríguez Juliá in 1981 and 1983, and *Encancaranublado* by Ana Lydia Vega in 1982. By 1983, two anthologies—one prepared by Efraín Barradas, *Apalabramiento*, and one by José Luis Vega, *Reunión de espejos*—presented the reading public with a sampling of the work of the new literary wave.

Among these works, *La guaracha del Macho Camacho* by Sánchez was undoubtedly a central text. Its use of the traffic jam as a metaphor for a colonial society in crisis after two decades of economic expansion; its intricate mix of street language, popular music and culture, and a refined baroque literariness; and its orality and irreverence made it the object of intense reactions, both positive and negative. This was not Sánchez's first work. He had published dramatic works and an innovative collection of stories, *En cuerpo de camisa*, in 1966, but *La guaracha* displayed some of the features of the new literary trends far more spectacularly than any previous text. It can justifiably be described as the major landmark of the beginning of a new literary moment.

Marqués had included no women in his anthology of a previous generation, *Cuentos puertorriqueños de hoy*, published in 1959. By contrast, women writers and feminist issues were a prominent aspect of the work of the new literary wave. The mid-1980s witnessed the appearance of new works by women writers. Rosario Ferré published *Maldito Amor*, Magali García Ramis *Felices Días, Tío Sergio*, and Ana Lydia Vega *Pasión de historia*. In 1980, Ferré had published *Sitio a Eros*, a collection of essays on women artists and activists such as Mary Shelley, George Sand, Virginia Woolf, Alexandra Kollontai, Sylvia Plath, and Julia de Burgos. This was a far cry from the authors of the previous generation, in whose texts women often acted as the emasculating agent of consumer society, draining the (male) artist's creative force.

As the titles of *La guaracha del Macho Camacho*, *El entierro de Cortijo*, and even *Zona de Carga y Descarga* suggest, these writers were interested in exploring diverse aspects of emergent Puerto Rican urban popular culture. The language of the Puerto Rican street now made its way into the literary text with unprecedented force. The playfulness of many of these texts was in part a protest against the solemnity and insistence of much past *independentista* discourse on renunciation and self-sacrifice as well as against the stark realist style typical of the previous generation of narrators. The juggling of diverse literary, filmic, pop music, or soap-opera conventions to sustain a parodic portrayal of diverse spheres of Puerto Rican society was a central aspect, for example, of the work of Vega. Authors now explored racial and above all sexual matters that in the past had been broached tangentially. It was as if Puerto Rican characters had acquired a more audacious language to refer to their bodies.[18]

The collection *El tramo ancla* edited by Vega is a representative gathering of texts (originally published in *Claridad*) by the new generation of authors. García Ramis's essay "Hostos, bróder, esto está difícil" is typical of some of the new attitudes, as the author informally addresses one of Puerto Rico's revered patriots as one would a good friend, using, furthermore, a hybrid Spanglish term of endearment (*bróder*, from "brother") while explaining that it is not always possible in contemporary Puerto Rico to act as ethically as he would have demanded. (The author explains how she was driven to buy some stolen auto parts to save some money after an accident.)

While writers engaged in their literary explorations, other artists worked in the renovation of the Puerto Rican stage and its graphic arts. Such was the case of the Taller de Histriones organized in 1971 by Gilda Navarra and the Taller Alacrán between 1968 and 1972, led by Antonio Martorell. Older artists continued their work, which often had an overt political character. In 1970, for example, the journal *La escalera* published a book of satirical political caricatures by Lorenzo Homar entitled *Aquí en la lucha*. Other graphic artists such as Nelson Sambolín, José Rosa, and Rafael Rivera Rosa were also involved in the student, labor, environmental, and independence activism of the time.

In 1979, José Luis González attempted to bring the developments across the literary and other artistic fields under a unifying category and present them as examples of shared sensibility. He thus described the work of Rosa along with *La guaracha del Macho Camacho* by Sánchez as examples of the cultural phenomenon he labeled *plebeyismo*. The term—borrowed from Ortega y Gasset—sought to explain how, according to González, the collapse of the culture of the old agrarian possessing classes had opened the path for the ascendance of a new popular culture, which the younger authors and artists were now using to refashion Puerto Rico's artistic production.

But, in spite of all the innovations, many authors of the 1970s and 1980s retained a shared objective with their predecessors: the desire to explain and define the Puerto Rican situation. Pedreira's question "What are we?" haunts many of these texts. Sánchez's elaborations around the life of popular singer and model of Latin masculinity Daniel Santos, Rodríguez Juliá's portrayals of the massive funerals of musical and political figures, Vega's stories of encounters between Haitian, Dominican, Cuban, and Puerto Rican characters, and García Ramis's portrayal of middle-class life in Santurce in the 1950s, to mention a few examples, can all be read as new installments in the tradition of national interpretation texts going back to Pedreira's *Insularismo*, Palés Matos's "Mulata Antilla," Matienzo Cintrón's "Pancho Ibero," and Lloréns Torres's "Canción de las Antillas."

In fact, the feminist iconoclasm and distancing from past literary generations did not prevent authors like Vega, Lugo Filippi, and García Ramis from engaging in some nostalgic moods of their own, evoking the wooden houses of their youth, the skill of traditional artisans and cooks, the slower life of Ponce as compared to San Juan, or even the ghostly presence of a Taino past.[19] By now this romantic escape from the existing form of "progress" should come as no surprise. This cultural-romantic aversion to the present, marked by a sense of loss and sustained by the evocation of an absent plenitude, is a theme running through Puerto Rican literature at least since the second decade of the twentieth century, even if what is longed for is quite different, depending on the author being considered. As we saw, even Flores's critique of Pedreira's vindication of an elite culture against the advance of mass civilization included its own Marxist-romantic vindication of the Taino past as a resource in the attempt to see beyond colonial capitalism.[20]

To be sure, while most members of the new wave shared with Pedreira and the *generación del treinta* a desire to define Puerto Rico's identity, they were increasingly aware of the difficulties inherent in such a project. A complex example of this tension can be found in the work of Rodríguez Juliá, beginning with his first novel, *La renuncia del héroe Baltasar*. *La renuncia* takes the form of a series of lectures delivered by historian Antonio Cadalso at the Ateneo in 1938.[21] The author thus makes his narrator a fictional member of the *generación del treinta*. But the story told by Cadalso is quite different from Pedreira's or Tomás Blanco's narratives. Instead of the story of the rise of Puerto Rican identity through the efforts of the nineteenth-century autonomists, we have the story of brutal class and racial conflicts in the little-known eighteenth century. There is no liberating synthesis at the end. At times, the narrative breaks down as the text becomes a description of diverse paintings. A series of juxtaposed images, a common occurrence in the texts of Rodríguez Juliá, is somehow expected to suggest a story that the narrator now feels unable to formulate but still yearns for. Similarly, in *El entierro de Cortijo*, Rodríguez Juliá explains how during Cortijo's funeral he tried to discover a panoramic vantage point, a place from which he could encompass the multitude within his field of vision, but the crowd present at the funeral was too protean to allow this.[22] The author thus turns to descriptions of diverse specific aspects of the event without ever completely abandoning the hope of turning it into a metaphor for Puerto Rico as a whole.

Through the 1980s and 1990s, Rodríguez Juliá was to issue essays and chronicles dealing with just about all matters Puerto Rican, from the place of baseball heroes in island culture to the murder by the police of *independentista* militants in Cerro Maravilla (see chapter 13), the work of composer Bobby Capó, the culture of the Puerto Rican middle class, the erotic rituals of diverse social sectors and generations, and the photographs of Jack Delano, among many topics too numerous to mention. These texts were and are often informed by a bittersweet sensibility, not opposed to the changes brought about by modernization yet not exempt from a sense of loss resulting from them. They offer an often disconcerting mix of cynicism and nostalgia. Not surprisingly, the figure of Muñoz Marín has been a recurrent theme in his writing, beginning with *Las tribulaciones de Jonás*, a hybrid text, part personal memoir, part interview with Muñoz Marín, part meditation on his historical significance. Its combination of understanding and rejection of Muñoz Marín's choices can be seen as initiating a more balanced examination of the life of a man who until then had largely been either exalted as the architect of Puerto Rico's progress or held in contempt as a traitor to his initial ideas.

But things were also stirring in the Puerto Rican diaspora. Often written about in the past, "Nuyoricans" now came forth to write themselves into the literary landscape.

The Nuyorican Explosion

In 1967, Piri Thomas published *Down These Mean Streets*, a vivid memoir of life in El Barrio, of the drug underworld and prison system, and, most significantly, of Puerto Rican (and not only American) racism. *Down These Mean Streets* was preceded by *Puerto Rican Sketches*, also written in English by Communist activist Jesús Colón. But Colón was a member of an earlier generation, those who had arrived in New York City around 1920, while Thomas's narrative reflects more fully the circumstances of the postwar migration. Thomas's text, furthermore, was the first book by a Puerto Rican to attain fame and critical acclaim in the United States. Before this, Puerto Ricans had been represented in U.S. text and film—most lastingly in the 1957 musical play and 1961 film *West Side Story*—mainly as a delinquent, at best exotic, at worst degraded and dangerous, other.

As indicated, Thomas's memoir is a vivid portrait and protest against racism, not only toward but among Puerto Ricans. It is an affirmation of his blackness as much as his Puerto Ricanness. The text suggests how contact with U.S. racism has helped make Puerto Rican racism more visible, an experience that is also narrated in the memoirs of New York community activist Antonia Pantoja. Realizing that in the United States their situation as darker Puerto Ricans was different from that of their lighter-skinned compatriots sharpened their perception of the more subtle—but no less real—discriminations that mark the Puerto Rican racial system.

In 1969, poet Víctor Hernández Cruz published *Snaps*, followed by *Mainland* in 1973, the same year in which Pedro Pietri issued *Puerto Rican Obituary* and

Author Piri Thomas, whose memoir *Down These Mean Streets* ushered in the work of Puerto Rican authors in English. (Proyecto digitalización fotos El Mundo–Biblioteca José M. Lázaro, Universidad de Puerto Rico–Río Piedras)

Nicholasa Mohr published *Nilda*, followed by *El Bronx Remembered* in 1975. In 1974, Miguel Piñero published his play *Short Eyes*, written while he was in Sing Sing prison. In 1975, he and Miguel Algarín published the anthology *Nuyorican Poetry*. These authors were soon joined by such writers as Tato Laviera, Sandra María Esteves, Judith Ortiz Cofer, and Ed Vega. Among other traits, the work of these writers boldly asserted the existence of a Puerto Rican literature in English.[23] The Nuyorican Poets Café in Manhattan's Lower East Side created by Algarín and others in 1974 became a gathering place for this emergent sensibility.[24] "Puerto Rican Obituary" by Pietri was as good a summary as any of the lives of the Puerto Rican proletariat in the United States. The first lines read:

They worked
They were always on time
They were never late
They never spoke back
when they were insulted
They worked
They never took days off
that were not on the calendar
They never went on strike
without permission
They worked ten days a week
and were only paid for five
They worked
They worked
They worked
and they died
They died broke
They died owing

In 1970, several artists/activists founded Taller Boricua in El Barrio with the objective of using art (music, dance, poetry, visual arts) to promote community activism. During the 1970s, the Taller was led by graphic artist Jorge Soto, who developed what has been called an Afro-Taino Nuyorican style. As the name indicates, it mixed pre-Columbian, African, and New York (graffiti) motifs, which the artist deployed to reinterpret classical Puerto Rican works or official emblems, such as Francisco Oller's *El Velorio* and the logo of the Institute of Puerto Rican Culture.[25]

By 1973, the demand for bilingual education and for recognition of Puerto Rican concerns in the universities led to the creation of the Centro de Estudios Puertorriqueños at Hunter College of the City University of New York. During the 1970s, Puerto Rican studies programs were established at other campuses of the CUNY system, of the State University of New York, and of the Rutgers University system in New Jersey, as well as in Northeastern (Illinois) and Wayne State (Indiana) universities.[26] This was a time of militant activism, which included the 1975–76 strike to prevent the closing of Hostos Community College in the South Bronx, which had opened its doors in 1968. Meanwhile, the work of the Centro, led by Frank Bonilla, Ricardo Campos, and Juan Flores, soon became a major challenge to the "island centered canon of Puerto Rican culture."[27]

The publication by Huracán of the *Memorias de Bernardo Vega*, edited by veteran Puerto Rican Marxist Andreu Iglesias, was an extraordinary contribution to the reconsideration of the Puerto Rican experience in New York, indeed the Puerto Rican experience everywhere. Bernardo Vega had left Puerto Rico in 1915. A Socialist and a cigarmaker, he was a product of Puerto Rico's early labor movement. His memoir tells the story of the formation of the Puerto Rican community in New York from a working-class, socialist, and internationalist perspective. Thanks to these diverse contributions, it became harder to deny that New York had been the home of many key contributions to Puerto Rican culture. Such was the case of much of the work of composers Rafael Hernández, Pedro Flores, and Bobby Capó; the *plena* and other recordings of Manuel Jiménez; the singing career of Daniel Santos; the apprenticeship of painter and graphic artist Lorenzo Homar; important portions of the lives of Juan Antonio Corretjer and Julia de Burgos; the anarchist writings of Luisa Capetillo; and the activism of the Puerto Rican cigarmakers in favor of Cuban and Puerto Rican independence before 1898.

There was one very visible cultural process unfolding since the late 1950s and early 1960s that combined contributions from diverse locations leading to creations that in many cases could only be described as emerging between Puerto Rico and the United States. No description of the 1960s and 1970s can fail to note the spectacular insurgence of salsa as a new musical fusion of Cuban, Dominican, and Puerto Rican Afro-Caribbean forms with a dosage of North American jazz. This development had been preceded by the work of bandleaders Tito Puente and Tito Rodríguez, among others, in the 1950s and early 1960s. These were the peak years of migration to New York, which turned clubs such as the Palladium, inaugurated in 1949, into showcases for Puente and Rodríguez. Meanwhile, Rafael Cortijo and Ismael Rivera had revolutionized island music, modernizing Afro–Puerto Rican forms in the late 1950s and early 1960s. These trends interacted in ways too complex to discuss here with the bands led by pianists Charlie and Eddie Palmieri, Richie Ray, and Larry Harlow, percussionists Ray Barreto and Roberto Roena, trombonist Willie Colón, bassist Bobby Valentín, the voices of Cheo Feliciano, Bobby Cruz, and Ismael Miranda, and the compositions of Catalino (Tite) Curet to create the new sound of salsa. Salsa was not a musical genre but a "particular way of making music" that in one piece could combine *jíbaro*-associated forms such as *aguinaldos* or *seis*, Afro–Puerto Rican *plenas* and *bombas*, Cuban *sones* and *guajiras*, and upper-class *danzas* in an eclectic mix difficult to classify according to traditional categories.[28]

By the early 1970s, a recording company in New York, FANIA, had become synonymous with the diffusion of salsa, and the concerts of the FANIA All-Stars were attended by thousands of enthusiastic fans. While the Palladium had been associated with the mambo age of Puente and Rodríguez, the FANIA concert at the Cheetah Club on August 26, 1971, and the resulting film (*Our Latin Thing*) and LPs were boldly marketed and widely accepted as the beginning of a new musical era. The music itself was, more often than not, not explicitly political, but it soon became a new emblem of Puerto Rican identity, both on the island and in the United States.

In balance, all these elements—the new independence and student movements, the emergence of a new history and a new literary discourse attuned to popular culture, the rise of a Nuyorican literature, and musical innovations such as the new song movement and the salsa explosion—yielded a widely shared perception that Puerto Rican culture was very much alive. The debates of the 1990s, in a different context (marked by the frustration of the hopes for social and political change), would oppose diverse attitudes regarding this fact, from celebratory declarations of Puerto Rican pride to postmodern rejections of the very notion of national identity as exclusionary and authoritarian.

ECONOMIC STAGNATION AND POLITICAL DEADLOCK, 1976-1992

The 1974–75 recession had a lasting impact on Puerto Rico. It marked the end of the rapid postwar expansion. Real yearly gross national product growth fell from 7 percent in the 1960s to 3.3 percent in the 1970s to 2.1 percent in the 1980s. The official unemployment rate had never dipped below 10 percent, but by 1980 it had risen to 17 percent. A further recession in 1981–83 raised it to 23.5 percent.[1] These numbers, combined with a 43 percent labor force participation rate, were clear indexes of the incapacity of the colonial economy to secure an adequate source of income for a sizable portion of the population. As in the past, unemployment was higher in the interior and in small towns. Only the influx of federal funds and an increase in government employment prevented greater hardship for many. Between 1970 and 1990, federal transfers to individuals in Puerto Rico—through food stamps and other programs—rose from $500 million to $6 billion. Their share of personal income went from 15 percent to 30 percent.[2] Meanwhile, Estado Libre Asociado government employment (not including municipalities and public corporations) more than doubled from 106,000 in 1970 to 222,000 in 1990.[3]

In that context, a new statehood movement, armed with a new discourse and led by Carlos Romero Barceló, now rose to become an equal partner/opponent in a political deadlock with the once invincible Partido Popular Democrático. But before the elections of 1976 placed Romero Barceló in the governor's mansion, PPD governor Rafael Hernández Colón had to immediately devise ways of responding to the 1974–75 shock. Some of his initiatives shaped the evolution of the Puerto Rican economy during the next two decades. It is to this that we now turn our attention, before examining the rise of the pro-statehood Partido Nuevo Progresista under Romero Barceló and the conflicts that it provoked.

The Age of "Section 936"

Faced with a looming fiscal crisis, in 1974 the Hernández Colón administration appointed a commission led by well-known economist James Tobin to prepare a report on Puerto Rico's finances. Tobin's *Report to the Governor* included reflections on long-term trends and recognized that "poverty and unemployment are still immediate problems for a large portion of Puerto Rico's population." It admitted that "dependence" was an appropriate description of the Puerto Rican economy: half of the "tangible reproducible assets" located in Puerto Rico were "externally owned."[4] This meant that a considerable portion of the income generated was not reinvested on the island. Furthermore, the report warned that Puerto Rico's ability to attract U.S. capital was being eroded. In the past, U.S. capital had been attracted by low wages, unrestricted access to the U.S. market, and the security afforded by the political link with the United States. But other areas could offer lower wages, many were gaining access to the U.S. market, and not all were insecure or unstable. The report concluded that Puerto Rico should formulate an economic program less reliant on U.S. capital. Yet, the insular government responded to the crisis by deepening its tax exemption policy, confirming its commitment to U.S. direct investments as the agent of Puerto Rico's development.

In 1976, the Hernández Colón administration successfully lobbied Congress to amend Section 931 of the U.S. Internal Revenue Code, which regulated the operations of U.S. corporations in U.S. possessions, including Puerto Rico. Under Section 931, U.S. manufacturing corporations in Puerto Rico could place their profits in island banks or move them to other possessions and, upon liquidation of their operations, transfer them to the mainland without paying federal taxes. While waiting for the best moment to repatriate their profits, some corporations moved their funds to Guam (another U.S. possession) and used them to speculate in the rising Eurodollar market. PPD lobbyists convinced Congress that allowing U.S. corporations to transfer their profits tax-free to the mainland at any moment (without having to liquidate their operations on the island) would recuperate millions of wayward dollars for the U.S. economy while enhancing Puerto Rico's industrial project. The changes were embodied in a new Section 936 of the Internal Revenue Code, adopted as part of the Tax Reform Act of 1976. The corresponding "936 corporations" were to become the mainstay of the Puerto Rican economy until the phasing out of Section 936 in 1996–2006. Most such operations in Puerto Rico functioned as subsidiaries of a U.S. corporate parent. The yearly "possession tax credit" claimed by 936 corporations gradually increased until it peaked at $5.8 billion in 1993.[5]

The new disposition was particularly attractive to high-tech, capital intensive operations such as pharmaceutical and precision instrument manufacturing. It thus fostered a rapid increase in the already high value of direct U.S. investments in Puerto Rico. By 1978, these stood at $10.8 billion, already the highest figure for all of Latin America, followed by Brazil with $7.1 billion and Mexico with $3.7 billion.[6]

Besides not paying taxes for income generated in Puerto Rico, 936 corporations could and did shift income generated elsewhere to Puerto Rico, thus avoiding the payment of federal corporate taxes. Thus, at one point or another, several major corporations registered a considerable part of their total income in Puerto Rico (for example, Pepsi Co., 21 percent; Union Carbide, 25 percent; Baxter Travenol, 37 percent; Abbott Laboratories, 71 percent).[7] Pharmaceuticals and other corporations often transferred to Puerto Rico profits derived from intellectual property and patents, also called "intangibles," developed elsewhere to shield them from federal taxes. At least one study concluded that, over time, the possibility of income-shifting to take advantage of tax breaks became the central attraction to investors.[8]

As indicated, many operations attracted by Section 936 employed fewer workers per unit of capital than past manufacturing activities. On balance, the measure was able to generate only a slight expansion in manufacturing employment, which hovered around 140,000–150,000 through the 1980s. While a small portion of the labor force secured relatively well-paying jobs, unemployment remained the lot of a substantial sector. Through the 1980s, the unemployment rate rarely fell below 15 percent, and the labor force participation rate did not reach 45 percent.

Furthermore, as had occurred during the golden age of Operation Bootstrap, the new capital-intensive operations did not produce significant industrial linkages on the island. Most of the inputs were imported and most of the output exported, accentuating Puerto Rico's export industry's enclave character.

Under the auspices of Section 936, the denationalization of the Puerto Rican economy—another facet of its colonial, dependent nature—continued apace. Puerto Rican capital remained a marginal force in export manufacturing. The largest locally owned exporter (the pharmaceutical company MOVA) had yearly revenue of $116 million in 2002, which was equal to less than 1 percent of pharmaceutical exports.[9] A recent report by the United Nations Economic Commission for Latin America concluded that "Puerto Rico is a great exporter, but Puerto Ricans are not."[10] Indeed, by the 1980s the Puerto Rican capitalist class mostly operated in non-export sectors, namely financial, insurance, and real estate operations, followed by importers and commercial firms devoted to wholesale and retail trade. The largest firm, Banco Popular de Puerto Rico, is a financial conglomerate and the single most successful insular capitalist enterprise. This is followed by an insurance company, a commercial and mortgage banking corporation, a financial holding company, and a food and beverage distributor. Of the top twenty-five firms ranked by assets, not one is a manufacturing firm. (Ten are financial, thirteen commercial, one a private university, and one a newspaper.) Largely acting as intermediaries or representatives of U.S. producers (as importers, dealers-distributors, wholesalers-retailers, or providers of financial or transportation services), the Puerto Rican capitalist class is a dependent, subordinated stratum, a modern-day version of the comprador bourgeoisie that in the nineteenth century acted as agents of metropolitan capital within the areas being reduced to colonial or semicolonial control or influence. Meanwhile, Puerto Rico has no lack of managerial personnel, qualified technicians, or skilled workers,[11] but the dependent, one-sided nature of the insular economy blocks the realization of its productive potential. Not surprisingly, many migrate to the United States in search of employment or better-paying positions.

In 1975, Tobin's *Report to the Governor* had pointed out that the outflow of profits resulting from external control of much of the Puerto Rican economy was statistically reflected in the widening gap between the gross domestic product and the gross national product, that is to say, between the measure of the island's income-generating activity and that of the income received by its residents.[12] The less the expansion of the GDP was reflected in the growth of the GNP, the less the island's economic expansion would translate into the welfare of its inhabitants. The report predicted that "growing dependence on external resources" and the shift to capital-intensive investments, which spent relatively less in wages per unit of capital and extracted considerable profits, would tend to widen this gap.

Tobin's prediction was to be fully confirmed. Since the 1970s, the difference between GNP and GDP has grown. Between 1971 and 1991, the GNP and GDP grew at an annual rate of 2.2 percent and 3.5 percent, respectively. Their evolution between 1947 and 2000 may be appreciated in Figure 13.1. By the year 1990, the flow of profits and dividends out of the island stood at almost $11 billion or 35 percent of the insular GDP.[13] An important caveat must be appended here: as indicated, a considerable but difficult to determine portion of Puerto Rico's

FIGURE 13.1. GNP and GDP in Puerto Rico, 1947–2000

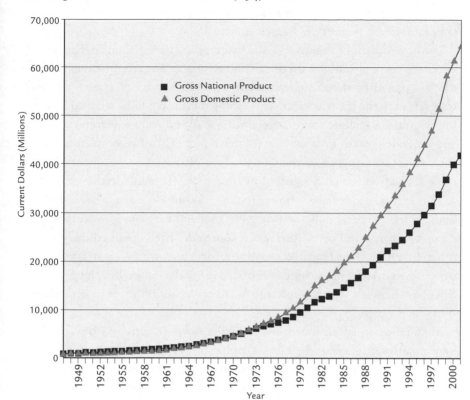

Source: Puerto Rico Planning Board.

GDP is made up of profits declared in Puerto Rico but not generated in Puerto Rico. Thus, part of the GDP/GNP gap must have been due to price manipulations and "transfer prices" and not to the outflow of income generated on the island.

This dynamic, as U.S. government agencies have admitted, has made the GDP an unreliable index for measuring Puerto Rico's economic performance in general (since part of the GDP corresponds to pricing manipulations for tax purposes and not actual economic activity) or of its impact on island residents in particular (since part of it is income that leaves the island as payments to external investors).[14] The most recent study on this issue argues that "much of what is recorded as production in Puerto Rico is a simple paper transaction in which income is transferred to Puerto Rico and then taken back out as dividend payments to mainland corporations." If adjustments are made for the income of corporations that is reported in Puerto Rico but not really generated there, manufacturing output in 2004 is actually 45 percent lower and the GDP is 17 percent lower than official figures indicate.[15]

The government of Puerto Rico did attempt to channel some of the profits of the 936 corporations toward the insular economy. The enactment of Section 936 was paired by the ELA government with the levying of a tax on profits transferred to the United States. This "toll-gate" tax could be reduced by placing the funds in public corporation, municipal, and state government bonds and other designated instruments in Puerto Rico. This was complemented by the passage by Congress of the Qualified Possessions Source Investment Income legislation, which designated income from other financial investments as also exempt from federal taxes. These provisions created a large mass of liquid assets ($8 or $9 billion at any given moment between 1986 and 1991) on deposit in banks in Puerto Rico and a source of cheap credit to the government.[16] At first, the island's Association of Bankers expressed dissatisfaction with the small share of 936 funds deposited in insular banks. But the growth of this share between 1977 and 1987 cemented the coalition eager to defend Section 936 in Washington.

An alliance, which included multinational corporations and the island financial, insurance, and real estate sectors, thus developed around the defense of Section 936. U.S. corporations created the Puerto Rico–USA Foundation to ensure the continuation of their tax privileges. The Association of Industrialists, the Association of Bankers, and the Chamber of Commerce all did the bidding of 936 corporations, insisting the well-being of the Puerto Rican economy depended on them.[17]

Of course, Section 936 applied to Puerto Rico only to the extent that the island remained a "possession," that is, under U.S. rule but not part of the United States. Its provisions would cease to apply if Puerto Rico were to become a state. Thus, 936 corporations had an interest in perpetuating Puerto Rico's existing status and consequently had an objective affinity with its proponent, the PPD. Indeed, through the 1980s and 1990s, the PPD acted as the political representative of the 936 coalition, which included multinational capital that benefited from Section 936 and its local allies.

Managing the Crisis: Federal Funds and Public Sector Expansion

Given the insufficiencies of the private sector, higher levels of unemployment and hardship for many were avoided only through the influx of federal funds that helped secure a minimum purchasing power and, along with increased government borrowing, helped sustain an expansion of government employment. In the past, Puerto Rico had received federal funds, most of which were earned income: they corresponded to programs (Social Security, veterans' benefits, pensions) to which Puerto Ricans had contributed via payments or services.[18] Beginning with the recession of the mid-1970s, which coincided with the extension to the island of the federal food stamps program, Puerto Rico witnessed a sharp rise in unearned federal transferences, which rose to 37 percent of all federal funds flowing to the island in 1980. While the unearned transfers are a drain on the federal budget, they are hardly a drain on the U.S. economy, as the funds are spent mostly on imports from the United States. Furthermore, between 1980 and 2000, the share of unearned transfers of the total federal transfers to the island fell to 23 percent.[19]

Meanwhile, federal funds received by the ELA government grew from $257 million in 1970 to $1.4 billion in 1990.[20] ELA government employment doubled between 1970 and 1990. But this was also financed by a rapid expansion in government borrowing. Public debt thus rose from $1.66 billion in 1970 to $7 billion in 1980 to $12.57 billion in 1990.[21] The limits of this type of crisis management are evident: government borrowing could not increase indefinitely, while economic stability depended on a flow of federal funds and the industrial and financial structure erected by Section 936, both of which were vulnerable to fiscally conservative political shifts in Washington. By the turn of the twenty-first century, Section 936 would be on the way out, public borrowing would be at its limit, and the insular government would be thrown into a deep fiscal crisis.

After the Golden Age: The Structural Continuity of Colonial Development

In 1938, the PPD had been organized partly under the banner of reducing absentee control of the Puerto Rican economy. In the mid-1940s, it had shifted to a strategy centered on attracting U.S. direct investments while reasserting its other objectives: reducing unemployment, outgrowing dependence on U.S. relief funds, and approaching U.S. living standards. Yet by 1975, the island still exhibited exceedingly high unemployment and very low labor force participation rates. It remained acutely dependent on U.S. investments and federal funds. Its relative per capita income, which in 1950 had been a fifth of the U.S. figure, had risen, but only to a third of U.S. per capita income or about one half of Mississippi's, the poorest state of the Union.

FIGURE 13.2. Index of Personal Income in Puerto Rico and U.S. Regions, 1930–2000

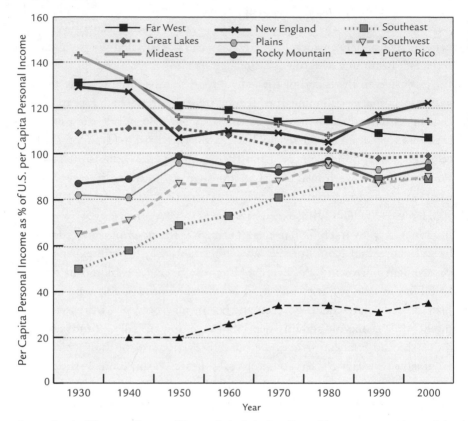

Sources: For the fifty states, Bureau of Economic Analysis, *State Personal Income 1929–2000* (RCN-0284) (U.S. Department of Commerce, Economics and Statistics Administration, Bureau of Economic Analysis, CD-ROM); for Puerto Rico, Junta de Planificación de Puerto Rico, "Table 1—Selected Series of Income and Product, Total and Per Capita: Fiscal Years." Thanks to Alejandro Díaz Marrero of Producto Bruto, Análisis Económico, Junta de Planificación de Puerto Rico, for e-mailing us the spreadsheet with the entire historical series (January 2005).

The extent to which Puerto Rico remains a distinct colonial area within the U.S. economy and polity can be graphically appreciated in Figure 13.2, which traces the evolution of personal income in different regions of the United States and Puerto Rico. While the figures of all regions tended to converge during the postwar boom (1940–80) and have diverged only slightly since then, Puerto Rico's personal income, after slightly converging with the rest between 1950 and 1970, has remained on the other side of a wide and intractable gap. The persistence of that gap, of course, was and is compatible with improving living standards in Puerto Rico. It has also been compatible with an improvement of Puerto Rico's living standards relative to the rest of Latin America. In other words: seen from the United States, Puerto Rico appears as a chronically depressed area, while seen from Latin America, it appears relatively well off. There are of course many problems when making international comparisons, including fluctuating exchange rates, differences in cost of living in each country, and basic issues of comparability of goods, as in medical services or university educations. With all due caution, Figure 13.3 shows an estimate of Puerto Rican incomes relative to the United States and some Latin American countries.

In terms of per capita income, U.S. colonialism has neither made the island converge with other U.S. regions nor allowed it to fall below a certain level. In an increasingly polarized international economy, U.S. colonialism keeps Puerto Rico perched about halfway between the developed North and the underdeveloped South. While the comparison with independent republics of the region leads most Puerto Ricans to favor continued political links with the United States, this does not erase the fact that under U.S. rule, the Puerto Rican economy can hardly be described as a healthy organism.

This diagnosis is equally valid thirty years after the end of the postwar boom. By 1999, Puerto Rico's per capita GNP was $14,412, compared to the U.S. figure of $41,994. An estimated 44.6 percent of all families in Puerto Rico lived under the poverty line, compared to 9.2 percent in the United States. In the United States, 9.5 percent of all households had a yearly income of less than $10,000; the corresponding figure for Puerto Rico was 37.1 percent.[22]

In recent decades, neoliberal authors and policy makers have argued that free trade and capital mobility will lead less-developed regions to converge with their more advanced counterparts. A century of U.S.–Puerto Rico relations invites caution regarding such claims. The Puerto Rican economy has developed under a regime of free trade with the United States since 1901, U.S. capital has had perfectly unimpeded entrance into the insular economy, the island functions with the U.S. dollar, and the banking system operates under the supervision of the U.S. Federal Reserve. Moreover, since 1904, Puerto Rico exhibits one feature that none of the countries of Latin America or the signatories of recent free trade agreements with the United States enjoy: unrestricted mobility of its labor force into the United States. Puerto Ricans have utilized this escape valve massively, to the point that the Puerto Rican population in the United States is now larger than that on the island. And yet, despite such unprecedented freedom of movement for capital *and* for labor, the island's economy has not converged with other regions of the United States.

FIGURE I3.3. GDP per Capita of Puerto Rico, the United States, and Latin America, 1950–1998

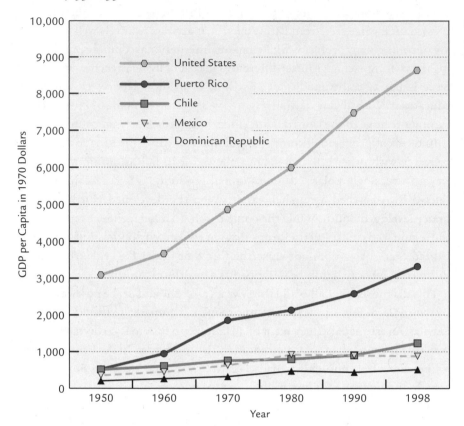

Sources: Figures for Latin America and the United States—in dollar exchange rates—are from James W. Wilkie, Eduardo Alemán, and José Guadalupe Ortega, eds., *Statistical Abstract of Latin America*, vol. 37 (Los Angeles: UCLA Latin American Center Publications, 2001), 1052; Puerto Rico figures for 1950–80 are from Puerto Rico Planning Board, *Income and Product, Puerto Rico* (San Juan: Puerto Rico Planning Board, May 1985), 30–33; figures for 1983–93 are from Junta de Planificación de Puerto Rico, *Ingreso y producto 1993* (San Juan: Junta de Planificación de Puerto Rico, 1994), 1; figures for 1992–98 are from Junta de Planificación, *Informe económico al gobernador: apéndice estadístico* (Feb. 1999): table 1.

Note: Figures in current dollars for Puerto Rico were converted to 1970 dollars using the Consumer Price Index published by the Federal Reserve Bank of Minneapolis in <http://minneapolisfed.org/Research/data/us/calc/hist1913.cfm>.

The influx of federal funds to Puerto Rico is often presented as one of the benefits of U.S. rule for Puerto Rico. But an economy that requires such subsidies is hardly a success story: if U.S. rule has made such subsidies possible, it has also made them necessary. If the solution to Puerto Rico's problems is not a sudden cut in federal funds, neither is it a mere continuation of the century-long reliance on foreign direct investment and free trade. Meanwhile, afflicted by low growth, increased unemployment, and persistent poverty, the island also acquired a growing informal and often illegal economy with all its attendant violent byproducts, including higher levels of street violence, which we discuss in chapter 14.

Politics in an Age of Stagnation: The Statehood Offensive, 1976–1984

The economic and social sea change of the mid-1970s coincided with a lasting political shift. Soon after engineering the passage of Section 936, the PPD, hard-hit by the 1974–75 recession, lost the 1976 elections to the pro-statehood PNP, now led by Carlos Romero Barceló. Unlike its earlier victory in 1968, this time the PNP gained control of both houses of the legislature. The era of almost uncontested PPD control gave way to the alternation in government of two evenly matched parties. Of the eight elections held between 1976 and 2004, the PNP and the PPD each won four races for governor. In those eight elections, the PNP received an average 47.6 percent of the vote to the PPD's 47.02. On two occasions (1980 and 2004), the party winning the governorship failed to win one or both houses of the legislature.

The onset of the period of economic slowdown not only accelerated the rise of the PNP but also shaped its discourse and strategy. As indicated, the economic downturn brought about an influx of federal funds in a U.S. political context that had been transformed by the civil rights and related movements. Hoping to capitalize on these new currents, Romero Barceló refashioned the statehood project in the mold of a welfare-based populism, borrowing some of the rhetoric of the antipoverty and civil rights struggles. Indeed, since before the founding of the PNP, Romero Barceló had pushed for changes that he felt would make statehood more attractive to the less well-off sectors of Puerto Rican society.[23] His innovations cannot be understood if the context of the upheavals of the 1960s is not taken into account.

By the mid-1970s, the upsurges of the previous decade had created a new political landscape in the United States. The civil rights movement had dismantled the segregated regimes of the South. Black resistance in the South and in northern cities had helped reveal the plight of the poor in the largest of the wealthier nations. The combined impact of these struggles had pushed the Johnson administration to pass the Civil Rights Act of 1965, declare a "War on Poverty," and launch the project of the Great Society while acknowledging the state's responsibility in solving long-standing social ills. For many activists in the social movements, these measures were not sufficient. But there is no question that by the early 1970s, a new language of equality, civil rights, welfare, antidiscrimination, integration, and cultural diversity had gained considerable legitimacy in the U.S. political arena, despite the rise of a New Right. Conditions therefore existed for combining the demand for statehood with the civil rights discourse. Statehood could now be presented in terms of equality, the ELA denounced as a form of discrimination, and the growing recognition by the United States of its cultural diversity considered a guarantee for Puerto Rican cultural identity under statehood. Expanding federal social programs could be presented as proof of statehood's benefits for Puerto Rico's poor.

It was in this context that Romero Barceló articulated a new statehood discourse, best summarized in the title of his 1972 pamphlet *Statehood Is for the Poor*. Romero Barceló denounced the fact that some federal programs were not extended to the island as a form of discrimination. He insisted that statehood would increase federal funds received by poor Puerto Ricans and criticized the PPD for placing the interests of those who did benefit from the existing status—namely, the tax-exempt corporations—above the well-being of the poor.

In the past, Puerto Rican parties had identified with opposing dominant parties in the United States. The PPD had links with the Democratic Party, going back to the New Deal, while the statehooders were close to the Republican Party. Romero Barceló broke that alignment in 1964–65, arguing that the statehood message was being hindered by its association with the socially conservative Republicans.

In a 1980 article in *Foreign Affairs*, during his first term as governor, Romero Barceló explained his agenda: after winning the elections of 1980, he would sponsor a plebiscite on the status question. Armed with the mandate for statehood he expected to obtain, he would begin an aggressive campaign in Congress to ensure the rapid admission of Puerto Rico as a state.[24]

It is not hard to enumerate some of the obstacles that the ascendant statehood movement would confront in the United States. They included racist opposition to the annexation of a territory whose population is considered nonwhite; nativist or nationalist opposition to the incorporation of an island

PNP leader Luis A. Ferré (governor, 1968–72) (left) and Carlos Romero Barceló (governor, 1976–84). Under their leadership, the statehood movement reformulated its tactics and discourse in the late 1960s. (Proyecto digitalización fotos El Mundo–Biblioteca José M. Lázaro, Universidad de Puerto Rico–Río Piedras)

whose inhabitants' vernacular is not English; and conservative opposition to the annexation of a territory whose population is markedly poorer than that of any other state and whose full eligibility for federal assistance programs would imply a considerable added burden. Not the least contradiction of the statehood movement was and is the fact that the economic gap that makes statehood attractive to many in Puerto Rico makes it unpopular in Washington: insistence on increased federal funds under statehood may get votes in Puerto Rico but not in Congress. Moreover, even if statehood obtained majority support, political caution dictated careful consideration before admitting a state that would predictably include a sizable minority opposed to annexation. This led to talk of the need for a "super-majority" to make statehood viable. And finally, the statehood movement had to devise a strategy to confront the opposition to annexation by sectors of U.S. capital that benefited from features of the existing status, such as the "936 corporations," whose tax benefits would vanish if Puerto Rico became a state.

Most of these obstacles to annexation had existed since 1898. The Foraker

Act of 1900 was itself an indication that Congress at the time did not wish to make Puerto Rico a state or a future state, which is what both the Partido Federal and the Partido Republicano had requested. Similarly, the extension of U.S. citizenship to Puerto Rico in 1917 had been emphatically described by its proponents as not constituting a promise of future statehood. The U.S. Supreme Court later determined that the measure had not altered Puerto Rico's status as a nonincorporated territory. During the 1930s, several statehood bills introduced by Resident Commissioner Santiago Iglesias had received no attention in Congress. During the 1940s, Congress had shown reluctance to place statehood among the options in a possible plebiscite.

But there is logic to the persistence of the statehood movement. From its inception, it made a wager on the long-term, objective effects of U.S. rule over Puerto Rico. Thus, statehooders felt, and feel, that Congress would and will eventually have to search for a more permanent option to the existing arrangement. Meanwhile, the mesh of economic, social, migratory, and cultural links between Puerto Rico and the United States continues to thicken, tending to make statehood a more viable option than independence. Thus, free trade as established by the Foraker Act and citizenship as extended by the Jones Act would prove to be objective steps toward statehood, even if Congress had not conceived them as such. This, of course, calls for patience. It implies waiting for as many decades as it takes for Congress to adjust its collective mind to the objective trends it has put in motion. As Juan B. Huyke argued in 1945: "*Independentistas* are in a hurry. It is natural. They wish to turn their fatherland into a republic as soon as possible to prevent the slow process of Americanization from having its effect on the people." For the very same reason, statehooders need not hurry. "Time," he explained, "is omnipotent."[25]

By 1976, Romero Barceló seemed to herald the arrival of a more impatient annexationism. But the PNP, in spite of its rhetoric, was not, and is not, a poor people's or an insurgent civil rights movement or coalition. It is a political party, like the PPD, led and controlled by sectors of the local possessing classes. Its links to the poor are typically clientelist. Thus, the demand for welfare benefits and the promise of higher minimum wages or of more funds for students was expected to translate into votes for the PNP, not into the growth of social movements to sustain such demands. As a party committed to the preservation of the existing economic and property relations acting in a period of austerity, the PNP could not but turn against militant labor, student, community, and poor people's struggles when they did emerge. The discrepancy between its defense of statehood as good for the poor and its policies within

Puerto Rico was considerable. Thus, if we take the 1976–84 period, Governor Romero Barceló, while favoring the extension to the island of the federal minimum wage, moved against unions demanding higher wages from his government, such as the electrical-power system union, the Unión de Trabajadores de la Industria Eléctrica y Riego (UTIER), in its 1977–78 and 1981–82 strikes. While speaking of the benefits that statehood would secure for students, university tuition hikes during his administration provoked a long and militant student strike in 1981. While speaking of statehood's benefits for the poor, he severely repressed poor people's movements, such as Villa Sin Miedo (a squatter community in Río Grande), which was violently dislodged by the police in May 1982. In February 1980, a similar eviction had resulted in the death of Adolfina Villanueva in the town of Loíza, an event that became an emblem of the brutal behavior of the police toward dispossessed sectors.

A similar dynamic operated in other fields. While speaking about the guarantees to Puerto Rican culture under statehood, Romero Barceló was in fact worried that insistence on a distinct Puerto Rican identity could be construed as anti-American. He thus moved to limit even such domesticated vehicles of Puerto Rican cultural affirmation as the Instituto de Cultura Puertorriqueña. Similarly, while sometimes boldly affirming that he would favor independence if Congress denied statehood, he was in fact worried that the actions and visibility of the independence movement would make many congressmen and U.S. policy makers less likely to support statehood.

These actions guaranteed considerable opposition to the PNP and the Romero Barceló government, including that of a persistent Left. The Left, in spite of its small electoral presence, retained significant influence and visibility as a participant in student, community and labor mobilizations, including those provoked by Romero Barceló's heavy-handed policies. For example, the 1977–78 UTIER strike of some 6,000 electrical workers was led by Luis Lausell, a member of the Partido Socialista Puertorriqueño, while the main leader of the 1981 student strike against tuition hikes was Roberto Alejandro, a militant of the Movimiento Socialista de Trabajadores. Furthermore, this was a period of intensified actions both in Puerto Rico and the United States by groups advocating armed struggle against U.S. rule.

A Small War: Armed Struggle and Repression in the 1970s

In the mid-1970s, several *independentista* groups opted to follow the path of the earlier Comandos Armados de Liberación and the Movimiento Revolucionario

One of many marches during the 1980–81 student strike against tuition increases at the University of Puerto Rico. The strike was one of several major conflicts that marked the administration of Governor Carlos Romero Barceló. The main strike leader, Roberto Alejandro, is fifth from the left in the first row. (Proyecto digitalización fotos El Mundo–Biblioteca José M. Lázaro, Universidad de Puerto Rico–Río Piedras)

Armado, which had been active in the late 1960s. They sought to make U.S. colonial rule increasingly costly to the federal government and less secure for U.S. investors.

On the island, Socialist *independentistas* organized the Ejército Popular Boricua-Macheteros in 1978. In 1974, *independentistas* and community activists in Chicago had organized the Fuerzas Armadas de Liberación Nacional. Between 1974 and 1981 the FALN took responsibility for close to 120 bombings, mostly directed at U.S. government agencies (Department of Defense, FBI, military recruiting stations) or the offices of multinational corporations (Sears, Mobil, Citibank, Chase Manhattan). Five persons were killed as a result of this campaign. One action was particularly controversial. In 1975, after a bomb placed by an unidentified right-wing group near an *independentista* rally in Mayagüez killed two, the FALN responded by placing a bomb in a New York City restaurant, killing four customers. This action was criticized even by some who defended the legitimacy of armed actions as an attack on civilians who had no say in U.S. policy.

In December 1979, an attack on a U.S. Navy bus by the Macheteros resulted in the death of two servicemen. In January 1981, a Machetero operation destroyed eight fighter planes, valued at $40 million, at the National Guard Air Force Base in San Juan. By 1983, it became public that the multimillion-dollar holdup of the Wells Fargo facilities in Hartford by employee Victor Gerena had also been a Machetero operation directed at financing further *independentista* initiatives. Labor struggles were also marked by acts of sabotage, such as those preceding and coinciding with the 1977–78 electrical workers' strike, during which militant groups sought to paralyze the electric grid, while the government increased vigilance to prevent a blackout.

Meanwhile, federal grand jury investigations seeking information on clandestine activities led to the incarceration of activists who refused to testify. Between 1980 and 1983, several raids led to the arrest and conviction of fifteen Chicago *independentistas* accused of belonging to the FALN. Considered security risks by prison authorities because of their political views and unrepentant attitude, FALN prisoners were from the start kept in almost complete isolation, denied all but the most limited contact with friends and family. After their conviction, they were kept in maximum security and special control units, such as those in Lexington, Kentucky, and Marion, Illinois.

In August 1985, the FBI arrested twenty-one persons in Puerto Rico and the United States, including Filiberto Ojeda and well-known labor lawyer Jorge Farinacci, who were accused of participating in the diverse actions claimed by the Macheteros. The trials resulted in eleven new convictions. The liberation of the *independentista* prisoners and the denunciation of the inhuman conditions to which many were subjected became part of the agenda of *independentista* organizations through the 1980s and 1990s.

The counterpart to all this was Romero Barceló's active harassment of the Left as he sought to portray it as a terrorist, externally financed fringe. During the late 1970s, traditional government monitoring of left activists was complemented by the creation of specialized "antiterrorist" units and the emergence beyond them of autonomous groups of police officers who combined harassment of the *independentista* and union Left with profitable smuggling, extortion, and kidnapping operations. The activities of this mesh of police "intelligence" activity and ganglike intimidation culminated in the killing of two *independentistas* at Cerro Maravilla on July 25, 1978. Led by a police undercover agent who had gained their trust, young activists Arnaldo Darío Rosado and Carlos Soto Arriví attempted to destroy government television transmission towers in the central mountain range of Puerto Rico. Captured alive by the police, they were executed on the spot. The official version, which claimed they had been killed during the initial gun battle, was contradicted by Julio Ortiz Molina, the *público* driver who had been commandeered to Cerro Maravilla by the two *independentistas* and the undercover agent. According to Ortiz Molina, Soto and Rosado had been captured alive by the police. Governor Romero Barceló stood by the official version. Bitter controversy erupted as many felt that the incident had been a well-planned entrapment, conducted for political and propagandistic effect.

These events plagued Romero Barceló through his second administration. After taking control of the Senate in the 1980 elections, the PPD sponsored an investigation that by 1983 confirmed, in televised hearings watched by a deeply shaken public, that the two *independentistas* had indeed been killed after being taken alive. The investigation unveiled the repeated attempts by insular prosecutors and federal agents, above all the San Juan office of the FBI, to cover up what had taken place in Cerro Maravilla.[26] The undercover agent involved in the case was himself killed in April 1986 by a clandestine *independentista* group.

None of these often dramatic conflicts implied that the PNP ceased to be a major political force that enjoyed considerable support. But they did generate substantial opposition from wide sectors. In the end, Romero Barceló's anti-*independentista* campaign backfired, as many who did not sympathize with independence still came to see its supporters as the victims of illegal government repression and persecution.

Romero Barceló and Section 936: From Denunciation to Accommodation

In the area of economic policy, the Romero Barceló administration at first seemed ready to make good on its promise of phasing out the tax exemptions enjoyed by U.S. corporations in order to lay the groundwork for an economy more compatible with statehood. Thus, in 1978, the PNP administration amended tax incentive legislation to impose some insular taxes on U.S. investments. But by the time Congress began considering proposals to reduce benefits provided by Section 936, the recession of the early 1980s had dealt another blow to the insular economy. At a critical moment, Romero Barceló decided not to challenge the entrenched economic structure created by Puerto Rico's industrialization program. With official unemployment rates reaching 23 percent, he now chose to lobby in favor of Section 936, thus helping preserve what he had long described as one of the pillars of the ELA.

Already in 1980, electoral results had demonstrated that the embattled Romero Barceló had not been able to build the electoral majority he needed for the push for statehood. Not only was he reelected by a very slim margin (.2 percent, or just over 3,000 votes), but the PNP lost control of the legislature. In that context, a sector of the PNP led by San Juan mayor Hernán Padilla, perceiving Romero Barceló's falling support and isolation, sought to provide a new option to statehood voters by organizing the Partido de Renovación Puertorriqueña in 1983. This party disappeared after the elections of 1984 but not without contributing to the defeat of the PNP by taking around 70,000 votes away from it. After eight years in the opposition, the PPD was back in office.

Crisis on the Left

The rise of an aggressive statehood movement led by Romero Barceló and the faltering of the labor movement after the 1974 recession helped to accentuate debates within the Left. While some followed the path of armed struggle mentioned above, differences widened between the Partido Independentista Puertorriqueño and the PSP and within the PSP itself.

Since its birth, the PSP included two currents: on the one hand, a left-nationalism that, for all its sympathies for labor and poor people's struggles, retained independence as its central goal,[27] and, on the other hand, a more class-oriented perspective that tended to see independence as one aspect, although a central one, of the struggle for socialism. If the first wing could be easily drawn toward an alliance with the PPD to confront the threat of annexation, the second group, without denying the need for alliances, tended to emphasize the need to build an independent working-class movement.

Under the PPD administration of 1969–75, the first position seemed to dominate party policy. Secretary General Juan Mari Brás argued in 1973 that the PPD's demand for autonomy in specific areas—minimum wage, the environment, and coastwise shipping—corresponded to its desire to enhance the prerogatives of U.S. corporations in Puerto Rico. It was, he argued, a pseudo-autonomism that could only deepen the island's dependence on the United States.[28] Similarly, the party's most complete programmatic statement, *La alternativa socialista*, issued in 1974, had argued that the overthrow of capitalism was a precondition for true independence. A capitalist independence would imply continued subordination to the United States. The document described the PPD as the representative of the most powerful imperialist interests in Puerto Rico.[29] Such considerations seemed to foreclose any alliance with the PPD.

But the political context after 1976 facilitated the reassertion of the left-nationalist orientation. The aggressiveness of the PNP statehood offensive after 1976 evidently had an impact. By early 1978, both Mari Brás and other PSP leaders were promoting the idea of a broad anti-annexation front and initially mentioned former governor Sánchez Vilella as its possible figurehead. The notion was gradually broadened to include the possibility of an alliance with a wing of the PPD.[30]

This inclination was facilitated by shifts within the PPD. By 1978, former governor Hernández Colón, defeated in the elections of 1976, dispirited by the failure of the "New Compact," and humiliated by President Ford's 1976 pro-statehood declaration, became more critical of U.S. policies. He now explained in his "New Thesis" that growing federal intervention had progressively eroded the ELA's autonomy. The ELA not only had failed to grow but had shrunk. It was necessary to reinitiate the struggle for autonomy.[31] Meanwhile, the PPD, faced with the PNP statehood offensive, accentuated the cultural/*puertorriqueñista* dimension of its political discourse.[32]

For PSP leader Mari Brás, these and other developments—such as Hernández Colón's participation (contrary to past PPD policy) in the 1978 U.N. Decolonization Committee's hearings on Puerto Rico—opened the path for a PPD-*independentista* alliance.[33] By way of contrast, the PIP insisted that the slight reforms sought by the PPD and Hernández Colón would only help perpetuate the existing colonial arrangement. Statehood, according to the PIP, was not an immediate danger, given the lack of support for it in U.S. policy-making circles. The threat of a lightly made-over colony, and not statehood, should be the main concern of the independence movement.[34] Needless to say, an increased *independentista* vote for the PPD to allegedly block statehood would have threatened the PIP with the loss of its ballot status, a dire prospect for a party that was already then a fundamentally electoral organization. A combination of anticolonial conviction and the imperatives of electoral self-preservation thus drove PIP leaders to a more critical view of the PPD.

By 1982, Mari Brás had embraced the idea of an alliance with the "patriotic" wing of the PPD. Since the Puerto Rican bourgeoisie was becoming increasingly annexationist, he argued, the PPD's enduring support was a reflection of the workers' attachment to their *puertorriqueñidad*.[35] An opposition to this orientation crystallized inside the PSP, led by Wilfredo Mattos and Héctor Meléndez, among others, which favored an alternate emphasis on the construction of a workers' party and a more cautious approach to possible alliances with the PPD. The debate concluded with the expulsion of the opposition during the 1982 party congress. Mari Brás left the PSP to pursue the possibility of a broad national liberation front. As the 1984 electoral battle intensified, the PSP formulated thinly disguised calls for a vote for the PPD in order to defeat Romero Barceló's bid for reelection. By 1985, the party was a shadow of its former self. The crisis of the PSP marked the end of a phase in the history of the independence movement that had begun with the creation of the Movimiento Pro Independencia in 1959 and reached its peak around 1975, at the height of the PSP's visibility and influence and the PIP's revitalization.

Déjà Vu: The PPD and Hernández Colón Back in Government, 1984–1992

Beginning in 1985, the new PPD administration under Hernández Colón deployed an agenda that reproduced its 1972–76 orientation, namely, a systematic defense of the tax-exemption policy around Section 936, an accentuation of the *puertorriqueñista* discourse that differentiated it from the PNP, and a new attempt to reform the existing status. Regarding the latter, the objectives of the PPD were again frustrated.

In 1989, Senator Bennett Johnston (D-La.), head of the Energy and Natural Resources Committee (entrusted with issues related to territories and possessions), announced his intention of devising legislation that would lead to a resolution of the status question. For some, this initiative confirmed a theory that political analyst Juan M. García Passalacqua had put forth in 1984 to the effect that influential U.S. policy-making circles had decided to steer Puerto Rico toward independence, which would take the form of an "associated re-

Rafael Hernández Colón, governor in 1972–76 and 1984–92 and the main leader of the PPD during the 1970s and 1980s. Beside him is Sila M. Calderón, PPD governor, 2000–2004. (Proyecto digitalización fotos El Mundo–Biblioteca José M. Lázaro, Universidad de Puerto Rico–Río Piedras)

public." This orientation was allegedly based on the realization that by making Puerto Rico a republic, the United States could secure its interests there at a lesser expense than in the existing arrangement. Other analysts questioned this appreciation. They felt that concern with federal expenditures in Puerto Rico was not critical enough to drive an attempt to alter the status quo, which remained politically stable.[36] Events between 1984 and 1992 tended to confirm the view that the vector of congressional and federal executive policy still leaned toward perpetuating the status quo.

Senator Johnston favored a mechanism that would include a plebiscite presenting options previously negotiated with Congress, which would abide by the result. By September 1989, he submitted the first piece of legislation along these lines (S. 712). In the meantime, President George H. W. Bush had affirmed his support of this effort and his personal commitment to statehood for Puerto Rico. A problem soon emerged as it appeared that many congressmen would not commit in advance to statehood, while others questioned the viability and constitutionality of the expanded ELA favored by the PPD. Nor was there any sign of a decided congressional drive to move Puerto Rico toward independence. By February 1991, S. 712 had become S. 244, which failed to gain majority support in committee. In the end, no legislation was approved.

In a sense, this could be construed as a victory for the PPD, since the ELA was to remain in place by default. Yet the erosion of the social situation under it kept feeding a growing dissatisfaction that could be capitalized on by its critics. Furthermore, federal tax exemptions, embodied in Section 936, and the axis of the PPD economic policy were coming under attack in Washington from both the Treasury Department and conservative congressmen committed to a balanced budget. In 1985, faced with such an attack led by influential Senator Robert Dole (R-Kans.), the Hernández Colón administration was able to save Section 936 only by committing some of the 936 funds deposited in Puerto Rico to the development of the Caribbean Basin Initiative, which the Reagan administration was then deploying as a response to the revolutions in Nicaragua and Grenada and to the revolutionary insurgency in El Salvador.[37] Barely saved in 1985, Section 936 was sure to come under fire in the future.

As in the past, the PPD mixed affirmations of Puerto Rican identity with close collaboration with U.S. corporate sectors interested in the privileges made possible by the island's status as a territory of the United States, a possession but not part of it. This double orientation—toward the nationalization of culture and a denationalization of the economy—was dramatically demonstrated in 1990–91 when the Hernández Colón administration simultaneously approved legislation establishing Spanish as Puerto Rico's sole official language while seeking to privatize the Puerto Rico Telephone Company. The most likely buyer of the company would be a U.S. multinational corporation. Of course, this combination of economic reliance on U.S. capital with an accentuated *puertorriqueñista* discourse had characterized autonomism from the 1950s.

In 1991, after the legislation promoted by Senator Johnston failed, the desire to strengthen the ELA against the statehood forces led Governor Hernández Colón to propose several amendments to the ELA constitution, which reaffirmed Puerto Rico's culture as "non-negotiable" under any status. The maneuver backfired. The PNP denounced the amendments as favoring separation from the United States despite the fact that the proposal included a reaffirmation of U.S. citizenship as equally "non-negotiable." Many within the majority of Puerto Ricans who opposed separation from the United States were thus skeptical about the proposed amendments. *Independentistas*, in spite of the position of the PIP and the PSP in favor of a Yes vote, could hardly be very enthusiastic about them either, given their affirmation of U.S. citizenship. On December 8, 1991, ratification of the proposed amendments was rejected by a 53 percent to 45 percent margin. It was a preamble to the statehood party's victory in the general elections of 1992.

Thus, two decades after the end of the postwar boom, Puerto Rican politics were at a stalemate. The relation of nonincorporation, reorganized as the ELA in 1952, implied an increasingly close material connection to the United States while also promoting the feeling of a distinct Puerto Rican identity. It was fertile ground for the existence of currents pushing both in the direction of statehood and of greater political autonomy, without either being able to achieve a clear majority. The PPD, of course, tried to manage those crosscurrents into the continued existence of the ELA, which allowed for a distinct Puerto Rican political and cultural space in close connection to the United States. But the new governor, Pedro Rosselló, promised a new statehood offensive as well as the full incorporation of Puerto Rico into the wave of neoliberal privatization and deregulation sweeping through the capitalist world. The stage was thus set for the political and labor battles of the 1990s.

POLITICS AND SOCIAL CONFLICT IN THE
EPOCH OF NEOLIBERALISM, 1992–2004

In Puerto Rico, the 1990s were years of sharpened political and social conflict. After eight years of Partido Popular Democrático administration, the pro-statehood Partido Nuevo Progresista won the elections of 1992. The new governor, Pedro Rosselló, was committed to a new push for statehood. This led him to organize plebiscites on the status question in 1993 and 1998. Between these initiatives, his administration, with the help of friendly congressmen, lobbied for federal legislation that it hoped would also open the path for statehood. Furthermore, the Rosselló administration embraced what its opponents denounced as a neoliberal economic agenda. In this area, the Rosselló government was part of an international trend.

The response of capitalist states to the end of the postwar boom was quite different from the reaction elicited by the preceding global slowdown of the 1930s. In the 1930s, the crisis led to loss of faith in the tenets of laissez-faire capitalism and legitimized diverse forms of state intervention and regulation of the market economy. Thus, the rise of the PPD in the 1930s had been linked to New Deal regulatory policies. Between 1976 and 1984, Carlos Romero Barceló had tried to link the statehood movement to the last wave of social reforms arising within that framework from the upheavals of the 1960s. But the deepening crisis provoked a rejection, by the late 1970s and early 1980s, of those regulatory and redistributive policies. The rise of the New Right in the United States fostered the adoption of antiwelfare, privatization, free trade, monetarist, and neoliberal policies. For the PNP to insist on the pro-statehood discourse elaborated in the early 1970s was to set itself against the new dominant currents in U.S. politics. This it was not willing to do. Thus, the PNP that took office in 1992 was not a mere extension of the welfare-statehood populism of Romero Barceló but rather a party that had embraced the neoliberal gospel of entrepreneurial initiative, competition, deregulation, and privatization.

Puerto Rico has a sizable public sector. It had been created by the PPD in the 1940s when public corporations were organized to provide electricity, running water, transportation, and other services. Over the years, public school and health systems expanded, providing services and generating vast bureaucracies. As underlined by James Dietz, it was this type of direct government action, and not the trickle-down impact of foreign direct investments, that was largely responsible for the improved living standards of most Puerto Ricans during the 1950s and 1960s. In 1974, the government acquired the island facilities of International Telephone and Telegraph and also organized its own shipping company. After the economic slowdown of the 1970s, public employment grew, financed by an inflow of federal funds and by government borrowing. Between 1970 and 1988, government employment doubled to almost 225,000. By 1990, almost 25 percent of the labor force was employed by the government.[1]

Arguing that a large public sector hinders entrepreneurial initiative and hurts competitiveness, the Rosselló government embarked on a project of privatization in such areas as jails and school cafeterias; the training of new employees; and shipping, public transport, health, water, electrical, and telephone services. It set out to sell government-operated hotels, convention centers, and agricultural enterprises. Diverse models were employed: privatization of the management of agencies, subcontracting, outright sale of facilities, construction of private installations parallel to public facilities, private operation of toll bridges, and, in the case of education, financial autonomy for schools and school vouchers. Some of these measures were undoubtedly popular. The reform of the health system implied the privatization of public facilities and the creation of a government health insurance for those not covered by private plans. Even if the government-paid plans rationed services, they still gave clients a choice of private providers instead of confining them to public facilities, which had been allowed to decay over the years.

In a similar vein, Rosselló tried to rewrite labor legislation, making it more flexible to employers' needs; to cut back the regulatory power of public agencies (such as the Department of Consumer Affairs); and to speed up the processes of granting permits for building projects (the so-called fast track), thus making it more difficult for community or ecological groups to object or raise questions regarding them. Governor Rosselló's "Nuevo Modelo Económico," issued in February 1994, was a summary of this wide-ranging neoliberal orientation. This project had a clear anti-union dimension: unions are precisely one of the "rigidities" that neoliberalism seeks to eliminate, one of the obstacles to the type of flexibility it would like to guarantee each and every entrepreneur. Rosselló's policies thus implied a confrontation with a labor movement that culminated with the battle over the privatization of the telephone system in 1997–98.

By 1999, two additional issues erupted into Puerto Rican politics. A series of scandals revealed an unprecedented level of corruption amid mid- and high-level government officials. Meanwhile, the killing of a civilian guard during bombing practices conducted by the U.S. Navy on the island of Vieques led to the occupation of the bombing range by protesters. While the camps of civil disobedience paralyzed the navy's operations, initiatives both on the larger island and in the United States built what eventually became mass support for an end to navy operations in Vieques.

Weakened by corruption scandals, the mishandling of the Vieques crisis, and the repression of the phone workers' strike, Rosselló, who had easily won reelection in 1996, chose not to run in 2000. But the PPD, which won the elections of 2000, also faced a major challenge. In 1996, Congress had mandated the phaseout of Section 936 of the U.S. Internal Revenue Code, which had been the centerpiece of the PPD tax exemption policy. The PPD was thus faced with the need of devising a new economic strategy not based on the policies followed since 1947.

A New Statehood Offensive: Plebiscite and Congressional Moves

Soon after taking office and seeking a mandate for statehood, PNP governor Rosselló sponsored a three-way plebiscite (statehood, Estado Libre Asociado, independence) in 1993. The objective of the PNP was a plurality for statehood, sufficient to demonstrate that it now enjoyed more support than any other option. Negotiations with Congress would ensue, leading to the future victory of statehood with even wider support. But the ELA defeated statehood, as it received 48.6 percent of the vote to statehood's 46.3 percent. The bright spot for the PNP leaders was the fact that the ELA failed to reach 50 percent of the vote. While the Partido Independentista Puertorriqueño participated in the plebiscite, other *independentista* groups did not. Independence received 4.4 percent of the vote, a share roughly corresponding to PIP support in regular elections. During the campaign, the PPD ably and effectively linked the ELA to the defense of Puerto Rican culture and identity, a task made easier by the rise of the "English-only" movement in the United States.

The Rosselló administration did not abandon its push for statehood, but it shifted its campaign to Congress. The vehicles for this effort were the bills presented by Representative Don Young of Alaska between 1993 and 1998 (H.R. 3715 in 1993, H.R. 4442 in 1994, H.R. 3024 in 1996, and H.R. 856 in 1998).[2] In its final version, the bill replaced the three options included in previous plebiscites (statehood, ELA, independence) by a choice between three alternative paths: (1) a path toward statehood beginning with incorporation as a territory of the United States; (2) a path toward separate sovereignty to be later defined as either independence or free association; and (3) a reaffirmation of the existing status as an unincorporated territory. The intent of this legislation was evident: it excluded the status option favored by the PPD, that is to say, the ELA defined as a "compact" between Puerto Rico and the United States. The PPD would have to either not participate or choose between endorsing colonialism (path 3) or separation (path 2). This time the measure was brought to a vote in the U.S. House of Representatives in March 1998. It passed by only one vote. A new push was needed if the bill was to pass in the Senate. Thus, in an attempt to speed up the consideration of such legislation, Rosselló decided to call another plebiscite in December 1998. Statehood was again defeated, receiving 46.5 percent of the vote.

But this defeat cannot be divorced from the other dimension of Rosselló's agenda: his policies toward the labor movement, which were in turn shaped by his neoliberal economic program on the one hand and by short-term political considerations on the other. While the neoliberal economic agenda led him into a sharp conflict with sectors of the union movement, short-term considerations pushed him to make some concessions in the hope of gaining the support—or at least the neutrality—of some unions.

Privatization and "La Huelga del Pueblo"

After the 1969–75 upsurge, the labor movement sank into a period of demobilization. The electrical power workers' strikes in 1977–78 and 1981 were significant exceptions. While the 1977–78 strike ended in a draw, the 1981 conflict resulted in a defeat for the electrical workers' union, the Unión de Trabajadores de la Industria Eléctrica y Riego. In the private sector, the 1985 strike at the *San Juan Star* newspaper, during which the strikers published an alternative biweekly (the *San Juan Sun*), provided a brief interlude of labor militancy and creativity. The labor movement remained fragmented into several currents: the AFL-CIO affiliates, the officially social-Christian Central Puertorriqueña de Trabajadores (CPT, organized in 1982) and the more left-wing Concilio General de Trabajadores (CGT, organized in 1983), and independent unions, such as UTIER. Some unions belonging to the CGT were linked to AFL-CIO unions—such as the Federación de Maestros, affiliated with the American Federation of Teachers—but were more active in the insular confederation.

During the 1980s, the labor movement retreated in the private sector, hard hit by the closing of shoe, garment, tuna, oil refining, and other operations that had been unionized before the crisis of Operation Bootstrap in the mid-1970s. The pharmaceutical, electronics, and precision instruments industries that expanded through the 1980s employed a relatively small labor force, paid wages considerably higher than other sectors, and implemented strict anti-union policies—barriers that unions have so far been unable to surmount. The level of unionization in manufacturing collapsed from 30 percent in 1970 to 2 percent in 2000. The bulk of the labor movement thus came to be located in the public sector. The rate of organization in the public sector went from 7 percent to 29 percent during the same period.[3] But in this case, organization did not necessarily mean unionization, since public sector workers faced different legal dispositions that shaped the type of organizations that emerged.

The public sector in Puerto Rico includes public corporations and regular government agencies. Public corporations are government-owned operations that enjoy fiscal and financial autonomy. Their workers are covered by Law 130 of May 8, 1945, which recognizes their right to organize, collectively bargain, and strike. Regular state employees were not granted these rights, although another law (134 of July 19, 1960) allowed for dues checkoff to employee associations. This implied widely varying situations, from agencies where organizations did not exist or were very weak, to those with strong associations (non-teaching staff at the University of Puerto Rico, for example) capable of forcing their employers to sign agreements, to associations organizing a minority of their sector but still capable of effective mobilizations, such as the (then) 10,000-member strong Federación de Maestros. By 1996, around 62,000 employees, or close to 25 percent of the government workforce, belonged to associations organized under Law 134.[4]

Across these varied contexts, the neoliberal privatizing and subcontracting project had an immediate anti-union effect in that it could weaken, fragment, reduce, or destroy key labor organizations. In 1993, Rosselló's proto-privatization project of "community schools" led to a confrontation with the main teachers' organizations. Many judged this to have been an ingredient in his defeat in the 1993 status plebiscite.

But in his attempt to obtain support for his administration and for the push for statehood, Rosselló was also willing to make concessions. He thus sought to obtain the endorsements, or at least neutrality, of some unions by combining his privatization policies with legislation that would allow public employees to unionize and bargain collectively. In January 1995, he introduced an initial bill recognizing the right of public employees to organize and bargain collectively while prohibiting strikes and similar actions.

The initiative was expected to have several positive effects from Rosselló's perspective. It could soften the opposition of some unions to privatization (and split the labor movement), to the extent that some considered organizing a reduced public labor force more attractive than an all-out fight against privatization. While recognizing the right to bargain, it allowed the government to restrict the activities of the existing associations, which, for the very same reason that they were not officially recognized unions, were not subject to penalties for their initiatives. Rosselló could even hope that some AFL-CIO unions, in exchange for the unionization bill, would help him lobby for some of his initiatives in Congress. While there is no proof that the AFL-CIO lobbied directly for the Young bill sponsored by Rosselló, researcher César Rosado has documented that some of its affiliates helped open doors for Rosselló in Washington. For their part, some AFL-CIO unions invested considerable effort in getting action from Puerto Rico's legislators, to the point of getting Vice President Al Gore to urge the latter to approve the proposed bill. It must have been evident to PNP legislators that adoption of the proposed legislation could help whatever agenda they wished to take to Washington under the Clinton administration.[5] More immediately, the 1995 initiative was an attempt to gain support in preparation for the 1996 elections.

Nevertheless, in 1995, Rosselló's policy-mix failed to strike the right balance: while the unionization bill was being discussed, his administration introduced a series of neoliberal amendments to existing labor legislation granting employers greater flexibility in determining employment and working conditions and eroding workers' rights and protections, a move that generated strong opposition within the union movement. In this context, the unionization bill—opposed by some in the labor movement who considered it too restrictive and questioned by private employers who felt it was not restrictive enough—failed to obtain sufficient support during the legislative session.

While the negotiations around a public sector unionization bill went on, the struggle over privatization entered a new stage in April 1997 after the governor announced his intention of privatizing the Puerto Rico Telephone Company (PRTC).[6] As the largest, most successful public corporation, the PRTC was the prize of Rosselló's privatization program. Rafael Hernández Colón, PPD governor between 1984 and 1992, had already proposed privatizing it in February 1990, but the proposal had generated widespread opposition. Most Puerto Ricans could remember the expensive and poor services offered by private provider ITT before 1974. Opposition to Hernández Colón's proposal led to a public employees' one-day general strike (*paro*) on March 28, 1990, which included a 50,000-strong march in San Juan. Hernández Colón was not able to sell the PRTC at the time, although the smaller long distance service of Telefónica Larga Distancia was sold to a Spanish firm in 1992.

Rosselló's 1997 privatization initiative generated even wider opposition. A new Comité Amplio de Organizaciones Sociales, Sindicales, Políticas, Comunales, Estudiantiles y Religiosas, or CAOS for short, was created on August 3, 1997. CAOS was a broad coalition coordinated by the telephone unions open to all social, political, student, environmental, women's, and religious organizations opposed to privatization. The teachers' federation, the association of nonteaching university staff, and the electrical workers' union were the backbone of the more militant wing of CAOS, which also included revived student organizations. Student activists turned the university campus in Río Piedras into the site of antiprivatization protests, all the more intensely after the Rosselló administration announced plans to finance its school voucher program through reduction in the funds available for the university.

At its height, CAOS functioned as a broad front against privatization that insisted on the responsibility of the state to provide essential services for all, questioned the expansion of multinational corporate control of key sectors of the insular infrastructure, and affirmed the right of citizens to have a say on key policy decisions. The popular slogan "Puerto Rico no se vende," which can be translated as both "Puerto Rico is not for sale" and "Puerto Rico does not sell out," synthesized the mix of labor, social, democratic, and national demands that informed the antiprivatization campaign between October 1997 and July 1998. CAOS carried out a successful *paro* on October 1, 1997, which greatly surpassed its 1990 predecessor. This time the strikers could count on the support of the PPD, which opposed privatization of the phone company as proposed by Rosselló, although not privatization in general.

CAOS was nevertheless seen by part of the labor leadership, particularly sectors of the CPT and some AFL-CIO unions, as a threat. Some AFL-CIO unions considered it an impediment to their hopes of obtaining favorable actions from the PNP administration, namely the passing of public employee union legislation. In the midst of the debates over the privatization of the PRTC, the

Union protest against privatization in 1998. In 1997–98, the battle over the privatization of the Puerto Rico Telephone Company shook the island more than any other labor conflict in decades. It was led by a broad coalition under the motto "¡Puerto Rico no se vende!" (Puerto Rico is not for sale or Puerto Rico will not sell out). (JAM)

intense AFL-CIO lobbying for a public employees' union law bore fruit with the passing of Law 45 in February 1998 (Puerto Rico Public Service Labor Relations Act). Law 45 recognized the right of public workers to bargain collectively, but it denied them the right to strike and severely penalized any action intended to interrupt the labor process. Thus, at least initially, the quantitative growth of many unions corresponded to a lower level of mobilization and activism. Furthermore, the need to select union representatives and the competitive dynamic within a fragmented labor movement led to bitter clashes between independent unions and AFL-CIO affiliates and, in some cases, between AFL-CIO affiliates. By 2000, unions certified under the new legislation had organized about 23 percent of all public sector workers.[7] Many, as indicated, had been already organized under Law 134, which did not include the restrictions enunciated in the new legislation but had not allowed them to negotiate binding collective agreements.

But union organizing, or reorganizing, under Law 45 was barely beginning in 1998. Meanwhile, as the centennial year of the U.S. occupation progressed, CAOS gathered considerable support, in spite of internal conflicts. By May 1998, Governor Rosselló announced that the PRTC would be sold to U.S. communications giant GTE (later acquired by Verizon) and a group of Puerto Rican investors headed by Banco Popular.

In spite of the systematic delaying actions of some labor leaders, a telephone workers' strike against privatization began on June 18. It was marked by widespread support for the strikers and culminated in a two-day general strike on July 7–8, which shook the island like no other labor action in recent history. The strike was also marked by repeated violent clashes between riot police and striking workers. Defeated by exhaustion and by the disorganization and disorientation fostered by leaders who had opposed the strike from the start, telephone workers ended the strike on July 21. CAOS did not survive much longer. The labor movement emerged weakened and divided from its largest mobilizations in decades, even if the popularity of Governor Rosselló had also suffered deeply as a result of the battle over the privatization of the PRTC.[8]

It was in this context that Governor Rosselló, hoping to reinvigorate the Young bill in Congress, decided to call a plebiscite on the status question in December 1998. And like the Young bill, he tried to ensure the defeat of the ELA by excluding it from the ballot. The ballot included four options: statehood, independence, free association (which most autonomists reject), and the existing status, defined as an unincorporated territory (a definition supporters of the ELA also reject). With the autonomists not voting or dividing their vote between the last two options, statehood would win the plebiscite. Nevertheless, as a result of a lawsuit and a decision of the Puerto Rico Supreme Court on the occasion of the 1993 plebiscite, the ballot included a fifth option: "None of the above."

The PPD decided to call for a vote for "None of the above." So did others wishing to express their opposition to the governor's policies, such as the handling of the telephone workers' strike. The vote for "None of the above," far from representing a rejection of politics, as it is sometimes construed, was as political a statement as any made in previous elections. The result was a defeat for Rosselló: statehood received 46.5 percent of the vote to 50.3 percent for "None of the above." The former was a slight improvement over the 46.3 percent obtained in 1993 (a loss of 61,000 votes in absolute terms) but hardly the show of strength needed to impress Congress. Then in April 1999, a further latent conflict exploded with unexpected force.

Since before 1898, Puerto Rico had been considered of significant strategic importance to the United States military. During World War II, the U.S. military presence significantly increased. A vast navy base was built in Ceiba (Roosevelt Roads), which also incorporated portions of Vieques and Culebra. By 1947, the navy controlled two-thirds of Vieques. The emergence of an active resistance to the navy presence in Culebra was one of the significant mobilizations of the late 1960s. The navy withdrew from Culebra in 1975 but intensified its use of Vieques.[9]

Beginning in 1975, protests grew in Vieques with fishermen playing a leading role, culminating with the arrest of twenty-one activists on May 19, 1979. Found guilty of trespassing, they were sentenced to several months in federal prison. One of them, Angel Rodríguez Cristóbal, member of the *independentista* Liga Socialista, was killed in a federal prison in Tallahassee, Florida. The protests continued through the 1980s and 1990s, sustained by local activists and mostly *independentista* supporters from the larger island. Then, on April 19, 1999, a navy F-18 plane missed its target and killed civilian guard David Sanes. Coming in the wake of months of agitation—marches, *paros*, two general strikes—against privatization of the PRTC and building on decades of activism against the navy, the local reaction of indignation soon became an island-wide movement demanding the end of the navy occupation of Vieques. Hundreds of civilian protesters built camps on the navy-held beaches. The campaign was led by, among others, public school teacher Ismael Guadalupe, fishermen Carlos Zenón and Carlos Ventura, resident North American activist Robert Rabin, and groups such as the Comité Pro Rescate y Deasarrollo de Vieques and the Alianza de Mujeres Viequenses, coordinated by Nilda Medina. Thousands visited or stayed in the encampments during the following thirteen months. Even Governor Rosselló called for the withdrawal of the navy. A special commission appointed by him in May 1999 recommended an immediate and permanent end of bombing practices in Vieques.

Given the strength of the movement, President Clinton had instructed the secretary of defense to name a Vieques Comprehensive Review Commission to study the situation. A final proposal was announced by Clinton in February 2000 in an unprecedented broadcast by a U.S. president to the Puerto Rican people: a referendum would be held in Vieques on the continuation or termination of navy operations. If termination was the favored option, the navy would leave by May 2003. Protesters in the bombing areas would be removed,

A march against the U.S. Navy presence in Vieques in 2000. Protesters carry a photo of Angel Rodríguez Cristobal, a socialist activist killed in a U.S. prison in Florida. After the killing of civilian guard David Sanes during bombing practice in April 1999, the movement to end the use of Vieques by the U.S. Navy grew to encompass mobilizations in Vieques, the larger island, and the United States. (JAM)

and bombing practices with "inert bombs," limited to ninety days per year, would resume.

The offer of withdrawal in three years' time was no mean achievement, given the navy's past declarations. Governor Rosselló agreed to Clinton's terms. But the large and still growing movement was in no mood for compromise. The idea of dismantling the peace encampments so the bombing could resume was simply not acceptable. Rosselló was widely denounced for accepting Clinton's terms. On February 21, 2000, the largest march in Puerto Rico in recent times (estimated at 150,000) reasserted the demand that the navy quit Vieques. Puerto Rican activists in the United States mobilized to demand the pullout of the navy. The federal government, aware of the widespread support for the protesters, did not act to remove them from the navy-held beaches until May 4, 2000. Confrontations continued as every set of bombing practices brought new acts of civil disobedience. Between May 2000 and May 2003, around 1,300 persons were arrested for their participation in acts of civil disobedience related to the Vieques conflict.

Participants in civil disobedience activities plant a palm tree on one of the navy-held beaches in 2001. (JAM)

The Rosselló administration faced another crisis. Beginning with the No-vember 1998 indictment of Toa Alta PNP mayor Angel Rodríguez for extortion and illegal use of federal hurricane relief funds, a series of scandals revealed how the elevation of individual enrichment to the status of a new social ideal had produced a veritable explosion of government corruption. Investigations, principally by the federal prosecutor in San Juan, eventually led to the arrest and conviction of the secretary of education, the president of the House of Representatives, the head of the Ports Authority, and the director of the AIDS Institute, among other high officials of the Rosselló administration, as well as several PNP mayors and legislators or former legislators for their role in diverse fraud and payback schemes. Many of the fraud and embezzlement ploys in-volved federal funds. It certainly did not help the case for statehood that the party supporting it was so deeply involved in the illegal appropriation of fed-eral monies.

The combined and cumulative impact of the telephone workers' strike, the defeat in the 1998 plebiscite, the ongoing Vieques conflict, and the growing corruption scandals led to Rosselló's decision not to run for reelection as well as to the eventual defeat of the PNP in the 2000 elections.[10] A new PPD administration was thus inaugurated in 2001, now headed by Puerto Rico's first woman governor, Sila Calderón.

Neoliberalism in El Barrio and Beyond

While the labor movement in Puerto Rico was faced with the insular version of privatization and deregulation policies, poor and working-class Puerto Ricans in the United States were hit by cuts in state social and welfare programs. For the oldest Puerto Rican communities in the U.S. mainland, the intensification of this neoliberal offensive was signaled by the election of Rudolph Giuliani as mayor of New York City in 1993 and of George Pataki as state governor in 1994. Under their combined efforts, programs serving the poor, homeless, and unemployed were drastically cut. Tuition hikes were decreed for the City University of New York. All of these measures had a disproportionate impact on a Puerto Rican population already hard hit by the collapse of manufacturing in New York, in which many had been employed in the past.

Federal cutbacks in subsidized housing construction and the failure of municipalities to maintain low-cost housing heightened the vulnerability of low-income sectors to displacement by the process—commonly referred to as gentrification—of upgrading decayed housing for renting or selling to higher income sectors or for commercial or corporate use. The debates and struggles around gentrification, like the battles over privatization, opposed two divergent social and economic orientations: on the one hand, a corporate agenda that promoted the subordination of all economic decisions to the criteria of private profitability (as reflected in the choices of financial investors, real estate interests, and developers), and on the other, a demand for public curbing of the destructive consequences of the "free market" in the interest of community needs for employment, housing, and other basic services.

In the case of Puerto Rican communities in New York and Chicago, the fight over gentrification took on a national-cultural dimension. State policies favoring gentrification through privatization of housing and city services have often been defended, according to Arlene Dávila's study of El Barrio, through a critique of ethnic (in this case Puerto Rican) claims to space (El Barrio) as a narrow "discourse of the past" that should now give way to a broader multi-culturalism.[11] Renewal through the attraction of new private investments is in turn presented as a route to success in a new global economy. Against this, as Gina M. Pérez has put it (referring to Chicago), community activists have deployed "cultural symbols to construct a 'Puerto Rican space' that preserves neighborhood use value."[12] Such struggles affirm, Dávila adds, that in spite of neoliberal pretensions, "people and places are never easily reducible into commodities." In a sense, this has been a barrio version of the island cry against the privatization of the PRTC: *Puerto Rico no se vende*.[13] In Chicago, these efforts led to the transformation of a stretch of Division Street into Paseo Boricua, book-ended by two steel sculptures of the Puerto Rican flag, as monumental a claim to Puerto Rican space as one could think of. Less grandiose but no less important and perhaps more fully linked to community activism has been the trend in New York, Boston, and Chicago itself to reclaim vacant lots to construct *casitas* (small houses) as community centers that reproduce traditional Puerto Rican rural dwellings as well as the taking over of decayed structures and walls to paint murals depicting aspects of Puerto Rican culture, history, and past social struggles.

Nevertheless, as Pérez, Dávila, and Ana Y. Ramos-Zayas have chronicled, not all Puerto Ricans are poor or working-class, and there has been contention about how to confront gentrification in particular and how to face the neoliberal, antiwelfare, privatizing offensive in general. Upwardly mobile, middle-class Puerto Rican professionals often criticize inner-city activists for promoting a narrow-minded nationalist outlook instead of teaching the skills needed for a professional career or for successful entrepreneurship. For them, Nationalist leader Pedro Albizu Campos, an icon of community struggles, is a convicted inspirer of attacks on a U.S. president and Congress and hardly an adequate emblem for Puerto Ricans in the United States. "Barrio nationalism," argues Ramos-Zayas, was deployed in the 1990s not only against the surrounding Anglo culture but also against what are seen as middle-class "assimilated" Puerto Ricans, disconnected from the problems of "la gente pobre" (the poor people).[14]

In the case of Chicago, conflicts continued to unfold around Roberto Clemente High School. In 1988–89, a new set of community protests led to a reorganization of the school under a largely Puerto Rican Local School Council. The school's new curriculum and programs of parent participation, student trips to Puerto Rico, and legal counsel for immigrants were attacked by critics as inappropriate and even illegal. Conservative sectors insisted that the school had been taken over by *independentistas* who were using it to promote their anti-American agenda. *Independentista* activists have indeed been a visible and influential force in Chicago's Puerto Rican community since the early 1970s.

Foremost among these was the Movimiento de Liberación Nacional (MLN), led by José López, and the Puerto Rico Cultural Center and Pedro Albizu Campos High School linked to it. Furthermore, through the 1990s, Chicago *independentista* activists campaigned for the liberation of the fifteen Puerto Ricans incarcerated in the early 1980s accused of belonging to the clandestine Fuerzas Armadas de Liberación Nacional. For conservative sectors and the FBI, organizations like the MLN and the Puerto Rico Cultural Center, and even the work around Roberto Clemente High School, were fronts for "terrorist organizations." In 1995, Roberto Clemente High School was placed on financial and academic probation, and the programs instituted since 1989 were dismantled.

The campaign to free the Puerto Rican *independentista* prisoners continued. The abnormally long sentences imposed and the mistreatment to which they were subjected generated support for this demand far beyond the confines of the independence movement. In 1999, thirteen of the fifteen FALN prisoners regained their freedom under clemency offers issued by President Clinton. Two prisoners remained incarcerated while both houses of Congress passed resolutions condemning Clinton for this concession to "terrorism."

The community mobilizations of the 1990s described by Dávila, Pérez, and Ramos-Zayas have all taken place within a stark North American political landscape. At the start of the twenty-first century, there is no mass social movement in sight capable of reversing the neoconservative attacks on social legislation. This larger absence limits Puerto Rican initiatives. After all, neoliberal measures and economic depression affect not only Puerto Ricans but all poor and working people in the United States. They cannot be reversed without the emergence of a broad movement able to encompass a hitherto fragmented working class. Regarding this, Andrés Torres has underlined the need for "class unity" capable of bringing together "working and poor people of all races and ethnicities" in a struggle for an economy that "subordinates profit motive to social criteria." "Ethnically oriented interventions," he adds, "would be less necessary in the presence of a broad-based challenge to the capitalist accumulation process." But it is the absence of such class unity that has most evidently characterized U.S. politics in the American Century.[15]

Indeed, the most salient aspect of U.S. politics when compared to western Europe has been the absence of a mass party identified with the labor movement. All attempts to generate a significant trans-ethnic, class-based political force, from the Debsian Socialist Party to the push by some leftists to make the CIO the basis of a labor party, have failed, due to reasons that have been the subject of considerable debate. In other words, Puerto Ricans have migrated into a metropole where, in the words of Perry Anderson, "capital has always lorded it over labor to an extent unknown in other advanced industrial societies."[16] In the absence of a broad-based politics of class, organization along racial and ethnic lines, often headed by what Gabriel Kolko has called "specialized ethnic bureaucracies," has remained a big part of the struggle for political and economic advancement.[17] Evidently, the forms taken by Puerto Rican organizations in the United States cannot be divorced from this central aspect of U.S. politics in the twentieth century.

Given the absence of independent working-class politics, Puerto Ricans, entering the United States as a colonial people and suffering specific forms of discrimination, have adopted many of the strategies of past ethnic activism, even if most have so far refused the hyphenated American identity that has historically gone with them. Thus, thirty years after the explosions of the late 1960s and the early 1970s, Puerto Rican politics in the United States still exhibits the differentiation already discernible in the 1960s: (1) mainstream, largely Democratic Party electoral politics; (2) nonprofit, self-help associations or advocacy groups; (3) government-funded community projects (now faced with budget cuts and privatization policies); and (4) noninstitutional radical activism.

As on the island, radical activism has not been able to regain the influence and visibility it attained in the 1970s. Meanwhile, in both New York and Chicago, redistricting battles, fought on the principle of constituting ethnic electoral blocs, allowed for the election of three Puerto Ricans to Congress: José Serrano was elected in 1990 for the Bronx; Nydia Velázquez was elected in 1992 for portions of Brooklyn, Manhattan, and Queens; and Luis Gutiérrez was elected in 1992 in Chicago. Gutiérrez, former member of the Partido Socialista Puertorriqueño, initially rose to prominence as part of Mayor Harold Washington's coalition, which briefly suggested the possibility of a broad working-class, multi-ethnic, multinational, anticorporate political movement. The movement, still trapped in the framework of the Democratic Party, collapsed after Washington's death in 1987. Nevertheless, the presence of a few Puerto

MAP 14.1. Puerto Rican Population in the Fifty States, 2004

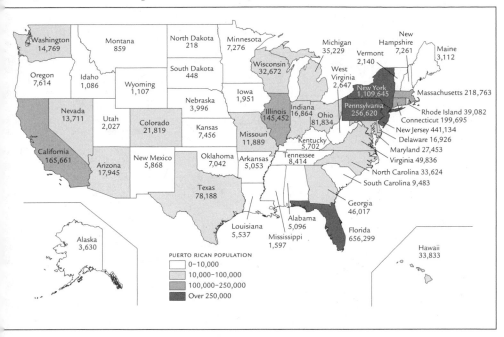

Source: U.S. Census Bureau, 2004 American Community Survey.

Ricans in the halls of Congress as members of the party that instituted a ruthless reduction in welfare programs and proved incapable of implementing even a mild health reform is hardly a substitute for the mass working and poor peoples' movement needed to roll back the conservative/neoliberal offensive. The absence of such a broad movement challenging neoliberalism within the United States also limits political and economic options in Puerto Rico and not only the alternatives available to Puerto Ricans in the United States. The development of *independentista* programs for reconstructing the Puerto Rican economy in a more autonomous, planned, and egalitarian direction is made all the more difficult by this absence, as it deprives such projects of potential metropolitan allies and of a more hospitable international context.

Meanwhile, through the 1990s, Puerto Rican migration has shifted to new locations, a development that social scientists have only recently begun to examine.[18] By 2003, Florida had become the state with the second-largest number of resident Puerto Ricans, and Orlando now has more Puerto Ricans than Chicago (see Maps 14.1 and 14.2). Seemingly better off than past Puerto Rican

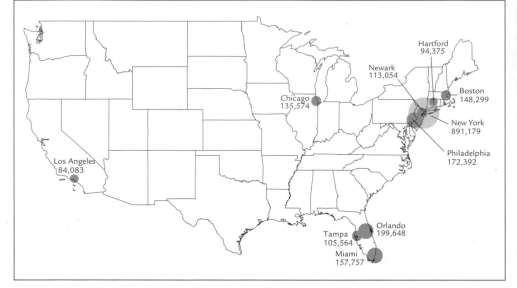

Source: U.S. Census Bureau, 2004 American Community Survey.

migrants and moving into a sociocultural and political context of the Sun Belt, very different from the older northeastern and midwestern urban-industrial centers, the cultural and political dynamics of this flow are not yet clear.

Business as Usual: Governor Sila Calderón's
PPD Administration, 2000–2004

Taking over the insular government after eight years of PNP administration, PPD governor Sila Calderón did not attempt to undo the most significant measures introduced by her predecessor and by and large left the privatized firms created by Rosselló untouched. The only exception was the aqueduct authority, whose contract with private administrators was rescinded. Regarding labor, no substantial amendments of the public employees' unionization law were introduced. In her last year as governor, Calderón took advantage of the negative public image of the corrupt leadership of the water system workers' union to mount an offensive that sought to break the union. With little support from the labor movement, the 4,000 members of the union struck, returning to work after a compromise was reached.

Calderón's administration proved disappointing with respect to Vieques.

Having promised to speed up the withdrawal of the navy, it adopted the calendar agreed upon by Governor Rosselló and President Clinton. The ELA government held a local referendum in Vieques on July 29, 2001, in which 68.2 percent voted for a rapid navy withdrawal, but the Calderón administration failed to use the results to demand a reconsideration of the existing timetable for the navy's departure. In the meantime, activists kept the pressure on the navy by interfering with each set of maneuvers at the price of weeks and months in jail.

The PPD failed another major challenge. Section 936 of the U.S. Internal Revenue Code had been the key mechanism for attracting U.S. capital to the island. But Section 936 had been under heavy attack in Congress from the start of the Reagan era. In 1996, Congress opted to phase out Section 936 by the year 2006. The phaseout of Section 936 was part of the Small Business Job and Protection Act of 1996. Thus, when the PPD returned to office in 2000, it did so in a changed institutional landscape. The main piece of its economic strategy, federal tax exemption for U.S. corporations, was in the process of being dismantled in preparation for its programmed demise in 2006. The PPD was evidently in need of a new "economic model," but it could do no better than attempt to revive the tax-exemption strategy. Specifically, it lobbied unsuccessfully for bills (H.R. 2550 and S. 1475 of 2001) that expanded the benefits that U.S. investors in Puerto Rico can now obtain under Section 901 of the U.S. Internal Revenue Code by registering as "controlled foreign corporations." Some critics in the corporate press argued that by concentrating on this effort, the PPD failed to ensure the extension to Puerto Rico of other federal measures that may have been a better substitute for Section 936.[19]

In the midst of this lackluster performance, Governor Calderón announced that she would not seek reelection. At the same time, former governor Pedro Rosselló, who had been living in the United States since the end of his term in 2000, returned to Puerto Rico and announced his intention of seeking the PNP nomination for governor.

The Independence Movement in the 1990s

Through the status, privatization, and labor struggles of the 1990s, the *independentista* and socialist movements went through new turns and differentiations. In the past, *independentista* organizations had argued that for any referendum or plebiscite to be a true means of self-determination, its results had to be binding on the U.S. Congress. Otherwise, the ultimate decision would remain in the hands of U.S. officials. The PIP broke with this position in 1993 by agreeing to participate in the plebiscite sponsored by PNP governor Rosselló. The PIP reasoned that statehood was unviable, given persistent opposition to it in Congress. The ELA was losing support in Washington as its cost to the federal government increased.[20] Conditions were thus ripe for gaining support in Washington for independence, as long as its proponents adopted a flexible, nonthreatening orientation. In this fashion, the PIP hoped to negotiate an attractive independence proposal that would include such rights as free mobility of citizens between Puerto Rico and the United States, for example. In the medium or long run, since statehood was impossible given opposition to it in the United States, any weakening of the existing status would effectively be a step toward independence, which would eventually come to be seen as the only viable option to the existing arrangement.

This was combined with the transformation of the PIP into an almost exclusively electoral organization with few activist links with the social and labor movements. As an electoral apparatus, the PIP had settled into a limited niche. It received on average 4.46 percent of the votes (5.35 percent when it ran its best-known leader, Rubén Berríos, for governor, and 3.86 when it did not) in the five elections between 1984 and 2000. It also managed to elect two at-large candidates to the House and the Senate. The PIP remained the largest organization of the independence movement.

Many *independentistas* were apprehensive of the PIP's participation in the PNP-sponsored plebiscites. While some were wary of its assumption that statehood was not possible, others emphasized their rejection of the PIP's strictly electoral politics unconnected to social and labor struggles. The PIP was able to obtain 4.4 percent of the vote (75,620) for independence in the 1993 status plebiscite, which the rest of the *independentista* organizations boycotted. This share dropped to 2.5 percent in the 1998 plebiscite (39,838). Nevertheless, as a result of its activism in the Vieques struggle, the party was able to reorganize its core militants and its periphery, avoiding a major crisis. It received 5.2 percent of the vote in 2000 (104,705).

Another wing of the independence movement gravitated toward de facto alliance with the PPD. This orientation had been advancing since the late 1970s during the governorship of Romero Barceló. During the 1990s, this broad unofficial coalition was redeployed against the PNP government of Rosselló. In the process, many placed their socialist aspirations on the backburner. Thus, former PSP secretary general Juan Mari Brás argued in the 1990s that it was necessary to postpone any socialist vision to an indefinite future while seizing the possibility of turning Puerto Rico into an effective player in an emergent globalized market. Such a project, he argued, required a considerable dosage of realism, including the search for an alliance with the PPD to obtain a larger measure of autonomy under the ELA if independence were to prove impossible.[21]

Yet a third current, best represented by the Frente Socialista, warned (like the PIP) that mere national affirmations easily played into the hands of the PPD, which skillfully turned Puerto Rican national pride into a means for furthering its own brand of autonomist-colonial politics. But this current (unlike the PIP) insisted on the need to build an anticolonial movement, a movement for self-determination, as an expression of the growing organization and mobilization of labor and other oppressed sectors. While maintaining some influence in sectors of the labor and student movement and playing a major role in the creation and development of CAOS in the 1997–98 antiprivatization campaign, this current was nevertheless unable to qualitatively increase its size or influence to levels comparable to those of the PSP in the early 1970s.

Clandestine *independentista* organizations had largely abandoned their armed actions after the mid-1980s. Some, such as the wing of the Macheteros associated with well-known labor lawyer Jorge Farinacci, had retained their former clandestine structure but had redirected their efforts to union and coalition work with other forces, such as the Frente Socialista. Filiberto Ojeda, leader of another wing, had gone underground while awaiting trial in a U.S. district court. For years he had successfully avoided FBI attempts to capture him and regularly issued public statements. On September 23, 2005, Ojeda was cornered in his house in the town of Hormigueros. Shot by an FBI sharpshooter, he was left unattended for hours. Ojeda bled to death. The date on which these events took place, the day of the 1868 rebellion against Spanish rule annually commemorated by the independence movement, was widely interpreted as adding insult to injury. An indication of the considerable prestige enjoyed by Ojeda, his wake and funeral were the occasion of massive expressions of admiration and condemnation of the FBI incursion.

Ojeda's life mixed many of the varied facets of the Puerto Rican experience in the American Century. Born in 1933 in the coastal town of Naguabo, he worked in the sugar industry as a young man before spending long stretches in New York in the 1940s and 1950s, where he joined the independence movement and played the trumpet with some of the best-known orchestras of the time. By the early 1960s, he moved to Cuba, where he actively joined the ongoing revolution before returning to Puerto Rico while he began his political organizing efforts and also played for a season with the Sonora Ponceña, one of the precursors of the salsa wave. By the late 1960s, he went underground to spend the rest of his life building a clandestine urban guerrilla movement against U.S. colonial rule.[22]

Elections and Economic Uncertainty

The result of the elections of 2004 confirmed the impasse of Puerto Rican party politics in a dramatic fashion. Former governor Rosselló was able to rally PNP followers. Yet his association with corruption and militant annexationism led an unprecedented number of *independentistas* to vote for the PPD. Through the campaign, the PPD all but admitted it could not win without the *independentista* vote, thus tacitly confirming that annexationism was the single largest voting bloc on the island.

The results of the election were mixed and created the ground for further conflicts. Aníbal Acevedo Vilá, the PPD candidate for governor, was elected by the slimmest of margins (3,566 votes or .18 percent of the vote). The PNP took control of the legislature. It also won the straight party vote with 49.3 percent to the PPD's 48.4 percent. Vote for the PIP collapsed to 54,551 or 2.74 percent of the vote (from 104,705 or 5.2 percent in 2000) as many *independentistas* chose to cast their ballots for the PPD.

Meanwhile, the phaseout of Section 936 was beginning to have an impact. Puerto Rico experienced a net loss of about 22 percent of its manufacturing jobs, from 162,475 in 1992 to 126,707 in 2006.[23] This loss has been uneven across different sectors. Labor intensive operations, such as food, electrical equipment, textiles and apparel, computer and electronic equipment, plastic and rubber products, and beverage and tobacco products, all suffered losses in employment.[24] Other sectors, particularly chemicals and, within that category, the capital-intensive pharmaceutical industry, have experienced a modest expansion in employment.[25] Corporations that have remained in Puerto Rico have been reorganizing under the provisions of the U.S. Internal Revenue Code that allows them to function in Puerto Rico as "controlled foreign corporations." This status offers lower benefits than those granted by Section 936, but it does give U.S. corporations in Puerto Rico the same U.S. tax deductions they enjoy when operating in foreign countries.[26] A recent study suggests that income shifting through transfer pricing to Puerto Rico subsidiaries by U.S. corporations to avoid or limit tax liability has continued under this alternate mechanism.[27]

The phaseout of Section 936 also had financial repercussions. The deposits of

936 corporations, which had nurtured the banking sector, departed en masse. Puerto Rico lost $7.4 billion, or 90 percent of the deposits of the 936 corporations, since the phaseout of 936 began in 1996. Of the eleven largest banks in Puerto Rico, only one, Banco Popular, generates sufficient deposits to lend; the rest rely on what are known as "brokered deposits." Whereas in the United States banks get only 5 percent of deposits from brokers, in Puerto Rico, with the exception of Banco Popular, 25 percent of deposits are from brokers. This creates a volatile situation since, in the words of one analyst, unlike the more stable retail deposits, "rapid transfers by investors looking for a better rate could cause a liquidity crisis."[28]

Outlaw Capitalism

No portrait of Puerto Rican society since the 1970s can afford to ignore the increase over this period of street and domestic violence. Limited unemployment in the formal economy and state prohibitionist policies have led to the steady expansion of the illegal drug trade. Like all unregulated market economies, it is characterized by fierce competition, which in this case takes a particularly ruthless and violent character. Illegality and heightened police repression has the perverse effect of bringing up drug prices and thus potential profit margins, making this line of trade both riskier and financially more rewarding. Conflicts over sales territories (*puntos*), the collection of debts, the silencing of witnesses and informers, and the financing of drug purchases produce deaths on a daily basis. State repression and illegal entrepreneurship thus produce a mutually reinforcing dynamic that has further collateral effects. Criminalization of drug use makes the search for treatment more difficult. Street violence or the fear of it leads to the fragmentation of urban areas into controlled access units, segregated according to income level. Repressive policies mixed with racism lead to the stereotyping of certain sectors (public housing residents, young black males, "rappers") as "criminal" elements. Prison population grows. By 2004, Puerto Rico had 402 persons in jail per 100,000 inhabitants, the twelfth-highest rate of imprisonment in the world, although lower than U.S. rates.

The shifts in state penal policies fit the periodization we have followed in this narrative. The postwar boom was characterized by the influence of a discourse of rehabilitation and the use of minimum security jails and penal farms. The coming of economic stagnation and heightened social crisis led to the hardening of a punitive logic and the reliance on more restrictive prison regimes.[29] The inmates organized to resist. The most important organization to emerge was the Asociación de Confinados, led by prisoner Carlos Torres Iriarte ("La sombra"), who was assassinated in 1981. The association struggled to move out of the mold of a traditional gang to become an organization of prisoners, although the dynamic of conflict with existing gangs has never allowed it to complete that transition. Close to forty prisons are "controlled" by diverse organizations such as the Asociación de Confinados (Ñetas) and Los Veintisiete (associated with the large public housing project Manuel A. Pérez), in tense conflict with each other and with prison authorities.

State repression in the 1990s took diverse forms. The most spectacular was the *mano dura* policy of the Rosselló administration, which included the semi-occupation of housing projects and neighborhoods by the National Guard. State repression, as indicated, has often fostered what it sought to eliminate. The occupation of *puntos* in the San Juan area by the National Guard in the mid-1990s led to increased competition for a reduced number of outlets and therefore to acute violence. Eventually the occupation produced the spread of the network of distributors to areas where the drug trade had been nonexistent or weak until then. As part of the *mano dura* approach, in 1994 the Rosselló administration proposed an amendment to limit the right to bail recognized by the ELA constitution. The amendment was defeated in a referendum. Its opponents, a coalition of labor, community, and left organizations, argued that curtailing democratic rights was neither an acceptable nor effective way of dealing with the problems posed by addiction or street violence.

Repressive policies were hardly exclusive to the island. In 1994, President Clinton signed the Federal Death Penalty Act that provided for capital punishment for certain federal offenses. This meant that federal courts in Puerto Rico could now impose the death penalty for certain offenses committed on the island. This raised two issues. Politically, it posed the question of Puerto Rico's relation to the United States and of the nature of the present status. The ELA constitution explicitly forbids the death penalty, which had been abolished in Puerto Rico in 1929. The fact that the federal courts in Puerto Rico can nevertheless impose the death penalty is a stark commentary on the limited reach of the insular constitution. Furthermore, the constitutional provision is a reflection of a long tradition of opposition to the death penalty, going back to the early 1900s.[30] In 1902, for example, the execution of four prisoners convicted for murder and rape committed during the disturbances related to the *partidas sediciosas* of 1898 had to be delayed due to opposition to the death penalty. According to the *San Juan News* of June 3, 1902, "No carpenter could be found to build the platform nor would anyone sell board or nails. The platform had to be made by soldiers."[31] Perpetuating this honorable legacy, civil rights, trade union, community, religious, and political organizations have opposed the newest attempts to impose the death penalty in Puerto Rico.

More than a hundred years after the Spanish-American War, Puerto Rico is still de facto and, according to at least some court decisions, de jure an unincorporated territory of the United States. Puerto Rico's economic miracle ended in the mid-1970s. Its economy, plagued by chronic unemployment, has not been able to generate any autonomous dynamic and still depends on the inflow of U.S. capital, while federal welfare funds provide a minimum of relief for the poorer sectors. Sharp social inequalities subsist and the insufficiency of the formal economy fosters the emergence of a significant informal economy, including a thriving illegal drug trade with all its ramifications. Industry, wholly oriented to export markets; a ruined agricultural sector; and an urban expansion subordinated to the interests of developers and land speculators, largely reproducing the unsustainable model of automobile-centered suburban sprawl, have an increasingly devastating social and ecological impact. Puerto Rico undoubtedly needs a new politics and a new economy, a means to determine collectively and democratically its social and economic evolution. A similar balance sheet may be formulated regarding the situation of the majority of Puerto Ricans in the United States, who, in spite of the emergence of middle-class communities in Florida and other states, are still located on the lower ranks of the North American social order.

NEONATIONALISM, POSTMODERNISM, AND OTHER DEBATES

A brief overview of the Puerto Rican literary and cultural landscape since the late 1980s cannot do justice to the many individual contributions and debates that have shaped it. What we can do here is sketch a map locating the main tendencies, touching on some interventions, without in any way implying they are the only significant ones. Some areas, genres, and authors are inevitably, if unjustly, left out.

Forced to choose some trends, we limit ourselves to three that played a major role in recent debates. The first is a current, sometimes labeled neonationalist (although there are many variations within it), that enthusiastically embraces affirmations of Puerto Rican nationhood and largely builds its political and/or cultural intervention around it. A parallel trend takes critical distance (again with many variations) from past or present visions of Puerto Rican national identity but does not—or at least does not fully or explicitly—abandon the vision of political and social change associated with the anticolonial Left in the past. Finally, there is the current that favors a reconsideration of Puerto Rico's situation from what it describes—as a participant of the postmodern sensibility—as the collapse of the "master narratives" of modernity. As we consider these interventions, we will refer to works by authors on the island and in the United States.

By the late 1970s, many of the more influential Puerto Rican intellectuals had embraced some brand of socialism. Whether as "new historians," old Marxists, or left-nationalists, the influence of Marxism was present across the differences that otherwise existed between authors such as Angel Quintero Rivera, José Luis González, Manuel Maldonado Denis, or Juan Flores, to name a few. As the 1980s and early 1990s progressed, this sensibility was subjected to increasing strains. The Reagan presidency marked the start of a formidable right-wing backlash. Optimistic expectations for radical change in the United States and

Europe now proved to be unrealistic. The Soviet Union and the regimes allied to it—which many on the Left had seen, if not as a model, at least as a counterweight to U.S. hegemony—collapsed. The Nicaraguan Revolution stalled. The Salvadoran insurgency had to settle for negotiations short of a revolutionary victory. The Cuban regime found itself isolated. Activists were now forced to address the sense, articulated by many in Europe and the United States, that the socialist project was at an impasse. This debate coincided in Puerto Rico with the continuing electoral deadlock between the Partido Popular Democrático and the Partido Nuevo Progresista, with the former playing the cultural card, seeking to portray itself as the defender of Puerto Rican identity. But national affirmation was a much wider phenomenon than PPD cultural politics.

Neonationalisms

The two decades after 1980 witnessed the rise of what some critics call neonationalism. The 1990s was a decade of newfound pride in being Puerto Rican, from the PPD anti-statehood emphasis on identity to national motifs in commercials and pop music lyrics. The reissue of Rafael Hernández's classic patriotic song "Preciosa" by salsa star Marc Anthony and the adoration of athletes or performers as emblems of the Puerto Rican nation all reflected the rising neonationalist cultural élan. Annual TV specials on Puerto Rican culture sponsored by the Banco Popular or the cry of "Puerto Rico no se vende" during the 1998 phone workers' strike represented the same sentiment from opposite sides of the privatization battles of the 1970s.

Already in 1993, statehood ideologist Luis Dávila Colón denounced what he labeled a neonationalist wave, which led, through the presence of *independentistas* in government and private publicity agencies, to the permeation of the public sphere with anti-American messages.[1] Sociologist Arlene Dávila explored the sponsoring of identity by government agencies and private enterprise while also noting its undeniable popularity. The manufacturers of Winston cigarettes, for example, found it convenient to change the slogan "Yo y mis Winston," which associated the cigarette with the myth of U.S. individualism, for "Winston y Puerto Rico, no hay nada major," which sought to tap the potential buyer's national self-identification.[2] Different sectors of the Puerto Rican intelligentsia provided diverse explanations of the new cultural trends.

For many *independentistas*, the so-called neonationalist wave was a welcome development that strengthened the struggle against annexation. These *inde-*

pendentistas were inclined to favor an alliance with the PPD around cultural issues. In 1991, PPD governor Rafael Hernández Colón sponsored legislation making Spanish the official language of Puerto Rico, replacing a law dating back to 1902 that had made both Spanish and English official languages. The revocation of the measure by the incoming PNP administration in January 1993 led to a massive march in defense of Spanish with the support of both the PPD and the independence movement. Similarly, in July 1996 a U.S. governors' conference in Puerto Rico in the midst of the pro-statehood offensive led by PNP governor Pedro Rosselló became the occasion for another march under the slogan "la nación en marcha," which again brought together autonomists and many *independentistas*.[3]

José Luis Méndez, an author associated with the Partido Socialista Puertorriqueño in the past, pointed out the paradoxical coincidence of a growing political annexationist movement and a receding cultural assimilationist sentiment. Since the 1960s, the support for statehood had grown along with the feeling of Puerto Rico as a distinct cultural entity. Such were the elements of a deadlock in which pro- and anti-annexation forces had blocked each other's preferred political options. Méndez proposed the search for a "national consensus"—including a capital-labor consensus—as the basis for a resolution of the status impasse.[4] The starting point of the desired consensus, he argued, had to be the widely shared feeling of nationhood. If statehood could not be discarded, the United States should be made to understand that it would imply incorporating another nation and would thus transform the Union into a multinational state.

While some authors placed their socialist sympathies on hold, others sought to combine national affirmation with a socialist vision. Juan Manuel Carrión considered that the persistence of nationalism over time in diverse social formations argued against considering it a bourgeois ideology, as many Marxists had done in the past. Nor was the resilience of national feeling something to be lamented. According to Carrión, the feelings of solidarity needed for a break with capitalism depend on a sense of community larger than the sum of its parts, an idea that is often lived in the modern world as nationhood. Carrión's analysis led to the conclusion that the feeling of Puerto Rican nationhood should not be weakened by attempts to discredit it as bourgeois, Hispanophile, or racist. Instead of deepening the "racial fissures" that may divide the nation, it was necessary to struggle to strengthen the "links of solidarity that give it life."[5] His analysis thus tended to downplay the need to address issues such as racism, while the feeling of nationhood claimed center stage in the struggle against the enticements of U.S. capitalism and consumer culture.

Meanwhile, through a series of short texts on different cultural trends ranging from government publicity to the work of "traditional" artisans, Ramón López sketched a subtle positive vision of Puerto Rican culture. López criticized both the representations of Puerto Rico in government ads as well as defenses of Puerto Rican culture that have idealized a rural and artisanal past. López insisted on the need to see culture not as a search for origins but as a constant process of re-elaboration. Just as the protest singers of the 1970s had taken what they found useful from Bob Dylan or Argentinean singer Atahualpa Yupanqui, it was a sign of vitality that new generations were doing as much with African American hip-hop. Similarly, Puerto Rican culture in the United States could not be expected to be a repetition of island culture; it is instead an ever-changing and distinct creation.[6] The situation of López as an artisan seems to have shaped his vision of cultural traditions not as a limiting heritage but as a set of practices that subsist only in a process of constant redefinition. His brief texts seek to combine a vindication of the artisan, a critique of the degradation of his or her work by capitalism, and openness to new cultural trends and re-elaborations. Varied as the views of Méndez, Carrión, and López were, they shared a relatively positive view of nationhood, a tendency to celebrate affirmation of Puerto Rican identity as a liberating, empowering expression in the face of colonial domination.

In some cases, the defense of Puerto Rico's identity led to rejections of new cultural trends. Thus, poet Edwin Reyes denounced the influence of rap, an expression he described as a dark and primitive form emanating from the North American ghettos.[7] In his defense of Puerto Ricanness, he thus deployed metaphors traditionally used by colonial discourse to describe African and other conquered populations. The combination of national affirmation and moral conservatism was also present in the reaction to performer Madonna's sexually suggestive use of the Puerto Rican flag during a 1993 concert on the island. While many saw it as an insult to a cherished emblem, what scandalized some was the openly sexual attitude of the performer. As in the reaction to hip-hop, the incident evidenced how affirmations of Puerto Rican identity could act as vehicles for conservative fears of cultural forms transgressive of dominant definitions of taste or morality.

The clearest example of this was the pastoral letter on national identity issued by San Juan bishop Roberto González Nieves.[8] The document began by recognizing the separation of church and state, but Gonzalez Nieves's particular affirmation of Puerto Rican culture allowed him to deftly weaken this separation in the name of the nation. The state, the document argues, has the duty to defend Puerto Rican identity, which, according to González Nieves, is essentially Catholic. From this position, it is easy to conclude that the state has the duty to stem the advance of abortion rights, gay marriage, or contraceptives, all in the name of Puerto Rican identity. An antifeminist, homophobic, conservative agenda was thus presented in terms of national affirmation against the menace of a denationalizing globalization. González Nieves even criticized nineteenth-century separatist Eugenio María de Hostos for his materialist inclinations and disregard for religion in the construction of his ethical system. The notion of Puerto Rico as a Catholic nation was, of course, based on the erasure from history of the many Puerto Ricans who have been or are spiritualists, freethinkers, atheists, or *santeros*, as well as the large number who belong to the many Protestant churches.

Nationalism under Scrutiny

Meanwhile, other currents took a more critical view of nationalism. One strand of this critical sensibility built its work on the ideas of the "new historians" of the 1970s. These interventions were less interested in examining the impact of U.S. colonialism as in exploring the blind spots of the reigning notions of Puerto Rican identity and unveiling the discursive strategies through which particular social groups had constructed it. These critics tended to privilege intellectuals like themselves and above all the *generación del treinta* and its continuators. In the process, they drew on the work of Uruguayan critic Angel Rama (who had worked in Puerto Rico during the early 1970s) on the role of literary, intellectual, and textual circuits, what he called the "lettered city," on the evolution of Latin American societies.[9]

These authors often saw representations of Puerto Rican culture as a definite canon whose rules of inclusion and exclusion it was necessary to explore. Sociologically inclined scholars, like Juan Gelpí, linked such practices to specific classes, drawing, as indicated, on the work of the "new historians" and critics of the 1970s. For Gelpí, María Elena Rodríguez Castro,[10] and others, much of Puerto Rican literature—from Luis Lloréns Torres in the second decade of the twentieth century to Antonio S. Pedreira in the 1930s and René Marqués in the 1950s—corresponded to the perspective of a receding *hacendado* class centered on the paternalistic vision of a "great Puerto Rican family."[11] In the 1970s, the works of José Luis González and Luis Rafael Sánchez had been hailed (or criticized) as a break with the *generación del treinta*. Gelpí argued that much of their work had in fact retained part of their predecessors' paternalistic stance, as exemplified by the magisterial voice through which they spoke in their texts about Puerto Rico's cultural situation.[12] Searching for a clearer break with what he described as the dominant paternalist canon, Gelpí singled out the work of women such as Ana Lydia Vega and of gay author Manuel Ramos Otero. With them, Gelpí argued, it became evident that social phenomena generated by the modernization of Puerto Rico had finally undermined the basis of the long-reigning paternalistic discourse.

Newer critics have insisted on the need to recognize new emergent voices, ignored or excluded from the nationalist discourse and even from that of its left critics of the 1970s. Past research that had focused on working-class and women's struggles was reexamined with an ear to what were judged to be its telling silences. Eileen J. Suárez Findlay nuanced the notion of a labor movement open to women's demands and in particular demonstrated how male working-class ideologists built the image of the honest, hard-working laborer through the articulation of the counterimage of the immoral prostitute.[13] Kelvin Santiago-Valles, in a similar vein, argued how even proletarian, wage-labor identities and moralities had been built in opposition to excluded, marginalized, and criminalized others.[14]

Attention to silenced, ignored voices also meant a vindication of queer or transgressive gay and lesbian identities and culturally hybrid subjects or trends (from Spanglish to transvestism), generated via cultural remixing through migration or the reworking of global media currents. The enthusiastic reception of Mayra Santos's 2000 novel *Silena Serena vestida de pena*, with its transvestite protagonist, is an evident example, which we discuss in more detail below. But this openness to the hybrid and the impure could also be perceived in contributions by authors who had played a key role in the rise of the "new history" in the 1970s.

Quintero Rivera, for example, shifted his interventions toward the study of popular music and the cultural and racial configuration of Puerto Rico. In the early 1970s, he and other "new historians" had denounced how in the past the *jíbaro* had been privileged as representative of Puerto Rican culture. Against this they underlined the importance of the Afro-Caribbean coastal component as a parallel cultural current. Quintero Rivera now argued that it is necessary to question the very notion of a white *jíbaro. Jíbaro* culture had emerged from a racially mixed peasantry made up of displaced small farmers, runaway slaves, stowaways, army deserters, and fugitives, united in the desire to avoid subordination by an advancing state and plantation economy.[15] African forms were present not only on the coast but also in the interior, as part of *jíbaro* culture itself. Indeed, they were also present in the culture of the *criollo* possessing classes. The *danza*, often seen as the insular evolution of European dances, had its own African or mulatto dimension. This was a formal parallel to the sociological fact that it was music for prosperous white *criollo* families but was often played and written by black or mulatto musicians, such as Juan Morell Campos.

Arcadio Díaz Quiñones, another member of the 1970s generation, argued that the work of Puerto Rican graphic artist Lorenzo Homar must be understood as a product of experiences both in Puerto Rico and New York and of his mixing of currents as diverse as jazz, modern European painting, medieval calligraphy, and his *independentista* politics. But such borrowings, he added, could be found in even the more emblematically national Puerto Rican texts. Mixed origins, such as the influence of Tennessee Williams in the dramas of Marqués, are often erased in the process of turning a text into a national icon. Thus, Puerto Rican identity, both Quintero Rivera and Díaz Quiñones seemed to suggest, need not and must not be discarded, but it must truly begin to see itself as hybrid, impure, and ever-changing.

Juan Flores, one of the pioneers of the studies of the Puerto Rican diaspora, embraced the postmodern vindication of hybridity and its rejection of essentialist notions of identity, placing them at the service of his consideration of the situation of the Puerto Rican migrant. He thus explored the work of the pioneering New York Puerto Rican hip-hop performers while denouncing both conservative censors and commercial manipulators who sought to domesticate its subversive edge. (Interest in hip-hop was shared by other authors, as we shall see.) Flores similarly pointed to earlier texts on the diasporic dimension of the Puerto Rican experience, including Luis Rafael Sánchez's "La guagua aérea" and Sandra María Esteves's "Not Neither" as examples of the growing understanding of the unviability of anything but an unstable, troubled definition of the Puerto Rican self.[16] Meanwhile, Jorge Duany and Arlene Dávila explored changing perceptions of *puertorriqueñidad* and concluded that Puerto Rico is an emergent example of cultural nations: a feeling of nationhood that has not translated into a desire for state formation and political independence, a feeling of collective belonging that spans two territories, the island and the United States.[17]

Duany also pioneered the study of migrant communities in Puerto Rico. Indeed, by the 1990s, the deepening crisis of the region's capitalist economies was having a new type of impact on Puerto Rican society: growing migration *into* Puerto Rico from the neighboring Dominican Republic. As the decade advanced, thousands braved the rough seas of the Mona passage to reach Puerto Rico. The 2000 census registered 61,000 resident Dominicans, but the real figure is certainly much higher, if difficult to calculate. Reproducing a well-known dynamic, Dominicans have been incorporated into the lower-paid, more precarious sectors of the labor force. In a sad irony, some Puerto Ricans have reacted to Dominican immigration with xenophobic expressions (blaming them for taking away jobs, deteriorating services, or crime), not unlike those directed at Puerto Ricans in the United States. Racism has been part of that reaction, as the perception of Dominicans as darker allows for the self-perception of some Puerto Ricans as whiter. Yet Dominican presence has continued to expand and is progressively reshaping several zones of the San Juan metropolitan area while adding new elements to Puerto Rico's cultural (dietary, musical, lexical, for example) mix. Disagreeable as it may be to those who would rather have it otherwise, Dominican presence vividly reasserts the fact that Puerto Rico is in the Caribbean and that its evolution, regardless of its particular relation to the United States, cannot be divorced from it.[18]

Like Flores, Mayra Santos and Raquel Z. Rivera were drawn to the study of the evolution of Puerto Rican hip-hop and rap. Rivera produced a history of the Puerto Rican role in the rise of hip-hop culture. Her text is a polemic both against accounts that overlook the participation of Puerto Ricans in the emergence of hip-hop and conceptions that exclude hip-hop from the evolving map of Puerto Rican culture. By the early 1960s, most Puerto Ricans in New York City lived in Brooklyn and the Bronx. It was there, and above all in the Bronx, that hip-hop emerged in the late 1970s. It was an invention of African American and Puerto Rican youth familiar with the realities of shrinking employment or low-paying part-time jobs, gang life, police brutality, eroding housing and public services, and long-standing forms of discrimination. Rivera did not shy away from the hope that her work would contribute to "cultural and political collective ends" or from linking her own sense of self with the object of her research: "I certainly have come to realize my involvement with hip hop has been linked to a frantic need to reclaim myself, feel part of a community." Thus, Rivera's work, in spite of the radical differences in context, style, and content (beginning with the vindication of African American cultures), cannot but remind us of Pedreira's quest of collective "soul" through the recovery of a particular Puerto Rican cultural itinerary. Recent authors are often not as distant from long-standing debates as it may appear.[19]

Meanwhile, Santos studied the evolution of rap on the island. Island rap was an adaptation by poor urban youngsters of Afro-American and Afro-Caribbean forms, such as hip-hop and reggae, asserting cultural connections that run contrary to the way many prefer to think of Puerto Rico as fundamentally Hispanic and white. What Santos called the "territorio rapero" was originally an archipelago of poor barrios and *caseríos* (housing projects).[20] Puerto Rican rap reportedly began in the Las Acacias housing project and José Julián Acosta High School in Puerta de Tierra in 1981, and its first noncommercial phase lasted until 1985. By 1985, it entered the commercial mainstream with the first studio recordings by Rubén DJ, Vico C, and Lisa M.[21] Since then, its popularity and commercialization have steadily increased, eventually leading to the emergence of a new musical form called reggaetón.

Vindicating these forms as the latest in a long series of Afro-Caribbean expressions in Puerto Rico, Santos warns that the market subjects them to the pressures of dominant cultures, which prescribe nonpolitical lyrics and moralizing approaches to social problems. Even more limiting, we would argue, is the fact that while the culture of rap is largely antibourgeois, it is hardly anticapitalist: plebian in its rejection of bourgeois manners, styles, and respectability, it also embraces the mores of capitalist accumulation and competitive masculinity. The video images of a moneyed "gangsta" fuses the ideal of the corporate magnate and the underground entrepreneur and neutralizes the oppositional force of this creation of the dispossessed.

Many contemporary critics would reject the appreciation just enunciated as a perpetuation of the elitism they detect in the rejection of mass culture by the *generación del treinta* or in the notion of "colonial mentality" used by nationalists or of "false consciousness" deployed by Marxists. In some cases, this inclination is part of a wider repudiation of the vision of radical social change historically associated with the Left in general and anti-imperialist and socialist movements in particular.

From the New to the Post

While the authors mentioned above departed from the work of "new historians" of the 1970s without repudiating it, others saw themselves as signaling a sharper break with past intellectual projects. If the new historiography of the

1970s had criticized nationalism from a class-socialist perspective, some of the newer currents now saw not only nationalism but also Marxism and anti-imperialism as examples of the "master narratives" and "totalizing visions" behind which lurked, not emancipatory projects, but the power of those articulating such discourses. Marxism speaking in the name of the working class, anti-imperialism speaking in the name of the people/nation, and feminism speaking in the name of women were repudiated as inherently authoritarian. The "totalitarian" logic of such projects was already present in the elitist claim to a privileged access to the truth by nationalist, Marxist, or feminist vanguards.[22]

Writing in 1995, for example, Arturo Torrecilla explained how the "new historians" had criticized nationalist historiography but only to replace the nation with a new myth: the myth of the working class, which allowed them to present themselves as representatives of those they hailed as such. But the heroic working class, Torrecilla argued, had not behaved as expected: the revolution did not materialize, while new social subjects (ecological, postwork) not contemplated by Marxism emerged.[23] Marxism and the privileging of the working class as transformative social agent now stood exposed as complicit with many of the oppressive features of capitalism, including "productivism" (the imperative of constantly expanding production) or the work ethic (the link of dignity to labor).[24]

Several journals, including *Postdata* in 1990 and *bordes* in 1995, emerged as vehicles for the postmodern, post-Marxist, post-Enlightenment sensibilities. Carlos Gil described the creation of *Postdata* as a response to the dissolution of the "strong subjects of Modernity (the Proletariat, the People, the Masses, the Insurrection, the Revolution, Progress)" as well as the end of "messianic" aspirations to a radically different society.[25] The antipathy of many authors within this current toward the mix of nationalist and Marxist metanarratives they identified with the independence movement shaped their analysis of diverse social struggles to the point of subordinating all other considerations.

Thus, the editors of *bordes* found the main reason for the defeat of the telephone workers' struggle against privatization in the alleged takeover of it by the nationalist Left and the preemption of the flexible strategies needed for victory by the all-or-nothing logic typical of the *independentista* discourse. A similar fate had been imposed on the struggle to stop U.S. Navy use of Vieques, as a local social struggle was turned into a stage to play out the Left's patriotic drama with itself as protagonist. Taking this argument further, Juan Duchesne Winter argued that the struggle in Vieques was, in fact, redundant, since the U.S. Navy had already decided to cease activities there. The "struggle" in Vieques was, in fact, a pseudoprotest, a form of authorized protest, a spectacle whose real effect was to make the opening of Vieques to corporate investment seem like a liberation while generating support for the PPD under a solidified national consensus.[26] In both cases, the analysis seemed to suggest that abstaining from participating in the ongoing mobilizations was a more subversive stand than the Left's usual "manipulative" activism.

The critique of Puerto Rican nationalism from this perspective was further developed by Carlos Pabón and Frances Negrón-Muntaner. Pabón, in the essays gathered in *Nación postmortem* in 2002, offers a portrait of what he calls Puerto Rican neonationalism. According to him, neonationalism reduces the Puerto Rican nation to its Hispanic "roots" and a linguistic essence (Spanish). It implies a paranoid attitude, constantly policing the borders of Puerto Rican culture. Nationalists cannot but insist on the image of a Puerto Rican culture on the verge of disintegration under the blows of imperialism. It is that story which allows them to present themselves as guardians of the nation. But this elitist, conservative, essentialist, and authoritarian neonationalism is fighting a losing battle. Pabón argues that the mixing of cultural trends in a globalized planet makes the pretensions of national intellectual elites increasingly untenable.[27]

Negrón-Muntaner developed her own critique of nationalism in her 2004 collection *Boricua Pop: Puerto Ricans and the Latinization of American Culture*. According to her, affirmations of Puerto Ricanness are not innocent reiterations of identity but are fueled by an unspoken shame. They are "constitutively shameful." Descriptions of 1898 as trauma, for example, do not stem from the fact that Puerto Rican resistance was crushed or from the devastating effects of the war but rather from the shame that there was no resistance and hardly a war at all. The actual trauma is the shameful realization that there was no trauma. Pride in Spanish as central to Puerto Rican identity is fueled not by the need to save it from imminent demise but by the shame of being considered an African, hybrid people. As in much recent literature, in this work the term "nationalism" expands to include just about any concern with Puerto Ricans considered as a distinct people, from radical Albizuista political nationalism to Pedreira's *Insularismo* to PPD language legislation. Across such differences, Negrón-Muntaner's conclusion is clear: far from being a liberating force, nationalism blocks a less guilt-ridden consideration of the Puerto Rican condition, of Puerto Rican history, and of the "status" question.

Puerto Rico, she argues, has been a queer nation that has not followed the "normal" path toward independence. Intellectuals have criticized that in the way that "real" men would, hence their obsession with Puerto Rican identity, a preoccupation that has less, if anything, to do with resisting U.S. colonialism than with the preservation of certain privileges within Puerto Rico: white, male, heterosexist, elite-educated privilege, which is blind to the fact that most Puerto Ricans have benefited from the conditions created by U.S. rule. This reduction of nationalism to a conservative force intent on preserving past hierarchies parallels the analysis put forth by modernization theory in the 1950s. Proponents of capitalist modernization and heralds of the postmodern thus join hands in dismissing the possibility that anticolonial nationalism may have something to say about the particular course of colonial modernization. While Pabón's critique led to a vague aspiration to "radical democracy," Negrón-Muntaner rejected independence and embraced what we may call a pluralist annexationism as the best alternative to colonialism. She had adopted this position in 1997, along with other authors who had followed their own politico-intellectual road to the same conclusion.

For example, in 1990, Duchesne Winter had advanced the notion of a "lite" independence, which required a break with the notions of revolution or direct confrontation with imperialism. Revolutions, faced with imperial aggression, inevitably led to the erection of a "new despotism." He now favored molecular, cumulative change from below, devoid of the moral imperatives and the calls to sacrifice typical of *independentista* discourse.[28] Somewhat earlier, Ramón Grosfoguel had relayed the views of Sandinista leader Victor Tirado, who after the Sandinista electoral defeat of 1990 concluded that the epoch of antiimperialist revolutions was over. Like Duchesne Winter, Grosfoguel argued for a strategy of "seduction" instead of a direct confrontation with imperialism.

By 1997, Duchesne Winter, Grosfoguel, and Negrón-Muntaner came over to the pro-statehood position mentioned above. Independence, they warned, would imply continued subordination to the United States without the compensating features resulting from direct U.S. rule, such as unrestricted migration to the United States and federal funding for government agencies and individuals.[29]

The notion of statehood as economically more advantageous than independence was hardly new. It has been the statehood movement's key argument for annexation since 1898.[30] What was new was the conviction among radicals that the socialist transformation they had once envisioned as an alternative to both colonialism and capitalist independence had become—and perhaps had always been—an unrealizable and/or undesirable utopia. For the very same reason, they now embraced not a socialist annexationism but rather the notion of "radical democratic" initiatives under U.S. rule and within a capitalist world hierarchy taken as fundamentally unshakeable.[31]

Individuals holding this position do not agree on all issues. While some, like Grosfoguel, have stuck to an anti-imperialist orientation, others tend to see "imperialism" as one of the necessary fictions of the nationalist discourse.[32] Even Grosfoguel has tended to conflate his "radical" perspective with the existing support for statehood or Puerto Rico's present status. He writes that "the Puerto Rican people's strategy has been pragmatic rather than utopian; that is they are not struggling to be freed from imperialist oppression (which is highly improbable under the present circumstances), but are instead attempting to struggle for a milder version of this oppression."[33] Reading this, one has the impression that a majority of Puerto Ricans see the condition of Caribbean or Latin American republics as the result of imperialist or neocolonial subordination and that they have astutely opted to resist U.S. imperialism from within. In fact, existing annexationist inclinations more often than not see the poverty of independent republics not as the result of imperialist domination but rather as self-inflicted or natural malady they have been unable to escape. Racist explanations of their persistent poverty and underdevelopment are not uncommon. The United States is regarded as a country that, having attained a high level of material well-being, has fortunately allowed Puerto Rico to partake of its prosperity. In other words, popular rejection of independence does not reflect at present a cunning or pragmatic anti-imperialist or anticolonial consciousness but rather an adoption of the ideological explanations and justifications of existing international hierarchies and inequalities.

For Pabón, as opposed to Grosfoguel, imperialism was but one of the threatening "others" deployed by nationalism in order to justify itself. Duchesne Winter similarly described resistance to globalization as the expression of backward-looking nationalism.[34] This tendency to see the world situation in terms of a clash between the democratic forces propitiated by globalization and a fundamentalist nationalist rejection of it shaped the reaction of Pabón, Duchesne Winter, Torrecilla, and others to the attack on Afghanistan launched by the United States in response to the September 11 attacks.[35] Describing fundamentalism as an authoritarian response to the more democratic and emancipatory aspects of modernity and globalization and rejecting the denunciation of U.S. imperialism coming from the Left as a product of either kneejerk anti-Americanism or perhaps of sympathy for fundamentalism, they concluded it was necessary to critically support U.S. intervention. The notion was preposterous: nobody in Puerto Rico sympathized with Islamic fundamentalism, although socialists and *independentistas*—and it was this that made their position different from that of the signers of the declaration—did refuse to turn their rejection of fundamentalism or terrorism into an endorsement of U.S. intervention in central Asia.

On a less strident note, the aversion to nationalism was also compatible with a positive re-valorization of Luis Muñoz Marín's turn away from independence in 1946, as an early attempt to rethink the Puerto Rican situation beyond the norm of the nation-state. Silvia Alvarez Curbelo thus argued that the context of World War II allowed "Muñoz Marín, always libertarian and internationalist, to more effectively and legitimately organize a proposal for Puerto Rico without the straitjacket of nationalism."[36] She similarly proposed a recovery of nineteenth-century reformism, abolitionism, and autonomism, not as a return to the "origins of the nation" or to recover "prophetic voices," but as a project of modernity—a look back that seemed to correspond in the present to the turn away from visions of radical political or economic rupture (of the Nationalist or Socialist type) to a search for reforms of a liberal-democratic nature.[37]

A New Aestheticism?

By 2000, the notion of the end of the "master narratives" had itself become a "master narrative" cutting across the Puerto Rican intellectual terrain. Prefacing their anthology of Puerto Rican poetry of the 1980s, Mario R. Cancel and Alberto Martínez-Márquez certified the death of several narratives: of the nation (embraced by the *generación del treinta*), of the West (favored by the Jaime Benítez wing of the PPD), and of the revolution (formulated by the new Left). In 2003, critic Luis Felipe Díaz described this as a context in which "the narratives that promise liberating futures are abandoned." What had come about by the 1990s was not the revolution but the end of the "Marxist Utopia." This was not to be lamented, since such utopias had been the "treacherous other side (the same as) the grand imperialist narratives they despised so much."[38]

Mayra Santos's *Sirena Selena vestida de pena* has been hailed, most prominently in a symposium published in the journal *Centro*, as the most representative emblem of new literary sensibilities in Puerto Rico.[39] Nevertheless, the novel has been the object of diverse readings. The protagonist of the novel is a young transvestite performer who travels to the Dominican Republic in the hope of negotiating a contract in one of the plusher hotels there. The story touches on a series of complex and related issues: gender identities and by implication other identities as social constructions, tourist industries in the context of international hierarchies of wealth and power, the complex links between Puerto Rico and the Dominican Republic, and the commodification of sex and the survival strategies of those seeking entrance into the First World.

A postmodern reading sees the novel as liberating Puerto Rican literature from its obsessions with national identity, colonialism, imperialism, or the vision of some nationalist or socialist utopia. It is a queer novel, which challenges "heteronormality," portrays gender as a "performative act," and proposes a "total liberation of the body, repressed desire, and eroticism." The opposite of a pretended national or working-class epic, it is the chronicle of dispersion away from the rule of the written or unwritten law.[40]

An alternative approach is suggested, tentatively, by Efraín Barradas.[41] He sees the novel as indeed criticizing essentialist, static notions of gender and, by implication, national identity. Yet the novel does not ignore the fact that alternative "fluctuating" identities are constructed in a world marked by gender, class, race, and national inequalities, forms of subordination that do not leave the new unstable identities untouched. The tourist industry, for example, can have a liberating *and* a subordinating impact, eroding oppressive traditional structures, opening spaces for a transvestite challenging of "heteronormativity," and yet also subordinating such performances to the needs of First World consumers. Drag performances, in that context, can be both vehicles of liberation and compromises with the oppressors. While the novel recognizes the strategies employed by Sirena Selena to survive in a world in which money—and more specifically, U.S. money—rules, it does not pretend that such navigations abolish the subordination of the feminine, the black, the Caribbean, or the dispossessed by the masculine, the white, the North American, the moneyed. In this reading, the novel does not necessarily renounce anticolonialism and anticapitalism as so many dead utopias but at least leaves the door open to their reformulation in non-nationalist, non-essentialist, queerer terms.[42]

The same may be argued regarding another text representative of newer trends: Rafael Acevedo's *Exquisito cadáver*.[43] To limit ourselves to one detail, the phrase "all light unleashes a barbarism" ("toda luz desencadena una barbarie"), which appears in the text several times, cannot but remind the reader of the postmodern critique of the Enlightenment as a promise of progress leading to sinister results. Yet the novel is set in a future fully privatized world in which corporate capital regulates all activities: an evident reference to neoliberal capitalism taken to the limit. There are also subtle references to a sense of loss (of feeling, of intensity of experience, of companionship) amidst a "system" that, the novel reminds us, looks "like a net" but is in fact a "hierarchy." References to old *boleros*, a romantic popular musical genre, give many passages a nostalgic undercurrent. Through the description of a futuristic urban landscape, the novel seems to reformulate rather than simply leave behind many of the concerns of Puerto Rican literature since 1898 and the Left's agenda in the age of market globalization.

Purer examples of the postmodern sensibility are perhaps the texts of Pedro Cabiya. In Cabiya's "fantastic worlds," argues Luis Felipe Díaz, "there is no place for utopia," "(presumably) liberating truths," or "projects of social redemption." These texts, argues Díaz, can be read as parodies. But they are parodies of parody itself.[44] They parody the belief that parody can be a liberatory force as it unmasks some aspect of the ruling order. This corresponds to Fredric Jameson's definition of "pastiche" as that which replaces parody within the postmodern sensibility. Pastiche, he argues, is parody "without parody's ulterior motive, without the satirical impulse."[45] Indeed, if the work of Cabiya and other young authors exhibits the typical modernist desire of breaking with tradition, they are a "vanguard without a mission,"[46] since the idea of mission, whether nationalist, socialist, or feminist, is what they find most objectionable in their predecessors. Interestingly, the type of critical realism cultivated by José Luis González or Pedro Juan Soto in the past has found continuators, not on the island (where many now see it as infected with elitism/populism and as detrimental to aesthetic freedom and play), but in its diaspora. There is, for example, no equivalent in recent island fiction of Abraham Rodríguez Jr.'s representation of the thriving drug underworld in his 1993 novel *Spidertown*.[47]

Tensions have continued, on the other hand, among authors of the diaspora, perhaps rooted in an objective dynamic beyond personal preferences or opinions. Authors writing in English tend to move in the U.S. publishing world and are shaped by it, either as willing, unwilling, or oppositional participants. Authors writing in Spanish tend to keep as a central reference Latin American literature in Spanish, of which many feel part. While many among the former would affirm a Nuyorican identity, at least some among the latter see it as a surrender to the North American model of hyphenated ethnic assimilation, which they feel can be successfully resisted only by writing in Spanish. Tension, in this case, would be a positive sign, as it indicates a continuing debate, as opposed to each side treating the other with growing indifference.[48]

To summarize: in spite of the presence of some nuanced, intermediate positions, mentioned above, much of the Puerto Rican debates on culture, identity, and history became polarized in the 1990s around two sensibilities. For some, the rise of a heightened sense of Puerto Rican identity was a welcome development. It represented the coming to fruition of years of cultural resistance. For others, such neonationalism was a conservative reaction to the growing erosion of fixed identities in a context shaped by the passage to an increasingly globalized postmodernity.

Yet, in spite of their opposite views on nationhood, either embracing or allegedly superseding it, neonationalists and postmoderns share an implicit premise: their parallel farewells to an anticapitalist, socialist vision. Seen as irrelevant to an urgent national project, or as one of the failed "master narratives" of modernity, Marxism and more broadly the socialist ideals vanish from both nationalist and postmodern horizons.

This suggests a possible alternative to both nationalism and its postmodern critics: a perspective that largely shares the postmodern critique of nationalism, fully shares its enthusiasm for an increasingly transnational culture, and makes the struggle against nonclass forms of oppression (gay/lesbian, for example) its own, but that, unlike *both* the nationalist and postmodern creeds, insists on the need for a radical transformation of existing political, social, and economic structures as part of a global anticapitalist project. This perspective argues that radical democracy, if it hopes to be truly radical, must of necessity question the social and ecological consequences of capitalist competition and private control of productive assets. If it is to remain a subversive, oppositional force, it cannot afford to ignore the limits that capitalism sets to all emancipatory proposals, whether it is the progressive reduction of the working day and the expansion of free time, the institution of a guaranteed livelihood for all, or the adoption of sustainable forms of production and consumption. Nothing approaching these goals is attainable as long as the imperatives of capitalist accumulation and of survival in a competitive market remain the fundamental regulators of economic—indeed, of all social—activities and relations.[49]

This perspective enjoins us to reject and resist both oppressive gender and sexual categories *and* the market and its attendant cultures; to deconstruct nationalism while *also* opposing globalization in its existing neoliberal form; to denounce the oppressive uses of national sovereignty *as well as* the negative consequences of its erosion to the benefit of multinational capital. While the postmodern sensibility effortlessly embraces the first term in each of these couplings, it is at best lukewarm regarding the second, seeing in them the danger of nationalism or of Marxist teleology. But if this third vision can indeed be identified as Marxist, it implies no teleology. While capitalism may create the material basis for emancipation and abundance, it does not make them inevitable.

Nor does this perspective imply a belief in a self-proclaimed vanguard. It does insist that a freer world will not emerge spontaneously from the workings of capitalist globalization, from the spread of a non- or postwork ethic in informal economies, or from merely molecular forms of resistance. Emancipation must be achieved by the oppressed themselves, but it requires the conscious collective elaboration of an anticapitalist alternative. For this orientation, the resolution of Puerto Rico's colonial problem would be part of a radical social transformation that would be viable only in connection with currents moving in the same direction beyond Puerto Rico: a process made up of social, political, and economic struggles from below in Puerto Rico and the United States (including the many Puerto Ricans who live there), as well as in the rest of the Caribbean.

In this regard, there are grounds for cautious optimism. Indeed, the apogee of neoliberalism in the mid-1990s seemed to justify a deep pessimism about the possibility of progress understood as the capacity of radical collective action to increase general welfare. But the recent rise of strong oppositional movements to neoliberalism in Latin America, Europe, and the United States, including the "Bolivarian Revolution" in Venezuela, the Argentine insurrections of 2001–2, the election of the Movimiento al Socialismo government in Bolivia, the mass student and labor mobilizations in France, and the new activism among immigrants in the United States, not to speak of the anti- or alter-globalization movement ushered in by the Seattle protests of 1999, bring to the fore old questions that some postmodern commentators had dismissed as belonging to the past. For the movements against neoliberalism must all struggle with issues pertaining to concerted mass action as opposed to atomized individual activity. The postmodern trend may have confused a cyclical decline of oppositional movements with an "end of history" in which collective antisystemic action was forever doomed.

CONCLUSION

The history of Puerto Rico in the American Century breaks down into four periods, which closely coincide with the phases of the U.S. and world capitalist economies since the mid-1890s. (See Table I.1 in the introduction.) Puerto Rico, as a possession of but not part of the United States, has been pulled along by its metropole as U.S. capital and market demand repeatedly remade the Puerto Rican economy and the lives of Puerto Ricans, including the millions who moved north in search of employment. The specific form taken by the long-term fluctuations of capitalism within Puerto Rico cannot be divorced from the framework imposed by U.S. colonial rule and shifting state policies within that framework. Thus, each cycle of expansion of the economy has combined the development of an exporting sector with certain exceptional political measures that favor its growth.[1] Summarizing the evolution examined in the preceding chapters, we can posit the following elements of this cycle:

1. Expansion of an export sector due to certain "exceptional measures" in the context of an upswing in the international capitalist economy
2. Growing difficulties in the main export sector due to the results of the ongoing expansion of the international capitalist economy
3. Additional "exceptional measures" that attempt to alleviate the growing difficulties in the main export sector
4. Jettisoning the existing pattern of incentives and "exceptional measures" and searching for a new "economic model"

Puerto Rico has traversed this cycle twice during the American Century. Between the Spanish-American War and World War II, as the United States evolved from a regional to world power, the process unfolded as follows:

1. Between 1900 and the early 1920s: rapid expansion of the sugar export sector stimulated by the privileged access to the protected North American market

2. After the early 1920s: growing crisis of the world sugar industry due to overproduction and overcapacity
3. During the 1920s: protectionist measures adopted by the U.S. Congress in response to falling prices that stimulated production in Puerto Rico, the Philippines, and the beet-producing states
4. After 1930: deepening of the world sugar crisis and revolution in Cuba, leading to the adoption of the quota system and other means of crop-reduction, combined with the Plan Chardón in Puerto Rico

In the post–World War II period, when U.S. influence became truly global, the cycle took the following form:

1. During the 1950s and 1960s: expansion of light manufacturing for export stimulated by tax exemption, nonapplicability of the federal minimum wage, and unrestricted access to the U.S. market, followed by the attempt to construct a petrochemical project around special import privileges
2. By the 1960s: rise of manufacturing in semi-industrializing countries that compete with Puerto Rico in the U.S. market and sharp rise in oil prices after the mid-1970s
3. In 1976 in the midst of generalized recession: adoption of Section 936 tax provisions that sought to expand tax incentives to confront faltering growth
4. Through the 1980s and 1990s: adoption of free trade models that reduce the exceptionality of Puerto Rico's access to the U.S. market and the inability of Section 936 to launch a rapid expansion, concluding with the phaseout of Section 936 in 1996–2006

Between the first and second cycle, Puerto Rican New Dealers, led by Luis Muñoz Marín, elaborated a project of agrarian reform and diversification, production for insular consumption, and a more independent economic dynamic. This interlude began with the Plan Chardón in 1934 and concluded in 1947 with the adoption of the model of tax incentives to U.S. capital known as Operation Bootstrap. There was nevertheless some continuity between both periods as the state kept control of a significant array of public agencies.

Neither participation in the growth periods of the world capitalist economy nor the special features of its relation to the United States has allowed Puerto Rico to escape a condition of extreme dependence on foreign direct investments or its status as a relatively impoverished region under U.S. rule. Since this is the result of a century of unrestricted trade and unimpeded capital and labor mobility between Puerto Rico and the United States, it can hardly be blamed on an unwarranted limitation of the "natural laws" of the market, as neoliberal doctrines are wont to do. On the contrary, Puerto Rico's continued precarious economic and worsening social and ecological situation, secularly high unemployment rates, and lack of organic linkage between industry and agriculture are the result of this long colonial experiment in "free trade" as a recipe for development. The inability of its economy to generate anything resembling a self-sustaining dynamic or to free itself of the need for U.S. federal funds to sustain a minimum purchasing power for most of its people testify to the limitations of the free market approach to development. What Puerto Rico needs—as the New Dealers of the 1930s, to their credit, understood —is a program of planned economic and social reconstruction. That crucial decade, with its sharpened social clashes and wide-ranging debates, can still throw some light on the dilemmas of our troubled present.

In the 1930s, New Deal functionaries such as Henry Wallace and Rexford Tugwell in the Department of Agriculture were quite conscious that, in contrast to precapitalist economic crises, capitalist crises were not characterized by scarcity but rather by overproduction. Their most dramatic feature was the paradoxical presence of poverty, insecurity, and misery in the midst of potential abundance. Millions of laborers willing, desperate, to work stood destitute not far from closed factories. The unemployed went hungry while farmers went bankrupt as their crops decayed unsold. As a historian of the Agricultural Adjustment Administration has argued, "The lack of adequate food and clothing which afflicted so many in the nation was not related in any way to an actual shortage, for the nation was blessed—cursed, some thought—with an abundance of food and fiber."[2] Capitalism, driven by the search for higher profits, had created productive forces it could not operate profitably, and capitalism, profit being its objective, was thus led to reduce or paralyze production. To increase production was to further depress prices and profits and send the system deeper into its crisis. "As our economic system works," argued Wallace, ". . . it seems the greater the surplus of wheat on Nebraska farms, the longer the breadlines in New York."[3] The criteria of capitalist profitability thus stood starkly counterposed to the logic of the full utilization of existing resources to satisfy human needs: under the distorted logic of capitalism, potential abundance became the source of accentuated material hardship.

Tugwell, on his part, worried lest the "contrast between what we are and what might be will lodge itself firmly in every worker's mind."[4] "What might be" was not difficult to fathom: freed from the need to function as sources of private profit for competing capitals in a market economy, productive resources could be operated as a means of directly satisfying human needs as fully and efficiently as possible. Increased productivity would then lead, as one may rationally expect, not to misery but to adequate consumption, not to unemployment but to progressive reductions in the working time required of the producers, thus freeing time for other pursuits. But such a solution would have required the transformation of land and machines from private into collective or state property. The antidogmatic pragmatism regarding economic problems of which Wallace and Tugwell (and in Puerto Rico, Muñoz Marín) often boasted was in fact wedded to the unmovable dogma of private property. The middle ground they sometimes claimed to seek between laissez-faire capitalism and socialism was in fact a reformed version of the former. Unwilling to free production from the limits of capitalist property, they had little choice but to attempt to limit production in the hope of reviving capitalism. The most extreme example of such policies was the plowing-up of planted crops in order to reduce the pressure of surpluses on the market. As Wallace commented, "To have to destroy a growing crop is a shocking commentary on our civilization."[5] Indeed.

Between 1940 and 1948, the impact of war and fascism on the world labor movement and the capitalist economies created the context, at a terrible cost for humanity, for a new wave of capitalist expansion: the long postwar boom. In the United States, the more audacious considerations of the need for economic reform and of curbing the dynamics of capitalism, beyond mild Keynesian monetary and fiscal manipulations, were shelved. In Puerto Rico, Muñoz Marín and the Partido Popular Democrático abandoned the vision of a planned, increasingly independent Puerto Rican economy as counterpart to the New Deal in the United States and embraced the notion of industrialization driven by U.S. direct investments.

But since the contradictions vividly described by Wallace and Tugwell are inherent to capitalism, they eventually reasserted themselves globally by the late 1960s, bringing to a close the period of rapid postwar expansion. With this turn, the Puerto Rican "miracle" also came to an end. Since then, inequalities have increased both in the world economy and within states, and in Puerto Rico social and economic crisis has deepened. Enhanced tax incentives offered to U.S. investors under Section 936 stabilized but did not reduce unemployment significantly and have implied increased dependence on federal funds and borrowing for state financing.

Meanwhile, the political impasse has been unmovable. Regarding the status issue, Ramón Grosfoguel has argued that in their attempt to reorganize the world economy and salvage capitalism from its troubles, U.S. policy makers now seek to transform Puerto Rico into an independent neocolony. According to Grosfoguel, in Puerto Rico "there are four reactions to this new colonial strategy." While we should be cautious regarding the intentions of U.S. policy makers toward Puerto Rico, the currents described by Grosfoguel provide a useful map of sociopolitical options not limited to the traditional status preferences. The first three currents can be summarized as follows:

1. Blind support of a "neo-colonial republic," which would allow "the local and transnational bourgeoisie to better compete . . . while pauperizing Puerto Rican workers" (ending federal programs costly to capital)
2. Support for the present status, which is compatible with reduction in federal funds that benefit the island
3. "Right-wing neoliberal statehood," which attempts to make statehood viable by linking it to cuts in federal programs and other attacks on working and poor people

Grosfoguel favors a fourth option:

Resist neoliberal privatizations and cuts in federal transfers. . . . Any decolonization of the island should claim a "historic indemnification" from the United States to rebuild Puerto Rico's economy after one hundred years of colonialism. Decolonization should also imply a radicalization of the existing democratic structures in alliance with social movements and oppressed groups in the metropole, mobilizing U.S. citizenship as means to fight and demand social justice and equality within the U.S. empire. This is a new type of social struggle that attempts to expand Puerto Ricans citizenship rights and democratic representation within the U.S. empire. Some have called this approach "statehood from a radical-democratic perspective."[6]

There are several admirable aspects to the fourth perspective. It recognizes the need for radical social and political change from below in the United States, if the needs of its vast working majority are to be met. It does not take American society as an unchangeable monolith but as a complex social formation split against itself by latent or open social conflicts that may yet clear the path to radical change. It affirms, furthermore, that the evolution of progressive social and political struggles in Puerto Rico cannot be divorced from social struggles in the United States. In addition, this perspective optimistically bets on the eventual emergence, from a myriad of ongoing social struggles, of a movement wide and strong enough to revert the policies dominant in Washington at least since the beginning of the Reagan era, which run contrary to any form of "indemnification" for the consequences of oppression or of reform programs geared to achieve greater equality between individuals and between regions.

But this vision calls forth two evident questions that Grosfoguel fails to pose. The first is whether such a movement in the United States would limit itself to proposing a reorganization of the areas politically within the U.S. "empire" and for the benefit of those who can "mobilize U.S. citizenship" on their own behalf. Should this movement concern itself only with the internal provinces of the empire, or should it question the imperial projection of the state within which it struggles? The answer, of course, is that if this orientation's "democratic radicalism" is to be consistent, it must embrace not only the notion of reform within the empire but also a new type of relation of the United States with the rest of the world, beginning with the area where it first projected its imperial power: the Caribbean and Central America. It is hard to imagine a radical shift within the United States capable of securing some form of indemnification for a century of colonial rule in Puerto Rico without it also implying a radical shift in U.S. global policies.

The second question flows from the answer to the first question. If a "radical democratic" movement in the United States must include the vision of a new type of relation with the independent Caribbean (and other areas), must the Puerto Rican counterpart of such a movement of necessity embrace the perspective of statehood for Puerto Rico, to which Grosfoguel's list of options restricts it? Does not the movement needed to build a "radical democratic statehood" and to make a "historical indemnification" a viable option also make possible a radical democratic independence in growing integration with the surrounding Caribbean?

The notion of a struggle for a socially progressive independence in conjunction with social struggles in the United States that we are advancing here is, of course, not new. Socialist activists such as Jesús Colón and Bernardo Vega long ago saw participation in the social struggles in the United States and the struggle for an independent Puerto Rico not as alternate programs (as both nationalist *independentistas* and "radical" statehooders tend to see them) but as interdependent aspects of a single project of international anticapitalist social and political transformation. Eugenio María de Hostos and Rosendo Matienzo Cintrón did as much regarding the struggle for independence and the fight to curtail the power of big capital within the United States. Nationalists are wrong in thinking that the evolution of social struggles in the United States is a matter of indifference for a future Puerto Rican republic. The options open to such a republic would largely depend on the policies irradiating from Washington. But it is also a mistake to conclude that the relevance of U.S. struggles for Puerto Rico's future precludes the transformation of future working and poor peoples' mobilizations and self-organization on the island into a movement for political sovereignty in close association with progressive forces in the United States.

From this perspective, the struggle of immigrant communities (including Puerto Ricans) in the United States and Dominican immigrants in Puerto Rico, the fight to remake the economies and polities of the independent Caribbean (such as the Dominican Republic), and the search for Puerto Rico's self-determination can be seen as facets of a complex international movement to remake, indeed unmake, the hierarchies erected by more than a century of colonial, imperial, and capitalist rule. Culturally, what corresponds to this perspective must be an open, porous notion of Puerto Rican culture and identity, a *puertorriqueñidad* in the tradition of the ideas of Matienzo Cintrón and Rubén del Rosario, to mention two figures discussed earlier, capable of critically embracing the diverse experiences and remixes emerging from migrations out of and into Puerto Rico.

As things stand in 2006, the state of social and labor movements in Puerto Rico offers little prospect for radical change in the near future. Yet such change is necessary. At the time of writing, the decrease in manufacturing employment continues, pubic debt has reached unprecedented levels, and Wall Street rating agencies are close to reducing Puerto Rico's government financial instruments to the level of junk bonds. More critically, government agencies have run out of funds two months before the end of fiscal year 2005–06. An impasse between the PPD-controlled executive and a PNP-led legislature forced a two-week layoff of close to 100,000 public employees. Coinciding with this, Congress is conducting hearings on possible mechanisms of dealing with the status question. Erosion of the prestige of the major political parties, fiscal crisis, and growing exasperation on the island, on Wall Street, and in Washington with Puerto Rico's overall situation: Puerto Rican society is at the end of an era. Meanwhile, amid a depressingly atomized social landscape, symptoms of resistance from below to existing dominant policies can be discerned in dozens of community, environmental, labor, and other initiatives. All of these movements share one characteristic: they all embody the struggle of people to more directly control part of their lives, from their work environment, the air they breathe, the way their communities are policed, or how the state budget is distributed. They are all, in that sense, struggles for self-determination. It is the task of all those involved to help turn these fragmented initiatives into a wider movement for growing public democratic sovereignty over key economic decisions.

Therein lies the basis for a radical break with the past. The exit from colonial subordination and misdevelopment, the achievement of true self-determination, cannot be detached from a renewed questioning of private accumulation and the market as the central regulators of social reproduction arising from such struggles. Nor is the need for this exclusive to Puerto Rico: the impact of late capitalist crisis and social deterioration cannot but pose the same problem within the United States. From that angle, as indicated, the interests of the Puerto Rican, Caribbean, and North American working people are, and can only become, increasingly interdependent. But to offer a blueprint for the future exceeds the boundaries of this book. The authors will be satisfied if it ever so modestly contributes to that effort through a clearer understanding of a complex past.

NOTES

ABBREVIATIONS

EI	*El Imparcial*	*LD*	*La Democracia*	*NYT*	*New York Times*
EM	*El Mundo*	*ND*	*El Nuevo Día*	*UO*	*Unión Obrera*
LC	*La Correspondencia*				

INTRODUCTION

1. Ernest Mandel, *Long Waves of Capitalist Development: The Marxist Interpretation* (Cambridge: Cambridge University Press, 1980); Eric J. Hobsbawm, *The Age of Extremes: A History of the World, 1914–1991* (New York: Pantheon, 1994); Angus Maddison, *The World Economy in the 20th Century* (Paris: Development Centre of the Organisation for Economic Co-operation and Development, 1989). For a nuanced exploration of the fluctuations and shifting location of working-class militancy and capital-labor conflicts largely compatible with this periodization, see Beverly J. Silver, *Forces of Labor: Workers' Movements and Globalizations since 1870* (Cambridge: Cambridge University Press, 2003).

CHAPTER ONE

1. Theodore Roosevelt, *Selections from the Correspondence of Theodore Roosevelt and Henry Cabot Lodge 1884–1918*, 2 vols. (New York: Charles Scribner's Sons, 1925), 1:299–300, 301.

2. Qtd. in Walter Lafeber, *The New Empire: An Interpretation of American Expansionism, 1860–1898* (Ithaca: Cornell University Press, 1963), 110.

3. Angel Rivero, *Crónica de la guerra hispano-americana en Puerto Rico* (Río Piedras: Edil, 1972), 623, 624.

4. The term "trauma of 1898" was used by Francisco Manrique Cabrera in his 1956 *Historia de la literatura puertorriqueña* (New York: Las Américas Publishing Co., 1956).

5. Henry K. Carroll, *Report on the Island of Porto Rico* (Washington: GPO, 1899), 296.

6. Events in Ciales on August 13, 1898, have been much debated. Some consider it a separatist and others a pro-American uprising. Another debate surrounds the group led by José Maldonado ("Aguila Blanca"). Evidence indicates he was a rural bandit, not politically motivated. "El 'Aguila Blanca' fue capturado . . . ," *LD*, Aug. 3, 1907. See Juan Manuel Delgado, *El levantamiento de Ciales* (Guasábara, 1980); and Mariano Negrón

Portillo, *Cuadrillas anexionistas y revueltas campesinas en Puerto Rico, 1898–1899* (Río Piedras: Centro de Estudios Sociales–Universidad de Puerto Rico, 1987).

7. Eileen J. Suárez Findlay, *Imposing Decency: The Politics of Sexuality and Race in Puerto Rico, 1870–1920* (Durham, N.C.: Duke University Press, 1999).

8. Carroll, *Report*, 678, 687. See also Nancy J. Herzig Shannon, *El Iris de Paz: el espiritismo y la mujer en Puerto Rico* (Río Piedras: Huracán, 2001).

9. "A diestro y siniestro," *LD*, Jan. 22, 30, 1895; Mariano Abril, "Las Huelgas," *LD*, Jan. 22, 1895; "El conflicto de Arecibo," *LC*, Jan. 22, 1895.

10. Bailey K. Ashford, *A Soldier in Science: The Autobiography of Bailey K. Ashford* (1934; San Juan: Universidad de Puerto Rico, 1998), 38. For references and caution regarding the San Juan–Ponce dialectic, see María de los Angeles Castro, "De Salvador Brau a la 'novísima' historia: un replanteamiento y una crítica," *Op.Cit.* 4 (1988–89): 52–54.

11. Carroll, *Report*, 151, 144.

12. Some created secret groups to boycott Spanish merchants. This led to repression in 1887 (known as *compontes*), including arrests of autonomist leaders.

13. "Si; reflexionemos," Dec. 15, 1870, in Reece B. Bothwell, ed., *Puerto Rico: cien años de lucha política*, 4 vols. (San Juan: Editorial de la Universidad de Puerto Rico, 1979), 2:20.

14. Alejandro Tapia, "Puerto Rico visto sin espejuelos por un cegato" (1876), in *Obras completas* (San Juan: Instituto de Cultura Puertorriqueña, 1968), 55–60; Román Baldorioty, *Exposición Universal de París en 1867. Memoria presentada a la Comisión Provincial de Puerto Rico* (San Juan: Acosta, 1868).

15. Luis A. Figueroa, *Sugar, Slavery and Freedom in Nineteenth-Century Puerto Rico* (Chapel Hill: University of North Carolina Press, 2005), 171.

16. Annexationist sympathies were strong among professionals, such as José J. Henna and Roberto H. Todd. They, not the *independentistas* such as Sotero Figueroa, Francisco Marín, and Antonio Vélez Alvarado, became the official leaders of the Puerto Rico Section of the PRC.

17. Luis Muñoz Rivera, "Las causas del mal," "Los remedios del mal" (1891), in *Campañas Políticas*, 2 vols. (Madrid: Puerto Rico, 1925), 1:20–39, 40–47.

18. "Manifiesto de los dirigentes liberales" (1899), in Bothwell, *Puerto Rico* 1:267.

19. For example, E. M. de Hostos, introduction to *Moral Social* (1888; Madrid: Archipiélago, 1965).

20. The subtitle of Kipling's poem was "The United States and the Philippine Islands." It was first published in *McClure's*, Feb. 1899. For Mark Twain, see Jim Zwick, ed., *Mark Twain's Weapon of Satire: Anti-imperialist Writings on the Philippine-American War* (Syracuse: Syracuse University Press, 1992).

21. Some labor anticolonialists adopted racist views: they opposed colonialism as a means of blocking the influx of alien labor, judged to be inferior.

22. *Loughborough v. Blake*, 1820 5 Wheat. 317, 5 L. ed. 98 (1820).

23. *Downes v. Bidwell*, 182 U.S. 244 (1901).

24. Supreme Court justice John Marshall Harlan eloquently opposed the doctrine of nonincorporation. But his commitment was to the integrity of the U.S. Constitution,

not to the conquered peoples' right to self-determination. He felt Puerto Rico had been incorporated by the ratification of the Treaty of Paris, a view that rejected retaining it as a colony but gave it no role in the determination of its political future.

25. Pedro A. Cabán, *Constructing a Colonial People: Puerto Rico and the United States, 1898–1932* (Boulder: Westview Press, 1999), 99.

26. Richard Levins, "Review of Gordon Lewis' Puerto Rico: Freedom and Power in the Caribbean," *Science and Society* 29, no. 1 (Winter 1965): 96–101.

27. David Healy, *U.S. Expansionism: The Imperialist Urge in the 1890s* (Madison: University of Wisconsin Press, 1970), 12.

28. Before the war, the U.S. Naval Board underlined the importance of controlling Puerto Rico in the case of a war with Spain. In his *Lessons of the War with Spain*, Mahan insisted that Puerto Rico would be to an isthmian canal what Malta was to the Suez Canal. A. T. Mahan, *Lessons of the War with Spain and Other Articles* (Boston: Little, Brown and Co., 1899).

29. Qtd. in Cabán, *Constructing a Colonial People*, 16. See similar views by Foraker in Everett Walters, *Joseph Benson Foraker: An Uncompromising Republican* (Columbus: Ohio History Press, 1948), 153.

30. See Rogers Smith, *Civic Ideals: Conflicting Visions of Citizenship in U.S. History* (New Haven: Yale University Press, 1997). In the late 1880s, Puerto Rican separatist Hostos denounced the discrepancy between U.S. republican ideals and the policy of Chinese exclusion, which he likened to European anti-Semitism. Hostos, *Moral Social*, 32–33.

31. Eric Foner, *The Story of American Freedom* (New York: W. W. Norton, 1998), 131, 132.

32. Mark S. Weiner, "Teutonic Constitutionalism: The Role of Ethno-Judicial Discourse in the Spanish-American War," in *Foreign in a Domestic Sense: Puerto Rico, American Expansion and the Constitution*, ed. Christina Duffy Burnett and Burke Marshall (Durham: Duke University Press, 2001), 48–81.

33. George Davis, *Report of the Military Governor of Porto Rico on Civil Affairs* (Washington: GPO, 1902), 115–16. Not all U.S. functionaries held such views. Commissioner Carroll drew a fairly positive view of the island's inhabitants. His proposals for an insular government were more liberal than those of General Davis or of the eventual dispositions of the Foraker Act.

34. Lanny Thompson, "The Imperial Republic: A Comparison of the Insular Territories under U.S. Dominion after 1898," *Pacific Historical Review* 71, no. 4 (Nov. 2002): 539–40.

CHAPTER TWO

1. Miguel Guerra Mondragón, "The Legal Background of Land Reform in Puerto Rico," in *Portrait of a Society: Readings on Puerto Rican Sociology*, ed. Eugenio Fernández Méndez (Río Piedras: University of Puerto Rico Press, 1972), 167.

2. Municipalities are classified according to which of the three export crops—sugar, tobacco, or coffee—occupied more land.

3. Clara Lugo Sendra, "The Sugar Industry in Puerto Rico" (Ph.D. diss., University of California at Los Angeles, 1943), 117.

4. Henry K. Carroll, *Report on the Island of Porto Rico* (Washington: GPO, 1899), 134, 182.

5. Qtd. in Edward J. Berbusse, *The United States in Puerto Rico, 1898–1900* (Chapel Hill: University of North Carolina Press, 1966), 174.

6. César J. Ayala, *American Sugar Kingdom: The Plantation Economy of the Spanish Caribbean, 1898–1934* (Chapel Hill: University of North Carolina Press, 1999).

7. Esteban Bird, *Report on the Sugar Industry in Relation to the Social and Economic System of Puerto Rico* (San Juan: Government Office of Supplies, Printing and Transportation, 1941), 67.

8. Sidney W. Mintz, *Sweetness and Power: The Place of Sugar in Modern History* (New York: Viking, 1985), xviii.

9. Joseph Marcus, *Labor Conditions in Puerto Rico* (Washington, D.C.: GPO, 1919); Erick Pérez Velasco, "La condición obrera en Puerto Rico (1898–1920)," *Plural* (University of Puerto Rico) 3, nos. 1–2 (1984): 157–70; Frank Tannenbaum, "Los últimos treinta años: 1898–1928," *Op.Cit.* 7 (1992): 145–207.

10. See Ramón Aboy, "Vida económica de Puerto Rico bajo la dominación de Estados Unidos," *Revista de las Antillas* 2, no. 5 (July 1914): 74–78.

11. Carmen González Muñoz, *El tiempo de los príncipes del azúcar: la discursividad azucarera en Puerto Rico, 1920–1929* (Ph.D. diss., Universidad de Puerto Rico, 254), 80, 81.

12. Iris López, "Borinkis and Chop Suey: Puerto Rican Identity in Hawaii, 1900 to 2000," in *The Puerto Rican Diaspora: Historical Perspectives*, ed. Carmen T. Whalen and Víctor Vázquez-Hernández (Philadelphia: Temple University Press, 2005), 43–67.

13. For an overview of the Puerto Rican economy, see Victor S. Clark et al., *Porto Rico and Its Problems* (Washington, D.C.: Brookings Institution, 1930).

14. Juan José Baldrich, *Sembraron la no siembra: los cosecheros de tabaco puertorriqueños frente a las corporaciones tabacaleras, 1920–1934* (Río Piedras: Huracán, 1988), 118.

15. See Arturo Bird-Carmona, "Between the Insular Road and San Juan Bay: The Cigar World of Puerta de Tierra" (Ph.D. diss., University of Iowa, 1998).

16. Miguel Meléndez Muñoz, "El estado social del campesino puertorriqueño" (1913), in *Obras Completas*, vol. 1 (Barcelona: Ediciones Rumbos, 1963). This collection includes his major works.

17. For Zeno, see his *El obrero agrícola o de los campos* (San Juan: La Correspondencia, 1922).

18. See Baldrich, *Sembraron la no siembra*.

19. Juan José Baldrich, "Gender and the Decomposition of the Cigar-Making Craft in Puerto Rico, 1899–1934," in *Puerto Rican Women's History: New Perspectives*, ed. Linda C. Delgado and Félix Matos Rodríguez (Armonk, N.Y.: M. E. Sharpe, 1998), 105–25.

20. See works by Laird W. Bergad and Fernando Picó in the Bibliographical Essay.

21. "El café de Puerto Rico y la iniciativa industrial," *LD*, Aug. 20, 1915.

22. "La asamblea de cultivadores de café," *LD*, Nov. 9, 1909; "Los alcaldes y la 'Asociación nacional de productores de café,'" *LD*, Jan. 18, 1910; "A los cafetaleros de Puerto

Rico," *LD*, June 16, 1910; "Asociación Nacional de Productores de Café," *LD*, Aug. 29, 1914; "El café de Puerto Rico," *LD*, Aug. 20, 1915.

23. See Caroline Manning, *The Employment of Women in Puerto Rico*, Bulletin of the Women's Bureau 18 (Washington, D.C.: U.S. Department of Labor, 1934).

24. Pedro Albizu Campos, "Comentarios del Presidente del Partido Nacionalista al margen del informe rendido por el Instituto Brookings" (1930), in *Obras escogidas: 1923–1936*, ed. J. Benjamín Torres, 4 vols. (San Juan: Editorial Jelofe, 1975–87), 1:103.

25. Qtd. in Bolívar Pagán, *Historia de los partidos políticos puertorriqueños (1898–1956)* (San Juan: n.p., 1972), 1:290.

26. Luis Muñoz Marín, "What Next in Puerto Rico?" *Nation*, Nov. 20, 1929, 608.

27. Samuel R. Quiñones, "El discurso radiometido el viernes . . . ," *LD*, Jan. 30, 1936.

28. José Enamorado Cuesta, *Porto Rico: Past and Present* (1929; New York: Arno Press, 1975), 118; Clara Lugo Sendra, "Comentarios a la actitud económico-social del nacionalismo puertorriqueño," *EM*, June 28, 1936; Sendra, "Sugar Industry," 102.

29. Carroll, *Report*, 524, 48.

30. See U.S. Department of Commerce, Bureau of the Census, *Fourteenth Census of the United States Taken in the Year 1920*, vol. 6, part 3 (Washington, D.C.: GPO, 1922), 385.

31. César J. Ayala and Laird Bergad, "Rural Puerto Rico in the Early Twentieth Century Reconsidered: Land and Society, 1899–1915," *Latin American Research Review* 37, no. 2 (2002): 65–97. This article examines records for Aguas Buenas, Utuado, Cayey, Humacao, San Germán, Lares, Manatí, Fajardo, Yauco, and Santa Isabel in the years 1905 and 1915. The database contains 11,383 properties in 1905 and 16,103 in 1915 and includes regions that specialized in sugar, coffee, and tobacco production.

32. See V. I. Lenin, "New Data on the Laws Governing the Development of Capitalism in Agriculture. Part One. Capitalism and Agriculture in the United States of America," in *Lenin on the United States: Selected Writings* (New York: International Publishers, 1970), 114–205.

33. Manuel A. Pérez, *Living Conditions of Small Farmers in Puerto Rico* (San Juan: Bureau of Supplies, Printing and Transportation, 1942), 10.

34. A Puerto Rican *cuerda* is equal to .9712 acres. Figures from Puerto Rico Reconstruction Administration, *Census of Puerto Rico, 1935* (Washington, D.C.: GPO, 1938), 112–13 and other tables.

CHAPTER THREE

1. See, for example, Mariano Negrón Portillo, *Las turbas republicanas, 1900–1904* (Río Piedras: Huracán, 1990).

2. Probably many Afro–Puerto Ricans saw the coming of U.S. rule with sympathy. Racist U.S. practices could not appeal to them, but neither could they look back to Spanish rule as anything but an epoch of oppression. But Barbosa's annexationism should not be turned into a function of his "blackness." It was initially shared by most Puerto Rican liberals, white or black.

3. José Celso Barbosa, "El problema del color" (1909), 31–34, and "En nuestro terreno" (1915), 42, in *Problema de razas*, ed. Pilar Barbosa (San Juan: Obra de José Celso Barbosa, 1984).

4. See, for example, Rosendo Matienzo Cintrón, "La dureza del lenguaje" (1911), in Luis Díaz Soler, *Rosendo Matienzo Cintrón*, 2 vols. (Río Piedras: Instituto de Literatura Puertorriqueña, Universidad de Puerto Rico, 1960), 2:25.

5. José Celso Barbosa, "Notas políticas" (1916), 115, and "Siempre leales a la fe jurada" (1920), 179, in *Orientando al pueblo*, ed. Pilar Barbosa de Rosario (San Juan: Imprenta Venezuela, 1939).

6. Barbosa, "Hipócritas" (1920), in *Orientando*, 163. Also see in the same work "Perseverancia en los ideales" (1915), 111, and "Con motivo de las elecciones . . . ," (1920), 189–90.

7. "Convention in Puerto Rico," *NYT*, Dec. 20, 1898, 3; Henry K. Carroll, *Report on the Island of Porto Rico* (Washington: GPO, 1899), 236; "El 25 de julio. Por qué no lo celebramos" (1900), in Reece B. Bothwell, ed., *Puerto Rico: cien años de lucha política*, 4 vols. (San Juan: Editorial de la Universidad de Puerto Rico, 1979), 2:144–45; "Opiniones del Sr. Muñoz Rivera" (1898), in Bothwell, *Puerto Rico*, 2:108–11.

8. Leo S. Rowe, *The United States and Porto Rico* (New York: Longmans, Green, 1904), 248, 157.

9. "Muñoz Rivera establece . . . ," *LD*, Apr. 13, 1914; "Lo que escribe Muñoz Rivera," *LD*, Sept. 4, 1909; "Por la autonomía," *LD*, Aug. 4, 1909; Bolívar Pagán, *Historia de los partidos políticos puertorriqueños (1898–1956)* (San Juan: n.p., 1972), 1:154.

10. "Una carta de Luis Muñoz Rivera," *LD*, Aug. 9, 1912.

11. Mariano Abril, "Más patriotismo," *LD*, Nov. 3, 1915.

12. José A. Cabranes, *Citizenship and the American Empire: Notes on the Legislative History of the United States Citizenship of Puerto Ricans* (New Haven: Yale University Press, 1979), 60, 69, 82; Pedro A. Cabán, *Constructing a Colonial People: Puerto Rico and the United States, 1898–1932* (Boulder: Westview Press, 1999), 199–200. Such was also the position of President Taft, "Porto Ricans Must Wait," *NYT*, Apr. 17, 1912, 16. It has been argued that U.S. citizenship sought to make Puerto Ricans eligible for the U.S. armed forces, but they were already eligible. Nor is there indication, Cabranes argues, that this played a role in the adoption of the Jones Act.

13. "En la reunión de anoche . . . ," *LD*, Mar. 8, 1921; "Un notabilísimo artículo . . . ," *LD*, Dec. 31, 1921. See also Antonio R. Barceló, *The Acute Political Crisis of Porto Rico* (San Juan: Tipografía La Democracia, 1921), 13, 14.

14. *Balzac v. Puerto Rico*, 258 U.S. 298 (1922).

15. "Unión de Puerto Rico invita . . . ," (1914), in Bothwell, *Puerto Rico* 1:343; Gonzálo Córdova, *Luis Sánchez Morales* (San Juan: Académica, 1991), 96.

16. Luis Araquistáin, *La agonía antillana: El imperialismo yanqui en el Mar Caribe* (Madrid: Espasa-Calpe, 1928), 97.

17. Most influentially in Angel G. Quintero Rivera, *Conflictos de clase y política en Puerto Rico* (Río Piedras: Huracán, 1976).

18. "La cuestión magna," *LD*, Apr. 21, 1913; "El debate sobre azúcares," *LD*, May 9, 1913; "Los intereses creados," *LD*, June 18, 1913; "Discurso del Sr. Muñoz Rivera . . . ," *LD*, Mar. 28, 1912; "Labor de sierpes," *LD*, Mar. 23, 1912.

19. "Benigno Fernández García comenta . . ." (1919), in Bothwell, *Puerto Rico*, 2:289–97.

20. "La limitación a 500 acres," *LC*, Feb. 15, 1910.

21. The Partido Popular Democrático, which would dominate island politics from 1940 to 1968, would further develop this orientation.

22. "Labor Union in Porto Rico," *NYT*, Dec. 8, 1901, 3.

23. Angel G. Quintero Rivera, "Clases sociales e indentidad nacional; notas sobre el desarrollo nacional puertorriqueño," in *Puerto Rico: identidad nacional y clases sociales (Coloquio de Princeton)*, ed. Angel G. Quintero Rivera, José Luis González, Ricardo Campos, and Juan Flores (Río Piedras: Huracán, 1981), 31.

24. "Iglesias Says He Is Persecuted," *San Juan News*, Nov. 14, 1901.

25. Rafael Alonso Torres, *Cuarenta años de lucha proletaria* (San Juan: Imprenta Baldrich, 1939), 263.

26. A. Hyatt Verrill, *Porto Rico Past and Present and San Domingo Today* (New York: Mead, 1919), 148.

27. *American Federationist* 22, no. 4 (Apr. 1915): 267; 23, no. 12 (Dec. 1916): 1163.

28. "Habla el gobernador," *LD*, Feb. 22, 1915; "Se pide la supresión . . . ," *LD*, Feb. 4, 1920; "La supresión de la bandera . . . ," *EM*, Oct. 21, 1920; M. Abril, "Incendios y huelgas," *LD*, Feb. 18, 1915; M. Abril, "El maximalismo criollo," *LD*, Jan. 26, 1920; "Provocaciones de los Bolshevikis . . . ," *LD*, Jan. 30, 1920; Bolívar Ochart, *La noche del 12 de marzo de 1919* (Fajardo: Conciencia Popular, 1919). See also Kelvin Santiago-Valles, *"Subject People" and Colonial Discourses: Economic Transformation and Social Disorder in Puerto Rico, 1898–1947* (Albany: State University of New York Press, 1994).

29. Sandalio Alonso, "¿Quiénes deben ocupar la dirección de las secciones socialistas?" *Justicia*, Dec. 25, 1922.

30. See "Manifiesto dirigido al pueblo de Puerto Rico . . ." (1924), 1:426–31; "Importante reunión del Comité Territorial Republicano . . ." (1924), 2:362–65; and "Manifiesto del Presidente del Partido Republicano . . ." (1924), 1:432–39, all in Bothwell, *Puerto Rico*.

31. Puerto Ricans had been allowed to enter the United States without going through immigration procedures since 1904.

32. See Virginia Sánchez Korrol, *From Colonia to Community: The History of Puerto Ricans in New York City, 1917–1948* (Westport, Conn.: Greenwood Press, 1983), and Bernardo Vega, *Memoirs of Bernardo Vega: A Contribution to the History of the Puerto Rican Community in New York*, ed. César Andreu Iglesias, trans. Juan Flores (New York: Monthly Review Press, 1984).

33. Vega, *Memoirs of Bernardo Vega*, 153, 128.

34. See María Barceló Miller, *La lucha por el sufragio femenino en Puerto Rico, 1896–1935* (Río Piedras: Huracán/Centro Investigaciones Sociales, 1997).

35. Yamila Azize, *La mujer en la lucha* (Río Piedras: Editorial Cultural, 1985), 126, 131.

36. "Senor E. M. Hostos Talks," *NYT*, July 22, 1898, 2. This was the opposite of Barbosa's perspective, summarized above, premised on the fact that Puerto Rico's status would be determined by Congress.

37. Eugenio María de Hostos, "El gobierno civil en Puerto Rico," *Madre Isla*, in *Obras Completas* (La Habana: Cultural, 1939), 5:223. See discussion in Rafael Bernabe, *Respuestas al colonialismo en la política puertorriqueña, 1899–1929* (Río Piedras: Huracán, 1996), 35–46.

38. "Discurso del patriota Rosendo Matienzo . . ." (1902), in Bothwell, *Puerto Rico*, 2:194.

39. Rosendo Matienzo Cintrón, "Colonia inglesa" (1911), in Díaz Soler, *Rosendo Matienzo Cintrón*, 2:154.

40. Matienzo Cintrón, "El 30 de noviembre . . ." (1911), "Sacrílegos," in ibid., 2:67, 42; Hostos, *Madre Isla*, in *Obras Completas*, 5:108, 197–98, 245, 258, 274, 308.

41. There were brilliant aspects as well as contradictions and even eccentricities and bizarre turns in the work and deeds of Matienzo Cintrón, which we cannot go into here. For a discussion of these debates, see Bernabe, *Respuestas al colonialismo*, 183–92.

42. "Claúsulas de incorporación . . . Partido de la Independencia" (1912), in Bothwell, *Puerto Rico*, 1:305–33. The program was largely taken from the New Zealand Liberal Party. See discussion in Bernabe, *Respuestas al colonialismo*, 265–78.

43. Rafael López Landrón, "La plutocracia norteamericana," *Revista de las Antillas* 1, no. 2 (Apr. 1913). For López Landrón, see Bernabe, *Respuestas al colonialismo*, 249–65.

44. López Landrón, "Seleccionemos," *La Independencia* 1, no. 1 (Feb. 1913); "Los bancos y la crisis," *LC*, Aug. 6, Sept. 2, 1912; "Mitin político en Bayamón," *LC*, Mar. 23, 1912; "La plutocracia norteamericana," *Revista de las Antillas* 1, no. 2 (Apr. 1913). See also his *Cartas abiertas para el pueblo de Puerto Rico* (San Juan: Tip. Venezuela, 1928). López Landrón was an enthusiastic defender of women's rights; see *La mujer puertorriqueña ante el Bill Jones* (San Juan: Tip. Boletín Mercantil, 1916).

45. "Ambiente social. Notas de duelo," *LC*, Apr. 13, 1917; Arturo Bird-Carmona, *A lima y machete* (Río Piedras: Huracán, 2001), 128–29. Among the supporters of the Partido de la Independencia were novelist Matías González García and painter Ramón Frade, creator of the best-known painting of the period in Puerto Rico: *El pan nuestro* (1904); "A la independencia . . . ," *LC*, Feb. 16, 1912.

CHAPTER FOUR

1. See Christopher Schmidt-Nowara, *Empire and Antislavery: Spain, Cuba, and Puerto Rico, 1833–1874* (Pittsburgh: University of Pittsburgh Press, 1999).

2. Salvador Brau, "La campesina" (1886), and "Rafael Cordero," in *Disquiciones sociológicas*, ed. Salvador Brau (Río Piedras: Instituto de Literatura, 1956), 234, 261–73.

3. Qtd. in Nancy Morris, *Puerto Rico: Culture, Politics, and Identity* (Westport, Conn.: Praeger, 1995), 26.

4. Victor S. Clark et al., *Porto Rico and Its Problems* (Washington, D.C.: Brookings Institution, 1930), ix.

5. Rosendo Matienzo Cintrón, "Patriotismo" (1911), in Luis Díaz Soler, *Rosendo Matienzo Cintrón*, 2 vols. (Río Piedras: Instituto de Literatura Puertorriqueña, Universidad de Puerto Rico, 1960), 2:231.

6. Ibid., "Violada el alma jurídica" (1911), 2:194.

7. Ibid., "Seamos caballeros" (1912), 2:347.

8. Ibid., "La posición que ocupamos" (1911), 2:277.

9. Ibid., "La posición que ocupamos" (1911), 2:278.

10. Ibid., "Las colonias extranjeras," 2:174.

11. Qtd. in Morris, *Puerto Rico*, 26.

12. Aida Negrón de Montilla, *La americanización de Puerto Rico y el sistema de instrucción pública, 1900–1930* (Río Piedras: Editorial Universitaria, 1977).

13. De Diego, to be fair, embraced central elements of modern republicanism, such as the separation of church and state. See José De Diego, "Por la fe y por la patria," in De Diego, *Obras completas* (San Juan: Instituto de Cultura Puertorriqueña, 1966), 85–89. For a more consistent conservative, pro-Spanish Catholic critique of the United States, it is necessary to turn to Vicente Balbás's *Puerto Rico a los diez años de americanización*, published in 1910 (San Juan: Tipografía Heraldo Español). Balbás was a Spanish resident in Puerto Rico. His text was a critique of sugarcane monoculture and of U.S. corporations and a conservative denunciation of the separation of church and state and of what he took to be the erosion of Catholic morals after 1898. As part of his opposition to U.S. corporations, Balbás grudgingly recognized that it would be necessary to make an alliance with the labor movement and even collaborated with anti-Catholics Matienzo Cintrón and López Landrón and with the FLT in cooperative initiatives.

14. Luis Lloréns Torres, "El zapatismo en México" (1913), in *Obras Completas*, 3 vols. (San Juan: Instituto de Cultura Puertorriqueña, 1969), 3:415–18.

15. Noel Luna, "Paisaje, cuerpo e historia: Luis Lloréns Torres," *La Torre* 4, no. 11 (1999): 53–78.

16. For the works of Nemesio Canales, see *Paliques* (1915; Barcelona: Editorias Vosgos, 1974) and *Antología de Nemesio Canales*, ed. Servando Montaña Peláez (San Juan: Editorial de la Universidad de Puerto Rico, 2000). See also Rafael Bernabe, *La maldición de Pedreira: aspectos de la crítica romántico-cultural de la modernidad en Puerto Rico* (Río Piedras: Huracán, 2002).

17. See, for example, "Puerto Rico, cementerio de vivos" (1920), 318–20; "El negro" (1916), 153–54; "La Conferencia de Londres" (1922), 230–233; "El futurismo" (1912), 45–47; "¡Quien fuera burro!" (1912); "Adiós, 1915" (1915), 141–42; "Nuestras mujeres y la cuestión feminista" (1917), 166–69; "Réplica a una carta de A. Pérez Pierret" (1917), 172–77; and "Guijas y guiños" (1919), 185–88, all in Montaña Peláez, *Antología*.

18. Miguel Guerra Mondragón, *Oscar Wilde. Estudio y traducciones* (San Juan: Editorial Antillana, 1914), xii.

19. Miguel Guerra Mondragón, "San Juan de Puerto Rico. Su movimiento literario," *Revista de las Antillas* 2, no. 4 (June 1914): 83.

20. Miguel Guerra Mondragón, "El poeta" (1914), in *Antonio Pérez Pierret, Obra poética*,

ed. Antonio Colberg Pérez (Río Piedras: Editorial de la Universidad de Puerto Rico, 1998), 3–16.

21. Manuel Rojas, *Cuatro siglos de ignorancia y sevidumbre en Puerto Rico* (San Juan: Imprenta La Primavera, 1914).

22. Bernardo Vega, *Memoirs of Bernardo Vega: A Contribution to the History of the Puerto Rican Community in New York*, ed. César Andreu Iglesias, trans. Juan Flores (New York: Monthly Review Press, 1984), 34.

23. Eileen J. Suárez Findlay, *Imposing Decency: The Politics of Sexuality and Race in Puerto Rico, 1870–1920* (Durham, N.C.: Duke University Press, 1999), 38.

24. The group included Betances and Segundo Ruiz Belvis, inspirers of the Lares rebellion of 1868, and Alejandro Tapia, the island's foremost literary figure until his death in 1883.

25. Arthur A. Schomburg, "The Negro Digs Up His Past" (1925), in Alain Locke, ed., *The New Negro: Voices of the Harlem Renaissance* (New York: Touchstone, 1997), 231.

26. Jesse Hoffnung-Garskof, "The Migrations of Arturo Schomburg: On Being *Antillano*, Negro, and Puerto Rican in New York, 1891–1938," *Journal of American Ethnic History* 21, no. 1 (Fall 2001): 36–46. In an interesting work, Winston James indicts Socialist cigarmaker Bernardo Vega of a subtle racism, attributing to him the feeling that Schomburg had ceased to be a Puerto Rican once he identified with the struggle for African American liberation. But it seems to us that Vega was acknowledging Schomburg's chosen affiliation while affirming a bond with him as a fellow fighter against oppression. Writing in the early 1960s, Vega was, after all, trying to bring back to memory a figure which had been forgotten in Puerto Rico. The contrast drawn by James between Schomburg's Pan-Africanism to New York activist Jesús Colón's Socialist *independentismo* also seems to us one-sided. It gives the impression that Colón was indifferent to the problem of racism. In fact, he often wrote on this issue while insisting that the eradication of racism would require the installation of a radically different social order. See Winston James, "The Peculiarities of Afro-Hispanic Radicalism in the United States: The Political Trajectories of Arturo Schomburg and Jesús Colón," in *Holding Aloft the Banner of Ethiopia* (London: Verso, 1998), 195–231. For Colón's comments, see Jesús Colón, *Lo que el pueblo me dice—: crónicas de la colonia puertorriqueña en Nueva York*, ed. Edwin Karli Padilla Aponte (Houston: Arte Público Press, 2001).

27. "La carta del Comisionado de Instrucción sobre los estudiantes . . . ," *LD*, Jan. 18, 1919. See also "La petición de los estudiantes," *LD*, Jan. 20, 1919.

28. Albizu Campos, whose ideas we explore later, was, according to Soto Vélez, sympathetic to the literary efforts of the Atalayistas in the late 1920s.

29. Luis Hernández Aquino, *Nuestra aventura literaria: los ismos en la poesía puertorriqueña, 1913–1948* (Río Piedras: Editorial de la Universidad de Puerto Rico, 1980).

30. Emilio R. Delgado, "La isla de humo y caramelo," in ibid., 92.

31. Luis Araquistáin, *La agonía antillana: El imperialismo yanqui en el Mar Caribe* (Madrid: Espasa-Calpe, 1928).

32. In Cuba and the Dominican Republic, such views had tragic consequences. In

Cuba, they fostered xenophobic laws. In the Dominican Republic, they were linked to the 1937 massacre of at least 12,000 Haitians ordered by President Trujillo.

33. Vicente Géigel Polanco, "Un libro de Araquistáin," *LD*, Apr. 20, 1928.

34. Luis Muñoz Marín, "Tom-Toms and Rotarians," *Nation*, Aug. 8, 1928, 136, 138. Left-nationalist José Enamorado Cuesta similarly adopted Araquistáin's racist views in his 1937 book (written in 1935) *El imperialismo yanqui y la revolución en el Caribe* (3rd ed., San Juan: Ediciones Puerto, 1974). Enamorado Cuesta traveled to Spain in 1936 where he rapidly moved further left in the context of the civil war. By the time he published his book in 1937, he appended an introduction in which he repudiated the racist views contained in the main text.

35. For the debates around the University of Puerto Rico as a center of Pan-Americanism leading to the creation of *Indice*, see Laura Rivera Díaz and Juan G. Gelpí, "Las primeras dos décadas del Departamento de Estudios Hispánicos de la Universidad de Puerto Rico: ensayo de historia intelectual," in *Los lazos de la cultura. El Centro de Estudios Históricos de Madrid y la Universidad de Puerto Rico, 1916–1939*, ed. Consuelo Naranjo, María Dolores Luque, and Miguel A. Puig-Samper (Madrid: Centro de Investigaciones Históricas de la Universidad de Puerto Rico/Consejo Superior de Investigaciones Científicas, 2002), 94–120.

CHAPTER FIVE

1. James Dietz, *Economic History of Puerto Rico: Institutional Change and Capitalist Development* (Princeton: Princeton University Press, 1986), 139.

2. José Enamorado Cuesta, "Se necesita un comité de huelga," *EM*, Feb. 13, 1934. See also Rafael Bernabe, "Luchas obreras en Puerto Rico, 1933–34," *Pensamiento Crítico* 12, no. 63 (May–July 1989): 1–12.

3. María del Carmen Baerga Santini, "La defensa del trabajo industrial a domicilio: mujeres en contra de la sindicalización en Puerto Rico, 1920–1940," *Historia y sociedad* 7 (1994): 33–57.

4. The Puerto Rico Emergency Relief Administration issued a valuable report on the impact of U.S. tariff policies on Puerto Rico: Darwin De Golia, *The Tariff of Puerto Rico* (San Juan: Tariff Survey Division of PRERA, 1935).

5. Qtd. in Thomas Mathews, *Puerto Rican Politics and the New Deal* (Gainesville: University of Florida Press, 1969), 112.

6. Qtd. in María de los Milagros Pérez, "Nacimiento y arraigo del vanguardismo en Puerto Rico, 1919–1925" (Ph.D. diss., University of Puerto Rico-Río Piedras, 2003), 206, 209, 226. See also Carmelo Rosario Natal, *La juventud de Luis Muñoz Marín: vida y pensamiento, 1898–1932* (Río Piedras: Editorial Edil, 1989).

7. Cary Nelson, *Revolutionary Memory: Recovering the Poetry of the American Left* (New York: Routledge, 2001).

8. Marcelino J. Canino Salgado, ed., *La obra literaria de Luis Muñoz Marín* (San Juan: Fundación Luis Muñoz Marín, 1999), 419.

9. "Notas editoriales. Lobos y corderos," *LD*, July 21, 1926; "Es preciso evitar . . . ," *LD*, Sept. 19, 1926; "Notas editoriales. Las garantías del capital," *LD*, Aug. 14, 1926. See the discussion in Rafael Bernabe, *Respuestas al colonialismo en la política puertorriqueña, 1899–1929* (Río Piedras: Huracán, 1996), 115–24.

10. "Guerra Mondragón ha dirigido . . . ," *LD*, Aug. 23, 1933.

11. The relevant documents may be consulted in Reece B. Bothwell, ed., *Puerto Rico: cien años de lucha política*, 4 vols. (San Juan: Editorial de la Universidad de Puerto Rico, 1979), 1:470–82.

12. John E. Dalton, *Sugar: A Case Study of Government Control* (New York: Macmillan, 1937), 3.

13. Qtd. in Mathews, *Puerto Rican Politics*, 151. See on this "La sombra del maestro," *LD*, Jan. 22, 1934.

14. "Barceló y Muñoz Marín conferenciaron . . . ," *LD*, Nov. 16, 1934.

15. "Puerto Rico pasa a la dirección . . . ," *LD*, May 30, 1934; "Puerto Rico en la ruta del 'New Deal,'" *LD*, May 31, 1934; "Ernest Gruening," *LD*, Aug. 18, 1934.

16. "Los trabajadores de café acordaron el domingo . . . ," *LD*, Oct. 15, 1935.

17. The PRRA spent around $72 million in Puerto Rico between 1935 and 1941. Harvey S. Perloff, *Puerto Rico's Economic Future* (Chicago: University of Chicago Press, 1950), 31; Dietz, *Economic History*, 154–58; "Un resumen de la labor realizada . . . ," *EM*, Mar. 22, 1936.

18. For Fernós's critique of the idea that poverty was caused by overpopulation, see "Alibi," *LD*, May 19, 1938; "El problema de población . . . ," *LD*, May 2, 1937; "Preguntas y respuestas," *LD*, Oct. 7, 1937.

19. "Manifiesto de los Partidos Coalicionistas a Puerto Rico" (Oct. 1935), in Bothwell, *Puerto Rico*, 1:519–48.

20. "Gruening contesta el manifiesto de la Coalición" (1935), in Bothwell, *Puerto Rico*, 1:549–63.

21. "Ickes preguntó ayer . . . ," *EM*, Jan. 10, 1936; "Ickes considera terrible . . . ," *EM*, Jan. 12, 1936.

22. "Que el plan de cooperativas . . . ," *EM*, Sept. 17, 1936; "El Dr. Carlos Chardón contesta la carta . . . ," *LD*, Sept. 22, 1936; "De comunistas tacha Fernández García . . . ," *EI*, Aug. 22, 1936; "Una carta injusta de Mr. Bourne," *LD*, Feb. 19, 1936. Angel Quintero Rivera has argued that the movement headed by Muñoz Marín constituted a "class in the making," a group that, having lost its economic basis as the children of the ruined *hacendados*, sought to remake itself as a new class. In this view, this class brought itself into existence through its political project. Angel Quintero Rivera, "La base social de la transformación ideológica del Partido Popular en la década del 40," in *Cambio y desarrollo en Puerto Rico: la transformación ideológica del Partido Popular Democrático*, ed. Gerardo Navas Dávila (Río Piedras: Editorial de la Universidad de Puerto Rico, 1985), 35–119. We find this unconvincing. Social classes in Puerto Rico were those typical of a colonial capitalist social formation: U.S. and insular capitalist interests, landowning and other

propertied sectors, small independent producers, and a large mass of proletarians and semiproletarians. A condition such as "children of the *hacendado* class" does not constitute a group into a class, although it may designate a cultural or generational milieu. There existed in Puerto Rico in the 1930s an educated social layer, not a class in the making, made up of professionals and university graduates. Many came from *hacendado* families. As the U.S. government managed the economic crisis, it was from this sector that most functionaries were recruited. Working within the limits of the U.S. state structures, they were committed to the reproduction of the existing social order. They had to seek the support of sectors of the existing social classes. But that did not turn them, or New Deal functionaries in the United States, into a "class in the making."

23. Pedro Albizu Campos, "Manifiesto ante la visita del presidente de Estados Unidos" (1934) in *Obras escogidas: 1923–1936*, ed. J. Benjamín Torres, 4 vols. (San Juan: Editorial Jelofe, 1975–87), 2:40. See also from the same work "La esclavitud azucarera" (1934), 2:15–19; "La huelga agrícola" (1934), 2:11–14; and "Pedro Albizu Campos critica manifestaciones . . ." (1934), 2:62. See also "La independencia en la Unión . . . ," *EM*, Nov. 27, 1930.

24. It seems Albizu Campos held pro-U.S. views until 1918. He volunteered to serve in World War I. It was in the period 1919–21 that he began denouncing U.S. imperialism. There were excellent reasons to reject U.S. rule, but the specific mix of experiences behind his personal shift is little known.

25. "Racismo contra Albizu retrasa independencia," *Correo de la Quincena* (Guaynabo, Puerto Rico) 9 (Sept. 30–Nov. 1, 1972): 165–67.

26. Ramiro Guerra y Sánchez, *Sugar and Society in the Caribbean* (New Haven: Yale University Press, 1964).

27. "El mitin nacionalista de Hato Rey," *EM*, Apr. 21, 1931.

28. "El Sr. Ramón S. Pagán reta al Senador Iglesias . . . ," *LD*, June 12, 1931; José Enamorado Cuesta, "No hay redención obrera fuera del nacionalismo," *EM*, Feb. 5, 1934; "La independencia en la Unión, dijo Albizu Campos . . . ," *EM*, Nov. 27, 1930; Martín Avilés Bracero, "Socialismo y nacionalismo," *EM*, Jan. 28, 1934; E. Sánchez Ortiz, "Nacionalismo de izquierda," *EM*, Sept. 8, 1932; "Actos nacionalistas celebrados en San Juan . . . ," *EM*, Feb. 16, 1934.

29. In 1937, Enamorado Cuesta argued that Puerto Rico, not having followed other countries into political independence, could not repeat the stages of their past evolution. A "double revolution," both anticolonial and anticapitalist, was needed. José Enamorado Cuesta, *El imperialismo yanqui y la revolución en el Caribe*, 3rd ed. (San Juan: Ediciones Puerto, 1974), 137–41.

30. For ideas summarized here, see Pedro Albizu Campos, "Importante acto político" (1923), 1:12–13; "El estado federal para Puerto Rico no es aceptable . . ." (1923), 1:14–15; "Hablando con Albizu Campos" (1930), 1:64–70; and "Independencia económica" (1930), 1:111–64, all in *Obras escogidas*. We borrow here from the analysis of Rafael

Rodríguez Cruz, "El Nacionalismo ante la crisis económica mundial: 1929–1932," *Pensamiento Crítico* 33 (July–Aug. 1983): 1–15, and 35 (Nov.–Dec. 1983): 1–15.

31. Gordon K. Lewis, *Puerto Rico: Freedom and Power in the Caribbean* (New York: Monthly Review Press, 1963), 136; Luis Angel Ferrao, *Pedro Albizu Campos y el Nacionalismo puertorriqueño* (San Juan: Editorial Cultural, 1990).

32. Juan Antonio Corretjer, "Desvivirse es vivir," *EM*, June 21, 1936.

33. "El nacionalismo ante la huelga," *LD*, Jan. 17, 1938.

34. "Albizu campos contra el fascismo y el comunismo," *LD*, May 3, 1938. The letter is dated Dec. 24, 1937.

35. Arcadio Díaz Quiñones, *Conversación con José Luis González* (Río Piedras: Huracán, 1976), 117–18. Transcript of intervention in Suzy Castor, ed., *Puerto Rico, una crisis histórica* (Mexico City: Nuestro Tiempo, 1979), 179–80.

36. See Ramón Medina Ramírez, *Verbo encadenado* (San Juan: n.p., 1955); Medina Ramírez, *Discurso a la llegada de Julio H. Velázquez* (Santurce: Editorial Betances, 1940).

37. "Anti-imperialist Struggle Is Key to Liberation" (1938), 35; "Tasks of the Trade Union Movement in Latin America" (1938), 82; both in *Writings of Leon Trotsky (1938–39)*, ed. Naomi Allen and George Breitman (New York: Pathfinder, 1974).

38. "La muerte del coronel Riggs . . . ," *LD*, July 17, 1936.

39. Ernest Gruening, *Many Battles: The Autobiography of Ernest Gruening* (New York: Liveright, 1973), 200–201.

40. "Snyder rinde informe" (1937), in Bothwell, *Puerto Rico*, 3:182.

41. Harold L. Ickes, *The Secret Diaries of Harold L. Ickes*, 3 vols. (New York: Simon and Schuster, 1953–54), 1:547–48.

42. Vicente Géigel, "Géigel Polanco insta . . ." (1936), in Bothwell, *Puerto Rico*, 2:584.

43. "Texto de la importante conferencia," *LD*, May 10, 1936; "El discurso del Presidente del Partido Liberal," *LD*, May 16, 1936; "Los incidentes tumultuosos," *EM*, May 15, 1936.

44. "El Lcdo. Pedro Albizu Campos pide al Frente Unido . . . ," *LD*, July 14, 1936.

45. Carmelo Rosario Natal, ed., *Albizu Campos: preso en Atlanta* (San Juan: Producciones Históricas, 2001), 65–66.

46. Clara Lugo Sendra, "Comentarios a la actitud económico-social del nacionalismo puertorriqueño," *EM*, June 28, 1936.

47. Clara Lugo Sendra, "The Sugar Industry in Puerto Rico" (Ph.D. diss., University of California at Los Angeles, 1943), 96.

48. "10,000 Parade Here for Puerto Ricans," *NYT*, Aug. 30, 1936, 24.

49. Besides press reports, for Marcantonio and the Communist Party in El Barrio, we rely on Gerald Meyer, *Vito Marcantonio: Radical Politician, 1902–1954* (Albany: State University of New York Press, 1989), and Bernardo Vega, *Memoirs of Bernardo Vega: A Contribution to the History of the Puerto Rican Community in New York*, ed. César Andreu Iglesias, trans. Juan Flores (New York: Monthly Review Press, 1984).

50. Roberto Rodríguez-Morazzani, "Linking a Fractured Past: The World of the Old Puerto Rican Left," *Centro: Journal of the Center for Puerto Rican Studies* 7, no. 1 (Spring 1995): 20–30.

51. "El Partido Comunista de Nueva York . . . ," *LD*, Aug. 29, 1934; "Entidades comunistas hispanas de NY . . . ," *LD*, Aug. 31, 1934.

52. "Los actos celebrados por el Partido Nacionalista," *EM*, Oct. 20, 1932.

53. "Carta abierta a López Antongiorgi," *EI*, Aug. 31, 1936; "Marcantonio con el retraimiento . . . ," *EI*, July 27, 1936; "De poco decentes . . . ," *EI*, Aug. 14, 1936.

54. Mathews, *Puerto Rican Politics*, 257–58.

55. "Del Dr. Francisco Susoni al Señor Barceló . . . ," *LD*, Dec. 5. 1936. The main documents of this polemic may be found in Bothwell, *Puerto Rico*, 3:13–36.

56. Qtd. in Mathews, *Puerto Rican Politics*, 307.

57. For these events, see "Más detalles de la matanza de Ponce," *LD*, Mar. 24, 1937; "Tres mil personas asistieron a un mitin . . . ," *LD*, Apr. 1, 1937; and "Por razones políticas . . . ," *LD*, Apr. 24, 1937.

58. "Americanismo versus Panamericanismo," *LD*, May 27, 1937.

CHAPTER SIX

1. The editors of *Indice* were Antonio S. Pedreira, Vicente Géigel, Samuel R. Quiñones, and Alfredo Collado Martell.

2. Antonio S. Pedreira, *El periodismo en Puerto Rico* (Río Piedras: Edil, 1982), 17.

3. John Hutchinson, "Cultural Nationalism and Moral Regeneration," in *Nationalism*, ed. John Hutchinson and Anthony D. Smith (New York: Oxford University Press, 1994), 123, 124.

4. José J. Rodríguez Vázquez, *El sueño que no cesa. La nación deseada en el debate intelectual y político puertorriqueño* (Río Piedras: Callejón, 2004), 100–101.

5. Antonio S. Pedreira, *Insularismo* (Río Piedras: Edil, 1988), 23, 76–77, 79, 80–84, 94.

6. "El regionalismo del licenciado Emilio S. Belaval," *LD*, Feb. 14, 1937.

7. See Magali Roy-Féquière, *Women, Creole Identity, and Intellectual Life in Early-Twentieth-Century Puerto Rico* (Philadelphia: Temple University Press, 2004).

8. See the stories "Exaltación de Bebé Pacheco," "Tony Pérez es un niño flan," "La tesis de amor de Gracia Torres," and "La fórmula de la felicidad de Luciano Aldavín" in Emilio S. Belaval, *Los Cuentos de la universidad* (1935; Río Piedras: Editorial Cultural, 1977).

9. Roy-Féquière, *Women, Creole Identity, and Intellectual Life*, 168.

10. Abelardo Díaz Alfaro's collection of stories *Terrazo* constituted a coda to the literary efforts of the *generación del treinta*. It was a poignant portrait, part evocation and part denunciation, of the plight of the rural worker and farmer. Drama was not a major genre at the time. The emblematic work was Manuel Méndez Ballester's 1938 *Tiempo muerto*, a tragedy set among the sugarcane proletariat.

11. Tomás Blanco, "Comunismo y fascismo," *LD*, Mar. 17, 1938.

12. "Elogio de la plena," in *Revista del Ateneo* 1, no. 1 (1935): 97–106.

13. Luis Palés Matos, "El dadaísmo" (1922) in *Obras 1914–1959*, ed. Margot Arce (Río Piedras: Editorial de la Universidad de Puerto Rico, 1984), 211–14.

14. See Juan Antonio Corretjer, "Spengler: una proyección criolla," *EM*, June 25, 1936.

15. Palés Matos, "El arte y la raza blanca" (1927), 229–232; "Nuestras entrevistas" (1926), 283–91; both in *Obras*. The quote is from p. 230.

16. Mercedes López-Baralt, ed., *La poesia de Luis Palés Matos* (Río Piedras: Editorial de la Universidad de Puerto Rico, 1995), 533–35, 541–42.

17. Palés Matos, "Hablando con don Luis Palés Matos" (1932), in *Obras*, 299.

18. See articles collected in Jose De Diego Padró, *Luis Palés Matos y su trasmundo poético* (San Juan: Ediciones Puerto, 1973).

19. Arcadio Díaz Quiñones, "La poesía negra de Luis Palés Matos: realidad y conciencia de su dimensión colectiva," *Sin Nombre* 1, no. 1 (1970): 7–25.

20. For example, Roy-Féquière in *Women, Creole Identity, and Intellectual Life*.

21. Alan West-Duran, "Puerto Rico: The Pleasures and Traumas of Race," *Centro: Journal of the Center for Puerto Rican Studies* 17, no. 1 (Spring 2005). See also Frances R. Aparicio, *Listening to Salsa: Gender, Latin Popular Music, and Puerto Rican Cultures* (Middletown, Conn.: Wesleyan University Press, 1998), 42.

22. José M. Toro Nazario, "El gobierno de las Diez B's," *LD*, July 8, 1938; José Paniagua Serracante, "Hostos, ciudano de America," *EM*, Sept. 11, 1932, and "Meditaciones interpretativas de nuestra cultura," in *Antología del pensamiento puertorriqueño, 1900–1970*, ed. Eugenio Fernández Méndez (Río Piedras: Editorial Universitaria, Universidad de Puerto Rico, 1975), 1:527–46.

23. Juan Antonio Corretjer, "Desvivirse es vivir," *EM*, June 21, 1936.

24. See Roy-Féquière, *Women, Creole Identity, and Intellectual Life*.

25. The poem by Clara Lair criticizing Palés Matos is "Trazos del vivir sombrío."

26. Julia de Burgos, "Farewell in Welfare Island," in *Song of the Simple Truth: The Complete Poems of Julia de Burgos*, ed. and trans. Jack Agüeros (Willamantic, Conn.: Curbstone Press, 1997), 357.

27. See Ruth Glasser, *My Music Is My Flag: Puerto Rican Musicians and Their New York Communities, 1917–1940* (Berkeley: University of California Press, 1995).

28. Some interpreters commented on political events. Manuel ("Canario") Jiménez, who had moved to New York in 1914, protested against the "Río Piedras massacre" in his 1935 recording "Héroes de Borinquen."

29. See Marithelma Costa and Alvin Figueroa, *Kaligrafiando: conversaciones con Clemente Soto Vélez* (Río Piedras: Editorial de la Universidad de Puerto Rico, 1990).

30. Graciany Miranda Archilla, "La decadencia de Mussolini," and the poems "Haile Salassie" and "Cristo, por Etiopía," *Alma Latina*, Aug. 15–30, 1935. We thank Melissa Figueroa for bringing this text to our attention.

31. Graciany Miranda Archilla, *Hungry Dust/Polvo hambriento*, ed. Orlando José Hernández (New York: Latino Press, 2004).

32. Emilio R. Delgado, "Conciencia de nuestro mestizaje" (1956), in *Antología*, ed. Vicente Géigel Polanco (San Juan: Instituto de Cultura Puertorriqueña, 1976), 103–5.

33. Ibid., "La América mestiza" (1963), 119.

34. Ibid., "Del epistolario de Emilio R. Delgado," 176–77.

35. Margot Arce, "La misión de la universidad," in *Problemas de la cultura en Puerto Rico: foro del Ateneo Puertorriqueño, 1940* (Río Piedras: Editorial Universitaria, Universidad de Puerto Rico, 1976), 238–39.

36. Jaime Benítez, "Definiciones de cultura," in ibid., 13, 15.

CHAPTER SEVEN

1. "La primera obra del Partido Popular," *LD*, Aug. 18, 1938.

2. "El Partido Popular celebra asambleas . . . ," *EM*, Aug. 4, 1940.

3. "La cuestión del status . . . ," *LD*, Jan. 17, 1940.

4. "Géigel Polanco cree impropio descartar . . ." (1940), in Reece B. Bothwell, ed., *Puerto Rico: cien años de lucha política*, 4 vols. (San Juan: Editorial de la Universidad de Puerto Rico, 1979), 3:222–23.

5. "Partido Popular declara que no está en issue . . . ," *LD*, July 22, 1940.

6. "Vida Obrera. Francisco Colón Gordiany," *Pueblos Hispanos*, Nov. 6, 1943; "600 personas comprendidas en la huelga . . . ," *LD*, Jan. 13, 1937.

7. Laura Briggs, *Reproducing Empire: Race, Sex, Science, and U.S. Imperialism in Puerto Rico* (Berkeley: University of California Press, 2002), 91.

8. For Vergne Ortiz: Rafael López Landrón, *La ciencia y el arte de la filosofía* (San Juan: Cantero Fernández, 1915); "El separatismo y la juventud," *LD*, Jan. 21, 1915; "La convención socialista . . . ," *EM*, Oct. 7, 1920; "La independencia en la Unión . . . ," *EM*, Nov. 27 1930; "El mitin nacionalista . . . ," *EM*, Apr. 21, 1931; "La junta nacional del partido nacionalista . . . ," *LD*, Feb. 23, 1932; "Un nacionalismo que gobierna . . . ," *EM*, Feb. 20, 1932; "Se constituye en San Juan . . . ," *EM*, Nov. 4, 1932; José Hernández, "Entrevista a Clemente Soto Beles," *Areito* 9, no. 35 (1983): 47–49.

9. José A. Lanauze Rolón, *Por qué somos comunistas* (Ponce: n.p., c. 1932), 21, 22.

10. "El Partido Comunista de la isla no acepta . . . ," *EM*, Sept. 7, 1934.

11. In October 1934, Sánchez led a meeting in Ponce of twenty delegates from twelve sugar *colonias* and the Guánica, Aguirre, and Mercedita mills who called for the creation of a national union of workers in the sugar industry. "Autodefensa para el cañaveral," *Correo de la Quincena* 9, nos. 165–67 (Sept. 30–Nov. 1, 1972): 18.

12. "Los comunistas independientes," *LD*, Nov. 7, 1934; "Mitin comunista esta noche," *EM*, Oct. 4, 11, 18, 25, 1935; Jan. 17, 31, 1936; Mar. 7, 14, 1936; "El administrador de la capital . . . ," *LD*, Feb. 29, 1936; "Incidentes en torno al mitin . . . ," *EM*, Feb. 29, 1936.

13. "Para ingresar . . . ," *EM*, Apr. 24, 1936; "Mitin Comunista," *EM*, May 22, Oct. 8, 1936; *Chispa* 1, no. 1 (June 15, 1937), organ of the PCI (Fourth International).

14. "Declaraciones de Juan Santos Rivera . . . ," *Pueblos Hispanos*, Dec. 4, 1943.

15. "Los resultados de la primera cruzada . . . ," *LD*, May 11, 1929.

16. Andreu Iglesias's text in the *Album*, "Las luchas iniciales de la clase obrera," included a brief attempt to outline a Marxist analysis of Puerto Rico's evolution, from

the rise of a *criollo* bourgeoisie in the struggle against the triple evils of slavery, Spanish commercial interests, and the "semifeudal" Spanish state, to its accommodation to U.S. rule.

17. Bernardo Vega, *Memoirs of Bernardo Vega: A Contribution to the History of the Puerto Rican Community in New York*, ed. César Andreu Iglesias, trans. Juan Flores (New York: Monthly Review Press, 1984), 194, 204.

18. "Constituyó un acto . . . ," *LD*, Mar. 1, 1939; "El Partido Popular ofrece su cooperación" and "La marcha de hambre," both in *LD*, Sept. 19, 1939; "La protesta de los choferes" and "Es efectivo el paro . . . ," both in *LD*, June 14, 1939; "Los choferes son la llave . . . ," *LD*, July 1, 1939; "Un contraste significativo," *LD*, Feb. 13, 1939; "Discurso de Muñoz Marín . . . ," *LD*, Feb. 1, 1940; "Muñoz Marín exhorta . . . ," *LD*, Jan. 30, 1939; "Muñoz Marín en simpatías . . . ," *LD*, Aug. 28, 1937; "Ya están despertando los choferes . . . ," *LD*, Sept. 7, 1939.

19. "Fijan fecha tentativa para la Asamblea . . . ," *LD*, July 18, 1939; "¿No hay dignidad política?" *LD*, June 29, 1939.

20. "Muñoz Marín habla a todo Puerto Rico" (1940), in Bothwell, *Puerto Rico*, 3:275

21. *People of Puerto Rico v. Rubert Hnos., Inc.*, 309 U.S. 543 (1940).

22. Rexford G. Tugwell, *The Stricken Land* (Garden City, N.Y.: Doubleday, 1947), 148.

23. Harold L. Ickes, *The Secret Diaries of Harold L. Ickes*, 3 vols. (New York: Simon and Schuster, 1953–54), 2:6.

24. "Luis and Rex," *Time*, Aug. 18, 1941, 15.

25. See Norberto Barreto Velásquez, *Rexford Guy Tugwell. El último de los tutores* (Río Piedras: Huracán, 2004).

26. "CGT Crece Descomunalmente," *EI*, Oct. 26, 1940.

27. René Jiménez Malaret, *Organización obrera (Discursos en torno al movimiento obrero de Puerto Rico)* (San Juan: Editorial Esther, 1943); "Avilés Bracero no ve razón . . . ," *EM*, Jan. 12, 1942.

28. "Monseñor Haas gestiona . . . ," *EM*, Jan. 30, 1942; "Un muerto y nueve heridos . . . ," *EM*, Jan. 31, 1942.

29. See *Pueblos Hispanos*, June 26, 1943; and "Albizu Campos, Corretjer electos al Comité Nacional . . . ," *Pueblos Hispanos*, July 17, 1943. Two examples were often given of the progressive social reforms an independent Puerto Rican republic could take: Chile, which was then under a government of a left Popular Front, and Cuba, under President Batista, who was then allied to the Cuban Communist Party (the Partido Socialista Popular).

30. Carlos Rodríguez Fraticelli, "Pedro Albizu Campos: estrategias de lucha y luchas estratégicas," in *La nación puertorriqueña: ensayos en torno a Pedro Albizu Campos*, ed. Juan Manuel Carrión, Teresa C. García Ruiz, and Carlos Rodríguez Fraticelli (Río Piedras: Editorial de la Universidad de Puerto Rico, 1993), 130.

31. Jesús Colón, "Escribe esa carta" (1943), in *Lo que el pueblo me dice—: crónicas de la colonia puertorriqueña en Nueva York*, ed. Edwin Karli Padilla Aponte (Houston: Arte Público Press, 2001), 105–6.

32. Jesús Colón, "Lo que el pueblo me dice," *Pueblos Hispanos*, Apr. 14, 1943.

33. This idea was more fully fleshed out in the series "¿Cuál debe ser nuestra posición ante el problema político de Puerto Rico?" (1946), in Colón, *Lo que el pueblo me dice*, 196–213. Such a perspective had an antecedent in Hostos's interventions between 1898 and 1903, which, as we have seen, linked the prospects of self-determination in the Caribbean to the struggle against the "trusts" in North America, and in Matienzo Cintrón's and López Landrón's linkage in the second decade of the twentieth century of the struggle for independence with the fight against the plutocracy in the United States. Colón underlined that Puerto Ricans should not mistake the image offered by Hollywood for U.S. culture: while affirming their own culture against U.S. colonial rule and commercial fare, Puerto Ricans should not close themselves off to American radical democratic, labor, and revolutionary traditions, from Tom Paine to Eugene Debs. "¿Cuál debe ser nuestra posición. . . ?" (1946), 110.

34. See articles in Colón, *Lo que el pueblo me dice*. Nor did Colón avoid endorsing the Moscow show-trials that sealed Stalin's bureaucratic counter-revolution through the liquidation of much of the Bolshevik old guard.

35. See the telegram from Corretjer to Muñoz Marín in *Pueblos Hispanos*, Sept. 2, 1944.

36. Luis Muñoz Marín, "What Next in Puerto Rico," *Nation*, Nov. 20, 1929, 609.

37. For the idea that independence would complete New Deal reconstruction, see Antonio Fernós, "¿Quién en Puerto Rico aboga . . . ?" *LD*, Mar. 12, 1937. See also "Quezón, Barceló, Muñoz Marín," *LD*, Mar. 16, 1937; and Jaime Benítez, "El plan Chardón más la independencia," *LD*, May 17, 18, 1935.

38. This idea is in "Dos lecciones de McDuffie," *LD*, June 17, 1933; "Muñoz Marín dictó una conferencia . . . ," *LD*, Feb. 19, 1937; "Conferencia del Senador Muñoz Marín . . . ," *LD*, Dec. 17, 1934; and "Muñoz Marín contesta . . . ," *LD*, Dec. 30, 1937.

39. "Nuevos caminos hacia viejos objetivos" (June 1946), 3:496–505; "Alerta a la conciencia puertorriqueña" (Feb. 1946), 3:456–76; both in Bothwell, *Puerto Rico*.

40. U.S. Tariff Commission, *The Economy of Puerto Rico* (Washington, D.C.: U.S. Tariff Commission, 1946).

41. See "Nuevos caminos hacia viejos objetivos" (June 1946), in Bothwell, *Puerto Rico*, 3:496–505.

42. Muñoz Marín, "What Next in Puerto Rico?" *Nation*, Nov. 20, 1929, 608.

43. Leonardo Santana Rabell, *Planificación y política durante la administración de Luis Muñoz Marín: un análisis crítico* (Río Piedras: Análisis, 1984), 129, 131, 148; James Dietz, *Economic History of Puerto Rico: Institutional Change and Capitalist Development* (Princeton: Princeton University Press), 184.

44. Emilio Pantojas-García, "Puerto Rican Populism Revisited: The PPD during the 1940s," *Journal of Latin American Studies* 21, no. 3 (Oct. 1989): 521–57.

45. José A. Padín, "Imperialism by Invitation: Causes of a Failed Developmental State Project in Puerto Rico, 1940–1950" (Ph.D. diss., University of Wisconsin–Madison, 1998).

46. "Don Luis Muñoz Marín hace declaraciones . . ." (1937), 3:176–77; "Muñoz Marín

dirige un manifiesto . . ." (1936), 2:593–97; "Más sobre la autonomía" (1940), 3:210–11; all in Bothwell, *Puerto Rico*; Antonio Fernós, "El espectro de la autonomía" *LD*, Nov. 6, 1937.

47. Amalia Alsina Orozco, *Los congresos pro-independencia* (San Juan: Centro de Estudios Avanzados de Puerto Rico y el Caribe, 1994).

48. Muñoz Marín's statement read: "I wish the Congress complete success in the expression to the people and the Government of the United States of ideals that are undoubtedly those of a very many [*numerosísimos*] Puerto Ricans," *LD*, Aug. 17, 1943.

49. "Tydings le pidió a Muñoz que se definiese," *EM*, Nov. 30, 1943.

50. Juan Santos Rivera, *Puerto Rico, ayer, hoy y mañana: informe al Comité Central del Partido Comunista Puertorriqueño* (San Juan: n.p., 1944), 11, 30–31.

51. The Communist International (Comintern) dissolved itself on June 10, 1943, and many Communist parties of allied countries during World War II followed suit. Fernando Claudín, *The Communist Movement: From Comintern to Cominform* (New York: Monthly Review Press, 1975), 1:15.

52. Néstor R. Duprey Salgado, *Independentista Popular: las causas de Vicente Géigel Polanco* (San Juan: Editorial Crónicas, 2005), 120.

53. "Muñoz Marín declaró . . ." (1945), in Bothwell, *Puerto Rico*, 3:451–52.

54. Luis Muñoz Marín, "Alerta a la conciencia puertorriqueña" (Feb. 1946), in ibid., 3:456–76.

55. "Nuevos caminos hacia viejos objetivos" (June 1946), in ibid., 3:496–505.

56. "Liderato popular se reunió . . . ," *EM*, July 4, 1946; "Los populares incluyen . . . ," *EM*, July 5, 1946; "Géigel afirma . . . ," *EM*, July 1, 1946; "Fernós sugiere . . . ," *EM*, July 4, 1946.

57. "Muñoz habló anteanoche," *EM*, May 28, 1945.

58. "Chapman anuncia examinarán en breve . . . ," *EM*, Feb. 8, 1947.

59. Luis Muñoz Marín to Undersecretary Chapman, June 14, 1947, qtd. in Carlos Zapata Oliveras, *Nuevos caminos hacia viejos objetivos: Estados Unidos y el establecimiento del Estado Libre Asociado de Puerto Rico, 1945–1953* (Río Piedras: Comisión Puertorriqueña del Quinto Centenario, 1991), 226.

60. See Ruth M. Reynolds, *Campus in Bondage: A 1948 Microcosm of Puerto Rico*, ed. Carlos Rodríguez-Fraticelli and Blanca Vázquez Erazo (New York: Centro de Estudios Puertorriqueños–Hunter College, CUNY, 1989).

61. "Discurso de Luis Muñoz Marín . . ." (1948), in Bothwell, *Puerto Rico*, 3:535–41.

62. Morris Kaplan, "Muñoz Marín's Foe Comes to Steer Puerto Rican Vote to Marcantonio," *NYT*, Oct. 27, 1949, 1.

63. See Gerald Meyer, *Vito Marcantonio: Radical Politician, 1902–1954* (Albany: State University of New York Press, 1989), 162, 169; "Puerto Ricans" in *Encyclopedia of the American Left*, ed. Mari Jo Buhle, Paul Buhle, and Dan Georgakas (Urbana: University of Illinois Press, 1992), 614–17.

CHAPTER EIGHT

1. Congress would also be asked to abide by the result of a two-way (statehood/independence) plebiscite to be organized at a future date to be determined by the insular government. This second aspect of the proposal was soon forgotten. Luis Muñoz Marín, "Discurso completo del 4 de julio de 1948," in Reece B. Bothwell, ed., *Puerto Rico: cien años de lucha política*, 4 vols. (San Juan: Editorial de la Universidad de Puerto Rico, 1979), 3:525–34.

2. Muñoz Marín's strategy and the negotiations with Washington are discussed in José Trías Monge, *Como fue: Memorias* (Río Piedras: Universidad de Puerto Rico, 2005).

3. 81 P.L. 600, 64 Stat. 319, 48 U.S.C.S. §731b–731e (1950).

4. For example "La independencia y el proyecto Tydings," *EM*, May 27, 29, 1936. "Don Luis Muñoz Marín hace declaraciones. . . ." (1937), in Bothwell, *Puerto Rico*, 3:176–77.

5. See Antonio Fernós, *Estado Libre Asociado de Puerto Rico. Antecedentes, creación y desarrollo* (Río Piedras: Editorial de la Universidad de Puerto Rico, 1974). See also José Trías Monge, "El significado de la ley de constitución y convenio" (1951), in Bothwell, *Puerto Rico*, 4:56–61.

6. For the Nationalist insurrection, see Miñi Seijo Bruno, *La insurrección nacionalista en Puerto Rico 1950* (San Juan: Edil, 1997).

7. Ibid., 245.

8. Néstor R. Duprey Salgado, *Independentista Popular: las causas de Vicente Géigel Polanco* (San Juan: Editorial Crónicas, 2005), 513–15, 520.

9. Ibid., 536–38.

10. P.L. 447, 66 Stat. 327 (1952).

11. Qtd. in Carlos Zapata Oliveras, *Nuevos caminos hacia viejos objetivos: Estados Unidos y el establecimiento del Estado Libre Asociado de Puerto Rico, 1945–1953* (Río Piedras: Comisión Puertorriqueña del Quinto Centenario, 1991), 284.

12. Qtd. in David M. Helfeld, "Congressional Intent and Attitude toward Public Law 600 and the Constitution of the Commonwealth of Puerto Rico," *Revista Jurídica de la Universidad de Puerto Rico* 21, no. 4 (May–June 1952): 265. This article quotes similar statements by Fernós. See also Zapata Oliveras, *Nuevos caminos*, 279.

13. Helfeld, "Congressional Intent," 293.

14. Qtd. in ibid., 277, 314.

15. Qtd. in Zapata Oliveras, *Nuevos caminos*, 223, 277.

16. See an example of such an exchange in 1950 in Fernós, *Estado Libre Asociado de Puerto Rico*, 100.

17. Qtd. in Zapata Oliveras, *Nuevos caminos*, 391–92. See also José Trías Monge, *Historia constitucional de Puerto Rico* (Río Piedras: Editorial Universitaria, 1980–83, 1994), 4:15.

18. Qtd. in Zapata Oliveras, *Nuevos caminos*, 396–97, 413–15.

19. Qtd. in ibid., 429–30.

20. Qtd. in ibid., 446; Trías Monge, *Historia constitucional*, 4:43, 53.

21. *Figueroa v. People of Puerto Rico*, 232 F.2d 615 (1st Cir. 1956).

22. *Hernández Agosto v. Romero Barceló*, 748 F.2d 1 (1st Cir. 1984); *United Stated v. Quiñones*, 758 F.2d 40 (1st Cir. 1985); *Harris v. Rosario*, 446 U.S. 651 (1980); *U.S. v. López Andino*, 831 F.2d 1164 (1st Cir. 1987).

23. *United States v. Sánchez*, 992 F.2d 1143 (11th Cir. 1993); General Accounting Office, *U.S. Insular Areas. Application of the U.S. Constitution. Report to the Chairman, Committee on Resources, House of Representatives*, GAO/OGC-98-5 (Washington, D.C., Nov. 1997); *United States v. Pérez-Pérez*, 72 F.3d 224 (1st Cir. 1995).

24. The Task Force was appointed by President Clinton and took five years to prepare its ten-page report.

25. Pedro Muñoz Amato, "Congressional Conservatism and the Commonwealth Relationship," *Annals of the American Academy of Political and Social Science* 285 (Jan. 1953): 27–29, 31.

26. Carl J. Friedrich, *Puerto Rico: Middle Road to Freedom* (New York: Rinehart, 1959), 36–37, 66.

27. Trías Monge, *Historia constitucional*, 4:127.

28. Néstor R. Duprey Salgado, *Crónica de una guerra anunciada* (Río Piedras: Cultural, 2002), 171, 182.

29. See also José Trías Monge, *Puerto Rico: The Trials of the Oldest Colony in the World* (New Haven: Yale University Press, 1997).

30. Between 1940 and 1950, life expectancy increased from forty-six to sixty-one years and real per capita income grew by 48 percent. James Dietz, *Economic History of Puerto Rico: Institutional Change and Capitalist Development* (Princeton: Princeton University Press, 1986), 204.

31. Friedrich, *Puerto Rico*, 61, 62. This same hope was held by Muñoz Marín: "El Gobernador Luis Muñoz Marín explica la nueva posición . . ." (1959), in Bothwell, *Puerto Rico*, 4:249–57.

CHAPTER NINE

1. Eric J. Hobsbawm, *The Age of Extremes: A History of the World, 1914–1991* (New York: Pantheon, 1994), 286.

2. See Carmen T. Whalen and Víctor Vázquez-Hernández, eds., *The Puerto Rican Diaspora: Historical Perspectives* (Philadelphia: Temple University Press, 2005).

3. U.S. Commission on Civil Rights, *Puerto Ricans in the Continental United States: An Uncertain Future* (Washington, D.C.: U.S. Commission on Civil Rights, 1976), 5, 21.

4. Carmen T. Whalen, *From Puerto Rico to Philadelphia: Puerto Rican Workers and Postwar Economies* (Philadelphia: Temple University Press, 2001).

5. Emilio Pantojas-García, *Development Strategies as Ideology: Puerto Rico's Export-Led Industrialization Experience* (Boulder: Lynne Rienner, 1990), 86.

6. Harvey S. Perloff, *Puerto Rico's Economic Future* (Chicago: University of Chicago Press, 1950), 34.

7. José Padín, "Puerto Rico in the Post War: Liberalized Development Banking and the Fall of the 'Fifth Tiger,' " *World Development* 31, no. 2 (2003): 281–301.

8. James Dietz, *Economic History of Puerto Rico: Institutional Change and Capitalist Development* (Princeton: Princeton University Press, 1986), 193.

9. Clara Lugo Sendra, "The Sugar Industry in Puerto Rico" (Ph.D. diss., University of California at Los Angeles, 1943), 130.

10. Mathew D. Edel, "Land Reform in Puerto Rico," part 2, *Caribbean Studies* (Jan. 1963): 32; Dietz, *Economic History*, 201.

11. Nathan Koenig, *A Comprehensive Agricultural Program for Puerto Rico* (Washington, D.C.: GPO, 1953), 262.

12. Rexford Tugwell, "Report on the 'Five Hundred-Acre Law,' " in *Puerto Rican Public Papers of R. G. Tugwell, Governor* (San Juan: Service Office of the Government of Puerto Rico, Printing Division, 1945), 291–347. On land reform, see Mathew D. Edel, "Land Reform in Puerto Rico," pts. 1 and 2, *Caribbean Studies* (Oct. 1962): 22–60 and (Jan. 1963): 28–50.

13. Keith Rosenn, "Puerto Rican Land Reform," *Yale Law Journal* 73 (1963): 355; Koenig, *Comprehensive Agricultural Program*, 257–58.

14. A Special Correspondent, "Puerto Rico: The Necessity for Socialism," *Monthly Review* 2, no. 10 (Feb. 1951): 457. This text, perhaps written by Gordon Lewis, adheres to the description of the nationalist movement as fascist or semifascist, which we criticize in chapter 5.

15. Koenig, *Comprehensive Agricultural Program*, 257.

16. Angel David Cruz Báez, "Export Agriculture under Economic Development: A Geographic Analysis of the Decline of Sugarcane Production in Puerto Rico" (Ph.D. diss., University of Wisconsin–Madison, 1977), 39.

17. Rubén Nazario Velasco, "Pan, casa, libertad: de la reforma agraria a la especulación immobiliaria," in *Luis Muñoz Marín: perfiles de su gobernación*, ed. Fernando Picó (San Juan: Fundación Luis Muñoz Marín, 2003), 145–64. See Félix Córdova, "El desarrollo del capitalismo en Puerto Rico durante el Siglo XX y su impacto sobre la naturaleza," *Pensamiento Crítico* 7, no. 40 (Sept.–Oct. 1984): 2–8.

18. Pantojas-García, *Development Strategies*, 48.

19. Thomas Hibben and Rafael Picó, *Industrial Development of Puerto Rico and the Virgin Islands* (Port of Spain, Trinidad: Caribbean Commission, 1948), 123.

20. See Pantojas-García, *Development Strategies*, 62–72, 107–9.

21. Palmira Ríos, "Export Oriented Industrialization and the Demand for Female Labor: Puerto Rican Women in the Manufacturing Sector, 1952–1980," *Gender and Society* 4, no. 3 (Sept. 1990): 321–37.

22. Dennis Merrill, "Negotiating Cold War Paradise: U.S. Tourism, Economic Planning, and Cultural Modernity in Twentieth Century Puerto Rico," *Diplomatic History* 25, no. 2 (Spring 2001): 179–214. See also David F. Ross, *The Long Uphill Path: A Historical Study of Puerto Rico's Program of Economic Development* (San Juan: Editorial Edil, 1976), 100–105.

23. César J. Ayala, "The Decline of the Plantation Economy and the Puerto Rican Migration of the 1950s," *Latino Studies Journal* 7, no. 1 (Winter 1996): 61–90.

24. C. Wright Mills, Clarence Senior, and Rose Kohn Goldsen, *Puerto Rican Journey: New York's Newest Migrants* (New York: Harper and Row, 1950), 44, 186.

25. Michael Lapp, "Managing Migration: The Migration Division of Puerto Rico and Puerto Ricans in New York City, 1948–1968" (Ph.D. diss., Johns Hopkins University, 1991), 46.

26. Perloff, *Puerto Rico's Economic Future*, 225.

27. Andrés Torres, *Between Melting Pot and Mosaic: African Americans and Puerto Ricans in the New York Political Economy* (Philadelphia: Temple University Press, 1995), 87.

28. Pantojas-García, *Development Strategies*, 145.

29. Dietz, *Economic History*, 266.

30. U.S. Commission on Civil Rights, *Puerto Ricans in the Continental United States*, 44, 47.

31. Torres, *Between Melting Pot and Mosaic*, 144–45, 151.

CHAPTER TEN

1. "Democracy's Laboratory in Latin America," *Time*, June 23, 1958, cover.

2. Fernando Sierra, "Antonio S. Pedreira: buceador de la personalidad puertorriqueña" (1942), in *Antología del pensamiento puertorriqueño, 1900–1970*, ed. Eugenio Fernández Méndez (Río Piedras: Editorial Universitaria, Universidad de Puerto Rico, 1975), 1:597–606.

3. Jaime Benítez, "Doce años después," in Luis Palés Matos, *Tuntún de pasa y grifería* (San Juan: Cultural, 1988), 9–41.

4. In 1941, Rexford Tugwell had been named chancellor of the UPR, just before his appointment as governor was announced. Muñoz Marín insisted that he take a leave of absence from the UPR post, to which he would thus return whenever his term as governor ended. The move ignited a student strike, which rejected the notion of an interim chancellor and demanded wider university autonomy from the political establishment. For once, the very charismatic and eloquent Muñoz Marín was unable to obtain the endorsement for his proposal from a serene but steadfast student assembly. Tugwell resigned from his post at the UPR, but the success of the student protest may well have convinced Muñoz Marín that stricter controls of this potential source of opposition were in order. See Nereida Rodríguez, *Debate universitario y dominación colonial (1941–1947)* (San Juan: n.p., 1996).

5. Henry K. Wells, *The Modernization of Puerto Rico* (Cambridge: Harvard University Press, 1969); Charles T. Goodsell, *Administration of a Revolution* (1967; Río Piedras: Editorial de la Universidad de Puerto Rico, 1978). Not all academic efforts had an apologetic slant. A study cosponsored by the University of Chicago and the University of Puerto Rico and carried out by (then) young anthropologists Sidney Mintz and Eric Wolf, among others, resulted in a remarkable portrait of Puerto Rican society as it

stood poised on the threshold of economic transformation. See Julian H. Steward, *The People of Puerto Rico* (Urbana: University of Illinois Press, 1956). Mintz also published *Worker in the Cane: A Puerto Rican Life History* (New Haven: Yale University Press, 1960), a pioneering ethnography of a sugarcane worker.

6. See Michael Lapp, "Managing Migration: The Migration Division of Puerto Rico and Puerto Ricans in New York City, 1948–1968" (Ph.D. diss., Johns Hopkins University, 1991).

7. C. Wright Mills, Clarence Senior, and Rose Kohn Goldsen, *Puerto Rican Journey: New York's Newest Migrants* (New York: Harper and Row, 1950), 97. A previous study, *The Puerto Rican Migrant in New York* (New York: Columbia University Press, 1938) by Lawrence R. Chenault, went largely unnoticed. Left-nationalist José Enamorado Cuesta reviewed it favorably, praising its documentation of the discrimination suffered by Puerto Ricans, but criticized it for its explanation of migration as a result of overpopulation and not the economic distress resulting from colonial rule. "Un libro sobre la emigración puertorriqueña en Nueva York," *LC*, July 12, 1939.

8. Mills, Senior, and Goldsen, *Puerto Rican Journey*, vii, 123.

9. Edgardo Meléndez Vélez, "*The Puerto Rican Journey* Revisited: Politics and the Study of Puerto Rican Migration," *Centro: Journal of the Center for Puerto Rican Studies* 17, no. 2 (Fall 2005): 193–221.

10. Nathan Glazer and Daniel P. Moynihan, *Beyond the Melting Pot: The Negroes, Puerto Ricans, Jews and Irish of New York City*, 2nd ed. (Cambridge: MIT Press, 1970); Oscar Lewis, *La Vida: A Puerto Rican Family in the Culture of Poverty, San Juan–New York* (New York: Random House, 1966).

11. Carmen T. Whalen, *From Puerto Rico to Philadelphia: Puerto Rican Workers and Postwar Economies* (Philadelphia: Temple University Press, 2001), 220, 224, 227–28; Edgardo Meléndez, "Puerto Rican Politics in the United States: Examination of Major Perspectives and Theories," *Centro: Journal of the Center for Puerto Rican Studies* 15, no. 1 (Spring 2003): 8–39.

12. Laura Briggs, *Reproducing Empire: Race, Sex, Science, and U.S. Imperialism in Puerto Rico* (Berkeley: University of California Press, 2002)

13. María Mercedes Alonso, *Muñoz Marín vs. the Bishops: An Approach to Church and State* (San Juan: Publicaciones Puertorriqueñas Editores, 1998).

14. See Annette B. Ramírez de Arellano and Conrad Seipp, *Colonialism, Catholicism and Contraception* (Chapel Hill: University of North Carolina Press, 1983).

15. Eugenio Fernández Méndez, "Más allá del insularismo: hacia una civilización puertorriqueña" (1954), in *Antología del pensamiento*, 1:843–48.

16. Luis Muñoz Marín, "La personalidad puertorriqueña en el Estado Libre Asociado" (1953), in *Del cañaveral a la fábrica: cambio social en Puerto Rico*, ed. Eduardo Rivera Medina and Rafael L. Ramírez (Río Piedras: Huracán-Academia, 1994), 99–108.

17. Labor Gómez Acevedo, *Organización del trabajo en el Puerto Rico del siglo xix (proletarios y jornaleros)* (San Juan: Instituto de Cultura Puertorriqueña, 1970), 434. On the evolution of Puerto Rican historiography, see María de los Angeles Castro, "De Sal-

vador Brau a la 'novísima' historia: un replanteamiento y una crítica," *Op.Cit.* 4 (1988–89): 9–55.

18. Eric J. Hobsbawm, *Nations and Nationalism since 1780: Programme, Myth, Reality* (Cambridge: Cambridge University Press, 1991), 143.

19. John K. Galbraith in the introduction to *The Affluent Society* (Boston: Houghton Mifflin, 1958) credited Muñoz Marín's ideas in this area as stimulants for his own critique of U.S. society.

20. Margot Arce de Vázquez, "Reflexiones en torno a *Insularismo*" (1943), in *Obras Completas*, vol. 1, ed. Hugo Rodríguez Vecchini (Río Piedras: Editorial de la Universidad de Puerto Rico, 1998), 285–96.

21. Angela Negrón Muñoz, *Mujeres de Puerto Rico* (San Juan: Imprenta Venezuela, 1935), 256–57.

22. René Marqués, "Pesimismo literario y optimismo: su coexistencia en el Puerto Rico actual" (1959), in *El puertorriqueño dócil y otros ensayos* (Río Piedras: Antillana, 1977), 64.

23. The story mentioned is "Otro día nuestro," in *Cuentos puertorriqueños de hoy*, ed. René Marqués (Mexico City: Club del Libro Puertorriqueño, 1959), 109–28. Quote is from p. 122.

24. René Marqués, "El cuento puertorriqueño en la promoción del cuarenta" and "El puertorriqueño dócil," in *El puertorriqueño dócil*, 87–115, 153–215. On women in particular, see 174–76.

25. Pedro Juan Soto, *Ardiente suelo, fría estación* (1961; San Juan: Cultural, 1993), 238. It should be pointed out that Soto defended Puerto Rican literature in English against those who would reject it as un–Puerto Rican.

26. César Andreu Iglesias, "Pedro Albizu Campos," in *Cosas de aquí: una visión de la decada del '60 en Puerto Rico* (San Juan: Publicaciones Atenea, 1975), 279–80. Between 1959 and 1967, Andreu Iglesias wrote a column, "Cosas de aquí," in *El Imparcial*. Simply written, often penetrating, at times problematical (for example, when he ridiculed the Spanish of the Puerto Rican migrant), the essays were a sustained commentary on Puerto Rican life, unseen since the essays of Canales in the second decade of the twentieth century.

27. Nilita Vientós Gastón, "Comentarios a un ensayo sobre Puerto Rico" (1964), in *Indice cultural* (Río Piedras: Ediciones Universidad de Puerto Rico, 1984), 4:116, 120.

28. She thus defended Spanish as Puerto Rico's vernacular while proclaiming her love for literature in English. Her longest critical text was not about a Puerto Rican author but about Henry James.

29. See Rafael Bernabe, *La maldición de Pedreira: aspectos de la crítica romántico-cultural de la modernidad en Puerto Rico* (Río Piedras: Huracán, 2002).

30. Qtd. in Francisco Matos Paoli, *Canto de la locura*, ed. Angel Darío Carrero Morales (Carolina, P.R.: Terranova, 2005), xii.

31. José A. Pérez Ruiz, "A 50 años del Centro de Arte Puertorriqueño," *Revista del Instituto de Cultural Puertorriqueña*, 2nd ser., 1, no. 2 (July–Dec. 2000): 7.

32. See Jack Delano, *Puerto Rico Mío: Four Decades of Change* (Washington, D.C.: Smithsonian Institution Press, 1990).

33. See photos included in Library of Congress, *America from the Great Depression to World War II, 1935–1945*, <http://rs6.loc.gov/ammem/fsahtml/fahome.html>.

34. Steven Loza, *Recordando a Tito Puente* (New York: Random House, 2000).

35. Rubén del Rosario, "Nacionalidad y lengua" (1955), in *La lengua de Puerto Rico* (Río Piedras: Cultural, 1985), 29; "Tres errores en la interpretación de la lengua en Puerto Rico," *Mundo Libre* 1, no. 3 (1943): 21. See Rafael Bernabe, " 'Un Puerto Rico distinto y futuro': lengua, nacionalidad y política en Rubén del Rosario," *Revista de Estudios Hispánicos* 24, no. 1 (1997): 221–36.

36. Rubén del Rosario, "La crisis del lenguaje" (1947), in *Selección de ensayos lingüísticos* (Madrid: Partenón, 1985), 53.

37. Rubén del Rosario, "Un libro de De Granda" (1969), in *Ser puertorriqueño* (Madrid: n.p., 1984), 33–34.

38. Rubén del Rosario, "El destino de la lengua," *Isla* 1, no. 2 (1939).

39. Del Rosario, "Un libro de De Granda," 39, and "Cultura, política, universidad" (1948), 18, both in *Ser puertorriqueño*.

CHAPTER ELEVEN

1. See Severo Colberg, "Desafueros del industrialismo" (1959), in Reece B. Bothwell, ed., *Puerto Rico: cien años de lucha política*, 4 vols. (San Juan: Editorial de la Universidad de Puerto Rico, 1979), 4:226–27; Juan M. García Passalacqua, *La crisis política en Puerto Rico (1962–1966)* (San Juan: Edil, 1970).

2. Jenaro Baquero, "La importación de fondos externos y la capacidad absorbente de nuestra economía," *Revista de Ciencias Sociales* 7 (Mar.–June 1963): 79–92; "Magnitud y características de la inversión exterior en Puerto Rico," *Revista de Ciencias Sociales* 8 (Mar. 1964): 5–13.

3. "Vanguardia repudia resolución del PPD" (1967), in Bothwell, *Puerto Rico*, 4:430–32.

4. Edgardo Meléndez, *Puerto Rico's Statehood Movement* (Westport, Conn.: Greenwood Press, 1988), 89.

5. Andreu Iglesias eventually left the MPI in 1970 over its position on attacks on individual U.S. soldiers, which he rejected as counterproductive acts of terrorism. Among his important works of the 1960s, see "El movimiento obrero y la independencia de Puerto Rico," *La escalera* 2, nos. 8–9 (Jan.–Feb. 1968): 1–34.

6. Ronald Fernández, *The Disenchanted Island: Puerto Rico and the United States in the Twentieth Century* (New York: Praeger, 1992), 220.

7. Carmen Gautier Mayoral and Teresa Blanco Stahl, "Documentos Secretos F.B.I.," *Pensamiento Crítico*, Summer 1979, 1–32.

8. See Rubén Berríos, *La independencia de Puerto Rico. Razón y lucha* (Mexico City: Editorial Línea, 1983); "El Partido de la Independencia y el Socialismo. Propuesta de la Oposición en el P.I.P." (n.d.), signed by Aarón Ramos, Luis A. Torres, Norman Pietri,

César Andreu Iglesias, Samuel Aponte, Michel Godreau, and Angel Villarini, among others; Norma Iris Tapia, *La crisis del PIP* (Río Piedras: Editorial Edil, 1980).

9. See Migdalia Guzmán Lugo, "El debate público sobre la participación puertorriqueña en Vietnam" (M.A. thesis, University of Puerto Rico, 1997).

10. Carmen Concepción, "The Origin of Modern Environmental Activism in Puerto Rico in the 1960s," *International Journal of Urban and Regional Research* 19, no. 1 (Mar. 1995): 113.

11. Julio Llanes Santos, *Desafiando al poder: las invasiones de terrenos en Puerto Rico* (Río Piedras: Huracán, 2001); Lilliana Cotto, "The Rescate Movement: An Alternative Way of Doing Politics," in *Colonial Dilemma: Critical Perspectives on Contemporary Puerto Rico*, ed. Edwin Meléndez and Edgardo Meléndez (Boston: South End Press, 1993), 119–30; Eduardo Bonilla-Silva, "Squatters, Politics, and State Responses: The Political Economy of Squatters in Puerto Rico, 1900–1992" (Ph.D. diss., University of Wisconsin–Madison, 1993).

12. Our discussion of labor relies on Raul Guadalupe, "Sindicalismo y lucha política en Puerto Rico, 1969–1972" (M.A. thesis, University of Puerto Rico, 1995); César F. Rosado Marzán, "Dependent Unionism: Resource Mobilization and Union Density in Puerto Rico" (Ph.D. diss., Princeton University, 2005); Carlos Carrión, "Hacia una historia del Movimiento Obrero Unido," *Pensamiento Crítico* 18, nos. 82–83 (Nov. 1995–Feb. 1996): 35–72; Luis Rafael Matos Díaz, *La fragua del plomo y el papel* (M.A. thesis, University of Puerto Rico, 1992); and Miles E. Galvin, *The Organized Labor Movement in Puerto Rico* (Cranbury, N.J.: Associated University Presses, 1979).

13. Pedro A. Cabán, "Industrial Transformation and Labour Relations in Puerto Rico: From 'Operation Bootstrap' to the 1970s," *Journal of Latin American Studies* 21, no. 3 (Oct. 1989): 588.

14. Carrión, "Hacia una historia," 56; "La política sindical del PSP," *Claridad*, Mar. 11–17, 1977, 6.

15. We rely on Elizabeth Crespo Kebler and Ana Irma Rivera Lassen, *Documentos del feminismo en Puerto Rico: facsímiles de la historia*, vol. 1 (1970–79) (Río Piedras: Editorial de la Universidad de Puerto Rico, 2001).

16. Antulio Parrilla Bonilla, "Aborto y control poblacional," Mar. 11, 1973; "Protección de la vida y la persona," May 13, 1973; Raúl González Cruz, "Una imposición colonial," Feb. 13, 1973; all in *Claridad*.

17. In 1975, the Federación de Mujeres Puertorriqueñas, which had a close, although not official, connection to the PSP, briefly joined MIA in raising the issue of women's rights.

18. See José D. Rodríguez Allende, "El movimiento homosexual puertorriqueño y su impacto" (M.A. thesis, University of Puerto Rico, 2000); Frances Negrón-Muntaner, "Echoing Stonewall and Other Dilemmas: The Organizational Beginning of a Gay and Lesbian Agenda in Puerto Rico, 1972–1977," pts. 1 and 2, *Centro: Journal of the Center for Puerto Rican Studies*, 4, no. 1 (Winter 1991–92): 76–95 and no. 2 (Spring 1992): 98–115.

19. Lawrence La Fountain-Stokes, "1898 and the History of a Queer Puerto Rican

Century: Gay Lives, Island Debates, and Diasporic Experience," *Centro: Journal of the Center for Puerto Rican Studies*, 11, no. 1 (Fall 1999): 91–109.

20. Luis Aponte-Parés and Jorge B. Merced, "Páginas Omitidas: The Gay and Lesbian Presence," in *The Puerto Rican Movement: Voices from the Diaspora*, ed. Andrés Torres and José E. Velázquez (Philadelphia: Temple University Press, 1998), 296–315.

21. "People-Mi gente. Gilberto Gerena Valentín," *Centro: Journal of the Center for Puerto Rican Studies*, 2, no. 5 (Spring 1989): 32–36.

22. Antonia Pantoja, *Memoir of a Visionary* (Houston: Arte Público Press, 2002).

23. Michael Lapp, "Managing Migration: The Migration Division of Puerto Rico and Puerto Ricans in New York City, 1948–1968" (Ph.D. diss., Johns Hopkins University, 1991), 323–24.

24. Puerto Rican Forum, *The Puerto Rican Community Development Project* (1964; New York: Arno Press, 1975), 9.

25. Ibid., 91.

26. What follows relies largely on Torres and Velázquez, *Puerto Rican Movement*.

27. See Gina M. Pérez, *The Near Northwest Side Story: Migration, Displacement and Puerto Rican Families* (Berkeley: University of California Press, 2004); and Ana Y. Ramos-Zayas, *National Performances: The Politics of Class, Race, and Space in Puerto Rican Chicago* (Chicago: University of Chicago Press, 2003).

28. U.S. Commission on Civil Rights, *Puerto Ricans in the Continental United States: An Uncertain Future* (Washington D.C.: U.S. Commission on Civil Rights, 1976), 119.

29. Ruth Glasser, "From 'Rich Port' to Bridgeport: Puerto Ricans in Connecticut," in *The Puerto Rican Diaspora: Historical Perspectives*, ed. Carmen T. Whalen and Víctor Vázquez-Hernández (Philadelphia: Temple University Press, 2005), 181–83.

30. "Desde las entrañas. Declaración Política de la Seccional de Estados Unidos del PSP" (1974), *Nueva Lucha*, Jan.–Feb. 1974, 25.

31. El Comité–MINP, *El proceso de emigración puertorriqueña y la clase obrera norteamericana* (New York: El Comité–MINP, 1975).

32. Our account of Philadelphia follows Carmen T. Whalen, *From Puerto Rico to Philadelphia: Puerto Rican Workers and Postwar Economies* (Philadelphia: Temple University Press, 2001).

33. "Anteproyecto del Pacto de Unión Permanente . . . ," in Bothwell, *Puerto Rico*, 4:604–16.

34. José Trías Monge, *Puerto Rico: The Trials of the Oldest Colony in the World* (New Haven: Yale University Press, 1997), 133.

CHAPTER TWELVE

1. Manuel Maldonado Denis, "El futuro del movimiento independentista" (1965), in *Puerto Rico: mito y realidad* (Barcelona: Península, 1973), 89, and *Puerto Rico, una interpretacion historico-social* (1969; Mexico City: Siglo XXI, 1974), 124–25, 217.

2. It was sustained over the years by Edwin Reyes, Andrés Castro Ros, José Manuel

Torres Santiago, and Vicente Rodríguez Nietszche, among others. Other important poets such as José María Lima and Angelamaria Dávila, whose work we cannot consider here, were at times close but did not belong to the *Guajana* group.

3. Gervasio García, "Apuntes sobre una interpretación de la realidad puertorriqueña" (1970), in *Historia crítica, historia sin coartadas: algunos problemas de la historia de Puerto Rico* (Río Piedras: Huracán, 1985), 107–18. See also María de los Angeles Castro, "De Salvador Brau a la 'novísima' historia: un replanteamiento y una crítica," *Op.Cit.* 4 (1988–89): 9–55.

4. Georg Fromm, "El Grito de Lares," *La escalera* 3, no. 2 (Sept.–Oct. 1968): i–iv.

5. Richard Levins, "De rebelde a revolucionario," *La escalera* 1, nos. 3–4 (Apr.–May 1966): 3–18.

6. Angel G. Quintero Rivera, José Luis González, Ricardo Campos, and Juan Flores, eds., *Puerto Rico: identidad nacional y clases sociales (Coloquio de Princeton)* (Río Piedras: Huracán, 1979).

7. Angel G. Quintero Rivera, *Conflictos de clase y política en Puerto Rico* (Río Piedras: Huracán, 1976).

8. Fernando Picó, *Libertad y servidumbre en el Puerto Rico del siglo XIX: los jornaleros utuadeños en vísperas del auge del café* (Río Piedras: Huracán, 1979).

9. Laird W. Bergad, *Coffee and the Growth of Agrarian Capitalism in Nineteenth-Century Puerto Rico* (Princeton: Princeton University Press, 1983), 196.

10. Juan Flores, "The Insular Vision: Pedreira and the Puerto Rican Misere," in *Divided Borders: Essays on Puerto Rican Identity* (Houston: Arte Público Press, 1993), 21, 28–29, 32–33; see also in the same work "The Puerto Rico that José Luis González Built," 66.

11. Isabelo Zenón Cruz, *Narciso descubre su trasero: el negro en la cultura puertorriqueña*, 2nd ed., 2 vols. (Humacao, Puerto Rico: Editorial Furidi, 1975).

12. Efraín Barradas, *Sin nombre* 4, no. 1 (July–Sept. 1975): 73–75.

13. See appendix to the second edition (1975) of Zenón Cruz, *Narciso*, 1:347–64.

14. Zenón Cruz, *Narciso*, 2:185.

15. Alan West-Duran, "Puerto Rico: The Pleasures and Traumas of Race," *Centro: Journal of the Center for Puerto Rican Studies* 17, no. 1 (Spring 2005): 58, 62.

16. Francisco Scarano, *Sugar and Slavery in Puerto Rico: The Plantation Economy of Ponce, 1800–1850* (Madison: University of Wisconsin Press, 1984).

17. They include Aixa Merino, Palmira Ríos, Juan Giusti, Raul Mayo, Mariano Negrón Portillo, Joseph Dorsey, and Luis Figueroa.

18. For some critics, this language was the main achievement of this literary wave. Rubén Ríos, "El arte de dar lengua en Puerto Rico," in *Polifonía salvaje*, ed. Irma Rivera Nieves and Carlos Gil (San Juan: Postdata, 1995), 331. This is where José Luis González distanced himself from the new orientations. He rejected what he felt was the exaltation of what he termed lumpen figures and was uncomfortable with the work of avowedly homosexual author Manuel Ramos Otero. Arcadio Díaz Quiñones, *Conversación con José Luis González* (Río Piedras: Huracán, 1976), 46–47.

19. See Ana Lydia Vega, ed., *El tramo ancla* (Río Piedras: Editorial de la Universidad de Puerto Rico, 1988).

20. Rosario Ferré criticized what she felt was an obsession with material goods in terms reminiscent of the views of Pedreira and Marqués. "Ferré dice porqué es independentista," *EI*, Sept. 18, 1972.

21. Edgardo Rodríguez Juliá, *La renuncia del héroe Baltasar: Conferencias pronunciadas por Alejandro Cadalso en el Ateneo Puertorriqueño, del 4 al 10 de enero de 1938* (San Juan: Editorial Antillana, 1974).

22. Edgardo Rodríguez Juliá, *El entierro de Cortijo* (Río Piedras: Huracán, 1983), 77.

23. Meanwhile, poets such as David Cortés Cabán, Marithelma Costa, Pedro López Adorno, Myrna Nieves, Carmen Valle, Lourdes Vázquez, Alfredo Villanueva Collado, and Iván Silén continued the long tradition of New York Puerto Rican literature in Spanish.

24. In 1980, Efraín Barradas and Rafael Rodríguez published *Herejes y mitificadores: muestra de poesía puertorriqueña en los Estados Unidos* (Río Piedras: Huracán, 1980), an anthology of works by Puerto Rican authors in the United States. See also by Barradas *Partes de un todo. Ensayos sobre literatura puertorriqueña en los Estados Unidos* (Río Piedras: Editorial de la Universidad de Puerto Rico, 1998).

25. See Yasmín Ramírez, "Nuyorican Visionary: Jorge Soto and the Evolution of an Afro-Taino Aesthetic at Taller Boricua," *Centro: Journal of the Center for Puerto Rican Studies* 17, no. 2 (Fall 2005): 23–41.

26. Edna Acosta-Belén, "The Building of a Community: Puerto Rican Writers and Activists in New York City (1890s–1960s)," in *Recovering the U.S. Hispanic Heritage*, ed. Ramón Gutiérrez and Genaro Padilla (Houston: Arte Público Press, 1993), 190.

27. Jorge Duany, *The Puerto Rican Nation on the Move: Identities on the Island and in the United States* (Chapel Hill: University of North Carolina Press, 2002), 167.

28. Salsa is an international musical phenomenon headquartered in the Afro-Caribbean Latino communities of New York City, with vigorous centers in Venezuela, Puerto Rico, Dominican Republic, Panama, and Colombia, among others. See César Miguel Rondón, *El libro de la salsa: crónica de la música del caribe urbano* (Caracas: Editorial Arte, 1980). For the Puerto Rican dimension of this larger musical complex, see Angel G. Quintero Rivera, *Salsa, sabor y control: sociología de la música tropical* (Mexico City: Siglo XXI, 1999), 22. There is a growing literature on salsa. See Frances R. Aparicio, *Listening to Salsa: Gender, Latin Popular Music, and Puerto Rican Cultures* (Middletown, Conn.: Wesleyan University Press, 1998); and Juan Flores, *From Bomba to Hip-Hop: Puerto Rican Culture and Latino Identity* (New York: Columbia University Press, 2000).

CHAPTER THIRTEEN

1. Eliezer Curet Cuevas, *Economía política de Puerto Rico: 1950–2000* (San Juan: Ediciones M.A.C., 2003), 38. Edwin Irizarry Mora, *Economía de Puerto Rico: evolución y perspectivas* (Mexico City: Thomson Learning, 2001), 88, 219.

2. Francisco L. Rivera-Batiz and Carlos E. Santiago, *Island Paradox: Puerto Rico in the 1990s* (New York: Russell Sage Foundation, 1996), 10–11, 14–15.

3. Irizarry Mora, *Economía de Puerto Rico*, 135.

4. James Tobin et al., *Report to the Governor: The Committee to Study Puerto Rico's Finances* (n.p., 1975), 6, 62.

5. U.S. Government Accounting Office, *Puerto Rico: Fiscal Relations with the Federal Government and Economic Trends during the Phaseout of the Possessions Tax Credit*, GAO-06-541 (Washington, D.C.: General Accounting Office, 2006), 4, 6, 15.

6. Irizarry Mora, *Economía de Puerto Rico*, 293.

7. Emilio Pantojas-García, *Development Strategies as Ideology: Puerto Rico's Export-Led Industrialization Experience* (Boulder: Lynne Rienner, 1990), 153. On this, see General Accounting Office, *Tax Policy: Puerto Rico and the Section 936 Tax Credit*, GAO/GGD-93-109 (Washington, D.C.: General Accounting Office, 1993), 10.

8. Harry Grubert and Joel Slemrod, "The Effect of Taxes on Investment and Income Shifting to Puerto Rico," *Review of Economics and Statistics* 80, no. 3 (Aug. 1998): 365.

9. Caribbean Business, *The Book of Lists* (San Juan: Caribbean Business, 2004), 29–30.

10. Comisión Económica para América Latina, *Globalización y desarrollo: desafíos de Puerto Rico frente al siglo XXI* (Mexico City: CEPAL, 2004), 79.

11. The point is made by Orlando Sotomayor, "Development and Income Distribution: The Case of Puerto Rico," *World Development* 32, no. 8 (Aug. 2004): 1403.

12. Tobin et al., *Report to the Governor*, 15.

13. Government Development Bank for Puerto Rico, *Puerto Rico in Figures* (San Juan: Government Development Bank, 2000), 3; Curet Cuevas, *Economía política*, 124; Irizarry Mora, *Economía de Puerto Rico*, 156.

14. U.S. Government Accounting Office, *Puerto Rico: Fiscal Relations with the Federal Government*, 11, 49, 64–68.

15. Barry P. Bosworth and Susan M. Collins, "Economic Growth," chapter 2 of *The Economy of Puerto Rico: Restoring Growth*, ed. Barry P. Bosworth, Susan M. Collins, and Miguel A. Soto-Class (Washington, D.C.: Brookings Institution and Center for the New Economy, 2006), 28.

16. This is equal to about 55 percent of Puerto Rico's GNP at the time. Curet Cuevas, *Economía política*, 359.

17. An excellent analysis of the coalition that defended the 936 tax benefits can be found in Sarah Grusky, "Political Power in Puerto Rico: Bankers, Pharmaceuticals and the State" (Ph.D. diss., Howard University, 1994).

18. Puerto Rico residents, it should be remembered, pay no federal taxes on income from insular sources, but they pay Social Security and Medicaid taxes.

19. See Emilio Pantojas-García, "Los 'fondos federales' y la economía de Puerto Rico: mitos y realidades" (typed ms., University of Puerto Rico, 2005).

20. Irizarry Mora, *Economía de Puerto Rico*, 226.

21. Curet Cuevas, *Economía política*, 178

22. U.S. Government Accounting Office, *Puerto Rico: Fiscal Relations with the Federal Government*, 79.

23. Edgardo Meléndez, *Puerto Rico's Statehood Movement* (Westport, Conn.: Greenwood Press, 1988), 91, 93.

24. Carlos Romero Barceló, "Puerto Rico, USA: The Case for Statehood," *Foreign Affairs* 59, no. 1 (Fall 1980): 60–81.

25. Juan B. Huyke, "Estadidad" (1945), in *Las ideas anexionistas en Puerto Rico bajo la dominación norteamericana*, ed. Aarón Gamaliel Ramos (Río Piedras: Huracán, 1987), 90–91.

26. Manuel "Manny" Suárez, *Two Lynchings on Cerro Maravilla: The Police Murders in Puerto Rico and the Federal Government Cover Up* (San Juan: Instituto de Cultura Puertorriqueña, 2003).

27. Héctor Meléndez, *El fracaso del proyecto PSP de la pequeña burguesía* (Río Piedras: Editorial Edil, 1984), 23.

28. Juan Mari Brás, "Tres meses del nuevo gobierno," Apr. 1, 1973; "Autonomismo asimilista," Aug. 5, 1973; "El jaque mate," Aug. 12, 1973, 8; all in *Claridad*. Pedro Juan Rúa, "Notas sociológicas sobre el Puerto Rico de hoy," *Nueva Lucha* 6 (Apr.–June 1973): 29–36; and "¿Confrontación? ¿Qué confrontación?" *Claridad*, Nov. 12, 1976. See also Juan Mari Brás, "La autodeterminación y el superpuerto," May 20, 1973, and "Con la guardia en alto" June 26, 1973, both in *Claridad*.

29. *La Alternativa Socialista*, 1974, 87, 95.

30. Juan Mari Brás, "Muñoz y Sánchez," Feb. 24–Mar. 2, 1978; Carlos Gallisá, "Partido y frentes," Mar. 10–16, 1978; both in *Claridad*.

31. The idea of the new thesis was announced in July 1978, and the text was made public in July 1979.

32. See Rafael Hernández Colón, "Defensa de la libre asociación," in *Puerto Rico, una crisis histórica*, ed. Suzy Castor (Mexico City: Nuestro Tiempo, 1979), 58.

33. Daniel Nina, *Por la libre: conversaciones con Juan Mari Brás* (Santo Domingo–San Juan: Isla Negra, 1998), 101.

34. Rubén Berríos, "El problema colonial de Puerto Rico y la estrategia independentista" (1978), and "La historia de la lucha independentista" (1978), in *La independencia de Puerto Rico. Razón y lucha* (Mexico City: Editorial Línea, 1983), 195–217.

35. See for example, Juan Mari Brás, "Los populares y nosotros I–III," *Claridad*, Aug. 27–Sept. 2, Sept. 3–9, 10–16, 1982.

36. Carmen Gautier Mayoral, "Por qué no viene la república en 1992" (1985), in *República Asociada y libre asociación: documentación de un debate*, ed. Marco Antonio Rigau and Juan Manuel García Passalacqua (San Juan: Atlántico, 1987), 245–47.

37. Gary Martin, "Industrial Policy by Accident: The United States in Puerto Rico," *Journal of Hispanic Policy* 4 (1989–1990): 105.

CHAPTER FOURTEEN

1. James Dietz, *Puerto Rico: Negotiating Development and Change* (Boulder: Lynne Rienner, 2003), 11; Leonardo Santana Rabell, *Fulgor y decadencia de la administración pública en Puerto Rico* (San Juan: La Torre del Viejo–DEGI, 1994), 82, 84, 182–83.

2. The 1996 bill was retired over the language issue. Congressman Gerald B. H. Solomon (R-N.Y.) amended it to link statehood with the adoption of English as language of instruction. Aware that anything but a clear recognition of Puerto Rico's culture would hinder statehood in a plebiscite, proponents withdrew the bill.

3. César F. Rosado Marzán, "Dependent Unionism: Resource Mobilization and Union Density in Puerto Rico" (Ph.D. diss., Princeton University, 2005), 16; Carlos Alá Santiago, "The Puerto Rican Labor Movement in the 1990s," in *Colonial Dilemma: Critical Perspectives on Contemporary Puerto Rico*, ed. Edwin Meléndez and Edgardo Meléndez (Boston: South End Press, 1993), 143.

4. Rosado Marzán, "Dependent Unionism," 103.

5. Ibid., 121–23.

6. The PNP justified privatization pointing to the future impact of the Federal Telecommunications Act of 1996, which opened Puerto Rico's phones to private providers.

7. Rosado Marzán, "Dependent Unionism," 104.

8. The evolution of the Federación de Maestros, Puerto Rico's largest union, is a microcosm of the conflicts within the labor movement. Officially affiliated to the American Federation of Teachers (AFT) since 1974, its victory in representation elections under Law 45 could be seen as an addition of 40,000 new members to the AFL-CIO ranks. Yet the Puerto Rican union has a strong independent identity, built by activists who had little contact with the dynamics or style of the AFT. By 2003, scandals related to the management of the union's health insurance plan led to the victory in internal elections of an opposition current, which by 2005 led the union out of the AFT. This opposition tendency was the initiative of an activist current, largely connected but not reducible to the Movimiento Socialista de Trabajadores, which has pushed for changes since the early 1980s. At the time of writing, the legal battle over economic issues arising from the disaffiliation is still unfolding.

9. Katherine T. McCaffrey, *Military Power and Popular Protest: The US Navy in Vieques, Puerto Rico* (New Brunswick: Rutgers University Press, 2002); César Ayala, "Recent Works on Vieques, Colonialism, and Fishermen," *Centro: Journal of the Center for Puerto Rican Studies* 15, no. 1 (Spring 2003): 212–25.

10. Rosselló's decision may have been part of his hopes for a cabinet post if Al Gore won his bid for the presidency. For this and a summary of the corruption cases, see Eliezer Curet Cuevas, *Economía política de Puerto Rico: 1950–2000* (San Juan: Ediciones M.A.C., 2003).

11. Arlene M. Dávila, *Barrio Dreams: Puerto Ricans, Latinos, and the Neoliberal City* (Berkeley: University of California Press, 2004), 30, 98, 65, 64, 96, 11, 62.

12. Gina M. Pérez, *The Near Northwest Side Story: Migration, Displacement and Puerto Rican Families* (Berkeley: University of California Press, 2004), 130.

13. In Chicago, the battle against gentrification led to the creation of the Humboldt Park Empowerment Partnership in 1995, a coalition to demand affordable housing and community-led development projects. These movements had an antecedent in Boston. In 1965, city government plans to a turn a Puerto Rican area into the location for new

malls and other structures led to the creation of an Emergency Tenants Council. Its efforts led to the establishment of Villa Victoria, a renovated, largely Puerto Rican community. Félix V. Matos-Rodríguez, "Saving the Parcela: A Short History of Boston's Puerto Rican Community," in *The Puerto Rican Diaspora: Historical Perspectives*, ed. Carmen T. Whalen and Víctor Vázquez-Hernández (Philadelphia: Temple University Press, 2005), 200–226.

14. See Ana Y. Ramos-Zayas, *National Performances: The Politics of Class, Race, and Space in Puerto Rican Chicago* (Chicago: University of Chicago Press, 2003).

15. Andrés Torres, *Between Melting Pot and Mosaic: African Americans and Puerto Ricans in the New York Political Economy* (Philadelphia: Temple University Press, 1995), 19–20, 167–68.

16. Perry Anderson, "Force and Consent," *New Left Review* 17 (Sept.–Oct. 2002): 22.

17. Gabriel Kolko, *Main Currents in Modern American History* (New York: Pantheon, 1984), 67, 91.

18. Jorge Duany and Felix V. Matos Rodríguez, *Puerto Ricans in Orlando and Central Florida* (New York: Centro de Estudios Puertorriqueños Policy Report, vol. 1, no. 1, Spring 2006).

19. A wage credit provision known as "Section 30A" was not extended to Puerto Rico, for example. See Marialba Martínez, "The End of an Era: Congress Recently Passed Bills Making Federal Taxes for Manufacturing Operations on the Island Higher Than Those on the Mainland . . . ," *Caribbean Business*, Oct. 14, 2004, 18–25.

20. Luis Varela Ortiz, "El PIP y la estadidad: una diferencia estratégica," *Claridad*, Sept. 9–15, 2004.

21. Juan Mari Brás, "La renovación del discurso independentista," pts. 1–4, *Claridad*, May 20–26, May 27–June 2, June 10–16, June 17–23, 1994.

22. José Elias Torres, *Filiberto Ojeda Ríos: su propuesta, su visión* (San Juan: Ediciones Callejón, 2006).

23. For debates on these figures between the government of Puerto Rico and the U.S. Census Bureau, see José A. Delgado, "Cuadran cifras en la manufactura," *ND*, Oct. 21, 2005; and U.S. Census Bureau, *Puerto Rico Manufacturing: 2002 Economic Census of Island Areas*, IA02-001-PRM (RV) (Washington, D.C.: U.S. Department of Commerce, 2005), 9. See also U.S. Government Accounting Office, *Puerto Rico: Fiscal Relations with the Federal Government and Economic Trends during the Phaseout of the Possessions Tax Credit*, GAO-06-541 (Washington, D.C.: General Accounting Office, 2006).

24. Martínez, "End of an Era," 22.

25. Daniel R. Garza, "A Pleasant Surprise: Manufacturing Is Not Down and Out," *Caribbean Business*, June 8, 2000, 30–34; Martínez, "End of an Era," 22.

26. Ralph J. Sierra and Margarita Serapión, "Puerto Rico's Tax Incentives in the New Millennium," *Tax Notes International*, Oct. 13, 2003: 181–86.

27. U.S. Government Accounting Office, *Puerto Rico: Fiscal Relations with the Federal Government*, 65.

28. Laura K. Thompson, "Tax Plan Offered to Reverse Deposit Drain in Puerto Rico,"

American Banker 168, no. 187 (Sept. 9, 2003): 4–8; Matthias Rieker, "What's behind Puerto Rico Mortgage Mess," *American Banker* 170, no. 83 (May 2, 2005): 7–11.

29. Fernando Picó, *El día menos pensado: historia de los presidiarios en Puerto Rico (1793–1993)* (Río Piedras: Huracán, 1998).

30. On the opposition to the death penalty in Puerto Rico in the early twentieth century, see Nahomi Galindo Malavé, "Entre el garrote y la horca. La oposición a la pena de muerte en Puerto Rico, 1898–1910" (B.A. thesis, University of Puerto Rico, 2006). A shorter piece under the same title can be found in *Pensamiento Crítico* 28, no. 97 (Fall 2006): 4–12.

31. "Ponce Murderers Will Die This Morning," *San Juan News*, June 3, 1902; "The Death Penalty," *San Juan News*, June 4, 1902.

CHAPTER FIFTEEN

1. Luis Dávila Colón, "La virazón del No," pts. 1 and 2, *ND*, Nov. 8 and 9, 1994; "El neonacionalismo," *ND*, Dec. 8, 1993. For a celebration of "cultural nationalism," see Juan M. García Passalacqua, "El plañido de la torre," *Nómada* 2 (Oct. 1995): 89–95.

2. Arlene M. Dávila, *Sponsored Identities: Cultural Politics in Puerto Rico* (Philadelphia: Temple University Press, 1997), 179–80, 182.

3. There were divergences within the neo-nationalist current. In 1988, many criticized Governor Hernández Colón after he minimized the African aspect of Puerto Rican culture. Rafael Hernández Colón, "España, San Antón y el ser nacional," *ND*, June 6, 1988. For a left-nationalist critique, see Manuel Maldonado Denis, "Ni hispanófilos ni hispanófobos: puertorriqueños," *EM*, June 13, 1988.

4. See José Luis Méndez, *Entre el limbo y el consenso: el dilema de Puerto Rico para el próximo siglo* (San Juan: Milenio, 1997).

5. Juan Manuel Carrión, "Etnia, raza y la nacionalidad puertorriqueña," in *La Nación puertorriqueña: ensayos en torno a Pedro Albizu Campos*, ed. Juan Manuel Carrión, Teresa C. Gracia Ruiz, and Carlos Rodríguez Fraticelli (San Juan: Editorial de la Universidad de Puerto Rico, 1993), 8–11, 13, 18. See also Juan Manuel Carrión, *Voluntad de nación: ensayos sobre el nacionalismo en Puerto Rico* (San Juan: Nueva Aurora, 1996).

6. Ramón López, *Historia de la artesanía puertorriqueña* (San Juan: Instituto de Cultura Puertorriqueña, 2003); *Puerto Rico, USA: historia de un país imaginario* (Río Piedras: Huracán, 2000); and *La cultura puertorriqueña en Estados Unidos* (San Juan: Instituto de Cultura Puertorriqueña, Cuadernos de Cultura, n.d.).

7. Edwin Reyes, "Rapeo sobre el rap en Ciales," *Claridad*, Dec. 29, 1995–Jan. 4, 1996. For a response, see Rafael Bernabe, "Rap: soy boricua, pa'que tú lo sepas," *Claridad*, Jan. 19–25, 1996.

8. Roberto Gonzáles Nieves, *Carta pastoral: Patria, nación e identidad: don indivisible del amor de Dios* (San Juan: 2003).

9. Angel Rama, *La ciudad letrada* (Hanover, N.H.: Ediciones del Norte, 1984).

10. María Elena Rodríguez Castro, "Tradición y modernidad: el intelectual puertorriqueño ante la década del treinta," *Op.Cit.* 3 (1987–88): 45–65; and "Las casas del porvenir: nación y narración en el ensayo puertorriqueño," *Revista Iberoamericana* 59, nos. 162–63 (Jan.–June 1993): 33–54.

11. Juan Gelpí, *Literatura y paternalismo en Puerto Rico* (Río Piedras: Editorial de la Universidad de Puerto Rico, 1993).

12. Juan Gelpí "El clásico y la reescritura: *Insularismo* en las páginas de *La guaracha del macho camacho*," *Revista Iberoamericana* 59, nos. 162–63 (Jan.–June 1993): 55–71. See also his "Historia y literatura en *Página en blanco y staccato* de Manuel Ramos Otero," in *Globalización, nación, postmodernidad*, ed. Luis Felipe Díaz and Marc Zimmerman (San Juan: Ediciones La Casa, 2001), 281–89.

13. Eileen J. Suárez Findlay, *Imposing Decency: The Politics of Sexuality and Race in Puerto Rico, 1870–1920* (Durham, N.C.: Duke University Press, 1999).

14. Kelvin Santiago-Valles, *"Subject People" and Colonial Discourses: Economic Transformation and Social Disorder in Puerto Rico, 1898–1947* (Albany: State University of New York Press, 1994).

15. Angel G. Quintero Rivera, *Salsa, sabor y control: sociología de la música tropical* (Mexico City: Siglo XXI, 1999).

16. Juan Flores, "Cortijo's Revenge: New Mappings of Puerto Rican Culture," in *Divided Borders: Essays on Puerto Rican Identity* (Houston: Arte Público Press, 1993), 104. See also Flores, *From Bomba to Hip-Hop: Puerto Rican Culture and Latino Identity* (New York: Columbia University Press, 2000).

17. Jorge Duany, *The Puerto Rican Nation on the Move: Identities on the Island and in the United States* (Chapel Hill: University of North Carolina Press, 2002). Frances Negrón-Muntaner takes a similar position describing "modern boricuas" as "a 'cultural subject,' an ethno-nation," hailed and imagining themselves "alternately as an 'ethnicity' (defined by a specific culture across national-state boundaries) and a 'nationality' (defined in relationship to a specific territory, with full or partial claims to independent sovereignty)." Frances Negrón-Muntaner, *Boricua Pop: Puerto Ricans and the Latinization of American Culture* (New York: New York University Press, 2004), 6.

18. See Jorge Duany, "La diáspora dominicana en Puerto Rico. Su persistente exclusión étnica, racial y genérica," in *Desde la diversidad humana: un acercamiento interdisciplinario*, ed. Rosalie Rosa (San Juan: Gaviota, forthcoming).

19. Raquel Z. Rivera, *New York Ricans from the Hip Hop Zone* (New York: Palgrave-Macmillan, 2003), xii–xiii.

20. Mayra Santos, "Geografía en decibeles: utopías pan-caribeñas y el territorio rap," *Revista de Crítica Literaria Latinoamericana* 23, no. 45 (1997): 351–63.

21. Rubén DJ, Vico C, and Lisa M are the artistic names of Rubén Urrutia, Luis A. Lozada Cruz, and Marilisa Marrero Vázquez.

22. For the postmodern as loss of credibility of the master-narratives, see Jean-Francois Lyotard, *La condition postmoderne: rapport sur le savoir* (Paris: Minuit, 1979).

23. See Arturo Torrecilla, "Litekapitalismus intelligentsia," 69–148, and with Carlos Pabón, "La clase obrera de Marx, ¿para qué?," 49–67, in *El espectro posmoderno: ecología, neoproletario, intelligentsia* (San Juan: Publicaciones Puertorriqueñas, 1995); "Watermelon Intelligentsia: Intellectuals in the Party-State," *Social Text* 38 (Spring 1994): 135–47; and "Los protocolos del consigliere," *Nomada* 2 (Oct. 1995): 89–95. Roberto Alejandro, leader of the university student strike in 1981, founder with Torrecilla of the group Autogestión in the early 1980s, formulated a similar diagnosis in 1987. See Alejandro, "La generación acomodada," *ND*, June 23, 1987; "La generación desgastada," *ND*, June 6, 1987; and "El eco de Washington . . . ," *ND*, Aug. 1, 1985.

24. Other versions of this search for alternatives both to capitalism and Marxist discourses (considered to be equally infected by the repressive work-ethic) can be found in *Social Text* 38 (Spring 1994), which includes articles by Kelvin A. Santiago-Valles, María Milagros López, and Miriam Muñiz Varela, among others.

25. Carlos Gil, "Postdata o 'ni pastores ni sepultureros,'" *Revista de Estudios Hispánicos* 22 (1995): 491–92, 498; and "Intellectuals Confront the Crisis of Traditional Narratives in Puerto Rico," *Social Text* 38 (Spring 1994): 97–104. See also Juan Duchesne Winter, "Del prólogo al pórtico: criticar un texto llamado Rodríguez Juliá," in *Las tribulaciones de Juliá*, ed. Juan Duchesne Winter (San Juan: Instituto de Cultura Puertorriqueña, 1992), 14.

26. Juan Duchesne Winter, "Vieques: la protesta como escenario espectacularizado y consensual." This article appeared on the Web site of Foro Civil Sobre Vieques, moderated by Professor Juan Giusti Cordero of the University of Puerto Rico, <www.red betances.com>, accessed May 21, 2001.

27. Carlos Pabón, *Nación postmortem* (Río Piedras: Ediciones Callejón, 2002). See Michael Mann, "Has Globalization Ended the Rise and Rise of the Nation State?" *Review of International Political Economy* 4, no. 3 (Autumn 1997): 472–96.

28. Juan Duchesne Winter, "Convalescencia del independentimso de izquierda," *Postdata* 1 (1990).

29. Juan Duchesne Winter, Chloe Georas, Ramón Grosfoguel, Agustín Lao, Frances Negrón, Pedro Angel Rivera, and Aurea María Sotomayor, "La estadidad desde una perspectiva democratica radical," *Diálogo*, Feb. 1997, 30–31.

30. Opposition to independence based on a negative view of U.S. control over independent states also has precedents. See the consideration on José Celso Barbosa and Muñoz Marín in chapters 3 and 7.

31. Not the least contradiction of this current is its combination of a celebration of the alleged growing irrelevance of the nation-state in a globalized world with its insistence on the particular advantages of retaining U.S. citizenship.

32. See, for example, Ramón Grosfoguel, "La 'campaña' militar del posmoderninsmo eurocéntrico," *Diálogo*, Apr. 2002, 20–21.

33. Ramón Grosfoguel, *Colonial Subjects: Puerto Ricans in a Global Perspective* (Berkeley: University of California Press, 2003), 2, 68.

34. Juan Duchesne Winter, "La globalización explicada a los adultos," *Claridad*, Feb.

21–27, 1997. For a response, see Rafael Bernabe, "Acuerdos y diferencias sobre la globalización," *Claridad*, Mar. 14–20, 1997.

35. Jaime Benson, Juan Duchesne Winter, Heidi Figueroa, Javier Figueroa, Emilio González, Laura Ortiz, Carlos Pabón, Madeline Román, Marlene Duprey, Luis Avilés, Ivette N. Hernández, Juan L. Bonilla, and Roberto Rodríguez Morazzani, "La amenaza fundamentalista global: un punto de vista independiente," *Diálogo*, Dec. 2001, 26–27. Duchesne reversed his position in "Debatir la guerra . . . el silogismo de la bestia," *Diálogo*, Sept. 2002, 21.

36. Silvia Alvarez Curbelo, "Las lecciones de la guerra: Luis Muñoz Marín y la Segunda Guerra Mundial, 1943–1946," in *Luis Muñoz Marín: ensayos del centenario*, ed. Fernando Picó (San Juan: Fundación Luis Muñoz Marín, 1999), 31–59.

37. Silvia Alvarez Curbelo, *Un país del porvenir: el afán de modernidad en Puerto Rico (Siglo XIX)* (San Juan: Ediciones Callejón, 2001), 9, 15.

38. See the introductions in Mario R. Cancel and Alberto Martínez-Márquez, eds., *El límite volcado: antología de la generación de los poetas de los ochenta* (San Juan–Santo Domingo: Isla Negra, 2000). Luis Felipe Díaz, "La narrativa de Mayra Santos y el travestismo cultural," *Centro: Journal of the Center for Puerto Rican Studies* 15, no. 2 (Fall 2003): 28, 30.

39. Mayra Santos, *Sirena Selena vestida de pena* (Barcelona: Mondadori, 2000).

40. Alberto Sandoval-Sánchez, "*Sirena Selena vestida de pena*: A Novel for the New Millennium . . . ," *Centro: Journal of the Center for Puerto Rican Studies* 15, no. 2 (Fall 2003): 9, 8, 19.

41. Efraín Barradas, "*Sirena Selena vestida de pena* o el Caribe como travestí," *Centro: Journal of the Center for Puerto Rican Studies*, 15, no. 2 (Fall 2003): 53–61.

42. See Mayra Santos, "El universalismo y yo," *Claridad*, Apr. 10–16, 1996, 20–21.

43. Rafael Acevedo, *Exquisito cadáver* (San Juan: Ediciones Callejón, 2001).

44. Luis F. Díaz, "Postmodernidad discursiva en *Historias tremendas* de Pedro Cabiya," in *Modernidad literaria puertorriqueña* (San Juan: Isla Negra, 2005), 257–58, 260.

45. Fredric Jameson, "Postmodernism and Consumer Society," in *The Cultural Turn: Selected Writings on the Postmodern, 1983–1998* (London: Verso, 1998), 5.

46. Perry Anderson, *The Origins of Postmodernity* (London: Verso, 1998), 109.

47. Abraham Rodríguez Jr., *Spidertown* (New York: Hyperion, 1993).

48. For an inkling of these debates, see Pedro López-Adorno, ed., *Papiros de Babel. Antología de la poesía puertorriqueña en Nueva York* (Río Piedras: Editorial de la Universidad de Puerto Rico, 1991). To further nuance this landscape, Victor Hernández Cruz, one of the pioneers of Nuyorican literature, now resides in Puerto Rico and continues to write in both English and Spanish. See, for example, his *Panoramas* (Minneapolis: Coffee House Press, 1997).

49. This orientation is defended through a polemic with other authors in Rafael Bernabe, *Manual para organizar velorios. Notas sobre la muerte de la nación* (Río Piedras: Huracán, 2003).

CONCLUSION

1. Emilio Pantojas, "Puerto Rico post-936: ¿existen alternativas?" *Diálogo*, Mar. 2001.

2. Van L. Perkins, *Crisis in Agriculture: The Agricultural Adjustment Administration and the New Deal, 1933*, University of California Publications in History 81 (Berkeley: University of California Press, 1969), 6.

3. Henry Wallace, *New Frontiers* (New York: Reynal and Hitchcock, 1934), 172.

4. Qtd. in Bernard Sternsher, *Rexford Guy Tugwell and the New Deal* (New Brunswick: Rutgers University Press, 1964), 145.

5. Wallace, *New Frontiers*, 138–39.

6. Ramón Grosfoguel, *Colonial Subjects: Puerto Ricans in a Global Perspective* (Berkeley: University of California Press, 2003), 66.

BIBLIOGRAPHICAL ESSAY

There are hundreds of books and articles on Puerto Rico since 1898. To list the works cited in this book would take more space than we have at our disposal. We have selected around 250 titles from those that have been more helpful to us and that we feel may help others. We have not privileged those texts with which we agree but rather those that provide overviews of a period or an issue and that help map out the main debates. Many provide useful references. Our own views are expressed in this book and other publications from which the reader may discern where we agree or disagree with any particular interpretation. Through the pages that follow, we use three abbreviations: EUPR for Editorial de la Universidad de Puerto Rico, ICP for Instituto de Cultura Puertorriqueña, and *Centro* for *Centro: Journal of the Center for Puerto Rican Studies*.

The most comprehensive general history of Puerto Rico is Francisco Scarano's *Puerto Rico: cinco siglos de historia* (Bogotá: McGraw Hill Interamericana, 1993). James Dietz's *Economic History of Puerto Rico: Institutional Change and Capitalist Development* (Princeton: Princeton University Press, 1986) is the best general economic history up to the 1980s. His *Puerto Rico: Negotiating Development and Change* (Boulder: Lynne Rienner, 2003) brings the discussion to the late 1990s. The classical anthropological work edited by Julian H. Steward, *The People of Puerto Rico* (Urbana: University of Illinois Press, 1956), is still useful as historical background and portrait of the island in the late 1940s. *Puerto Rico: cien años de lucha política*, edited by Reece B. Bothwell in four volumes (San Juan: EUPR, 1979), is a useful collection of political texts from 1876 to 1976. *Puerto Rico: arte e identidad* (Río Piedras: EUPR, 1998), edited by the Hermandad de Artistas Gráficos de Puerto Rico, covers the evolution of Puerto Rican art through the twentieth century. The standard reference book for Puerto Rican literature is Josefina Rivera de Alvarez, *La literatura puertorriqueña: su proceso en el tiempo* (Madrid: Partenón, 1983), but it stops around 1980.

For photographic registers of Puerto Rico's evolution, the reader may begin with Jack Delano, *Puerto Rico Mío: Four Decades of Change* (Washington, D.C.: Smithsonian Institution Press, 1990); Osvaldo García, *Fotografías para la historia, 1844–1952* (Río Piedras: EUPR, 1989); and Félix V. Matos-Rodríguez and Pedro J. Hernández, *Pioneros: Puerto Ricans in New York City, 1896–1948* (Charleston, S.C.: Arcadia, 2001).

The reader may approach economic and social evolution and struggles in Puerto Rico during the nineteenth century by consulting Francisco Scarano, *Sugar and Slavery in Puerto Rico: The Plantation Economy of Ponce, 1800–1850* (Madison: University of Wisconsin Press, 1984); Manuel Moreno Fraginals, Frank Moya Pons, and Stanley L. Engerman, eds., *Between Slavery and Free Labor: The Spanish-Speaking Caribbean in the Nineteenth Century* (Baltimore: Johns Hopkins University Press, 1985); Joseph C. Dorsey, *Slave Traffic in the Age of Abolition: Puerto Rico, West Africa, and the Non-Hispanic Caribbean, 1815–1859* (Gainesville: University of Florida Press, 2003); Luis A. Figueroa, *Sugar, Slavery and Freedom in Nineteenth-Century Puerto Rico* (Chapel Hill: University of North Carolina Press, 2005); Laird Bergad, *Coffee and the Growth of Agrarian Capitalism in Nineteenth-Century Puerto Rico* (Princeton: Princeton University Press, 1983); Fernando Picó, *Libertad y servidumbre en el Puerto Rico del siglo XIX: los jornaleros utuadeños en vísperas del auge del café* (Río Piedras: Huracán, 1979); and Sidney W. Mintz, "The History of a Puerto Rican Plantation," in his *Caribbean Transformations* (Chicago: Aldine, 1974).

The debates on social, economic, and political issues linked to the questions of slavery and the search for liberal reforms may be explored beginning with Silvia Alvarez Curbelo, *Un país del porvenir: el afán de modernidad en Puerto Rico (Siglo XIX)* (San Juan: Ediciones Callejón, 2001), and Christopher Schmidt-Nowara, *Empire and Antislavery: Spain, Cuba, and Puerto Rico, 1833–1874* (Pittsburgh: University of Pittsburgh Press, 1999). The best introduction to the Grito de Lares is Francisco Moscoso, *La revolución puertorriqueña de 1868: el Grito de Lares* (San Juan: ICP, 2003). The history of the separatist movement is told in Germán Delgado Pasapera, *Puerto Rico: sus luchas emancipadoras (1850–1898)* (Río Piedras: Editorial Cultural, 1984).

The debates and issues at stake in the new territorial policy instituted through the Foraker Act and the Insular Cases are discussed in Christina Duffy Burnett and Burke Marshall, eds., *Foreign in a Domestic Sense: Puerto Rico, American Expansion and the Constitution* (Durham, N.C.: Duke University Press, 2001). For a brief introduction, see James E. Kerr, *The Insular Cases: The Role of the Judiciary in American Expansionism* (Port Washington, N.Y.: Kennikat Press, 1982). Background for past U.S. territorial policy may be found in Jack Ericson Eblen, *The First and Second United States Empires: Governors and Territorial Government, 1784–1912* (Pittsburgh: University of Pittsburgh Press, 1968). Differential U.S. attitudes toward the populations conquered in 1898 are discussed by Lanny Thompson in "The Imperial Republic: A Comparison of the Insular Territories under U.S. Dominion after 1898," *Pacific Historical Review* 71, no. 4 (November 2002): 535–74. A summary of the violent events following the U.S. invasion is in Fernando Picó's *La guerra después de la guerra* (Río Piedras: Huracán, 1987).

The massive *Report on the Island of Puerto Rico* (Washington, D.C.: GPO, 1899; repr., New York: Arno Press, 1975) prepared by Henry K. Carroll is an abundant source of material on the economic, social, and political situation of Puerto Rico in 1898. The expansion of the sugar industry after 1898 is covered within a broader international context by César J. Ayala, *American Sugar Kingdom: The Plantation Economy of the Spanish Caribbean, 1898–1934* (Chapel Hill: University of North Carolina Press, 1999), and from a perspective favorable to the sugar companies by Arthur D. Gayer et al., *The Sugar Economy of Puerto Rico* (New York: Columbia University Press, 1938). For the life of the sugarcane proletariat, see the work by Steward cited above and Sidney W. Mintz, *Worker in the Cane: A Puerto Rican Life History* (New Haven: Yale University Press, 1960). Arturo Bird-Carmona offers a view of the cigarmakers in "Between the Insular Road and San Juan Bay: The Cigar World of Puerta de Tierra" (Ph.D. diss., University of Iowa, 1998). The garment and home-needlework industry is discussed in the collection edited by María del Carmen Baerga, *Género y trabajo: la industria de la aguja en Puerto Rico y el Caribe hispánico* (Río Piedras: EUPR, 1993). The economy of Puerto Rico is surveyed in the late 1920s and early 1930s from a pro-market orthodox view in Victor S. Clark et al., *Porto Rico and Its Problems* (Washington, D.C.: Brookings Institution, 1930), and from an anti-imperialist critical perspective in Bailey K. Diffie and Justine Diffie's *Porto Rico: A Broken Pledge* (New York: Vanguard Press, 1931).

Sugar: A Case Study of Government Control (New York: Macmillan, 1937) by John E. Dalton is still a good overview of the sugar crisis framing reform programs in Puerto Rico in the 1930s. For a study of the early planning efforts under the Plan Chardón and Governor Tugwell, see Leonardo Santana Rabell, *Planificación y política durante la administración de Luis Muñoz Marín: un análisis crítico* (Río Piedras: Análisis, 1984). For a critical history of Operation Bootstrap and its different stages, see Emilio Pantojas-García, *Development Strategies as Ideology: Puerto Rico's Export-Led Industrialization Experience* (Boulder: Lynne Rienner, 1990). On the same topic, besides his *Economic History* and *Negotiating Development* quoted above, see James Dietz's "Puerto Rico: The 'Three-Legged' Economy," *Integration and Trade* (Institute for Integration of Latin America and the Caribbean, Buenos Aires) 5, no. 15 (2001): 247–73. For a stimulating analysis of the contradictions of the PPD industrialization policy and underlying social dynamics, see José A. Padín, "Imperialism by Invitation: Causes of a Failed Developmental State Project in Puerto Rico, 1940–1950" (Ph.D. diss., University of Wisconsin–Madison, 1998). His argument is further developed in "Puerto Rico in the Post War: Liberalized Development Banking and the Fall of the 'Fifth Tiger,'" *World Development* 31, no. 2 (2003): 281–301.

Originally published by the University of Chicago Press in 1950, *Puerto Rico's Economic Future* (New York: Arno Press, 1975) by Harvey S. Perloff registers the main ideas of Puerto Rico's economic strategists at the start of Operation Bootstrap. David F. Ross's *The Long Uphill Path: A Historical Study of Puerto Rico's Program of Economic Development* (San Juan: Editorial Edil, 1976) is a glowing presentation of the tax exemption–based policy of industrialization. For an admiring biography of the main executive in charge of the industrial promotion program in the golden years of Operation Bootstrap, see A. W. Maldonado, *Teodoro Moscoso and Puerto Rico's Operation Bootstrap* (Gainesville: University of Florida Press, 1997). An introduction to the agrarian side of the PPD reform program may be obtained from Nathan Koenig, *A Comprehensive Agricultural Program for Puerto Rico* (Washington, D.C.: GPO, 1953); Mathew D. Edel, "Land Reform in Puerto Rico," pts. 1 and 2, *Caribbean Studies* (October 1962): 22–60 and (January 1963): 28–50; Keith Rosenn, "Puerto Rican Land Reform," *Yale Law Journal* 73 (1963): 334–56; and Angel David Cruz Báez, "Export Agriculture under Economic Development: A Geographic Analysis of the Decline of Sugarcane Production in Puerto Rico" (Ph.D. diss., University of Wisconsin–Madison, 1977).

For a historical exploration of Puerto Rico's postwar economy leading to proposals for the future, see Edwin Irizarry Mora, *Economía de Puerto Rico: evolución y perspectivas* (Mexico City: Thomson Learning, 2001). Francisco L. Rivera-Batiz and Carlos E. Santiago present a statistical summary of past trends and a portrait of Puerto Ricans in *Island Paradox: Puerto Rico in the 1990s* (New York: Russell Sage Foundation, 1996). Richard Weisskoff's *Factories and Food Stamps* (Baltimore: Johns Hopkins University Press, 1985) is a mathematically oriented study of the tendencies of the Puerto Rican economy after the mid-1970s slowdown and the influx of federal funds. Two collections of essays provide different contributions to an understanding of Puerto Rico's cultural, political, and economic dynamics in the 1990s. They are Edwin Meléndez and Edgardo Meléndez, eds., *Colonial Dilemma: Critical Perspectives on Contemporary Puerto Rico* (Boston: South End Press, 1993), and Aarón Gamaliel Ramos and Angel Israel Rivera, eds., *Islands at the Crossroads: Politics in the Non-independent Caribbean* (Kingston, Jamaica: Ian Randle Publishers; Boulder: Lynne Rienner, 2001). For the benefits of Section 936 to U.S. corporate capital and to the Puerto Rican banking sector and the relation between these two interests, see Sarah Grusky, "Political Power in Puerto Rico: Bankers, Pharmaceuticals and the State" (Ph.D. diss., Howard University, 1994). The evolution of public administration in an epoch of privatization and deregulation is discussed in Leonardo Santana Rabell, *Fulgor y decadencia de la administración pública en Puerto Rico* (San Juan: La Torre del Viejo–DEGI, 1994).

An overview of Puerto Rico's economy was commissioned by the United Nations Economic Commission for Latin America and published as *Globalización y desarrollo: desafíos de Puerto Rico frente al siglo XXI* (Mexico City: CEPAL, 2004). An overview of issues and debates is available in Emilio Pantojas-García, "End-of-the-Century Studies of Puerto Rico's Economy, Politics and Culture: What Lies Ahead?" *Latin American Research Review* 35, no. 3 (2000): 227–40. The work of Eliezer Curet Cuevas includes ample empirical material and covers the policies of Governor Pedro Rosselló in detail. See *El desgobierno de Rosselló y Cifuentes* (San Juan: Ediciones M.A.C., 1996) and *Economía política de Puerto Rico: 1950–2000* (San Juan: Ediciones M.A.C., 2003). Orlando Sotomayor explores the issue of social inequality in recent years in "Development and Income Distribution: The Case of Puerto Rico," *World Development* 32, no. 8 (August 2004): 1395–406 and "Poverty and Income Inequality in Puerto Rico," *Review of Income and Wealth* 42 (1996): 49–61. The Brookings Institution has recently issued a massive report on Puerto Rico's economy: Barry P. Bosworth, Susan M. Collins, and Miguel A. Soto-Class, eds., *The Economy of Puerto Rico: Restoring Growth* (Washington, D.C.: Brookings Institution and Center for the New Economy, 2006).

Puerto Rican politics have been examined in dozens of books and hundreds of articles. The twists and turns of party politics between 1898 and 1912 are told in Luis Díaz Soler, *Rosendo Matienzo Cintrón*, 2 vols. (Río Piedras: Instituto de Literatura Puertorriqueña, Universidad de Puerto Rico, 1960), which is centered on the figure of Matienzo. A very influential vision of island politics between 1898 and 1930 has been Angel G. Quintero Rivera, *Conflictos de clase y política en Puerto Rico* (Río Piedras: Huracán, 1976). Rafael

Bernabe offers a critique and alternate views in *Respuestas al colonialismo en la política puertorriqueña, 1899–1929* (Río Piedras: Huracán, 1996). Yet another overview is Pedro A. Cabán, *Constructing a Colonial People: Puerto Rico and the United States, 1898–1932* (Boulder: Westview Press, 1999), which places strong emphasis on the importance of the period of military rule of 1898–1900. For the issues surrounding the extension of U.S. citizenship to Puerto Rico, see José A. Cabranes, *Citizenship and the American Empire: Notes on the Legislative History of the United States Citizenship of Puerto Ricans* (New Haven: Yale University Press, 1979). The early U.S. military presence is discussed in María Eugenia Estades Font, *La presencia militar de Estados Unidos en Puerto Rico, 1898–1918: intereses estratégicos y dominación colonial* (Río Piedras: Huracán, 1988). For an overview up to the 1980s, see José Rodríguez-Beruff, *Política militar y dominación* (Río Piedras: Huracán, 1988).

For a story of the early New Deal with emphasis on party politics and an unhidden admiration for Muñoz Marín, see Thomas Mathews, *Puerto Rican Politics and the New Deal* (Gainesville: University of Florida Press, 1969). The history of the PPD has been the subject of much debate. A critical summary discussion is Emilio Pantojas-García, "Puerto Rican Populism Revisited: The PPD during the 1940s," *Journal of Latin American Studies* 21, no. 3 (October 1989): 521–57. Luis Muñoz Marín tells the story of the route to the creation of the PPD in *Memorias: autobiografía pública, 1940–1952* (San Juan: Fundación Luis Muñoz Marín, 2003). His ideas may also be discerned from his *Historia del Partido Popular Democrático* (San Juan de Puerto Rico: El Batey, 1984). For a vision of the rise of the PPD, which we have strongly criticized here, see Angel Quintero Rivera, "La base social de la transformación ideológica del Partido Popular en la década del 40," in *Cambio y desarrollo en Puerto Rico: la transformación ideológica del Partido Popular Democrático*, edited by Gerardo Navas Dávila (Río Piedras: EUPR, 1985).

For an account of the debates and initiatives on the status question from the Tydings bill to the plebiscite of 1967, see Surendra Bhana, *The United States and the Development of the Puerto Rican Status Question, 1936–1968* (Lawrence: University of Kansas Press, 1975). A detailed and informative history of the making of the ELA and the PPD's shifting policies is Carlos Zapata Oliveras, *Nuevos caminos hacia viejos objetivos: Estados Unidos y el establecimiento del Estado Libre Asociado de Puerto Rico, 1945–1953* (Río Piedras: Comisión Puertorriqueña del Quinto Centenario, 1991). For a survey of the main judicial issues regarding Puerto Rico's status question since 1898, see José Trías Monge, *Puerto Rico: The Trials of the Oldest Colony in the World* (New Haven: Yale University Press, 1997). Frank Otto Gatell argues that the drift of Muñoz away from independence began with the Tydings bill of 1936. See his "Independence Rejected: Puerto Rico and the Tydings Bill of 1936," *Hispanic American Historical Review* 38, no. 1 (February 1958): 25–44. For a contemporary critique of the ELA, largely validated by later events, see Vicente Géigel Polanco, *La farsa del Estado Libre Asociado* (1951; Río Piedras: Editorial Edil, 1981). An early and thorough study of the congressional debates surrounding the creation of the ELA is found in David M. Helfeld's "Congressional Intent and Attitude toward Public Law 600 and the Constitution of the Commonwealth of Puerto Rico," *Revista Jurídica de la Universidad de*

Puerto Rico 21, no. 4 (May–June 1952): 255–315. For a study of the limits of the ELA by one of the advisors who helped devise it, see Carl J. Friedrich, *Puerto Rico: Middle Road to Freedom* (New York: Rinehart, 1959).

The statehood movement has been studied much less than the rival political currents. A sampling of the ideas of the leaders of the movement in different epochs is to be found in Aarón Gamaliel Ramos, ed., *Las ideas anexionistas en Puerto Rico bajo la dominación norteamericana* (Río Piedras: Huracán, 1987). The most complete study is Edgardo Meléndez, *Puerto Rico's Statehood Movement* (Westport, Conn.: Greenwood Press, 1988). The orientation of one of its main leaders in its period of ascendance from the 1960s to the 1980s can be consulted in Carlos Romero Barceló, "Puerto Rico, USA: The Case for Statehood," *Foreign Affairs* 59, no. 1 (Fall 1980): 60–81. The ideas of its most prominent leader after Romero may be gathered from Pedro Rosselló, *The Unfinished Business of American Democracy* (San Juan: n.p., 2005).

The independence movement has included many currents. The ideas of Albizu Campos may be discerned from his *Obras escogidas: 1923–1936*, edited by J. Benjamín Torres in four volumes (San Juan: Editorial Jelofe, 1975–87). The most ambitious biography of Albizu is Marisa Rosado, *Las llamas de la aurora: acercamiento a una biografía de Pedro Albizu Campos* (Santo Domingo: Corripio, 1992). A very complete history of the 1950 Nationalist insurrection is Miñi Seijo Bruno, *La insurrección nacionalista en Puerto Rico 1950* (San Juan: Edil, 1997). For a vision of the nationalist movement as conservative and semifascist, see Luis A. Ferrao, *Pedro Albizu Campos y el nacionalismo puertorriqueño* (Río Piedras: Cultural, 1990). For a response to Ferrao, see Taller de Formación Política, *Pedro Albizu Campos: ¿conservador, fascista o revolucionario?* (Río Piedras: Taller de Formación Política, 1991).

The works of Manuel Maldonado Denis are representative of the *independentista* historiography of the 1950s and 1960s. See, for example, *Puerto Rico: A Socio-historic Interpretation* (New York: Vintage, 1972). For the ideas of the main leader of the Independence Party since the late 1960s, see Rubén Berríos, *La independencia de Puerto Rico* (Mexico City: Editorial Línea, 1983). The ideas and trajectory of a Marxist *independentismo* linked to the communist movement can be gathered from Georg Fromm, *César Andreu Iglesias* (Río Piedras: Huracán, 1977); Arcadio Díaz Quiñones, *Conversación con José Luis González* (Río Piedras: Huracán, 1976); and José Luis González, *El país de cuatro pisos y otros ensayos* (Río Piedras: Huracán, 1980). For a history of the independence movement as seen by the main leader of the MPI and PSP in the 1960s and 1970s, see Juan Mari Bras, *El independentismo en Puerto Rico: su pasado, su presente y su porvenir* (Santo Domingo: Cepa, 1984), and Daniel Nina, *Por la libre: conversaciones con Juan Mari Brás* (Santo Domingo–San Juan: Isla Negra, 1998). For critical histories of the PSP by members of the opposition to Juan Mari's current in the early 1980s, see Héctor Meléndez, *El fracaso del proyecto PSP de la pequeña burguesía* (Río Piedras: Editorial Edil, 1984), and Wilfredo Mattos Cintrón, *Puerta sin casa: crisis del PSP y encrucijada de la izquierda* (San Juan: La Sierra, 1984). For some of the groups involved in armed struggle, see Ronald Fernández, *Los Macheteros: The Wells Fargo Robbery and the Violent Struggle for Puerto Rican Independence* (New York: Prentice Hall, 1987).

The independence movement has been the subject of diverse forms of overt and covert repression. Some aspects of this are discussed in Ivonne Acosta, *La mordaza* (Río Piedras: Edil, 1987); Manuel "Manny" Suárez, *Two Lynchings on Cerro Maravilla: The Police Murders in Puerto Rico and the Federal Government Cover Up* (San Juan: ICP, 2003); Ramón Bosque-Pérez and José Javier Colón-Morera, eds., *Las carpetas: persecución política y derechos civiles en Puerto Rico: ensayos y documentos* (Río Piedras: Centro para la Investigación y Promoción de los Derechos Civiles, 1997), and, by the same editors, *Puerto Rico under Colonial Rule: Political Persecution and the Quest for Human Rights* (Albany: SUNY Press, 2005); Ronald Fernández, *Prisoners of Colonialism: The Struggle for Justice in Puerto Rico* (Monroe, Maine: Common Courage Press, 1994); and José Paraliticci, *Sentencia impuesta: cien años de encarcelamiento por la independenceia de Puerto Rico* (San Juan: Puerto, 2004).

For general histories of the labor movement, see Angel G. Quintero Rivera and Gervasio L. García, *Desafío y solidaridad: breve historia del movimiento obrero puertorriqueño* (Río Piedras: Huracán, 1982), and Miles E. Galvin, *The Organized Labor Movement in Puerto Rico* (Cranbury, N.J.: Associated University Presses, 1979). A collection of documents from the beginnings of the union movement and a bibliography may be found in Angel G. Quintero Rivera, *Lucha obrera en Puerto Rico: antología de grandes documentos en la historia obrera puertorriqueña* (Río Piedras: CEREP, 1971). For the links with the AFL, see Carlos Sanabria, "Samuel Gompers and the American Federation of Labor in Puerto Rico," *Centro* 17, no. 1 (Spring 2005): 141–61. The main leader of the early labor movement tells his story in Santiago Iglesias, *Luchas emancipadoras; crónicas de Puerto Rico*, 2nd ed. (1929; San Juan: Imprenta Venezuela, 1958). For a biography of Iglesias, see Gonzalo F. Córdova, *Resident Commissioner Santiago Iglesias and His Times* (Río Piedras: EUPR, 1993). For the cultural world of the early labor movement, see Rubén Dávila Santiago, *El derribo de las murallas: orígenes intelectuales del socialismo en Puerto Rico* (Río Piedras: Cultural, 1988); and Carmen Centeno Añeses, *Modernidad y resistencia: literatura obrera en Puerto Rico (1898–1910)* (San Juan: Ediciones Callejón, 2005). The major sugarcane workers' and dockworkers' strikes of 1934 and 1938 are recounted in detail by Taller de Formación Política in *Huelga en la caña: 1933–34* (Río Piedras: Huracán, 1982) and *No estamos pidiendo el cielo: huelga portuaria de 1938* (Río Piedras: Huracán, 1988). Basic facts about the history of the Confederación General del Trabajo may be found in Higinio Feliciano Avilés, "Origen, desarrollo y división de la Confederación General de Trabajadores de Puerto Rico" (B.A. thesis, University of Puerto Rico, 1976). A good overview of the evolution of the labor movement in the 1950s and 1990s with provisional strategic conclusions is César F. Rosado Marzán, "Dependent Unionism: Resource Mobilization and Union Density in Puerto Rico" (Ph.D. diss., Princeton University, 2005). For a survey of labor activism in the late 1960s and early 1970s, see Pedro A. Cabán, "Industrial Transformation and Labour Relations in Puerto Rico: From 'Operation Bootstrap' to the 1970s," *Journal of Latin American Studies* 21, no. 3 (October 1989): 559–91. The history of the rise and fall of the Movimiento Obrero Unido is told in Carlos Carrión, "Hacia una historia del Movimiento Obrero Unido," *Pensamiento Crítico* 18, nos. 82–83 (November 1995–February 1996): 35–72.

The number of works on the history of women in Puerto Rico is growing. For diverse early struggles, see Yamila Azize, *La mujer en la lucha* (Río Piedras: Editorial Cultural, 1985). The history of the suffrage movement in particular is told in María Barceló Miller, *La lucha por el sufragio femenino en Puerto Rico, 1896–1935* (Río Piedras: Huracán/Centro Investigaciones Sociales, 1997). *Imposing Decency: The Politics of Sexuality and Race in Puerto Rico, 1870–1920* (Durham, N.C.: Duke University Press, 1999) by Eileen J. Suárez Findlay explores the connection between class and racial privilege, the regulation of sexuality, and the definitions of decency in the early years of U.S. rule. Women's activism in the tobacco industry is analyzed by Ivette M. Rivera-Giusti in "Gender, Labor, and Working-Class Activism in the Puerto Rican Tobacco Industry, 1898–1924" (Ph.D. diss., Binghamton University, 2004). Facts and considerations on the life and ideas of labor and women's emancipation activist Luisa Capetillo may be gathered from Norma Valle Ferrer, *Luisa Capetillo* (Río Piedras: Cultural, 1990); Julio Ramos, ed., *Amor y anarquía: los escritos de Luisa Capetillo* (Río Piedras: Huracán, 1992); and Nancy A. Hewitt, *Southern Discomfort: Women's Activism in Tampa, Florida, 1880s–1920s* (Urbana: University of Illinois Press, 2001). The role of women in the Puerto Rican intellectual sphere as well as other aspects of the work of the *generación del treinta* are explored by Magali Roy-Féquière in *Women, Creole Identity, and Intellectual Life in Early Twentieth-Century Puerto Rico* (Philadelphia: Temple University Press, 2004). For the position of women in the post-1945 process of industrialization, see Palmira Ríos, "Export Oriented Industrialization and the Demand for Female Labor: Puerto Rican Women in the Manufacturing Sector, 1952–1980," *Gender and Society* 4, no. 3 (September 1990): 321–37. For a study of debates and policies regarding contraception, sterilization, and women's sexuality from the 1920s to the 1950s, see Laura Briggs, *Reproducing Empire: Race, Sex, Science, and U.S. Imperialism in Puerto Rico* (Berkeley: University of California Press, 2002). Annette B. Ramírez de Arellano and Conrad Seipp in *Colonialism, Catholicism and Contraception* (Chapel Hill: University of North Carolina Press, 1983) provide the chronology and basic history of population control efforts and the promotion of family planning by private and public agencies. For a documentation of the rise of the new feminism in the late 1960s and 1970s, see Elizabeth Crespo Kebler and Ana Irma Rivera Lassén, *Documentos del feminismo en Puerto Rico: facsímiles de la historia* (San Juan: EUPR, 2001).

Besides the labor and women's movements, the late 1960s witnessed other important mobilizations. For the land occupation and *rescate* movement, see Juan Llanes Santos, *Desafiando al poder: las invasiones de terrenos en Puerto Rico* (Río Piedras: Huracán, 2001), and, over a longer period, Eduardo Bonilla-Silva, "Squatters, Politics, and State Responses: The Political Economy of Squatters in Puerto Rico, 1900–1992" (Ph.D. diss., University of Wisconsin–Madison, 1993). On the environmental movement, see Carmen Concepción, "The Origin of Modern Environmental Activism in Puerto Rico in the 1960s," *International Journal of Urban and Regional Research* 19, no. 1 (March 1995): 112–28. A chronology of the 1960s student movement may be constructed from David Rodríguez Graciani, *¿Rebelión o protesta? La lucha estudiantil en Puerto Rico* (Río Piedras: Puerto, 1972). The 1981 student strike at the University of Puerto Rico is covered in *Las vallas rotas,* edited by Fernando Picó, Milton Pabón, and Roberto Alejandro (Río Piedras: Huracán, 1982). The gay movement has been the object of several studies, including José D. Rodríguez Allende, "El movimiento homosexual puertorriqueño y su impacto" (M.A. thesis, University of Puerto Rico, 2000); Luis Aponte-Parés and Jorge B. Merced, "Páginas Omitidas: The Gay and Lesbian Presence," in *The Puerto Rican Movement: Voices from the Diaspora*, edited by Andrés Torres and José E. Velázquez, 296–315 (Philadelphia: Temple University Press, 1998); and Frances Negrón-Muntaner, "Echoing Stonewall and Other Dilemmas: The Organizational Beginning of a Gay and Lesbian Agenda in Puerto Rico, 1972–1977," pts. 1 and 2, *Centro* 4, no. 1 (Winter 1991–92): 76–95 and no. 2 (Spring 1992): 98–115.

The struggle against the U.S. Navy in Vieques between 1999 and 2003 sparked a resurgence of academic interest in the topic. The reader may begin explorations with Katherine T. McCaffrey, *Military Power and Popular Protest: The US Navy in Vieques, Puerto Rico* (New Brunswick: Rutgers University Press, 2002); César Ayala, "Recent Works on Vieques, Colonialism, and Fishermen," *Centro* 15, no. 1 (Spring 2003): 3–16; and Amílcar Antonio Barreto, *Vieques, the Navy and Puerto Rican Politics* (Gainesville: University of Florida Press, 2002).

Puerto Rican literary debates since 1898 have been numerous and complex. For the policies of Americanization, see Aida Negrón de Montilla, *La americanización de Puerto Rico y el sistema de instrucción pública, 1900–1930* (Río Piedras: Editorial Universitaria, 1977). A picture of the intellectual life in the second decade of the twentieth century can be discerned from Sócrates Nolasco, *Escritores de Puerto Rico* (Manzanillo, Cuba: Editorial El Arte, 1953). The work by Bernabe, *Respuestas al colonialismo* (cited above), discusses the views and political activism of poet Luis Lloréns Torres. For additional views on this influential figure, see Arcadio Díaz Quiñones, "La isla afortunada: sueños liberadores y utópicos de Luis Lloréns Torres," *Sin nombre* 6, no. 1 (July–September 1975): 5–19, and 6, no. 2 (October–December 1975): 5–32; and Noel Luna, "Paisaje, cuerpo e historia: Luis Lloréns Torres," *La Torre* 4, no. 11 (January–March 1999): 53–78. For a biography of Arturo Schomburg, see Flor Piñero de Rivera, *Arturo Schomburg. Un puertorriqueño descubre el legado histórico del negro* (San Juan: Centro de Estudios Avanzados de Puerto Rico y el Caribe, 1989). See also Jesse Hoffnung-Garskof, "The Migrations of Arturo Schomburg: On Being *Antillano*, Negro, and Puerto Rican in New York, 1891–1938," *Journal of American Ethnic History* 21, no. 1 (Fall 2001): 3–49.

A good introduction to the work of the main essayists of the *generación del treinta* are the studies by Arcadio Díaz Quiñones, "Recordando el futuro imaginario: la escritura histórica en la decada del treinta," *Sin Nombre* 14, no. 3 (April–May 1984): 16–35, and "Tomás Blanco: racismo, historia, y esclavitud," in Tomás Blanco, *El prejuicio racial en Puerto Rico*, 19–91 (1942; Río Piedras: Huracán, 1985). *Insularismo*, by Antonio S. Pedreira, the most debated essay in Puerto Rican literary history, may be read along with the marginal notes by one of its main interlocutors (Tomás Blanco) in Mercedes López-Baralt, ed., *Sobre ínsulas extrañas. El clásico de Pedreira anotado por Tomás Blanco* (Río Piedras: EUPR, 2001). Diverse views on Pedreira may be considered by consulting the essays by Díaz Quiñones cited above as well as those included in his *El arte de bregar* (Río Piedras: Callejón, 2000) and the essays by Juan Flores in *Divided Borders: Essays on Puerto Rican Identity* (Houston: Arte Público Press, 1993). In the influential *Literatura y paternalismo en Puerto Rico* (Río Piedras: EUPR, 1993), Juan Gelpí discusses the work of Pedreira and other authors as examples of the paternalist outlook that he argues pervades much of Puerto Rican literature, from the collapse of the world of the *hacienda* to the full impact of urban modernization in the 1970s. Beginning with a consideration of the work of Pedreira, Rafael Bernabe's *La maldición de Pedreira: aspectos de la crítica romántico-cultural de la modernidad en Puerto Rico* (Río Piedras: Huracán, 2002) examines the work of Nemesio Canales, Pedro Albizu Campos, René Marqués, César Andreu Iglesias, Nilita Vientós, and others as sharing a romantic-cultural critique of modernity.

For the poetry of Luis Palés Matos, see *La poesía de Luis Palés Matos*, edited by Mercedes López-Baralt (Río Piedras: EUPR, 1995). The literary work of Muñoz Marín is collected in Marcelino J. Canino Salgado, *La obra literaria de Luis Muñoz Marín* (San Juan: Fundación Luis Muñoz Marín, 1999).

For the relation between the University of Puerto Rico, Columbia University, and the Centro de Estudios Históricos in Madrid in the 1930s, see Consuelo Naranjo, María Dolores Luque, and Miguel A. Puig-Samper, eds., *Los lazos de la cultura. El Centro de Estudios Históricos de Madrid y la Universidad de Puerto Rico, 1916–1939* (Madrid: Centro de Investigaciones Históricas de la Universidad de Puerto Rico/Consejo Superior de Investigaciones Científicas, 2002).

The work by Henry K. Wells, *The Modernization of Puerto Rico* (Cambridge: Harvard University Press, 1969), is the most complete analysis of Puerto Rico since 1898 from the perspective of modernization theory. The *Annals of the American Academy of Political and Social Science* published a special issue (285, of January 1953) dedicated to Puerto Rico. It contains a sampling of the work of sociologists, demographers, economists, political scientists, historians, literary critics, and political leaders linked to the PPD and its project of modernization. The collection *Del cañaveral a la fábrica: cambio social en Puerto Rico* (Río Piedras: Huracán-Academia, 1994), prepared by Eduardo Rivera Medina and Rafael L. Ramírez, is a useful anthology of works in the social sciences from the 1950s and 1960s. Eugenio Fernández Méndez, *La identidad y la cultura* (San Juan: ICP, 1970), is a good example of the ideas of the *puertorriqueñista* wing of the PPD cultural establishment in the 1950s. A sense of the intellectual, artistic, and academic atmosphere of the 1950s may be obtained from Emilio Díaz Valcárcel, *En el mejor de los mundos* (Río Piedras: Cultural, 1991), and Arcadio Díaz Quiñones, "La vida inclemente," in *La memoria rota*, 17–66 (Río Piedras: Huracán, 1993). *Cuentos puertorriqueños de hoy*, edited by René Marqués (Mexico City: Club del Libro Puertorriqueño, 1959), was the preeminent anthology of narrative texts of the main authors of the 1950s. The work of Marqués may be approached from Díaz Quiñones, "Los desastres de la guerra: para leer a René Marqués," *Sin Nombre* 10, no. 3 (October–December 1979): 15–44, or in the chapter dedicated to him in Bernabe, *La maldición de Pedreira*, quoted above. Some elements of the Puerto Rican graphic art efforts of the 1950s may be discerned from J. A. Torres Martinó, *Mirar y ver.*

Textos sobre arte y artistas en Puerto Rico (San Juan: ICP, 2001), as well as in the collection *Puerto Rico: arte e identidad*, mentioned above. *Sponsored Identities: Cultural Politics in Puerto Rico* (Philadelphia: Temple University Press, 1997) by Arlene M. Dávila lucidly discusses government and corporate cultural policies in Puerto Rico. For an attempt to document popular perceptions of culture and identity in Puerto Rico, see Nancy Morris, *Puerto Rico: Culture, Politics, and Identity* (Westport, Conn.: Praeger, 1995).

For the contributions of Rubén del Rosario to a non-nationalist opposition to U.S. colonialism, linked to an open conception of Puerto Rican culture, see Rafael Bernabe, " 'Un Puerto Rico distinto y futuro': lengua, nacionalidad y política en Rubén del Rosario," *Revista de Estudios Hispánicos* 24, no. 1 (1997): 221–36.

Flor de lumbre. Antología poética del grupo Guajana, 1962–2002, edited by Reynaldo Marcos Padua (San Juan: Guajana-ICP, 2004), is a selection of the poetry linked to the journal *Guajana*. For an introduction to the literary innovations and debates of the late 1960s and early 1970s, see Arcadio Díaz Quiñones, "Introducción a *La Guaracha del Macho Camacho*," in Luis Rafael Sánchez, *La guaracha del Macho Camacho* (Madrid: Cátedra, 2000); the collection *Apalabramiento: diez cuentistas puertorriqueños de hoy* (Hanover, N.H.: Ediciones del Norte, 1983), edited by Efraín Barradas, and his critical essay *Para leer en puertorriqueño: acercamiento a la obra de Luis Rafael Sánchez* (Río Piedras: Cultural, 1981). For a colloquium including many of the key authors writing in the 1970s and 1980s both from the island and in the United States, see Asela Rodríguez-Seda de Laguna, ed., *Images and Identities: The Puerto Rican in Two World Contexts* (New Brunswick: Transaction Books, 1987).

El tramo ancla, edited by Ana Lydia Vega (Río Piedras: EUPR, 1988), is a collection of essays by many well-known island authors in the 1980s. Essays by one of the most influential authors since the early 1970s are included in Luis Rafael Sánchez, *No llores por nosotros, Puerto Rico* (Hanover, N.H.: Ediciones del Norte, 1998). For a consideration of the role of women in the emergent literature of the 1970s and 1980s, see Ramón Luis Acevedo, *Del silencio al estallido: narrativa femenina puertorriqueña* (Río Piedras: Cultural, 1991).

The article "De Salvador Brau a la 'novísima' historia: un replanteamiento y una crítica," *Op.Cit.* 4 (1988–89): 9–55, by María de los Angeles Castro, is a very useful overview of the evolution of Puerto Rican historiography. The collection *Puerto Rico: identidad nacional y clases sociales (Coloquio de Princeton)* (Río Piedras: Huracán, 1981), edited by Angel G. Quintero Rivera, José Luis González, Ricardo Campos, and Juan Flores, includes examples of the three strands of the new history of the 1970s: old Marxist and new Left currents and new migration studies, linked to CEREP and the Center for Puerto Rican Studies in Hunter College. For key articles and overviews on the emergence of a new history in the 1970s, see Gervasio García, *Historia crítica, historia sin coartadas: algunos problemas de la historia de Puerto Rico* (Río Piedras: Huracán, 1985). Many of the ideas of one of the more influential new historians are included in Angel G. Quintero Rivera, *Patricios y plebeyos: burgueses, hacendados, artesanos y obreros: las relaciones de clase en el Puerto Rico de cambio de siglo* (Río Piedras: Huracán, 1988). The issue of racism in Puerto Rican culture was most emphatically raised in the 1970s in Isabelo Zenón Cruz, *Narciso descubre su trasero: el negro en la cultura puertorriqueña*, 2nd ed., 2 vols. (Humacao, Puerto Rico: Editorial Furidi, 1975). There is a growing literature on these issues, including Lydia M. González, ed., *La tercera raíz: presencia africana en Puerto Rico* (San Juan: CEREP, 1993); Juan A. Giusti, "Afro–Puerto Rican Cultural Studies: Beyond *Cultura negroide* and *Antillanismo*," *Centro* 8, nos. 1–2 (1996): 57–77; and the work by Roy-Féquière referenced above.

There is an expanding literature on salsa and related genres and practices. See Frances R. Aparicio, *Listening to Salsa: Gender, Latin Popular Music, and Puerto Rican Cultures* (Middletown, Conn.: Wesleyan University Press, 1998); Angel G. Quintero Rivera, *Salsa, sabor y control: sociología de la música tropical* (Mexico City: Siglo XXI, 1999); and Juan Otero Garabis, *Ritmo y nación* (Río Piedras: Callejón, 2000). An introduction to the life of salsa legend Ismael Rivera is Aurora Flores, "Ecua jei! Ismael Rivera, el sonero mayor," *Centro* 16, no. 2 (Fall 2004): 63–67. The life and work of Tito Puente is explored in Steven Loza, *Recordando a Tito Puente* (New York: Random House, 2000). See also the texts by Juan Flores mentioned below.

Salsa was largely born in New York and reminds us of the huge diasporic dimension of the Puerto Rican experience since 1898. The history of the early Puerto Rican *colonia* in New York is told by Virginia Sánchez Korrol, *From Colonia to Community: The History of Puerto Ricans in New York City, 1917–1948* (Westport, Conn.: Greenwood Press, 1983). In *The Puerto Rican Diaspora: Historical Perspectives* (Philadelphia: Temple University Press, 2005), editors Carmen T. Whalen and Víctor Vázquez-Hernández assemble abundant material on Puerto Ricans in New York and beyond. A fascinating personal and political memoir of the same process is Bernardo Vega, *Memoirs of Bernardo Vega: A Contribution to the History of the Puerto Rican Community in New York*, edited by César Andreu Iglesias and translated by Juan Flores (New York: Monthly Review Press, 1984). The pioneering academic study of Puerto Rican migration done by commission of the Puerto Rican government is C. Wright Mills, Clarence Senior, and Rose Kohn Goldsen, *Puerto Rican Journey: New York's Newest Migrants* (New York: Harper and Row, 1950). Like *Puerto Rican Journey*, the study of Nathan Glazer and Daniel P. Moynihan portrayed Puerto Ricans as having no organizational traditions in New York; see their *Beyond the Melting Pot: The Negroes, Puerto Ricans, Jews and Irish of New York City* (Cambridge: MIT Press, 1963). The vision of Puerto Ricans as mired in a culture of poverty was advanced by Oscar Lewis, *La vida: A Puerto Rican Family in the Culture of Poverty* (New York: Random House, 1966). A pioneering and still sound analysis of the mass migration of the postwar years and its link to capitalist accumulation is Centro de Estudios Puertorriqueños/History Task Force, *Labor Migration under Capitalism: The Puerto Rican Experience* (New York: Monthly Review Press, 1979).

Government migration policies are explored in Michael Lapp, "Managing Migration: The Migration Division of Puerto Rico and Puerto Ricans in New York City, 1948–1968" (Ph.D. diss., Johns Hopkins University, 1991). For an abundant source on the history of Puerto Ricans in New York and extensive bibliographies, see Gabriel Haslip-Viera, Angelo Falcón, and Félix Matos-Rodríguez, *Boricuas in Gotham: Puerto Ricans in the Making of Modern New York City* (Princeton: Markus Wiener, 2005). The history and present of Puerto Rican Chicago is studied in Gina M. Pérez, *The Near Northwest Side Story: Migration, Displacement and Puerto Rican Families* (Berkeley: University of California Press, 2004), and Ana Y. Ramos-Zayas, *National Performances: The Politics of Class, Race, and Space in Puerto Rican Chicago* (Chicago: University of Chicago Press, 2003). Carmen T. Whalen studies Puerto Ricans in Philadelphia in *From Puerto Rico to Philadelphia: Puerto Rican Workers and Postwar Economies* (Philadelphia: Temple University Press, 2001). The process of incorporation of Puerto Ricans to U.S. politics and theories that seek to explain it are discussed in Edgardo Meléndez, "Puerto Rican Politics in the United States: Examination of Major Perspectives and Theories," *Centro* 15, no. 1 (Spring 2003): 8–39. For a statistical portrait of the socioeconomic situation of the Puerto Ricans in the United States at the end of the postwar boom, see U.S. Commission on Civil Rights, *Puerto Ricans in the Continental United States: An Uncertain Future* (Washington, D.C.: U.S. Commission on Civil Rights, 1976). The process of incorporation of Puerto Ricans into North American society is discussed from a comparative perspective in Andrés Torres, *Between Melting Pot and Mosaic: African Americans and Puerto Ricans in the New York Political Economy* (Philadelphia: Temple University Press, 1995). For an empirically rich refutation of theories of a Puerto Rican underclass, see Marta Tienda, "Puerto Ricans and the Underclass Debate," *Annals of the American Academy of Political and Social Science* 501 (January 1989): 105–19.

The role of Vito Marcantonio and of the Puerto Rican Left in New York in the 1930s and 1940s is explored by Gerald Meyer in *Vito Marcantonio: Radical Politician, 1902–1954* (Albany: State University of New York Press, 1989). For the life of a key community activist of the 1950s and 1960s, see Antonia Pantoja, *Memoir of a Visionary* (Houston: Arte Público Press, 2002). The rise of a new Puerto Rican activism in the late 1960s is explored in all its variants in *The Puerto Rican Movement: Voices from the Diaspora*, edited by Andrés Torres and José E. Velázquez (Philadelphia: Temple University Press, 1998). For a memoir of the Young Lords, see Miguel "Mickey" Meléndez, *We Took the Streets: Fighting for Latino Rights with the Young Lords* (New York: St. Martin's Press, 2003). For aspects of life in El Barrio in the epoch of neoliberal privatization and social cutbacks, see Arlene M. Dávila, *Barrio Dreams: Puerto Ricans, Latinos, and the Neoliberal City* (Berkeley: University of California Press, 2004). Some of the cultural debates arising from the constant flow of Puerto Ricans to and from the United States, as well as official cultural policy in Puerto Rico, are explored in Jorge Duany, *The Puerto Rican Nation on the Move: Identities on the Island and in the United States* (Chapel Hill: University of North Carolina Press, 2002).

Ruth Glasser has written a fascinating account of Puerto Rican music in New York during the 1920s and 1930s: *My Music Is My Flag: Puerto Rican Musicians and Their New York Communities, 1917–1940* (Berkeley: University of California Press, 1995).

Nuyorican Poetry, edited by Miguel Algarín and Miguel Piñero (New York: William Morrow, 1975), is a pioneering anthology. See also Pedro Pietri, *Puerto Rican Obituary* (New York: Monthly Review Press, 1973). Over the years, critic Efraín Barradas has concerned himself with Puerto Rican literature in the United Status. His articles are collected in *Partes de un todo. Ensayos sobre literatura puertorriqueña en los Estados Unidos* (Río Piedras: EUPR, 1998). Juan Flores has been one of the most prolific and influential commentators on the life and culture of the Puerto Rican diaspora and Puerto Rico in general. His essays may be consulted in several collections he has edited: *Divided Borders: Essays on Puerto Rican Identity* (Houston: Arte Público Press, 1993); *From Bomba to Hip-Hop: Puerto Rican Culture and Latino Identity* (New York: Columbia University Press, 2000); and *La venganza de Cortijo y otros ensayos* (Río Piedras: Huracán, 1997). For interviews with Puerto Rican authors writing in English in the United States, see Carmen Dolores Hernández, *Puerto Rican Voices in English* (Westport, Conn.: Praeger, 1997). For a survey of the evolution of Puerto Rican work in the academia, from its insurgence in the 1960s to possible neutralization, see Pedro A. Cabán, "From Challenge to Absorption: The Changing Face of Latina and Latino Studies," *Centro* 15, no. 2 (Fall 2003). The essays by Lisa Sánchez González in *Boricua Literature: A Literary History of the Puerto Rican Diaspora* (New York: New York University Press, 2001) provocatively argue for the constitution of a Boricua canon, separate from the Puerto Rican (island) counterpart. It contains a sharp critique of the best-selling work by a Puerto Rican in the 1990s, Esmeralda Santiago's memoir of the 1950s, *When I Was Puerto Rican*.

To map out the different intellectual trends in Puerto Rico commonly identified as postmodern or post-Marxist, it is useful to consult the collection *Globalización, nación, postmodernidad*, edited by Luis Felipe Díaz and Marc Zimmerman (San Juan: Ediciones La Casa, 2001). A representative set of essays by a prominent Puerto Rican post-Marxist is Arturo Torrecilla, *El espectro posmoderno: ecología, neoproletario, intelligentsia* (San Juan: Publicaciones Puertorriqueñas, 1995). The journal *Social Text* (issue 38, Spring 1994) is in part dedicated to Puerto Rico and contains a varied sampling of what we would term postmodern/post-Marxist approaches. Some of the most stimulating interventions from a cultural studies perspective politically sympathetic to the radical statehood position may be found in Frances Negrón-Muntaner, *Boricua Pop: Puerto Ricans and the Latinization of American Culture* (New York: New York University Press, 2004). For a consideration of Puerto Rico's and Puerto Ricans' status from a world-system perspective also sympathetic to the radical statehood position, see Ramón Grosfoguel, *Colonial Subjects: Puerto Ricans in a Global Perspective* (Berkeley: University of California Press, 2003). A critique of nationalism from a post-Marxist perspective is Carlos Pabón, *Nación postmortem* (Río Piedras: Ediciones Callejón, 2002). For a left-nationalist response to Pabón, see Luis F. Coss, *La nación en la orilla* (San Juan: Punto de Encuentro, 1996). For a Marxist response to Pabón and other post-Marxist/postmodern currents, see Rafael Bernabe, *Manual para organizar velorios. Notas sobre la muerte de la nación* (Río Piedras: Huracán, 2003).

A collection of essays by one of Puerto Rico's postmodern critics is Luis F. Díaz, *Modernidad literaria puertorriqueña* (San Juan: Isla Negra, 2005). On theater and performance, see the reviews by Lowell Fiet in *El teatro puertorriqueño reimaginado* (Río Piedras: Callejón, 2004). The interest of Puerto Rican authors in hip-hop and related genres may be explored in the collections by Juan Flores cited above and in Raquel Z. Rivera's *New York Ricans from the Hip Hop Zone* (New York: Palgrave-Macmillan, 2003). The debates on Mayra Santos's novel *Sirena Selena vestida de pena* and some of the currents in Puerto Rican cultural studies may be discerned from the contributions included in the special issue dedicated to the novel by the journal *Centro* 15, no. 2 (Fall 2003).

INDEX

Amalgamated Meatcutters Union, 233
American Birth Control League, 207
American Civil Liberties Union (ACLU), 116
American civil rights movement, 7, 256, 277–78
American Colonial Bank, 41
American Communist Party, 114, 131, 139, 141, 147, 156
American Federation of Labor (AFL), 7, 17, 62, 64, 98, 146. *See also* AFL-CIO
American Federation of Teachers, 295, 376 (n. 8)
Americanization: clashes over, 3; and Matienzo Cintrón, 70, 77, 78, 84; failure of, 76; and public education, 76, 88; and avant-garde, 90; and Muñoz Marín, 93; and nonincorporation, 210; consolidating Puerto Rican culture against, 212; and Soto, 213; and loss of Puerto Rican culture, 221; and independence movement, 280
American Jewish Congress, 239
American Labor Party (ALP), 95, 114, 133, 147, 161, 238
American Metal Climax, 192
American Railroad Company, 42
American Sugar Refining Company, 36, 38
American Tobacco Company, 42
Anarchist activists, 64, 66
Anderson, Perry, 306
Andreu Iglesias, César: and Marxism, 139, 359–60 (n. 16); and socialism, 141; and *Pueblos Hispanos*, 147; and independence movement, 153, 226, 369 (n. 5); *Los derrotados*, 214; on Puerto Rican culture, 214, 216, 368 (n. 26); and labor movement, 234; and *La escalera*, 248; and Puerto Rican historiography, 252; and Zenón, 257; *Memorias de Bernardo Vega*, 265
Angiolillo, Michele, 24
Angleró, Teresa, 97
Anglo-Saxonism, 31
Annexationism: and New York revolutionaries, 23, 344 (n. 16); and free trade, 25, 28; and Partido Republicano, 52–53; and Partido Unión, 57; and U.S. citizenship, 57–58; and U.S. colonial policies, 108; and

Puerto Rican culture, 152, 318; and Puerto Rican identity, 208; and Estado Libre Asociado, 211; and Romero Barceló, 280; and voting bloc, 312; and neonationalism, 317; and postmodernism, 327, 328; and Afro–Puerto Ricans, 347 (n. 2). *See also* Statehood
Anthony, Marc, 317
Anti-Americanism, 204
Anticolonialism, 158, 159, 170, 242, 251, 257, 311
Anticommunism, 205
Antiegalitarianism: in U.S., 31
Antillean identity, 75, 125
Aponte, Samuel, 248
Arab-Israeli War (1973), 192–93
Araquistáin, Luis, 59, 92–93, 353 (n. 34); *La agonía antillana*, 92
Arbello, Fernando, 132
Arbenz, Jacobo, 151, 173
Arce, Margot, 91, 117, 128, 134, 135, 203, 211–12
Argentina, 333
Arjona Siaca, Rafael, 112, 134, 154
Arnold, Matthew, 83
Arroyo, Lupercio, 68
Ashford, Bailey K., 19
Asociación de Banqueros, 272
Asociación de Choferes (AC), 140–41
Asociación de Colonos, 103, 104
Asociación de Confinados, 314
Asociación de Maestros, 78
Asociación de Mujeres Graduadas de la Universidad de Puerto Rico, 129
Asociación de Trabajadores Agrícolas (ATA), 243
Asociación de Trabajadores de Hoteles y Restaurantes, 141
Asociación Puertorriqueña de Mujeres Sufragistas, 69
Asociación Puertorriqueña Pro-Bienestar de la Familia, 207–8
Asomante, 129, 216
Aspinall Bill of 1963, 224
ASPIRA, 224, 238–40, 241, 245
Assimilation, 249, 304, 318
Association of Bankers, 272
Association of Coffee Growers, 46

Bryan, William Jennings, 25
Burgos, Julia de: recuperation of itinerary, 11; and cultural/literary debates, 117, 128, 129, 133, 259, 265; "A Julia de Burgos," 129; *Canción de la verdad sencilla*, 129; *Poema en veinte surcos*, 129; "Yo misma fui mi ruta," 129; "Ay Ay de la grifa negra," 129, 131; "Río Grande de Loíza," 131; and *Pueblo Hispanos*, 147
Bush, George H. W., 288

Cabán, Pedro, 27
Cabán Vale, Antonio: "Verde Luz," 250
Cabiya, Pedro, 331
Cabranes, José A., 348 (n. 12)
Cabrera, Francisco Manrique, 91, 218–19, 343 (n. 4)
Cadetes de la República, 109, 110, 116
Cádiz Constitution of 1812, 256
Calderón, Sila, 303, 308–9
Calypso, 220
Campos, Ricardo, 264
Canales, Nemesio: misrepresentation of, 11; and *modernismo*, 79, 80–81; political views of, 80, 81–83; critical spirit of, 89; and Muñoz Marín, 98; Pedreira compared to, 119, 120; and *Juan Bobo*, 129; and cultural-romantic aversion to capitalism, 216; Andreu Iglesias compared to, 368 (n. 26)
Cancel, Mario R., 329
Cancel Miranda, Rafael, 201
Canción protesta, 250. *See also* New song movement
Cánovas, Antonio, 23, 24
Capetillo, Luisa, 11, 44, 63, 66, 85, 252, 265
Capitalism: evolution of international capitalism, 3, 8; capitalist agriculture, 38, 49–50; and Canales, 83; and Blanco, 123; and Corretjer, 127; and labor movement, 139; and Muñoz Marín, 152, 161; role in poverty, 207; cultural critique of, 212; cultural-romantic aversion to, 216–17; and Partido Independentista Puertorriqueño, 228; and imperialism, 249; and deregulation, 290, 291; laissez-faire capitalism, 291, 338; outlaw capitalism, 313–14, 315; and neona-

tionalism, 319; limits on emancipatory proposals, 332–33; and overproduction, 337–38. *See also* U.S. capitalism; World capitalist economy
Capitalist accumulation: competitive logic of, 31; in agriculture, 38, 49; and Canales, 82; Torres on, 305; Santos on, 324; persistence of, 332
Capó, Bobby, 220, 261, 265
Caribbean, 7, 29, 30, 340, 342
Caribbean Basin Initiative, 289
Caribbean Refining Corporation, 192
Carpetas, 227
Carrión, Juan Manuel, 318, 319
Carroll, Henry K., 15, 16, 19, 37, 48, 345 (n. 33)
Casa de las Américas, 248
Casals, Pablo, 203
Castro, Américo, 91
Castro Ros, Andrés, 371 (n. 2)
Catecismo del pueblo, 137
Catholicism and Catholic Church, 16, 84, 105–7, 110, 126–27, 207, 208, 320
Cautiño, Eduardo, 60
Ceiba, 231, 300
Central Aguirre, 30
Central America, 14, 29, 340
Centrales, 36, 38–39, 44, 186
Central Fajardo, 38, 145, 186
Central Puertorriqueña de Trabajadores (CPT), 294, 297
Centro de Arte Puertorriqueño, 219
Centro de Estudios Económicos y Sociales, 17
Centro de Estudios Históricos, 91
Centro de Estudios Puertorriqueños, 251–52, 264
Centro de Investigaciones Históricas, 209
Centro de Investigaciones Sociales (CIS), 203–4, 205
Centro para el Estudio de la Realidad Puertorriqueña (CEREP), 251, 252
Chamber of Commerce, 145, 272
Chapman, Oscar, 158–59, 170, 172
Chardón, Carlos, 101, 102–3, 104, 184, 185, 204
Chávez, Frank, 232–33
Chavez, Linda, 206–7

Chenault, Lawrence R., 367 (n. 7)

Chicago, Illinois, 2, 241–42, 244, 303–5, 307, 376 (n. 13)

China: revolution of 1911, 81

Chinese exclusion, 32, 345 (n. 30)

Church/state separation, 16, 70, 320, 351 (n. 13)

Cigarette industry, 33, 42, 43, 44

Cigar industry, 33, 42–43, 44, 63, 64, 66

Civil Rights Act of 1965, 278

Claridad, 226, 227, 259

Clark, John, 86

Clark, Victor S., 76, 78

Clinton, Bill, 296, 300–301, 305, 309, 314

Coalición, 65, 69, 95, 100, 103, 104, 115, 142, 145

Coffee industry: and social class, 19, 23, 45–46, 252; and U.S. colonial policies, 19–20; stagnation and collapse of, 33, 35, 46; cultivated land devoted to, 35, 45; tobacco industry compared to, 42; boom in, 45, 253; and U.S. market, 46; and Partido Unión, 59, 60, 61; and Laguerre, 128; and Puerto Rican historiography, 253

Cold War, 148, 152, 193

Colectivo Orgullo Gay (COG), 236

Collado Martell, Alfredo, 93, 357 (n. 1)

Collazo, Oscar, 165

Colombia, 29

Colón, Jesús: and labor movement, 44, 85; and Spanish language, 68; and socialism, 87, 238, 340, 352 (n. 26); and International Workers Order, 114, 141; writings of, 147–48; *Puerto Rican Sketches*, 262; and Moscow show-trials, 361 (n. 34); and Puerto Rican culture, 361 (n. 33)

Colón, Noel, 225, 243

Colón, Willie, 265

Colón Gordiany, Francisco, 140, 141, 146, 154

Colonialism: noncolonial imperialism, 1, 2, 30, 162; and U.S. policies toward political relationship with Puerto Rico, 7, 10, 19–20, 24–28, 29, 32, 52–55, 58–59, 61, 73, 75–76, 78, 108, 158, 164, 167, 251, 283, 344 (n. 21); and economics, 7, 182, 204, 205, 268–70, 273–75, 277; and Puerto Rican identity, 10, 61, 75; and U.S. English language policies, 10, 61,

75–76, 78; accommodation of U.S. colonial policies, 15, 53, 55, 56, 59, 73, 108; and coffee industry, 19–20; democracy incompatible with, 25; and Foraker Act, 52; and U.S. citizenship, 57–58; and cultural/literary debates, 75, 258–59; and Muñoz Marín, 85, 176; and U.S. corporations, 108; and United Nations debate, 172–73; role in poverty, 205, 207, 275; and Puerto Rican culture, 210, 212, 213, 222, 249; Marqués on, 212; and Partido Independentista Puertorriqueño, 228; and student movements, 230; and Fanon, 248; and Maldonado Denis, 250; and neonationalism, 319; and Puerto Rico as independent neocolony, 339

Colonos (cane growers): and consolidation of rural proletariat, 36; links to *centrales*, 38–39; subordination to capital, 42, 50; pressures on, 43; and Plan Muñoz Marín, 101; and Plan Chardón, 103, 104; opposition to agrarian reform, 183, 184, 185, 186

Columbia University, Bureau of Applied Social Research, 205

Comandos Armados de Liberación, 281

El Comité, 243

Comité Amplio de Organizaciones Sociales, Sindicales, Políticas, Comunales, Estudiantiles y Religiosas (CAOS), 297–99, 311

Comité de Apoyo del Migrante Puertorriqueño, 243

Comité de Defensa Republicano, 54

Comité Homosexual Latino, 237

Comité Pro Rescate y Deasarrollo de Vieques, 300

Committee of Pacific Islands and Puerto Rico, 37

Commonwealth of Puerto Rico. *See* Estado Libre Asociado

Commonwealth Oil Refining Company, 192, 193

Communist International, 139, 362 (n. 51)

Communist Party, 110, 114

Communist Party of Puerto Rico, 138–39, 154

Community activism, 237, 304, 305

Competition, 291, 292, 313

Concepción de Gracia, Gilberto, 116, 141, 161, 228

Concilio de Organizaciones Hispanas (COH), 245

Concilio General de Trabajadores (CGT), 295

Conde, Eduardo, 17

Confederación General del Trabajo (CGT), 95, 136, 141, 145–46, 154, 156, 161, 183, 202, 232

Confederación General del Trabajo (CGT) Auténtica, 154

Congreso de los Pueblos, 238

Congreso Pro Independencia (CPI), 153, 154, 156–57

Congress of Industrial Organizations (CIO), 7, 109, 138, 146, 306. *See also* AFL-CIO

Conservatism: and Albizu Campos, 105, 112, 254; and Partido Nacionalista, 109, 139; and Puerto Rican identity, 121, 122, 319, 320; and Pedreira, 127; and *generación del treinta*, 133; and Marqués, 212; and Puerto Rican culture, 221–22; and feminism, 235, 236; and gay organizations, 236; and Partido Unión, 253; and possessing classes, 254–55

Construction industry, 39, 64

Consumer boycotts, 96, 97

Contraception, 180, 207–8, 235, 236, 320. *See also* Birth control

Cooperatives, 104, 185

Copper deposits, 192, 231

Cordero, Rafael, 75

Córdova Dávila, Félix, 57

La Correspondencia, 16

Corretjer, Juan Antonio: and avant-garde, 88; and Partido Nacionalista, 90, 107, 109, 147; indictment of, 110; on modernity, 127; and *Pueblos Hispanos*, 131, 147–48; and new middle age, 216; *Alabanza en la torre de Ciales*, 218, 256; and Brown, 250; Fromm on, 251; and racism, 257; and Zenón, 257; and Puerto Rican culture in New York, 265

Cortés Cabán, David, 373 (n. 23)

Cortijo, Rafael, 220, 257, 265

Costa, Marithelma, 373 (n. 23)

Cost of living issues, 233

Criollo culture, 19, 45, 74–75, 322

Cruz, Bobby, 265

Cruz Monclova, Lidio, 209, 251

Cuadrillas, 15

Cuba: as U.S. protectorate, 7, 56, 96; revolution of 1959, 7, 193, 202, 226, 227, 247–48; revolution of 1933, 7, 336; and Spanish-American War, 14; sugar industry in, 18, 36, 38, 41, 92, 96, 100, 336; and Puerto Rican coffee, 19, 45; Spanish administration of, 20; insurgency of, 23; and free trade, 25; U.S. recognition of independence, 27; and Platt Amendment, 29, 102; U.S. interventions in, 30; Africanization of, 92; and U.S. capital, 150; isolation of, 317; xenophobic laws in, 353 (n. 32)

Cuban identity, 20

Cuban War of Independence of 1868–78, 18, 21

Culebra, 1, 231, 300

Cultural/literary debates: developments in, 9, 73, 202; and Puerto Rican identity, 12, 93, 117, 134, 332; and colonialism, 75, 258–59; and Americanization, 76; and Spanish language, 76, 326; and *modernismo*, 79–85, 119; and realism, 84; and labor movement, 85–86; and Schomburg, 86–88; and avant-garde, 88–91, 93; and foreign visitors, 91–94; and Great Depression, 94, 116, 247; and Pedreira, 117, 118–20; and women, 117, 128–29, 247, 259; and Ateneo forum, 134; and social science, 202, 203–4; and modernization, 202, 213, 321, 327; and popular culture, 202, 255, 259, 260; and social movements, 247; and popular music, 259, 265–66; and neonationalism, 316, 317–20; and postmodernism, 316, 325–29, 332, 333; and new aestheticism, 329–33

Cultural nationalism, 118, 121

Cultural universalism, 134–35, 203

cummings, e. e., 133

Curet, Catalino "Tite," 257, 265

Danzas, 123–24, 265, 322

Darío, Rubén, 79, 124

Dávila, Angelamaria, 372 (n. 2)

Dávila, Arlene, 303, 304, 305, 317, 322

Dávila Colón, Luis, 317

Davis, George W., 31–32, 345 (n. 33)

Debs, Eugene, 62

Decolonization, 179, 248, 256, 339

De Diego, José: and Partido Autonomista, 23; and independence, 57, 109; and Hispanophile rejection of U.S. rule, 60; and *radicales*, 72; and cultural/literary debates, 73, 79, 89, 351 (n. 13); and English language, 78; and Puerto Rican identity, 79, 84, 89; and Cadetes de la República, 110; Maldonado Denis on, 249; and Puerto Rican historiography, 252, 253; Lloréns Torres compared to, 253

De Diego Padró, José, 89

De Granda, Germán, 221

Delano, Irene, 219

Delano, Jack, 219, 261

Del Castillo, José, 231

De Leon, Daniel, 62

Delgado, Emilio R., 89, 90, 132, 133

De los Ríos, Fernando, 91

Del Rosario, Rubén, 11, 91, 112, 153, 221–22, 341

La Democracia, 16, 46, 92, 99, 116, 128, 136

Democracy: and U.S. colonial role, 25; and Iglesias, 62; and Matienzo Cintrón, 70, 77, 78, 253; and Hostos, 70–71; and López Landrón, 72–73, 253; and Canales, 81; and Ateneo forum, 134; and Public Law 600, 170; and draft, 230; radical democracy, 332, 339–40

Democratic Party (U.S.), 25, 68, 278, 306

De Onís, Federico, 91

Development Bank of Puerto Rico, 184

Díaz, Luis Felipe, 329, 331

Díaz Alfaro, Abelardo: *Terrazo*, 357 (n. 10)

Díaz González, Abraham, 230

Díaz Quiñones, Arcadio, 125, 252, 254, 322

Díaz Soler, Luis, 209

Díaz Valcárel, Emilio, 212, 218

Diepalismo, 89

Dietz, James, 199, 292

Dockworkers: strikes of, 63, 64, 109, 138, 141

Dole, Robert, 289

Dominican Republic, 7, 20, 23, 30, 38, 41, 102, 323, 341, 353 (n. 32)

Dorfman, Benjamin, 150

Downes v. Bidwell (1901), 27

Draft: opposition to, 225, 229, 230

Drug trade, 313–14, 315

Duany, Jorge, 322–23

Dubinsky, David, 232

Du Bois, W. E. B., 161

Duchesne Winter, Juan, 325–26, 327, 328

Dumont, Pedro J., 141–42

Dylan, Bob, 319

Echevarría, Moisés, 63

Economic Development Administration (Fomento), 190, 191, 192

Economics: alternating phases of, 2, 3, 8; slowdown cycles, 2, 3, 12, 291; expansion cycles, 2, 12, 38, 66, 88, 177–78, 179, 267, 274, 275, 291, 335–36, 338; and Puerto Rican migration, 3, 161, 179, 194, 270; and colonial dependent structure, 7, 182, 204, 205, 268–70, 273–75, 277; and U.S. capital, 10, 149, 151, 178, 179, 182, 193, 205, 268, 275, 315, 335; influence of U.S. invasion on, 32; and aftermath of Spanish-American War, 33; Carroll's diversification recommendation, 37; and Sugar Act of 1934, 101, 102; and Plan Chardón, 102–3; and Partido Nacionalista, 105; and independence, 111, 149–50, 307; and Muñoz Marín, 113, 149, 150, 153, 179–80, 189, 201; and Pedreira, 120; and Blanco, 123; and Puerto Rico's political relationship with U.S., 149, 150, 151, 153, 178, 275, 336–37; and Partido Popular Democrático, 179–80, 189, 198–99, 201, 231, 237, 245, 273, 289, 293, 309; slow growth of 1970s, 198; denationalization of economy, 199; reconfiguration of 1960s, 223; and Partido Independentista Puertorriqueño, 229; and recession of 1974, 233, 245–46, 267, 336; and recession of 1981–83, 267; and Hernández Colón, 267, 268–72; and gross national product, 267, 270–71, 275; and gross domestic product, 270–72, 276; and federal funds, 272–73, 277, 278, 338; informal economy, 277, 313–14, 315; and statehood movement, 279, 327; and Romero Barceló, 285; and Rosselló, 292, 294. *See also* World capitalist economy

Education. *See* Public education; University of Puerto Rico

Eisenhower, Dwight D., 173, 175

Ejército Popular Boricua-Macheteros, 283–84, 311

Ellington, Duke, 132

El Salvador, 289, 317

Emmanuelli, Juan, 114, 141, 238

Enamorado Cuesta, José, 48, 97, 107, 141, 153, 353 (n. 34), 355 (n. 29), 367 (n. 7)

English language: as vernacular of Puerto Rican diaspora, 2; U.S. colonial policies on, 10, 61, 75–76, 78; protests over imposition of, 76, 78–79, 88–89; and Puerto Rican literature, 133, 222, 263, 331, 368 (n. 25); and Vergne Ortiz, 138; end of imposition of, 201, 210; U.S. "English-only" movement, 293; and statehood, 376 (n. 2)

Ensayo Obrero, 17

Entrepreneurial initiative, 291, 292, 293

Environmental issues, 192

Environmental movement, 231, 237, 245–46, 247, 292, 297

Episcopal Church, 231, 243

La Escalera, 248, 250, 251, 260

Escudero, Ralph, 132

Escuela Ferrer, 85

Espartaco, 98

Espiritistas, 16

Estadistas Unidos, 225

Estado Libre Asociado (ELA; Commonwealth of Puerto Rico): and Guerra Mondragón, 84; creation of, 153, 161, 162, 179; and Muñoz Marín, 153, 157, 161, 162–63, 168–69, 171, 175–76; and Partido Popular Democrático, 162, 163, 171, 172, 173, 174, 175, 200; and Public Law 600, 163–65, 167–70; and self-government, 168, 169, 171–73, 175, 176, 179; and statehood, 173, 178, 278, 288–89; autonomism, 173, 178, 286, 311; continuing debate on, 173–78; support for, 177;

and Puerto Rican migration, 194–95; and Casals, 203; and Puerto Rican identity, 208–9, 211, 293; and Fernós-Murray bill of 1959, 224; and plebiscites, 224, 293, 294, 299; and ASPIRA, 239; and Puerto Rican diaspora, 243; and New Compact, 246; José Luis González on, 255; and government employment, 267, 273, 292; and toll-gate tax, 272; and federal funds, 273; and nonincorporation, 290; and Vieques, 309; lack of U.S. support for, 310; and Federal Death Penalty Act, 314

La Estampa puertorriqueño, 219

Estampas de San Juan, 219

Esteves, Pedro, 85

Esteves, Sandra María, 263; "Not Neither," 322

Euforismo, 89

Europe, James Reese, 132

Export production, 19, 33, 41, 179–80, 335

FANIA, 266

Fanon, Frantz, 242, 248

Farinacci, Jorge, 283–84, 311

Farm Security Administration, 219

Fascism: nationalist movement as fascist, 105, 109, 250, 251, 365 (n. 14); and Albizu Campos, 109–10, 147; and Corretjer, 127–28, 148; and Miranda, 133; and Muñoz Marín, 161; and labor movement, 338

FBI, 283, 305, 311

Federación de Maestros, 295, 376 (n. 8)

Federación de Mujeres Puertorriqueñas, 370 (n. 17)

Federación de Universitarios Pro Independencia, 226, 230

Federación Libre de Trabajadores (FLT): organization of, 17; and U.S. colonial policies, 53; *turbas*' targeting of, 54, 61; and Partido Unión, 55, 61, 63, 64; and American Federation of Labor, 62, 64, 98; membership of, 63; and women's suffrage, 66; journal of, 85; dominance of, 95; and Great Depression, 97; and Muñoz Marín, 98; and Albizu Campos, 105; and Partido Laborista Puro, 142; and Confederación

General del Trabajo, 145–46; recovery of history of, 252

Federación Regional de los Trabajadores (FRT), 17

Federal Death Penalty Act, 314

Federal Emergency Relief Act, 97

Federal Labor Standards Act, 141

Federal Relations Act, 163, 168, 173, 174, 175. *See also* Jones Act of 1917

Federal Telecommunications Act of 1996, 376 (n. 6)

Feliciano, Cheo, 265

Feliú, Angel María, 114

Feminism: social feminism, 68–69; and Belaval, 121–22; and sterilization programs, 208; second-wave feminism, 235–37; and cultural/literary debates, 259, 260

Fernández, Annie, 248

Fernández García, Benigno, 60, 103, 136, 141, 145–46

Fernández García, Rafael, 102

Fernández Méndez, Eugenio, 208

Fernández Retama, Roberto: *Calibán*, 255

Fernós, Antonio, 104, 162, 163, 164, 165, 169, 171, 172, 175, 176

Fernós-Murray bill of 1959, 224

Ferrao, Gerardo, 140

Ferrao, Luis Angel, 109

Ferré, José A., 104, 145

Ferré, Luis A., 225, 231, 232, 233, 245

Ferré, Rosario: *Papeles de Pandora*, 258; *Maldito Amor*, 259; *Sitio a Eros*, 259; on Pedreira, 373 (n. 20)

Ferrer, Francisco, 77

Ferrer y Ferrer, José, 17, 63

Figueroa, Luis A., 23

Figueroa, Sotero, 88, 344 (n. 16)

Figueroa Cordero, Angel, 201

Figueroa v. People of Puerto Rico (1956), 173–74

First National City Bank, 42

Fitzsimmons, Patrick J., 145

500-acre law: and beet lobby pressure, 36–37; enforcement of, 37, 64, 84, 103; and labor movement, 43, 64; and agrarian reform, 50–51, 186; and Partido Unión, 72; and U.S. Supreme Court, 143–44; and Fitzsim-

mons, 145; and Partido Popular Democrático, 182; and sugar industry, 184

Flores, Irving, 201

Flores, Juan, 255–56, 261, 264, 316, 322, 323

Flores, Pedro, 131, 265

Florida, 41, 307

Flynn, Elizabeth Gurley, 85

Fomento (Economic Development Administration), 190, 191, 192

Foner, Eric, 31

Font Suárez, Eugenio, 141

Foraker Act of 1900: and civilian government, 25–26, 28; and tariffs, 26, 36; and U.S. market, 26–27, 36; and free trade, 33; González Muñoz on, 40; and U.S. colonial policies, 52; and Partido Unión, 55; implications of, 56; and Hostos, 70; and Matienzo Cintrón, 70; and rolling over of budget, 72; and Public Law 600, 163; as Organic Act of Congress, 174; and opposition to statehood, 279–80; and Carroll, 345 (n. 33)

Ford, Gerald, 231, 246, 286

Foster, William Z., 147

Frade, Ramón, 350 (n. 45)

France, 29, 47, 333

Free association status, 287–88, 299

Free market, 303

Freemasons, 16

Freethinkers, 16, 19, 320

Free trade: and annexation, 25, 28; effects of, 33, 35, 277, 336; and sugar industry, 35, 36–37, 40; and Muñoz Marín, 150; and neoliberalism, 275; and statehood, 280; and New Right, 291

Frente Socialista, 311

Frente Unido Femenino Pro Convención Constituyente, 129

Frente Unido Pro-Constitución de la República, 112

Friedrich, Carl, 175, 177, 204

Fromm, Georg, 248, 251

Frost, Robert, 133

Fuerzas Armadas de Liberación Nacional (FALN), 244, 283, 305

Fuerzas Vivas, 99

Fuller, Melville W., 31, 177
Fundamentalism, 328–29

Gag Law of 1948 (Law 53), 160, 167, 218
Galbraith, John K., 204
Gamble, Clarence J., 207–8
García, Gervasio, 248, 250, 251
García, Oscar, 114
García Passalacqua, Juan M., 287–88
García Ramis, Magali: *La familia de todos
    nosotros*, 258; *Felices Días, Tío Sergio*, 259;
    "Hostos, bróder, esto está dificil," 259–60;
    and nostalgia, 260
Garvey, Marcus, 87
Garveyism, 7
Gay Liberation Front, 236
Gay organizations, 236–37
Gays: and Puerto Rican identity, 320, 321
Géigel, Vicente: and avant-garde, 88; and
    Partido Nacionalista, 89; and University
    of Puerto Rico, 92, 203; and *Indice*, 93, 357
    (n. 1); and independence, 100, 112, 153, 157,
    167, 211; and Ateneo, 134; and Partido Pop-
    ular Democrático, 138, 144, 157, 211; and
    Muñoz Marín, 138, 157, 167, 176; *La farsa del
    Estado Libre Asociado*, 167, 211; *El despertar de
    un pueblo*, 211; and feminism, 236
Gelpí, Juan, 320–21
Gender issues: and Nuyoricans, 247
Generación del cuarenta, 209
Generación del treinta: and *plena*, 86; and
    Puerto Rican identity, 117, 261, 320–21; and
    Puerto Rican migration, 131, 132–33; and
    periodization, 142; and Partido Popular
    Democrático, 202, 208, 211; and Great
    Depression, 247; and Maldonado Denis,
    249; literary canon of, 252, 357 (n. 10);
    rejection of mass culture, 324
Gentrification, 303–4, 376–77 (n. 13)
George, Catherine, 86
Georgetti, Eduardo, 60, 72, 99, 100
Gerena, Victor, 283
Gerena Valentín, Gilberto, 238
Germany, 29
Gil, Carlos, 325
Gilded Age, 31

Gil de la Madrid, José, 159, 233
Giuliani, Rudolph, 303
Glazer, Nathan, 206
Globalization, 311, 320, 328, 331, 332–33
Gómez, Carmen, 68
Gómez, José Gualberto, 88
Gómez, Labor, 209
Gompers, Samuel, 7, 17, 62, 63
González, José Luis: on Albizu Campos, 109;
    En la sombra, 128; and *Pueblos Hispanos*, 147;
    and colonialism, 212; "El ausente," 213; and
    Hemingway, 213; *Paisa*, 213; "La noche que
    volvimos a ser gente," 214; and Puerto
    Rican migration, 214; and Puerto Rican
    historiography, 252, 254; "El país de cuatro
    pisos," 254, 255; *Balada de otro tiempo*, 255;
    and Zenón, 257; and *plebeyismo*, 260; and
    Marxism, 316; and break with *generación
    del treinta*, 321; and realism, 331
González, Josemilio, 218
González, Juan, 242
González García, Manuel: *Gestación*, 84
González García, Matías, 350 (n. 45)
González Muñoz, Carmen, 40
González Nieves, Roberto, 319–20
Goodsell, Charles T., 204
Gore, Al, 296, 376 (n. 10)
Grant, Pedro, 233, 235
Grau, Ramón, 96
Great Depression, 43, 44, 48, 51, 94, 95–97,
    116, 247
Grenada, 289
Grillo, Frank, 220
Grito de Lares, 18
Grosfoguel, Ramón, 327, 328, 339–40
Gruening, Ernest, 102, 103, 104, 110, 111, 115–
    16, 144
Guadalupe, Ismael, 300
Guajana, 248, 250, 371–72 (n. 2)
Guam, 1, 7, 24, 268
Guánica Sugar Company, 186, 193
Guatemala, 173
Guerra, Ramiro, 92, 107
Guerra Mondragón, Miguel, 33, 79, 80–81, 83,
    84, 89, 98, 100, 103
Guevara, Ernesto, 242, 247–48

Johnson, Lyndon B., 175–76, 240, 241, 278
Johnston, Bennett, 287, 288, 289
Johnston, Olin D., 170
Jones, William A., 58
Jones Act of 1917, 37, 57–59, 143–44, 163, 165, 174, 188, 280, 348 (n. 12)
Juan Bobo, 129

Kafka, Franz, 217
Kelly, Frank, 85
Kennecott Copper, 192
Kennedy, John F., 175–76, 202, 224
Keynesian synthesis, 204, 338
Kipling, Rudyard, 24, 28
Kolko, Gabriel, 158, 306
Kollontai, Alexandra, 259
Korean War, 161

Labor force mobility, 275
Labor force participation rates, 267, 269, 273
Labor movement: in U.S., 7, 25, 29, 31, 306, 344 (n. 21); rise of, 16–17; and World War I, 35, 64; and sugar industry, 39; and tobacco industry, 44; and reformist colonial politics, 53, 61–66; *turbas'* targeting of, 54; and Partido Unión, 55, 56; and American Federation of Labor, 62; right to assemble and strike, 63; mobilizations of, 63–64; and women, 64, 66, 85–86, 321; autonomous cultural sphere generated by, 76; De Diego on, 79; and Lloréns Torres, 80, 141; and Capetillo, 85; alternative cultural initiatives of, 85–86; and Great Depression, 95; and Muñoz Marín, 98–99, 141–42, 145–46, 154, 224, 232; and Partido Nacionalista, 105, 109, 138, 139; and Left, 138–42, 233; and Partido Popular Democrático, 138, 141–42, 145–46, 154, 156, 202, 232; and independence movement, 139, 154, 227, 233, 252; and Partido Communista, 140; and isolation of radicals, 154; fragmented structure of, 156; and Delano, 219; coordinating efforts of, 223; remobilization of, 232–35, 237, 246, 247; and violence, 233, 283, 299; and Maldonado Denis, 249; and Puerto Rican historiography, 252; Quintero

Rivera on, 252; and Partido Nuevo Progresista, 281, 297–98; and recession of 1974, 285; and Rosselló, 292–93, 294, 295–96; demobilization of, 294–95, 299; and privatization, 297–98; and Calderón, 308; and Frente Socialista, 311; and fascism, 338. *See also* Strikes
Lafeber, Walter, 249
La Follette, Robert M., 68, 98
Laguerre, Enrique, 117, 134, 231; *La llamarada*, 128
Lair, Clara, 128, 129
Lanauze Rolón, José, 116, 138, 139, 141, 142, 153, 207
Land Authority, 145, 184–85
Landing, Jorge Luis, 159
Land tenure: and free trade, 33; and capitalist agriculture, 38, 49–50; concentration of landownership, 47–48; and pre-1898 era, 47–49, 113; reduction in concentration of landownership, 49, 347 (n. 31); land reforms, 137, 182, 184–87; and Partido Popular Democrático's agrarian reform, 186; comparative data for, 186, 187; and *rescates*, 231–32; and Partido Unión, 253
Lares rebellion of 1868, 18, 80, 119, 123, 251, 311, 352 (n. 24)
Lassalle, Beatriz, 68
Latin America: U.S. policies on, 68; and Matienzo Cintrón, 77; student activism in, 89; populism in, 151; and unity, 248; and Puerto Rico's living standards, 275; gross domestic product in, 275, 276; Rama on, 320
Latin American Development Organization, 241
Lausell, Luis, 281
Laviera, Tato, 263
Law 45, 298–99, 376 (n. 8)
Law 53 (Gag Law of 1948), 160, 167, 218
Law 130, 295
Law 134, 295, 298
Lebrón, Lolita, 201
Lee, Consuelo, 147
Left: and Puerto Rican *colonia* in New York, 95, 202; in Cuba, 96; and Muñoz Marín,

138; and labor activism, 138–42, 233; Puerto Rican Left in New York, 147–48; and Partido Independentista Puertorriqueño, 229; and *rescates*, 232; and feminism, 235; and Emmanuelli, 238; and Puerto Rican diaspora, 244; and cultural/literary debates, 248, 316; impact of, 251; and racial issues, 256; and Partido Nuevo Progresista, 281; and Romero Barceló, 284; debates within, 285–87; and Soviet Union, 317; and Vieques, 325, 326; and imperialism, 328

Lenin, V., 49

Leontief, Wassily, 204

Lesbianism, 235, 320, 321

Lesser Antilles, 254

Levins, Richard, 27–28, 248, 251

Levis, José Elías, 85

Lewis, Gordon K., 109, 248, 249–50, 251, 365 (n. 14)

Lewis, John L., 148

Lewis, Oscar, 206

Liberalism: in Spain, 20, 21, 22; in Puerto Rico, 20–22, 27, 30; and U.S. colonial policies, 27–28, 251; and Acosta, 86. *See also* Neoliberalism

Liga Femínea, 68

Liga Internacionalista de los Trabajadores, 236

Liga Puertorriqueña e Hispana, 68

Liga Socialista, 300

Liga Social Sufragista, 68, 69

Lima, José María, 372 (n. 2)

Lindsay, Vachel, 98

Literacy rate, 74, 180

Living standards, 177–78, 181, 182, 198–200, 201, 226, 240, 273–75, 292, 364 (n. 30)

Lloréns Torres, Luis: misrepresentation of, 11; and *radicales*, 71, 72; leaving active politics, 73, 80; and cultural/literary debates, 73, 90; and *modernismo*, 79, 80–81; "Canción de las Antillas," 79, 260; *El grito de Lares*, 80; "Un sermón en la bolsa," 80; "Banquete de gordos," 80, 141; "Soliloquio del soldado," 80, 141; and *hacendado* class, 80, 141, 320; and independence, 109; and Partido Popular Democrático, 138; De

Diego compared to, 253; paternalistic ideology of, 253, 320

Lodge, Henry Cabot, 14, 29

Lodge, Henry Cabot, Jr., 173

López, José, 305

López, Ramon, 319

López Adorno, Pedro, 373 (n. 23)

López Cruz, Francisco, 131

López de Victoria, Tomás, 165

López Landrón, Rafael: as critic of U.S. colonial policy, 25; and Partido de la Independencia, 72, 141; and democracy, 72–73, 253; and women, 73, 350 (n. 44); and Vergne Ortiz, 138–39; and Font Suárez, 141; and independence, 361 (n. 33)

Lora, Federico, 243

Louisiana, 41

Löwy, Michael, 119

Luce, Henry, 1

Luciano, Felipe, 242

Lugo, Clara, 48, 112–13, 129, 153

Lugo Filippi, Carmen, 260; *Vírgenes y mártires*, 258

Maceo, Antonio, 88

Machado, Gerardo, 96

Macías, Manuel, 15

Maddison, Angus, 3, 8

Madonna, 319

Magruder, Calvert, 174, 175

Mahan, Alfred Thayer, 29, 345 (n. 28)

Malcolm, George A., 145

Maldonado, José, 343 (n. 6)

Maldonado Denis, Manuel, 248–49, 250, 316

Mambo, 220, 266

Mandel, Ernest, 3, 8

Manufacturing sector: and Moscoso, 179–80; and expansion of factory production, 181, 336; and Section 936, 269, 312; and labor movement, 295; unemployment in, 341

Mao Tse-Tung, 242

Marcano, Juan S., 63, 85

Marcantonio, Vito, 95, 113–15, 116, 133, 141, 147, 161, 205, 238

Marcus, Joseph, 39

Marcuse, Herbert, 248

Mariátegui, José Carlos, 255

Mari Brás, Juan, 159, 226, 286, 287, 310–11

Marichal, Carlos, 219

Marín, Francisco, 88, 344 (n. 16)

Marín, Ramón Juliá: *La gleba*, 84

Markham, Edwin, 98–99, 141, 202

Marqués, René: and Partido Popular Democrático, 120; *Cuentos puertorriqueños de hoy*,
212, 259; and Puerto Rican culture, 212–13;
La carreta, 213; narrations and essays of,
216; and independence, 218; and Centro de
Arte Puertorriqueño, 219; paternalistic
ideology of, 253, 320; and Williams, 322;
Rosario Ferré on, 373 (n. 20)

Martell, Esperanza, 243

Martínez, Antonia, 230

Martínez-Márquez, Alberto, 329

Martínez Nadal, Rafael, 65

Martorell, Antonio, 260

Marxism: and capitalist agriculture, 49; and
Muñoz Marín, 98; and Andreu Iglesias,
139, 359–60 (n. 16); and Corretjer, 218; and
Partido Independentista Puertorriqueño,
229; and Maldonado Denis, 249; and
Levins, 251; and Puerto Rican migration,
252; and cultural/literary debates, 316, 333;
and Puerto Rican historiography, 325; and
utopia, 329

Marxism-Leninism, 227

Masters, Edgar Lee, 98

Matienzo Cintrón, Rosendo: misrepresentation of, 11; and Puerto Rican self-
determination, 12, 52; political leadership
of, 23, 80; as critic of U.S. colonial policy,
25, 52–53, 70, 77, 78–79; and independence,
52, 70, 77, 109, 341, 361 (n. 33); on Barbosa,
54–55; and Partido Unión, 55, 61, 71–72, 79;
initiatives of, 69–70, 350 (n. 41); and Americanization, 70, 77, 78, 84; and democracy,
70, 77, 78, 253; and cultural/literary debates, 73, 89; and Puerto Rican culture,
77–78, 79, 341; and Partido de la Independencia, 141; "Pancho Ibero," 260

Matos Paoli, Francisco: *Canto de la locura*, 218

Mattos, Wilfredo, 287

May Day celebrations, 17

McCarthyism, 202

McIntyre, Frank, 58

McKinley, William, 14, 25, 62

Meader, George, 170

Medicaid taxes, 273, 374 (n. 18)

Medina, Nilda, 300

Medina Ramírez, Ramón, 109

Melendes, Joserramón: *Desimos désimas*, 258

Meléndez, Concha, 128

Meléndez, Héctor, 287

Meléndez, Miguel, 242

Meléndez Muñoz, Miguel: "Portalatín in
Bankruptcy," 43; "Portalatín's Uncertainty," 43; "Prosperity," 43; and tobacco
industry, 43; *Yuyo*, 84

Meléndez Vélez, Edgardo, 206

Men: unemployment rate of, 181–82, 191;
labor force participation rates of, 191

Méndez, José Luis, 318, 319

Méndez Ballester, Manuel: *Tiempo*, 357 (n. 10)

Menéndez Ramos, Rafael, 102

Menon, Lakshami N., 172–73

Mestizaje, 92

Mexico, 26, 173, 269

Middle class: and Muñoz Marín, 99, 100; and
Partido Popular Democrático, 137; and
statehood movement, 226; and self-help
organizations, 238; and Puerto Rican–
Hispanic Leadership Forum, 239; and
Puerto Rican identity, 240–41; and cul-
tural/literary debates, 260, 261; and
Puerto Rican diaspora, 304, 315

Miller, Paul, 89

Millet, Jean-François, 98

Mills, C. Wright, 205, 249

Minimum Wage Board, 146

Minimum wage laws, 141, 189, 280–81, 336.
See also Wages

Mining industry, 192, 231

Mintz, Sidney, 39, 366–67 (n. 5)

Miranda, Ismael, 265

Miranda Archilla, Graciany, 132–33; *Hungry
Dust*, 133

Misión Industrial, 231, 243, 245

Modernismo, 79–85, 119, 124

Modernity: and Puerto Rico, 22; and

Nationalist movement: and wage labor, 47; and Albizu Campos, 95, 105–9, 165, 254; clash with U.S. authorities, 104; as fascist, 105, 109, 250, 251, 365 (n. 14); and Puerto Rican identity, 126–27, 247; Muñoz Marín compared to, 152; insurrection of 1950, 160, 162, 165, 167–71; and Estado Libre Asociado, 162, 174; Wells on, 204; and sterilization, 208; and Andreu Iglesias, 214; Lewis on, 250, 251; Levins on, 251; and idealized vision of pre-1898 era, 253; and neonationalism, 316, 317–24; and postmodernism, 326–29, 332

National Maritime Union, 109, 138

National Recovery Administration, 97

National Sugar Refining Company, 36, 38

Native Americans: U.S. displacement of, 26, 32

Navarra, Gilda, 260

Navarro Tomás, Tomás, 91

Navas, Gerardo, 225

Needlework industry: and U.S. market, 33; expansion of, 35, 46–47; and idle season of sugar industry, 39; in New York, 68; and strikes, 96; organization of, 97; wages of, 179; reduced employment in, 181, 190, 193

Negrón Muñoz, Mercedes, 129

Negrón-Muntaner, Frances, 326–27, 379 (n. 17)

Nelson, Cary, 99

Neoconservatives, 305

Neoliberalism, 11, 275, 290–92, 294–96, 303–8, 332, 333, 337, 339

Neonationalism, 316, 317–24, 326, 332

New Deal: and tobacco industry, 44; and Partido Liberal, 95, 102; and Muñoz Marín, 101, 103, 104, 115, 119, 149, 151, 152, 224, 336; consequences of, 115–16, 337; and Partido Popular Democrático, 182, 224, 291

New Right, 236, 278, 291

New song movement, 248, 250, 266

New York, New York: and Puerto Rican diaspora, 2, 41, 66, 68, 202; and Puerto Rican separatists, 23; and Puerto Rican cigarmakers, 66; and Puerto Rican migration, 66, 68, 161, 180, 197, 349 (n. 31); Puerto

Rican cultural expressions in, 76, 85, 220, 262–66; and Puerto Rican music, 86; and Schomburg, 86–88; and Partido Nacionalista, 113–15, 116; and Burgos, 131; and cultural/literary debates, 131–33; Puerto Rican Left in, 147–48; and support for Marcantonio, 161; Puerto Rican activism in, 205, 237–45; and neoliberalism, 303. *See also* Nuyoricans

Nicaragua, 7, 30, 89, 289, 317

Nieves, Myrna, 373 (n. 23)

Nineteenth Amendment, 69

Nixon, Richard, 246

Noísmo, 89–90

Nolla, Olga: *El ojo de la tormenta*, 258

Noncolonial imperialism, 1, 2, 30, 162

Nonincorporation doctrine, 27, 28, 31, 344–45 (n. 24)

Nonincorporation status, 32, 53, 56, 177, 210, 280, 290, 299, 315

Nuyorican Poets Café, 263

Nuyoricans, 247, 249, 262–66

Oil processing operations, 181–82, 191, 192–93, 245–46

Ojeda, Filiberto, 283–84, 311–12

Oller, Francisco: *El Velorio*, 264

O'Mahoney, Joseph O., 163, 170

Operación Serenidad, 210–11, 217

Operation Bootstrap: and Muñoz Marín, 153; pace of changes, 180; petrochemical project of, 181–82, 191, 192–93, 245–46; and Partido Popular Democrático industrial policy, 187–94, 200; and tourist industry, 193; and growth of production, 210–11; and Puerto Rican culture, 212, 218; and shifts in industry, 225; and environmental movement, 231; and labor movement, 232, 295; and Hernández Colón, 245; Maldonado on, 248; Section 936 compared to, 269; and tax incentives, 336

Oppenheimer, Joselino "Bun Bun," 86

Oral histories, 11

Organización Puertorriqueña de la Mujer Trabajadora, 236

Ortega y Gasset, José, 119, 120, 255, 260

138, 141–42, 145–46, 154, 156, 202, 232; and
elections of 1940, 142–44, 182; wartime
bloc of, 144–46; and elections of 1944, 153–
54; and independence, 153–54, 156, 201,
286–87, 310–11, 312, 318; breakup of bloc,
153–54, 156–61; and Marcantonio, 161; and
Estado Libre Asociado, 162, 163, 171, 172,
173, 174, 175, 200; and Public Law 600, 164;
improvements under, 167; and Puerto
Rican constitution, 168; and colonialism,
176; and economics, 179–80, 189, 198–99,
201, 231, 237, 245, 273, 289, 293, 309; and
social reform, 182–84, 224, 250; and industrialization, 183, 186, 187–94, 200, 204, 268,
338; and University of Puerto Rico, 203–4,
230; and Puerto Rican identity, 208, 209–
11, 289, 293, 317; and Puerto Rican culture,
208, 211–14, 216–19, 286, 293, 317; and elections of 1968, 223, 224–26, 230; division of,
230, 231; and New Compact, 246, 286; Maldonado Denis's counternarrative to, 249;
and Partido Nuevo Progresista, 267, 286,
287, 317; and U.S. corporations, 268, 272,
278, 286, 287, 289, 293, 309; and elections of
1976, 277; investigations of Romero Barceló, 284; and elections of 1984, 285; and
Partido Socialista Puertorriqueño, 286–87;
and elections of 1992, 291; and elections of
2000, 293, 303; and privatization, 297; and
plebiscites, 299; and Calderón, 308–9; and
elections of 2004, 312
Partido Republicano: and U.S. relations, 20,
26; and sugar industry, 40, 53; and U.S.
colonial policies, 52–55, 59, 73; *turbas* tied
to, 54, 61; and Jones Act, 58; and Partido
Socialista, 65, 100; Matienzo Cintrón's
abandonment of, 70; and Great Depression, 95; and Plan Chardón, 103; split in,
142; and statehood, 280
Partido Revolucionario Cubano, 23
Partido Socialista: and reformist colonial
policies, 53, 65, 73; program of, 64–65;
and Partido Republicano, 65, 100; and
women's suffrage, 69; and López Landrón,
73; journal of, 85; and Great Depression,
95; and Muñoz Marín, 98, 99; and Plan

Chardón, 103; and Albizu Campos, 107;
and labor movement, 138, 139; split in, 142;
recovery of history of, 252
Partido Socialista Puertorriqueño (PSP):
and Movimiento Pro Independencia, 227;
and *terceristas*, 229; and labor movement,
233, 234, 235; and gay activism, 237; island-
centered orientation of, 243; crisis after
1976, 244; and Puerto Rican Alliance, 245;
and Lausell, 281; and Partido Independentista Puertorriqueño, 285; and Partido
Popular Democrático, 286–87; and Gutiérrez, 306
Partido Unión: and sugar industry, 40, 60–
61; and independence, 53, 55, 58–59, 89, 116,
177; and U.S. colonial policies, 53, 58–59;
and Federación Libre de Trabajadores, 55,
61, 63, 64; and Matienzo Cintrón, 55, 61,
71–72, 79; rise of, 55–57; and Miramar
rules, 57; and Jones Act, 58; misconceptions of, 59–60; dissident voices within,
61; and Guerra Mondragón, 84; and Zeno
Gandía, 84; vacillations of, 89; and Great
Depression, 95; and Albizu Campos, 106;
and *hacendados*, 253; Quintero Rivera on,
253
Pastiche, 331
Pataki, George, 303
Paternalistic ideology, 253, 320–21
Patriotic discourse, 56, 62, 80, 105, 253
Pedreira, Antonio S.: and autonomism, 83,
118, 119, 255; impact of, 88, 118–20, 133; and
Centro de Estudios Históricos, 91; and
Puerto Rican culture, 92, 210, 260, 324; and
Índice, 93, 117, 118, 134, 211, 357 (n. 1); *Insula-
rismo*, 117, 118–19, 120, 121, 122, 123, 202, 208,
211, 255, 260, 326; and Spengler, 120, 124;
and Belaval, 122; and Palés Matos, 125; and
conflict between culture and civilization,
127, 216; and Morales Carrión, 209; and
Géigel, 211; Maldonado Denis compared
to, 249; paternalistic ideology of, 253, 320;
Flores on, 255, 261; and *hacendado* class,
320; Rosario Ferré on, 373 (n. 20)
Penal policies, 313–14
People's Party (U.S.), 25

Pérez, Gina M., 304, 305

Pérez Velasco, Erick, 39

Perloff, Harvey S., 194–95, 204

Perón, Juan, 151–52

Pettigrew, Richard, 25

Pharmaceutical industry, 199, 207–8, 269, 295, 312

Philadelphia, Pennsylvania, 2, 244–45

Philippines: U.S. colonial government in, 1, 7, 24, 25, 56; independence of, 1, 7, 96, 102, 147, 150, 158; and Spanish-American War, 14; Spanish administration of, 20; and free trade, 25; Puerto Rico compared to, 32; sugar industry in, 36, 40, 41, 96, 97, 101

Philips Petroleum, 192

Phillips, Wendell, 21

Picó, Fernando, 253, 254

Pietri, Pedro: *Puerto Rican Obituary*, 262, 263–64

Piñero, Jesús T., 103, 154, 156, 157, 158, 163

Piñero, Lorenzo, 114, 226

Piñero, Miguel: *Nuyorican Poetry*, 263; *Short Eyes*, 263

Pinto Gandía, Julio, 116

Plan Chardón, 102–3, 119, 240, 336

Plan Muñoz Marín, 101, 102

Plantations, 18, 33, 49, 185, 258

Plath, Sylvia, 259

Platt Amendment, 29, 102

Plenas, 86, 123–24, 220, 265

Plessy v. Ferguson (1896), 7, 31, 177

Plutocracy, 70–71, 72, 73, 99–100, 107, 108, 361 (n. 33)

Poe, Edgar Allan, 124

Political issues: and Lloréns Torres, 79–80, 84; and Canales, 80, 81–83; and Guerra Mondragón, 84; and Partido Nacionalista, 105; and Albizu Campos, 108–10; and Blanco, 123; and Puerto Rican diaspora, 223, 237–45, 301, 303–7; and Maldonado Denis, 250; and Quintero Rivera, 252–53; and scandals, 293, 302–3. *See also* Annexationism; Autonomism; Independence movement; Statehood

Political parties: and labor movement, 17; leadership of, 20–21, 23; formation of, 21;

and Great Depression, 95; history of, 142, 143; impasse of, 312. *See also specific political parties*

Ponce, 19, 42, 47

Ponce Massacre, 116

Popular culture: and cultural/literary debates, 202, 255, 259, 260

Popular music: and Puerto Rican identity, 12, 219–21, 266, 322, 323–24; Puerto Rican music in New York, 86, 131–32; and Afro-Puerto Ricans, 157, 220–21; and salsa, 221, 265–66, 312, 373 (n. 28); and new song movement, 248, 250; and cultural/literary debates, 259, 265–66; and neonationalism, 319; Quintero Rivera on, 321–22

Population: density of, 1–2; and sugar industry, 33, 35; poverty and overpopulation, 41, 149, 150, 205, 206, 207; and Puerto Rican migration, 41, 194–95, 205–6, 307–8, 367 (n. 7); of small farmers, 48–50; unemployment and overpopulation, 194, 205, 206; study of, 204; and contraception, 207–8; and abortion, 236; prison population, 313; migrants from Dominican Republic, 323

Populists, 25

Porto Rico American Tobacco Company, 43, 64

El Porvenir Social, 17

Possessing classes: as political class, 22; and statehood, 52; and accommodation of U.S. colonial policies, 53; and Partido Unión, 57; patriotic discourse of, 62; and labor movement, 62, 68; and independent party of labor, 65; and Partido de la Independencia, 73; political subordination of, 76; and Lloréns Torres, 80; and Fuerzas Vivas, 99; paternalistic ideology of, 253; José Luis González on, 254–55, 260; and Partido Nuevo Progresista, 280

Post, Regis, 58, 72

Postcolonial theory, 40

Postdata, 325

Postmodernism: and Puerto Rican identity, 266; and cultural/literary debates, 316, 325–29, 332, 333; and new aestheticism, 329–33

Poverty: role of sugar industry in, 39, 104; role of overpopulation in, 41, 149, 150, 205, 206, 207; and Great Depression, 96; structural determinations of, 199–200; role of colonial economy in, 205, 207, 275; culture of poverty, 206–7; and Puerto Rican diaspora, 247; Tobin on, 268; and statehood movement, 277, 278, 280; in U.S., 277–78; and Partido Nuevo Progresista, 280–81; and racism, 328. *See also* Rural poor

Prado, Pérez, 220

Pragmatism, 84

Private property, 18, 185, 338

Privatization, 11, 289, 291, 292–300, 303–4, 308, 317, 325, 339, 376 (n. 6)

Progressivism, 72

Property rights, 182, 183

Property taxes, 37–38, 49

Proportional profit farms, 184, 185

Public debt, 273, 292, 341

Public education: and Matienzo Cintrón, 70; and English language, 75–76, 78, 79, 88–89; and Americanization, 76, 88; and Clark, 78; and Belaval, 122; and Pedreira, 127; growth in, 223, 292; and Rosselló, 295, 297

Public Law 600, 163–65, 167–70, 172

Public sector, 292, 295

Public sector employment, 267, 273, 292, 295, 296, 298, 308, 341

Public sphere, 76

Pueblos Hispanos, 131, 147–48

Puente, Tito, 220, 265, 266

Puerto Rican Alliance, 245

Puerto Rican Community Development Project (PRCDP), 240, 241

Puerto Rican constitution, 163, 164, 168–70, 173–74, 176, 314

Puerto Rican culture: institutionalization of, 3, 208–11, 218–19; and U.S. colonial policies, 10; and *criollo* culture, 19, 45, 74–75, 322; and Taino culture, 74, 255, 260, 261; and Matienzo Cintrón, 77–78, 79, 341; African dimension of, 78; and De Diego, 79, 351 (n. 13); and Guerra Mondragón, 83; and Afro–Puerto Ricans, 86, 93, 124, 125, 254, 255, 321–22, 324, 326, 378 (n. 3); and Ateneo

forum, 134; and Muñoz Marín, 152; and migration, 205, 206–7, 213–14, 321; Arce on, 211–12; variations of oppositional culture, 211–14, 216–19; Marqués on, 212–13; Andreu Iglesias on, 214, 216, 368 (n. 26); cultural hybridity, 214, 222, 247, 249, 321, 322; del Rosario on, 221–22; and gay activism, 237; and statehood, 281, 318, 376 (n. 2); and privatization, 304; and neonationalism, 318–19, 326; and paternalistic ideology, 320–21. *See also* Puerto Rican identity

Puerto Rican Day parade, 237, 238, 245

Puerto Rican diaspora: experience of, 2; and New York, 2, 41, 66, 68, 202; evolution of, 9; interaction with events on island, 11; and economics, 178, 315; political activism of, 223, 237–45, 301, 303–7; and gay activism, 236–37; mixed culture of, 249; and cuts in state social and welfare programs, 303; and neoliberalism, 304; and middle class, 304, 315; and Puerto Rican culture, 319, 322; and Puerto Rican literature, 331–32. *See also* Nuyoricans; Puerto Rican migration

Puerto Rican Forum, 238, 240–41

Puerto Rican–Hispanic Leadership Forum, 238–40

Puerto Rican historiography: and political evolution, 3, 9, 10, 17, 28, 32, 335; and pre-1898 era, 47, 48, 49–50, 113, 216, 253; and cultural/literary debates, 80, 247, 248, 321; reconsideration of, 80, 250–56; and Nuyoricans, 247; Lewis on, 248, 249–50, 251; Maldonado Denis on, 248–49, 251; Fromm on, 251; and Centro para el Estudio de la Realidad Puertorriqueña, 251–52; and neonationalism, 320, 324–25

Puerto Rican identity: debates of, 3, 11, 224, 247, 248; and U.S. colonial policies, 10, 61, 75; emphasis on, 11–12; and cultural/literary debates, 12, 93, 117, 134, 332; and popular music, 12, 219–21, 266, 322, 323–24; and Spanish administration, 20; and Afro–Puerto Ricans, 74, 91, 117, 121; and racial issues, 74, 91, 117, 210; vitality of, 76; and Spanish language, 76, 222, 326; and Puerto

Rican literature, 77; and Matienzo Cintrón, 77, 79; and *modernismo*, 79; and De Diego, 79, 84, 89; and Guerra Mondragón, 83; and Schomburg, 87; and Muñoz Marín, 100; and *generación del treinta*, 117, 261, 320–21; and Pedreira, 118–19; and Belaval, 120–21; and Catholicism, 126–27, 320; and Partido Popular Democrático, 208, 209–11, 289, 293, 317; double-edged affirmations of, 210; definition of, 218; permeability of, 222; and Puerto Rican Forum, 240; and postmodernism, 266; and statehood, 278, 281, 290; and neonationalism, 319, 320, 322, 379 (n. 17); González Nieves on, 319–20; and new aestheticism, 330. *See also* Puerto Rican culture

Puerto Rican literature: renewal of, 77; and English language, 133, 222, 263, 331, 368 (n. 25); Cabrera on, 218–19; context for literary departures, 224; and Nuyoricans, 247, 262–66, 331; racism of, 256; and literary insurgencies, 258–62; and aversion to present, 261; and neonationalism, 320–21; and new aestheticism, 329–30; and Puerto Rican diaspora, 331–32; and Spanish language, 331–32, 373 (n. 23). *See also specific authors*

Puerto Rican migration: geographic spread of, 2, 180–81, 197, 307–8; and economics, 3, 161, 179, 194, 270; and recruitment of Puerto Rican workers, 35, 41; and New York, 66, 68, 161, 180, 197, 349 (n. 31); and unemployment, 179, 181, 193, 194, 195, 270, 275; general trends in, 194, 196; and Estado Libre Asociado, 194–95; effects of, 200; management of, 205; and Puerto Rican culture, 205, 206–7, 213–14, 321; study of, 205–6; and Centro de Estudios Puertorriqueños, 251–52. *See also* Puerto Rican diaspora

Puerto Rican self-determination: and Matienzo Cintrón, 12, 52; and Albizu Campos, 12, 109; and Puerto Rico's political relationship with U.S., 158, 341–42; and Public Law 600, 170; and United Nations

debate, 172; and plebiscites, 224, 309; and feminism, 236; and Frente Socialista, 311; and Hostos, 361 (n. 33)

Puerto Rican separatists, 23, 24, 126, 345 (n. 30)

Puerto Rican society: tensions within, 15–17, 343 (n. 6); and Americanization, 70; and affirmations of Puerto Rican identity, 210; and economic reconfiguration of 1960s, 223; impact of plantations on, 258; Vega on, 259

Puerto Rican Student Union (PRSU), 223–24, 242–43

Puerto Rico Cultural Center, 244, 305

Puerto Rico Department of Education, 218; Community Education Division, 219

Puerto Rico Department of Labor, Migration Division, 195–96, 205

Puerto Rico Development Company, 188–89, 190

Puerto Rico Emergency Relief Administration, 97

Puerto Rico Policy Commission, 102

Puerto Rico Railway Light and Power Company, 42

Puerto Rico Reconstruction Administration (PRRA), 102–3, 104, 119, 184, 185

Puerto Rico's political relationship with U.S.: and insular politics, 2, 20, 23, 28; and U.S. colonial policies, 7, 10, 19–20, 26–28, 29, 32, 52–55, 58–59, 61, 73, 75–76, 78, 108, 158, 164, 167, 251, 283, 344 (n. 21); and political subordination, 7, 149, 153, 210; nonincorporation status, 32, 53, 56, 177, 210, 280, 290, 299, 315; and economics, 149, 150, 151, 153, 178, 275, 336–37; and plebiscites, 156–58, 162, 168, 224, 225, 227, 246, 278, 280, 291, 293–94, 299, 363 (n. 1); and Public Law 600, 163–65, 167, 168–70, 176; and United Nations debate, 171–73; and Federal Relations Act, 173; and Estado Libre Asociado, 175–76, 179; and nonincorporation, 210, 290; and U.S. armed forces recruitment, 230; and associated republic status, 287–88, 299; and Federal Death Penalty Act, 314; and radical democracy, 339–40

Puerto Rico Telephone Company (PRTC), 42, 289, 296–98, 299, 300, 304, 376 (n. 6)

Puerto Rico–USA Foundation, 272

Pullman strike, 63

Qualified Possessions Source Investment Income legislation, 272

Quiñones, Francisco Mariano, 21, 256

Quiñones, Samuel R., 48, 89, 92, 93, 100, 357 (n. 1)

Quintero Rivera, Angel, 62–63, 251, 252–54, 316, 321–22, 354 (n. 22)

Rabin, Robert, 300

Racial mixing, 54, 118–19, 256

Racism and racial issues: and U.S. annexation of Puerto Rico, 25; and statehood movement, 25, 278; and imperialism, 30–32; Barbosa on, 54; and Puerto Rican identity, 74, 91, 117, 210; and *criollo* culture, 74–75; and Puerto Rican culture, 78, 92–93, 238; and Zeno Gandía, 84; and Araquistáin, 92–93, 353 (n. 34); toward Albizu Campos, 107; and Pedreira, 118–19, 120, 249; and Belaval, 122; Blanco on, 123; and Palés Matos, 124, 125, 129; and Burgos, 129, 131; Delgado on, 133; and linguistic purism, 221; and Puerto Rican diaspora, 241; and Nuyoricans, 247; and independence movement, 252; race as cultural construction, 256; Zenón on, 256–57; and Puerto Rican historiography, 256–58; Albizu Campos on, 257; and Thomas, 262; and illegal drug trade, 313; and neonationalism, 318–19; and Dominican Republic migration, 323; and poverty, 328; and Colón, 352 (n. 26)

Radicales, 71–72

Radicalism: and labor movement, 65, 66; and Vega, 85; isolation of, 154; and Puerto Rican diaspora, 306–7; and postmodernism, 327–28, 333; and democracy, 332, 339–40

Radical nationalism, 91

Radical Reconstruction, 30

Railroads, 41, 42, 64

Rama, Angel, 320

Ramírez, Armando, 114

Ramírez, Rafael W., 256–57

Ramos Antonini, Ernesto, 100, 116, 141, 154

Ramos Otero, Manuel, 321, 372 (n. 18); *La novelabingo*, 258

Ramos-Zayas, Ana Y., 304, 305

Raw materials: production of, 28, 38–39, 41, 43, 45, 49

Ray, Richie, 265

Readers, 44, 63, 64

Reading circles, 16

Reagan, Ronald, 289, 309, 316, 340

Realism, 84, 128, 259, 331

Reily, E. Mont, 10, 58–59, 68

Report by the President's Task Force on Puerto Rico's Status, 174–75

Report of the Puerto Rico Policy Commission, 102

Republican Party (U.S.), 30, 54, 278

Rescates, 231–32

Reserve Officers Training Corps (ROTC), 229, 230

Resistance: diverse forms of, 7, 341–42; to privatization, 11; to imposition of English language, 76, 78–79, 88–89; to Americanization, 88; working-class resistance, 252; Flores on, 255

Rexach, Silvia, 217–18

Reyes, Edwin, 319, 371 (n. 2)

Riggs, Francis E., 110–11, 115, 144

Right, 184, 316. *See also* New Right

Rincón, Felisa, 161

Rivera, Ismael, 220, 257, 265

Rivera, Josefina, 218

Rivera, Raquel Z., 323–24

Rivera, Ray "Silvia," 236

Rivera de Alvarado, Carmen, 129, 207, 226

Rivera Izcoa, Carmen, 254

Rivera Martínez, Prudencio, 44, 63, 142

Rivera Rosa, Rafael, 260

Rizzo, Frank, 245

Roberto Roena y su Apollo Sound, 220

Robinson, Harry, 115

Rodó, José Enrique: *Ariel*, 255

Rodríguez, Abraham, Jr.: *Spidertown*, 331

Rodríguez, Adrián, 230

and Muñoz Rivera, 56, 57, 158; and U.S. citizenship, 58; and Barceló, 64; and Partido Socialista, 65; and Matienzo Cintrón, 70; and U.S. colonial policies, 158; and Estado Libre Asociado, 168, 169, 171–73, 175, 176, 179

Self-help organizations, 238

September 11 attacks, 328

Serrano, José, 306

Sexism, 119, 120, 252

Shakespeare, William, 255

Shelley, Mary, 259

Sherman Anti-Trust Act, 31

Sierra Berdecía, Fernando, 89–90, 202

Silén, Iván, 373 (n. 23)

Slavery: abolition of, 18, 21, 74, 123, 258; and Puerto Rican historiography, 257, 258

Small Business Job and Protection Act of 1996, 309

Small farmers: displacement of, 47, 49, 50, 92; population of, 48–50; and Muñoz Marín, 104; and Partido Nacionalista, 105; and Guerra, 107; and Belaval, 122; and Hernández, 132; and Partido Popular Democrático, 137, 138; and land reform, 184, 185, 186

Small property holders, 47

Smith, Rogers, 30

Smith Act, 158

Social class: and coffee industry, 19, 23, 45–46, 252; effect of U.S. invasion of 1898 on, 32; and sugar industry, 38–39; and Iglesias, 61–62; and self-government, 65; and political parties, 73; and Puerto Rican identity, 210; and Nuyoricans, 247; and Puerto Rican migration, 252; and Puerto Rican historiography, 252, 253; and Partido Socialista Puertorriqueño, 285; and class unity, 305; and colonial capitalist social formation, 354–55 (n. 22). See also *Hacendado* class; Middle class; Possessing classes; Working class

Social Darwinism, 31

Social feminism, 68–69

Socialism: and labor movement, 66; and Lloréns Torres, 80; and Canales, 82; and

Vega, 87, 238, 265, 340; and Colón, 87, 238, 340, 352 (n. 26); and Puerto Rican identity, 91; and Muñoz Marín, 98, 99; and Partido Nacionalista, 107; and Lanauze Rolón, 139; and Cuban Revolution, 227; and feminism, 235; and Young Lords, 242; and Lares rebellion, 251; and Lewis, 251; and cultural/literary debates, 316–17; and neonationalism, 318. *See also* Partido Socialista; Partido Socialista Puertorriqueño

Socialist Labor Party (U.S.), 62

Socialist Party (U.S.), 62, 68, 306

Social movements: rise of, 223, 341–42; student movements, 229–31, 237, 242, 247, 264, 281, 297, 311, 366 (n. 4); and Culebra, 231; environmental movement, 231, 237, 245–46, 247, 292, 297; and *rescates*, 231–32; in U.S., 256, 277–78

Social science: and cultural/literary debates, 202, 203–4

Social Security taxes, 273, 374 (n. 18)

Sociedad Albizu Campos, 242

Solá, Mercedes, 68

Soltero Peralta, Rafael, 153

Soto, Jorge, 264

Soto, Pedro Juan, 212, 218, 331, 368 (n. 25); *Ardiente suelo, fría estación*, 213–14

Soto Arriví, Carlos, 284

Soto Vélez, Clemente, 90, 107, 110, 132, 147

South Porto Rico Sugar Company, 38

Soviet Union, 128, 129, 158, 317

Spain: revolution of 1868, 16, 80; and Puerto Rican coffee market, 19; liberalism in, 20, 21, 22; political parties of, 23, 24; Puerto Rican differentiation from, 74–75

Spanish Action Committee of Chicago, 241

Spanish administration: of Puerto Rico, 15–16, 20, 36, 48, 61, 76, 80. *See also* Lares rebellion of 1868

Spanish-American War of 1898, 1, 3, 7, 14–15, 29, 167, 219, 315, 335

Spanish Civil War, 129, 211

Spanish Communist Party, 133

Spanish intellectuals, 203

Spanish language: as vernacular of Puerto Ricans, 2; and Puerto Rican identity, 76,

222, 326; and public education, 89; and American Communist Party, 114; and linguistic purism, 221, 222; as official language, 289, 318; and Puerto Rican literature, 331–32, 373 (n. 23)

Spanish Republic, 123, 129, 211; of 1873–74, 21

Spengler, Oswald, 120, 124, 255

Sports, 209

Stalin, Josef, 110

Stalinism, 139–40

Standard of living. *See* Living standards

STAR (Street Transvestite Action Revolutionaries), 236

Statehood: and Partido Autonomista, 24; and racial issues, 25, 278; and U.S. territorial expansion, 26, 28; and U.S. citizenship, 28, 56, 57, 58, 280; demands for, 32; and sugar industry, 40; and U.S. colonial policies, 52, 59; and Barbosa, 54–55; and Matienzo Cintrón, 54–55, 70, 77; and Partido Unión, 55, 57, 58; feasibility of, 56; and Muñoz Rivera, 57; and Albizu Campos, 108–9; tax burden of, 152; and Muñoz Marín, 152, 156; and Estado Libre Asociado, 173, 178, 278, 288–89; and Partido Popular Democrático, 202, 225, 288–89; and elections of 1968, 223; and plebiscites, 224, 225, 278, 280, 291, 293–94, 295, 299, 303; growth of movement, 225–26; and Partido Nuevo Progresista, 225–26, 267, 277, 286; and Romero Barceló, 246, 267, 277, 285, 291, 299, 303; and Section 936, 272; and civil rights discourse, 278; U.S. opposition to, 278–80, 288–89, 291, 310; and Puerto Rican culture, 281, 318, 376 (n. 2); and Rosselló, 290, 291, 293–96, 299, 318, 376 (n. 2); and postmodernism, 327; and radical democracy, 340

State repression, 314

State-run enterprises, 189

Steinem, Gloria, 235

Sterilization, 208, 236

Street language, 259–60

Strikes: of January–February 1895, 16; general strikes, 17, 299; and labor mobilization, 63–64; and Great Depression, 96–97;

and Albizu Campos, 109, 159; and labor activism of 1937, 138; and Communist Party of Puerto Rico, 138–39; and Partido Popular Democrático, 183; and University of Puerto Rico, 229, 281, 366 (n. 4); and reactivation of labor movement, 232–33; and Partido Nuevo Progresista, 281; and labor demobilization, 294–95; and public sector employees, 296; and privatization, 299; and neonationalism, 317

Student movements, 229–31, 237, 242, 247, 264, 281, 297, 311, 366 (n. 4)

Student Non-violent Coordinating Committee, 241

Students for a Democratic Society, 244

Suárez Findlay, Eileen J., 16, 85–86, 321

Subsistence farmers, 18, 19

Suez Canal, 29

Suffrage: universal suffrage, 28, 55–56, 69, 120, 212; and Muñoz Rivera, 55–56; women's suffrage, 64, 66, 68–69, 81; and Pedreira, 120; and Quiñones, 256

Sugar Act of 1934, 100, 101–2, 103

Sugar industry: economic importance of, 10, 18, 35; and U.S. sugar market, 17, 19, 25, 33, 35, 36, 38, 40, 53, 60, 96, 101, 113, 335; competition with beet sugar, 25, 35–37, 41, 96, 100, 111; and population shifts, 33, 35; and wage labor, 35, 38–39; cultivated land devoted to, 35, 39; and irrigation system, 37, 38, 49, 60; and property taxes, 37–38; expansion of, 38–40; tobacco industry compared to, 44, 45; and small farmers, 50; and strikes, 63, 64, 96–97, 145–46; impact of, 92; and Great Depression, 95–97; and Plan Muñoz Marín, 101, 102; and Plan Chardón, 103–4, 336; and Laguerre, 128; and Muñoz Marín, 150; wages of, 179; and Partido Popular Democrático, 183; and 500-acre law, 184; gradual decline in, 186; and industrialization, 188; reduced employment in, 193–94; and U.S. colonial rule, 252

Sugar Trust, 36, 38

Sun Oil, 192

Sweezy, Paul, 249

162, 171–73, 175; and nationalist insurrection, 165; and independence movement,
227; Decolonization Committee, 227, 286
United Nations Economic Commission for
Latin America, 269–70
United Porto Rico Sugar Company, 38, 96,
101
U.S. armed forces recruitment, 230
U.S. capital: and economics of Puerto Rico,
10, 149, 151, 178, 179, 182, 193, 205, 268, 275,
315, 335; influence of, 10, 193; and sugar
industry, 33, 37, 38, 41; and tobacco industry, 33, 41–45; and banking, 41–42, 268–69;
competitive pressure of, 61; and trusts, 70;
and Muñoz Marín, 161; and manufacturing sector, 179; and Operation Bootstrap,
190, 211; and statehood movement, 279;
and Partido Popular Democrático, 289
U.S. capitalism, 7, 68, 199, 220
U.S. citizenship: and statehood, 28, 56, 57, 58,
280; definitions of, 30, 31, 339–40; and
Jones Act, 57–58, 348 (n. 12); and Public
Law 600, 163; and Partido Nuevo Progresista, 289; and independence movement, 289–90
U.S. Civil War, 18, 31
U.S. Constitution, 26–27, 164
U.S. corporations: and U.S. colonial policies,
25, 167; and irrigation system, 60; and
Albizu Campos, 108; and Muñoz Marín,
149, 151; tax exemptions for, 189, 190, 268,
285, 293, 309; and tourist industry, 193; and
contraception, 207–8; and Puerto Rican
middle class, 226; and Partido Popular
Democrático, 268, 272, 278, 286, 287, 289,
293, 309; and 936 corporations, 268–69,
271–72, 293, 312–13; and neoliberalism, 303;
Balbás on, 351 (n. 13)
U.S. Department of Agriculture, 100, 101, 104
U.S. Department of Interior, Division of
Insular Territories and Possessions, 102,
104, 162, 171, 172
U.S. Department of Justice, 110
U.S. Department of Labor, 47
U.S. Department of State, 162–63, 170, 172,
227

U.S. global power, 1, 14, 30
U.S. Internal Revenue Code: Section 901,
309; Section 936, 268–73, 277, 279, 285, 287,
289, 293, 309, 312–13, 336, 338
U.S. labor movement, 7, 25, 29, 31, 344 (n. 21).
See also specific unions
U.S. military bases, 144
U.S. Naval Board, 345 (n. 28)
U.S. Navy: and industrialization, 29; and
Vieques, 231, 293, 300–301, 309, 325–26; in
Culebra, 231, 300; violence against, 283
U.S. North, 30
U.S. South: institutionalized racism in, 7;
Jim Crow doctrines in, 30–31, 123, 158; dis-
enfranchisement in, 31; segregation in, 54,
277
U.S. Supreme Court: and segregation, 7, 31;
on U.S. territories, 26, 27, 31; and Puerto
Rico as unincorporated territory, 59, 174,
177, 280, 315; and 500-acre legislation, 143–
44
U.S. Tariff Commission, 150
U.S. territorial expansion, 26–28, 29, 30
United States v. López Andino (1987), 174
United States v. Quiñones (1985), 174
United States v. Sánchez (1993), 174
U.S. working class, 31
University of Puerto Rico: transition of, 91–
92; and Pedreira, 118; and cultural univer-
salism, 134–35, 203; and Albizu Campos,
159; and Benítez, 203; and Partido Popular
Democrático, 203–4, 230; and moderniza-
tion, 204, 366–67 (n. 5); and population
studies, 205; and Puerto Rican culture,
209; critical voices within, 218; expansion
of, 223; and student strikes, 229, 281, 366
(n. 4); and *La escalera*, 248
Urbanization, 180, 187, 193, 201, 219–20, 315
Urban League, 239
Usera, Ramón, 132
Utopianism, 66, 329, 330, 331

Valentín, Bobby, 265
Valle, Carmen, 373 (n. 23)
Valle, Norma, 235, 252
Vanguardia Popular, 225, 231

223; and Puerto Rican historiography, 252.
See also Feminism

Woolf, Virginia, 259

Workbook (*libreta*), 18, 21

Working class: ethnic hierarchies of, 7; and
Afro–Puerto Ricans, 75; and Muñoz
Marín, 100; and Partido Nacionalista, 105;
and International Workers Order, 114; and
Partido Popular Democrático, 137; and
labor movement, 156; changes in, 202;
musical traditions of, 220; and cost of living issues, 233; and Movimiento Izquierda
Nacional Puertorriqueña, 244; and Puerto
Rican historiography, 251, 252; and *hacendado* class, 253; and neoliberalism, 305;
myth of, 325

World capitalist economy: turning points
of, 3; Puerto Rico's integration into, 3, 177;
phases of, 8; and imperial states, 28–29;
depression after 1873, 35–36; and sugar
industry, 40–41; and Great Depression, 95;
organization of, 178, 179; slow growth of
mid-1970s, 182, 198. *See also* Capitalism

World War I: and labor mobilization, 35, 64;
and sugar industry, 35, 95; and coffee
industry, 46; and needlework industry,

46–47; and U.S. control over Puerto Rico,
57; economic expansion during, 66

World War II: economic slowdown after, 2, 3,
12, 291; economic expansion after, 2, 12,
177–78, 179, 267, 274, 275, 291, 336, 338; economic expansion before, 2, 12, 335–36; economic slowdown before, 3, 291; and
Ateneo forum, 134; and government economic initiatives, 188, 189

Yager, Arthur D., 58, 64

Young, Don, 294, 296, 299

Young Lords, 223, 241–43, 245

Young Lords Party, 242

Yugoslavia, 173

Yupanqui, Atahualpa, 319

Zalduondo, Celestina, 207

Zapatismo, 80

Zeno, Francisco M., 43, 47

Zeno Gandía, Manuel: *El negocio*, 19; *La
charca*, 46; and *radicales*, 71; and cultural/
literary debates, 73, 89; *Redentores*, 84–85

Zenón, Carlos, 300

Zenón, Isabelo, 256–57

Zona de Carga y Descarga, 258, 259